Columbian Lodge

Also from Westphalia Press

westphaliapress.org

A Historical Account of Columbian Lodge of Free and Accepted Masons of Boston, Mass.

By John T. Heard

WESTPHALIA PRESS
An imprint of Policy Studies Organization

A Historical Account of Columbian Lodge of Free and Accepted Masons of Boston, Mass.

Westphalia Press
An imprint of Policy Studies Organization
1527 New Hampshire Ave., NW
Washington, D.C. 20036
info@ipsonet.org

ISBN-13: 978-1-63391-237-3
ISBN-10: 163391237X

Cover design by Taillefer Long at Illuminated Stories:
www.illuminatedstories.com

Daniel Gutierrez-Sandoval, Executive Director
PSO and Westphalia Press

Updated material and comments on this edition
can be found at the Westphalia Press website:
www.westphaliapress.org

A

HISTORICAL ACCOUNT

OF

COLUMBIAN LODGE

OF

Free and Accepted Masons of Boston, Mass.

BY JOHN T. HEARD.

TO WHICH ARE ADDED, THE CHARTER, THE BY-LAWS ADOPTED
NOVEMBER 28, 5854; CATALOGUES OF OFFICERS, MEMBERS
AND INITIATES OF COLUMBIAN LODGE, AND OF THE
PRINCIPAL OFFICERS OF THE GRAND LODGE OF
THE COMMONWEALTH OF MASSACHUSETTS.

BOSTON:

1856.

REPORT.

At the regular communication of Columbian Lodge for the present month, the following resolution was unanimously adopted :

" *Resolved*, That the subject of amending, altering or repealing the Constitution and By-Laws of this Lodge, and the formation of a new Code of By-Laws which shall take the place of the present Constitution and By-Laws, be referred to a Committee, who shall report thereon on or before the regular communication in December next."

The undersigned having been appointed the Committee under the above resolution, ask, respectfully, to Report :

On examining the existing Constitution and By-Laws of Columbian Lodge, the Committee observe that they embrace only partially the regulations to which the Lodge owe obedience; that many and important printed edicts of the Grand Lodge, designed for the government of subordinate Lodges, are not included therein; rendering a frequent reference to the statutes of the parent Institution indispensable to ascertain various duties and obligations that no well regulated Lodge would disregard. The inconvenience of seeking out the path of duty through the medium of the code of the Grand Lodge, which includes regulations not material to the government of a subordinate Lodge, would seem to demand such a change in the By-Laws of this Lodge as would obviate this difficulty. A remedy that suggests itself is to render the By-Laws as full and comprehensive, as, under prudent Masonic limitations, is practicable. The embodying of all written regulations applicable to a Lodge into their By-Laws, would tend to facilitate business, and insure accuracy in their proceedings; as, the officers and members having the legal guide always at hand in a convenient form, could rightly inform themselves as to their respective duties and powers.

In view of these facts and considerations, the Committee,—having first carefully collated the provisions contained in the statute regulations of the Grand Lodge of this Commonwealth, and in the Constitutions and By-Laws of this Lodge,—have prepared, chiefly from these authorities, a Code of By-Laws, which they have the honor herewith to present. To alter or amend, merely, the present By-Laws seeming impracticable consistently with clearness and the method of arrangement it was thought desirable to adopt, determined the Committee to recommend their repeal.

Regarding the time-honored Charter of the Lodge,—derived more than half a century ago from the Grand Lodge,—as the real Constitution of Columbian Lodge; and viewing the present Constitution, so called, as being essentially no more the fundamental law than are the By-Laws themselves, the undersigned would recommend its entire repeal, also; especially as this act will not practically abrogate it: all its main provisions having been incorporated into the proposed By-Laws.

There are several sections in Article XXII containing parliamentary rules, the adoption of which the committee do not urge, though they might be occasionally serviceable, perhaps, to the presiding officer in confining debate to its just limits. These rules are almost universally regarded by deliberative bodies, and are the same which the Grand Lodge have adopted to govern their deliberations.

The change proposed in the title of the Master, is what seems to be demanded by the practice existing not only in this Masonic jurisdiction, but generally throughout the United States.

A copy of the Charter is herewith communicated; and it is respectfully suggested that should the proposed By-Laws, (if adopted,) be printed, the Charter would be an appropriate accompaniment.

All of which is respectfully submitted,

JOHN T. HEARD,
GEO. M. THACHER,
PETER C. JONES,
WM. W. BAKER,
WM. D. COOLIDGE,
WM. B. FOWLE, JR.

} COMMITTEE.

Boston, Nov. 24th, 5854.

CHARTER.

—

To all the FRATERNITY

To whom these Presents shall come:

THE GRAND LODGE of the Most Ancient and Honorable Society of FREE and ACCEPTED Masons, for the Commonwealth of MASSACHUSETTS, send Greeting:

⎡SEAL.⎤

WHEREAS a Petition has been presented to us by Joseph Churchill, James Eaton, John Rittenhouse, Joshua Hardy, Nicholas Kindness, Snelling Powell, Henry Wickham, Thomas Tannatt, T. McCoristine, Thomas Leatham, Henry Lord, John Perkins, John Pingree, John Coles, James L. Connings, Samuel Hayden, and James Dodge,

all ANCIENT, FREE and ACCEPTED Masons---praying that they, with such others, as shall hereafter join them, may be erected and constituted a regular

PAUL REVERE, Grand Master.
SAM'L DUNN, Deputy Grand Master.

Lodge of FREE and ACCEPTED Masons, which petition appearing to us as tending to the Advancement of Masonry and the Good of the Craft:

NOW Ye therefore That We the Grand Lodge aforesaid, reposing special Trust and Confidence in the Prudence and Fidelity of our beloved Brethren aboved named, have Constituted and Appointed, and by these Presents, do Constitute and Appoint

them the said Joſeph Churchill, James Eaton, John Rittenhouſe, Joſhua Hardy, Nicholas Kindneſs, Snelling Powell, Henry Wickham, Thomas Tannatt, T. McCoriſtine, Tho's Leatham, Henry Lord, John Perkins, John Pingree, John Coles, James L. Connings, Samuel Hayden, and James Dodge, a regular 𝕃𝕠𝕕𝕘𝕖 of FREE and ACCEPTED 𝕄𝕒𝕤𝕠𝕟𝕤, under the Title and Deſignation of COLUMBIAN 𝕃𝕠𝕕𝕘𝕖, hereby giving and granting unto them and their Succeſſors, full Power and Authority to convene aſ 𝕄𝕒𝕤𝕠𝕟𝕤, within the Town of BOSTON, in the County of SUFFOLK, and Commonwealth aforeſaid---to receive and enter Apprentices, paſſ Fellow Crafts, and raiſe Maſter Maſons, upon the payment of ſuch moderate Compenſation for the same as may be determined by the ſaid 𝕃𝕠𝕕𝕘𝕖; alſo to make choice of a MASTER, WARDENS, and other OFFICE BEARERS, annually, or otherwiſe, as they ſhall ſee cauſe; to receive and collect FUNDS for the relief of poor and diſtreſsed BRETHREN, their WIDOWS, or CHILDREN, and in general to tranſact all matters relating to Masonry, which may to them appear to be for the Good of the 𝕮𝕣𝕒𝕗𝕥, according to the ancient Uſages and Cuſtoms of 𝕄𝕒𝕤𝕠𝕟𝕤.

And 𝖂𝖊 do hereby require the said conſtituted Brethren, to attend the 𝕲𝕣𝕒𝕟𝕕 𝕃𝕠𝕕𝕘𝕖 at their QUARTERLY COMMUNICATIONS, and other Meetings, by their MASTER and WARDENS, or by Proxies regularly appointed; also to keep a fair and regular Record of all their Proceedings, and to lay them before the 𝕲𝕣𝕒𝕟𝕕 𝕃𝕠𝕕𝕘𝕖 when required.

And we do enjoin upon our Brethren of the ſaid 𝕃𝕠𝕕𝕘𝕖, that they be punctual in the quarterly Payment of ſuch Sums as may be aſſeſsed for the Support of the 𝕲𝕣𝕒𝕟𝕕 𝕃𝕠𝕕𝕘𝕖----

that they behave themfelves respectfully and obediently to their Superiors in Office, and in all other refpects conduct themfelves as good 𝕸𝖆𝖘𝖔𝖓𝖘.

And we do hereby declare the PRECEDENCE of the faid 𝕷𝖔𝖉𝖌𝖊, in the 𝕲𝖗𝖆𝖓𝖉 𝕷𝖔𝖉𝖌𝖊 and elsewhere, to commence from the ninth day of June, five thoufand, seven hundred and ninety-five.

𝕴N 𝕿𝖊𝖘𝖙𝖎𝖒𝖔𝖓𝖞 𝖜𝖍𝖊𝖗𝖊𝖔𝖋, We the 𝕲𝖗𝖆𝖓𝖉 𝕸𝖆𝖘𝖙𝖊𝖗 and 𝕲𝖗𝖆𝖓𝖉 𝖂𝖆𝖗𝖉𝖊𝖓𝖘, by Virtue of the Power and Authority to us committed, have hereunto fet our Hands, and caufed the 𝕾𝖊𝖆𝖑 of the 𝕲𝖗𝖆𝖓𝖉 𝕷𝖔𝖉𝖌𝖊 to be affixed, at BOSTON, this ninth Day of June, Anno Domini one thousand, seven hundred and ninety-fix, and of 𝕸𝖆𝖘𝖔𝖓𝖗𝖞 five thoufand seven hundred and ninety-fix.

By order of the Grand Lodge,

Daniel Oliver, GRAND SECRETARY.

Isaiah Thomas, SENIOR GRAND WARDEN.
Joseph Laughton, JUNIOR GRAND WARDEN.

CONTENTS OF HISTORICAL ACCOUNT.

Chapter VIII.

Chapter IX.

Chapter X.

Chapter XI.

Chapter XII.

Chapter XIII.

Chapter XIV.

CHAPTER XV.

CHAPTER XVI.

CHAPTER XVII.

CHAPTER XVIII.

CHAPTER XIX.

———

INDEX TO BIOGRAPHICAL NOTICES.

BY·LAWS.

ARTICLE I.
THE LODGE.

COLUMBIAN LODGE shall be composed of a Worshipful Master, a Senior and a Junior Warden, (constituting the Executive government,) a Treasurer, a Secretary, a Senior and a Junior Deacon, a Senior and a Junior Steward, with such other officers as the Master, with the advice and consent of the Wardens, may appoint, and of as many Master Masons as shall be regularly admitted members.

ARTICLE II.
ELECTIONS.

The first nine officers shall be chosen by written ballots, at the stated meeting in December, annually, by a majority of the members present, and shall perform the duties of their offices, respectively, until others are elected and installed in their stead. Any vacancy shall be filled in

like manner, and at such times as the Lodge may
direct. All other officers shall be appointed by
the Master, with the advice and consent of the
Wardens.

ARTICLE III.

MEMBERS.

SECTION 1. Each applicant for membership
shall stand proposed at least to a subsequent meeting, and his name shall be upon the notifications
for the meeting at which the application is to be
acted upon : he must receive the unanimous consent by ballot of the members present, shall pay
the established fee, before his application shall be
acted upon, and shall sign the By-Laws before he
shall be recorded a member. Should the applicant be accepted, and he neglect for three months
to sign the By-Laws, he shall renew his application, before he can be recorded a member.

SECTION 2. Any member about to leave town
for one or more years, may, at his own request,
have his membership suspended, provided all his
periodical dues are paid ; but from the time of
suspension, all his privileges of membership shall
cease, until, on his return, he shall, in writing, in-

form the Lodge, of his wish to exercise the rights of membership.

SECTION 3. Any member neglecting to pay his periodical dues for eighteen months, may be suspended or expelled from the rights of membership by a majority of the members present at any regular meeting.

SECTION 4. No member shall be elected or appointed to office, unless he shall have paid all assessments due by him to the Lodge.

SECTION 5. If any deceased member leave a widow or orphans, notwithstanding he may owe the Lodge, such widow or orphans shall forthwith be presented by the Master and Wardens, with the sum of twenty dollars. Provided, however, the widow or orphans of a member not residing in Boston at the time of his decease, shall inform the Lodge of her or their place of residence.

SECTION 6. Every member in balloting upon an application for membership or degrees may vote as he thinks proper, and no member can be caused to divulge how he voted, nor can he be questioned at all, nor called on to give a reason for his vote.

SECTION 7. Any member having complied with the provisions of the By-Laws, shall, at his request, be honorably discharged.

SECTION 8. No Bróther shall be made an honorary member, unless his name for such membership shall be on the notifications for the meeting at which the application is to be acted upon, and he be unanimously accepted.

SECTION 9. Any member who shall purchase an exemption from periodical assessments during life, shall never be affected by any future vote or by-law relative to quarterages or periodical assessments.

SECTION 10. No Brother who has been discharged from any other Lodge for non-payment of dues, shall be admitted to membership in this Lodge, until the same shall be paid or remitted. The receipt or certificate from the Secretary of the Lodge of which the applicant was last a member, shall be satisfactory evidence that his dues have been liquidated.

SECTION 11. No member shall hold more than one office in the Lodge at the same time.

SECTION 12. Each member, (honorary excepted) shall be assessed sixteen and two-thirds cents each month, which shall be payable at the stated meeting in December, annually, except when the membership is withdrawn or suspended, in which case, all dues shall be paid. But, as a full compensation for all assessments, any member may pay twenty dollars, which shall exempt him from the payment of all periodical dues during life.

A deceased member, whose periodical dues shall have been paid to the preceding December, shall not be considered a delinquent : his account shall be balanced.

SECTION 13. No note of hand shall be taken for fees, nor shall any term of credit be given for the payment thereof.

SECTION 14. The fee for membership shall be five dollars from a Brother who received his degrees in this Lodge, and ten dollars if he received them in another Lodge.

ARTICLE IV.
MEETINGS.

SECTION 1. Stated or regular meetings, or communications, shall be held on the first Thursday of each month, at such time as the Master shall order, and specially at the pleasure of the Master ; in his absence, at the pleasure of the S. Warden ; and in the absence of both, at the pleasure of the J. Warden :   Provided, nevertheless, that the Lodge may adjourn over the summer months, should it be deemed expedient.

SECTION 2.   At called or special meetings no other business shall be transacted except that named in the notifications for such meetings.

SECTION 3.   Notifications of every meeting shall be sent to the members residing in Boston, in which the time and place of meeting shall be stated.

SECTION 4.   At the time appointed, the Lodge shall be opened in due form, seven members being present, one of whom being qualified to preside.

SECTION 5.   No business, other than that appertaining to the work and lectures, shall be transacted in the Lodge while open on the first or second degree.   All general business, such as the election and installation of officers, the discussion of questions relating to the general interests of the Fraternity, and the local affairs of the Lodge, shall be transacted in a Master's Lodge.

ARTICLE V.

MASTER.

SECTION 1. The Worshipful Master, as the head and Governor of the Lodge, shall at all times have in his possession, the Charter from the M. W. G. Lodge, and shall enjoy all the rights, privileges and immunities of Ancient Craft Masonry; and by the same shall govern his Lodge, constantly having in view the Constitution and By-Laws of the M. W. Grand Lodge of Massachusetts, and By-Laws of this Lodge.

SECTION 2. He may call special meetings of the Lodge whenever the interests of the Lodge or of Masonry, may in his judgment require it.

SECTION 3. The decision of the Master, upon any question or point, is final and conclusive, and there is no appeal from it, except to the Grand Lodge or Grand Master.

SECTION 4. It shall be the duty of the Master, when notified of the intended official visit of the District Deputy Grand Master, to convene the Lodge, receive him as the representative of the Grand Lodge, resign the chair to him while making his official communications, submit to his inspection the by-laws, records and mode of work, and deliver to him the return of the Lodge, and the dues to the Grand Lodge.

SECTION 5. He shall appoint all committees except those herein provided for.

ARTICLE VI.
SENIOR AND JUNIOR WARDENS.

The Senior and Junior Wardens will assist the Master in the work and government of the Lodge.

The S. Warden, in the absence of the Master, shall preside, with all his powers and prerogatives.

The J. Warden in the absence of the Master, and S. Warden, will preside in like manner.

ARTICLE VII.
TREASURER.

The Treasurer shall be exempted from quarterages; he shall have charge, and keep an inventory of all funds and property of the Lodge, the Charter, Books, Records and Papers excepted.

The inventory shall express every species of property belonging to the Lodge; the time of purchase; the cost; if a donation, the time, the name of the donor, and the value; and all property worn out, altered, or disposed of, shall be noted. This inventory shall be revised by a committee, and reported by the Treasurer at the stated meeting in December annually. He shall pay all bills approved by the Financial Committee, and all orders drawn by the Committee on Charity. He shall annually attend the meeting of the Financial Committee, and exhibit an accurate statement of the receipts, expenditures, monies voted by the Lodge to applicants for charity, and the amount of funds. He shall deliver to his successor, within fifteen days after his installation, all funds and property of the Lodge. He shall at all times be under the special direction of the Lodge. He shall, within twenty days after his installation give bonds to the Master and Wardens, with satisfactory sureties, for the faithful discharge of his duties.

ARTICLE VIII.

SECRETARY.

The Secretary shall be exempted from quarterages. He shall have charge of all books, records, and papers, (the Charter, Treasurer's accounts, and inventory excepted.) He shall attend the meetings of the Lodge, with all necessary books and papers. He shall make a just and fair record of the proceedings of each meeting. He shall record all applications for the degrees and membership,—all degrees conferred, and by whom received,—all who shall be admitted members,—all members withdrawn, suspended, or renewed,—all names of members who shall purchase an exemption from periodical assessments during life. He shall receive all monies due to the Lodge, and before the next meeting, pay the same to the Treasurer. He shall fill, for each meeting, notifications for all members residing in Boston, inserting thereon the names of all candidates for the degrees and membership, and all special business coming before the Lodge ; and shall continue to do the same until the work shall be completed ; and shall deliver the notifications to the Tyler for distribution.

He shall make correct Annual Returns to the M. W. G. Lodge. On the rejection of a candidate for the degrees, he shall forthwith notify every Lodge in the First Masonic District of such rejection.

He shall notify the chairman of each committee of his appointment, the names of his associates, and the business committed to them. He shall immediately after the stated meeting in November, annually, render to the Financial Committee an accurate statement of the work done, of the monies received, of the memberships commenced, suspended, renewed, or withdrawn. He shall, at the stated meeting in December, annually, and before the choice of officers, read the names of all delinquents, the sum due from each, and shall record the same with the doings of the meeting. He shall, before the closing of the Lodge, at each meeting, read the minutes of the proceedings by him kept. He shall permanently record said minutes before the next succeeding meeting. He shall, previous to initiation, receive the signatures, in a book kept for that purpose, of all applicants for the degrees, with their respective places of birth, residence, age and occupation. He shall be paid for each meeting two dollars and fifty cents, and for each diploma one dollar.

ARTICLE IX.

SENIOR AND JUNIOR DEACONS.

The Senior Deacon is exclusively under the orders of the Master. The Junior Deacon is under the orders of the Master and Senior Warden.

ARTICLE X.

SENIOR AND JUNIOR STEWARDS.

The Stewards are under the orders of the Master and Wardens, but particular under the direction of the Junior Warden.

ARTICLE XI.

CHAPLAIN.

There shall be a Chaplain appointed by the Master and Wardens, who shall perform such clerical duties as are suitable to his station and as are established by the usages of the Fraternity. He shall be exempted from quarterages.

ARTICLE XII.

MARSHAL.

The Marshal shall be appointed by the Master and Wardens. He shall direct the organization of the Lodge before it is opened; collect from the members and petitioners all communications for the Lodge and place them before the Secretary; shall introduce visitors; form and direct processions; and communicate and execute all orders of the Master, not otherwise provided for.

ARTICLE XIII.

SENTINEL.

The Sentinel shall be exempted from quarterages. He shall be exclusively under the orders of the presiding officer. He shall permit none to pass or repass without leave from said officer.

ARTICLE XIV.

TYLER.

The Tyler shall be exempted from quarterages. He shall deliver the notifications for the meetings. He shall keep a list, and have the care of the jewels, clothing, and furniture of the room. He shall at each meeting, deposit the several jewels at their respective stations, and at the close of each meeting shall collect and carefully secure the same. He shall have charge of the lights, fuel, hall, and rooms. When lights or fuel are wanted, he shall inform the Master and Wardens. He shall see the hall and rooms properly cleansed and lighted. He is exclusively under the orders of the presiding officer. He shall be paid for delivering the notifications, superintending, and tyling, the sum of five dollars.

ARTICLE XV

INSTALLATION.

SECTION 1. The officers of the Lodge, elected and appointed, shall be annually installed on or before the stated meeting in January, at such time as the Lodge shall direct.

SECTION 2. In case the Master elect cannot attend at the time appointed for his installation, he may be installed by proxy, on signifying his acceptance of the office; but such proxy must be a Past-Master. Other officers elected or appointed, who are absent, may also be installed by proxies, who must be members of this Lodge.

SECTION 3. The several officers, previous to their installation, shall make the following declaration:

"I solemnly promise upon the honor of a Mason, that in the office of ———, I will, to the best of my abilities, strictly comply with the Constitutions and Regulations of the Grand Lodge of this Commonwealth, all other Masonic usages, and the By-Laws of this Lodge, so far as the same shall come to my knowledge."

SECTION 4. All officers, elected or appointed, when installed, shall be proclaimed by the Marshal, and shall retain their stations until their successors are duly appointed and installed.

The proclamation shall be substantially as follows, viz.:

"I am directed by the Worshipful Master to proclaim, and I do now, therefore, proclaim, that the officers of Columbian Lodge, elected and appointed, having been installed, the said Lodge is duly organized, and is ready to transact any business that may lawfully come before it. This," &c.

SECTION 5. No elected officer shall act as such, until he is duly installed.

ARTICLE XVI.

BOARD OF RELIEF.

At the stated meeting in December, annually, there shall be chosen by ballot a committee, to consist of such a number as the Lodge shall determine at the time, whose duty it shall be to act as the representatives of this Lodge in the body known as the "Board of Relief."

ARTICLE XVII.

FINANCIAL COMMITTEE.

The Master and Wardens shall constitute the Financial Committee. They shall superintend the prudential concerns of the Lodge. They shall examine and approve in writing, all bills before they can be paid. They, with two other members to be chosen at the stated meeting in November, annually, shall form a committee to require of the Secretary and Treasurer accurate statements of their doings, and they shall report the same at the stated meeting in December, annually, before the choice of officers, including the precise state of the Lodge, of its funds, the number of members, of what class, the degrees given, on whom conferred, the receipts and expenditures, memberships commenced, withdrawn, suspended, or renewed; and all other things relating to the welfare of the Lodge.

All bills shall be presented to the Financial Committee within twelve days after the stated meeting in November, annually.

ARTICLE XVIII.

PROPERTY.

The funds or property of the Lodge shall never be divided among its members, but shall be exclusively devoted to charitable purposes, except such as shall be absolutely necessary for the support and government of the Lodge. And whenever its members become so few, scattered, or negligent, that there shall not be, during six months, a sufficient number to fill the first nine offices, it shall be the duty of the members forthwith to surrender to the M. W. G. Lodge of Massachusetts, the charter, books, records, jewels, funds, and all other property of Columbian Lodge.

ARTICLE XIX.

CANDIDATES.

SECTION 1. Each candidate for the degrees shall make a printed or written application, at a stated meeting, in the following form, viz. :

To the Worshipful Master and Brethren of Columbian Lodge.

The subscriber entertaining a favorable opinion of your ancient Order, is desirous of receiving the several degrees conferred in your Lodge.

Place of birth.
Residence.
Age.
Occupation.
Date.

[NAME.]

The application shall enclose thirty dollars, and shall be read in open Lodge ; and the applicant's name shall be inserted on the notifications for the meeting at which the application is to be acted upon, and when he may be balloted for. If he be rejected, the sum enclosed shall be returned.

SECTION 2. Any Brother who shall have received the first degree, or the first and second degrees, in any other Lodge, may receive the other degree or degrees by applying as other candidates are required to do, and paying for the second and third degrees, ten dollars for each degree ; and for the third degree only, ten dollars.

SECTION 3. No applicant shall receive the degrees but by the unanimous ballot of the members present.

SECTION 4. Any Brother raised to the sublime degree of Master in this Lodge, shall be entitled to a Diploma by placing his signature in the margin, in presence of the Master, one of the Wardens, or Secretary.

SECTION 5. The expense of meetings, called exclusively to accommodate candidates, shall be paid by them, unless remitted by the Master and Wardens.

SECTION 6. It shall not be regular to give more than one degree to the same individual on the same day, nor at a less interval than one month from the time of his receiving a previous degree, unless a dispensation shall have been obtained therefor.

SECTION 7. No candidate shall in any event be balloted for, into whose moral character a strict inquiry has not been made by an investigating committee, and whose name has not been borne on the notifications for the meetings at which he is to be balloted for.

SECTION 8. No candidate whose application for the degrees has been rejected by another Lodge, shall be initiated in this Lodge, without a recommendation from six members of the Lodge rejecting his application, of whom the Master and Wardens of such Lodge shall be three.

SECTION 9. No person residing in a town within this Commonwealth, wherein a Lodge is held, shall be admitted a candidate by this Lodge, without the approbation of the Master and Wardens of a Lodge in the town of his residence. Nor shall any candidate be received from any other State, (he being a resident thereof,) where a regular Grand Lodge is established, without the written permission of the Grand Master of such State.

Section 10. No Entered Apprentice or Fellow Craft, initiated or passed in another Lodge within the United States, shall be passed or raised in this Lodge, without the consent of the Master and Wardens of the Lodge in which he was first admitted, or a dispensation from the Grand Master.

Section 11. Any member of any Lodge within this Commonwealth may object to the initiation, passing, or raising of a candidate at any time before a degree is conferred.

Section 12. In the absence of the Master and Wardens, it is not lawful to initiate, craft or raise a candidate, unless a Past Master be present.

Section 13. No petition can be withdrawn, unless the report of the investigating committee be favorable.

ARTICLE XX.
REPRESENTATION IN GRAND LODGE.

Section 1. The majority of the members of the Lodge at any meeting, have the privilege of giving instructions to the Master and Wardens, for their government at the next meeting of the Grand Lodge; these officers being their representatives in the Grand Lodge, and are supposed to speak their sentiments in reference to its proceedings.

SECTION 2. As it is the duty, as well as the privilege of this Lodge to be represented at the communications of the Grand Lodge, by its Master and Wardens, at all times when they can attend, or by proxy, when their attendance is impossible or inconvenient, this Lodge therefore claims the right to appoint such proxy, according to the Constitutions of the Grand Lodge, whenever deemed expedient or necessary. And the letter by which the appointment is made, shall be substantially as follows, viz. :

To the Most Worshipful Grand Lodge of Massachusetts.

BE IT KNOWN,

****
* SEAL. *
****
—— ——,
Master of
—— *Lodge.*

That Brother —— ——, of ——, having been chosen by the members of Columbian Lodge, in Boston, to represent said Lodge in Grand Lodge the ensuing year : I do, by these presents, in their behalf, constitute and appoint him their representative ; for them to appear, and upon all subjects relating to the Craft in general, and to said Lodge in particular, to act and decide as fully as though we were personally present.

Confirming the acts of our beloved Brother, in his capacity aforesaid—We pray that he may enjoy all the privileges and protection to which we are entitled.

In witness whereof, I have hereunto subscribed my name, and caused the seal of our Lodge to be affixed, this —— day of ——, A. L. 58—.

Attest,

—— ——, *Secretary.*

ARTICLE XXI.

VISITING DEPUTATIONS.

All Lodges being particularly bound to observe the same usages and customs, every deviation, therefore, from the established mode of working is highly improper, and ought not to be countenanced; and in order to preserve uniformity of work, as well as to cultivate a good understanding among the Craft, the Master may from time to time, appoint visiting deputations, composed of the members of this Lodge, to visit other Lodges in this Commonwealth, as in his judgment shall appear requisite to promote the objects above named.

ARTICLE XXII.

MISCELLANEOUS REGULATIONS.

SECTION 1. No Brother shall leave the Lodge during the session without permission of the presiding officer.

SECTION 2. No refreshment shall be provided except by special vote of the Lodge, from time to time.

SECTION 3. No officer or member of this Lodge shall, under any circumstances, give a certificate or recommendation, to enable a Mason to proceed from Lodge to Lodge, as a pauper, or, in an itinerant manner, to apply to Lodges for relief.

SECTION 4. It shall not be permitted to introduce political or other exciting topics for discussion into the Lodge.

SECTION 5. A visiting Brother, having produced his Grand Lodge certificate, or Diploma, has a right to see the Charter of the Lodge; but this privilege shall not be granted to him except in the Lodge, and after the Lodge shall be satisfied that he is a worthy Mason.

SECTION 6. No Mason, not a member of another Lodge, and who is a resident of Boston, shall be allowed to visit this Lodge twice without permission of the Master.

SECTION 7. The Lodge may take cognizance of the conduct of any sojourning Brother or Brethren, not attached to any particular Lodge, upon a charge of unmasonic conduct.

SECTION 8. The removal of a Brother into another masonic jurisdiction, does not, of itself, authorize his name to be stricken from the roll of the Lodge of which he is a member.

SECTION 9. No other business can be transacted at any meeting to which the Lodge may be called off, except such as was announced or begun on the day or night of the stated monthly meeting and could not be finished ; and such unfinished business must be specified on the minutes, and announced to the members present, when the Lodge is called off.

SECTION 10. The minutes of a preceding meeting cannot be altered at any subsequent meeting. If any change or alteration should be desired, it must be submitted to the Lodge, by a resolution, for its action.

SECTION 11. No vote or resolution is valid, if it conflict with the Constitution, Usages, or Regulations, established for the government of the Fraternity ; nor any By-Law or amendment, until approved by the Grand Lodge ; nor can any Section or Article of the By-Laws be suspended for any purpose, except by Dispensation.

SECTION 12. All resolutions shall be submitted in writing, before there shall be any debate upon them ; as shall all motions, if the Master or any member desire it.

SECTION 13. The Master shall be entitled to vote on all questions, and may also give the casting vote, whenever there shall be an equal division.

SECTION 14. No vote shall be reconsidered at the same meeting, by a less number than were present when it passed, provided a return of the number of votes was made and recorded ; nor at a subsequent meeting, unless the words, "*reconsideration of a vote*," be inserted on the notifications for the meeting at which the same is to be acted upon.

SECTION 15. No member shall speak more than twice to the same question, unless in explanation, or the mover in reply, without permission of the Master.

SECTION 16. Every member present shall vote on all questions, unless excused by the Lodge.

SECTION 17. Every member shall stand while speaking, and address himself to the Master ; and no Brother shall interrupt him, unless to address the Master on a point of order, or the Master shall call him to order.

SECTION 18. When a question is under debate, no motion shall be received, except to amend, commit, lay upon the table, or adjourn.

Section 19. A motion to amend, until decided, shall preclude all other amendments of the main question.

Section 20. Any member may call for a division of the question, where a division is admissible.

Section 21. No new motion, which totally changes the subject matter on which the original motion was intended to operate, shall be admitted, under color of amendment, as a substitute for the motion under debate.

Section 22. No member, except one of the majority which decided the question, shall be allowed to move for a reconsideration.

Section 23. After a motion is stated by the Master, it shall be deemed to be in possession of the Lodge, but may be withdrawn by the mover at any time before decision or amendment.

Section 24. There shall be no debate upon any question after it has been put by the Master.

Section 25. All motions and reports may be committed at the pleasure of the Lodge.

Section 26. While the Master is addressing the Lodge, or putting a question, or a Brother is speaking, no member shall entertain any private discourse, nor pass between the speaker and the chair.

SECTION 27.   All communications, petitions, appeals, resolutions, propositions and motions, shall be couched in decent and respectful language, or they shall not be entertained by the Lodge.

ARTICLE XXIII.
AMENDMENT AND REPEAL.

No By-Law of this Lodge shall be amended or repealed, at the meeting at which a repeal or an amendment is proposed, nor until the proposition has been duly considered by a committee ; and all propositions to amend or repeal shall be made and committed at a stated meeting, but shall not be acted upon until a subsequent meeting ; nor then, unless the subject shall have been entered on the notifications for such meeting.   A majority of three-fourths of the members present shall be requisite for the adoption of any amendment or repeal.

ARTICLE XXIV.
REPEALING ARTICLE.

The Constitution and all former By-Laws of this Lodge are hereby repealed.

I HEREBY certify that the foregoing By-Laws were unanimously adopted at a special meeting of COLUMBIAN LODGE, held at Masonic Temple, November 28, 5854. It was also

Voted, That said By-Laws be presented to the M. W. Grand Lodge of the Commonwealth of Massachusetts, for approval.

JOHN McCLELLAN,
SECRETARY.

———

AT the Regular Communication of the Grand Lodge of the Commonwealth of Massachusetts, held at Masonic Temple in Boston, on the 13th of December current, the undersigned were appointed a Committee, with full powers, to examine a code of By-Laws adopted by Columbian Lodge on the 28th of November last, and to approve the same if in their judgment entitled thereto.

The Committee having examined the said By-Laws, and found them conformable to Masonic law and usage, do hereby certify their approval of them.

PAUL DEAN,
EDWARD A. RAYMOND,
SIMON W. ROBINSON,
COMMITTEE.

Boston, December 27, 5854.

HISTORY

OF

COLUMBIAN LODGE,

OF

BOSTON, MASS.

HISTORY.

———❦———

CHAPTER I.

INTRODUCTION.

A desire having been frequently expressed by
many of the present members of Columbian
Lodge for convenient means of information concerning the transactions of their predecessors, first
suggested the preparation of an Historical Account
of the Lodge. To supply this want it was originally contemplated to give little more than the
annals of the Lodge, which might have been
embraced within the limits of a few pages. But,
on the examination of their voluminous records,
covering a period of sixty years, and reciting the
doings of nearly a thousand meetings, it became
obvious that something more than the plan at
first thought of was required to do justice to the
brethren whose labors they evidenced, and convey to Masons of the present day an adequate
conception of the extent and effects of those
labors. It became soon apparent that all the proceedings could not be given, fully and coherently,
without collateral aid from other sources, and that
though the records and files of the Lodge were in
a remarkable degree full and well preserved, something additional was necessary to render the ac-

count complete.   The records of the Grand Lodge were then resorted to, and various publications, Masonic and historical, consulted.   The materials thus obtained, having been connected in their order as to time and character, furnish the work now presented.

Another important reason for compiling and printing the transactions of the Lodge is, that their records and papers, from which mainly they are to be ascertained, are liable momentarily to be destroyed or seriously injured by fire.   Neither the records nor the papers on file are in duplicate; their loss, would, therefore, be irreparable—the means of determining the historical facts of the Lodge would be almost totally annihilated.

Again, the publication is demanded because the proceedings afford material of interest and instruction.   The existence of the Lodge has been in a period of time distinguished for great and important changes in the affairs of men—in nations, in governments, in theologies, in the arts and sciences, the past half century has teemed with change and innovation.   And although the Masonic Order are eminently conservative in their customs, and their principles are immutable, yet in many things they have not escaped the influences surrounding them.   Aside, therefore, from what it is desired to learn of the Masonic career of the Lodge, it will be interesting to trace the effects of such influences.

The Lodge may be regarded as ancient in its origin when the growth of the metropolis and the increase in the number of societies therein, since

5795, are considered. When the Lodge was established, in that year, the population of Boston numbered about 19,000; there were only nineteen churches; the Societies for charitable purposes, exclusive of Masonic, were about seven. The Massachusetts Charitable Mechanic Association was only instituted in 5795, and nearly all the Associations whose titles now fill pages of the Directories of Boston have since been established.

The general plan of the work is to treat, so far as is practicable or convenient, each subject separately. For this purpose it is divided into chapters, each chapter to include one or more subjects. Such an arrangement will tend to secure clearness and prevent confusion, and will enable the reader to refer readily to any particular transaction treated. It is designed also to let the record speak for itself whenever it can do so without extending the work beyond reasonable limits. A mere transcript or publication of the records is not intended; still, in some considerable degree, this may be advisable.

Several of the proceedings of the Grand Lodge are given at length. The account of ceremonies by this body on occasions interesting to the fraternity generally have been introduced. At first, this may seem to be foreign to a work of this kind; having for its main purpose a description of a particular subordinate Lodge; but it will be remembered that each Lodge within the jurisdiction of the Grand Lodge is a constituent part of the latter, participating in its proceedings, by its officers or other representatives, on all occasions.

For convenient reference, a catalogue of the higher officers of the Grand Lodge is appended to the historical account. It may be useful in determining who filled these offices at any time on occasions therein alluded to. And for a similar purpose as well as for others that are obvious, a list of the members and initiates of Columbian Lodge, prepared with care and labor by the Secretary of the Lodge, is also appended.

———o o———

CHAPTER II.

ORIGIN OF THE LODGE.

The incipient measures which resulted in the establishment of Columbian Lodge, originated in the "Columbian Society of Master Masons;" a committee of its members having been charged with the duty of procuring a charter for the Lodge from the Grand Lodge. What were the precise objects of this Society, who composed it, when it was instituted, and when it ceased to exist? Are questions that the most careful investigation will probably fail satisfactorily to answer. That its character was Masonic, its title, its instrumentality in obtaining the charter for the Lodge, its participation, in Masonic order, in the funeral ceremonies of a deceased member of the Lodge, would seem clearly to substantiate. It could not have been formed for the sole purpose of aiding in the establishment of the Lodge, as it preserved its identity, as a distinct organization, during several years after the Lodge had been in operation, and as late as November, 5802, when its financial relations with the Lodge were, only then, terminated. It may be reasonably supposed, that the design of the Society was to advance the interests and welfare of the Craft, and especially that sociability and good fellowship among them, which the sodality-meetings of the fraternity at the present time tend so effectually to promote. The President of the Society, in 5795, was John H. Meckell, who appears to have been an active Mason, and an unsuccessful petitioner to the Grand Lodge for a charter to erect a Lodge. The application to the Grand Lodge for a Dispensation to hold a Lodge, to be called Columbian Lodge, was made by " Joseph Churchill, and others." The petition was, probably, also signed by the original members of the Lodge, whose names, with Brother Churchill's, are embraced in the Dirpensation.

The following extracts from the records of the Grand Lodge, will afford a view of what took place between the parent institution and the petitioners previous to the granting of the Dispensation. At a meeting held at Concert Hall, December 12, 5794, M. W. John Cutler, G. Master:

"A Petition from Joseph Churchill and others praying for a dispensation for holding a Lodge, under the style and title of Columbian Lodge, of Boston, was read,—whereupon *Voted*, that the petitioners have leave to withdraw their petition. And that the Grand Lodge adhere to their vote of last Monday evening, and that the Grand Secretary inform them of the passing of the vote."

This vote had reference to the petition of Alexander Peters and others, praying the Grand Lodge to grant them a charter to assemble as a regular Lodge of Masons, in Boston, by the name of Melchizedeck. The vote is as follows:

"That the petitioners have leave to withdraw their petition—and that it is the sense of this Grand Lodge that the number of Lodges already constituted, in Boston, renders it inexpedient at present to increase the Lodges, by granting any new charters of erection."

Again, at a meeting of the Grand Lodge, held March 9th, 5795:

"A letter from Joseph Churchill and others was read, whereupon *Voted*, That a committee be appointed to confer with them respecting their petition: Brothers Donnison, Little and Windship were chosen for that purpose."

At a subsequent meeting of the Grand Lodge, M. W. Paul Revere, G. Master:

"The Committe appointed to confer with Joseph Churchill and others, reported: that they had attended to that service; had heard the petitioners and agreed to the following Report, viz: that a Dispensation be granted them to hold a regular Lodge in the Town of Boston, under such regulations and restrictions as the Grand Lodge shall see fit, for the term of twelve months, which report was accepted."

It is gratifying to observe that the rejection of the petition by the Grand Lodge rested upon no distrust of the character or motives of the petitioners, but was the consequence of a rule, previously adopted, that a sufficient number of Lodges already existed in Boston to accommodate the brethren then residing there. And it may be inferred that the consideration of their high qualifications as masons and standing as citizens, induced the Grand Lodge to suspend the regulation in their favor in order to secure the erection of a Lodge, the character of whose members afforded a pledge that it would become an ornament to the Order, and a faithful exponent of masonic principles.

———

CHAPTER III.

DISPENSATION AND CHARTER.

It has been shown in the preceding chapter, that the Grand Lodge, at their Quarterly Communication of June, 8th, 5795, granted a Dispensation to Columbian Lodge for the term of twelve months. This Dispensation, which the Lodge still possess in good preservation, declares that the "precedence" commences from June 9th, 5795. The precedence should have been given from the date when the Dispensation was granted, and the Grand Lodge seem so to have viewed it ; for in a list giving the rank assigned to the several Lodges within the jurisdiction, and recorded by the Grand Lodge, September 10, 5804, precedence is given to Columbian Lodge from June 8th, 5795. So slight a difference in the date merits notice only from the fact that it appears to have caused the brethren a little uneasiness some months later.

The first meeting, June 22d, 5795, is termed in the records "the first meeting of the Lodge by Charter." The Dispensation, corresponding almost word for word with the charter, might be regarded by one not acquainted with the nature of the two instruments, as one and the same thing. The Secretary who made the record, it may be presumed, was unaware that the former document limits the time in which it empowers a Lodge to work, while the latter does not, and hence arose his mistake.

The Lodge, at their first meeting, conferred distinguished favors upon Bros. Nicholas Kindness and John Coles, "on account of their exertions in obtaining the Charter of this Lodge." At the meeting of July 2d, 5795, a further recognition of acceptable services of the same kind was made in these words:

"The Committee of Ways and Means for obtaining a Charter, (which was appointed by the Columbian Society,) reported that a Charter had been obtained, which the Secretary, by order of the Master, read.

Voted, To accept the report ; and tender the thanks of the Lodge to the Committee."

The ravages of time are so rapidly destroying the documentary relics remaining in possession of the Lodge and belonging to their history, that their transcription into this work so far as its plan will allow, will be warranted. For this reason, the Dispensation, the earliest legal paper received from the Grand Lodge, is here introduced. The original is now protected with glass, and secured in a frame, and will be preserved for generations to come, should no serious accident occur to it. It is entire, excepting that the lower margin has been worn off. On this margin should have been the names of Isaiah Thomas and Richard Salter, Grand Wardens, and Daniel Oliver, Grand Secretary.

𝕿𝖔 𝖆𝖑𝖑 𝖙𝖍𝖊 𝕱𝖗𝖆𝖙𝖊𝖗𝖓𝖎𝖙𝖞 𝕿𝖔 𝖜𝖍𝖔𝖒 𝖙𝖍𝖊𝖘𝖊 𝕻𝖗𝖊𝖘𝖊𝖓𝖙𝖘 𝖘𝖍𝖆𝖑𝖑 𝖈𝖔𝖒𝖊:

[SEAL.]

PAUL REVERE, *Grand Master.*
W. SCOLLAY, *Dep. Grand Master.*

The GRAND LODGE of the Most Ancient and Honorable Society of FREE and ACCEPTED MASONS for the Commonwealth of MASSACHUSETTS, sends Greeting:

WHEREAS a Petition has been presented to us by Joseph Churchill, James Eaton, John Rittenhouse, Joshua Hardy, Nicholas Kindnes, Snelling Powell, Henry Wickham, Thomas Tannatt, T. McCoristine, Thomas Leatham, Henry Lord, John Perkins, John Pingree, John Coles, James L. Comings, Samuel Hayden, and James Dodge, all Ancient, Free and Accepted Masons, praying that they, with such others, as shall hereafter join them, may be erected and constituted a regular Lodge of Free and Accepted Masons—which Petition appearing to us as tending to the advancement of Masonry and the good of the Craft:

𝕶𝖓𝖔𝖜 𝖞𝖊 therefore, That We, the Grand Lodge aforesaid, reposing special trust and confidence in the prudence and fidelity of our beloved Brethren above-named, have constituted and appointed, and by these Presents, do constitute and appoint them the said Joseph Churchill, James Eaton, John Rittenhouse, Joshua Hardy, Nicholas Kindness, Snelling Powell, Henry Wickham, Thomas Tannatt, T. McCoristine, Thomas Leatham, Henry Lord, John Perkins, John Pingree, John Coles, James L. Comings, Samuel Hayden, and James Dodge, a regular Lodge of Free and Accepted Masons, under the Title and Designation of COLUMBIAN LODGE, hereby giving and granting unto them and their Successors, full Power and Authority to convene as Masons, within the Town of BOSTON. in the County of SUFFOLK, and Commonwealth aforesaid—to receive and enter Apprentices, pass Fellow-Crafts, and raise Master-Masons, upon the payment of such moderate compensations for the same as may be determined by the said Lodge ; also to make choice of a Master, Wardens, and other Office-Bearers, annually or otherwise, as they shall see cause ; to receive and collect Funds for the relief of poor and distressed Brethren, their Widows or Children, and in general to transact all Matters relating to Masonry, which may to them appear to be for the good of the Craft, according to the ancient usages and customs of Masons, for the term of one year.

And We do hereby require the said constituted Brethren, to attend the Grand Lodge at their Quarterly Communications, and other Meetings, by their Master and Wardens, or by Proxies regularly appointed ; also to keep a fair and regular Record of all their Proceedings, and to lay them before the Grand Lodge when required.

And we do enjoin upon our Brethren of the said Lodge, that they be punctual in the quarterly payment of such sums as may be assessed for the support of the Grand Lodge—that they behave themselves respectfully and obediently to their Superiors in Office, and in all other respects conduct themselves as good Masons.

And we do hereby declare the precedence of the said Lodge, in the Grand Lodge and elsewhere, to commence from the ninth day of June, Five thousand seven hundred and ninety-five.

In Testimony whereof, WE, THE GRAND MASTER and GRAND WARDENS, by virtue of the Power and Authority to us committed, have hereunto set our Hands, and caused the Seal of the GRAND LODGE to be affixed, at BOSTON, this sixteenth Day of June, Anno Domini 1795, and of Masonry, five thousand seven hundred and ninety-five.

At the Quarterly Communication of the Grand Lodge, held March 14, 5796, it is recorded :

" On motion, it was voted,—upon further consideration of the petition of the officers and members of Columbian Lodge,— That a Charter of Incorporation be granted at large, and to take date from the 8th of June, 5796, to the Columbian Lodge."

At a meeting of Columbian Lodge, March 22,
5796 :

" " The R. Worshipful Master informed the Lodge that a full
Charter was granted them by the M. W. G. Lodge."

At the meeting of August 9, 5796 :

" The Charter was presented by Bro. Perkins, not signed
by the Grand Master, and after some debate, *Voted*, That
these matters do subside."

At the meeting of August 3, 5797 :

" A motion was made and seconded that the Charter be
read—passed in the affirmative—was accordingly read by
Secretary."

" A motion was also made and seconded that the Secretary
be directed to bring forward, at the next meeting of the
Lodge, the Dispensation from which the Charter has been
copied, that the same may be compared."

Again, August 10, 5797, it is recorded :

" The following members were also unanimously chosen as
a Committee to examine and compare the Charter with the
Dispensation, viz : Bros. Gouldsbury, Dodge and Coles."

Again, September 7, 5797 :

" The committee appointed to examine and compare the
Charter, as having been copied from the Dispensation, made
the following report, viz : That having attended to that
service, they find the Charter to be a true copy of the Dispensation, except a trifling difference in the date, which, on
motion, was unanimously voted to remain."

The curious can, by a comparison of the two
documents, determine for themselves what the
discrepancy was which exercised the criticism of

the primitive brethren of the Lodge, and which did not permit them to be satisfied with the charter for more than a year after it came into their possession.

----⸲⸲----

CHAPTER IV.

PLACES OF MEETINGS.

CONCERT HALL—GREEN DRAGON TAVERN—AT A MEMBER'S HOUSE—IN MARKET SQUARE—IN ANN STREET.

CONCERT HALL.—Meetings of the Lodge were held in Concert Hall, from June 22, 5795, to May 5, 5796, with five exceptions, i. e., that of November 10, 5795, at Green Dragon Tavern, and those of December 5, 5795, March 22 and 27, and April 12, 5796, which were held at the house of Bro. John Perkins, in Ann Street. At his house degrees were conferred, and the usual business of the Order transacted.

From its erection until 5807, Concert Hall was the regular place of meeting of one or more of the Masonic bodies of Boston. This fact, as well as that of its having been the scene of the earlier days of Columbian Lodge, will render a description of it interesting, if not to the present generation, at least to our successors. The requirements of a rapidly growing metropolis are fast obliterating the monuments of the past, and the day may be near when this ancient edifice will be known only in history. Its location, on the corner of

Court and Hanover Streets, was, sixty years ago, nearly in the centre of the inhabited part of Boston, and was, consequently, most convenient for the purposes for which it was employed. It was described, in 5817, as follows:

" It is a large, handsome building, at the head of Hanover Street. It was erected in the year 1756, by Mr. Stephen Deblois, a musician, for the purpose of concerts, dancing and other entertainments. A few years since the building was enlarged and improved, at a great expense, by Mr. Amory, the proprietor. The front hall is about sixty feet by thirty, in the second story, and is justly admired for its correct proportions and the richness of its architecture, It is highly finished in the Corinthian style, with an orchestra, and the walls are ornamented with superb mirrors. In the rear is another hall, on the same story, finished in a plainer style, and well calculated for public entertainments and large parties."

The statement, in this account, that this Hall was erected in 5756 is erroneous; for, after the installation of the Right Worshipful Jeremy Gridley as Grand Master of Masons in North America, October 1, 5755, and after divine service on that occasion, "the Brotherhood returned to Concert Hall, and celebrated the day in harmony and joy." Its completion, in 1756, was probably what the writer should have recounted.

" The Saint John's Grand Lodge " held their communications here from 5755 until the union of the Grand Lodges in 5792; and from this year until 5807, " The Grand Lodge of Massachusetts " also assembled here. In 5763, " The Saint John's Grand Lodge " contemplated purchasing the Hall.

"An opportunity offering for the purchase of Concert Hall, it was judged that the possession of it would contribute to the 'honor, convenience and benefit of the Society;' accordingly a special meeting was called, October 28, 5763, at which the Brethren unanimously voted to purchase it at the rate at which it was offered, £1,200, and to open immediately a subscription for the purpose. But, notwithstanding the agreement made with its possessor, it was sold the next day, to their great disappointment."

GREEN DRAGON TAVERN.—The Green Dragon Tavern, where Columbian Lodge met, November 10, 5795, was demolished many years since, to give place to other structures. It stood at the corner of Hanover and Union Streets, on the north side of the former street. It was the property of Saint Andrew's Lodge, of Boston, and was occupied by them, for Masonic purposes, until its demolition. Tradition attributes to this Tavern the fame of its having been the place of important meetings in Revolutionary times.

It is evident that Columbian Lodge did not view Concert Hall as their permanent home, for as early as November 16, 5795, they adopted the following vote:

"*Voted*, That the R. W. Master, with Bro. Eaton and Bro. Perkins, be a Committee to procure rooms for the use of the Lodge, and report next Lodge night."

The committee reported progress from time to time, until April 12, 5796, when they appear to have completed the business for which they were appointed.

"The Committee on Rooms reported, as per file, which was accepted, and a committee chosen to make the contract and prepare the rooms for the reception of the Lodge as soon as may be. Bros. Churchill, Folsom and Coles were the committee."

COLUMBIAN HALL, MARKET SQUARE.—This Hall was occupied by the Lodge, from May 5, 5796, to June 23, 5800. It was in a building opposite the north side of Faneuil Hall, and which was taken down at about the time the great improvements were made in 5825 and 5826, which resulted in the removal of the market shed between it and Faneuil Hall, the filling up of the dock, and the opening of what is now North Market Street. A portion of this building was used at one time, probably in 5807 and previous, for a museum.

The committee appointed to make the contract performed their duty with exemplary dispatch, for, on the day following that of their appointment, April 13, 5796, the following lease was executed:

Be it known, that I, Bradstreet Story, merchant, of Boston, do bargain and agree to lease to the Society of Free Masons, called the Columbian Lodge, the upper chamber of the building improved by me, situated in Market Square, for the term of five years, upon the following condition: That the said Society do pay me, B. Story, one hundred dollars per annum, in quarterly payments; provided, should any complaint be made by an occupant of any part of said building, that the improvement of said upper chamber by the said Columbian Lodge, is dangerous or injurious in any respect, the complaint shall be referred to five persons, whose decision shall be final and conclusive. The five persons shall be chosen in the following manner, viz: two shall be chosen by the Society, two by the complainant, and the remaining one by me; provided, I am not the complainant, otherwise by the four first chosen. Should their decision be in favor of the complainant, it shall be at my option to make null and void the above lease.

The expense of plastering and making shutters to said chamber, and of making a door and closet in the entryway, and papering and painting the said room, to be deducted from the first year's rent.

The within instrument signed and sealed interchangeably this thirteenth day of April, in the year of our Lord one thousand seven hundred and ninety-six.

BRADSTREET STORY.

Witness : WM. STORY, JR.

At the meeting held at Concert Hall, May 5, 5796, after transacting a variety of business, the following vote was adopted :

"*Voted*, To adjourn the Lodge forthwith to our new Hall, in Market Square, and the visiting Brethren were requested, from the chair, to assist on the occasion, report having been made that said Hall was ready."

And, again, at the same meeting, it is recorded :

"The R. W. Master then appointed Bro. Powell, Marshal for the night, who accepted the office, and the procession was formed in regular order and form. Thus the Lodge moved forward in solemn pace, with all the apparatus, (tapers being lit,) to the Columbian Hall, in Market Square, where the Lodge was closed, after voting a request that the R. W. Master be pleased, at the next monthly meeting, to pronounce a discourse adapted to the consecration of the new Hall."

At the meeting of May 12, 5796, a Committee to take charge of the Hall were appointed.

"*Voted*, That the R. W. Master, Bros. Perkins, Folsom, Rittenhouse and Somes, are chosen a Standing Committee, to take all care of Columbian Hall, and dispose of it as they may think to the best advantage of the Lodge, until the next choice of officers."

This committee promptly and faithfully attended to the duty assigned to them. Their proceedings are recorded, at length, in one of the books of the Lodge, and are introduced here to show the means employed by the fathers of the Lodge to economically support their new hall, and at the same time devote it exclusively to Masonic purposes. The proceedings of the committee will also testify to what has already been averred in relation to the Columbian Society, that it was a Masonic body, having its own distinct organization.

" At a meeting of the Committee appointed to dispose of the Hall, on Saturday evening, May 12, 5796, *Voted*, This Committee have unanimously agreed to let the Hall, on such times as the Lodge do not meet, to any Lodge or Society of Masons, when applied for, and the terms are suitable."

" *Voted*, That Bros. Folsom and Perkins be chosen as a sub-committee to expedite the finishing of the Hall."

" *Voted* Also, that Bro. Jno. Coles is appointed Superintendent of the Hall and the property of the Lodge, and that he be paid therefor one dollar per month from the Treasury."

" *Voted*, To recommend to the Lodge to pass a vote that the Hall shall be locked up in half an hour after the Lodge is closed, and this vote to be recorded as a by-law from and after its being passed."

" At a meeting of the above Committee, May 23, 5796, to confer with a Committee from the Columbian Society, (appointed to inquire on the terms that the use of the Hall might be obtained,) Resolved, That agreeably to the power voted to said Lodge Committee by said Lodge, they are ready to let or re-lease the use of said Hall to the Columbian Society of Master Masons, at such times as the Lodge do not meet, on the following terms, viz:
The use of the Hall, together with common apparatus, also candles and firewood, free of any expense, and that good wine shall be provided to said Society at only one dollar per bottle, and punch in proportion, and the said contract to be binding on each party for one year. These terms were accepted by the Columbian Society's Committee, who agreed to make report to the said Society of their doings."

In the early days of our Institution, the Brethren, besides practicing charity, relieving the distressed, and studying into the mysteries of our
art, also, occasionally availed themselves of the
opportunities which their meetings afforded, to
promote social and friendly intercourse, and cultivate personal and intimate acquaintance with each
other; and, when labor was suspended, they consequently engaged in innocent festivity and cheerful, familiar conversation. They did not deem it
derogatory to their character, as men and Masons,
wisely and temperately to indulge in the pleasure
given by a generous glass of wine or a cheering
goblet of punch. Indeed, at this time it was the
universal custom, on all occasions, festive or grave,
when men were brought together, for them to
partake of either the juice of the fruit of the vine,
or of some other exhilarating beverage. At funerals, even, as well as at the marriage feast, it
would have been regarded as an incivility not to
have presented something of the kind to the assembled friends. The provision which our brethren proposed to make for the Society was, therefore, in conformity to a custom that then universally prevailed.

On the evening of June 2d, 5796, Columbian
Hall was consecrated; and agreeably to previous
arrangement, the Master, Bro. Joseph Churchill,
delivered an address and charge, when the Lodge
voted as follows:

" On motion, a Committee was chosen to wait on the R.
W. Master and return him the thanks of the Lodge for his
kind address and charge now delivered, and to request a Copy
for the use of the Lodge : the said Committee were Bros. Folsom, Coles, Perkins, Gouldsbury and Hayden."

The committee reported July 7, 5796 :

"The committee appointed to return the thanks of the
Lodge to the W. Master (Bro. Churchill) for his Masonic
charge delivered at consecrating Columbian Hall, Reported,
that they had attended to that duty, and had also requested
a Copy for the use of the Lodge ; which the W. Master was
pleased to say he would comply with, and deliver a Copy.
The above report was accepted."

The record for the special meeting of February
12, 5797, reads as follows :

" The Secretary then presented the Charge of the Right
Worshipful Master on behalf of the Committee who were
appointed to procure the same."

" On a Motion that a Subscription be opened in the Lodge
and if a sufficient number of Subscribers appears to defray the
Expenses of the same, to be printed. Passed in the affirmative."

Neither the manuscript nor a printed copy of
this address is in the archives of the Lodge ; and
it is doubtful whether it is now extant in any
form. It having been delivered by the first Master, and in the first year of the Lodge, would give
to it peculiar interest aside from any intrinsic
merit which it might have possessed, or any value
it might have had on account of the occasion it
celebrated. It is reasonable to suppose that it was
not printed ; because no further reference to it is
made in the records than what is contained in the
foregoing extracts. The early files of the Lodge
being far from perfect, it may be hoped that the
address as well as other important papers will yet
be found. This hope is based upon the proba-
bility that documents belonging to the Lodge will
be discovered among the private papers of some

6

one, of the many officers who from time to time have had the custody of them.

At the stated meeting held March 6, 5800, the following vote was adopted :

" *Voted*, That Bros. Folsom, A. Stetson, Baxter, Churchill and Pons be a Committee to procure a more eligible place for the meetings of Columbian Lodge during the Summer Months."

At a special meeting, March 15, 5800, it is recorded :

" The Committee appointed for procuring a more eligible situation for the meetings of Columbian Lodge, reported, that proposals being made by Messrs. Stetson & Thayer to accommodate the Lodge with a Hall in their store, they unanimously accepted the proposal, and the matter, being laid before the Lodge, it was universally approved of, and Bros. Folsom, Churchill, Baxter, S. Stetson and Pons, were appointed a Committee to make the Contract with Messrs. Stetson & Thayer for the above mentioned purpose."

The following vote was passed May 1, 5800. The hall is here termed Columbian Hall, but the records, generally, give it the name of Masons' Hall :

" *Voted*, That the Worshipful Master, Bros. Baxter, Hayden, Tower, Churchill, Eunson, and Sam. Stetson be a Committee to superintend the completion of Columbian Hall, so far as it respects papering and painting."

Again it is recorded, June 5, 5800 :

" *Voted*, That Columbian Lodge on St. John's day dedicate Columbian Hall, and invite the Grand Lodge to attend, and that Bros. Churchill, Jenks, S. Stetson, Rittenhouse and Folsom be a Committee for the purpose."

MASONS' HALL, *Ann Street.*—The first term that this Hall was occupied by the Lodge ex-

tended from June 23, 5800, to August 5, 5817.
On the evening of June 23, 5800, the Lodge met,
but transacted no other business than that of removing the records, emblems and other Masonic
property to the new Hall.

" The Lodge met at the new Hall, then adjourned to the
old Hall, the Right Worshipful Master in the Chair. The
Lodge was then opened, when the Ark and Paraphernalia
were removed to the new Hall in Masonic order, Bro. Purkitt
being Marshal."

Masons' Hall was immediately in the rear of
Columbian Hall, and fronted on Ann street. The
building now stands, it being the third from Union
street. The arched windows of its fourth story
may serve to designate the temple where our
fathers in Masonry assembled for many years.
The hall is now used as a mechanic's workshop,
and is in its last stages of existence. Still, its
proportions, form, ceiling, and the remains of
decorations, denote that it was once beautiful.
Its arched ceiling, with its centre stucco ornaments radiating from the point from which " the
chandelier" was suspended, its handsome and
elaborately worked cornices, its symmetrical form,
can yet be seen to some extent; not, indeed, as
in former times, in their freshness and elegance,
but blackened, broken and neglected.

The following is from the records:

" At a special meeting of Columbian Lodge, June 24, 5800,
for the purpose of dedicating Masons' Hall, Bro. John Murray made a prayer adapted to the subject, and Rev. Brother
Harris delivered an address pertinent to the occasion."

The following are the address and the invocation:

ADDRESS.

DELIVERED AT THE REQUEST OF THE OFFICERS AND MEMBERS OF COLUMBIAN LODGE, ON THE DEDICATION OF THEIR NEW HALL, JUNE 24, 1800.

Brethren : The ceremonies we are about to perform are not unmeaning rites, nor the amusing pageants of an idle hour, but have a solemn and instructive import. Suffer me to point it out to you, and to prepare your minds for those important sentiments they are so well adapted to convey.

This Hall, designed and built by *wisdom*, supported by strength, and adorned in *beauty*, we are first to consecrate IN THE NAME OF THE GREAT JEHOVAH,* which teaches us in all our works, begun and finished, to acknowledge, adore and magnify Him. It reminds us, also, in His fear to enter the door of the Lodge, to put our trust in Him while passing its trials, and to hope in Him for the reward of its labors.

Let, then, its altar be devoted to His service, and its lofty arch resound with His praise! May THE EYE WHICH SEETH IN SECRET witness here the sincere and unaffected *piety* which withdraws from the engagements of the world to silence and privacy, that it may be exercised with less interruption and less ostentation.

Our march round the Lodge reminds us of the travels of human life, in which Masonry is an enlightened, a safe and a pleasant path. Its *tassalated pavement of Mosaic work* intimates to us the checkered diversity and uncertainty of human affairs. Our step is time ; our progression, eternity.

Following our ancient constitutions, with mystic rites, we *dedicate* this Hall TO THE HONOR OF MASONRY.

Our best attachments are due to the craft. In its prosperity we find our joy ; and, in paying it honor, we honor ourselves. But its worth transcends our encomiums, and its glory will out-sound our praise.

Brethren, it is our pride that we have our names on the records of Masonry ; may it be our high ambition that they should shed a lustre on the immortal page !

The Hall is also to be *dedicated* TO VIRTUE.

This worthy appropriation will always be duly regarded while the *moral duties* which our sublime lectures inculcate with affecting and impressive pertinency, are cherished in our hearts and illustrated in our lives.

---

* See the ceremony of dedication, in the Book of Constitutions.

As Free Masonry aims to enliven the spirit of philanthropy and promote the cause of charity, so we *dedicate* this Hall to UNIVERSAL BENEVOLENCE, in the assurance that every brother will dedicate his affections and his abilities to the same generous purpose; that while he displays a warm and cordial affection to those who are of the Fraternity, he will extend his benevolent regards and good wishes to the whole family of mankind.

Such, my brethren, is the significant meaning of the solemn rites we are now to perform, because such are the peculiar duties of every Lodge. I need not enlarge upon them now, nor show how they diverge, as rays from a centre, to enlighten, to improve, and to cheer the whole circle of life. Their import and their application is familiar to you all. In their knowledge and their exercise may you fulfil the high purposes of the Masonic Institution!

How many pleasing considerations, my brethren, attend the present interview. Whilst in almost every other part of the world political animosities, contentions and wars interrupt the progress of humanity and the cause of benevolence, it is our distinguished privilege, in this happy region of liberty and peace, to engage in the plans and to perfect the designs of individual and social happiness. Whilst in other nations our Order is viewed by politicians with suspicion, and by the ignorant with apprehension, in this country its members are too much respected and its principles too well known, to make it the object of jealousy or mistrust. Our private assemblies are unmolested, and our public celebrations attract a more general approbation of the Fraternity. Indeed, its importance, its credit, and we trust its usefulness, are advancing to a height unknown in any former age. The present occasion gives fresh evidence of the increasing affection of its friends; and this noble apartment, fitted up in a style of elegance and convenience which far exceed any we have among us, does honor to Masonry, as well as the highest credit to the respectable Lodge for whose accommodation and at whose expense it is erected.

We offer our best congratulations to the *Worshipful* MASTER, WARDENS, OFFICERS and MEMBERS of the Columbian Lodge. We commend their zeal, and hope it will meet with the most ample recompense. May their Hall be the happy resort of PIETY, VIRTUE and BENEVOLENCE! May it be protected from accident, and long remain a monument of their attachment to

Masonry! May their Lodge continue to flourish, their union
to strengthen, and their happiness to abound! And when
they, and we all, shall be removed from the labors of the
earthly lodge, may we be admitted to the brotherhood of the
perfect, in the building of God, the hall not made with hands,
eternal in the heavens!

INVOCATION.

SUPREME ARCHITECT of all worlds! vouchsafe to
accept the solemn *dedication of this Hall*, TO THE GLORY OF
THY HOLY NAME! Make its walls salvation, and its arch
praise! May the brethren who shall here assemble meet in
unity, work in love, and part in harmony! May *Fidelity*
keep the door, *Faith* prompt the duties, *Hope* animate the
labors, and *Charity* diffuse the blessings of the Lodge! May
wisdom and virtue distinguish the Fraternity, and Masonry
become glorious in all the earth!

So mote it be!

AMEN!

Rev. John Murray was the first pastor of the
first Universalist Society in Boston, over which
he was settled in 5793. He has the reputation of
having been the first preacher in America of the
doctrines peculiar to his sect. He was born in
England, December 10, 5741, and came to this
country in 5770. He served as chaplain in the
American army in the war of the Revolution.
"In the month of May, 1775, the leading officers
of the Rhode Island Brigade, assembled in the
neighborhood of Boston, despatched a respectable
messenger with a letter soliciting the attendance
of the Promulgator as chaplain to their detach-
ment of the Revolutionary Army." Severe sickness did not permit him to remain long in the service, but while in it Gen. Washington honored

him "with marked and uniform attention." As a Mason, Brother Murray was devoted and zealous. He officiated one or more terms as Grand Chaplain of the Grand Lodge of Massachusetts. He died in Boston, Sept. 3, 5815.

Rev. Thaddeus M. Harris, D. D., was born in Charlestown, Mass., July 7, 5768, and graduated at Harvard University 5787. On the 23d of October, 5793, he was ordained over the Congregational Society in Dorchester. He died in Boston, April 3, 5842, in the 74th year of his age, and was buried in the cemetery at Dorchester. In the Eulogy pronounced before the Grand Lodge, by Rev. Bro. Huntoon, to commemorate the virtues of Bro. Harris, it is truthfully said: "His first great Masonic work was the editing of a collation, revision and publication of the 'Constitutions of the Ancient and Honorable Fraternity of Free and Accepted Masons,' a quarto volume, printed at Worcester, Mass., 1792; a work which he accomplished with the accustomed diligence and 'known fidelity' with which he performed every enterprise confided to his care. His various occasional addresses, while Grand Chaplain of the Grand Lodge, Masonic defences, and his volume of 'Masonic Discourses,' published in 1801, constitute a large part and valuable portion of the Masonic classic literature of America." Bro. Harris was Deputy Grand Master in 5812, and Corresponding Grand Secretary during eleven years.

The occupation of Masons' Hall by other Masonic bodies besides Columbian Lodge, must have

occurred not long after it came into the possession
of the latter institution.　The precise time when
the joint occupancy took place it is difficult to
determine.　The Royal Arch Chapter, Massachusetts and Mount Lebanon Lodges, were the first to
meet here.　The Grand Lodge held its first communication here in 5807.　Saint Andrew's Lodge
met at the Green Dragon Tavern, and Saint John's
Lodge at Concert Hall ; and it may be questioned
whether they held their meetings in this hall at
any time during the first term in which it was
used for Masonic purposes.

The further action of the Lodge in reference to
their places of meeting will be observed in the following transcript from their records :

October 2, 5800.　" Bros. S. Stetson, Churchill, and A.
Stetson, were appointed a special committee to settle with Mr.
Story for the Old Hall."

November 6, 5800.　"The Worshipful Master, Bros. A.
Stetson, Churchill, Baxter and Somes were chosen a Committee to adjust the accounts due from the Lodge to individuals
for services in finishing the Hall, and to settle and complete
the contract with the Proprietors."

December 18, 5800.　" *Voted*, That the business concerning
the Hall be postponed till the next regular night, and that a
committee be appointed to consult the proprietors concerning
the Lease, to consist of the following, viz., W. Master, Bros.
Baxter and Pons."

February 24, 5801.　" *Voted*, That the R. W. Master, Bros.
A. Stetson and Baxter be a committee to arrange the Hall for
the better accommodation of the Grand Lodge."

October 1, 5801.　"A communication being handed the
Worshipful Master from the Grand Lodge respecting the building of a Hall," a committee was appointed "to give in their
opinions on the business before the next regular communication of the Grand Lodge."

March 4, 5801. "The committee appointed in December last to survey and replace the Emblems of Columbian Hall and secure the Chandelier, gave in the following report, viz., That they have furnished new emblems designed on wood and much less liable to accident than those form'd in stucco work. They have also caused the chandelier to be so secured as to remove all apprehensions; all which is submitted,—A. Cutter, J. W. Folsom, S. Jenks, committee."

September 5, 5805. "R. W. Master, R. W. Bro. Stetson and Bro. Crooker were chosen to settle the bill of Bro. Davidson exhibited by him against the Lodge for repairing and cleaning the Lodge and adjacent rooms. *Voted*, That the said committee also determine on a mode of procuring fuel for the ensuing season in conjunction with other Lodges meeting in the same Hall or otherwise as they may judge most expedient. *Voted*, That the treasurer pay Bro. Davidson his charge for procuring the gilding of the candlesticks."

December 5, 5805. "On motion of Bro. Stetson, *Voted*, That a committee be chosen to confer with Mount Lebanon Lodge, and make an adjustment in regard to the furniture and flooring of the Lodge,—R. W. Bro. Baxter, Bro. Bean and R. W. Bro. Stetson were accordingly chosen for that purpose."

July 3, 5806. "It was moved by Bro. Davidson that a committee be raised to inquire the sum paid by Columbian Lodge for the rent of the Hall, and the sum paid by other Lodges who meet in the same Hall and report.—R. W. Bro. Daniel Baxter, W. Bro. Stephen Bean and Bro. Amos Binney were chosen accordingly."

April 2, 5807. "It was moved and seconded that a committee of three, viz., Bros Bean, Baxter and Binney be appointed to meet a Joint Committee from the various Lodges usually meeting in this Hall, to agree upon the proportional part of rent to pay for the same."

August 6, 5807. "A committee to inspect the repairs of the Hall, reported, that one hundred sixty-nine dollars and eleven cents had been expended, which report was accepted. *Voted*, That the thanks of the Lodge be presented to Bro. Sigourney for his attention in superintending the repairs of the Hall."

September 10, 5807. "A committee of three, viz, Bros. Bean, Baxter and Johnson were chosen to settle the last repairs on the Hall."

November 6, 5807. " *Voted*, That a committee of three, viz., Bros. Bean, Phillips and Binney be appointed to meet a committee from Saint John's Lodge, to agree upon terms to admit them to partake of the benefit of Mason's Hall."

November 8, 5807. " *Voted*, That Bro. Baxter be a committee to confer with the officers of the other Lodges who sit in this Hall, to provide a *Ventilator* to ease the Hall of smoke."

September 6, 5810. " *Voted*, To raise a committee to confer with committees from Lodges who meet in this Hall, respecting procuring new canvass for the use of said Lodges ; * * * or otherwise, as shall be thought by said committee most advisable. Bros. Moody, Jenkins and Smith were chosen for the above purpose."

January 17, 5811. " The committee of accounts reported that they had not finished the business of settlement with Bro. Seth Thayer and wished for liberty to sit again :

" *Voted*, That the committee of accounts have liberty to sit again, and that they report at the next regular meeting of the Lodge,—likewise that they be instructed to add one hundred dollars to the sum now in the hands of Brother S. Thayer ; provided he give sufficient security for the whole, and will receive the use thereof as an adequate compensation for the rent of Masons' Hall."

February 7, 5811. " The Committee of Accounts reported that they had received of Bro. Seth Thayer two hundred and forty dollars in cash, and taken his notes for the remainder of the nine hundred dollars in his hands, to-wit : A note of sixty dollars, payable on the first day of March next, with interest; and notes for the payment of one hundred dollars per month, until the whole shall be paid. Said notes are made payable to Bro. Daniel Baxter, Treasurer ; and the said Thayer, as collateral security for the payment of said notes, has assigned to the said Treasurer all the rent which shall become due on a lease of Masons' Hall, given by said Thayer to the St. Andrew's Royal Arch Chapter, Massachusetts, Columbian and Mount Lebanon Lodges, which rent will be three hundred dollars per year ; and said lease runs to the year A. D., 1814.

Voted, That the report of the Committee of Accounts be accepted."

March 7, 5811. " The Standing Committee reported that they, with the committees from the R. A. Chapter, Massachusetts and Mount Lebanon Lodges, had made some repairs upon Masons' Hall, and that the part of the expense to be borne by this Lodge is twenty-six dollars and seventy-one cents. The Treasurer was ordered to pay the same from the funds of the Lodge."

January 6, 5814. " A communication was received from a committee of Massachusetts Lodge, requesting that a committee might be chosen from this Lodge to confer with them and the committees of other Lodges, who at present occupy this Hall, to take into consideration the subject of lessening the expense of rent, after the present lease shall expire, or to procure some other place to meet in.

Voted, That the Standing Committee be requested to attend to that duty."

March 3, 5814. " The Committee on the renewal of the lease of Masons' Hall reported that they had made an agreement to renew the lease for two years, at two hundred dollars per year.

Voted, To accept the report, and the same committee were requested to finish the business."

May 5, 5814. " The Committee on the subject of the renewal of the lease of Masons' Hall, reported that they had signed a lease in behalf of the Lodge."

June 16, 5814. " The Hall undergoing some necessary repairs, the Lodge was adjourned to the first Thursday in September."

September 1, 5814. " Bro. Jenkins moved that a committee of three be appointed to take into consideration the necessity of procuring suitable flooring for the use of the Lodge. Said committee were instructed to confer with a committee of Mount Lebanon Lodge, and to see if they will be at part of the expense, and have them in common for the two Lodges. Bros. Jenkins, Collamore and Chandler, were chosen on the above committee, and they were instructed to report at the next regular meeting. The Standing Committee were authorized to superintend the repairs on the Hall and to settle the bills."

The committee appointed to procure the flooring, obtained that beautiful specimen of art which now adorns the Lodge room. Their report in relation to the flooring and their proceedings in connection with it, will be given in another chapter of this work. The transactions of the Lodge relative to the Hall, are continued as follows:

March 7, 5816. "*Voted*, That Daniel Baxter, Joseph Jenkins, and Benjamin B. Appleton, be a committee to confer with similar committees of the other Lodges in Boston, and the Chapter, on the subject of a convenient and proper place to hold their meetings when the present lease of Masons' Hall expires; and that said committee, on our part, and in conjunction with the other committees aforesaid, be authorized to conclude a bargain on such terms as they shall consider most for the interest and welfare of this Lodge, our sister Lodges, and the craft; and also on the necessity of hanging three curtains before the windows in the west."

March 6, 5817. "The committee, composed of the R. W. Master and Wardens, appointed at a former meeting, to consult with committees from the other Lodges in the town, respecting the procuring of some suitable place for our meetings, reported progress, and obtained full power, in conjunction with the committees from the other Lodges, to hire a place for this purpose."

March 20, 5817. "The committee raised for the purpose of procuring some convenient place for our meetings, informed the Lodge that, in pursuance to their instructions, they had, together with committees from the other Lodges, made an agreement with the proprietors of the Exchange Coffee House, for a Hall and the necessary ante-rooms, that the agreement only wanted the signatures of the parties in union with the committee from St. John's Lodge, to be ratified and duly executed; that the whole would be in readiness for consecration by the Grand Lodge on the 9th of June next. They also suggested the necessity of an extension of the power heretofore delegated, to embrace the views of the General Committee—whereupon it was

Voted, That said committee have full power to sell such of the decorations and fixtures in the old Hall as may not be wanted to complete the furniture of the new one; to apply the proceeds to the furnishing of the new Hall; to attend to the removal of the jewels, furniture and other property of the Lodge from the old Hall and see them properly deposited in the closets and wardrooms of the new one, and to meet and pay our proportion of the general expense of furnishing the new Hall.''

From the preceeding extracts from their records it appears that the regular place of meeting of the Lodge was at Masons' Hall in Ann street, from the time when they left Columbian Hall until they removed to the Exchange Coffee House; and it is remarkable that with one exception only, every meeting during this period was held in Masons' Hall. And on the evening which makes the exception, September 3, 5807, a regular meeting, they first met at their Hall, as will be observed by the following transcript from the record. The Mrs. Marean referred to was, according to the Boston Directory of that time, "Sarah Marean, Tavern Keeper, Elm street."

September 3, 5807. "The Brethren of Columbian Lodge met at Masons' Hall, and adjourned to Mrs. Marean's, where the Lodge opened in due form, R. W. Bro. Bean in the chair."

The first communication of the Grand Lodge held in Masons' Hall was that of December 14, 5807. Previous to this date their meetings were at Concert Hall regularly, until 5806, when several communications took place "at Vila's Hotel, No. 17 Court Street." They occupied Masons' Hall from 5807 up to the period when the Masonic rooms were provided in the Exchange Coffee House. The following are extracts from their records:

September 8, 5806. " On motion, *Voted*, That a committee be appointed to confer with the Masters of the several Lodges in Boston, on the expediency of agreeing with the proprietors of Masons' Hall (Hall of the Museum,) for the use of the Grand Lodge and the other Lodges in Boston, and know on what terms the Hall may be secured for a number of years, and report the next Lodge night.   Committee : R. W. Shubael Bell, Allen Crocker, and Stephen Francis."

December 17, 5810. " On motion, it was *Voted*, That the Committee of Accounts and Finance be empowered to determine what proportion of the expense of repairing and ornamenting Masons' Hall shall be paid by the Grand Lodge."

March 14, 5814. " *Voted*, That a committee of three be appointed and fully empowered to procure a suitable place for the future meetings of the Grand Lodge, and at their expense."

June 14, 5814. " The committee appointed by the Grand Lodge, to whom was referred the subject of providing, at the expense of the G. L., a suitable place wherein to hold their future meetings, have attended to the duty assigned them and ask leave to report—That they have procured of the lessees of Masons' Hall a right for the Grand Lodge to hold meetings therein during the term of the present lease, the Grand Lodge paying the lessees, or their agent, at the rate of thirty dollars per annum therefor."

March 10, 5817. " *Voted*, That a committee of three be nominated from the chair to contract for a place for this Grand Lodge to hold their meetings in in future, and to procure such furniture, in connection with other Lodges, as they shall deem expedient.   The M. W. Grand Master nominated the R. W. Brethren Robert Gould Shaw, Augustus Peabody, and Thomas Brown, who were accepted."

March 10, 5817. " *Voted*, That a committee be appointed, by nomination from the chair, to make arrangements for the consecration of the new Hall, at the next Quarterly Communication.   The M. W. Grand Master nominated the following R. W. Brethren, viz : The R. W. Masters of the Lodges (five in number,) in the town of Boston, together with the Presiding Officer of the Grand Royal Arch Chapter in said town, with the R. W. Shubael Bell—who were accepted by the Grand Lodge."

September 8, 5817. "The committee of the Grand Lodge appointed to procure a proper place for their future meetings, and to confer upon that subject with committees of other institutions, having attended to the duty assigned them, ask leave to report:—That they have procured a suitable place, upon a lease of ten years, in the Exchange Coffee House, upon the terms expressed in the report of the doings of the several committees of conference which accompanies this. All which is respectfully submitted.

AUGUSTUS PEABODY,
Per Order."

Hitherto, as has been seen, the Masonic institutions in Boston have not held their meetings in one hall. Each body has for itself provided its rooms independently of the others, though the conveniences afforded by Masons' Hall attracted thither a majority of them during the ten years previous to 5817. Henceforth, with a brief intermission, all these Masonic bodies will assemble in the same place and occupy the same apartments.

CHAPTER V.

PLACES OF MEETINGS, CONTINUED.

EXCHANGE COFFEE HOUSE — COMMERCIAL COFFEE HOUSE — ANN STREET, SECOND TERM — OLD STATE HOUSE — BOYLSTON HALL — WASHINGTON HALL — MASONIC TEMPLE.

EXCHANGE COFFEE HOUSE.—The meetings of Columbian Lodge, in the Hall provided in this Hotel for Masonic uses, began August 7, 5817, and terminated with their communication of October 1, 5818. The dedication of this Hall by the Grand Lodge occurred Tuesday, July 22, A. L., 5817, according to the following

ORDER OF SERVICES.

The GRAND LODGE will assemble in St. John's Hall—open. The guests will be admitted.

All other Masons will meet in the great Dining Hall.

The GRAND MARSHAL, in Grand Lodge, addresses the GRAND MASTER.

Most Worshipful,

The several Masonic Societies established in this town, being animated with a desire of promoting the honor and interest of the CRAFT, have, at great pains and expense, finished a Masonic Hall, for their convenience and accommodation ; they are now desirous that the same should be examined by the MOST WORSHIPFUL GRAND LODGE ; and if it should meet their approbation, that it should be solemnly dedicated to Masonic purposes, agreeably to ancient form.

The GRAND MASTER directs the GRAND MARSHAL to form a grand procession for the above purpose.

Procession formed by the left, as follows :

ORDER OF PROCESSION.

Tyler of a Blue Lodge.
Two Grand Pursuivants.
Two Stewards of Blue Lodges.
Entered Apprentices.
Fellow Crafts.
Master Masons.
Stewards, with Jewels.
Junior Deacons.
Senior Deacons.
Secretaries.

Treasurers.
Past Wardens.
Junior Wardens.
Senior Wardens.
Past Masters.
Presiding Masters.
Royal Arch Masons.
Knights Templars.
Grand Tyler.
Music.
Two Grand Stewards.
A Past Master bearing a golden vessel containing Corn.
Two P. Masters bearing silver vessels, containing Wine and Oil.
Singers.
Chief Architect.
Committee of Arrangements.
Grand Secretaries.
Grand Treasurer.
A Past Master bearing a Burning Taper.
Grand Steward. { A Past Master bearing Holy Bible, &c. } Grand Steward.
Two Past Masters, each bearing a Burning Taper.
Grand Chaplains and Orator.
Five Orders of Architecture borne by five Past Masters.
District Deputy Grand Masters.
Past Grand Wardens.
Past Deputy Grand Masters.
Past Grand Masters.
Two Past Masters bearing the Globes.
His Excellency and Suite.
Right Worshipful Grand Wardens.
Right Worshipful Deputy Grand Master, with Book of Constitutions.
Most Worshipful Grand Master.
Deacon.   Deacon.
Grand Sword Bearer.

GRAND LODGE, &c., fall in at their proper stations.

At the door of the new Hall the order will be reversed. Grand Lodge enter first, with their guests, and take their seats. All others take their seats. Furniture, &c., deposited on or near the ALTAR.

PRAYER, by Rev. Brother EATON.

ANTHEM, by BRETHREN.

The chief ARCHITECT rises and addresses the GRAND MASTER.

Most Worshipful,

Having been entrusted with the superintendence and management of the workmen employed in the construction of this Hall, and having, according to the best of my ability, accomplished the task assigned me; I now return my thanks for the honor of this appointment, and beg leave to surrender up the implements which have been committed to my care ; humbly hoping that the exertions which have been made on this occasion will be crowned with your approbation and that of the Most Worshipful Grand Lodge.

The GRAND MASTER replies :

Right Worshipful Brother Architect,

The skill and fidelity displayed in the execution of the trust reposed in you, at the commencement of this undertaking, have secured the entire approbation of this Grand Lodge, and they sincerely pray, that this Hall may continue a lasting monument of the taste, spirit and liberality of the Craft.

ORIGINAL ODE,

SUNG BY BROTHER EASTMAN.

Hail to the day, when, assembled in union,
   Springs, at the altar of friendship and truth,
Pledge of our fairest and dearest communion,
   The floweret which blooms in perennial youth ;
     E'er has it flourished fair,
     Sigh'd on by heaven's air,
Nurtur'd by dew drops distill'd from above ;
     Bright o'er its natal bed,
     Beams of gay light shall spread,
Strength'ning the rays of affection and love.

Hail to the Craft, whose light, broadly beaming,
   Streams from the loveliest *star* of the sky ;
O'er sorrows vale ever cheerfully gleaming,
   Guiding to yonder bright temple on high ;

Still may that holy ray,
Type of immortal day,
Light the lone path of the Pilgrim along,
Till the Grand Master's 'hest
Bid all his labours rest,
Attuning his harp to the mystical song.

Long may each Mason be firm in his duty,
  The grand and the useful in harmony join ;
Long in this Temple may wisdom and beauty,
  Stars of the high arch of Masonry shine :
Here may we often meet,
Each brother true to greet,
Time strewing flowers o'er the swift rolling year,
Here may fair union rise,
Here join the good and wise,
Charity, friendship and truth to revere.

Now to creation's Great Builder ascending,
  Loud let the chorus of gratitude swell ;
Here, as before Him, we humbly are bending,
  O ! may He deign in this Temple to dwell ;
Here may the sacred fire
Of Love, to heaven aspire,
Long from this Altar rise the incense of praise,
To the Eternal One,
Our ceaseless shining sun,
Master of *all ;* Holy,—"Ancient of Days !"

DEPUTY GRAND MASTER, addresses the GRAND MASTER.

Most Worshipful,

    The Hall in which we are now assembled, and the plan upon which it is finished, having met your approbation, it is the desire of the fraternity that it should be now dedicated according to ancient form and usage. The GRAND MASTER assents, and directs the GRAND MARSHAL to form procession for DEDICATION, which is done as follows :

Grand Sword Bearer.

A Past Master with a lighted Candle.

A Past Master with Bible, Square and Compasses.
Two Past Masters with each a lighted Candle.
Grand Treasurer and Secretary.
Junior Grand Warden bearing a vessel with Corn.
Senior Grand Warden bearing a vessel with Wine.
Deputy Grand Master bearing a vessel with Oil.
Grand Master.

Grand Deacon.   Grand Deacon.

All other Brethren keep their places.

Music plays a solemn march, while the procession moves once round the Altar, &c. The Junior Grand Warden then presents the vessel of Corn to the GRAND MASTER, who pours it out, pronouncing at the same time, "In the name of the Great Jehovah, to whom be all honor and glory, I do solemnly dedicate this Hall to Masonry." Flourish of Music. A March—Move once round as before. The Senior Grand Warden then presents the vessel of Wine to the GRAND MASTER, who sprinkles it out, at the same time saying, "In the name of Holy St. John, I do solemnly dedicate this Hall to Virtue." Flourish. A March—Move once round as before. The Deputy Grand Master presents the vessel of Oil to the GRAND MASTER, who, in sprinkling it out, says, "In the name of the whole Fraternity, I do solemnly dedicate this Hall to Universal Benevolence." Flourish. A solemn Invocation is made to heaven by the Grand Chaplain. Music plays while the GRAND MASTER, &c., resume their stations.

ODE.

All hail to the morning
That bids us rejoice ;
The Temple's completed,
Exalt high each voice ;
The cape-stone is finish'd,
Our labour is o'er ;
The sound of the gavel
Shall hail us no more.
To the Power Almighty, who ever has guided,
The tribes of old Israel, exalting their fame ;
To Him who hath govern'd our hearts undivided,
Let's send forth our voices to praise his great name.

Companions assemble
On this joyful day,
Th' occasion is glorious,
The key-stone to lay ;
Fulfill'd is the promise,
By the ANCIENT OF DAYS,
To bring forth the cape-stone,
With shouting and praise.
There's no more occasion for level or plumb-line,
For trowel or gavel, for compass or square ;
Our works are completed, the Ark safely seated,
And we shall be greeted as workmen most rare.

ALMIGHTY JEHOVAH,
Descend now, and fill
This Lodge with thy glory,
Our hearts with good will !
Preside at our meetings,
Assist us to find
True pleasure in teaching
Good will to mankind.
Thy wisdom inspired the great institution,
Thy strength shall support it, till nature expire ;
And when the creation shall fall into ruin,
Its beauty shall rise through the midst of the fire !

ORATION by Brother ALEXANDER BLISS.

PRAYER or BENEDICTION.

The Grand Procession proceed to Refreshment Hall.
After dinner the Grand Lodge will be escorted to their Hall
and close—all others will return to the Hall where they
assembled and unclothe.

By order of the Committee of Arrangements.
HENRY FOWLE, *Chairman.*

At the first meeting of Columbian Lodge in
this Hall, August 7, 5817, the Master made an
address appropriate to the occasion, when it was
voted :

"That a committee of three be appointed to wait on R. W. Bro. J. Jenkins and request of him a copy of the appropriate address delivered by him, from the chair, to be transcribed upon the records of the Lodge. This motion was seconded and a vote taken, and a committee raised, viz., J. McGaw, Charles Gray, Samuel Smith to wait upon the R. W. Master for the purpose expressed by said vote."

At the meeting of the Lodge of September 4, 5817, the above named committee reported as follows:

"That they deem it proper to present to the members of the Lodge some of the observations made by our R. W. Brother to your committee when performing the duty assigned them by your resolution, which were, viz.:

'That he considered this circumstance an additional evidence of your esteem. He regretted the many defects which might lessen its claim to your notice owing to the short time employed in writing the address. He assures you the favor and honor he has received are too deeply felt and gratefully cherished ever to be forgotten,—that in this instance, as in many others, he is guided by a sacred regard to your wishes; relying solely on the exercise of that candor which he has frequently experienced from you on similar occasions, and with renewed assurances of gratitude and fraternal affection, he furnishes the copy solicited by your committee.'

J. McGaw,
Samuel Smith,
Charles Gray."

"The foregoing report was accepted and directed to be recorded with the address, which is as follows, viz.:

"*Brethren*—Shall we not hail with pleasure the present era in the history of our Lodge? We have this evening for the first time assembled in this Hall, set apart and fitted up exclusively for the purpose of the Craft, and which has been recently dedicated in solemn form by the Most Worshipful Grand Lodge. We enter it also under circumstances which promise the happiest result. All the Masonic Societies of the metropolis of New England are united in one place for their future meetings, and this is the favored spot; this the centre of a constellation system from which we may hope to derive not only the light of science, but the purer and more heavenly effulgence of Masonic peace—benevolence—charity. Here, as from a living fountain, may streams of love and friendship issue to gladden and invigorate every legitimate plant in the vineyard of Masonry. And here, may every Brother *mark well* his duty, and strive to improve by this event in all that is good, in all that is manly, in all that is calculated to render our society the ante-past of those sacred and delightful convocations to which the immortal soul aspires beyond the grave.

" It were but wise, indeed it is the dictate of human prudence, to take advantage of every important occurrence of our lives for our improvement as individuals ; but when an epoch is presented fraught with so many valuable incentives and having so many favorable prospects as the present,— would it not be criminal indifference to neglect the improvements which it seems irresistably to inculcate ?

"The noble and generous heart will be deeply pierced if the union we have formed is not productive of the happiest consequences. It should serve to irradicate every local prejudice ; it should obliterate every feeling that savors of monopoly, or exclusive rectitude ; and persuade us to espouse one common cause ; to cut off from the narrow moorings of individual interest ; and launch magnanimously and triumphantly with our sister Lodges on the broad ocean of universal benevolence.

" We shall, I doubt not, see our character brightening from the date of this union, and each successive meeting furnish new and honorable evidence that we are not unmindful of our duty, and not ungrateful for our distinguished privileges. To realize these hopes we have much to do. Let us then be on our guard. We must be disinterested and sincere ; our conversation must be open and kind ; our appearance the true index of our hearts ; our prayers, humble, fervent, animated by a confidence that Infinite Justice will grant us the favors we ask. And may that Almighty Being who heareth prayer, have us each and all in His holy keeping, succeed our good intentions and build us up for His glory in one faithful and everlasting Brotherhood. ' So mote it be.' "

At the regular meeting of the Lodge, October 2, 5817, it was recorded as follows :

" A lengthy report from 'The sub-committee chosen by
the General Conference Committee,' on various subjects connected with furnishing the new Masonic Hall, arrangements
made with Lodges, agreements entered into, &c., accompanied
by an abstract account current of monies received and dis-
bursed by their Agent, was read, accepted and ordered to be
placed on file."

It will not be out of place to give here a description of an edifice of such magnificent proportions as to render it one of the most prominent
objects of its time of remark and curiosity. Besides, it has additional claims to the notice of
Masons on account of its having been a point of
pleasing anticipations and sudden disappointment
to the Fraternity. The description is from Snow's
History of Boston.

" THE BOSTON EXCHANGE COFFEE-HOUSE, whose name designates the purposes to which it was appropriated, was the
most capacious building and most extensive establishment of
its kind in the U. S. The early history of this structure is
that of an unsuccessful speculation, which involved individuals in ruin, and seriously injured a large portion of the
community. It cost the projector, and through him the public, upwards of $500,000, and was unfinished when he failed.
In other hands it was completed so far as to be tenantable,
and went into operation in 1808, two years and a half from
the time it was commenced.
" The E. C. H. was an immense pile of building, 7 stories
in height, with a cellar under the whole, and covering 12,753
square feet of ground. Its shape was an irregular square, or
that of an irregular triangle cut off at the acute angle, meas-
uring 132 feet in its broadest front, and only 94 feet on its
narrowest, from which the line of the sides diverged nearly
equally. The base of the building was of hammered granite
and the basement of white marble.
"The front in Congress street was highly ornamented. Six
marble pilasters, of the Ionic order, upon a rustic basement
supported an architrave and cornice of the same ; and the

whole front, which had an arched doorway, was crowned
with a Corinthian pediment. On this side there were 48
superb Venetian windows. There was another entrance towards State street, through an Ionic porch or vestibule, and
this front was ornamented with ten Ionic pilasters, and lighted by 58 windows. There was also an entrance, for the
lodgers in the hotel, on Salter's court, having a passage for
the ingress and egress of carriages. From this door there
was a circular stair-case, elegantly decorated, which led
without interruption to the attic story. There was also a
communication from Devonshire street, through an adjoining
house.

" Upon entering the house, you stood on an interior area 70
feet in length and 40 ft. wide, in the form of a parallelogram,
which was lighted from the top by means of a magnificent
dome, 100 ft. 10 inches in diameter. Around this area was
extended a portico, or rather several porticos, each consisting
of 20 columns, which reached from the ground floor to the
roof, and supported five galleries leading to the different
apartments. The height of the top of the dome from the
floor was 83 feet. Here was an assemblage of the different
orders of architecture, from the ornamental Doric to the
Corinthian, which produced a very agreeable impression upon
the eyes of the spectator, as he passed from the dome which
surmounted the whole, to the floor upon which he stood. The
interior space was as nearly as possible equi-distant from the
sides of the structure ; and the apartments, which surrounded
it upon the various stories, amounted to about 210.

" The house was divided into two species of rooms ; those
which belonged to the hotel, and those which were rented for
offices and shops to individuals. The basement story con-
sisted chiefly of an extensive kitchen, private lodging rooms,
larder, and the cellars, with some offices that were entered
from the street. The principal floor was originally intended
for a public Exchange, which design never was executed, as
the merchants, from long habit, prefer to stand in the street,
even during the inclement winter months. A public reading room, with a very large list of subscribers, was also upon
this floor, where the lodgers in the hotel had the privilege of
resorting, and in which was regularly kept a journal of the
most interesting occurrences of the times, whether of a political or commercial nature. A convenient Coffee room, a Bar

and withdrawing-room for boarders, were also on this floor ; besides various apartments occupied by public incorporations and private individuals. On the second floor chiefly devoted to the hotel, upon the southern side, there was a dining room sufficiently spacious to admit tables for three hundred persons ; about fourteen other apartments comprised the whole of the second story.

" The third and fourth floors belonged to the tavern. An arched ball-room, finished with great taste in the Corinthian order of architecture, extended through both stories, and was placed immediately over the large dining hall. The other apartments on these floors were either connected with the ball room, or were lodging chambers.

"Upon the northern side of the fifth and sixth floors, a large Masonic Hall was formed from a large number of lodging rooms, which were included in the apartments which we have just enumerated. The other rooms were appropriated for lodging chambers, with the exception of an observatory on the sixth floor, connected with the news room below."

This noble structure was doomed to a brief existence. On the night of Nov. 3d, 5818, it was destroyed by fire. It was not rebuilt. The public house lately taken down and bearing the same name, occupied but a part of the ground of that now described. The following account of the fire is taken from the history already cited from.

" This grand edifice was destroyed by fire, on Tuesday, Nov. 3, 1818. It was first discovered near the southwest corner of the attic story, about seven in the evening, and before ten o'clock the whole building was reduced to a melancholy heap of ruins. The most spirited and judicious efforts could only give a temporary check to the flames, which were hastily working their way behind the partition walls and round the cornices, in places beyond reach. In a very short time the greater part of the 2i0 halls, rooms, chambers, &c., exhibited a mass of intense fire seldom witnessed. About nine o'clock the noble dome came down with a frightful crash, and, soon after, nearly all the north and part of the south walls, each more than 80 feet in height, fell, and damaged many of the neighboring buildings. Several houses were much damaged, but none wholly burnt out, except the one on Devonshire Street, adjoining the Exchange. On Wednesday morning, the whole isolated front wall of the ruin, 90 feet high by 80 feet wide, with its marble columns and chimneys, appeared to stand tottering over the people's heads, and threatened in its fall to overwhelm the buildings opposite, which stood at the distance of 28 feet only from the wall. But in the course of that and the succeeding day they were levelled, without the least damage to the neighborhood or to the thousands of spectators who were witnesses to this sublime wreck of matter."

Our Brethren thus so suddenly deprivated of their ample Lodge room, and their regular communication to take place on the following Thursday, were compelled to make extraordinary exertions to provide another place of meeting and suitably furnish it. The place selected was the COMMERCIAL COFFEE HOUSE, situate at the corner of Milk and Batterymarch streets, lately occupying the site on which now stand extensive granite stores. Four meetings were held here, those of November 5 and 19, and December 2 and 17, 5818. How our Brethren sustained themselves in their misfortune will be judged by the succeeding extracts from their records:

November 5, 5818. "In consequence of the conflagration at the Exchange Coffee House on Tuesday evening last, Nov. 3, 5818, by which Masons' Hall was destroyed, in which this Lodge usually convened, a temporary arrangement was made to hold the meetings at the Commercial Coffee House for the present. Much praise is due the officers and brethren for their promptness in engaging, and their alacrity in fitting up the Hall in so short a time."

" On motion of the R. W. Bro. Baxter, *Voted, unanimously*, That the grateful thanks of this Lodge be expressed to R.

W. Bro. Thos. Power, D. D. G. M.; Bro. Spencer Thomas, Mass. Lodge; Bros. Daniel Johnson, Joel Smith, Jr., Columbian Lodge, for their active and successful exertions in rescuing from the fire, of Tuesday evening last, and their assistance in preserving the superb and valuable emblematic painting belonging to this Lodge. Also, *Voted*, That the same thanks be extended to Bro. Samuel Thaxter, of Mt. Lebanon Lodge, for the services rendered the Lodge in preserving the jewels on the same occasion; and to W. Bro. Calvin Howe, of Columbian Lodge, for his like successful exertions in saving the Charter of this Lodge; and that the Secretary be directed to transmit an abstract of this vote to all brethren and members of Columbian Lodge."

November 19, 5818. "*Voted, unanimously*, That the thanks of this Lodge be expressed to Bro. Oliver, for his persevering exertions in preserving the property of this Lodge from the fire at the Exchange Coffee House on the 3d instant, and that as a further testimony of the sense of the Lodge for the success of those exertions, the Treasurer be directed to present Bro. Oliver with five dollars."

The letter here copied is from a R. W. Brother, who now, as then, would wear no laurels belonging to another's brow. His long, arduous and faithful services in the Grand Lodge, in other Masonic bodies, and in the cause of the Order generally, entitle him to the fullest measure of gratitude and fraternal regard.

"R. W. Brother: I have received a copy of the vote passed in Columbian Lodge, in consequence of the preservation, at the late fire, of the painting, by Penniman, belonging to your Lodge.
"The services I may have rendered on that occasion can hardly deserve so liberal a testimonial. I am happy, however, in having this opportunity to do justice to a worthy individual, which I could not have done under other circumstances without the appearance of ostentation. Whatever merit there may have been in that affair belongs to Bro.

Daniel Johnson, a member of your Lodge, who first suggested the idea of saving the painting, and inquired whether any one would assist him.

" It will, however, be a pleasure to preserve the memorial, rather for the liberal sentiments of Columbian Lodge than for any merit I have in the event that occasioned it.

Respectfully, your Friend and Brother,
THOMAS POWER."

MASONS' HALL, *Ann Street—Second Term.* Columbian Lodge communications were held in this Hall the second term, from January 7, 5819, to March 15, 5821, when they removed to the Old State House. Concert Hall was again honored with the communications of the Grand Lodge for a short time after. the destruction of the Exchange, when they took place at Masons' Hall, in Ann street. The early action of both the Grand Lodge and Columbian Lodge in reference to another place in which to hold their meetings, denote that Masons' Hall was regarded as a temporary home; one provided for the emergency occasioned by the loss of the apartments in the Exchange. The following are from the records of Columbian Lodge:

April 1, 5819. "*Voted*, That the R. W. Master, Bros. David Moody, Amos Binney, Calvin Howe, and Gersham Cobb, be a committee to confer with similar committees from other Masonic Societies in Boston on the subject of erecting a Masonic Hall or Temple."

September 7, 5820. " The three first officers were appointed a committee to confer with other committees in procuring a place for future meetings, with full powers to act."

November 2, 5820. " A communication from the General Committee for fitting up the rooms in the Old State House as a Masonic Hall, was read and accepted, and the Treasurer directed to pay to the Treasurer of the M. W. Grand Lodge the sum of two hundred dollars, to carry the design into effect.''

March 1, 5821. '' Thecommittee chosen January 4, 5821, to take a schedule of the regalia, &c., were also '' to see the furniture, &c., removed to the new Hall.''

The proceedings of the Grand Lodge at this time, relative to Masonic apartments, may be gathered from the extracts from their records given below. It will be observed that the Fraternity came near being the proprietors of the now very valuable estate at the corner of Congress and Water streets, at that time known as Merchants' Hall, and will regard with curiosity and interest the causes that prevented the purchase.

December 28, 5818. '' *Voted*, That R. W. Brethren Elijah Morse, Joseph Jenkins, and Samuel Thaxter, be a committee to procure a place for the meeting of the Grand Lodge, and to consider the expediency of uniting with other Lodges in building a Hall.''

December 8, 5819. '' *Voted*, That Elijah Morse, Joseph T. Buckingham, L. G. Whitman, Charles Wells, and Henry Fowle, be a committee to procure a place of meeting for the Grand Lodge.''

December 27, 5819. '' Your committee, appointed to procure a suitable place for the future meetings of the Grand Lodge, respectfully report : That they can find no place more suitable for the meetings of this Lodge than the chambers in Merchants' Hall, when fitted for that purpose. The building called Merchants' Hall is for sale. It belongs to Thomas K. Jones, William Dehon, and Thomas Brown, who hold it in the name of the Proprietors of Merchants' Hall, by virtue of an Act of Incorporation passed February 15th, 1819. Your committee believe said proprietors have never held a meeting under said Act, nor have they transferred said estate to the corporation. This Act provides that the above named persons and their associates may hold said estate or corporate property, and shall divide the same into shares not exceeding five hundred.

" Your committee further report that said building can be purchased for twenty-five thousand dollars ; that it will cost thirteen thousand eight hundred and forty-four dollars to put the building in complete repair, as appears by the estimate of Brothers How and Wells, which accompanies this report.

" The interest on the cost of said building will be two thousand three hundred and thirty dollars and sixty-four cents annually. The rents of this building will be as follows, viz : The cellar will rent for five hundred dollars, the lower floor for eighteen hundred and fifty dollars, the second story for eight hundred dollars,—making eight hundred and nineteen dollars and thirty-six cents more than the interest on the first cost, exclusive of the third and fourth stories.

" Your committee further report that it is expedient for the Masonic institutions to purchase said building, to hold the same under said act of incorporation.

" They further recommend that a subscription paper be opened forthwith for the purpose of taking up the shares mentioned in said act, and that the shares be sold at eighty dollars each. That a committee be appointed to present such subscription paper to the several Masonic Institutions in town, and such others in the country as they may see fit ; then to the Brethren of this Institution ; not to allow any person to subscribe for shares not a Brother, unless it be absolutely necessary in order to dispose of the shares.

" They further recommend that the Grand Treasurer be directed to subscribe for —— shares in the name of the Grand Lodge.

" Your committee further recommend that the committee to procure subscriptions be directed to call a meeting of the subscribers, as soon as the shares are taken up, for the purpose of organizing themselves under the act of incorporation.

All which is respectfully submitted by

ELIJAH MORSE,
JOS. T. BUCKINGHAM, } *Committee.*
HENRY FOWLE,
CHARLES WELLS,

" The foregoing report was read and accepted.

" *Voted*, That Joseph T. Buckingham, Thomas Power and Elijah Morse, be a committee to obtain subscribers for the shares in Merchants' Hall.

" *Voted*, That the Grand Treasurer be authorized to subscribe for twenty shares in Merchants' Hall Corporation, at
eighty dollars each, in behalf of the Grand Lodge."

March 8, 5820. " The committee appointed at the last
communication of the M. W. Grand Lodge to procure subscriptions for the purpose of purchasing Merchants' Hall,
and converting the upper stories thereof into suitable halls
and rooms for Masonic purpose, respectfully report :

" That in order to carry into effect the intention of the
Grand Lodge, it was thought proper to consult the committees of the subordinate Lodges and other Masonic institutions
in the town of Boston, that the said committees might lay
the subject before the respective bodies which they represented.

" The committee found it difficult to procure so general a
meeting of the various committees as they wished. They
have, however, obtained several conferences with those committees, the result of all which is that in the opinion of your
committee it would have been an useless expenditure of time
to have opened a proposal and solicited subscriptions as contemplated by the Grand Lodge. Objections against the purchase existed in the minds of some influential brethren, which
were not easily to be overcome, and partialities in favor of
some other place for a Masonic Hall were strongly advocated
by others. Under these circumstances the committee judged
it most prudent to suspend any further attempts to prosecute
their commission without additional instructions from the
Grand Lodge.

" All which is respectfully submitted.

> JOSEPH T. BUCKINGHAM, ⎫
> ELIJAH MORSE,   ⎬ *Committee*.
> THOMAS POWER,   ⎭

" The foregoing report was read and accepted.

" On motion, *Voted*, That the committee appointed to
solicit subscriptions for the purchase of Merchants' Hall be
discharged."

March 8, 5820. " On motion, by the R. W. Elijah Morse,
Voted, That a committee of five be raised to attend the
next town meeting to be held in Boston on Monday next, to
state the views of this Grand Lodge upon an article in the

warrant then to be acted upon, respecting the subject of leasing to the Masons the Rooms in the Old State House, to confer with the committee of the town, if one should be appointed, upon the terms and conditions of a lease ; to devise the method of raising money to repair and alter said building; and to report the whole subject matter to this Grand Lodge at a special meeting to be called for that purpose, when the committee shall be ready to report—provided the M. W. Grand Master shall be pleased to call such meeting.

"Henry Fowle, Elijah Morse, —— Howard, Francis J. Oliver, and Andrew Sigourney were chosen, to whom the foregoing motion was referred·

June 14, 5820. " The committee appointed to confer with the Selectmen of Boston on the subject of the Old State House, reported progress."

September 13, 5820. " The committee appointed to confer with the Selectmen of Boston on the subject of the Old State House made a report that they were unable to make such terms as were expedient and acceptable to the Grand Lodge.

"Voted, That the same committee be continued in their authority to provide a suitable place of meeting for the Grand Lodge. Bro. Joseph T. Buckingham was added in place of Bro. Sigourney, deceased."

December 20, 5820. " The committee appointed to procure a place of meeting reported progress and obtained leave to continue their sitting "

December 27, 5820. " Voted, That a committee be raised to take such measures as may be necessary preparatory to dedicating the new Hall. M. W. John Dixwell, R. W's Ferdinand E. White, David Parker, Michael Roulstone, Samuel Smith, Charles Wells, Committee."

Old State House. In the preceding pages are given the proceedings of the Grand Lodge which resulted in the procuring of rooms in this ancient and celebrated building for the Masonic

Institutions of Boston. Columbian Lodge first met here, March 15, 5821, and afterwards until October 7, 5830, when they removed to Washington Hall. The record describes the hall in the Old State House as "splendid and appropriate."

"A regular meeting of Columbian Lodge was held at BOYLSTON HALL on Thursday evening, August 2, 5821, in consequence of Masons' Hall being occupied by the painters."

— The report of the General Committee of the Masonic Societies of Boston is here introduced, as it contains an authentic narration of facts and statement of figures highly interesting. It affords evidence, also, of the industry and fidelity with which the committee discharged their trust:

REPORT.

"The several Masonic Societies in the town of Boston, viz., M. W. Grand Lodge of Massachusetts, M. E. Grand R. A. Chapter, Boston Encampment of Knights Templars, Boston Council of Royal Masters, St. Andrew's R. A. Chapter, St. Paul's R. A. Chapter, St. John's, St. Andrew's, Massachusetts, Columbian and Mount Lebanon Lodges, having been deprived of their Masonic Hall in the Exchange Coffee House by fire, Nov. 3, 1818, chose, at their respective meetings, in the beginning of the year 1819, the following brethren as a general committee to procure a place for their future meetings, viz: Francis J. Oliver, Henry Fowle, Elijah Morse, Joseph T. Buckingham, Jonathan Howard, Daniel Baxter, Charles Wells, Nathaniel Alley, David Moody, Ferdinand E. White, Samuel Gragg, Calvin Howe, John Howe, Gershom Cobb, Robert Lash, Lucius Q. C. Bowles, Charles C. Nichols, Michael Roulstone, Amos Binney, Samuel Smith, Samuel Thaxter, Z. G. Whitman, Thomas Power, Joseph Jenkins, S. L. Knapp, Thomas P. Jackson, Rev. Paul Dean, J. L. Phillips, Henry Purkitt, John J. Loring, William Barry, Samuel Howe, Enoch Hobart.

" The above committee held their first meeting on the evening of April 2, 1819 ; afterwards various meetings were held and a number of sub-committees chosen to view several places which had been offered, supposed proper for the object of their appointment.

" At a meeting, January 8, 1820,—*Voted*, As the M. W. Grand Lodge is the only corporate Masonic body in Massachusetts, and, as the several committees, neither individually nor collectively, can proceed legally in the business committed to them,—that this " general committee " begin *de novo* and proceed under the direction and sanction of that body. A committee was chosen, who, after examining various places, particularly Merchants' Hall, Museum Hall, Dr. Robbins's building, on the site of the late Exchange Coffee House, and the chambers of the " Old State House " in State street—recommended the Old State House as the most eligible place ; and at a meeting May 22, 1820, a committee, consisting of the committee of the M. W. Grand Lodge, with R. W. Brothers Joseph Jenkins and Elijah Morse, was chosen to treat with the Selectmen for that place, ascertain the rents, expense of fitting up, &c., who, at a meeting held October 6, 1820, reported, " That the Selectmen had agreed that the Societies should have all the rooms above the first story (with the exception of the two rooms in the second story at the west end,) at a rent of six hundred dollars per annum, on a lease for ten years, with condition that, should the town in open meeting vote to take back the rooms for *town purposes,* they would allow the Grand Lodge ten per cent. of the expense of fitting them up for each year of the unexpired lease, when so taken back." This report being unanimously accepted, a sub-committee of one member from each society was selected to assist the committee from the M. W. Grand Lodge in carrying their intentions into effect—viz: for devising ways and means, contracting for repairs, superintending the work, and prosecuting with all possible despatch the desirable object.

COMMITTEE CHOSEN.

M. W. Grand Lodge,
{
R. W. Brothers, F. J. OLIVER,
.... HENRY FOWLE,
.... ELIJAH MORSE,
.... JONATHAN HOWARD,
.... J. T. BUCKINGHAM.

M. E. G. Chapter......R. W. Brothers, Henry Purkitt.
B. E. K. Templars................... Henry Fowle.
B. C. R. Masters.................... Thomas Payson.
St. Andrew's Chapter............... William Barry.
St. Paul's   do. .... Daniel Baxter.
St. Andrew's Lodge .... Benjamin Smith.
Massachusetts do. .... Michael Roulstone.
St. John's   do. .... Joseph Eveleth.
Columbian   do. .... Benjamin Stevens.
Mt. Lebanon   do. .... Charles Wells.

This committee appointed Gershom Cobb their Secretary.

At a meeting of the general committee, July 6, 1821, R. W. Brothers David Moody, Thomas P. Jackson and Gershom Cobb were chosen a committee to examine and audit the accounts of the Grand Treasurer.

The closets in the upper story were assigned to the several Societies as follows, viz :

No. 1—Grand Chapter, St. Andrew's and St. Paul's Chapters.
No. 2—St. Andrew's and Massachusetts Lodges.
" 3—Columbian and Mount Lebanon   do.
" 4—B. C. R. Masters.
" 5—B. E. K. Templars.
" 6—M. W. Grand Lodge.
" 7—St. John's   do.

At a meeting of the general committee, &c., Dec. 1, 1821, the sub-committee, chosen October 6, 1820, made the following report, which was accepted, and the sub-committee was discharged from further duty.

The sub-committee chosen on the evening of October 6, having attended to the duties assigned them, report, that at their first meeting they chose from among themselves four separate committees, viz :

One to superintend the fitting up of the Hall, &c., in the Old State House.

One for devising ways and means to meet the expenses.

One for assessing said expenses and apportion to each Society their just and equitable part—and

The other to provide furniture and furnish the Hall, &c.

Reports of each of these committees are subjoined.

The committee to superintend the fitting up of the Hall, &c., report, that they have attended to the duty assigned them; that they have procured materials and workmen, and finished the Hall, Refreshment Room, &c., according to approved plans; that the expenses arising in this work amount to $3,236 45, for which they have drawn on the Grand Treasurer.

Respectfully submitted,

FRANCIS J. OLIVER, *Chairman.*

The Committee of Ways and Means, in conjunction with the assessing committee, report, that having duly considered the business committed to them, have at three several times thought proper to assess the several Masonic Societies in the following sums, viz :

	1820.			1821.			1821.		Total.
Grand Lodge	$300	Oct. 21	250	March 26	250	July 21	800
Grand Chapter	160	" 21	100	" 26	100	" 21	360
Encampment	100	" 21	50	" 26	50	" 21	200
C. R. Masters	40	" 21	50	" 26	50	" 21	140
St. Andrew's Chapter,	200	" 21	150	" 26	150	" 21	500
St. Paul's do.	200	" 21	150	" 26	150	" 21	500
St. John's Lodge	200	" 21	150	" 26	150	" 21	500
Massachusetts Lodge..	200	" 21·	150	" 26	150	" 21	500
St. Andrew's do. ...	200	" 21	150	" 26	150	" 21	500
Columbian do. ...	200	" 21	150	" 26	150	" 21	500
Mt. Lebanon	200	" 21	150	" 26	150	" 21	500
	$2000		1500		1500		5000

Making the sum of Five thousand dollars, which has been paid over to the Grand Treasurer of the M. W. Grand Lodge. The assessing committee further report, separately, that they have apportioned the rent as follows, viz :

Grand Lodge, per annum.	$100	St. John's Lodge, per annum,	$ 60
Grand Chapter, do.	40	Massachusetts Lodge, do.	60
Encampment, do.	20	St. Andrew's do. do.	60
R. Masters, do.	20	Columbian do. do.	60
St. Andrew's R. A. C.do.	60	Mt. Lebanon do. do.	60
St. Paul's do. do.	60		$600

All which is respectfully submitted.

E. MORSE, *Ch'n Com. Ways and Means.*

H. PURKITT, *Ch'n Assessing Committee.*"

The committee appointed 6th July, 1821, made the following report:

The committee appointed by the general committee, July 6, 1821, to examine and audit the accounts of the Grand Treasurer, &c., beg leave to report, that they have attended to the duty assigned them, and find that the Grand Treasurer has received from the several Masonic Societies the sum of

$5,000

with which he has credited the Grand Lodge.

That he has answered drafts from the com-
mittee of repairs to the amount of..... $3,236 45
From the furnishing committee to the
  amount of........................ 1,660 56
For sundry small-bills, called miscellaneous,   67 50
Ventilating hall, printing, and stationery..   35 49
————$5,000

Your committee further report, that they find his accounts fairly kept, correctly cast, and properly vouched, and, as such, recommend that they be accepted and passed.

All which is respectfully submitted,

ATTEST: DAVID MOODY, *Chairman.*

True abstract of record,

ATTEST: G. COBB, *Secr'y Gen. Com.*

The committee for furnishing the Hall, report, that the expenses incurred in the materials, work, &c., of furnishing the Hall and Rooms, amount to................$1,660 56
And that sundry small expenses are 102 99

Making the whole amount of furnishing, &c...... $1,763 55
For which they have drawn on the Grand Treasurer.

Respectfully submitted,

FRANCIS J. OLIVER, *Chairman.*

The foregoing reports having been read, were respectively accepted, and report thereof ordered to be made to the general committee.

FRANCIS J. OLIVER, *Chairman.*

True abstract of record,

ATTEST: G. COBB, *Secr'y Sub. Com.*

The balance in the hands of the Grand Treasurer was placed to the order of R. W. Francis J. Oliver, Thomas

Power, and N. Alley, as a special committee, to be applied to ventilating the hall and for such other repairs and purposes as to them may seem proper.

R. W. Thomas Power and Gershom Cobb were appointed a special committee to prepare and superintend the printing of the proceedings of the general committee.

Voted, That 'the proceedings, when printed, be signed by the above committee, and copies given to each Masonic Society.

The general committee was then dissolved.

ATTEST : G. COBB, *Secr'y Gen. Com.*

The preceding is a true abstract of the proceedings of the general committee.

ATTEST : THOMAS POWER,
GERSHOM COBB.''

This Hall was dedicated by the Grand Lodge March 14, 5821. A procession was formed, and the ceremonies usually attending dedications took place; after which were—

Original Dedicatory Ode,
Oration by R. W. Samuel L. Knapp,
Anthem,
Prayer by Rev. Bro. Richardson.

The Grand Lodge then returned in procession to the small hall. On the same evening the following votes were passed by the Grand Lodge :

" *Voted*, That the thanks of the Grand Lodge be presented to R. W. Brother Knapp, for his Address at the dedication of Hall in the Old State House, and that a copy be requested for the press."

" After the above vote was passed, Brother Knapp rose and declined giving a copy. Thereupon it was— *Voted*, That a copy of the vote of thanks be presented to Brother Knapp by the Grand Secretary."

" *Voted*, That the thanks of the Grand Lodge be presented to Bro. John R. Penniman and Bro. Alexander Parris, for their assistance in finishing and decorating the new Masonic Hall, and that the same be done by the Grand Secretary."

The proceedings recorded in the extracts from
the Grand Lodge and Columbian Lodge here given
eventuated in the obtaining of Washington Hall.
In Grand Lodge—

March 10, 5830. "*Resolved*, That a committee of five be
appointed, on the part of this Grand Lodge, with authority,
in conjunction with the respective committees heretofore
appointed, or which may hereafter be appointed, by the several Masonic bodies in the city of Boston, for the purpose of
procuring a place for the meetings of the Grand Lodge and of
the other Masonic bodies in this city, forthwith to procure a
renewal of the lease of the Hall now in occupation of said
Grand Lodge, if it be possible, on such terms as they may
think expedient, or to procure some other convenient hall or
place for the use of this Grand Lodge and the other Masonic
bodies in Boston, for such time and on such conditions as they
shall think proper, and to take such other measures in relation to the subject matter of this resolution as they shall deem
expedient.   Committed to M. W. Joseph Jenkins, R. W.
Elijah Morse, Asa Eaton, Charles Wells, and John J. Loring.

Resolved, That the Grand Secretary be directed to inform
the Masonic bodies in this city that a committee has been
appointed by this Grand Lodge to procure a place of meeting,
and that they are requested by this Grand Lodge to co-
operate with them, by a committee or otherwise, in procuring
a place of meeting for the accommodation of this and other
Masonic bodies."

In Columbian Lodge:

April 1, 5830. " Bros. Flint, Appleton and Moody were
appointed a committee to act in conjunction with the Grand
Lodge and other committees, on the subject of procuring a
suitable place for the meetings of this and the other Masonic
Societies in this city."

Again, in Grand Lodge:

June 9, 5830. "*Voted*, That the Grand Master, by and
with the advice of the committee on the subject of procuring
a place of meeting, be authorized to cancel the lease now in

force between this Grand Lodge and the City of Boston, before the period at which it will by its terms expire, if requested to do so by the authorities of the city."

WASHINGTON HALL, *Washington Street.*—The Lodge adjourned from April 1 to October 7, 5830, when they met at this place. Their meetings were continued here until their removal to the Masonic Temple, January 5, 5832. The Quarterly Communication of the Grand Lodge, Sept. 8, 5830, occurred in this hall. During the summer of this year it is probable that the lease of the Old State House was cancelled, and the removal to Washington Hall took place, though the records of both the Grand Lodge and Columbian Lodge are silent as to any arrangement having been made with its proprietors relative to its occupancy by these bodies.

MASONIC TEMPLE, *Tremont Street.*—This spacious and magnificent Temple was dedicated to Masonic purposes May 30, 5832. The first meeting held in it by Columbian Lodge was that of January 5, 5832. It being the first building erected by the Fraternity in Boston for their uses, will render interesting an account of the action of the Masonic Societies, which resulted in its construction. At a very early date the Brethren first contemplated the erection of a Masonic edifice. At the meeting of Columbian Lodge, October 1, 5801, a communication was "handed the Worshipful Master from the Grand Lodge respecting the building of a Hall." Soon after, the Grand Lodge had this subject under serious consideration, as the subjoined extracts will show :

December 12, 5803. "*Voted*, That a committee be raised
to devise ways and means to erect a Hall for the use of the
Grand Lodge. Bros. Isaiah Thomas, Simon Elliot, Samuel
Dunn, Timothy Bigelow and John Soley were the committee."

December 10, 5804. "The committee appointed September
10, 5804, reported, and it was *Voted*, That a committee of
five be appointed to make application to the Legislature for
an Act to incorporate the officers of the Grand Lodge and
their successors so far as to enable them to hold real estate
sufficient whereon to build a Hall in which to hold their meetings, &c. The following were chosen a committee, viz:
Hon. Jonathan Maynard, Hon. Woodbury Storer, Hon. Timothy Bigelow, Esq., Hon. Perez Morton, and the Hon. John
Locke, Esq. And it was also *Voted*, That further proceedings on the important subject of a Hall, in which every
Mason in the Commonwealth must feel interested, be postponed to the next Quarterly Communication."

December 12, 5809. "The M. W. Isaiah Thomas directed
the Grand Secretary to call immediately on the committee who
were appointed in the year 5805, to petition the Honorable
Legislature of the State for the privilege of purchasing land to
erect a Temple, &c., and request their special attention to
that much desired object, and to report at the next Quarterly
Communication of the Grand Lodge."

December 10, 5810. "The committee on the application
to the Honorable Legislature, chosen in December, 5804,
were called upon for a statement of that business. R. W.
Bro. Maynard, chairman, being present, reported, that the
subject had been duly attended to, but without the desired
effect. On motion, *Voted*, That the committee be discharged
from any further duty on that subject."

At the meeting of Columbian Lodge, November
6, 5817, the following Circular from a Committee
of the Grand Lodge was presented. Though it
refers to other matters than the Act of Incorporation, yet its insertion entire will not be inappro-
priate.

CIRCULAR.

BOSTON, October 20, A. L., 5816.

Beloved Brethren, of Columbian Lodge:

The undersigned, a Committee of the M. W. GRAND LODGE, have the honor to address you on subjects intimately connected with the well-being of the Masonic Family in Massachusetts.

It is supposed that many Lodges in the interior are, from their remote situation, not acquainted with all the existing circumstances and important concerns of the Grand Lodge. Especially, it is believed, that they are not sufficiently informed respecting the act of incorporation granted the Grand Lodge by the Honorable Legislature, at their last session. To obviate the difficulties which would necessarily grow out of this want of information, we take the liberty to transmit you a statement of the measures pursued by the Grand Lodge in obtaining this act, and annex a copy of the same. At the communication of the Grand Lodge, December 27, 5816, a committee was appointed to take into consideration the expediency of petitioning the Legislature for an act of incorporation.

That committee faithfully considered the subject, and at the communication, March 10, 5817, reported in favor of petitioning as above ; their report being accepted, a committee of thirteen was appointed to carry the same into effect, who, by indefatigable attention to their duty, had the satisfaction to succeed in the object of their appointment.

You will perceive by the form of the act, that it incorporates the " Master, Wardens and Members of the Grand Lodge." You will pardon us in presuming a want of information, which we believe exists in some parts of our Commonwealth, when we suggest that your Lodge is a constituent part of the Grand Lodge ; that your Master and Wardens are members of that body, possessing equal rights and privileges, for the time being, with all others. You are then by this act virtually incorporated with all your sister Lodges of Massachusetts, in one body politic, under the name and title of the " Master, Wardens and Members of the Grand Lodge," and you have a right, in common with all others, to the benefits and immunities resulting from this new arrangement in the fiscal concerns of this Masonic compact.

It has long been a source of deep regret, that the actual members of the Grand Lodge do not more frequently attend its meetings. We sincerely hope that this event may prove a stimulant for future punctuality. The expense of sending at least one of the actual representatives to every session of the Grand Lodge would be but small, even to the most distant Lodges. But should that at any time be found impracticable, no Lodge is excusable in neglecting to appoint a suitable proxy, through whom they may make any communications with the Grand Lodge.

While on this subject permit us to remark, that in the appointment of proxies much judgment should be exercised; care should be taken that Commissions be made out in the form prescribed by the Constitution. Brethren should be appointed whose experience, information and talents would enable them to act understandingly and judiciously on all important subjects, and whose zeal and interest in the cause of the Craft would induce them to give their faithful attendance at all the communications of the Grand Lodge.

At the next Communication, which will be on the second Monday of December next, a committee appointed at the last meeting will report a code of By-Laws for the government of the Corporation, for the consideration of the Grand Lodge; and you will readily perceive the necessity that every Lodge should then be represented, that an arrangement of so much magnitude should be commenced in the best possible manner. It should be recollected that this event fixes an important epoch in the history of the Craft in Massachusetts; and that no Lodge may hereafter plead ignorance as an excuse for any delinquency, we ardently hope they will avail themselves of the opportunity which now offers to obtain all that information, and exercise all that independence of sentiment which are desirable on a subject so closely connected with their prosperity and honor.

With sentiments of affection and respect, we are

Your Brothers,

JOSEPH JENKINS,
ZACH. G. WHITMAN,
DANIEL L. GIBBENS, } *Committee.*
ELIJAH MORSE,
WM. BARRY,

COMMONWEALTH OF MASSACHUSETTS

In the year of our Lord one thousand eight hundred and seventeen.

AN ACT to Incorporate the Master, Wardens and Members of the Grand Lodge of Massachusetts.

SECTION 1. Be it enacted by the Senate and House of Representatives, in General Court assembled, and by the authority of the same, That Francis J. Oliver and his associates, and their successors be, and they hereby are incorporated and made a body politic, by the name of The Master, Wardens and Members of the Grand Lodge of Massachusetts, with the power to have a common seal, to sue and be sued, to make and ordain, from time to time, by-laws, rules and regulations, for the government and management of the Corporation ; Provided the same be not repugnant to the Constitution and Laws of this Commonwealth ; and that they have all the privileges usually given by acts of incorporation to charitable societies.

SECT. 2. Be it further enacted, That the said Corporation may take by purchase, gift, grant, or otherwise, and hold, real estate, not exceeding the value of twenty thousand dollars, and personal estate not exceeding the value of sixty thousand dollars, for charitable uses.

SECT. 3. Be it further enacted, That Francis J. Oliver be, and he is hereby authorized to call the first meeting of said Corporation, by advertisement, in two of the newspapers printed in Boston, three weeks previous thereto, and appoint the time and place thereof; at which meeting the mode of calling future meetings shall be regulated.

SECT. 4. Be it further enacted, That this act may be amended, revised, or terminated, at the pleasure of the Legislature.

In the House of Representatives, June 16, 1817. This Bill having had three several readings, passed to be enacted.

TIMOTHY BIGELOW, *Speaker.*

In Senate, June 16, 1817. This bill having had two several readings, passed to be enacted.

JOHN PHILLIPS, *President.*

June 16, 1817.—*Approved.* J. BROOKS.

A true copy.—*Attest :* ALDEN BRADFORD,
Secr'y of Commonwealth.

December 13, 5826. "*Voted*, That the Grand Secretary be directed to request the several Masonic Societies which usually hold their meetings in the city of Boston, to appoint a committee of three from their respective bodies, with authority to act with the committee of the Grand Lodge, appointed for the purpose of procuring a permanent place of meeting, and that a return of the names of said committees be forthwith made to the chairman of the Grand Lodge committee."

December 27, 5826. "The Grand Treasurer, R. W. Elijah Morse, in his annual report on the state of the Lodges in the Commonwealth, makes the following remarks relative to the erection of a Masonic Temple :

' A great desire among many of the Brethren has existed for a long time that a Masonic Temple should be erected under the Jurisdiction. A want of funds has been a great embarrassment to the enterprise. The G. Treasurer thought it an object to ascertain what funds were possessed by the Lodges, in order that the Grand Lodge might judge of the propriety of requesting them to coöperate in erecting an edifice. The Grand Treasurer flatters himself the above will be a sufficient explanation of his motives in making the recommendation he did. From the progress already made, he feels confident a Masonic Temple will soon be erected by this Grand Lodge ; and he is equally confident that the Subordinate Lodges would be pleased to invest a portion of their funds in the undertaking, on being satisfied that the investment would be secure and give a good income.' "

In Columbian Lodge—

February 1, 5827. "Bros. G. G. Smith, Appleton and Marden, were appointed a committee, with authority to act with the committee of the Grand Lodge, for the purpose of procuring a permanent place for the meetings of the several Masonic Societies of Boston."

March 14, 5827. In Grand Lodge, the following report was presented :

" The Committee appointed to inquire into the expediency and practicability of procuring a permanent place of meeting for the Grand Lodge, beg leave to report in part—That agreeably to the vote of the Grand Lodge, passed at the last quarterly communication, requesting the several Masonic Societies in Boston to appoint committees on their part to meet with your committee, delegates from these bodies were chosen, and at a meeting in general committee it was unanimously voted, that it is expedient to procure a permanent place of meeting ; and a sub-committee was appointed to devise measures to ascertain the practicability of procuring the funds necessary for the erection of a Temple which shall be an honor to the Craft and an ornament to the city. The labors of the committee, it is believed, will be much facilitated if the Grand Lodge will deem it expedient to declare what may be expected from them in aid of the undertaking ; and to bring the subject fairly before them, your committee recommend the adoption of the first vote following. And in order to remove certain jealousies which your committee are given to understand exist in relation to the views of the Grand Lodge, it is recommended that the second vote hereto annexed be also adopted.

Respectfully submitted, by order of the Committee,

FRANCIS J. OLIVER, *Chairman.*

1st. *Voted,* That whenever arrangements satisfactory to this Grand Lodge shall be made for the erection of a Masonic Temple, an amount not less than ten thousand dollars shall, if practicable, be invested therein from the funds of the Grand Lodge.

2d. *Voted,* That the Grand Lodge does not contemplate or wish for a controlling power in the direction of the measures necessary to insure the erection of a Masonic building, nor in the care thereof, but merely such an influence as they shall be equitably entitled to from the amount appropriated by the Grand Lodge for this desirable object.

Read and accepted, and further time granted."

Again, in Columbian Lodge :

April 5, 5827. "*Voted,* That the committee appointed to procure a permanent place for the meetings of the Masonic Societies, be empowered to proceed in concert with the committee of the other Masonic institutions."

The action of the Masonic Societies relative to the erection of a Hall for their uses, hitherto, has not resulted in the attainment of that long-cherished object. But their desires in this respect are at last to be gratified, and at a period in their history apparently the least propitious for so important and responsible an undertaking. At the moment when a fanatical persecution assailed the institution with its severest rancor, the erection of the Temple was, by the heroic constancy of the Craft, carried on triumphantly to its completion. The continuation here of extracts from the records will be interesting, as showing what were the preliminary measures that led to the building of this edifice:

June 9, 5830. "*Voted*, That the committee of this Grand Lodge, appointed at the last communication, be authorized and directed to procure a piece of real estate in the city of Boston, in the corporate name of this Grand Lodge, and proceed to construct thereon a building for the accommodation of this Grand Lodge and other Masonic bodies in Boston.

"*Voted*, That the committee of this Grand Lodge appointed to purchase land and construct a building thereon, be and they hereby are authorized, in the name and behalf of this Grand Lodge, to receive monies of Masonic bodies and other Brethren, for the purpose aforesaid, upon such terms and conditions as they shall believe most for the interest of this Grand Lodge in the aforesaid enterprise, but not exceeding fifteen thousand dollars. And they are hereby authorized to draw on the Treasurer for any unappropriated monies in his hands for the purposes aforesaid, and their receipts shall be his vouchers."

September 8, 5830. "*Voted*, That the Building Committee be authorized to borrow from any person or persons, and at such rate of interest as they shall consider fair and proper, the sum of fifteen thousand dollars named in the vote passed June 9, 5830, and for the purposes therein named."

The following extract is from the records of Columbian Lodge:

October 7, 5830. " An invitation was received from the Grand Lodge to unite in the ceremony of laying the corner-stone of the Masonic Temple, on the 14th instant, which was accepted.

" *Voted*, That Bros. Flint, Baxter, Sen., Moody, Jones, and Simpson, be a committee to send invitations to such Brethren as have received the degrees in this Lodge to unite with us in laying the corner-stone of the Masonic Temple on the 14th inst.

" *Voted*, That the above committee take into consideration what portion of the funds of the Lodge shall be appropriated to the erection of the Masonic Temple."

The description of the solemn and impressive ceremonies attending the laying of the corner-stone, and of the contents of the box placed under it, is from the records of the Grand Lodge, as follows :

October 14, 5830. " Pursuant to notice, the officers and members of the Grand Lodge assembled at Faneuil Hall, Boston, to unite in the ceremonies of laying the corner-stone of a Masonic Temple. A procession was formed at half-past 10 o'clock, A. M., and proceeded through Merchants' Row, State street, Court street, Tremont street, to the site of the Temple, next south of St. Paul's Church. The left of the procession having arrived at the platform, the ranks were opened to the right and left, and the whole marched through in reverse and took their position on the platform. Silence being proclaimed, an introductory prayer was made by Rev. Samuel Barrett. The inscriptions on the plate were read by the Treasurer. A box containing the following articles was deposited, viz. :

PLATE, WITH THE FOLLOWING INSCRIPTIONS.

Anno Lucis, 5830. On the 14th day of October, this corner-stone of the Masonic Temple, in Boston, was laid by the Most Worshipful Joseph Jenkins, Grand Master of Free Masons in the Commonwealth of Massachusetts, assisted by the Past Grand Masters and the Officers and Members of the Grand Lodge, and in presence of the Executive Officers of the

State and City, in the ninety-seventh year of the establishment of Free Maronry in this State, in the fifty-fifth year of the Independence of the United States, and in the year of our Lord and Saviour one thousand eight hundred and thirty. Andrew Jackson, President of the United States ; Levi Lincoln, Governor of Massachusetts ; Harrison Gray Otis, Mayor of Boston.

ORGANIZATION OF FREE MASONRY IN AMERICA.

5769.—Joseph Warren, of Boston, appointed Provincial Grand Master by George, Earl of Dalhousie, for Boston, New England, and one hundred miles of the same.

5772.—Joseph Warren appointed Provincial Grand Master for the Continent of America, by Patrick, Earl of Dumfries, Grand Master of Scotland.

5777.—An Independent Grand Lodge was established March 8, Joseph Webb, Grand Master.

5782.—John Warren, G. Master.

5784.—Joseph Webb, G. Master.

5787.—John Warren, G. Master.

5788.—Moses M. Hays, Grand Master, until the union of the Grand Lodges, March 5, 5792.

5733.—Henry Price, of Boston, appointed Provincial Grand Master for all North America, by the Right Honorable Anthony, Lord Viscount Montague, Grand Master of Masons in England.

5736. — Robert Tomlinson succeeded.

5744.—Thos. Oxnard succeeded.

5754.—Jeremy Gridley succeeded.

5767.—Henry Price succeeded.

5768.—John Rowe succeeded.

5775.—Hostilities commenced between Great Britain and America, April 19, and suspended the operations of this Grand Lodge.

5790.—John Cutler chosen Senior G. Warden, July 29, and exercised the authority of the chair until the union of the two Grand Lodges, March 5, 5792,

Constituting the Grand Lodge of Massachusetts.

GRAND MASTERS AFTER THE UNION.

5810.	Timothy Bigelow.	
5813.	Benjamin Russell.	
5816.	Francis J. Oliver.	
5819.	Samuel P. P. Fay.	
5820.	John Dixwell.	
5823.	John Abbot.	
5826.	John Soley.	
5829.	Joseph Jenkins.	

5792.	John Cutler.
5796.	Paul Revere.
5797.	Josiah Bartlett.
5799.	Samuel Dunn.
5802.	Isaiah Thomas.
5805.	Timothy Bigelow.
5808.	Isaiah Thomas.
5809.	Josiah Bartlett.

Here follow the names of the officers of the Grand Lodge. The following articles were also deposited :

Sundry coins of the United States.

Newspapers of the day.

Newspapers containing an account of the recent Revolution in France.

Book of Constitutions of Free Masonry.

By-Laws of the Grand Lodge and Charter of Incorporation.

Annual Communication of the Grand Lodge for 5829.

Constitution of the General Grand Encampment of Knights Templars of the United States of America.

Constitution of the General Grand Royal Arch Chapter of the United States of America.

Constitution and By-Laws of the Grand Royal Arch Chapter of Massachusetts.

Grand Master Jenkins' Address before the G. Lodge, Dec., 5829.

Companions Clark, Dean, Livingston and Poinsett's Addresses.

Colton's Address, in three numbers of Masonic Mirror.

A number of the Amaranth, or Masonic Garland, containing a chronological table, etc.

Old Continental Bills, of various denominations.

Otis' Address before the City Council, Sept. 17, 1830.

Quincy's Centennial Address, Sept. 17, 1830.

Sprague's Centennial Ode, Sept. 17, 1830.

Judge Story's Centennial Discourse, delivered in Salem.

An impression of the Seal of the Grand Lodge.

The stone being placed in its bed, the Grand Master applied the working tools and pronounced it to be " well formed, true and trusty." The Corn, Wine and Oil were poured out and the usual invocations followed.

An address was then pronounced by the Grand Master. After the address, a stanza was sung to the tune of Old Hundred. A benediction was pronounced by Dr. Ripley, of Concord.

A procession was again formed, and returned through Tremont street and Cornhill to Faneuil Hall.''

Below are extracts from the recorded proceedings of Columbian Lodge:

April 7, 5831. " The report of the committee on the disposal of the funds for the new Hall was accepted. See report on file.''

November 3, 5831. " A communication was received from the Masonic Board of Directors, requesting them to authorize their Representatives to that board to unite in contracting with the Grand Lodge for suitable apartments in the Masonic Temple : whereupon it was *Voted*, That the Master and Wardens be a committee on the above communication."

January 5, 5832. " *Voted*, That Bros. Moody, Appleton and Baxter be a Committee, with full power to dispose of such a portion of the funds of this Lodge as may be necessary to raise the amount voted by the Lodge towards the erection of the Masonic Hall, viz., $2,000, and any expenses that may have attended that appropriation."

The first Masonic communication held in Masonic Temple was the annual meeting of Mount Lebanon Lodge, which occurred December 26, 5831. The record of the Grand Lodge refers to the dedication of the Temple in these terms :

May 30, 5832. "At 10 o'clock, A. M., a special communication of the Grand Lodge of Massachusetts was held at the Masonic Temple, for the purpose of dedicating the same.

" A procession was formed and the Masonic Hall was consecrated to purposes of Masonry. Prayer by Bro. Eaton.

" The procession then proceeded to the Lecture Room, where the following exercises were had, viz :

Music.

Prayer, by Rev. Bro. Dean.

Anthem, composed for the occasion.

Dedication.

Prayer, by Rev. Bro. E. M. P. Wells.

Address, by Bro. Bernard Whitman.

Hymn.

Benediction, by Rev. Bro. Eaton."

A full description of the Temple and of the rooms into which it was at first divided, occurs in Bowen's " Picture of Boston," and is substantially the same which is entered on the records of the Grand Lodge. Its evident correctness will warrant its introduction here for the information of the Fraternity :

" MASONIC TEMPLE.—This building is situated in Tremont street, on part of the land that was formerly Washington Gardens. The land was purchased of the Hon. William Sullivan, and the corner-stone laid October 14, 1830, with appropriate Masonic ceremonies, by the Grand Lodge of Massachusetts. This Temple was dedicated May 30, 1832.

The location of this building is regarded as the most proper that could be selected, for the purpose for which it is intended. It is 60 feet wide, and 80 1-2 feet long ; and fronts westwardly on Tremont street. Its south boundary is Temple place, an avenue 40 feet wide, recently built up with handsome mansion houses. On the north, at 10 feet distance, is the elegant edifice, St. Paul's Church, and on the east, in the rear, is a six feet passage-way, for the accommodation of the tenants. The walls are 52 feet high, of stone, covered with a slated roof, 24 feet high, containing 16 windows to light the attic story. The gutters are of cast iron, and the water trunks are of copper. The basement is of fine hammered granite, 12 feet high, with a belt of the same. The towers at the corners next Tremont street are 16 feet square, surmounted with granite battlements, and pinnacles rising 95 feet from the ground. The door and window frames are of fine hammered granite, and the main walls from the basement to the roof are of *rubble* granite, disposed in courses, in such a manner as to present a finished appearance to the eye. The cellar, 55 by 75 feet in the clear, and 9 feet deep, is in a gravel bottom, perfectly dry, with sufficient light on two sides to render it an excellent place for many kinds of business. The basement story is divided into three apartments. The first, which is the chapel, 55 by 40 feet, and about 15 feet high, with a gallery on the long side, is capable of seating 600 persons. The second and third are two school rooms, one 16 by 14 feet, and the other 24 by 40, and 10 feet high.

In the second story is a spacious lecture room 65 by 55 feet, and 19 feet high, with circular seats upon a spherical floor, and lighted by eight windows ; capable of seating 1,000 persons. From 12 to 20 dollars rent per day is paid for the use of this hall, for about 100 days in the year. Over the vestibule are two lobbies, or school-rooms.

In the third story are, 1st, a spacious hall, 55 by 39 feet, and 16 feet high, well lighted, and capable of seating 400 persons ; 2d, a front hall 30 by 32 feet, and 16 feet high, well lighted, and capable of seating 200 persons. There are three lobbies attached to the halls of this floor, which are for the accommodation of the tenants.

In the attic story are, 1st, Masons' Hall, 46 by 26 feet, and 12 feet high, well lighted by six windows in the roof, and capable of seating 200 persons. Attached to this are 13 lobbies for the accommodation of the respective lodges; 2d, a drawing-room, 24 by 15 feet, and 8 feet high, sufficiently commodious to accommodate all the visiters of the lodges during their sessions, and over this last is a room for the purpose of storing their furniture, &c. Masons' Hall, with the other accommodations in this story, are appropriated to Masonic purposes.

From the street to all the stories are two flights of winding stairs in the towers, sufficiently spacious to admit a free entrance and departure of all persons from the different rooms. All the halls and rooms are provided with stove apparatus, for warming them in the winter season, and are lighted with gas. The whole cost, including the land, amounts to about 50,000.''

By the Act to incorporate the Master, Wardens and Members of the Grand Lodge of Massachusetts, they had power to hold real estate not exceeding in value twenty thousand dollars, and personal property not exceeding sixty thousand dollars. In 5831, after the building of the Temple had proceeded nearly to completion, and foreseeing that its cost would exceed the value of twenty thousand dollars, the Grand Lodge petitioned the Legislature for such change as would enable them to hold sixty thousand dollars of real and twenty thousand dollars of personal property. The prayer of the petitioners was rejected. At this time political Anti-Masonry had arrived at its culminating point, and such was the bitterness and malignity with which the opponents of the Craft were governed, that not only was this most reasonable request refused, but they even threatened to deprive the Fraternity of their chartered privileges. The Brethren met the crisis as became men and Masons, and in 5833, in a Memorial addressed to the Legislature, distinguished for its calmness, dignity and ability, they voluntarily surrendered their corporate rights. The proceedings of the Grand Lodge on this occasion, and in relation to the sale and repurchase of the Temple, will be read by every Mason with deep interest.

December 12, 5833. "The following Brethren were appointed a Committee to contract for the sale of the Masonic Temple, viz : R. W. Francis J. Oliver, Benjamin Russell, Augustus Peabody, Joseph Baker, and A. A. Dame, Esqs."

December 20, 5833. "*Voted*, That R. W. Francis J. Oliver, Augustus Peabody, Joseph Baker, John Soley, and Chas. W. Moore, be a committee to consider the expediency of surrendering the Act of Incorporation of the Grand Lodge, and report at the next meeting."

December 27, 5833. "The committee appointed, with full powers to make sale of the Temple, reported, that they had effected a sale to Robert G. Shaw, Esq.

"The committee appointed to consider the expediency of surrendering the Act of Incorporation of the Grand Lodge, reported the following Memorial, which was unanimously accepted :

MEMORIAL.

To the Honorable Senate and
  House of Representatives, in General Court assembled :

The Memorial of the undersigned, the Master and Wardens of the Grand Lodge of Freemasons, within the Commonwealth of Massachusetts, respectfully represents—

That the said Grand Lodge was established and organized in the then town of Boston, in said Commonwealth, as a voluntary association, on the 30th of July, A. D., 1733—assuming and exercising all the powers, rights and privileges which, by the ancient laws and usages recognized by the Fraternity of Freemasons, in their consociated capacity, it was empowered so to assume and exercise: That, in the legitimate exercise of those powers and privileges, and in its official capacity, as the head of a prosperous and growing BENEVO-

LENT ASSOCIATION, by the liberal donations of individual Freemasons, and by the usual contributions of the subordinate
Lodges, it was, in time, enabled to create and establish the
Fund known as the " CHARITY FUND OF THE GRAND LODGE OF
MASSACHUSETTS ;" subject to the provision that the income
thereof should be held in sacred trust for, and faithfully applied to, charitable purposes—to the relief of the distressed
and suffering.   And your memorialists have the gratification
to believe that the letter and spirit of this provision have ever
been, and they trust will long continue to be, scrupulously
observed and performed.

Your memorialists further represent: That from the period
of its establishment until the year 1817, this Fund was held
by, and under the control and direction of the said Grand
Lodge, acting as a voluntary association.   This tenure was
not only thought to be insecure, but the management of the
Fund was found to be attended with the various and unavoidable difficulties which are always incident to the conduct of
property thus situated.   Under these circumstances, and in
the belief that an act of incorporation would increase the security of the Fund, and facilitate the distribution of its charities,
FRANCIS J. OLIVER, Esq., and others, members of the said
Grand Lodge, petitioned and obtained of the Hon. Legislature,
on the 16th of June, 1817, an act, by which the Master,
Wardens and Members of the Grand Lodge were incorporated
and made a body politic, authorized and empowered to take by
purchase, gift, grant, or otherwise, and hold real estate, not
exceeding the value of twenty thousand dollars, and personal
estate, not exceeding the value of sixty thousand dollars ; and
to have and exercise all the privileges usually given by acts of
incorporation to charitable societies.   And so far as the knowledge of your memorialists extends, or their experience ena-
bles them to judge, they most confidently believe and affirm :
That all the transactions of the said Grand Lodge (with the
single exception hereafter noted,) have been conducted with
a scrupulous regard to the original purposes of its institution, and with an honorable endeavor to preserve the invio-
lability of the corporate powers with which it was invested by
the Hon. Legislature of the Commonwealth : That, in the
performance of the interesting duties pertaining to this connexion, its members have conducted as honest and peaceable
citizens, recognizing in the following " Ancient Charges " of
their Order unexceptionable rules of duty in all their social

and political relations : that they have "agreed to be good men and true, and strictly to obey the moral law; to be peaceable subjects, and cheerfully to conform to the laws of the country in which they reside; not to be concerned in plots or conspiracies against government, but patiently to submit to the decisions of the supreme legislature; to pay a proper respect to the civil magistrate, to work diligently, live creditably, and act honorably with all men."* And that, confidently relying on the protection guaranteed alike to all classes of citizens, by their written constitutions, they have rested quietly under their own vine and fig-tree, giving just cause of offence to none, and willing to believe they had none to molest or make them afraid.

Such was the condition of the affairs of the said Grand Lodge, prior to the summer of the year 1830, when, having previously been under the necessity of vacating the commodious apartments which it had for a long term of years occupied in one of the public buildings of the city, and experiencing much inconvenience from the want of suitable permanent accommodations for the transaction of Masonic business, it was proposed and determined, by an unanimous vote of its members, to erect an edifice, which, while it afforded ample accommodations for the fraternity, should also be an ornament to the city and a public convenience. Your memorialists would not disguise the fact, that considerations of revenue contributed to produce this determination on the part of the Grand Lodge. As the depository and guardian of a Charitable Fund, the Grand Lodge held itself morally responsible to the indigent recipients of the charities accruing from it, and felt bound to see that it was rendered as productive as a proper regard to its security would allow.

Under these circumstances, and not entertaining a suspicion that the Hon. Legislature would refuse, or that the most unyielding among the opponents of Freemasonry, could object to such a modification of its act of incorporation, as would enable it to hold a greater amount of real estate, and proportionally less of personal estate, than it was then empowered to do, the said Grand Lodge, in the autumn of 1830, laid the corner-stone of the building known as the " MASONIC TEMPLE," in the city of Boston.

The original purchase of this estate was far within the amount which the act of incorporation authorized the Grand

* Book of " Masonic Constitutions."

Lodge to hold; but foreseeing that the augmenting value of the rising structure would exceed this amount, a petition was presented to the Hon. Legislature, at the winter session of 1831, praying for such a modification of its corporate powers as would enable it to hold real estate, not exceeding the value of sixty thousand dollars, and personal estate, not exceeding the value of twenty thousand dollars. The petitioners did not ask for an extension of their corporate powers, nor to be invested with any additional ones; but simply for such a modification of the rights and powers which they already enjoyed as the Hon. Legislature has always shown itself willing to make for the accommodation of other corporate associations; a modification which, your memorialists humbly conceive, was calculated to lessen, rather than to increase the power of the corporation, and by which no principle of law or policy was to be surrendered or prejudicially affected. For reasons which impartial history will doubtless exhibit, but the pertinence of which the wisdom of the historian may not easily recognize, the prayer of these petitioners was not granted.

The embarrassment in which this unexpected result involved the corporation will readily occur to your Hon. body. The land on which the contemplated building was to be erected had been purchased, the foundation laid, and the contracts made for its erection. Your memorialists respectfully submit that there can be no difference of opinion among the ingenuous and unprejudiced portion of your Honorable body in respect to the course it was proper, under these circumstances, for the Grand Lodge to pursue. It determined to go on with the erection of the building it had commenced, and either to trust to the magnanimity and justice of a future Legislature, for the necessary modification of its act of incorporation, or to dispose of the property, as circumstances might dictate, when it should become saleable. For reasons, with which it is unnecessary to trouble the Legislature, the Grand Lodge have adopted the latter alternative.

Although your memorialists had observed in the proceedings of a former Legislature that certain citizens, professing to be jealous of the powers conferred by our act of incorporation, or of the manner in which they were exercised, had applied for a repeal of it, we had received no formal notice of any measure for that purpose until a few days ago, when a Circular, purporting to be a copy of a Memorial to your Hon. Body, was addressed and handed to all the principal officers of the said Grand Lodge, by a sheriff. The ultimate object of this petition seems to be a revocation of the act of incorporation of the Grand Lodge. On the face of it, however, is spread out a series of direct charges and scandalous insinuations against the principles and practices of that corporation. But, as they are true or supposable, only as a faithful representation of the spirit and proceedings of those who originated them, a due regard to the blamelessness and respectability of the said Grand Lodge, as well as a personal sense of self-respect, alike admonish your memorialists to refrain from any more particular notice of them. The Grand Lodge can enter into no discussion of the principles of Freemasonry with prejudiced and abusive partisans; but especially would it avoid the indecorum of obtruding such a controversy into the presence of the Legislature of the Commonwealth. All controversy which may be honorably avoided is inconsistent with the conciliatory precepts and beneficent designs of our association. We are required rather to suffer undeserved persecution and injury, than unnecessarily to maintain strife and bitterness. And although as citizens of a government of laws we can submit to nothing that is clearly wrong, as the friends of peace and order we can persist in nothing that is not clearly right. Actuated by these sentiments, and by a sincere desire to spare the Legislature the annoyance and unprofitable consumption of time, which the political party interested in the petition may otherwise occasion, the Grand Lodge has determined to make a voluntary surrender of its civil charter; and the undersigned, the present memorialists, have been duly appointed to inform the Honorable Legislature that by a vote, passed at a regular meeting of that Corporation, on the evening of December 27th, 1833, (a copy of which is hereunto annexed,) its corporate powers were relinquished, its act of incorporation vacated, and your memorialists instructed to return it to the Honorable Legislature, from whom it was derived.

Finally, that there may be no misunderstanding of this matter, either in the Legislature or among our fellow-citizens, we beg leave to represent precisely the nature and extent of the surrender contained in this memorial. By divesting itself of its corporate powers, the Grand Lodge has relinquished none of its Masonic attributes or prerogatives. These it claims to hold and exercise independently alike of popular will and legal enactment—not of toleration, but of right. Its members are intelligent freemen, and although willing to restore any gift or advantage derived from the government, whenever it becomes an object of jealousy, however unfounded, nothing is further from their intentions, or from their convictions of duty, than to sacrifice a private institution for social and benevolent purposes—the interests of which have been entrusted to them—in order to apease a popular excitement, of which that institution may have been the innocent occasion.

JOHN ABBOT, *Master*.
ELIAS HASKELL, } *Wardens*
BENJ. B. APPLETON, }
of the Grand Lodge of Massachusetts.

On motion, it was then " *Voted*, That the Master and Wardens of this Grand Lodge be authorized and directed to surrender to the Legislature the Act of Incorporation granted to the Master, Wardens and Members of the Grand Lodge of Massachusetts, June 16, 1817, and to present therewith the foregoing Memorial, signed by them."

The following vote was then offered and adopted : " *Whereas*, At the present communication of the Grand Lodge it has been voted to surrender to the Legislature the Act of Incorporation granted to the said Grand Lodge in 1817, and a Memorial has also by vote been adopted, to be presented to said Legislature, notifying them of the fact of said surrender : therefore, *Voted*, That the Grand Lodge of Massachusetts exists only as a voluntary association, having and possessing all and the same rights, powers, privileges and immunities, under its ancient charter, in relation to Freemasonry, which said Grand Lodge had and possessed before the aforesaid act of incorporation was granted ; and that the officers last elected have and retain their respective offices until the next annual communication of said Grand Lodge."

December 9, 5835. " The committee appointed on the property of the Grand Lodge generally, and with a special reference to the repurchase of the Masonic Temple, presented the following

REPORT.

That soon after their appointment they commenced negotiations, which have lately terminated in the transfer of the Masonic Temple, and the whole estate of which it is a part, from the gentleman to whom it was sold by the Grand Lodge, previous to the surrender of their Act of Incorporation, to a Board of Trustees, who hold and improve it for the benefit of the Grand Lodge, so long as it shall exist either as a voluntary association or an incorporated body, and, in the event of ' its final dissolution, are required to transfer the estate to the Grand Lodge of South Carolina, to be by them held for Masonic purposes, forever. The particular terms, conditions and limitations of this trust are explicitly set forth in the indenture by which it is instituted, and which is duly recorded in the Suffolk office. As the Grand Lodge is made in some respects a party to the execution of that instrument, the committee recommend that a fair and authentic copy of it be made in our Records or in some other book which will always be at hand at our communications.

The Board of Trustees, consisting of nine brethren—faithful, intelligent and zealous in their Masonic relations—has been organized for the present by the appointment of Bros. E. A. Raymond, B. B. Appleton and Winslow Lewis, Jr., respectively, to the offices of Chairman, Treasurer and Secretary ; and has adopted a code of by-laws, a copy of which will forthwith be placed in the hands of the Grand Secretary.

In effecting the repurchase of the Temple, an object so desirable and important to the Grand Lodge, your committee were obliged again to resort to the treasury of the Grand Charity Fund, and, of course, have incurred a debt there for which the Grand Lodge should immediately provide a suitable acknowledgment. And, as it appears that the debts of the Grand Lodge to that institution are at present represented in several notes of different dates and amounts, but all at the same rate of interest, it is recommended, as a measure of convenience, that the Grand Treasurer be authorized and instructed to execute a single note to the Trustees of the Grand Charity Fund, to the amount of all their actual dues from the Grand Lodge at the time of making it, and providing the same rate of interest as is now paid, and then to exchange the note thus made for the several notes against the Grand Lodge, now held by the Treasurer of the Grand Charity Fund.

The committee cannot refrain from congratulating their brethren upon the favorable termination of a negotiation which has restored this valuable estate to its original owners, and placed the financial concerns of the Grand Lodge in an unembarrassed and most promising condition.

A nation is deemed eminently fortunate to come out of a contest, either of aggression or defence, without an impoverished treasury. At the end of a controversy, as we believe, in which we have been engaged for several years past—a controversy which was stimulated in no inconsiderable degree by the expectation of booty—it is certainly a fair subject of self-satisfaction to find our treasury solvent and accumulating, and our resources adequate to the immediate and prospective wants of the Institution—and not only so, but what is still more tributary to our self-respect, a more precious treasure than this has been preserved. May we not be permitted to boast that we have come out of the struggle with honor untarnished, and the good faith of our Masonic engagements inviolate?

This Grand Lodge has neither made nor meditated any of those unworthy concessions which have compelled us to blush for our brethren in some other places. Regardless alike of the assaults of declared enemies, and the insidious suggestions of timid or time-serving friends, she has held on the even tenor of her way, amid opposition and contumely—her members determined to hold and exercise the unalienable right of association, and confident that their fellow-citizens would ultimately sustain them in this manly and worthy determination.

Nor have our fidelity and perseverance failed of an abundant reward in the auspicious circumstances to which this report particularly relates. Freemasonry has recovered her home—the Grand Lodge is no longer a tenant—this beautiful edifice, the object of our common interest and pride, is again our own, and we may well nigh realize the consciousness of the independence and security of those who sit under their own vine and fig-tree, having none to molest or make them afraid.

      *   *   *   *   *   *   *

The report was unanimously accepted and ordered to be placed on record.

The valuable papers, the jewels, and other property of the several Masonic Institutions, being deemed unsafe, from fire, in the ante-rooms of the Masonic apartments in the Temple, where they were usually deposited, it was determined to con-

struct a fire-proof safe, in which they might be
secured; and it is a subject of regret that this work
failed to be serviceable for what it was designed.
Its mode of construction was not calculated to
prevent that dampness which in a short time
would have destroyed what it was hoped it would
have preserved, and therefore it was abandoned.
The proceedings of Columbian Lodge in relation
to this depository are here given:

March 7, 5839. " On motion of Brother Appleton, *Voted*,
That the Treasurer of Columbian Lodge be empowered to pay
over to the proper authority any amount (not to exceed the
sum of twenty dollars,) which may be assessed as the proportion of the Lodge, towards building a fire-proof safe within
the Masonic Temple, for the deposit and safe-keeping of
records, jewels, &c., belonging to the several institutions of
the Fraternity, under the jurisdiction of the Grand Lodge or
other Masonic bodies of Massachusetts, in Boston."

September 17, 5839. " *Voted*, That R. W. Bros. Geo. G.
Smith and Benj. B. Appleton be a committee to attend to the
deposit of the jewels and other property of the Lodge in the
safe appropriated to the use of the Masonic bodies of this
city."

During the summer of 5842, the hall and adjoining rooms underwent some repairs, and an
organ was put up,—a present from R. W. Edward
A. Raymond. The action of the Lodge in relation thereto is thus recorded:

September 1, 5842. "R. W. Bro. Lewis, one of a committee appointed by the Trustees of the Temple to make repairs in the Masonic apartments during the summer recess,
stated that the repairs had been completed, and that a fine
organ had been presented for the use of the various Lodges
occupying the apartments, by R. W. Bro. E. A. Raymond,
whereupon it was
Voted, unanimously, That Columbian Lodge gratefully ac-
cepts and acknowledges the munificent and acceptable dona-

tion of Bro. Raymond ; and that the Secretary be directed to communicate to him this vote of the Lodge.''

In consequence of the increase of members of the several Masonic Institutions, it became necessary to enlarge the apartments devoted to Masonic uses. For this purpose the third story of the Temple was appropriated, and during the summer of 5846 it was converted into the spacious and elegant rooms where the brethren now assemble. Columbian Lodge acted in concert with the other institutions in the measures necessary to effect these additional accommodations, i. e.:

April 17, 5846. '' R. W. Master, from the Committee of Conference, reported in favor of joining the other Masonic Institutions in the enlargement of our apartments, which report was accepted ; and on motion of Bro. Baxter, the sum of two hundred dollars was appropriated towards the expense of furnishing the rooms.''

At the meeting of November 5, 5846, the following invitation, from the Committee of the Grand Lodge, was received :

BOSTON, October 27, 1846.

The Committee of Arrangements, on the Dedication of the new Masonic Hall, in the Temple, having fixed upon the evening of WEDNESDAY, the 11th of November next, for the performance of that ceremony, respectfully invite the officers and members of Columbian Lodge to be present on the occasion in their regalia.

Fraternally, yours,

WINSLOW LEWIS, JR.,
GEO. G. SMITH,
ENOCH HOBART,   } Committee.
RUEL BAKER,
WILLIAM EATON,

January 7, 5847. "A communication was received from Bro. G. G. Smith, in relation to the repairs of this Hall, asking for a further appropriation from the Lodge. The Treasurer, Secretary, Bro. Heard and the Master, were appointed a committee to pay to the Committee on Repairs the sum of one hundred and fifty dollars; and the Treasurer was authorized to make such arrangements with the stock of the Lodge as to meet any demands on him."

The following account of the dedication of this Hall, and description of it and the rooms contiguous, is from the Freemasons' Magazine:

DEDICATION OF THE NEW MASONIC HALL, IN THE MASONIC TEMPLE, BOSTON.

The new and beautiful Hall, recently fitted up in the Temple, for the use of the Lodges and other Masonic bodies in this city, was dedicated, in ancient form, by the Grand Lodge of this Commonwealth, on Wednesday, the 11th ult. The Hall was filled, at an early hour, to its utmost capacity, by Brethren of the city and neighboring towns. The Boston Encampment, the Grand Council of Princes of Jerusalem, the Chapters and several Lodges, were present in their regalia and jewels, and made a rich and imposing appearance.

The ceremonies were commenced by a voluntary on the organ, which was followed by an appropriate and fervent prayer by the Grand Chaplain. After which, the following Chant, from Bro. Power's "Masonic Melodies," was sung by the Choir, led by Bro. Wm. B Oliver:

REJOICE, all ye that are assembled in the Lord,
For in safety have we met again this day:
From the hands of our enemies He hath delivered us,
And the light of His countenance is here.

How beautiful are the gates of our Temple seen!
The incense of devotion we bring unto its courts:
With thankful hearts, before its altars we here appear,
To bow down and worship before His holy throne.

Let all the Brethren, in songs of praise, unite,
For all the goodness of God unto us shown:
We will rejoice in His mercy, evermore,
While together we journey through life. Amen. Amen.

The ceremonies of Consecration were then performed by the Grand Master, M. W. Simon W. Robinson, Esq., in a solemn and impressive manner, and in strict conformity with ancient Masonic form and usage; during which Nos. 21 and 22 of the Melodies were sung by the Choir. The dedicatory prayer by the Grand Chaplain concluded this part of the ceremonies.

The W. and Rev. Bro. Albert Case, of Worcester, then delivered an Address, of great beauty and excellence, in which he briefly alluded to the custom in all ages, of erecting structures for scientific, moral, religious and other purposes. He also referred to the ancient custom of dedication, the early erection of Masonic Halls in Europe, and gave an interesting narrative of the various efforts by the Grand Lodge of Massachusetts, for the erection or purchase of a suitable building for its own permanent use. This part of the address was full of interest, and new to most of the Brethren present. He next spoke of the erection and dedication of the Temple in which he was standing, referred to the adverse circumstances under which the enterprise was begun and carried though, and paid a just and merited compliment to its projectors. He then spoke of the beautiful apartments which they were then solemnly consecrating to Masonry, Virtue and Universal Benevolence,—complimented the Fraternity in the city on their liberality, and the committee on the good taste they had displayed in the arrangements and decorations, and the faithfulness with which they had discharged their responsible duties. He also referred to the generous donations of a beautiful chandelier, by the Grand Encampment of Massachusetts and Rhode Island—of three richly carved and costly chairs, for the East, by Bro. Jonas Chickering, and of a beautiful and valuable clock, by R. W. Bro. C. Gayton Pickman,— and concluded by an earnest caution to the Lodges against the too free admission of applicants, and the too hasty manner in which they were often passed through the degrees. The address was an able and eminently acceptable performance, and we are happy in having it in our power to state, that the Grand Lodge having requested a copy for its use, it will probably be published.

The "Concluding Melody," No. 23, was then sung:

> Our Temple reared, the cap-stone raised,
> Our altars blessed, Jehovah praised,
> Accept, O God, our solemn vow, -
> Before Thy holy name to bow.

O, let each heart a temple be,
Of heavenly truth and charity;
That life passed o'er, Thy Spirit, given,
May gather all to Thee, in Heaven.

After a Benediction by the Rev. and venerable Brother, Dr. ASA EATON, the Grand Lodge retired to their room, and the visiting Brethren to their homes.

The Masonic Fraternity in the city have heretofore occupied the upper apartments in the Temple; but, though of more than the ordinary capacity of Masonic Halls, and possessing many desirable conveniences, they were found, the last season, not to be sufficiently capacious to meet the increasing wants of the Lodges and other bodies which occupied them. It was, therefore, determined to fit up the apartments in the story next below, for Masonic purposes, for which they were originally designed. These consist of the main hall, 55 by 38 feet, a withdrawing room, 30 feet square, and several ante-rooms. This duty was committed to the superintendence of R. W. Bros. GEO. G. SMITH, EDWARD A. RAYMOND, and AMMI B. YOUNG. They have been fitted up, as nearly as could conveniently be done, with a Gothic finish. The ceiling and walls are richly frescoed, and embellished with appropriate emblems. This part of the work was executed by Bro. T. C. SAVORY, and is highly creditable to him as an artist. The canopy in the East, the drapery in other parts of the hall, and the permanent fixtures, are not less evincive of good taste in the committee, under whose direction the whole was designed, than of skill in the artist, Bro. EDWARD HENNESSEY. Indeed, all engaged in the undertaking have acquitted themselves in a highly acceptable manner, and our sincere prayer is, that they may long continue to enjoy the beautiful work of their own creation.

Besides the above apartments, the Fraternity will continue to improve, as heretofore, the rooms in the upper story of the building. These have been entirely renovated, and though much inferior to the new apartments, are, probably, in appearance and convenience, surpassed by few, if any, Masonic rooms in this country.

The amount expended will not, we understand, vary far from three thousand dollars. The whole of the apartments are lighted with gas, and in the evening present a brilliant appearance. The Brethren in Boston may be justly proud of their Masonic Temple.

In the narration embraced in this and the preceding chapters, every place that has been occupied by Columbian Lodge, for their communications, from the first meeting to the present time, has been clearly designated; and all their proceedings in relation to procuring places for meetings, are presented in detail. It is believed that no material fact has been omitted, and that the data here given, affords the means of determining the precise locality where each and every meeting was held. The transactions of the Lodge and of the Grand Lodge, and the concurrent action of the other Masonic bodies in Boston, which eventuated in the erection of the Temple, have also been so minutely described as to leave no important matter untold.

May it not be hoped that the Masonic Temple will remain forever in the possession of the Fraternity? Occupying a site unsurpassed for beauty and convenience, ornamental in its architecture, of solid and lasting materials, of ample dimensions, what more suitable place or structure can be desired? When economical considerations will allow of it, this edifice should be exclusively devoted to the purposes of Masonry; and it may be predicted that the day is not far distant when this will be realized.

CHAPTER VI.

BY-LAWS—CODES ADOPTED, 5795, &c.

The legislation of Columbian Lodge for their own government is replete with instructive information, and cannot fail to attract the attention of the enquirer who would know by what rules the brethren were in primitive times controlled. It being to a considerable extent illustrative of the history of the Lodge, and reflecting the views and feelings that have from time to time influenced them on important subjects, will justify a full account of it in this volume. It will be interesting, in tracing it, to observe the changes it indicates in the internal economy and customs of the Lodge, and, by comparing one code of laws with another, to note the probable or expressed cause of alteration or repeal.

The last two codes alone have been printed, while the others have existed only in manuscript, liable to irreparable injury or destruction. Already, it is feared has this misfortune occurred to the code of 5797, as no copy of it can be found on record or on file, though the strictest search for one has been made. The original copy of the By-Laws first adopted is also missing, but, happily, when the records were transcribed, in 5811, the faithful officer who performed that labor made a transcript of these laws, and by this means they have been preserved unshorn of a single provision.

What has befallen these important documents affords the strongest reasons for the multiplication of the remaining older laws in some form which shall ensure their preservation.

Seven codes of By-Laws have been adopted by the Lodge, i. e., the original and those of Feb. 12, 5797, May 2, 5799, April 7, 5808, August 1, 5816, June 22, 5821, and November 28, 5854. The various modifications to which the several by-laws have been subjected, by alteration or amendment of their provisions, will be inserted in their proper places, as to dates, to show their application, and the bearing they had upon the affairs of the Lodge.

The original by-laws contain provisions relative to the personal conduct of members towards each other, which could have had no practical application ; for a more harmonious and brotherly society of men or Masons than that composed of the founders of the Lodge, could not then or at this time be found within the bounds of civilization.

ORIGINAL BY-LAWS.

By-Laws for the Government of Columbian Lodge.

ARTICLE I.

Section 1. This Lodge will meet at such place as the majority shall think fit, on the first Thursday of every month, and in case of removal report shall be made to the Grand Lodge, at the next Quarterly Communication ; but the Master and Wardens, for the time being, shall have power to call Special Lodges on any Emergency.

Sect. 2. This Lodge may consist of *Thirty Members*, unless a majority may think it expedient to alter the number.

Sect. 3. That the greatest decency and good order may be observed, it is strongly recommended that every member appear cleanly dressed each Lodge night, and that no member presume to wear an apron, either in Lodge or at any procession, which has any paintings or decorations thereon, other than being lined, fringed, or trimmed with Ribbon. The Lodge conceiving any paintings or emblematic decorations to be highly inconsistent with the Masonic Art.

It shall be the duty of the Master to transact as much as possible all important Business of the Lodge previous to their being called to refreshment, and when he shall call to order there shall be profound silence, and the Lodge shall be closed when it is his pleasure.

Sect. 4. In all debates, every Brother, while speaking, shall stand and address the Master ; and whoever shall interrupt a Brother while speaking shall be reprimanded by the Master, and no Brother shall speak more than twice to the same question, unless to explain himself.

Sect. 5. If convenient, a Lecture shall be given by the Master, or his appointment, every Lodge night, during which the strictest attention shall be given, and no one shall be admitted into the Room.

Sect. 6. No Liquors shall be brought into the Lodge Room unless by order of the Master.

Sect. 7. No Brother shall quit the Lodge during Lodge hours without permission of the Master.

Sect. 8. Any Brother, while in the Lodge, or in the Lodge Room, after the Lodge is closed, who may be guilty of any quarrelling or fighting, shall use abusive or oprobrious language, or behave in any manner derogatory to the character of a good Mason, shall, for the first offence, be publicly admonished by the Master, the next time he comes into the Lodge, and for the second offence he shall be expelled the same.

ARTICLE II.

OF OFFICERS.

Sect. 1. The choice of officers shall be Annually, on the Evening preceding the Festival of St. John.

Sect. 2. The Master, Wardens, Treasurer and Secretary shall be chosen by Ballot, a majority of votes making a choice ; the other officers shall be chosen by the Lodge, by hand votes.

Sect. 3. It shall be the duty of the *Treasurer* to keep a just and fair account of all monies received and paid by him, on account of the Lodge, to account for the same when called upon by the Lodge, and to exhibit the Lodges' stock on the Table once in three months, give bonds, for the faithful discharge of his office, to the Master and Wardens, if required ; and when a new choice is made he shall deliver all the Lodges' property he possesses to the new Treasurer, and whenever the moneys in his hands shall amount to one hundred and fifty dollars, he shall acquaint the Lodge thereof, one hundred of which only shall be appropriated to the stock of the Lodge.

Sect. 4. It shall be the duty of the *Secretary* to keep a fair Record of the Transactions of the Lodge in a Book appropriated for that purpose ; to read the Records of the preceding meeting, as soon as the next Lodge is opened, if required. To send printed notifications to every member living in town, of the time and place of meeting each regular Lodge, noting on the summons the names of every candidate proposed to be made in this Lodge, and when any such names are inserted in the notification they shall be sealed ; to collect all monies in the Lodge, and pay the same to the Treasurer, taking his receipt for the same ; to Read the By-Laws and petitions when desired by the Master, and to attend, when required, on Committees of the Lodge, and when a new choice is made deliver an inventory of the furniture and utensils to his successor, to be placed on the files.

Sect. 5. The *Stewards* shall furnish the Tables when directed thereto by the Master, and on the Evening of the choice of officers they shall exhibit, in writing, to the Master, an inventory of the utensils and furniture belonging to the Lodge, and shall deliver the same to the *new Stewards*, and a copy of the inventory to the Secretary, for Record.

Sect. 6. The *Tiler* shall not be a member of any Lodge. He shall deliver the notifications to the members, and be subject to the direction of the Master.

ARTICLE III.

OF MEMBERS.

Sect. 1. Every *Brother* made in this Lodge desirous to become a member shall stand proposed one month, when he shall be balloted for, and if not more than three negatives appear against him he shall be admitted, after signing the By-Laws and paying the usual fees, but no Brother shall be proposed to become a member the same night he is made.

SECT. 2. Every *Brother* not made in this Lodge desirous to become a member shall be subject to the same proceedings as are requisite when a candidate made in this Lodge is proposed.

SECT. 3. No *Brother* shall enjoy the privileges of a member unless he complies with all the duties specified above.

SECT. 4. Every Member who shall propose a candidate to be made, shall deposit in the hands of the Secretary Five Dollars, which, if the candidate is accepted, shall be placed to his credit; if the candidate does not attend, the deposit shall be forfeited; but if he attends and is not accepted, it shall be returned.

SECT. 5. Every Member who shall neglect to pay his quarterages for three successive quarters, after being called thereon for, shall forever forfeit his privileges as a member, and all right to the Lodges' stock, unless he can give satisfactory reasons to the Lodge for his delinquency. Seafaring brethren shall be subject to these regulations only when at home.

ARTICLE IV.
OF CANDIDATES.

SECT. 1. Every Candidate to be made a Mason shall stand proposed one month, and if he obtains the unanimous consent of the Brethren present, he may be entered an apprentice; should two negatives appear against him, no further proceedings shall be had at the time of proposing. But if only one negative appears, he may have the Benefit of a second and third Trial. If proposed again, it shall be in the same manner as though he had never been mentioned in the Lodge. In cases of emergency, the dispensation of the Grand Master shall supercede the necessity of standing one month; and no candidate shall be made at a Lodge *specially* called for that purpose, unless he pays the expenses of that night, besides the usual fees.

SECT. 2. Every Brother made in this Lodge shall be passed a Fellow Craft whenever the Master shall judge him deserving that degree. But Brethren not made in this Lodge, desirous to be passed, must obtain the unanimous consent of the Brethren present; if obtained, he shall receive the degree, paying the usual Fees.

SECT. 3. Every Brother who desires to be raised to the Sublime Degree of Master Mason, shall be examined before the Lodge, respecting the proficiency he has made in his former degrees, after which, and obtaining the unanimous consent of the Brethren present, he shall receive that Degree, paying the usual Fee.

ARTICLE V.

OF VISITORS.

SECT. 1. No Brother, if he is a Foreigner, shall pay towards the expenses of the Evening, the first time he visits the Lodge, but every Brother belonging to Town, *or its vicinities*, shall pay for the first visit two shillings.

ARTICLE VI.

SECT. 1. Any Brother who discloses the Private transactions of the Lodge to any one who is not a member, shall, for the first offence, receive a public admonition by the Master, the first time he appears in Lodge, and for the second he shall be expelled the same.

SECT. 2. Any Brother who shall mention to any person not a member of this Lodge, the name of any person negatived in the same, shall be publicly reprimanded by the Master the first time he appears in the Lodge.

SECT. 3. Any Member of the Lodge who shall be present at the clandestine making of a Mason, or shall keep unlawful company, or shall frequent any Lodge not regularly and lawfully authorized, shall be expelled the Lodge.

ARTICLE VII.

OF FEES.

SECT. 1. Every Candidate made a Mason, shall, for being made and passed, pay.....................£3 16 6

Every Brother, not made in this Lodge, who shall be passed a Fellow Craft, shall pay................ 18 0

Every Brother raised to the sublime degree of Master Mason, if made in this Lodge, shall pay......... 1 4 0

Every Brother, *not made* in this Lodge, who shall be raised, shall pay	£1	10	0
Every Brother made in this Lodge, on his becoming a member, shall pay	3	0	0
Every Brother *not* made in this Lodge, on being admitted a member, shall pay	4	10	0
Every Member of this Lodge shall pay, every Quarter Year, (Secretary excepted,)	0	4	6
Every Brother visiting this Lodge shall pay		3	0
The Secretary shall receive, for every person made a Mason		6	0
The Closet Steward, for each meeting of the Lodge,		6	0
To Secretary, for each certificate given		12	0
The Tiler, for notifying the members		3	0
For Tiling the Lodge each night		3	0
For every person made a Mason		2	0
For every Brother made a Mason		2	0

ARTICLE VIII.

SECT. 1. All transactions in this Lodge, not specially regulated by the preceding By-Laws, shall be determined by the votes of the majority of the Brethren present, which votes shall be fairly recorded in the Book of By-Laws, with their dates, and shall be considered binding.

SECT. 2. Whenever the Breach of any of the preceding By-Laws shall come to the knowledge of the Secretary, he shall inform the Lodge of the same, under the penalty of paying forty shillings to the chest for each neglect.

SECT. 3. The foregoing Articles shall be considered as Binding on Columbian Lodge.

November 16, 5795. "*Voted,* That the By-Laws respecting the admission of members be so altered as to require an unanimous vote."

September 3, 5795. "The following Resolves then passed, (as By-Laws,) viz: *Resolved,* That the funds of this Lodge shall always be kept for the use of its members, and be applied as follows, viz:

"First—In case of the death of a member, it shall be the duty of the Master and Wardens (before the funeral, if possible,) to wait on the widow or nearest relation of the deceased member, or otherwise his administrator or assign, and present her, or them, the whole of said deceased's proportion of all the stock of the Lodge, deducting therefrom whatever he may have received before, if any, the same to be paid in cash, after deducting 2½ per cent. for the use of the Lodge. Passed unanimously.

"Second—In case any member of this Lodge shall remove from Boston, the distance of fifty miles, it shall be at his option to receive his proportion of all the stock of the Lodge, to be paid him in cash, after deducting 10 per cent. for the use of the Lodge, he giving proper notice of his removal, and in case such Brother shall again return to Boston, and wish to rejoin said Lodge as a member, he must refund the money so by him received. Passed unanimously.

"Third—No Petitioner shall at any one time receive more than ten dollars in silver, or the value thereof, out of said funds. Passed unanimously."

November 16, 5795. "Voted, That the visiting fee be raised from 2s. to 2s. 3d., or three-eighths of a dollar."

December 3, 5795. "Voted, as a By-Law, that any member hereafter admitted to the privilege of this Lodge shall, on his being received, pay to the Secretary, when demanded, his full and equal proportion of whatever all the stock of the Lodge may then amount to, over and above the sum in the former By-Laws."

March 22, 5796. "The By-Laws for members to stand one month proposed on the Book before they are admitted, was suspended by a vote of the Lodge, for this night, when Bro. Amasa Stetson and Bro. John James was balloted for to become members of this Lodge, and accepted."

April 12, 5796. "Voted, That no By-Law shall hereafter be acted upon unless two-thirds of the members are present."

May 7, 5796. "Voted, That each visiting Brother to the Columbian Lodge, after this night, is to pay half a dollar to the Secretary, for the expense of the evening."

December 1, 5796. "Voted, To choose a Committee to enquire and report on Fees of Secretary and Tyler. Bros. Goldsbury, Perkins and Raymond were chosen."

December 31, 5796. "*Moved and seconded*, That the Committee appointed to take into consideration the fees allowed the Secretary and Tiler, be requested to report, and that the Secretary furnish the chairman of that Committee with the names of the whole Committee."

On the evening of January 5, 5797, a Committee from the Grand Lodge visited Columbian Lodge and recommended a change in the By-Laws:

" The Committee also recommended to the Columbian Lodge a revision of their By-Laws, and to lay the same before them, that they may meet the approbation of the Grand Lodge at their next meeting."

And at the same meeting,—

" The Committee appointed to report the fees for the Secretary and Tyler gave in a report as follows, viz :

' The Committee appointed to take into consideration the fees of the Secretary and Tiler have attended to that service and made the necessary enquiries—that they are of opinion that the Secretary's fees for making, ought to be six shillings, and the like sum for issuing a certificate ; that the Tiler receive, for notifying the Lodge, fifty cents ; for Tiling the Lodge, fifty cents ; for each making and raising, thirty-three cents. All which is submitted.

Signed :   SAMUEL GOULDSBURY,
Chairman.' "

January 7, 5797. " On a motion to choose a Committee to take into consideration and make revision of the By-Laws, the following members were elected, viz : Worshipful Master Bros. Gouldsbury, Perkins, Folsom and Eaton."

February 2, 5797. " The Committee on the revision of the By-Laws reported progress, and requested leave to sit again, which was granted."

February 12, 5797. " The Committee appointed to alter and revise the By-Laws gave in their report.

" On a motion that the report of the Committee be read by the Secretary, passed in the affirmative. The articles were then accordingly read in gross.

"On a motion that the By-Laws read by the Secretary be again, by articles, read, debated and passed, this vote also passed in the affirmative. The articles were then accordingly taken up severally in their order debated, and with some small amendments passed unanimously.

"A motion was then made that the Laws now read and amended be received as the By-Laws of the Columbian Lodge. Passed in the affirmative.

"On a motion that the Secretary be directed to present the By-Laws to the Committee of the Grand Lodge, for their approbation—passed in the affirmative.

"On a motion, the Secretary be directed to copy the By-Laws of the Columbian Lodge, or procure them to be done, in a Book, for that purpose, at the expense of the Lodge— passed in the affirmative.

"On a motion to fix the hours of meeting and closing the Lodge at the monthly meetings—passed in the negative. This motion was overruled under the idea that such power remains only with the Master of the Lodge."

March 2, 5797. "The Secretary reported that agreeable to the vote of the Lodge, at their last meeting, to present the By-Laws (as they had been lately revised,) for the inspection of the Grand Lodge of Massachusetts, he had performed that service, and that they were accordingly unanimously approved."

As has been already stated, the By-Laws adopted in the transactions just narrated are not in the possession of the Lodge, and are, probably, irrevocably lost. This is the more to be regretted as their absence is the only link wanting in the chain of the legislation of the Lodge from the date of their origin to the present time. The succeeding extracts, from the records, will show what took place previous to the adoption of the By-Laws of May 2, 5799. The instructions from the Grand Lodge, alluded to in the records, were, without doubt, regulations for the Lodge; and, it may be presumed, they were the same which are recorded with the By-Laws of 5799, as will be seen hereafter.

August 10, 5797. " The Secretary having laid on the table instructions to all the Lodges under the jurisdiction of the Grand Lodge of Massachusetts, the same was read, and, on motion, *Voted*, That the Secretary be directed to have the same framed and placed in the Lodge Room."

February 8, 5798. " A motion was made to appoint a committee to examine and revise the By-Laws, and to make report at the ensuing monthly meeting. The following members were accordingly chosen, viz : Bros. Churchill, Eaton, Coles, H. Stetson and Hayden."

March 1, 5798. " The committee appointed to revise the By-Laws gave in the following report, viz :

' The committee appointed at the last meeting to take into consideration a revision of the By-Laws, having attended to that service, beg leave to report, that in their opinions the 10th article of the By-Laws be expunged. That that part of the 11th article, so far as annexes a penalty of one dollar, be also expunged.

" Your committee are of opinion that the present mode of loaning monies may tend to interrupt the harmony and create disunion in the Lodge; they do therefore recommend in future that the Lodge appoint a committee whenever it may become necessary to loan any part of the stock of the Lodge, so that the same may be put into such public stock as may be found to be most productive and safe.

JOS. CHURCHILL, }
S. HAYDEN,   } *Committee.*
AMASA STETSON, }

" The before mentioned report having been taken up, the same was read by paragraphs, unanimously accepted, and passed to be engrafted on the By-Laws.

" A Committee was then appointed, agreeable to the report, and for the purpose therein mentioned, consisting of the following members, viz : Bros. Churchill, Eaton, Folsom, A. Stetson and Hayden."

April 4, 5799.   '' The committee was then chosen to revise the By-Laws, viz : Bros. Coles, Folsom and Tannatt.''

May 2, 5799.   '' The committee appointed to revise and amend the By-Laws gave a report, which consists of a new draft, which being read by paragraphs, with amendments, the Secretary was directed to have the same copied in a Book provided for that purpose.

'' Bro. A. Stetson made a motion that an addition be made to the —— Article of our By-Laws, to provide that in all cases when a ballot is taken by the Lodge, for the admission of a candidate, or admittance of a member, and but two negatives appearing against him, that such candidate may have the advantage of the second and third trial. Should they persist, he or they so opposing shall be obliged to assign his or their reasons for so doing to the Master and Wardens for the time being, (in a room which the parties shall withdraw for that purpose,) where the Master and Wardens shall determine whether the reasons given shall amount to a negative ; but in case he or they shall refuse to give such information above mentioned, the vote shall be considered and pass unanimous.''

BY-LAWS

OF THE

COLUMBIAN LODGE,

Adopted May 2, 5799.

ARTICLE 1.   That this Lodge meet at Masons' Hall on the first Thursday of every month ; and in case of removal, report shall be made to the Grand Lodge at the next Quarterly Communication.   But the Master and Wardens for the time being shall have power to call special Lodges on any emergency.

ART. 2.   That the number of members for this Lodge shall consist of *fifty*, and no more, unless it should appear necessary for the benefit of Masonry, in which case it shall be determined by a majority of votes; *provided*, two-thirds of the members who are summoned are present, but not otherwise.

Art. 3. It shall be the duty of the Master to transact as much as possible the business of the Lodge previous to their being called to refreshment, and when he shall call to order there shall be profound silence.

Art. 4. In all debates every Brother while speaking shall stand and address the Master, and whoever shall interrupt a Brother while speaking shall be reprimanded by the Master, and no Brother shall speak more than twice to the same question unless to explain himself.

Art. 5. If convenient, a Lecture shall be given by the Master or his appointment every Lodge night, during which strict attention shall be given, and no one shall be admitted into the room.

Art. 6. No liquors shall be brought into the Lodge Room but by order of the Master.

Art. 7. No Brother shall quit the Lodge during Lodge hours without permission of the Master.

Art. 8. Any Brother while in the Lodge, or in the Lodge Room, after the Lodge is closed, who shall be guilty of any quarrelling or fighting, use abusive or opprobrious language, or behave in a manner derogatory to the character of a Mason, shall, for the first offence, be publicly admonished by the Master, the next time he comes into the Lodge, and for the second offence he shall be expelled the same.

Art. 9. No Brother shall visit or come into the Lodge who is disguised in liquor, whereby the harmony thereof may be disturbed.

Art. 10. The officers shall be chosen annually, on the first Thursday evening in December, preceding the festival of St. John.

Art. 11. The Master, Wardens, Treasurer, Secretary, Deacons and Stewards, shall be chosen by ballot, a majority of votes making a choice.

Art. 12. It shall be the duty of the Treasurer to keep a just and fair account of all monies received and paid by him on account of the Lodge, to account for the same when called upon by the Lodge, and give bonds for the faithful discharge of his office to the Master and Wardens if required, and whenever the monies in his hands shall amount to one hundred and fifty dollars, the same shall be laid on the table, and the Lodge made acquainted therewith, one hundred of which shall be appropriated to the stock of the Lodge and fifty remain in the Treasurer's hands, for the immediate uses of the Lodge, and when a new choice is made he shall deliver the Lodge's property he possesses into the hands of his successor.

ART. 13. It shall be the duty of the Secretary to keep a fair record of the votes and transactions of the Lodge in a Book appropriated for that purpose, to read the records of the preceding meeting as soon as the next Lodge is opened, if required, to send printed notifications to every member living in the town, of the time and place of meeting each regular Lodge, noting in the summons the names of the candidates proposed to be made in the Lodge, and of the Brethren proposed to become members, if not made in this Lodge, and whenever such names are inserted in the notification they shall be sealed; to collect the monies in the Lodge, and pay the same to the Treasurer, previous to the next regular meeting, taking his receipt for the same; to read the By-Laws and Petitions when desired by the Master, and to attend when required on committees of the Lodge, and when a new choice is made to deliver an inventory of the furniture and utensils to his successor, to be placed on the files. It shall also be the duty of the Secretary to call regularly on each member for his quarterages, when due, by noting it on the summons; should any member be found deficient to the amount of three quarters, the Secretary shall report the same to the Lodge on the next regular meeting, and a record made of the same. It shall then further be the duty of the Secretary to inform such delinquent member or members, in writing, that unless said arrearages are discharged previous to the next regular meeting of the Lodge report will be made and his name erased from the Books, and he will no longer be considered a member thereof. Seafaring Brethren shall be subject to these regulations only when at home.

ART. 14. It shall be the duty of the Stewards to furnish the tables when directed by the Master, and be subject to his directions while in the Lodge.

ART. 15. While the Lodge determines to procure their own stores there shall be a Closet Steward elected annually by the Master and Wardens, whose duty it shall be to take care of the stores, and acquaint the Treasurer from time to time, so that the closet may be properly supplied, and to keep the room and utensils of the Lodge in cleanly order, extinguish the fires and lights, and dispose of the keys under the direction of the Master, and to attend on committees when required; he shall be a member of the Lodge, and in case of necessary absence no other but a member of the Lodge shall supply his place, and be approved of by the Master. The compensation to be allowed him under the article of Fees.

ART. 16.   The Tiler shall not be a member of any Lodge; he shall deliver the notifications to the members, and be subject to the direction of the Master.

ART. 17.   Every Brother made in this Lodge and desirous to become a member, shall stand on the Books proposed one month, when he may be balloted for, and if it shall appear that he has an unanimous vote, he shall be admitted, on paying five dollars and signing the By-Laws; and every Brother not made in this Lodge and desirous to become a member, shall be admitted in like manner, on paying the sum of seven dollars.

ART. 18.   Every member who shall propose a candidate to be made shall deposit in the hands of the Secretary *five dollars*, which sum, if the candidate is accepted, shall be placed to his credit; if the candidate does not attend, and is not accepted, then the money shall be returned.

ART. 19.   Every candidate to be made a Mason shall stand proposed one month, and if he obtain the unanimous consent of the Brethren present, he may be entered an Apprentice; should three negatives appear against him, no further proceeding shall be had at that time of proposing, but if only one or two negatives appear, he may have the benefit of a second trial; if proposed again, it shall be in the same manner as though he had never been mentioned in the Lodge. In cases of emergency, the dispensation of the Grand Master shall supercede the necessity of standing one month, and no candidate shall be made at a Lodge specially called for that purpose unless he or they pay the expenses for that night besides the usual fees.

Art. 20. Every Brother made in this Lodge shall be passed a Fellow Craft whenever the Master shall judge him deserving that degree. But any Brother not made in this Lodge, desirous to be passed, must obtain the unanimous consent of the Brethren present; if obtained, he shall receive the Degree, paying the usual fees.

Art. 21. Every Brother desirous to be raised to the Sublime Degree shall obtain the consent of the Brethren present, and be recommended by the Master as qualified to receive it, when the degree may be conferred on him, he paying the usual fees.

Art. 22. No Brother shall pay a visiting fee the first time he appears in the Lodge, but all other visitors shall pay three shillings, unless excused by the Master.

Art. 23. Any Brother who discloses the private transactions of the Lodge to any one who is not a member, shall, for the first offence, receive a public admonition by the Master, the first time he appears in the Lodge, and for the second his name shall be erased from the Books.

Art. 24. Any member of this Lodge who shall be present at the clandestine making of a Mason, or shall keep unlawful company, or shall frequent any Lodge not regularly and lawfully authorized, his name shall be erased from the Books.

Art. 25. No sum exceeding five dollars shall at any time be taken from the funds of the Lodge unless two-thirds of the members who are summoned are present, in which case a majority of votes shall determine on any sum not exceeding ten dollars, as the case may require; *provided*, however, that when any such applicant may be a member, the widow or orphan of a member, then such number shall have power to grant twenty dollars, as the case may require.

Art. 26. Should it be found expedient to make any new By-Laws, or alter or amend any of the foregoing, such laws or alterations shall be committed to writing, at a meeting prior to its determination, and such notice given in the summons, and when two-thirds of the members of the Lodge who are summoned are present, a majority shall determine; then such law or alteration shall become permanent and binding.

ART. 27. The Stewards of the Lodge shall be exempt from quarterages when they attend the Lodge, and chargeable only when absent.

ART. 28. No vote shall be taken for the admission of a member when a less number than a majority of the Lodge that have been summoned are present ; and no vote of the Lodge shall be reconsidered by a less number than when the same was passed ; and the Master shall not be eligible to vote only when there is an equal division, in which case he shall have the casting vote.

ART. 29. All officers of the Lodge when absent on Lodge nights shall pay towards the funds of the Lodge a fine of fifty cents, unless confined by sickness or out of town.

------⦿------

INSTRUCTIONS

To all the Lodges under the Jurisdiction of the Grand Lodge of Massachusetts.

ARTICLE 1. By the Constitution of the Grand Lodge of Massachusetts, Chapter 5, Section 9, Article 1—The four quarterly communications in Grand Lodge shall be held on the evenings of the second Mondays in December, March, June and September.

ART. 2. The 6th, same section. Every Lodge under this jurisdiction shall, once every year, transmit to the Grand Lodge the names of their officers, &c., also the names of the Brethren who have been made Masons, passed Fellow Crafts, and raised to the sublime degree of Master Masons, in order that the same may be duly noticed in the Grand Lodge. By a vote which passed in the Grand Lodge June 11th, 5792, being the second Monday, every Lodge under this jurisdiction shall send a list of their members to the Grand Secretary, to be recorded in the Grand Lodge Book, in a page kept for that purpose, &c.; the names of every person made a Mason after this date, with three shillings for each person so made, to be kept as a Fund for Charity.

ART. 3. Article the 7th, same. Every Lodge shall be represented by their own Master and Wardens, or by proxy ;

and no proxy shall be received in the Grand Lodge except he
be a Master Mason and a member of some Lodge under this
Jurisdiction.

ART. 4.   April 2, 5792, A. L.   *Voted*, Every Lodge within this Jurisdiction shall pay *two dollars*, quarterly, for the
support of the Grand Lodge.

ART. 5.   When any Brother shall so misbehave as that the
Lodge of which he is a member shall expel him, his name,
with his crime, shall be transmitted to the Grand Lodge.

ART. 6.   That these instructions be recorded in the Lodge
Book of By-Laws of every Lodge under this Jurisdiction, and
read to the Lodge once in every quarter.

A true copy of Record.
　　Signed :　　　　　　　DANIEL OLIVER,
　　　　　　　　　　　　　　　Grand Secretary.

——◦◦——

FEES.

Every candidate made a Mason shall, for being made and passed, pay	$17 00
Every Brother not made in this Lodge who shall be passed a Fellow Craft	2 00
Every Brother raised to the Sublime Degree of Master Mason, if made in this Lodge, shall pay	3 00
Every Brother not made in this Lodge who shall be raised shall pay	5 00
Every Brother made in this Lodge, on his becoming a member, shall pay	5 00
Every Brother not made in this Lodge, on his becoming a member shall pay	7 00
Every member of this Lodge (Secretary excepted,) shall pay every quarter year	75
Every Visiting Brother to this Lodge shall pay	50
The Secretary shall receive for every person made a Mason in this Lodge	1 00
The Steward of the Closet shall receive at every meeting of the Lodge	2 00
The Secretary shall receive for every certificate, exclusive of the parchment	2 00
The Tiler shall receive for notifying members	50
For Tiling the Lodge each night	50
For every person made a Mason	33
For every Brother raised to the Sublime Degree	33

At the close of the year 5800 and subsequently several propositions were made to alter and revise the By-Laws, but no actual change occurred until December 3, 5801, when—

"The Committee * * * on By-Laws reported * * * * that the 28th Article of the By-Laws be so amended as to enable a majority of the members in town, summoned, to vote for the admission of a member. On motion, *Voted*, That the whole report be accepted, and that the By-Laws be altered accordingly."

At the meeting of January 7, 5802, a committee were "appointed to enquire into the circumstances of Brethren of the Lodge who had suffered by the late conflagration," and consider the propriety of dispensing with that part of the 25th Article of the By-Laws relating to the application of money to distressed members. The conflagration referred to was probably that which occurred in Ann street, December 16, 5801.

The report of the committee was made January 11, 5802, and ordered to be placed on file. It not being now on file, and the records being silent as to its purport as far as it related to the By-Law referred to their consideration, there remains not even the ground for conjecture as to what was the action of the Lodge in the matter, except that the report was accepted.

The subjoined extracts from the records have reference to proceedings consequent upon a communication from the Grand Lodge:

January 25, 5802. "The R. W. Master, Bro. Baxter and Bro. S. Stetson, were appointed a Committee to take into consideration the communication of the Grand Lodge, and to recommend what alteration (if any,) is necessary in our By-Laws to make them conformable thereto, and report the next regular night."

Feb. 4, 5802. " The committee appointed the last Lodge night to take into consideration the Regulations communicated from the Grand Lodge, and to recommend what alterations (if any,) are necessary in our By-Laws to make them conformable thereto, reported that they have attended to that duty, and beg leave to report:

1st. That the Regulations of the Grand Lodge render it indispensably necessary to alter the price of making a Mason to fifteen dollars, including the two dollars required by the Grand Lodge for every Initiate.

2d. That the price of passing to the Degree of Fellow Craft be two dollars.

3d. That every Brother raised to the Sublime Degree of Master shall pay three dollars.

4th. That the Secretary shall receive for every certificate (notwithstanding the regulations of the Grand Lodge,) one dollar, exclusive of the parchment, and that the Secretary be directed to alter the Table of Fees accordingly. All of which is duly submitted.

On motion, *Voted, unanimously*, That the above report be accepted."

Alterations of the By-Laws were proposed June 3, 5802, July 7, 5803, and November 21, 5803. The committee chosen at the date last named reported soon after their appointment, as will be seen by the following extracts:

December 1, 5803. " The committee appointed last Lodge night to alter the By-Laws and provide a permanent Fund, gave in the following report, viz:

" The Committee appointed to provide for a Fund, and for the management thereof, and to alter the By-Laws to conform thereto, have attended to that service and beg leave to report the following articles:

ARTICLE 1. To provide for the relief of the distressed is a prominent principle of our Order, therefore, all monies that arise from memberships, donations and assessments upon members, is appropriated for a sacred *permanent Fund*, for the benefit and relief of *widows and orphans of deceased members*.

ART. 2. There shall be chosen annually, on the evening for the choice of officers at the Lodge, three Trustees, for the management of the permanent fund; it shall be their duty, immediately upon the death of a member, to present to the legal heirs of the deceased his share of the said Fund.

ART. 3. Should any member remove twenty miles from Boston, he may draw nine-tenths of a share from the permanent fund, leaving the ten per cent. for the benefit of this Establishment; and should any member conduct himself so unbecomingly as to deprive him of his membership, he shall forfeit all claim to this fund.

ART. 4. That every Brother admitted a member shall deposit a sum equal to a full share in the permanent fund, in addition to the sum paid for membership.

ART. 5. That every member of the Lodge be assessed and pay quarterly one dollar, instead of seventy-five cents.

ART. 6. That the 27th Article of the By-Laws be expunged, excepting the Stewards from quarterages, and that Article 19 be so far altered as for a candidate to be proposed at a previous meeting, instead of standing proposed one month.

ART. 7. That the Table of Fees be altered to this report, and that the Secretary be allowed to receive two dollars, instead of one, for certificates.

All of which is duly submitted.

Signed: AMASA STETSON,
            DANIEL BAXTER,   } *Members.*
            WM. S. McDONNELL,

The above report was read and unanimously accepted by a vote of the Lodge—22 members present.

During a term of about three years no alteration of the By-laws was adopted, though several propositions were made during this period which were designed to change them in some respects, but not essentially. At the meeting of November 1, 5804, it was proposed to increase the number of the Trustees of the Permanent Fund to five in lieu of three.

13*

December 4, 5806. "The Committee chosen at the last meeting of Columbian Lodge to take into consideration the expediency of altering the by-laws establishing the permanent Fund, and also the fees of the Closet Steward, have attended to that service and report, that they are of opinion the following alterations of the by-laws are necessary, viz :

1st. That the 4th Article of the Laws regulating the permanent Fund be so far altered as that every Brother on becoming a member of this Lodge shall deposit a sum equal to one half of a full share in the fund in addition to the usual sum paid for membership.

2nd. That the 3rd Article be so altered that every Brother *hereafter* becoming a member, who shall withdraw his membership, in consequence of his removal more than twenty miles from Boston, shall have a right to receive nine tenths of a moiety of one share in the said fund, provided he has in all respects complied with the requisitions of the by-laws of the Lodge.

3rd. That the closet Steward shall be entitled to one dollar instead of two for his services every night he attends the Lodge.

Your Committee also recommend that the following Article be added to the by-laws, viz :

' That whenever an application is made by a Brother to become a member of this lodge, the R. W. Master shall call for a nomination of not more than *five* nor less than *three* members as a Committee to make enquiry of the qualifications of the candidate and report as soon as may be to the Lodge, when he may be balloted for, agreeably to the 28th article of the by-laws.'

All of which is duly submitted.

Signed :   TURNER CROOKER, } Committee.
                            STEP. BEAN,   }

BOSTON, Dec. 4, 5806.

This report was twice read and unanimously accepted.''

At the meeting of January 1, 5807, a revision of the By-laws was contemplated, and a Committee was appointed to consider the subject, but no action of the Lodge in reference thereto is recorded until the autumn of that year.

Nov. 12th, 5807. " *Voted*, That a Committee of five, viz : Brother Bean, Baxter, Phillips, Swett and Dunham be appointed to revise the by-laws and report their doings thereon."

April 7th, 5808. " The Committee appointed to revise and alter the by-laws, made their report which was accepted by a vote of the lodge. Twenty three members present.

Voted, That the Treasurer and Secretary be a Committee to procure a new book for the records and by-laws of the Lodge."

BY-LAWS

OF THE

COLUMBIAN LODGE

Unanimously adopted at a meeting held in MASON's HALL, on the evening of the 7th April, 5808.

ART. 1. This Lodge shall not exceed fifty members and shall meet at Mason's Hall, on the first Thursday of every month, the Master and Wardens for the time being may call special meetings on any emergency. In case of removal notice shall be given to the Grand Lodge.

ART. 2. The Lodge shall transact all the business of each meeting, previous to refreshment, and while at labor, the members shall pay the most exact obedience to the orders of the Master.

ART. 3. On every question before the Lodge each member has liberty to speak twice ; meanwhile standing and addressing the master, and shall not be interrupted except to call him to order.

ART. 4. A lecture shall be given at every meeting of the Lodge, by the master or his appointment, during which strict attention is enjoined, and no one admitted to the hall.

ART. 5. Any member or Brother who shall be guilty of ungentlemanlike conduct in the Lodge or in the hall after the Lodge is closed, shall be reprimanded by the master for the first offence, and for the second like offence, shall be expelled ; and no brother shall withdraw during Lodge hours without permission of the master.

ART. 6.   The officers of the Lodge shall be chosen by ballot on the first Thursday of December, annually, except the Tyler and Closet Steward, who shall be appointed by the master and Wardens.

ART. 7.   The Treasurer shall give bonds to the Master and Wardens, for the faithful discharge of his duty, and shall, at all times, when required by the Lodge, give a statement of its Funds ; when a new choice is made, he shall, within ten days transfer to his successor the books and funds in his hands.

ART. 8.   It is the duty of the Secretary to observe all the proceedings of the Lodge, and keep a faithful record thereof, to collect all moneys due the Lodge, keep a just account of the same, and pay it over to the Treasurer before the next meeting, to notify the members of every meeting, inserting in the notifications the names of candidates for initiation or membership, and be at all times under the direction of the Master.   He shall be entitled to a fee of one dollar for each initiation, and allowed to charge each Brother raised to the sublime degree of Master, three dollars, for which he shall furnish a diploma.

ART. 9.   Every candidate for membership shall stand proposed on the records one meeting previous to his being balloted for : if then admitted by an unanimous ballot, shall pay to the Secretary, fifteen dollars for the funds of the Lodge, and sign the By-Laws, he is then a member.

ART. 10.   Every member who proposes a candidate for initiation, shall deposit in the hands of the Secretary, five dollars, which sum shall be placed to the candidate's credit, and he shall be balloted for the next meeting of the Lodge, if he is unanimously accepted, and receive the first degree, shall pay a fee of fifteen dollars ; if he be accepted and refuse to attend he forfeits the deposit ; but if he be rejected, the Secretary shall refund the money, but the same candidate may be again proposed by another member, and if not then admitted can have no more trials.

ART. 11.   Candidates for the degree of Fellow Crafts, if made in this Lodge, shall be passed when the Master recommends him, he paying a fee of two dollars ; but if made in any other Lodge, must obtain the unanimous consent by ballot, and pay the same fee.

Art. 12. Every regular Fellow Craft may be raised to the sublime degree of Master, after obtaining the unanimous consent, by ballot, and shall pay a fee of three dollars, and three dollars to the Secretary, which shall entitle him to a diploma. When the Lodge is specially called to confer any of the degrees, the candidate shall pay the expense thereof in addition to the usual fees.

Art. 13. Every Visiting Brother shall pay a fee of fifty cents, unless he be excused by the Master.

Art. 14. Any member who shall disclose the private transactions of the Lodge to any one not a member, shall for the first offence, receive a public admonition in the Lodge, and for the second like offence, shall be expelled and his name erased from the books.

Art. 15. No money shall be voted from the funds of the Lodge, on any application, when the fund will thereby be reduced below one thousand dollars, except it be to a distressed member, his widow or orphans; and no sum exceeding five dollars, shall, at any time, be voted from the funds as a donation, unless two thirds the members summoned are present.

Art. 16. No vote of this Lodge shall be reconsidered by a less number than when it passed; the Master shall not vote unless there is an equal division when he shall have the casting vote to decide the question.

Art. 17. Every member shall pay quarterly to the Secretary one dollar for the funds of the Lodge; and if neglecting three quarters successively, the Secretary shall report the delinquent to the Lodge, and inform that member thereof by letter; if he then neglects to pay up his arrearages, previous to the next meeting, his name shall be erased and his membership forfeited. Members while at sea are exempt from forfeiture.

Art. 18. The Master and Wardens for the time being shall appoint some discreet Brother as Superintendant and Closet Steward, whose duty it shall be to take care of the Jewels &c., keep the hall clean, &c., and provide refreshments under the direction of the Master and Wardens. He shall be allowed two dollars for each meeting as a compensation for his services; but nothing more by way of perquisites.

ART. 19. A Tyler shall be appointed by the Master; he shall deliver the notifications to members, Tyle the Lodge and be under the direction of the Master; his fees shall be as follows: For delivering the notifications fifty cents, for Tyling each Lodge seventy five cents, for each initiation fifty cents, for every raising fifty cents.

ART. 20. Any member removing more than twenty miles from Boston, and withdrawing his membership, shall be entitled to receive from the Treasurer ten dollars as his proportion from the Fund, provided that sum shall not exceed two thirds of one share; and every member who shall decease, leaving a widow or orphans, shall be presented with twenty dollars from the funds, by the Treasurer, as soon as may be.

ART. 21. These By-Laws shall not not be altered, revised or amended, until a proposition to that effect be handed the Secretary in writing, the same read to the Lodge, and a Record thereof made, and the subject noted in the summonses; after which a majority of members present may adopt the amendment or alteration proposed.

ART. 22. All former By-Laws of this Lodge are hereby repealed; and the Master, Wardens, Treasurer and Secretary for the time being are charged with the execution of these.

—

March 2d, 5809. "Voted that a Committee of three be appointed to alter, revise and correct the By-Laws, who were Brothers Smith, Crooker, and Howard."

April 6th, 5809. "The Committee appointed to alter, revise and correct the By-Laws, made their report.
On motion, *Voted*, That the same be recommitted to the same Committee, with the addition of the three first officers of this Lodge for their consideration, and report next meeting."

May 4th, 5809. "The Committee chosen to alter or amend the By-Laws, made their report, *to wit:* that the thirteenth article of our By-Laws be so far altered that no fee shall be received of a Brother for his first visit.
On motion, *Voted*, To accept the report; seven in favor and two against it."

A Committee was chosen, November 1, 5810, to examine the By-Laws, and propose alterations therein, if by them deemed necessary. They reported December 6, 5810, as follows :

" After duly considering the subject, your Committee recommend that the 13, 17, 18, and 19 articles of the By-Laws be repealed and the following substituted therefor.

ART. 13. Every worthy Brother wishing to visit the Lodge, shall be admitted and made welcome, without money and without price.

ART. 17. Every member shall pay quarterly to the Secretary, fifty cents for the funds of the Lodge; and if neglecting three quarters successively, the Secretary shall report the delinquent to the Lodge and inform that member of his doings; if he then neglects to pay up his arrearages previous to the next meeting, his membership shall be forfeited, and it shall then be the duty of the Secretary to inform that brother by letter that his name is erased from the By-Laws, and that he is no longer a member of the Lodge.

Members while at sea shall be exempt from forfeiture.

ART. 18. The Master for the time being shall appoint some discreet Brother as Closet Steward, whose duty it shall be to take care of the Regalia, keep the hall clean, kindle the fires, and light the candles. He shall be allowed for his services not exceeding one dollar fifty cents for each meeting.

ART. 19. A Tyler shall be appointed by the Master, he shall deliver the notifications to members, Tyle the Lodge, and be under the direction of the Master, his fees shall be determined by the Master and Wardens, but not to exceed two dollars for each meeting.

Your Committee further recommend that the following articles be added to the By-Laws :

ART. 23. The Master and Wardens for the time being shall be a committee to provide all necessary articles for the use of the Lodge, and superintend the expenditures generally.

ART. 24. No refreshment shall, at any time, be used in the Lodge, except on particular occasions, nor then, but by the special direction of the Master and Wardens.

Signed : JOSEPH JENKINS, } Committee.
           D. MOODY, }

" After the whole report was read it was voted *nem. con.* to accept the report of the Committee on appointments. The articles proposed as alterations in the By-Laws were read again singly and accepted, as reported by the Committee, except article twenty third which was amended by Brother D. Baxter, and is recorded as amended by him."

December 5th, 5811. " The Committee appointed to report upon the propriety of making an alteration in the 10th article of the By-Laws reported as follows, viz : Every candidate for initiation in this Lodge shall make application in writing, and shall be balloted for at the next regular meeting ; if he be unanimously accepted, and receive the first degree, he shall pay a fee of fifteen dollars to the Secretary, for the funds of the Lodge,

Signed :   Jos Jenkins,
           Calvin Howe,   } *Committee.*"
           John Barker,

September 3d, 5812. " *Voted,* That Brothers Jenkins, Moody and Appleton be a committee to report upon the propriety of altering the 9th article of the By-Laws."

October 1st, 5812. " The following motion was laid upon the table, viz ; that the alteration of the 9th article of the By-Laws be recommitted to the Committee appointed at the last meeting, and likewise said committee be requested to take into consideration any other article of the said laws, and report as soon as may be, which motion passed in the affirmative."

October 15th, 5812. " The committee chosen to make alterations in the By-Laws reported as follows, viz. That the 9th article be so altered as that every Brother, admitted a member shall pay *ten* dollars instead of *fifteen* to the funds of the Lodge : also that the 20th article be so altered as that any member removing more than twenty miles from Boston, and withdrawing his membership, shall be entitled to receive from the Treasurer, only five dollars, and that the widow or orphans of any deceased member shall be presented with only *ten* dollars by the Treasurer.

" Your Committee would further recommend that in order to place every member upon a more equal standing in point of interest, in the Lodge, every member who has paid *fifteen* dollars for his membership shall be credited with five dollars for the payment of his quarterages as they become due.

All which is duly submitted.

Signed : JOS. JENKINS,
D. MOODY, } *Committee.*"
B. B. APPLETON,

March 7, 5816. " Brothers B. B. Appleton, Joseph Jenkins, Daniel Baxter, Elijah Morse and Samuel Smith were chosen a Committee to revise the By-Laws of Columbian Lodge."

April 4, 5816. " The Committee on By-Laws reported progress and obtained further indulgence."

May 2d, 5816. " The Committee on the By-Laws made a partial verbal report, which produced the following vote :

" That the Committee chosen on 7th March last to revise the By-Laws, be requested to continue their services, and that the Secretary be requested to insert in the notifications for the next meeting, that the By-Laws will be acted upon."

May 6, 5816. " The Committee on the By-Laws made their report, the consideration of the report was postponed to the next meeting."

June 6, 5816. " The consideration of the New By-Laws postponed to the next meeting."

August 1, 5816. " The New By-Laws acted on, firstly, article after article, in succession, and each singly accepted. Then voted unanimously that the whole be accepted. •

" *Voted*, That the Secretary record the new By-laws."

BY-LAWS

OF THE

COLUMBIAN LODGE

Adopted unanimously at a meeting held at MASONS' HALL, on the evening of the 1st August, 5816.

ART. 1. This Lodge shall not exceed seventy members, and shall meet at Masons' Hall, on the first Thursday of every

14

month. The Masters and Wardens for the time being may call special meetings on any emergency.

Art. 2. The Lodge shall transact the business of each meeting previous to refreshment, and while at labor, the members shall pay the most exact obedience to the orders of the Master.

Art. 3 On every question before the Lodge, each member has liberty to speak twice, at the same time standing and addressing the Master, and shall not be interrupted, except to call him to order.

Art. 4. A lecture, or part of a lecture, shall be given at every meeting of the Lodge, by the Master, or by some one by him appointed, when a strict attention shall be given.

Art. 5. Any member or brother who shall be guilty of unmasonic conduct in the Lodge, or in the Hall, after the Lodge is closed, shall be reprimanded by the Master, for the first offence, and for the second like offence, if a member, he shall be expelled, and no brother shall withdraw during Lodge hours without permission of the Master.

Art. 6. The officers of the Lodge shall be chosen by ballot on the first Thursday of December, annually, except the Tylers, inside Sentinel, and Closet Steward, who shall be appointed by the Master and Wardens.

Art. 7. The Treasurer shall give bonds to the Master and Wardens for the faithful discharge of his duty, and shall at all times when required by the Lodge, give a statement of its funds. When a new choice is made he shall within ten days transfer to his successor the books and funds in his hands.

Art. 8. The Secretary shall observe all the proceedings of the Lodge, keep a faithful record thereof, collect all monies due the Lodge, keep a just account of the same, and pay them over to the Treasurer before the next meeting. He shall notify the members of every meeting in sealed notifications, inserting therein the names of all candidates for initiation or membership, and be at all times under the direction of the Master ; he shall be entitled to a fee of one dollar for each initiation and three dollars for every brother raised to the sublime degree of Master Mason, and shall furnish him with a diploma.

ART. 9. Every candidate for membership shall make a written application, and stand proposed on the records one meeting previous to his being balloted for. If then admitted by a unanimous ballot, he shall pay the Secretary ten dollars for the funds of the Lodge, and sign the By-Laws; he will then be a member.

ART. 10. Every candidate for initiation in this Lodge shall make application in writing and be balloted for at the next meeting; if he be unanimously accepted, and receive the first degree, he shall pay a fee of fifteen dollars to the Secretary for the funds of the Lodge.

ART. 11. Every candidate for the fee of Fellow Craft, if made in this Lodge, shall be passed when the Master recommends him, he paying a fee of two dollars, but if made in any other Lodge, must obtain the unanimous consent by ballot and pay the same fee.

ART. 12. Every regular Fellow Craft may be raised to the sublime degree of Master after obtaining the unanimous consent of the Lodge, and shall pay a fee of six dollars for the funds of the Lodge, which shall entitle him to a diploma. When the Lodge is specially called to confer any of the degrees, the candidate shall pay the expense thereof in addition to the usual fees.

ART. 13. Every worthy brother wishing to visit the Lodge shall be admitted and made welcome without money and without price.

ART. 14. Any member who shall disclose the private transactions of the Lodge to any one not a member, shall, for the first offence receive a public admonition in the Lodge, and for the second like offence, shall be expelled and his name erased from the books.

ART. 15. No money shall be voted from the funds of the Lodge on any application, when the funds will thereby be reduced below *one thousand dollars*, except it be to distressed members, his widow or orphans, and no sum exceeding ten dollars shall at any time be voted from the funds as a donation unless twenty members are present.

ART. 16. No vote of this Lodge shall be reconsidered by a less number than were present when it passed; the master shall not vote unless there is an equal division, when he shall have the casting vote to decide the question.

ART. 17. Every member shall pay quarterly, to the Secretary, fifty cents for the funds of the Lodge, and if neglecting four quarters successively, the Secretary shall report the delinquent to the Lodge, and inform that brother of his doings ; if he then neglects to pay up his arrearages previous to or at the next meeting, his membership shall be forfeited, and it shall then be the duty of the Secretary to inform that brother, by letter, that his name is erased from the By-Laws, and that he is no longer a member of the Lodge.

Members absent from Boston one year or more, and distant thirty miles, shall be exempt from quarterages, during such absence.

ART. 18. The master for the time being shall appoint some discreet brother as a Closet Steward, whose duty it shall be to take care of the regalia, keep the hall clean, kindle the fires, light the hall, &c. ; he shall be allowed for his services not exceeding one dollar and fifty cents for each meeting.

ART. 19. A Tyler shall be appointed by the Master and Wardens ; he shall deliver the notifications to members, Tyle the Lodge and be under the direction of the master ; his fees shall be determined by the Master and Wardens ; but not to exceed one dollar and fifty cents for each meeting.

An Inside Sentinel shall also be appointed in the same manner, whose duty it shall be to see that no brother pass or repass without the permission of the Master ; for his services he shall be exempted from quarterages, or have such compensation as the Master and Wardens shall determine.

ART. 20. Any member, removing more than twenty miles from Boston, and withdrawing his membership, shall be entitled to receive from the Treasurer *five dollars*, or one half of his membership ; and every member who shall decease, leaving a widow or orphans, such widow or orphans shall immediately receive twenty dollars from the funds of the Lodge to be paid by the Treasurer, by the order of the Master and Wardens.

ART. 21. At the annual election of officers there shall be a committee chosen to be called the Standing Committee on Charity, consisting of the Rt. Worshipful Master for the time being, and two others, whose duty it shall be to receive and act upon all applications for pecuniary assistance.

Art. 22. The Master and Wardens for the time being shall be a Standing Committee to provide all necessary articles for the use of the Lodge, and superintend the expenditures generally, and no account against the Lodge shall be paid, except approved by the Master and Wardens.

Art. 23. No refreshments shall, at any time, be used in the Lodge, except on particular occasions, nor then, but by the special direction of the Master and Wardens.

Art. 24. These By-Laws shall not be altered, revised or amended until a proposition to that effect be handed the Secretary in writing, the same read to the Lodge, and a record thereof made and the subject stated in the notifications.

Art. 25. All former By-Laws of this Lodge are hereby repealed, and we, whose names are hereunto subscribed, promise a faithful compliance with the foregoing articles.

—

September 5, 5816. " *Voted,* That the thanks of Columbian Lodge be rendered Bro. Isaac McGaw, for his generously recording the New By-Laws of said Lodge, gratis.

May 7, 5818. " The following motion was laid on the table, viz : that a Committee be raised to take into consideration the expediency of altering that article of the By-Laws which regulates the fees of the Secretary ; which motion passed in the affirmative, and R. W. Bro. Joseph Jenkins, Brothers B. B. Appleton, Calvin Howe, Samuel Smith, and E. V. Glover were chosen a Committee for that purpose."

July 2, 5818. " The Committee appointed at the last meeting of the Lodge, to take into consideration the expediency of altering that article of the By-Laws which regulates the fees of the Secretary, report—That the eighth article be so far altered that the Secretary be allowed instead of the present fees, two dollars and fifty cents for each meeting of the Lodge that he attends.

Respectfully submitted by   Joseph Jenkins.
                             B. B. Appleton,
                             Calvin Howe,
                             Samuel Smith,
                             Elisha V. Glover.

The report being unanimously accepted."

April 1, 5819. " A Committee was appointed consisting of R. W. A. Bean, Bro. D. Baxter, and G. Cobb, to confer on the alteration of 10, 11 and 12 articles of the By-Laws, and to report at the next meeting."

May 6, 5819. " The Committee raised at the last meeting respecting the By-Laws, reported in favor of having the whole code revised and amended ; and a Committee for that purpose was appointed, consisting of the R. W. Bro. Aaron Bean, D. Baxter, J. Jenkins, D. Baxter, Jr., and G. Cobb."

April 5, 5821. " The Committee on the By-Laws then made a report that they had so far completed the duty assigned to them as to lay a Constitution and code of By-Laws before the Lodge for consideration, when the whole was read from the chair. The Constitution was then taken up (containing eleven articles) by single articles, considered, debated, and the first ten accepted by an unanimous vote ; the eleventh article after much debate was accepted, when Bro. Bender gave notice that he should move for the reconsideration of the vote on this article, at the next meeting."

April 25, 5821. " On motion from Bro. Bender, the vote accepting the 11th article of the Constitution taken at the last meeting was reconsidered, a substitute was offered by Bro. Bender,—various others were offered and negatived. Bro. Bender's was accepted and committed to R. W. Brothers Bender, Moody and Dean, to put in form and report at the next meeting on the By-Laws."

June 22, 5821. " Records of the last meeting were read. This meeting was specially called to consider and act upon the By-Laws. The committee chosen April 25th, 5821, to amend the 11th article of the Constitution, made a report which was accepted.

"The Constitution and By-Laws were then read by articles and accepted ; the whole was then taken in gross, unanimously accepted, and declared to be the Constitution and By-Laws of Columbian Lodge, and are as follows :

CONSTITUTION AND BY-LAWS

OF

COLUMBIAN LODGE,

ADOPTED, JUNE 22, 5821.

CONSTITUTION.

ART. 1. The title, style and name of this Lodge shall be, COLUMBIAN LODGE.

ART. 2. Columbian Lodge shall be composed of a R. W. Master, Senior and Junior Warden, (constituting the executive government) Treasurer, a Secretary, a Senior and Junior Deacon, and a Senior and Junior Steward, with such other officers as the R. W. Master, with the advice and consent of the Wardens, may appoint, and of as many Master Masons as shall be regularly admitted members.

ART. 3. Stated Meetings shall be held at least once in each month.

ART. 4. The nine first officers shall be chosen by written ballots, at the stated meeting in December, annually, by a majority of members present, and shall perform the duties of their offices respectively until others are elected and installed in their stead.

Any vacancy by death or otherwise, shall be filled in like manner, and at such time as the Lodge may direct. All other officers shall be appointed by the R. W. Master, with the advice and consent of the Wardens.

ART. 5. The Treasurer shall have charge of all the funds and property, the charter, books and records excepted ; and shall give bonds to the R. W. Master, and Wardens, with satisfactory sureties for the faithful discharge of his duties.

ART. 6. The funds or property of the Lodge shall never be divided among its members, but shall be exclusively devoted to charitable purposes, except such as shall be absolutely necessary for the support and government of the Lodge ; and whenever its members become so far scattered or negligent that there shall not be a sufficient number to fill the nine first offices during six months, it shall be the duty of the members forthwith to surrender to the M. W. G. Lodge of Massachusetts, the Charter, Books, Records, Jewels, Funds and all other property of Columbian Lodge.

ART. 7. Applicants for membership shall stand proposed at least to a subsequent meeting, and their names be inserted on the notifications for the meeting at which the application is to be acted upon. The same course shall be pursued with applicants for the degrees, unless overruled by a dispensation from the M. W. Grand Lodge.

ART. 8. Any member who shall purchase an exemption from periodical assessments during life, shall never be included in or affected by any future vote or By-Law relative to quarterages or periodical assessments.

ART. 9. No brother shall be made an honorary member unless his name for such membership shall be on the notifications for the meeting at which the application is to be acted upon, and he be unanimously accepted.

ART. 10. Additions not repugnant to any article of the Constitution at the time such addition is proposed, may be made in the following manner, viz : All proposed additions shall be in distinct articles, shall be read in open Lodge, shall be considered by a Committee, and the subject entered on the notifications for the meeting at which the proposition is to be acted upon ; and if the Committee report in favor of such article or articles, and three fourths of the members present shall vote to accept said report, then such article or articles shall be incorporated with and become part of the Constitution.

ART. 11. No article of this Constitution shall ever be repealed except in the manner herein provided, *to wit :* The subject of such repeal shall be considered by a special Committee, and be entered in the notifications for the meeting at which it is to be decided, when, if the committee report in favor of a repeal, and all the members present so notified do agree, it shall thenceforth be expunged and no longer considered a part of the Constitution.

BY-LAWS.

ART. 1. *Members.*—Each applicant for membership shall stand proposed at least to a subsequent meeting, and his name be inserted on the notifications for the meeting at which the application is to be acted upon ; he must receive the unanimous consent by ballot of the members present, shall pay all established fees, and shall sign the Constitution and By-Laws before he shall be recorded a member. Should the applicant be accepted and he neglect for three months to pay the fee and sign the Constitution and By-Laws, he shall make his application anew before he can be recorded a member.

Any member about to leave town for one or more years, may, at his request, have his membership suspended, provided all periodical dues are paid ; but from the time of his suspension, all privileges of membership shall *cease,* until, on his return he shall personally inform the Lodge of his wish to exercise the rights of membership.

Any member neglecting to pay his periodical dues for eighteen months may be voted out of the Lodge, by a majority of the members present. No member shall be elected or appointed to office unless he comply with the article regulating fees.

Any member deceasing, leaving a widow or orphans, notwithstanding he may owe the Lodge, such widow or orphans shall forthwith be presented by the R. W. Master and Wardens with the sum specified in the article of allowances.

No brother shall leave the Lodge while in session without leave from the presiding officer. Any member having complied with the Constitution and By-Laws, may, at his own request, be honorably discharged.

ART. 2. *Master.*—The R. W. Master as the head and governor of the Lodge, shall, at all times, have in possession the charter from the M. W. G. Lodge, and shall enjoy all the rights, privileges and immunities of Ancient Craft Masonry, and by the same shall govern his Lodge, constantly having in view the Constitution and By-Laws of the M. W. Grand Lodge of Massachusetts and the Constitution and By-Laws of this Lodge.

ART. 3. *Senior and Junior Wardens.*—The Senior and Junior Wardens will assist the R. W. Master in the work and government of the Lodge.

The Senior Warden in the absence of the R. W. Master will preside with all his powers and prerogatives.

The Junior Warden in the absence of the R. W. Master and Senior Warden, will preside in like manner.

ART. 4. *Treasurer.*—The Treasurer shall have charge and keep an inventory of all funds and property of the Lodge. The charter, books, records and papers, excepted.

The inventory shall express all species of property belonging to the Lodge, the time of purchase, the cost, if a donation, the time, the name of the donor, and the value; and all property worn out, altered or disposed of, shall be noted. This inventory shall be revised by a committee, and be reported by the Treasurer at the stated meeting in December annually; he shall pay all bills approved by the Financial Committee, and all orders drawn by the Committee on Charity; he shall annually attend the meetings of the Committee of Finance, and exhibit an accurate statement of the receipts, expenditures, moneys voted by the Lodge to applicants for charity, and the amount of funds. He shall deliver within fifteen days after his installation, to his successor, all funds and property of the Lodge. He shall at all times be under the special direction of the Lodge. He shall, within twenty days after his installation give bonds to the R. W. Master and Wardens, with satisfactory sureties for the faithful discharge of his duties.

ART. 5. *Secretary.*—The Secretary shall have charge of all books, records and papers; the charter, Treasurer's accounts and inventory excepted. He shall attend the meetings of the Lodge with all necessary books and papers; he shall make a just and fair record of the proceedings of each meeting; he shall record all applications for the degrees and membership, all degrees conferred, and by whom received, all who shall be admitted members, all memberships withdrawn, suspended or renewed, all names of members who have purchased an exemption from periodical assessments during life; he shall receive all moneys due the Lodge, and before the next meeting pay the same to the Treasurer; he shall fill for each meeting, notifications for all members residing in Boston, inserting thereon the names of all candidates for the degrees and membership, and all special business coming before the Lodge, and shall continue the same until it shall be completed, and shall deliver the notifications to the Tyler for distribution; he shall make correct annual returns to M. W. G. Lodge; he shall notify the chairman of each committee of his appointment, the names of his associates, and the business committed to them; he shall at the stated meeting in November, annually read the Constitution and By-Laws; he shall immediately after the stated meeting in November, annually, render to the Financial Committee an accurate statement of the work done, of moneys received, of memberships commenced, suspended, received or withdrawn; he shall, at the stated meeting in December, annually, and before the choice of officers, read the names of all delinquents, the sum due from each, and shall record the same with the doings of the meetings; he shall, before the closing of the Lodge, at each meeting read the minutes of the proceedings by him kept; he shall, previous to initiation, receive the signatures in a book kept for that purpose, of all applicants for the degrees, with their respective places of birth, residence, age, and occupation.

ART. 6. *Senior and Junior Deacons.*—The Senior Deacon is exclusively under the orders of the R. W. Master.

The Junior Deacon is under the orders of the R. W. Master and Wardens.

ART. 7. *Senior and Junior Stewards.*—The Stewards are under the orders of the R. W. Master and Wardens, but particularly under the direction of the Junior Warden.

ART. 8. *Sentinel.*—The Sentinel is exclusively under the orders of the presiding officer; he shall permit none to pass or repass without leave from said officer.

ART. 9. *Closet Steward.*—The Closet Steward is under the orders of the R. W. Master and Wardens; he shall keep a list and have the care of the Jewels, clothing, and furniture of the rooms; he shall, at each meeting, deposit the several Jewels at their respective stations, and at the close of each meeting, shall collect and carefully secure the same; he shall have charge of the Lights, Fuel, Hall and rooms. When lights or fuel are wanting he shall inform the R. W. Master and Wardens; he shall see the hall and rooms properly cleansed and lighted.

ART. 10. *Tyler.*—The Tyler shall deliver the notifications for the meetings; he is exclusively, under the orders of the presiding officer.

ART. 11. *Installations.*—The officers elected and appointed shall be installed at such time as the Lodge shall direct.

ART. 12. *Votes.*—No vote shall be reconsidered at the same meeting by a less number than were present when it passed, nor at a subsequent meeting unless the words "reconsideration of a vote," be inserted on the notifications for the meeting at which the same is to be acted upon.

ART. 13. *Refreshments.*—No refreshments shall be provided except by special vote of the Lodge from time to time.

ART. 14. *Charity.*—At the stated meeting in December, annually, there shall be chosen a committee to consist of such number as the Lodge shall determine at the time, who shall act on applications for charity. They shall have power to draw on the Treasurer for such sums as they find necessary. They shall keep a correct record in a book for that purpose, of the names of all applicants with the sums (if any) granted, and shall deliver the book to their successors. They shall, immediately after the stated meeting in November, annually, render a statement of their doings to the Financial Committee, —they are at all times under the special orders of the Lodge.

ART. 15. *Candidates.*—Each candidate for the degrees shall make a printed or written application in the following form, viz:

To the R. W. Master and Brethren of Columbian Lodge: The subscriber entertaining a favorable opinion of your ancient order is desirous of receiving the several degrees conferred in your Lodge.

Place of Birth........... Residence.................
Age.................... Occupation ....
Date ....
                         Signed :   D N.

Which application shall enclose the amount regulated in the Article of fees. The application shall be read in open Lodge, and the applicant's name shall be inserted on the notifications for the meeting, at which the application is to be acted upon, when he may be balloted for. (If he be rejected, the enclosed sum shall be returned.) If he be accepted, and on receiving the first degree, pays the further sum as regulated in the article of fees, he shall be entitled to the second degree, when recommended by the R. W. Master, and to the third when by the unanimous vote of the members present.—Any brother who shall have received the first degree, or the first and second degrees, in any other Lodge, may receive the other degrees by applying as other candidates, and paying the amount as regulated in the article of fees.

No applicant shall receive the degrees but by the unanimous ballot of the members present.—Any brother raised to the sublime degree of Master in this Lodge, shall be entitled to a diploma by placing his signature in the margin, in presence of the R. W. Master and Wardens or Secretary.

The expence of meetings called exclusively to accommodate candidates, shall be paid by them, unless remitted by the R. W. Master and Wardens.

ART. 16.—*Meetings.*—The members shall meet on the first Thursday of each month, at such time as the R. W. Master shall order, and specially, at the pleasure of R. W. Master; in his absence, at the pleasure of the S. W.; and in the absence of both, at the pleasure of the J. W. At the time appointed the Lodge shall be opened in due form, seven members present being qualified to preside.

ART. 17.—*Fees.*—Each applicant for membership, (honorary excepted,) before he can be recorded a member, shall pay ten dollars; each member (honorary excepted,) shall be assessed sixteen and two-thirds cents each month, which shall be payable at the stated meeting in November, annually, except when the membership is withdrawn or suspended, in which case all dues shall be paid. But as a full compensation for all assessments, any member may pay twenty dollars, which shall exempt him from all periodical dues during his life. Any member deceasing, whose periodical dues shall have been paid to the preceding November, shall not have been considered a delinquent; his accounts shall be balanced.

The application of each candidate for the degrees (clergymen excepted,) shall enclose fifteen dollars, and on receiving the first degree shall pay eight dollars more, and a Brother receiving the second and third degrees only, shall pay eight dollars, and any Brother receiving the third degree only, shall pay six dollars.

ART. 18.—*Allowances.*—The Secretary shall be allowed for each meeting two dollars and fifty cents, and for each diploma one dollar.

The Sentinel shall be allowed the amount of his periodical assessments.

The Closet Steward and Tyler shall be allowed according to the arrangement made with him by the presiding officers of the several Masonic Societies in this town, called the Boston Board of Directors. On the decease of any member, his widow or orphans shall receive twenty dollars; *provided*, however, the widow or orphans of any member not residing in Boston at the time of his decease, shall inform the Lodge of their place of residence. All bills shall be presented to the Financial Committee within twelve days after the stated meeting in November, annually.   •

ART. 19.—*Financial Committee.*—The R. W. Master and Wardens shall constitute the Financial Committee; they shall examine and approve, in writing, all bills, before they can be paid; they, with two other members to be chosen at the stated meeting in November, annually, shall form a committee to require of the Secretary and Treasurer accurate statements of their doings, and they shall report the same at the stated meeting in December, annually, before the choice of officers, including the precise state of the Lodge, of the funds, the number of members, of what class, the degrees given, on whom conferred, the receipts and expenditures, memberships commenced, withdrawn, suspended or renewed, and all other things relating to the welfare of the Lodge.

ART. 20.—*Alterations.*—Each proposed alteration of the By-Laws shall be read in open Lodge, shall be considered by a committee, and the subject entered on the notifications for the meeting, at which the proposition is to be acted upon; if the committee report in favor of said alteration, and a majority of the members present shall vote to accept said report, the same shall be entered with the records of the meeting, and the article altered shall be taken into a new form, containing the alteration, and shall retain the same number and name as the original article.

ART. 21.—*Additions.*—Each proposed addition of the By-Laws shall be read in open Lodge, shall be considered by a committee, and the subject entered on the notifications for the meeting at which the proposition is to be acted upon; if the committee report in favor of the proposed addition, and a majority of the members present shall vote to accept said report, the same shall be entered with the records of the meeting, shall be numbered and headed as the preceding articles, and shall be added to the By-Laws of Columbian Lodge.

ART. 22.—*Repeals.*—Whenever it is presumed that an article of the By-Laws is injurious to the harmony and welfare of the Lodge, the same shall be considered by a committee, and the subject entered on the notifications for the meeting at which the repeal is to be acted upon; if the committee report in favor of repealing said article, and a majority of the members present shall vote to accept said report, the same shall be entered with the records of the meeting, the repeal and date of the same shall be null and void. All former By-Laws of Columbian Lodge are hereby repealed.

"R. W. Bros. Moody, Baxter, G. G. Smith and Foster, were appointed a committee to procure suitable books, and to have the constitution and By-Laws fairly transcribed and brought forward for the signatures of the Brethren, and to consider the expediency of printing the Constitution and By-Laws for the use of the members."

July 5, 5821. "On motion of Bro. Appleton, the Constitution and By-Laws were recommitted to the original Committee to consider and report on the 14th article of the By-Laws."

September 6, 5821. "The Committee to whom the Constitution and By-Laws were recommitted on the evening of the 5th July last, made a report which was unanimously accepted, and incorporated with the By-Laws as on record."

September 26, 5821. "*Voted*, That the Secretary of this Lodge be requested to call on the Secretary of the M. W. G. Lodge of this Commonwealth and procure a copy of the alterations made in the 5th and 6th sections of the second chapter of the By-Laws of said G. Lodge, and endorse the same on the blank leaves of the copy of said By-Laws belonging to this Lodge."

August 1, 1822. "A committee of three was appointed for each quarter of the city to get the signatures of the members of this Lodge to the By-Laws:

In the Eastern, Brothers Fisher, Leman, Holmes. In the Western, Brothers Glover, Lovejoy, Bittle. In the Northern, Brothers Fisk, Bemis, G. G. Smith. In the Southern,

Brothers Daniel Baxter, Jr., Luther Corey, Benjamin M. Nevers were appointed."

September 4, 5823. " R. W. Bros. Baxter, Samuel Smith and Moody, were appointed a committee to determine what compensation shall be allowed Bro. G. Cobb, for making six copies of the New By-Laws, and for ascertaining, arranging, and transcribing the general proceedings of the Lodge, from the date of the charter to the present time."

October 2, 5823. " R. W. Geo. G. Smith, proposed an *addition* to the 4th Article of the Constitution relating to the choice of officers. After ' stated meeting in December, annually' insert, ' or at any special meeting duly notified in that month,' this proposition was committed to R. W. Bros. Samuel Smith, Daniel Baxter, and Daniel Baxter, Jr."

October 10, 5823. " The committee on the addition to the Constitution reported, ' That it is inexpedient to make said proposed addition.' See report on file."

January 6, 5825. " The Committee to whom was referred the expediency of an alteration in the 17th article of the By-Laws which says the application of each candidate for the degrees (clergymen excepted) shall enclose Fifteen dollars, and on receiving the first degree shall pay eight dollars more; Report—That the above clause be repealed and the following substituted instead, viz: The application of each candidate for the degrees (clergymen excepted) shall enclose twenty-three dollars.

" The above report was read and unanimously accepted, after due notice on the summons."

August 4, 5825. " *Voted*, That Bros. G. G. Smith, H. D. Wolcott, aud J. B. Flint, be a committee to confer with the Committee of St. John's Lodge on subjects of interest to the Brotherhood, and particularly on the subject of uniformity of fees for degrees of membership."

May 4, 5826. " Bros. G. G. Smith, S. Smith and Baxter, Jr., were appointed a committee to consider the expediency of altering the 17th article of the By-Laws regulating fees."

August 3, 5826. " *Voted*, That the 17th article of the By-Laws be so far altered as to bring the fees for initiation twenty-five dollars."

December 7, 5826. "Bros. Stevens, S. Smith, Baxter, Sen'r, Appleton and Baxter, Jun'r, were appointed a committee to take into consideration the alteration of the 18th article of the By-Laws, respecting the donation to the widow of a deceased member." ·

March 1, 5827. "The following report was made by the Committee on the 18th article of the By-Laws; they unanimously report that it is inexpedient to make any alteration in said 18th article of the By-Laws."

May 1, 5828. "Bros. S. Smith, Appleton and Wise were appointed a committee to consider the subject of amending Article 3d of the Constitution, relative to meetings."

July 3, 5828. "Bro. S. Smith, was excused from serving on the Committee on the 3d Article of the Constitution, and Bro. Moody was placed in his stead."

April 2, 5829. "The committee on the 3d Article of the By-Laws were requested to report at the next meeting."

June 4, 5829. "The Committee on the alteration of the Constitution made the following report which was accepted: That on a full consideration of the subject, they recommend that the 3d Article of the Constitution be repealed, and the following substituted, which shall be in future the 3d article, 'Stated meetings shall be held once in each month, unless the meetings are suspended by a vote of three quarters of the members present, which shall never be for more than six months at any one time,' all which is respectfully submitted. The three first officers were appointed a committee on the 10th article of the By-Laws, in order to propose such alteration therein as may render it conformable to the late alteration of the Constitution, with instructions to the report at the next meeting."

April 4, 5833. "R. W. J. B. Flint, with Bros. Appleton, D. Baxter, Jr., Neville and Allen were chosen a committee to consider the expediency of altering the 16th article of the By-Laws, with instructions to report at the next regular meeting."

February 5, 5835. "Bros. Appleton, Neville and Bittle, were appointed a Committee to consider the expediency of amending the 17th article of the By-Laws, or of annulling so much of said article as requires the payment of ten Dollars by each applicant for membership before he can be recorded a member.''

March 5. 5835. '' The following report was read, The committee on the alteration of the 17th article of By-Laws, having duly considered the same, ask leave to report that the said article be so far altered as to read, 'Each applicant for membership (honorary excepted) before he can be recorded a member shall pay five dollars.'

Submitted by   B. B. APPLETON, ⎫
                     W. W. NEVILLE, ⎬ *Committee.*
                     WM. BITTLE, ⎭
This report was accepted.''

October 6, 5836. '' On motion of Bro. Joel Nason, the following Brethren were appointed a committee for the purpose of considering the expediency of so amending the 17th article of the By-Laws as to abolish or reduce the quarterages by that article assessed on the members of this Lodge, to wit : Bros. Joel Nason, Benj. B. Appleton, Joseph Greeley, Benj. Converse, and Samuel A. Allen.''

April 15, 5837. '' The committee raised in October last to consider the expediency of altering the 17th article of the By-Laws, in regard to quarterages, was, by vote of the Lodge, discharged from further consideration of the subject.''

November 7, 5839. '' On motion of Brother Stevens,— *Voted*, That a committee of three be chosen to consider the expediency of so far altering the 16th article of the By-Laws as to give the master of the Lodge authority to postpone the regular meeting at a subsequent Thursday evening, if at any time found necessary for any cause, Bros. B. Stevens, Geo. G. Smith and William Ward were appointed for this purpose.''

November 2, 5843. '' On motion, it was *Voted*, That Bros. Baxter, and Smith, Jr., and the Secretary be a committee to consider the subject of a revision of the Constitution and By-Laws of the Lodge.''

December 15, 5843. '' The Committee on the revision of the Constitution and By-Laws, reported several proposed amendments,— *Voted*, That the report lay upon the table, and that the Secretary be directed to insert in the notifications for the next meeting, ' Alteration of Constitution and By-Laws.' "

January 2, 5845. " Bros. Baxter, Baker, Tillson, the Secretary, and P. C. Jones, were appointed a committee to enquire into the expediency of altering the evening of the regular meeting of the Lodge."

October 2, 5845. " On motion, it was *Voted*, That the three first officers be a committee to consider and report upon the expediency of amending Article 15 of the By-Laws."

January 15, 5846. " Brother Smith, from the committee on altering the By-Laws, recommended an alteration in *Art.* 1, the intent of which is that all applicants for membership shall pay the established *fee* before their application can be acted upon."

February 5, 5846. " The amendment of Article 1, of the By-Laws recommended by the committee at the last meeting to insert between the words ' fees and ' the words ' before his application shall be acted upon.' "

March 5, 5846. " Brother Senior Warden moved that the By-Laws of the Lodge be printed,—referred to the R. W. Master, Senior and Junior Wardens, with full powers."

April 2, 5846. " R. W. Master, R. W. Bros. Baxter and Smith were appointed a committee to revise the By-Laws and to report before printing."

September 3, 5846. " The committee on By-Laws reported several amendments, as follows : Amendment to Article 1, provides that a clergyman or other person, may, on special occasion, by vote of the Lodge be admitted without fee, and that the Treasurer, Secretary, Inside Sentinel and Tyler be exempt from quarterages, which amendments were severally adopted."

June 6, 1850. " Bro. Dupee gave notice that he should offer an amendment to the By-Laws, at the regular meeting in September, to limit the number of members to one hundred."

January 14, 5853. " R. W. Bro. Jones proposed the following additions to the Article of Fees, in the By-Laws :

The fee for membership for those not made in the Lodge, ' ten dollars.' The fee for membership for those made in the Lodge, ' five dollars '—which were referred to Bros. Jones, Ames, Fowle and McClellan.''

February 3, 5853. '' The Committee on By-Laws were granted further time.''

March 3, 5853. '' The Committee on By-Laws made a report proposing an additional clause to Article 16, as follows : Any Brother having received the unanimous vote of the members present at any meeting shall be entitled to all the privileges of membership upon payment of the sum of five dollars ; *provided*, said Brother shall have received his degree in this Lodge. Each applicant who shall have received the degrees elsewhere, the fee for membership shall be ten dollars—which report was unanimously accepted.''

May 4, 5854. '' Brothers Heard, Ames, Fowle, Jones and Coolidge were appointed a Committee on alteration of the By-Laws.''

May 19, 5854. '' R. W. Master from the Committee on By-Laws, reported that it was inexpedient to make any alteration at the present time.''

June 1, 5854. '' A communication was received from a committee from St. John's Lodge, on the subject of fees for the degrees, referred to R. W. Masters and Wardens.''

October 26, 5854. '' The Committee on the By-Laws reported that the words *twenty-five* in Article XVI, and in the Table of Fees, be struck out and the word *thirty* inserted.''

November 2, 5854. '' The Secretary offered the following resolution : *Resolved*, That the subject of amending, altering, or repealing the Constitution and By-Laws of this Lodge, and the formation of a new code of By-Laws, which shall take the place of the present Constitution and By-Laws, be referred to a committee, who shall report thereon on or before the regular communication in December next, which was adopted and referred to Bros. Heard, Jones, Baker, Fowle, Coolidge and Thacher.

November 28, 5854. '' R. W. Master from the Committee on By-Laws, reported an entire new code, which was by a unanimous vote adopted, and a copy sent to the M. W. Grand Lodge for its approval. The same committee was authorized to cause the same to be printed after its approval.''

January 4, 5855. ''The R. W. Master announced the approval by the M. W. Grand Lodge of the By-Laws adopted November 28, 5854.''

The By-Laws adopted November 28, 5854, having been presented in the first part of this volume, are, therefore, omitted here. Excepting these and the code of 5797, this chapter contains all the proceedings of the Lodge in relation to the rules they have established for their government; and it is a source of just pride to the members of the present day that all the deliberations of the brethren on this subject are characterized by a truly fraternal spirit, and manifest a firm attachment to the principles of Freemasonry. The votes passed as follows are not By-laws, but are given because of their intimate connection with them. Their character is executive, and they are designed to carry out effectually certain important provisions of the By-Laws.

May 3, 5855. '' On motion of Bro. Stetson it was *Voted*, That the place of business or residence of all candidates for the degrees shall be upon the printed notifications.''

May 3, 5855. ''*Voted*, That the Secretary is hereby instructed to notify each member of any committee, within the week ensuing, of his appointment, and the duties belonging to the same.''

It is unnecessary to comment here upon the modifications which have from time to time been made in the laws, or upon the motives or considerations which probably caused them to be made. In the succeeding pages the reasons for change will become apparent, and will lead the reader to consult this chapter as his inclination and objects of inquiry shall direct.

———○○———

CHAPTER VII.

RECORDS, BOOKS OF ACCOUNTS, PAPERS ON FILE.

The records of the proceedings of the Lodge are in a state of perfect preservation; the account of every meeting being evidently full and accurately rendered. They are a monument to the fidelity of the several Secretaries of whose labors they are the result. To the Lodge they are priceless; they being the original and only complete narration of their transactions. They are all contained in five handsome, durably-bound, large folio volumes. The penmanship throughout is clear and legible, most of it elegant, and to a considerable extent, affords specimens of the highest artistic character. The number of meetings thus recorded is nine hundred and seventy two. The dates embraced in each volume will be seen by the following table:

Vol. I. Begins June 22, 5795, and ends April 9, 5808.
" II. Begins April 9, 5808, and ends November 22, 5821.
" III. Begins March 15, 5821, and ends Dec. 20, 5838.
" IV. Begins January 3, 5839, and ends Nov. 2, 5848.
" V. Begins December 7, 5848, and ends June 7, 5855.

It will be observed by the dates here given that the proceedings of a few of the meetings have been twice recorded and are contained in two of the record books. The fifth volume is at present in use by the Lodge.

The first volume is a transcript of original records which are embraced in several small books or pamphlets. As early as 5811, this portion of the records was regarded as being in great danger of injury and loss as the books were, even at that time, much worn and defaced. This fact determined the Lodge to cause them to be transcribed into one book of suitable size and strength, as a prudential measure for the better preservation of the "ancient records." At the meeting of the Lodge held August 1, 5811, it was

" *Voted*, That the Secretary be requested to procure a suitable blank book to transcribe the old records of the Lodge upon,—to begin the transcription, and request the members of the Lodge to assist him."

Accordingly, the Secretary, Bro. Nathaniel Sawyer, commenced the work that year, but did not proceed further than to copy the records of the first two meetings. During the same year, Bro. George Bender, Jr., a member, continued the transcription and copied the transactions of the next seven meetings. Here the labor was suspended until March 14, 5814, when R. W. Bro. B. B. Appleton, Senior, who was then Secretary, recommenced it. With untiring energy and perseverence he completed the undertaking January 17, 5815, having transcribed during this short period of time, the records of two hundred and

eighty meetings. The Lodge being sensible of
their obligation to Bro. Appleton for this important
service, took measures to express to him their
appreciation of it. The subjoined extracts in
relation to this subject will be read with interest :

January 5, 5815. " On motion, *Voted*, That R. W. Bros.
Morse, Jenkins, and Moody be a committee to examine the
transcriptions of the ancient records of the Lodge, and report
what compensation be given to R. W. Bro. Appleton for his
services in the business."

February 2, 5815. " On motion, *Voted*, That the following Report be accepted and recorded :
" The committee appointed to examine the Transcript of
the Ancient Records of the Lodge by W. Bro. Appleton,
have attended to the duty and ask leave to report :
" That they find the records of the Lodge from 5795 to
5808, have been collected from sundry pamphlets and transcribed into an elegant folio volume, consisting of 420 pages.
That the same have been transcribed in a neat and elegant
style, and reflect much honor upon our worthy brother ; your
committee are satisfied that the transcript must have cost
Bro. Appleton much time and labor, and that he ought to be
remunerated for his faithful services.
" But as a good name is rather to be chosen than great
riches, and loving favor rather than silver and gold:
" Your committee recommend that the Lodge return him a
vote of thanks for his faithful and laborious services in transcribing said records. Your committee are happy also to
report that all the records of the Lodge since the date of the
charter are now contained in two volumes, and appear in
such a state as does much credit to our institution.
" All which is respectfully submitted.
ELIJAH MORSE, ⎫
JOSEPH JENKINS, ⎬ *Committee.*"
DAVID MOODY, ⎭

With the exception of the missing code already
referred to, all the By-Laws are recorded with the
records of proceedings. The code of 5821 was

also elegantly copied into small books for the use of officers and members by Bro. Gershom Cobb. Only two of these books are now in their possession. They are beautifully bound.

A list of the brethren who received the degrees in the Lodge, from 5795 to 5824, with the dates when they were conferred, is entire, as originally prepared.

The books of accounts, those of Treasurer and Secretary, will cover, very nearly, if not entirely, all the pecuniary transactions of the Lodge ; and should there be found a break in them, the annual reports, that are entered with the records, will supply the deficiency sufficiently to enable the enquirer to determine satisfactorily the nature and extent of these transactions. One of these books, the earliest, contains dates from June 5795 to the close of 5796 ; and embraces many entries of interest. It shows that the Grand Lodge were paid for "a dispensation to work $14 ;" and that " Bro. Revere's bill of Jewels, £8 12s. 6d.," was entered June 25, 5795. The Treasurer's book which that officer now uses, was opened in 5812, soon after the late Bro. Daniel Baxter, Senior, was elected to that office. This book, and that of the present Secretary, are kept with that system and correctness which show at a glance the exact condition of the finances.

The papers on file relate to various subjects. Some of them date from the origin of the Lodge ; and it is a remarkable fact that while the files for 5795 and 5796 are well filled, those of the succeeding twenty years are exceedingly deficient.

16

Still, there is much cause for rejoicing that so many of the ancient papers have been preserved to the present time. At the time of the destruction of the Exchange Coffee House by fire, it is not improbable that portions of the files were then destroyed. This event occurred in 5818; and the files now most defective would be those exposed to injury and destruction from this cause. But, the question arises, how came it that the papers of 5795 and 5796 escaped? Since 5819, most of the papers of subsequent dates exist, especially those of an official character; and the files formed by the present Secretary and his immediate predecessors may be regarded as complete. The principal papers now in the archives of the Lodge are: The Charter; Dispensation; Lease of Columbian Hall; Reports of Committees on Finance; "Minutes of Lodge from 5795 to 5796;" "various old minutes of meetings;" Reports of Committees; "Receipts prior to 5800;" "Receipts subsequent to 5800; "Communications, letters, &c.;" "Applications;" "Duplicate returns" and communications from D. D. G. Masters.

The books and papers, which have been briefly described, being of great value to the Lodge, should be the objects of the utmost care. No means should be neglected which will tend to their security and preservation. And it may be suggested that they be placed in a box, or safe, constructed in such a manner as to defy the effects of fire and moisture. The papers require, for easy reference, a more systematic arrangement, which could be effected with little labor. It would afford some satisfaction, perhaps, to have a statement of all books and papers, prepared at some length and in considerable detail, to be entered on the records of the Lodge. A general idea of their contents could thus be easily formed without recourse to the originals. The present imperfect file of the printed proceedings of the Grand Lodge, should, as far as possible, be provided with the documents of which it is deficient, and receive the protection of a substantial binding ; and, in future, these papers, as well as all other Masonic publications coming into the possession of the Lodge, should be carefully preserved for reference.

CHAPTER VIII.

MEETINGS — CHOICE OF OFFICERS — INSTALLATIONS — PUBLIC INSTALLATIONS — OTHER PUBLIC OCCASIONS — PUBLIC LECTURE, BY BRO. W. R. ALGER — MUSICAL ENTERTAINMENT — MASTERS' LODGES — SODALITY MEETINGS — SOCIAL MEETINGS.

The regular meetings have always been held on the first Thursday of the month. Until 5829, they occurred every month in each year, excepting in 5814, when the Lodge adjourned from June 16th, to the first Thursday in September following, in order to allow repairs to be made on the Hall. At the meeting of June 4, 5829, the by-laws were altered so that "stated meetings shall be held once in each month, unless the meetings are suspended by a vote of three-quarters of the members present, which shall never be for more than six months at any one time."

In 5829, 5835, 5838 and 5839, the adjournment was from May to October; in 5830, 5833 and 5836, from April to October; in 5831 and 5832, from April to September; in 5834, from March to October; in 5837, 5840 and 5842, from May to September; in 5841, from June to October; in 5843, 5844, 5846, 5847, 5850, 5853, 5854, and 5855, from June to September; and in 5845, 5848, 5851 and 5852, it was from July to September. In 5849, the regular meetings occurred in every month of that year. The principal reasons which caused a suspension of the meetings during the summer were the shortness of the evenings and warmth of the season; and the practice has been productive of much good in inducing a fuller attendance during the cool season, and relieving the brethren of a labor which would have caused personal discomfort to them, and which the calls of Masonry did not exact. The day of holding regular meetings has always been determined by the by-laws; and, excepting by a legal alteration of these laws, or a dispensation from the Grand Master, or by his authority, no other day could be substituted. In November 5839, and January 5845, the expediency of changing it was considered, but the ancient arrangement was continued. At the meeting of February 12, 5797, a proposition was made to fix the hours of meeting and closing at the monthly meetings, but it was rejected on the ground that it would be interfering with a prerogative of the Master. The time of opening has generally been at an early hour in the evening, and the duration of the sessions from two to four hours. The whole number of regular meetings held, beginning with the meeting of July 2, 5795 and ending with that of June 7, 5855, has been six hundred and forty-three.

The number of special communications that have taken place, including adjourned meetings, and terminating with the special meeting of May 30, 5855, is three hundred and twenty-nine. Very few meetings have been adjourned, and none at all for nearly ten years. Until 1821, the power to call special meetings rested with the Master and Wardens. By the by-laws adopted in that year, this authority was vested in the Master, and since then he alone has exercised it.

The by-laws, until 5816, provided that when the place of meetings should be changed, notice thereof should be given to the Grand Lodge. This provision is omitted in the code of 5816, and in those adopted subsequently. Originally, the places of meetings were determined by a majority of the Lodge; but afterwards, until 5821, they were designated by the by-laws. In the by-laws of 5821, the place of meeting is not provided for, nor does there appear to have been any regulation respecting it adopted by the Lodge. Such a regulation would however be unnecessary, as the Grand Lodge have the right to designate where the meetings of Subordinate Lodges shall be held.

TABLE OF MEETINGS,

INCLUDING THAT OF JUNE 7, A. L., 5855.

Year.	Regular.	Special.	Regular and Special.	Year.	Regular.	Special.	Regular and Special.
5795	6	7	13	5826	12	8	20
5796	12	21	33	5827	12	3	15
5797	12	12	24	5828	12	0	12
5798	12	10	22	5829	8	0	8
5799	12	11	23	5830	7	1	8
5800	12	12	24	5831	8	2	10
5801	12	13	25	5832	8	1	9
5802	12	6	18	5833	7	1	8
5803	12	5	17	5834	6	0	6
5804	12	9	21	5835	8	1	9
5805	12	4	16	5836	7	1	8
5806	12	11	23	5837	9	1	10
5807	12	10	22	5838	8	2	10
5808	12	6	18	5839	8	2	10
5809	12	5	17	5840	9	1	10
5810	12	8	20	5841	9	3	12
5811	12	3	15	5842	9	2	11
5812	12	5	17	5843	10	2	12
5813	12	1	13	5844	10	3	13
5814	10	5	15	5845	11	9	20
5815	12	2	14	5846	10	4	14
5816	12	4	16	5847	10	3	13
5817	12	9	21	5848	11	0	11
5818	12	7	19	5849	12	8	20
5819	12	5	17	5850	10	5	15
5820	12	6	18	5851	11	2	13
5821	12	15	27	5852	11	3	14
5822	12	8	20	5853	10	5	15
5823	12	4	16	5854	10	7	17
5824	12	6	18	5855	6	5	11
5825	12	14	26				
					279	85	364
	364	244	608		364	244	608
					643	329	972

The number of meetings held according to the days of the week, is as follows, viz.: seven hundred and ninety on Thursday, fifty-four on Friday, forty-two on Saturday, thirty-five on Tuesday, twenty-eight on Monday, twenty-two on Wednesday, and one on Sunday.

The first meeting was held at Concert Hall, June 22, 5795. The following partial account of it is taken from the records:

"On motion, the R. W. Master, Brother Joseph Churchill, took the chair. Bro. James Eaton, Senior Warden, and Bro. John Rittenhouse. Junior Warden, they having been recommended to Grand Lodge to fill said offices, and approved.

The Lodge chose the following officers, viz. :

Bro. JOHN COLES, Secretary.
" SAM. HAYDEN, Treasurer.
" S. POWELL, Senior Deacon.
" JAMES DODGE, Junior Deacon.
" NICHOLAS KINDNESS, First Steward.
" THOMAS LEATHAM, Second Steward.
" ——— JONES, Tyler.

The Lodge retired from labor to refreshment, when the R. W. Master gave the following Toast: ' The Most Worshipful Grand Lodge of Massachusetts, with all the Honors ;' also, ' The Columbian Lodge, of Boston.' "

Omission to transact business rarely occurred on Lodge nights. That instanced by the following extract taken from the record, was occasioned by the great manifestations of joy, in Boston, on account of the inauguration of General Harrison into the office of President of the United States.

March 4, 5841. "This meeting occurring on the 4th March, very many of the members were otherwise engaged. Consequently no business of importance was transacted, and the Lodge adjourned to Friday evening next, at 7 o'clock."

The first choice of Master and Wardens was made December 3, 5795, which was in conformity

to the by-laws, which provided that "the choice
of officers shall be annually on the evening preceding the Festival of Saint John." As this
festival occurs on the 27th of December, and the
annual meeting was held on the first Thursday of
that month, the word "evening" had reference
to the evening of the meeting of the Lodge, and
not to that next preceding the festival. Though
the exact language of the by-law might lead to
doubt on this point, yet the practice of the Lodge
in electing their officers on the first Thursday,
shows satisfactorily that the intention of the law
was that the choice should be made on the evening of the regular meeting next preceding St.
John's festival.

December 3, 5795. "The Lodge then proceeded to choose
their officers for one year next ensuing. A Master was bal-
lotted for, and the R. W. Bro. Jos. Churchill was chosen and
accepted the chair. Bro. James Eaton was chosen Senior
Warden, Bro. John Perkins was chosen Junior Warden, Bro.
Jno. W. Folsom was chosen Treasurer, Bro. Jno. Coles, Secretary, Bro. S. Powell and Bro. Sam. Gouldsbury, Senior and
Junior Deacons; Bro. Jno. Rittenhouse and Bro. Tannatt,
Stewards; Bro. Henry Wickham was appointed Tyler of the
Lodge, and accepted; and he withdrew his membership,
agreeably to the by-laws as therein provided."

The Dispensation having been granted for
twelve months, the Lodge could have worked
under it to the expiration of that time, retaining
the officers in office whose appointment was made
with the approbation of the Grand Lodge. Though
the "new officers took their jewels" at the meeting of December 5, 5795, they were not regularly
installed into office until April 14, 5796. At the

meeting of March 22, 5796, the Master having given information that a full charter had been granted, the following vote was adopted :

March 22, 5796. "*Voted*, That the installation take place on the first Thursday of April next, (being the next monthly meeting,) and a dinner be provided at the expense of the members, a band of music be procured, and a committee of three were chosen to conduct and arrange matters on the occasion. Bros. Churchill, Eaton and Folsom were the Committee."

This vote was reconsidered at the meeting of March 27, 5796, in these words :

"*Voted*, That the resolve passed at our last meeting, respecting a feast on the day of installation is now reconsidered.

Voted, That the Committee appointed for the purpose is dissolved, and that the whole be left with the W. Master, to be conducted agreeably to common usage in Boston."

April 12, 5796. "*Voted*, That the Secretary is directed to charge one dollar to each visiting brother, on the evening of our approaching installation."

On the 14th April, 5796, the Lodge was duly constituted by the Grand Lodge, and the Master, Wardens and officers were installed. A large number of visitors were present, the Rev. Bro. John Murray being one of them. This was the first visit of the Grand Lodge to Columbian Lodge.

The following account is all that the record affords relative to this important and interesting occasion :

"A Committee was chosen to wait upon the Grand Lodge, to inform them that Columbian Lodge was prepared to receive them as the Most Worshipful Grand Lodge of Massachusetts ; and Brothers Hayden, Folsom, Gouldsbury, Powell and Raymond, were chosen on said Committee.

The Grand Lodge having previously met in a room adjacent
to the Hall, on receiving the message as above, was so conde-
scending as to attend forthwith, being escorted by said Committee ; and on advancing within the walls of the Hall, were
received by Columbian Lodge, together with all the visitors
present, with all the Honors of Masonry ; and in Ample Form
the Columbian Lodge was installed and proclaimed as a regular Lodge of Free and Accepted Masons ; and at 10 o'clock
the Most Worshipful Grand Lodge retired with the same
honors as on entering, and three times three cheers.

Brothers Churchill, Eaton and Perkins were chosen a Committee to request a copy of the charge for record."

The choice of officers has been made with remarkable regularity at the stated meetings in
December, annually, as the by-laws have uniformly provided. Previous to the year 5832,
this provision was strictly adhered to, not a
single election having been postponed beyond the
regular night. The dates at which elections
occurred at adjourned meetings, were Dec. 29,
5832, Dec. 19, 5833, Dec. 15, 5836, Dec. 20,
5838, Dec. 19, 5839, Dec. 16, 5841, Dec. 9, 5842,
Dec. 15, 5843, Dec. 19, 5844, Dec. 13, 5845 and
Dec. 10, 5846; making only eleven times during
a period of sixty years, that they did not take
place at the stated meetings. The choice of officers in 5836, was deferred to Dec. 15, because the
annual Thanksgiving of that year occurred on
the day of the stated meeting, December 1, 5836.

The original by-laws provided that the Master,
Wardens, Treasurer and Secretary should be
chosen by ballot, a majority of votes making a
choice, and the other officers by hand vote. In
5799, it was established that the first five officers
and the Deacons and Stewards should be elected

by ballot, the majority to determine the choice; and that a Closet Steward should be elected annually, by the Master and Wardens. The by-laws of 5808 required all the officers to be chosen by ballot, excepting the Tyler and Closet Steward, who were appointed by the Master and Wardens. In 5816, this last named regulation was continued; and the office of Inside Sentinel was created, who was appointed by the Master and Wardens. The Constitution adopted in 5821, provided that the "nine first officers" should be chosen by written ballots: they were the Master, Wardens, Treasurer, Secretary, Deacons and Stewards. All other officers were "appointed by the Master, with the advice and consent of the Wardens." The by-laws of 5854, contain the same provisions as to the election of officers that existed in those adopted in 5821. A majority of members present has always determined the choice.

The installations of officers since 5796, fifty-nine in number, have occurred as follows, viz.: thirty-four at the stated meeting in January, ten at the stated meeting in December; ten at adjourned or special meetings in December; one February 17, 5820; one February 7, 5833; one February 6, 5840; one January 21, 5847; and one was commenced at the stated meeting in December, 5848, and completed at the succeeding stated meeting in January, 5849. No time was determined by the by-laws for installation previous to 5821. The code of that year provides that "the officers, elected and appointed" should be "installed at such time as the Lodge shall

direct." The interesting and impressive ceremonies of installation have been usually performed
only in presence of the Fraternity. Occasionally,
installations have been rendered additionally
attractive by addresses, music and the well-spread
festive board ; or when distinguished Masons have
honored them with their presence. Public installations, at which the members were permitted to
invite their acquaintances and friends, do not
appear to have received much encouragement at
any period of the existence of the Lodge. The
record descriptions of installations which have
been of a public character, or otherwise distinguished, and of proceedings connected therewith,
are contained in the subjoined extracts. The
officers elected in December 5804, were installed
at the Festival of St. John, December 27, of that
year :

November 1, 5804. " On motion, *Voted*, That Columbian
Lodge celebrate the Festival of St. John, in December next.

W. Master, Bros. Stetson, Folsom, Crooker and Benson,
were appointed a Committee of Arrangements on that day.

On motion, *Voted*, That R. W. Bro. Jno. W. Folsom be
requested to prepare and deliver a Masonic address on the
evening of the Festival of St. John."

December 27, 5804. " The Throne of Grace addressed in
prayer by the Rev. Bro. Eaton. An Ode being sung, the R.
W. Master proceeded to install, in due form, the several officers of the Lodge for the ensuing year.

A Masonic address was pronounced by R. W. Bro. J. W.
Folsom.

Voted, That the thanks of the Lodge, be tendered to the
Rev. Bro. Eaton for his services this evening.

Voted, That the thanks of the Lodge be given to R. W.
Bro. Folsom, for his appropriate, ingenious and interesting
address, by him this evening delivered. The R. W. Master,
R. W. Bro. Stetson and R. W. Bro. Benson, were chosen a

Committee to await on R. W. Bro. Folsom and request a copy of his address for the press."

The brother who acted as Chaplain at this celebration still lives, and is honored and beloved for his amiable and Christian character; and among the brethren, for his steady devotion to the principles of the Order. Rev. Asa Eaton, D. D. was born in Plaistow, N. H., July 25, 5778. He pursued his preparatory studies with Rev. Giles Merrill, the preceptor of Atkinson Academy in New Hampshire, and graduated at Harvard University in 5803. On leaving the University he became a lay reader in Christ Church, Boston, until 5805, when he was admitted to orders. From July, 5805 to May, 5829, he was the Rector of that Church. From 5829 to 5837, his untiring labors as City Missionary were crowned with abundant success, and secured for him the love and attachment of his parishioners. On retiring from this position, he became connected with a literary institution in New Jersey, which connection continued to the year 5841. Since his return to Boston, though having no parish, he has engaged actively in the service of the Church.

While a student at the University, he employed his vacations in keeping school. He was thus occupied at Groton, Mass., in 5802, when he was initiated into Masonry in Saint Paul's Lodge in that town. He received his first Masonic lesson from the late Hon. and R. W. Timothy Bigelow, who was then Master of the Lodge. On his removing his residence to Boston in 5803, he became a member of Saint John's Lodge. He

was Chaplain of the Grand Lodge; and he frequently officiated in this capacity for Subordinate
Lodges. In 5820, he was the Deputy Grand
Master, having received his appointment from
Hon. Samuel P. P. Fay, who was then the Grand
Master. After a connection with Freemasonry
for more than half a century, and much of that
time having been actively engaged in Lodge
duties, he fails not to bear hearty testimony to its
usefulness, and to express the sincerest approbation of its principles.

The installation that occurred January 4, 5810,
was celebrated by addresses from the R. W. Master, Bro. Jos. Jenkins, and from the Senior Warden,
Bro. Samuel Smith. The next succeeding installation, that of December 27, 5810, being connected with the Festival of St. John, was marked
with greater festivity; and R. W. Bro. Jenkins
was the orator of the occasion.

December 6, 5810. " *Voted*, That the R. W. Master and
Wardens be a Committee to make arrangements for celebrating St. John's Evening."

December 27, 5810. "It being the Festival of St. John,
an Ode suitable for the occasion was sung by the Brethren,
after which an address fraught with the principles of Masonry
was in an impressive manner delivered by the R. W. Master.
The Craft were then called from labor to refreshment, and
proceeded in due form under the direction of the Marshal to
the dining room, where they partook of a plentiful repast,
and drank a number of appropriate sentiments. They returned to the Hall in due order, and were called from refreshment to labor."

January 3, 5811. " *Voted*, That the thanks of the Lodge
be presented to the R. W. Joseph Jenkins for his truly Masonic address, delivered at the last meeting."

September 5, 5811. "*Voted*, That Bros. Sawyier, Moody and Howard be a Committee to take into consideration the expediency of having a Public Celebration, and report thereon at the next meeting of the Lodge."

October 3, 5811. "*Voted*, To discharge the Committee appointed upon the subject of a Festival.

Voted, That the same subject be committed to Bros. D. Baxter, Heard and Mills to report at the next meeting of the Lodge."

November 7, 5811. "The Committee to whom the subject of a Festival had been referred, reported that they had attended to that subject, but did not deem it advisable to have a Festival at the expense of the Lodge."

The first public installation was graced by the presence of ladies; and afforded great delight to a large auditory. The oration was pronounced by Bro. Elijah Morse, who was afterwards Master of the Lodge.

December 17, 5812. "The Standing Committee reported, that having considered of the propriety of having a Female Visitation of those connected with the members of the Lodge, conceive it proper; and recommend that it take place at the time of the next regular meeting of the Lodge; and that the officers elect, be installed on that evening, and that two members be added to the Committee, for the purpose of making arrangements.

Voted, To accept this report; also *Voted*, That Bros. Appleton and Mills be added to the said Committee."

January 7, 5813. "This being the evening assigned for installing the officers elect, and for the Female Visitation, the ladies were introduced and seated in the upper Hall.

The members and visiting brethren assembled in the lower Hall, opened the Lodge, and adjourned to 10 o'clock. They then proceeded in form to the Hall, with music by the band. The Rev. Bro. Kneeland addressed the Throne of Grace in a very able manner. The Officers Elect were then installed in due form by the W. Master, who delivered an appropriate charge to each. An excellent address was then delivered by

Bro. Morse, the concluding prayer by the Rev. Bro. Dean. In the course of the evening several appropriate songs were sung.

The company then formed in procession under the direction of the Marshal, and proceeded to the refreshment room ; when, after a plentiful repast and several appropriate sentiments, they again returned to the Hall in the same order as before, and spent the remainder of the evening in a social manner.

The Officers retired and closed the Lodge at half-past 10 o'clock, P. M.''

February 4, 5813. '' *Voted*, That the W. Master and Wardens be a Committee to wait on Bro. Morse, and in the name of the Lodge, to return him their thanks for his excellent address, delivered before them on their last meeting for the installation of the Officers ; and request of him a copy to be preserved with the Records of the Lodge.''

March 4, 5813. '' The Committee appointed on the last evening to wait on Bro. Morse, &c. reported verbally that they had attended to the duty assigned them and that Bro. Morse would comply with the wishes of the Lodge. Accepted.''

To the ceremonies of the installation of the officers elected to serve for the year 5817, performed December 19, 5816, were added that of the presentation of a Master's Jewel to R. W. Bro. B. B. Appleton ; and the transactions of the evening were throughout so interesting and of so high an order, that no abridgment of the record, would do justice to the occasion :

December 5, 5816. '' Bros. Jenkins and Morse were appointed a Committee to prepare and present R. W. B. B. Appleton something suitable as a mark of distinction, and approbatory for his faithful services in Columbian Lodge.''

December 19, 5816. '' At 8¾ o'clock, P. M., the Marshal introduced R. W. Bro. Joseph Jenkins, Master elect of this Lodge, to R. W. Bro. Appleton, Master the past year, who inducted him into office in due form.

R. W. Bro. Jenkins then as Chairman of the Committee chosen at the last meeting, availed himself of that opportunity to present to R. W. Bro. Appleton, the Jewel of a Past Master, with an engraving expressive of the grateful and affectionate sense the members entertained of his past faithful services, and his unremitted exertions, for the honor and interest of the Lodge ; at which time he also expressed in concise but comprehensive language, his personal approbation of his past conduct, and warmest wishes for his future peace, prosperity and happiness. To all which, R. W. Bro. Appleton made a suitable and Masonic reply, by reciprocating the good wishes of Bro. Jenkins, and testifying to the members in the strongest terms his gratitude for this additional evidence of their esteem.

R. W. Bro. Jenkins then proceeded to the installation of R. W. Bro. Morse as Senior Warden, R. W. Bro. Appleton as Junior Warden, R. W. and Rev. Bro. Paul Dean as Chaplain, R. W. Daniel Baxter as Treasurer, R. W. Isaac M. Gaw as Secretary, R. W. Samuel Smith, Senior Deacon, R. W. Nathaniel Hammond, Junior Deacon, Bro. George Guild, Senior Steward, Bro. Daniel Baxter, Jr., Junior Steward, and Bro. E. V. Glover, Tyler. To all whom he forcibly, solemnly and affectionately explained their several duties, enjoining upon each and every one of them to act becoming their stations and faithfully to perform their respective duties.

After which he delivered an address exhibiting the qualities, designs and effects of Free Masonry, proving by a chain of events the intimate connection it has with Christianity, and that both were kindly and wisely instituted by one Almighty Parent, to make man happy here and prepare him for joys unspeakable hereafter.

Several appropriate Odes were sung on the occasion, and a Masonic Prayer made by R. W. and Rev. Bro. Dean, Chaplain, after which the craft were called from labor to refreshment, when a procession was formed under the direction of Bro. Binney, the acting Marshal, and members and visitors assembled round the festive board to partake of the bounties of Providence. Several original and appropriate toasts were drank; and after a short interval the craft resumed their labor."

January 2, 5817. " Bros. Morse, Appleton, Baxter, Smith and Howard were, on motion of the Secretary, chosen a Committee to wait upon R. W. Joseph Jenkins, and, as the organ of the Lodge, to tender their thanks to him for his instructive and lucid address delivered on the evening of his last installation, and to request of him a copy thereof to be placed on the file with the records of the Lodge.''

February 6, 5817. '' The report of the Committee appointed to wait on the R. W. Bro. Jenkins and to present to him the thanks of the Lodge for the lucid and instructive address delivered at the installation of officers, and to request a copy of the same to be placed upon the files of the Lodge, was received and read by the Secretary. The Committee in that report state that upon their own responsibility they have extended the power vested in them, and requested of Bro. Jenkins a copy of the charge given to the respective officers; and they also state that our R. W. Bro. Jenkins, with great modesty, complied with the request of the members, and also with that of the Committee,—and this report was also accepted.''

On the evening of December 22, 5817, the second public installation took place in the Masonic Rooms in the Exchange Coffee House :

'' At seven o'clock the Committee of Arrangements for the public installation of the officers, announced the arrival, in the rooms adjoining the Hall of the Coffee House, of the ladies and other invited guests; upon which the chairman was requested to introduce them to the Hall. On their entering, the band played some appropriate music, and after being accommodated with seats, the Chaplain, Bro. P. Dean, advanced to the altar and implored the blessing of the Supreme Architect on all present. R. W. Bro. Baxter, after examining the Master elect, proceeded to install him in his office. The R. W. Master then installed all the officers in the usual form, giving to each an appropriate charge, concluding with a pertinent address to the Brethren, Visitors and particularly to the Ladies. Several pieces of sacred music were sung; after which W. Bro. Morse arose and delivered an address with his usual animation and elegance of diction, which was listened to with much delight.

The ladies and visitors were then formed into a procession

and conducted to the Hall of the Coffee House where the tables were covered with a variety of fruit, wine &c., and all partook of the repast which had been prepared by the Committee from the voluntary subscription of some of the members. A great number of toasts were drank, and some songs sung. Among the visitors were the first officers of the Grand Encampment of Knight Templars, of the Royal Arch Chapter and of the several Lodges in this town, together with many clergymen and Bro. Gen. James Miller. The exact number was not ascertained, but was calculated to be, 170 to 180 ladies, 100 to 120 gentlemen, in the whole 300 or upwards."

The installation of January 21, 5847, was the third public one. The address by R. W. John H. Sheppard, was able and eloquent. It was printed in pamphlet form ; but as very few copies of it are probably accessible to the present members of the Lodge, a part of it is introduced into the account of the ceremonies of the evening :

January 7, 5847. R. W. Master on behalf of the Committee on Installation, reported that it was expedient to have a public installation ; report accepted, and the four first officers and Brother Ball were appointed a Committee to make the necessary arrangements.

January 21, 5847. A special meeting of Columbian Lodge was held this evening at the Masonic Temple, at 7 o'clock. The Lodge opened in the upper Hall, and then proceeded to the lower Hall where a large number of ladies and gentlemen were seated. The Grand Master attended by the officers of the Grand Lodge and a delegation from the other Masonic Institutions, then entered the Hall. After a prayer by the Rev. Bro. Taylor.—the Grand Master installed R. W. George M. Thacher, as Master.

The R. W. Master then made the following appointments :

Rev. Bro. E. T. Taylor, as Chaplain.
"   Newell A. Thompson, Marshal.
"   William W. Wood, Inside Sentinel.
"   William C. Martin, Tyler.

R. W. Geo. G. Smith, then installed W. Peter C. Jones, as Senior Warden, W. Wm. D. Coolidge, as Junior Warden, Rev. Edward T. Taylor, as Chaplain, R. W. Ruel Baker, as Treasurer, John McClellan, as Secretary, William W. Baker, as Senior Deacon, John T. Heard, as Junior Deacon, George Tucker, as Senior Steward, Hiram Simmons, as Junior Steward, Newell A. Thompson, as Marshal, William W. Wood, as Inside Sentinel, William C. Martin, as Tyler; proclamation was then made by the Marshal, that Columbian Lodge was duly organized; after an Ode, R. W. John H. Sheppard delivered an eloquent and instructive address.

The Grand Master and the other visiting Brethren then retired, after which the Lodge proceeded to the upper Hall and closed in due form at 10 o'clock.''

BRO. G. G. SMITH'S ADDRESS.

And now, Brethren of Columbian Lodge, permit me in completing this, probably my last official act among you, to thank you from the bottom of my heart, for all those tokens of sympathy and confidence which I have received from you during a membership of more than twenty years. We have experienced varied fortunes together—sometimes the Masonic horizon has been clouded; and yet, while we have been vehemently assailed by the storms of bigotry and detraction from without, within our Lodge all has been peace; and so far as I know, there has been no personal disagreement between any two of our members since I have been connected with you. Even our elections, where, if ever, the preferences of personal friendship are apt to generate unkind feelings towards opponents, and especially successful opponents—have passed off, so far as I know with perfect cordiality, and the will of the majority has been obeyed without the least cavil or dissatisfaction.

And from this truly Masonic union it would have been easy to predict the prosperity which followed. Look at your Lodge, now, my Brethren! second, perhaps, to none in the Union, in numbers, and certainly second to none in the only true element of Masonic strength, the moral worth of its members; you have before you, so far as human reason may venture to predict, a long course of prosperity and usefulness. Let me entreat you then, as I have done many times before, to avoid the common and pernicious error of regarding Masonry as a mere system of ceremonies and ordinances, or that he who is most lip-learned in mere technicalities is the brightest Mason. It is not so, my Brethren! Masonry is a life—and, however important may be a thorough knowledge of our ritual, which I would not in the least undervalue—remember that he alone is a true son of Masonry who conscientiously and habitually lives out its precepts.

Wherefore, my Brethren, let this Lodge be, as every Lodge ought to be, a bright point in the dark waste of human selfishness and contention ; let its members so live, that those who are not of us, seeing us united by bonds which neither the jealousies of trade, nor the divisions of politics, nor the quarrels of contending sects can sever,—in short, that, under every discouragement we are as a body and as individuals, doing what we can to bring all mankind into that true fraternal union of which Christianity, properly understood, is the perfection. Let them see this, and they may perhaps, at last be made to unstand that in opposing an institution which, as society is now organized, alone has the power to bring these antagonist elements of sects, and parties, and conditions into harmonious contact—they are opposing one of God's chief appointed means of human progress, whose necessity is inherent in man's nature, and therefore essential, so far as human means can avail, to his attaining that perfection which the laws of his being indicate, and which the Word of God has solemnly foretold and promised.

Brethren, with sincere wishes for the continued welfare of Columbian Lodge, I now bid you an affectionate farewell.

February 4, 5847. " On motion of Brother Hall the Committee on installation were directed to return the thanks of the Lodge to R. W. Bro. J. H. Sheppard for the interesting address delivered by him at the installation of the officers, on the 21st January, and request a copy for the press."

The subject of the eloquent and instructive production of Brother Sheppard, was " THE DISCIPLINE OF THE SECRET, by which the mysteries of Freemasonry were cherished, preserved, and handed down by the first followers of our Divine Master—by the *Fathers of the Church.*" The following extract, being the conclusion of the address, affords a specimen of the style of the orator.

" W. MASTER—The Installation of this evening has been singularly interesting. You have been invested with your jewel of office by the Grand Master of Masons in Massachusetts, and your Brethren elect, have received theirs in due form. These ceremonies have been witnessed by visitors of high rank in the Fraternity. In looking round this superb Hall, you behold representatives of several Lodges—of the Grand Lodge of this State, the Royal Arch Chapters, and the Encampment of Knights Templars—of all the Ineffable degrees, even to the highest, which are recognized in foreign countries—and each in the rich costume, and splendid regalia of their respective Orders. Strangers, too, and fair guests have been invited, and many beautiful eyes have been gazing upon a spectacle which has seldom, if ever, been so imposing in this country. This is no small testimony of the estimation in which Columbian Lodge is held by the Brethren at large, and your history richly deserves it.

Chartered June 9, 1796, it is now more than half a century since your Lodge was consecrated by PAUL REVERE, then Grand Master of Massachusetts ; a name dear to Masons and to the public. He was the father of the Massachusetts Charitable Mechanic Association, which has done so much good in this city ; and the *Revere House,* dedicated by them to his memory, affords fresh evidence that eminent Masons are often no less distinguished by the confidence of their fellow citizens. I might add, too, ISAIAH THOMAS, S. G. Warden, at that ceremony—another excellent man and Mason, greatly esteemed by the public, and the Patriarch of the Press in New England. Of seventeen Past Masters who have presided over this Lodge, only six are now living—two of whom we have the pleasure to meet on this occasion, Brother BAKER, who officiated four, and Brother SMITH, seven years, to the honor and increase of your Fraternity. Of 862 Masons, who were made here, but 250 are now surviving. St. Paul's R. A. Chapter originated from petitioners belonging to Columbian Lodge, nine of whom were chosen officers of that Order. Many who once presided here, have filled the Chair in the Grand Lodge of Massachusetts; and long before the great Temperance cause had drawn the attention and the efforts of the philanthropist, Columbian Lodge set the example of a reform which was soon followed by other Lodges.

During the long night when persecution raged against the

Brotherhood, a period we all remember too well, your Lodge never suspended their meetings; and on the first dawn of peace, it was at your door the candidate was received and initiated. Such recollections must be pleasing, and endear your memory to all our Fraternities. You have our warmest wishes, that Columbian Lodge may always sustain its high reputation, and preserve inviolate the ancient land-marks of the Order.

When I recall, my Brother, that period in our history, when there was darkness that could be felt, and it seemed as though the pillars of the temple were shaken from their foundation by the violence of the storm; when I remember that time, in which more than *six thousand* Masons pledged their names and their characters, but in vain, in behalf of an institution unjustly accused; and when I look back on my own situation, and anxieties, like a mariner on the hurricane deck of a steamer, amidst the darkness and roar of the elements—it is with heartfelt sensibility, 1 recur to the noble course pursued by the Fraternities of Boston. Nor did one of her five Lodges, nor either Chapter, nor the Encampment of Knights Templars, waver in the trial. They stood firm. They endured unto the end. To them the Masons of New England looked up. By their example, with few, very few exceptions, every Lodge, on every hill, and in every low vale, was sustained and encouraged.''

Bro. Sheppard was born in Cirencester, County of Gloucester, England, and accompanied his father to this country when three years old. He resided in Wiscasset, Maine, until 1843, when he removed to this city. He was a representative from Boston in the Massachusetts Legislature of 5854. His first lessons in Masonry he received in Lincoln Lodge, Wiscasset. His contributions to Masonic literature in the Freemason's Magazine and other publications, evince profound research, and display an ardent attachment to Masonry. He is the present Grand Corresponding Secretary of the Grand Lodge of Massachusetts.

The fourth and last public installation of officers was equally as interesting as either of those preceding it. On the evening of December 21, 5849, the ceremonies of this attractive occasion were witnessed by a numerous assembly of Masons and their families and friends. Bro. George M. Randall delivered a masterly and brilliant address, having for his subject "The History of Freemasonry." It is much regretted that this admirable production was not preserved in some form. It was pronounced without notes, and cannot, therefore, now be obtained, except through "the reproducing power of the author."

December 21, 5849. "A special meeting of Columbian Lodge was held this evening at the Masonic Temple at 6½ o'clock, and was opened in the upper Hall. The Lodge then proceeded under the direction of Bro. Newell A. Thompson, to the lower Hall, escorting the M. W. Grand Master, and a delegation from the M. W. Grand Lodge; Grand Chapter; Grand Encampment of Mass., and R. I.; Princes of Jerusalem; St. Andrews and St. Paul's Chapters; St. John's, St. Andrews, Massachusetts, and Mt. Lebanon Lodges, where about three hundred ladies and gentlemen were seated. After an invocation to the deity, R. W. Bro. Jones, announced the object of the meeting, and asked the permission of the R. W. Grand Master to proceed with a public installation of the officers. The M. W. Grand Master signifying his assent, the R. W. Bro. G. G. Smith, at the request of the R. W. Master, proceeded to install in that chaste and elegant style for which he is so justly celebrated. Proclamation was then made by the Marshal that the Lodge was duly organized for the ensuing year. The Rev. and R. W. Bro. Geo. M. Randall, D. G. Master, then delivered an eloquent and impressive address upon the History of Free Masonry. The Brethren and visitors separated all highly pleased with the ceremonies of this interesting occasion."

ORDER OF EXERCISES

AT THE

Installation of the Officers of Columbian Lodge,

At the Masonic Temple, Friday Evening, Dec. 21, 1849.

INTRODUCTORY PRAYER.

OPENING ANTHEM, FROM POWER'S MASONIC MELODIES.

Rejoice, all ye that are assembled | in the | Lord,
For in safety have we | met a- | gain this | day :
From the hands of our enemies He hath de- | livered | us,
And the light of His | counte- | nance is | here.

How beautiful are the gates of our | Temple | seen !
The incense of devotion we | bring un- | to its | courts :
With thankful hearts, before its altars, we | here ap- | pear,
To bow down and worship be- | fore His | holy | throne.

Let all the Brethren, in songs of | praise, u- | nite,
For all the goodness of | God un- | to us | shown :
We will rejoice in His mercy | ever- | more,
While together we journey through | life, A- | men, A- | men.

INSTALLATION OF OFFICERS.

POWER'S MASONIC MELODIES.

Installation of the Master.

Support to the Master, that rules by the Square !
Let sons of the Light to the East now repair ;
With hearts for his aid, now united and free,
Obedient we labor and kindly agree,
    Chorus.—With hearts for his aid, &c.

Installation of Senior Warden.

Support to the Warden installed in the West,
Who works by the Level, where sorrows may rest !
With hearts for his aid, now united and free,
Obedient we labor, and kindly agree.
    Chorus.—With hearts for his aid, &c.

Installation of Junior Warden.

Support to the Warden, by Plumb still upright,
Whose sun, in the South, never hides its fair light!
With hearts for his aid, now united and free,
Obedient we labor, and kindly agree.
CHORUS.—With hearts for his aid, &c.

Installation of other Officers.

To our Brother, now before THEE, | LORD, our | GOD,
Grant thy holy pro- | tection | all his | days.   ‖ A- | men.

———

ODE.

POWER'S MASONIC MELODIES.

Your voices lend, to hail the friends
 We welcome here to-night,
For Friendship's chain, with Brothers true,
 Is seen more fair and bright;
And hours that kindness treasures here
 The night-song still shall find,
While every heart shall catch the strain
 That tells of thoughts most kind.
CHORUS.—And kindly thus shall Brothers know
 True hearts will joyous be,
:‖: Where notes of love responsive rise,
 In hours of social glee. :‖:

O, who, with thought and heart so cold,
 The joyous hour would miss,
That brings, amid time's changing scenes,
 The truest source of bliss!
One whispered word shall kindly tell,
 One gentle hand shall bear,
A pledge that time shall never waste,
 That changes ne'er impair.
CHORUS.—And kindly thus shall Brothers know,
 True hearts will joyous be, &c.

When dreams of other days return,
 And mark departed joys,
We'll treasure then their brightest forms,
 That distance ne'er destroys:

Though other climes their charms disclose,
    And newer hopes may bring,
Our memory then shall trace, once more,
    The welcome friends now sing.
CHORUS.—And kindly thus shall Brothers know
    True hearts will joyous be, &c.

ADDRESS BY R. W. REV. GEORGE M. RANDALL.

CLOSING PRAYER.—CLOSING ODE.

POWER'S MASONIC MELODIES.

We met in love ; we part in peace ;
    Our council-labors o'er,
We'll ask, ere life's best days shall cease,
    To meet in time once more.
CHORUS.—'Mid fairest scenes to memory dear,
    In change of joy and pain,
We'll think of friends assembled here,
    And hope to meet again.

Though changes mark time's onward way,
    In all we fondly claim,
Fraternal hopes shall ne'er decay,
    Our landmarks still the same.
CHORUS.—'Mid fairest scenes, &c.

Our Faith unmoved, with Truth our guide,
    As seasons mark our clime,
Through winter's chill, or summer's pride,
    We'll hail the Art sublime !
CHORUS.—'Mid fairest scenes, &c.

When life shall find its silent close,
    With Hope's kind promise blest,
In that Grand Lodge may all repose,
    Where joys immortal rest !
CHORUS.—'Mid fairest scenes to memory dear,

    In change of joy and pain,
We'll think of friends assembled here,
And hope to meet again.
    'Mid fairest scenes, &c.
BENEDICTION.

January 3, 5850. "On motion of R. W. Bro. Thacher, it was voted, that the thanks of the Lodge be presented to R. W. and Rev. Bro. G. M. Randall for his eloquent and impressive address at the installation of the officers of the Lodge, on the evening of December 21st."

" On motion of the Secretary, it was voted that the thanks of the Lodge be presented to the ladies and gentlemen of the choir, for the valuable and gratuitous services rendered by them, on the evening of December 21st."

" On motion of R. W. Bro. Thacher, it was voted that the thanks of the Lodge be presented to our R. W. Bro. Geo. G. Smith, for the valuable and efficient services rendered by him on the same occasion."

In 5851, it was proposed to have a public installation, but the proposition was not favorably entertained.

December 4, 5851. "Bros. Coolidge, Heard, Adams and Baker were appointed a Committee to take into consideration the subject of a public installation of the officers."

December 20, 5851. " Bro. Coolidge, from the Committee on installation, reported that it was inexpedient to have a public installation the present year, and that the installation take place at the next regular meeting of the Lodge."

The Masonic address delivered by Bro. Joseph B. Kelley so far back as 5804, would be for its antiquity alone, a valuable acquisition to the library of the Lodge ; but no manuscript of it is to be found, and as it was not printed, all hope of obtaining it is lost. The occasion on which it was uttered is referred to in the records, as follows :

January 5, 5804. " R. W. Bros. Folsom, Stetson and the W. Master were appointed a Committee to request Bro. Joseph B. Kelley to deliver an oration on Masonry, in this Lodge."

January 19, 5804. " W. Bros. Folsom, Stetson and Baxter were appointed a Committee to request Bro. Kelley to deliver an address on Masonry the next Lodge night; and also make arrangements for such an occasion."

February 2, 5804. " Bro. Kelley then delivered a Masonic address, agreeably to the request of the Lodge. W. Bro. Folsom, W. Master and Bro. Stetson were appointed a Committee to request of Bro. Kelley a copy of his address delivered in the Lodge this evening."

The first visit of ladies to the Lodge occurred in 5807; and was an occasion of more than ordinary interest to the brethren; and the "select party of ladies" could not have failed to find pleasure in witnessing ceremonies which were to them novel, and in sharing in the attending festivities. The record account, though lengthy, is worth presenting entire to the reader:

August 6, 5807. " *Voted*, That Bros. Bean, Jenkins and Phillips appoint an orator from their Committee to deliver an appropriate address at our next regular meeting."

September 3, 5807. " A Committee of five, viz.: Bros. Baxter, Bean, Binney, Johnson and Jenkins were appointed to consider the propriety, and if they see cause, to make arrangements for the entertainment of a select party of ladies at our next regular Lodge night, and report at a special meeting appointed on Thursday evening next."

September 10, 5807. " The Committee appointed to make arrangements for the ladies, reported, and the report was accepted. *Voted*, That the same Committee make the necessary arrangements.
Voted, That no member be admitted into the lower Hall for refreshment, but with permission from the Worshipful Master."

October 1, 5807. " Brother Bean reported the doings of the Committee for a special meeting, and the report was accepted by the Lodge."

October 8, 5807. " At a special meeting of Columbian Lodge, held at Masons' Hall, for the purpose of introducing the near connected ladies of the members of this Lodge, members all present, with their wives, &c in the lower Hall. Proceedings as follows : The Right W. Bro. Bean in the chair.—The Lodge opened in due form, and the Throne of Grace addressed by the Rev. Brother Eaton.—A Committee was appointed to introduce the visiting ladies into the Hall ; music by the band ; ladies seated.—An introductory prayer by the Rev. Bro. Eaton. — Music. — An Address on the occasion was delivered by the Right W. Master, John W. Folsom.—A Masonic song was sung by Bro. Joshua Eaton, accompanied by the band.—Music.—A song by Bro. Coolidge, accompanied by the band.—Music.—The Committee escorted the ladies to the lower hall from whence they came, for refreshment. The Lodge closed in due form at 9 o'clock, and retired below to pass a cheerful hour with the ladies."

The recollection of the pleasures afforded by this reception of their female friends, induced the brethren, in 5809, to give a similar entertainment. The proceedings attending the second visit of the ladies are described in the extracts from the records, which here follow :

October 12, 5809. " The Committee chosen at the last meeting of Columbian Lodge, recommend that the members of this Lodge introduce their ladies into this Hall at a future time ; and they have spoken to a Brother who will deliver an address at the meeting, should it meet their approbation."

October 26, 5809. " The Lodge was opened in due form. Bro. Samuel Smith was desired to serve as Marshal for the evening. This being the evening appointed for the purpose of introducing the ladies, they accordingly met in the lower Hall. Proceedings as follows : The visiting ladies were introduced into the upper Hall ; while advancing, music by the band ; after the ladies were seated, the R. W. Master gave a short address from the chair. Entered apprentices' song ac-

companied by the band. An introductory prayer by R. W.
P. M. Bro. John W. Folsom. A song written by the Rev.
Bro. Harris, and sung by Bro. Horsman, accompanied by the
band. An address on the occasion delivered by Bro. Joseph
Jenkins. A song by Bro. Horsman, accompanied by the band.
Concluding prayer by the R. W. Master; after which a
Committee waited on the ladies to the lower Hall, from
whence they came, for refreshment. The Lodge then closed
in due form at nine o'clock, and retired below to pass a cheer-
ful hour with the ladies.''

After a lapse of seven years, the Halls of the
Lodge were again, and for the third time, enliv-
ened with the company of ladies at entertainments
of a festive character, specially designed for them.
At installations and at other times, they have
graced the Masonic Hall with their presence, but
then neither the banquet nor the dance offered
attractions; "the feast of reason and the flow of
soul" appear to have succeeded the less intellect-
ual enjoyments of earlier days:

February 1, 5816. "This being the evening assigned by
the Standing Committee to introduce ladies into Masons'
Hall, the Lodge at 7 P. M. was closed in due form, and at
7½ the ladies entered, conducted by the Marshal. The company being seated, the performances were the following, and
their order: a voluntary by the band; an excellent prayer by
the Rev. P. Dean; an address by our R. W. Bro. Joseph
Jenkins, very appropriately representing the principles and
benefits of Freemasonry, as it respects this or a future existence. Music, vocal and instrumental; prayer by Bro. P.Dean;
a trio by Bros. Eastman, Jewett and Williams. At 8½ the
ladies were conducted to refreshment Hall, where they partook
of fruit of several kinds, also of the wine, and other things
suited to the occasion. The brethren were accommodated
in an adjoining hall, where they regaled themselves. At 9½
returned from refreshment to Masons' Hall. A solo was performed with great eclat by Bro. Jewett; another solo by Bro.
Welsh; a third by Bro. Bray; a duet by Bros. Jewett and

Eastman closed the hilarity of the evening, and at 10 P. M. the company retired.''

March 7, 5816. '' *Voted*, That the thanks of this Lodge be presented to Bro. Jenkins for his elegant and Masonic address delivered before this Lodge at our last meeting, a copy be requested to be preserved with our records ; and also that the thanks of this Lodge be presented to our R. W. and Rev. Bro. Paul Dean for his services in the solemnities of the evening, and that the Secretary be requested to present Bros. Jenkins and Dean with a copy of the foregoing votes.''

May 2, 5816. '' The following communication was made by R. W. Joseph Jenkins, which was voted to be inserted with the records of Columbian Lodge.

'BOSTON, May 2, 1816.

DEAR SIR :

A variety of secular engagements have prevented my answering till this late day, your favor covering a vote of thanks from Columbian Lodge for the address I had the honor to pronounce before them at their late festival, and also a request that I would furnish a copy to be preserved with their records. Be sure this kind expression of friendship and approbation from a Lodge I so much love and venerate, excites more gratitude than I am capable of expressing, and the polite manner in which these expressions were communicated, adds, if possible, to every grateful sensation. Would compliance with the request in my opinion promote in any sense the interest of the Craft, I should not hesitate to furnish the copy requested ; but fraught as it is, with so many imperfections, I dare not submit it to the inspection of any but the candid eye of private friendship, and individual brethren. With sentiments of fraternal esteem and the highest consideration, I have the honor to be your sincere friend and Brother,

JOSEPH JENKINS,' ''

On the evening of January 30, 5854, an address was delivered before the members of the Lodge and their friends, by Rev. Bro. William R. Alger, but not in open Lodge. It was not written, but merely meditated and spoken extemporaneously.

The benefits of so valuable and elegant an effort ought not to have been confined to those who heard it, alone ; they should have been extended to the reader and to all who seek for knowledge from the history of the Order. The following vote was passed by the Lodge at their next meeting :

February 2, 5854. " On motion, it was *Voted*, That the thanks of the Lodge be presented to Rev. Bro. W. R. Alger for the very able and interesting lecture, delivered by him before the Lodge on the 30th ult."

Bro. Alger was born at Freetown, Mass., in 5825. He did not graduate at any college, but received the honorary degree of A. M. from Harvard University in 5850. He was initiated into Masonry in Washington Lodge, Roxbury, Mass., on the recommendation of that worthiest of men, and of Masons, the late venerable Winslow Lewis, Senior; and has served as Chaplain in various branches of the Masonic Institution.

In 5854, a desire having been manifested among the brethren to extend civilities to those members of the Legislature and State Government, who were Masons and residing temporarily, only, in Boston, measures to that end were taken by the Lodge. A large number of gentlemen responded to an invitation to meet the Lodge opened in due form at their Hall. The evening was spent in an agreeable and social manner and terminated with a banquet:

April 14, 5854. " The Council were appointed a Committee to invite such members of the Legislature as are members of the Fraternity, to attend a special meeting of the Lodge on

Tuesday evening next, April 18.   Bros. Thacher, Jones, Baxter, Dupee and Cotting were appointed a Committee with full powers, to make the necessary arrangements for their reception."

Tuesday, April 18, 5854.   "A special meeting of Columbian Lodge was held this evening at the Masonic Temple.

Lodge opened at 7 o'clock; present, R. W. J. T. Heard, seventy-six members and eighty-three visiting brethren.   The Lodge with its invited guests, among whom were His Honor the Lieut. Governor, several Senators and Representatives of the General Court, proceeded to the festive board and passed a social hour."

In the following year a like ceremonial took place; and after an interchange of fraternal greeting between the members and their guests, it also was terminated in a festive manner.

Several of the brethren having a fondness for fine music, proposed, in 5855, that the Lodge should authorize a musical entertainment to be given in the Lodge room.   Others of the brethren being professional musicians of a high order, whose aid had been promised, seemed to render the novel undertaking most desirable.   The proposition was adopted; and the concert gave great satisfaction to the audience.   The weather was unpropitious, but there was nevertheless a considerable attendance.   M. W. Winslow Lewis, Grand Master, was present.   The Lodge was opened without form:

March 1, 5855.   "Bros. Coolidge, Bigelow, Baker and McClellan were appointed a Committee with full powers, on the subject of a musical entertainment, for the members of the Lodge and their ladies."

MUSICAL ENTERTAINMENT.—COLUMBIAN LODGE, AT MA-
SONIC TEMPLE, SATURDAY EVENING, MARCH 17, 1855.—
CONCERT BY THE MENDELSSOHN QUINTETTE CLUB,
AND MR. J. TRENKLE, PIANIST.

PROGRAMME.—PART I.

1. Overture, " La Gazza Ladra,"   *Rossini.*

2. Adagio, from the Clarinette Quintette in A,   *Mozart.*

3. Grand Trio, in B flat, Messrs. Trenkle, A. & W. Fries,
   For Piano, Violin and Violincello.   [*Beethoven.*
   Four Movements—
      Allegro, Scherzo, Adagio and Finale Presto.

PART II.

4. Trio Concertante, for Flute, Violin and Violincello, on
   Themes from " Zampa,"   *Kalliwoda.*
   Messrs. Krebs, A. & W. Fries.

5. Piano Solos,   Adagio,   *Chopin.*
                Song without words,   *Mendelssohn.*
      Mr. Trenkle.

6. First Concert for Violin.   A. Fries,   *De Beriot.*

7. Duo Concertante, for Piano and Violincello,   *Chopin.*
      Messrs. Trenkle & W. Fries.

8. Closing Music,—" Auld Lang Syne."

         We meet in love ; we part in peace ;
           Our kindly greeting o'er,
         We 'll ask, ere life's best days shall cease,
           To meet in time once more.
CHORUS.—'Mid fairest scenes to memory dear,
           In change of joy and pain,
         We 'll think of friends assembled here,
           And hope to meet again.

         When life shall find its silent close,
           With Hope's kind promise blest.
         In that Grand Lodge may all repose,
           Where joys immortal rest.
CHORUS.—'Mid fairest scenes, &c.

The brethren have frequently met together on other than Lodge nights, for instruction and sociability. Sometimes these reunions have not been in open Lodge ; and they have been called by various names. In the earlier days, they were termed Masters' Lodges ; afterwards, Lodges of Instruction, Sodality Meetings and Social Meetings. They have been productive of vast good, both in the inculcation of Masonic information and in extending personal acquaintance and friendship among the brethren. The series of citations from the records in reference to these meetings, will no doubt awaken the remembrance of pleasant associations in the minds of many of the elder members of the Fraternity :

April 7, 5796. " Bros. Churchill, Eaton and Hayden were chosen a Committee to appoint a time for a separate Lodge of Masters to be held, and report next monthly meeting."

May 5, 5796. " The Lodge being opened, the Committee on a Masters' Lodge, reported that it appeared to said Committee not expedient at present to appoint a regular stated meeting from time to time for a Masters' Lodge to be held, but that calling such meetings when occasion may require will best serve the interest of the Lodge."

" Voted, That the above report be accepted. Voted, That the Secretary be directed to summons for a Masters' Lodge to be held next Thursday evening at Columbian Hall."

June 2, 5796. " Voted, To appoint a Masters' Lodge to-morrow night."

March 6, 5817. " Voted, That the members of the Lodge meet every Thursday evening at this Hall, for the purpose of instructing themselves in the lectures and their relative duties, until further orders."

February 15, 5822. " Bros. G. G. Smith, Lovejoy and Fisk, were appointed to treat with the Suffolk Society for the use of their room for sodality purposes."

March 7, 5822. "Bros. Baxter, J. Jenkins and Moody were chosen a Committee to consider the propriety of defraying the expenses of any member joining the Suffolk Society to obtain the lectures."

October 3, 5822. "*Voted*, That seventy-five cents per week be appropriated from the funds of the Lodge for sodality purposes."

November 30, 5822. "*Voted*, That the Secretary notify the members at the next meeting, of the sodality meetings held on Monday evenings."

October 3, 5833. "*Voted*, That this Lodge conjoin with Mount Lebanon and St. Andrew's Lodges in a series of sodality meetings during the ensuing season."

November 5, 5846. "On motion of R. W. Bro. Smith, it was voted, that the Lodge hold sodalities on Saturday evenings of each week."

February 3, 5848. "A communication was received from R. W. Bro. Daniel Harwood and others, asking the consent of this Lodge to form a Lodge of instruction. Referred to Bros. Baxter, Coolidge, Tillson, Thacher and Ball."

March 2, 5848. "The Committee on the petition of R. W. Bro. Harwood and others, reported that it was inexpedient for this Lodge to move in the matter at present."

February 6, 5851. "Bros. Coolidge, Heard, McClellan, Thacher and Schouler, were appointed a Committee to take into consideration the expediency of the Lodge having a social meeting."

January 4, 5855. "The first three officers were appointed a Committee with full power on the subject of a social meeting."

During the anti-masonic period when the faithful of the craft were threatened and proscribed by that hydra headed monster,—a fanatical and misguided public opinion,—one of the means employed to while away the lonely hours of the dreary winter of persecution, was a series of lectures on scientific subjects. It was at this time that the lecturing system, now so prevalent, commenced; and the wants of the Fraternity seemed to point it out as a source of relief from that gloom which adversity had carried even into the sacred and ordinarily cheerful Lodge room. The recorded proceedings of the Lodge at that time are most significant; and will be perused with more than usual attention.

January 1, 5829. "*Voted*, That Bros. G. G. Smith, Baxter, Jr., Johnson, Appleton and Moody be a Committee to take into consideration, and if thought expedient, to have a course of philosophical lectures delivered by some Brother or Brothers, at our regular meetings; with a request that they procure some Brother to deliver an introductory lecture at our next regular meeting; provided it can be done without expense to the Lodge."

February 5, 5829. "The Committee on Philosophical Lectures, reported that they had called on Bro. Jenkins who had kindly consented to deliver an introductory lecture at the next regular meeting."

April 2, 5829. "Thanks were voted to R. W. Jerome V. C. Smith for his kindness in volunteering to deliver the introductory lecture this evening."

October 1, 5829. "Bros. G. G. Smith, D. Baxter, Jr. and P. Johnson were appointed a Committee to procure suitable Brethren to deliver a course of philosophical lectures at our meetings through the winter."

February 3, 5831. "*Voted*, That Brother Flint be a Committee to confer with other Lodges, and if thought expedient, to procure some person or persons to deliver a course of lectures at our regular meetings, commencing at the next one, if convenient."

March 1, 5832. "A communication was read by the R. W. Master from a Committee of St. Paul's Chapter, in relation to establishing a course of lecturing for the benefit of the Masonic Institution.

A Committee consisting of the three first officers of the Lodge, was raised to confer with the Chapters and Lodges upon the subject of the above communication."

April 6, 5832. "The R. W. Master as Chairman of a Committee raised at the last meeting to confer with Committees from the several Chapters and Lodges in this city on the subject of lectures during the ensuing fall and winter, reported in part the doings of the Committee."

September 6, 5832. "Bros. Tillson, W. Fisher and Allen were chosen a Committee to take measures in relation to obtaining a fuller attendance of our meetings, and for the further purpose of inviting some Brother to address the Lodge at its next regular communication."

October 4, 5832. "The Committee appointed at the last meeting, reported that the R. W. Master, Joshua B. Flint, had accepted an invitation to address the Lodge at the present meeting.

Voted, That a copy of the address, delivered this evening by the R. W. Master, be requested of him to be placed upon the records of the Lodge.

Voted, That the Committee appointed at the last meeting be authorized to invite some Brother of the Lodge to favor us with an address at the regular communication in December next."

The address of Brother Flint was only in part copied into the records; and there being no manuscript of it on file, precludes its being given to the reader. The small portion of it extant, shows that its subject had reference to the anti-masonic movement which had at that time only partially subsided.

December 6, 5832. "*Voted*, That Columbian Lodge accept the invitation from St. Andrew's and Mount Lebanon Lodges, to join with them in a series of social Masonic Lectures."

March 7, 5833. " The Lodge and visiting brethren listened to an address by the R. W. Bro. G. G. Smith.

Voted, That the thanks of the Columbian Lodge be presented to Bro. Smith for his able and instructive lecture of this evening."

October 3, 5833. " Bros. Appleton, Chas. Henshaw and Geo. G. Smith were chosen a Committee to obtain lecturers before this Lodge during the approaching winter season."

November 6, 5834. " A communication from Mount Lebanon Lodge was received, inviting Columbian Lodge to participate with them in a series of sodality meetings to be held on Thursday evening of each week."

Though it comes not within the scope of this work to relate the transactions of the brethren when assembled for social objects merely, and at other than Lodge hours ; yet it will not be deemed improper to allude to one of these occasions which afforded much enjoyment to those who participated in it. An excursion to the fishing grounds "down the harbor" had previously been proposed, but was not attempted until July 5847. Some of the brethren, to the number of about twenty, employing a pleasure yacht for the purpose, passed a day of innocent and agreeable recreation on the "deep and dark blue ocean."

July 3, 5845. " On motion, *Voted*, That Bros. Baxter, McClellan, Follansbee, Appleton, and J. W. Ward, be a committee to make arrangements for a fishing excursion for the Lodge, with power to invite whom they please."

September 4, 5845. " Bro. Baxter made some remarks on the fishing excursion proposed at a former meeting ; but on account of the season being so far advanced, it was voted that the matter subside."

June 3, 5847. "On motion of R. W. Bro. Baker, the Master, Senior and Junior Wardens, Secretary, Bro. Samuel McClellan and John Wright, were appointed a committee to make the necessary arrangements for a fishing excursion the present season."

In reviewing the proceedings of the Lodge, which are given in this chapter, the attention is attracted to their business-like, decorous, and dignified character. The large number of meetings promptly attended ; no adjournment of business incompatible with the requirements of the by-laws ; strict performance of the duties pertaining to the annual communications ; the unremitting regularity in the election of officers ; the appropriate and solemn ceremonies of installations, public and private ; the social tendencies of the occasional communications ; attest abundantly to the vigilance and wisdom of the brethren to whose guidance the welfare of the Lodge has been committed.

CHAPTER IX.

FLOORING — JEWELS — REGALIA — PRESENTS TO THE
LODGE.

The first recorded action of the Lodge in
relation to a Master's carpet or flooring, was on
the 18th of December, 5795. This important
emblematic fixture of a Lodge, appears to have
received at all times the attention it merited ;
and it will not be without profit to follow the proceedings of the Lodge which refer to it.

December 18, 5795. " *Voted*, That Bro. Jno. W. Folsom
be directed to provide the Lodge with a painted canvass, a
book for the records, a sword for the tiler, a balloting box, an
Ark for the apparatus and a board, and report thereon as
soon as may be.''

December 3, 5801. " *Voted*, That Bro. Cutter, Folsom &
Jenks be a committee to mend the emblems of the Lodge
and for securing the chandelier.''

March 4, 5802. " The committee appointed in December
last to survey and replace the emblems of Columbian hall and
secure the chandelier, gave in the following report, viz.: that
they have furnished new emblems designed on wood, and
much less liable to accident than those formed in stucco work.
They have also caused the chandelier to be so secured as to
remove all apprehension of its safety. All which is submitted.   AMMI CUTTER, } *Committee*.''
                   SAMUEL JENKS, }

December 5, 5805. " On motion of Bro. Stetson, *Voted*,
That a committee be chosen to confer with Mount Lebanon
Lodge and make an adjustment in regard to the furniture and
flooring of the Lodge. R. W. Br. Baxter, Br. Bean and R.
W. Bro. Stetson were accordingly chosen for that purpose.''

September 6, 5810. " *Voted*, to raise a committee to confer with committees from Lodges who meet in this hall, respecting procuring new canvass for the use of said Lodges with emblems for each degree on separate canvass or otherwise, as shall be thought by said committee most advisable. Bros. Moody, Jenkins and Smith were chosen for the above purpose."

In 5813 a committee were appointed on the subject of a flooring ; but it does not appear that they obtained one. In 5814, another committee were chosen, (see page 67) who adopted measures that resulted in procuring the elegant emblematic picture which is now a prominent object in the Masonic apartments. They were instructed to report at the next regular meeting.

October 29, 5814. " The committee on the subject of a flooring made a report, which after some debate was referred to the next regular meeting."

November 3, 5814. " The subject of a flooring for the use of the Lodge was taken up, debated, and finally referred to the yearly meeting."

December 1, 5814. " The committee on the subject of a flooring for the use of the Lodge, made a report as follows, viz. :

The committee to whom was referred the subject of a flooring, having attended to that duty ask leave to report : That the plan therewith proposed with some small alterations in point of proportion, is in their opinion best calculated to promote the object to be desired and expected by symbolic representations ; that it unites convenience and elegance ; and that while it serves to convey to the initiate the many necessary and salutary lessons by regular progression, it furnished the Lodge with an ornament worthy of its standing with its sister Lodges. Submitted respectfully by

JOSEPH JENKINS,
JOSEPH R. CHANDLER,   } *Committee.*
HORACE COLLAMORE,

The above report was read and a plan submitted for the inspection of the members.

Voted, That the report be accepted, and the same committee was instructed to procure the said flooring as soon as may be.

On motion, *Voted*, That Bro. Mills be added to the committee."

February 1, 5816. "The committee appointed to purchase and suspend the new flooring for this Lodge, having performed the duty assigned them, it was exhibited to public view. Its elegance commanded much attention and applause.

The committee appointed to ascertain the property of the Lodge, reported progress and obtained further indulgence."

March 7, 5816. "The committee appointed to purchase the new flooring were authorized to procure a covering for the same."

May 6, 5816. "Brs. Appleton, Glover and Stone were appointed to procure, immediately, a curtain to be suspended before the new flooring."

July 4, 5816. "The committee appointed to procure a curtain for the flooring, reported progress."

August 1, 5816. "The committee to purchase a curtain reported progress."

September 5, 5816. "The committee raised to purchase a curtain for the new flooring, reported that they had attended to their duty, and exhibited it suspended in its proper situation."

Jan. 2, 5817. "On motion of Bro. Appleton a vote was taken, appointing a committee, viz. : Bros. Appleton, Smith and Howard, to prepare a vote expressive of the thanks of this Lodge to the committee who superintended the execution of the Masonic flooring and to report the same for the acceptance of the Lodge at the next meeting."

February 6, 5817. "The report of the committee chosen on the 2d January, 1817, on the subject of the Masonic flooring, was received and read by the secretary, accepted and directed to be recorded ; and is as follows, viz :

The committee appointed at a meeting of Columbian Lodge, January 2d, 1817, to prepare a vote expressive of the thanks of said Lodge to the committee who superintended the execution of the Masonic flooring, and to report the same for the acceptance of the Lodge, have attended to that duty.

This committee are fully aware of the time and attention of the committee who superintended the execution of the said painting, particularly the Bros. Jenkins and Mills, and that it merits more than the mere thanks of the Lodge; and they are also aware that the said committee would decline any pecuniary remuneration for their services; they, therefore, ask leave to report the following vote of thanks, and that the secretary be requested to present each member of the committee with a copy of the same:

Voted, That the thanks of the Columbian Lodge be presented to the committee who devised and superintended the execution of the Masonic flooring for said Lodge, which not only adds to the embellishment of the hall, but to the instruction, and edification of the craft. Submitted by

B. B. APPLETON,
SAM'L SMITH,   } *Committee.*"
JONATHAN HOWARD,

March 15, 5821. " *Voted*, That R. W. Bros. Appleton, Fisk, Baxter and G. G. Smith be a committee to repair the flooring belonging to the Lodge, and place it under the direction of the B. M. B of Directors."

August 2, 5821. " A communication from the B. M. board of directors respecting the insurance of the property belonging exclusively to Columbian Lodge, was read, placed on file and the subject committed to R. W. Bros. S. Smith, Appleton and Baxter, Jr."

It will be remembered that the Lodge removed from Masons' Hall, Ann street, to the Old State house, March 15, 1821; and the repairs on the flooring and the insurance on property were made at that time. The flooring was undoubtedly tarnished by the fire of November 3, 5818, and it was natural that its restoration should be desired before placing it in new and fresh apartments.

September 6, 5821. "The committee chosen on the 2d August, to consider the propriety of insuring the property of Columbian Lodge, made a report recommending the insurance, in common with the Grand Lodge and other Lodges, of property to the amount of four hundred dollars, viz. :

On the grand flooring or emblamatic painting, $330
2 grand Masonic pitchers, highly ornamented,   25
12 jewels, belonging to the different officers,   25
2 large Masonic bibles,   20
                                                   _____
                                                    $400"

This work of art and valuable Masonic guide which the brethren have watched over and protected with so much vigilance, was the production of the late brother John R. Penniman, one of the first ornamental painters of his day—a man of rare natural abilities, though his acquirements in the line of his profession were not extensive. He was esteemed by his cotemporaries for his amiable and social character. His work shop at the time he was employed on the flooring was numbered two, in Warren street, and his residence was at number fifty-seven in the same street. The cost of the flooring was three hundred and eighty-nine dollars, including what was paid for the curtain, etc.

May 4, 5837. "The following brethren were appointed a committee to regild the frame of the flooring of the Lodge, and to make such repairs as may be deemed proper, viz. : R. W. Ruel Baker and W. Wm. Bittle."

October 5, 5837. "The committee on the subject of the regilding of the frame of the flooring of the Lodge, reported that they had attended to that duty, and that the object of their charge had been done at an expense of about twenty dollars."

June 1, 5854. "R. W. Master and Wardens were appointed a committee to procure two globes, for the master's carpet."

There being many interesting facts pertaining to the furniture, jewels, regalia and other Masonic clothing of the Lodge, justifies the liberal appropriation of space assigned to these subjects. The old documents introduced from the files, and the extracts from the records, comprise about all the information desirable in this connection. Paul Revere, Senior, of the house of Paul Revere & Son, who furnished the first jewels of the Lodge, was a goldsmith, and, in 5789, occupied a shop then numbered, 50, Cornhill. This street was at that time a part of the present Washington street. He was at a later date a bell-founder. He was master of the Grand Lodge in 5795.

" *The Columbian Lodge to Paul Revere & Son, Dr.*
To the Master's jewel,......................£0. 18s. 6d.
To the Sr. Warden's do.......................1. 0. 0.
To the Jr. Warden's do. ....0. 15. 0.
To the Sec'y,...... ....1. 2. 6.
To the Treasurer's,..........................1. 2. 6.
To Sr. Deacon's,.............................0. 17. 6.
To Jr. Deacon's,.............................0 17. 6.
To the Steward's, ...0. 13. 6.
To the do......................................0. 13. 6.
To the Tyler's,..............................0. 12. 0.

£8, 12s. 6d.

Boston, 25th June, 1795. Errors excepted.
Pr.   PAUL REVERE, JR.

Boston, June 30, 1795. Rec'd pay in full,
PAUL REVERE, JR."

The Columbian Lodge in acc't with Brother Rittenhouse.

Dr.					Cr.
21½ yds. lace at 2s. 8d,	£2. 17. 4	Cr. cash rec'd Br. Coles,		£3.	6. 9
2½ " silk at 6s.	15.	" "			1. 6
2½ " silk ribbon at 1s. 6d.	3. 9				
3 yds. ribbons to tye the) jewels with, }	1. 6			£3.	8. 3
		Paid balance,			9. 4
	£3. 17. 7.			£3.	17. 7

Boston, 25 June, 1795.   Errors Excepted.   JOHN RITTENHOUSE.
Balance rec'd in full,   JOHN RITTENHOUSE.

Columbian Lodge to Simon Hall, Dr.

To a common gavel, ... 3. 0.
To 2 columns at 1s. 6d........................... 3. 0.
To 2 wands at 1s................................ 2. 0.

                                              £0. 8. 0.
Boston 25th June, 1795.
             Rec'd Payment,   SIMON HALL.

November 16, 5795. " *Voted*, That Bros. Hayden, Folsom and Coles, be a committee to procure a seal and candlesticks for the Lodge."

Columbian Lodge to Eben Knowlton, Dr.

To a balloting box,.............................$2 00
To 50 white and black balls at 3d..................2 08

Boston, 7th Jan. 1796. $4 08
        Rec'd payment in full,
                      EBENEZER KNOWLTON.

Columbian Lodge to John Perkins, Dr.

1796. To cash pd. towards Charter,.............£0. 7. 0.
       To book of Constitutions,............... 0. 12. 0.
       To bible,............................... 0. 6. 7.
       To blank book for by-laws,.............. 0. 2. 6.
       To 2 bottles wine for committee,......... 0. 15. 0.

                                              £2. 3. 1.
To cash over pd. Secretary on acct. of Br. Somes, 1. 10. 0.

                                              £3. 13. 1.
     Feb'y 1796.   Rec'd Payment.   JOHN PERKINS.

Columbian Lodge to John Perkins, Dr.

To vellum for charter,........................£0. 12. 0.	
To writing the charter, ... 1. 16. 0.	
To ribbon, 1s. 6d.—wafers, &c., 1s. 6d.......... 0. 3. 0.	

£2. 11. 0.

1796.   Rec'd pay. of the treas'r.   JOHN PERKINS.

Boston, July 1, 1796. Rec'd of John Coles ten dollars, being in full for three large wooden candlesticks said to be for the Columbian Lodge. Rec'd in behalf of Messrs. How & Alexander.   WILLIAM HOPPING.

Columbian Lodge at their special meeting at their hall, Dec. 31, 5796, in the evening,—then Br. John Coles, late secretary of said Lodge, reported the apparatus in the secretary's department to be as follows, viz. :

One book of By-Laws, &c., No. 1.
One Book of Records, No. 2.
One Book of Accounts, No. 3.
One Blotter Book, No. 4.
One File of Manuscripts, No. 1.
One File of do. No. 2.
One File of Bills and Recpts }
  for the year 5795, No. 3. }

One File of Bills and Recpts. } No.
  for the year 5796.   } 4.
One green Bag for Books.
One Silver Seal.
One Ink Stand.

The above were delivered in open lodge to the Right W. Master, on date above. Attest, JNO. COLES, *late Secretary.*"

July 7, 5796. " The committee appointed some months past to provide candlesticks, (Bro. Hayden being chairman,) reported that the committee had attended to the duty assigned them, and had provided the large candlesticks then on the tables—accepted,—The same committee had also the charge of providing a silver seal for the Lodge, and the chairman reported that the seal was provided and delivered to the Secretary. Report accepted."

July 5796. " Bro. John Perkins proposed to supply the Lodge with aprons such as are commonly worn by Masons, at the rate of one shilling and sixpence each, that is twenty five cents, as long as he lives.

N. B. This proposal was accepted by the Lodge and ordered to be recorded."

June 7, 5798. "On motion, *Voted*, That a committee be appointed to take into consideration and examine the sashes and jewels of the Lodge, and make suitable alterations and additions, so that the same may appear respectable as well as do honor to the craft.—passed. The following brethren were appointed, viz. R. W. Master, Bro Folsom and Raymond."

December 3, 5801 "Application was made by brother Alford Richardson and associates for the purchase of the Ark : on motion, *Voted*, That the secretary be directed to inform Bro. Richardson that they were welcome to the use of the Ark until Columbian Lodge has occasion for it."

January 25, 5802. "The R. W. Master, Brs. Baxter and Cutter were appointed a committee to procure a suitable stamp for stamping aprons for the use of the Lodge, and to purchase two dozen aprons for the immediate use of the Lodge."

February 4, 5802. "The committee appointed to purchase two dozen Masonic aprons, and to procure a suitable stamp for marking them, have attended that service, and beg leave to report, that they have bought the aprons, but have not yet been able to procure a suitable stamp, presume in a few days to be able to furnish one to the satisfaction of the Lodge ; which report was accepted by a unanimous vote."

November 18, 5802. "The treasurer and secretary were appointed a committee to procure two dozen white dimity aprons for use of members."

September 5, 5805. "*Voted*, That the treasurer pay Br. Davidson his charge for procuring the gilding of the candlesticks."

February 13, 5806, "*Voted*, That the secretary procure for the use of the Lodge, thirty new white aprons."

March 6, 5806. "*Voted*, That Bros. Benson, Crooker, and Swett be a committee to take into consideration the expediency of procuring jewels for the Past Masters."

May 15, 5806. "Bro. Swett of the committee raised to procure Past Masters' jewels and a hat for the Lodge, reported in part ; and it appearing there was some misunderstanding between the members of the committee, *Voted*, unanimously,—

That the secretary be empowered to adjust the business fully, and report at the next meeting. *Voted*, That the secretary and Bro. Davidson be a committee to procure a bible, square and compasses, and a trunk for jewels."

June 5, 5806. "The secretary having been authorized at a late meeting of the Lodge to meet the committee raised to procure a hat and three Past Masters' jewels, and adjust the dispute between the members of that committee, also to procure for the use of the Lodge some necessary furniture,—reported that he had attended to the business, reconciled all misunderstandings between the committee, and procured for the use of the Lodge a hat for the W. Master,......$10 00

3 Past Master's Jewels,...........................	15 00
Trimmings for the Jewels,.......................	6 00
* * * *	7 81
Bible, Square and Compasses,.....................	4 56
Paid for cleaning Sword,.........................	2 00
Trunk for use of Jewels,.........................	2 25

All which is duly submitted. $47 62

Voted, That the Secretary's report be accepted."

April 19, 5810. "*Voted*, To choose a committee to enquire respecting the sale of the old jewels, belonging to this Lodge, and the purchase of the new ones, and that they report at the next meeting of the Lodge. Bros. Seth Thayer, Stephen Bean and John Swett were chosen, and the chairman served with a copy of the vote and their appointment."

May 17, 5810. "The committe respecting the jewels submitted the following Report:

Your committee appointed to enquire into the business respecting the sale of the old jewels, and the purchase of the new ones have attended that duty, and ask leave to report: That in their opinion, the exchange is a very necessary, proper and advantageous one; and that brother Moody, who effected the negociation, is entitled to receive the cordial approbation and thanks of the Lodge for his attention in the business.

Your committee further report, that, as the funds of the Lodge are now in a tolerably flourishing state, and as the expenditures thereof have in a considerable degree been retrenched, they think the balance due for the said new jewels, ought to be paid from the Lodge fund.

Your committee also beg leave to suggest as their opinion, that it is the duty of the Lodge to communicate to Miss Sarah Baxter, daughter of our R. W. brother Baxter, their sincere and respectful thanks, gratitude and esteem, for her judgment and taste displayed in making the collars for the jewels, as also for her generosity and friendly disposition manifested towards the Lodge in performing for them that very acceptable piece of service. All which is duly submitted.

SETH THAYER, }
STEPHEN BEAN, } Committee.
JOHN SWETT, }

Boston, May 16, 5810.

Voted, To accept the report of the committee respecting the jewels.

Voted, The report be recorded on the Lodge's book.

Voted, The Secretary present Miss Sarah Baxter a copy of the last section of the report of the committee respecting the jewels of the Lodge.

The substance of the report above alluded to has been presented to Miss Baxter by the Secretary."

November 15, 5810. " *Voted,* That Br. Binney be a committee to obtain and render a schedule of the regalia of Columbian Lodge, and report next meeting."

April 1, 5813. " Bros. Baxter and Appleton were appointed a committee to inquire into, and report, the situation of the Past Masters' jewels."

May 6, 5813. " The committee on the subject of the Past Masters' jewels, reported that they had not finished their duty, and asked further time on the subject,—granted."

November 4, 5813. " On motion of Bro. Morse, a committee was chosen to procure a Past Master's jewel, to be disposed of as the Lodge may hereafter direct. Bros. Morse and Moody was chosen on said committee."

December 2, 5813. " On motion of Bros. Morse, *Voted,* unanimously, that the Past Master's jewel which the Lodge ordered to be procured at the last meeting, be presented to R. Worshipful Joseph Jenkins, (by his successor in office) at the time he leaves the chair, in token of the gratitude we owe him for his distinguished services in this Lodge, and of our brotherly love and affection to which he is so justly entitled. The jewel to bear the following inscription :

PRESENTED TO

R. W. JOSEPH JENKINS,

BY THE UNANIMOUS VOTE OF

COLUMBIAN LODGE,

FOR HIS DISTINGUISHED AND SUCCESSFUL SERVICES

AS MASTER,

FROM DECEMBER 7, 1809 TO DECEMBER, 2, 1813.

June 2, 5814. " *Voted,* That the Secretary be directed to procure two dozen aprons for the use of the Lodge."

December 19, 5816. " Bros. Stewards were chosen a committee to select the regalia and effects of the Lodge from that of other Lodges, and to make out an inventory of the same."

September 7, 5820. " *Voted,* That a committee be appointed to inquire into the state of the regalia, and to make such additions as to them may seem proper. Committee, R. W. Master, R. W. Bro. Baxter and Bro. G. Cobb."

January 4, 5831. " That the Deacons and Stewards be a committee to examine and take an inventory of the regalia and other property belonging to the Lodge not in the hands of the Treasurer."

February 22, 5821. " The committee chosen 4th January to take a schedule of regalia, &c., made a report in part, which was recommitted to ——— and R. W. Bros. Smith and Stevens joined to complete the same, and see the furniture, &c. removed to the new hall."

March 15, 5821. " The committee on the regalia, furniture, &c. made a final report, which was accepted and ordered to be placed on file."

October 4, 5821. " On motion of W. Bro. Bittle, R. W. Bros. G. G. Smith, Appleton, D. Baxter, D. Baxter, Jr. and Cobb, were appointed a committee to consider the expediency of procuring new collars for the Lodge and to report as soon as convenient."

November 1, 5821. " The committee appointed at the last regular meeting to consider the expediency of obtaining new collars for the officers of the Lodge, made the following report, which was accepted, viz. :

'Boston, Nov. 1st, 1821.   The committee on the subject of collars beg leave to report, that taking into consideration the proposed visit of the R. W. D. D. G. M. and viewing it as of considerable importance that the regalia of the Lodge should be in perfect order on that occasion, they have in pursuance of the advice of some of the oldest members, taken the liberty to have them completed in a style of elegance, and durability suited to the standing which Columbian Lodge has ever held.

They are well aware that in taking this step, they have far exceeded the powers committed to them, and have only to ask the indulgence of their brethren, in consideration of the peculiar circumstances of the case.

They would also state to the Lodge, that the aprons for the officers, and a new gavel for the master have been presented by two of the members ; the articles they are sorry to say, could not be obtained in time for the present meeting.   All which is respectfully submitted.   G. G. SMITH,
                                            B. B. APPLETON,
                                            D. BAXTER,
                                            D. BAXTER, JR.
                                            G. COBB.'

Voted, That the thanks of this Lodge be expressed to R. W. Daniel Baxter, for the present of a new gavel, and to R. W. Francis Fisher for a dozen of aprons, particularly appropriate for the use of the officers.

Voted, Also, the thanks of the Lodge to the committee on collars, for the correct taste and good judgment in which the collars have been procured."

January 2, 5823.   " The committee to procure a Past Master's jewel for our late worthy Master, Samuel Smith, brought forward their doings, and the jewel was presented with an appropriate address from the chair, and an answer equally appropriate from the recipient."

January 1, 5824.   " The R. W. Master and Wardens were appointed a committee to consider the expediency of procuring badges to be worn by the members while in the Lodge, as a mark of distinction and recognition."

February 5, 5824. "The committee on procuring badges to be worn by members of Columbian Lodge, reported in favor of having them immediately, which report was unanimously accepted, and the same committee were authorized to provide them."

December 6, 5827. " *Voted*, That Bros. S. Smith and Flint be a committee to procure a Past Master's jewel for the present Master."

January 3, 5833. " *Voted*, That the Lodge relinquish its right in the chandelier belonging to the Masonic institutions of this city, and formerly used by them,—provided that the same be presented to the Bethel church, and accepted by them for the use of their building, now erecting in North Square."

December 3, 5833. "Bros. Samuel Smith, Horace Dupee and S. A. Allen were chosen a committee for the purpose of recovering certain lost and mislaid property belonging to the Lodge."

December 19, 5833. "Bro. William Bittle and William H. Neville were added to the committee on the property of the Lodge chosen at the last meeting."

February 2, 5837. "On motion it was *Voted*, That a committee of three be appointed to look up and preserve any such property as may be found in the hands of members of the Lodge or others, and the following brethren were appointed : William Bittle, Benjamin B. Appleton and David Tillson."

May 4, 5837. "The R. W. Master was chosen a committee to attend to the clothing and regalia of the Lodge, and to make any additions or repairs thereto that may be necessary."

December 7, 5837. "Brother Appleton in behalf of the committee on lost property, reported that certain books, papers and seals had been received and restored to the archives of the Lodge and the committee was discharged."

October 5, 5837. "The R. W. Master as committee on the subject of the clothing and regalia of the Lodge, reported that some twelve or fourteen new aprons had been added thereto."

June, 5841. "The Secretary acknowledged the receipt through the hands of Bro. Moore, of some books, the property of Columbian Lodge, which had been retained some time by a former Secretary."

June 8, 5841. "On motion of Bro. Ruel Baker, the three first officers of the Lodge were appointed a committee to put the regalia of the Lodge in order, and make any additions they may think necessary."

January 6, 5842. "*Voted*, That R. W. Bro. Baker, the Secretary and P. M. B. B Appleton be a committee to attend to such repairs in the regalia and aprons of the Lodge as they may deem necessary."

March 3, 5842. "Bro. Baker, chairman of the committee on the regalia, &c. reported, that that duty had been performed, that the clothing of the Lodge had been put in suitable order, and the jewels repaired and burnished. The report was accepted, but in order to place before the Lodge the exact condition and amount of the furniture belonging to it, the acceptance of the report was reconsidered ; and after some remarks by the brethren, it was finally ordered, that the subject be again committed to the same committee, with instructions to report a detailed list of all the furniture, &c. in the possession of the Lodge, and that said report when presented should be entered in the books of the Secretary. Br. Baker asked permission of the Lodge to procure a trunk to contain the clothing of the Lodge, which permission was granted."

May 5, 5842. "Brother Baker, from the committee on the condition of the furniture and property of the Lodge, reported that the committee had attended to their duty and submitted the accompanying schedule, in compliance with a vote of the Lodge, passed at a previous meeting.

Inventory of furniture, &c., belonging to Columbian Lodge, March, 1842.—Charter with case—one large Masonic flooring —one large bible—one small bible—one book of Constitutions —one book of By-Laws of Grand Lodge—four books of Columbian Lodge—one Masonic chart—one Masonic Monitor— one large ivory square—two small do—one pair of silver compasses—two pair of brass do—one master's mallet—two ebony truncheons for Wardens—one gilt do. for Marshal—

one silver mounted dirk—fourteen aprons for officers—fifty-six
do. for members—thirteen collars and jewels— * * * *
thirteen officers sashes—twenty-four members' sashes—two
mahogany trunks for jewels, sashes, &c.—one small trunk
for safe　*　*　*　*　one ballot box and balls—a
right in three transparencies belonging to St. John's Lodge—
a steel seal screw-press, with trunk for do.—three folio
record books—a large trunk with old books, papers, &c.—one
standard, &c., complete—one trunk for clothing, &c., new—
* * * * * a right in the iron safe in the basement of the
Temple.''

February 1, 5844. ''The committee on regalia had completed the duty assigned to them and made a final report of
their doings,—accepted.''

February 25, 5845. '' The Treasurer and Secretary were
appointed a committee, to consider the expediency of insuring
the regalia of the Lodge, with full power to effect such insurance, if necessary.''

February 6, 5851. '' Bro. Stevens was appointed a committee to procure a sign, with the name of the Lodge upon
it, to be hung upon the outside door on the evenings of the
Lodge meetings.''

December 16, 5851. '' Bros. Coolidge, Heard, Ames and
McClellan were appointed a committee to procure a new set
of collars.''

March 4, 5852. '' R. W. Master, Senior and Junior Wardens were appointed a committee on transparencies with full
power.''

February 1, 5855. '' The Executive of the Lodge were appointed a committee with full powers ; to act in conjunction
with the other Lodges in procuring a new organ.''

Besides the presents already referred to in the
preceding extracts, others were from time to time
received by the Lodge, from brethren whose generosity was duly acknowledged by their associates.
In copying from the records what relates to this
subject, an omission of some recorded act of lib-

erality may have happened ; but it is believed
that the extracts given below are a faithful trans-
script of every thing properly coming under this
head, not referred to elsewhere in this volume.

December 18, 5795. "Bro. Raymond presented the W.
Master with an implement of war, for the use of the Lodge,
for which present, he received the thanks of the Lodge."

June 2, 5796. " Bro. Folsom presented the Lodge with an
oil painting of a Grecian temple, and received the thanks of
the Lodge for the present : and the same was ordered to be
placed in the hall."

April 4, 5805. " *Voted*, To accept a mallet presented by
the Millennium Society to this Lodge for the use of the R.
W. Master, and to return them the thanks of the Lodge
therefor."

February 5, 5818. "R. W. Br. Benj. B. Appleton and
Horace Collamore, as evidence of their attachment to the
Lodge, presented three masonic pitchers,—on which it was
voted that the thanks of the Lodge be presented to Brs. Appleton and Collamore for their donation, with a promise to
preserve them as a memento of their liberality."

July 1, 5819. " A letter was received from R. W. Bro.
Horace Collamore, accompanying two Masonic pitchers,
which was immediately voted to be placed on the records of
the Lodge : it is as follows :—

' Boston, July 1st, 1819.
Right Worshipful Brother Bean,—Dear Sir—I have taken
the liberty to cause the two accompanying Pitchers to be
manufactured, with an intention of presenting them to Columbian Lodge in which I received the first rays of Masonic
light,—a Lodge endeared to me by a thousand nameless ties,—
a Lodge whose diffusive benevolence has so often dried the
widow's tears, and caused the orphan's heart to leap for gladness. Should they be found acceptable, I shall consider myself amply rewarded for procuring them. I am, dear Sir, with
great consideration, your Brother, &c.

HORACE COLLAMORE.'

Voted, That Columbian Lodge receive with sincere pleasure and heartfelt gratitude, the superb and valuable present of R. W. Bro. Horace Collamore, of two elegant pitchers with appropriate Masonic emblems, and that the thanks of the Lodge be particularly given to Bro. Collamore for this renewed expression of his good will, and particular attention to the adornment of the furniture of Columbian Lodge.

A committee was then chosen to present this vote to Br. Collamore, consisting of Bros Baxter, Jenkins and Appleton. The care and safe keeping of these pitchers were committed to the Treasurer, by vote."

June 1, 5820. " *Voted*, That the grateful thanks of this Lodge be presented to R. W. Bro. Daniel Baxter for a valuable present to the Lodge of a book of Constitutions.

Voted, also, That the grateful thanks of this Lodge be presented Bro. G. G. Smith for his very valuable present of a seal for the Lodge."

August 10, 5820. " *Voted*, unanimously, that ; as a token of the pleasure and approbation with which the officers and members of Columbian Lodge have received the present of a well designed, handsomely executed seal, from Bro. Geo. G. Smith, for the use of the Lodge, they compliment him with a free membership."

December 7, 5820. " *Voted*, That the thanks of this Lodge be expressed to R. W. Bro. D. Baxter and R. W. Geo. G. Smith, for a handsome set of truncheons presented to the Lodge by the former, with the name and cypher of the Lodge engraved by the latter."

March 15, 5821. " On motion *Voted*, That the thanks of Columbian Lodge be presented to R. W. Bro. Samuel Smith for the present of a superb Bible from him, for the use of the Lodge."

February 6, 5823. " *Voted*, That the grateful thanks of Columbian Lodge be expressed to R. W. Junior Warden for the present of a Masonic chart for the use of the Lodge."

December 4, 5823. " *Voted*, That the thanks of this Lodge be presented to W. Hy. D. Wolcott for the present of an elegant dirk for the use of the Lodge, and to R. W. Geo. G. Smith, for the appropriate and beautiful designs by him executed on the dirk, and on the new square and compasses belonging to the Lodge.''

January 15, 5846. ''Bro. Wood made a donation to the Lodge which was accepted, and the thanks of the Lodge were passed to him.''

The present here referred to, was a bell of fine tone and excellent workmanship. Bro. William W. Wood, the donor, became a member of the Lodge on the 29th May, 5840. He was appointed inside sentinel in 5844, which office he has most faithfully filled to the present time.

May 3, 5855. '' Mt. Lebanon Lodge presented a copy of its By-Laws to be placed in the archives of the Lodge.''

The three Past Masters' jewels which were purchased in 5806, (see page 227,) during the administration of W. Bro. D. Baxter, Sr. who was the fourth Master, were probably for Past Masters Churchill, Folsom and Stetson. The record is not explicit on this point; but as it has been the custom of the Lodge to present this jewel only on the retirement of the Master from office, and as Bro. Baxter did not retire in 5806, the fair inference is that the jewels were all intended for his predecessors. The practice has been to grant this mark of a P. M. at the close of the presidency of each Master. The jewel provided by Columbian Lodge is a heavy silver medal bearing appropriate devices.

CHAPTER X.

CORRESPONDENCE AND INTERCOURSE WITH OTHER
MASONIC BODIES.—IMPORTANCE OF SUCH COMMUNI-
CATION.—VISITING DEPUTATIONS.—THEIR ANTIQUITY.
—REFRESHMENTS.—MASONIC ETIQUETTE.

The importance of fraternal correspondence
and frequent intercourse between different Masonic bodies, has not been overlooked by the
Lodge. Such relations, established by the various organizations of the same Order, are productive of incalculable good upon all its members.
They tend to unite and weld together the entire
Fraternity; and insure harmony of action. They
give power and efficiency to all benevolent un-
dertakings; they stimulate and embolden the
weak and hesitating; and strengthen the strong
in whatever there is of labor to be performed for
the welfare of the Craft. In adversity, the brotherhood, thus united, could "overcome evil with
good" so effectually as to disarm oppression;
and at all times they would possess a rallying
point for coöperation in the diffusion of the benign influences of Brotherly Love, Relief and
Truth. The ritual and ceremonies, though solemn and instructive, are not alone what constitutes Freemasonry; these acquire their full unc-
tion, only, when the soul is moved by an enlightened appreciation of the tenets of Masonry, and
when brethren are made to realize by actual and
frequent communication with each other, both in

and out of the Lodge-room, that they are in truth members of a sacred band or society of friends and brothers. Columbian Lodge possess in their archives much that will demonstrate the truth of these remarks; many evidences of reciprocal acts of courtesy and kindness that have cheered them in the days of adversity and illumined the hours of their prosperity. Invitations for the Lodge to unite with other Masonic institutions in celebrating Saint John's festival, to attend installations of officers, and to participate in other ceremonies, have often been received; and periodical communications from other Lodges beyond this jurisdiction, transmitting lists of officers and fraternal congratulations, are among the most gratifying of the evidences of good fellowship existing in the Fraternity. The following is a list, not perfect perhaps, of invitations extended from Masonic bodies in Massachusetts to Columbian Lodge :

Amicable Lodge, Cambridgeport, Saint John's Festival, June 24, 5815.
Washington Lodge, Roxbury,   "   "   "   June 24, 5817.
Mount Hermon Lodge, Malden, Installation of Officers, May 20, 5818.
Constellation Lodge, Dedham,   Saint John's Festival,   June 24, 5819.
Constellation Lodge, Dedham,   "   "   "   June 24, 5820.
Mount Carmel Lodge, Lynn,   "   "   "   June 24, 5825.
Saint Jonn's Lodge, Boston, Centennial Anniversary,   April 30, 5833.
Saint John's Lodge, Portsmouth, Saint John's Festival, June 24, 5836.
Boston Encamp. of K. T., Boston, Installation of Officers, Dec. 21, 5836.
Saint John's Lodge,   Boston,   "   "   "   Feb'y   5838.
King Solomon's Lodge,   Charlestown, 17th of June,   5843.
Mt. Lebanon Lodge,   Boston, Visit of D. D. G. M.   Oct. 30, 5843.
St. Andrew's Lodge,   Boston,   "   "   "   Nov. 9, 5843.
King Solomon's Lodge,   Charlestown. Model Monument, June, 5845.
Star of Bethlehem Lodge, Chelsea,   Dec. 5845.
Massachusetts Lodge,   Boston, Installation of Officers, Jan. 29, 5846.
Aurora Lodge,   Fitchburg, St. John's Festival, June 24, 5846.
Morning Star Lodge,   Worcester,   "   "   June 24, 5847.
Star-in-the-East Lodge, New Bedford "   "   June 24, 5848.
Middlesex Lodge,   Framingham, "   "   June 24, 5850.
Essex Lodge,   Salem,   "   "   June 24, 5851.
Morning Star Lodge,   Worcester,   "   "   June 24, 5853.

Middlesex Lodge,	Framingham, St. John's Festival, June 24, 5854.
Montgomery Lodge,	Milford,	"	"	June 23, 5855.

It will be observed that the communications referred to below, have been principally of a complimentary character. The annual congratulations from the Canadian Lodges have been accompanied with the names of officers and such other information as would enable the brethren of Columbian Lodge, when in Canada, easily to find the Masonic hand so cordially extended to them.

Grand Lodge of Nova Scotia. Expulsions,	5796.
M. Seikas, Grand Master of R. I., St. John's Festival, June 24, 5803.
G. Lodge of Nova Scotia. List of officers and congratulations, 5822.
Windsor Lodge,	Baltimore,	March, 5827.
Masonic Convention, Portland, St. John's Festival,	June 24, 5844.
St. John's Lodge, No. 1, N. York, Representatives,	Aug. 13, 5846.
Grand Lodge of New York, Clandestine Lodges,	Feb. 18, 5847.
St. John's Lodge. No. 1, New York, List of officers
	and congratulations,	Dec. 27, 5847.
Ark Lodge, Geneva, N. Y. List of officers and
	congratulations,	July 5, 5848.
Grand Lodge of North Carolina, Charity,	Feb. 4, 5851.
New Caledonian Lodge, No. 1, Pictou, N. S. Saint
	John's Festival,	June 24, 5851.
Saint John's Lodge, 3-491, Kingston, C. W. List
	of officers and congratulations,	Dec. 27, 5851.
Trent Lodge, Trent Port, C. W. List of officers
	and congratulations,	Dec. 27, 5851.
Belleville Lodge, Belleville, C. W. List of officers
	and congratulations,	Dec. 27, 5851.
Grand Lodge of Kentucky, Clay's Monument,	Sept. 22, 5852.
Belleville Lodge, Belleville, C. W. List of officers
	and congratulations,	Jan. 1, 5853.
Saint John's Lodge, Hartford, Conn. List of offi-
	cers and congratulations,	Jan. 5, 5853.
Committee of Masons, New York. Masonic Ball,	March 9, 5853.
Grand Lodge of Louisiana. Board of Relief,	Sept. 1, 5853.
Saint John's Lodge, 3-491, Kingston, C. W. List
	of officers and congratulations,	Dec. 27, 5853.
Trent Lodge, Trenton, C. W. List of officers, &c.	Dec. 27, 5853.
Belleville Lodge, Belleville, C. W. "	"	"	Jan. 1, 5854.
Virgin Lodge, Halifax, N. S.	"	"	"	March 1, 5854.
Lafayette Lodge, Manchester, N. H. Saint John's
	Festival,	June 24, 5854.
Grand Lodge of Louisiana,	Oct. 3, 5854.
Saint John's Lodge, 3-491, Kingston, C. W. List
	of officers, &c.	Dec. 27, 5854.

A copy of the communication received from
the Grand Lodge of Nova Scotia, in 5796, is here
given, it being the oldest communication from a
Masonic body in the files of the Lodge :

To all Masters, Wardens, and Members, of the Most Ancient
and Honorable Fraternity of FREE AND ACCEPTED
MASONS, Greeting.

BE IT REMEMBERED,

THAT, in the Fifth Year of the Grand Mastership of the
Right Worshipful and Honorable RICHARD BULKE-
LEY, Member of His Majesty's Council, &c. &c. Grand Mas-
ter of the Most Ancient and Honorable Fraternity of FREE
AND ACCEPTED MASONS, in NOVA-SCOTIA, and Masonical Juris-
diction thereunto belonging :

[Here are the names of twenty-two persons.]

Late Members of Hiram Lodge, No. 17, held in the City of
St. John's, New-Brunswick, British North America, were all
and every of them, expelled for Apostacy : And, in Grand
Lodge, held on the 7th Day of September, 1796, unanimously
declared unworthy of Admittance into any regular Lodge ;
or holding any Masonical Conversation with any of the true
and faithful Fraternity.—Therefore, " Now we command
you, Brethren, in the Name of the Lord, &c. that you will
withdraw yourselves from every Brother that walketh disor-
derly, and not after the Tradition which he received of us."

By Order of the Right Worshipful Grand Lodge of NOVA-
SCOTIA,   JOHN SELBY, Grand Secretary.

The quarterly communications of the Grand
Lodge also present a most favorable opportunity
of bringing the Fraternity into more intimate relations. The first three officers of every Lodge
in the Commonwealth, being ex officio members
of that body, are several times in each year convoked for business ; and on these occasions it
might be profitable if a portion of time were assigned for festivities, and the cultivation of personal acquaintance among those who are the

proper representatives and legislators, masonically, of the whole State. The influences of such re-unions would be felt beneficially throughout the entire jurisdiction.

Another means of promoting concord and pro-ducing community of feeling and interests among the Craft, is by an interchange of kindly greet-ings between Lodges through the instrumentality of visiting delegations. Columbian Lodge have at different times sanctioned the appointment of such delegations. Their origin goes back to a remote date, but how far, it is not here proposed to enquire. In the general regulations of the Grand Lodge of England, "compiled first by Mr. George Payne, Anno 1720, when he was Grand Master, and approved on St. John Baptist's Day, Anno 1721, at Stationer's Hall, London; when the most noble Prince John Duke of Montagu was unanimously chosen Grand Master for the year ensuing;" there is the following regulation, it being Section X. of that compilation:

" All particular Lodges are to observe the same usages as much as possible; in order to which, and for cultivating a good understanding among Free Masons, some members out of every Lodge shall be deputed to visit the other Lodges as often as shall be thought convenient."

The regulations of the Grand Lodge of this Commonwealth contain a similar provision, which is clothed in nearly the same language. It may be found in Sec. 9, Art. 1, Part Fourth of the Con-stitutions of that body.

" All Lodges are particularly bound to observe the same usages and customs. Every deviation, therefore, from the established mode of working is highly improper, and ought not to be countenanced. In order to preserve this uniformity, and to cultivate a good understanding among the Craft, some members of every Lodge should be deputed to visit the other Lodges as often as may be convenient."

It is remarkable that a regulation so ancient and important has been suffered to be almost entirely disregarded. The requirements of the Grand Lodge ought to be complied with or they should be annulled. The "cultivation of a good understanding among the Craft," is surely an object of the utmost moment; and therefore any measure of the Grand Lodge, which in their wisdom they recommend for that purpose, ought in all fidelity to be adopted.

At a very early date, in 5804, Columbian Lodge appointed a visiting committee, probably in accordance with general regulations at that time existing; but the records do not show that the practice was of long continuance. Thirty years later, in 5833, the appointment of such a committee is again recorded; and from that year until 5854, visitations by delegates were entirely neglected. In that year, they were again revived, and have been continued, apparently with beneficial results, until the present time. By reference to the extracts here given, the reader will see what have been the proceedings of the Lodge in relation to this subject.

December 27, 5804. "The R. W. Master, R. W. Bro. Stetson, R. W. Bro. Folsom, W. Bro. Benson, W. Br. Crooker, W. Br. Swett and Bro. Cutter were appointed a committee for the period of six months for the purpose of visiting each of the Lodges in this district, in order the more effectually to cultivate friendship and harmony among the Brethren, as well as to assimilate the modes of working in the several Lodges."

November 7, 5833. "W. David Tillson, W. Bro. B. B. Appleton, Bros. W. H. Neville, David Marden and Ruel Baker were chosen a committee of visitation to the different Masonic Lodges in the first Masonic district, at such of their meetings as may occur between the present and the next regular communication of this Lodge."

December 5, 5833. "The committee appointed at the last meeting to visit the different Lodges in the first Masonic district, reported that they had in pursuance of the duty assigned them, waited upon those Lodges, and were highly gratified with their general good condition and spirit.

The following Brethren were appointed a visiting committee for the ensuing month : Samuel A. Allen, Joel Nason, Warren Fisher, B. M. Nevers, Joseph Grelee."

March, 2, 5854. "On motion of R. W. Bro. Coolidge, the R. W. Master was authorized to appoint a deputation to visit our sister Lodges."

April 6, 5854. "R. W. Bro. Coolidge in behalf of the visiting committee reported that the committee had visited four of our sister Lodges, and had been received with the usual civilities extended on such occasions."

May 4, 5854. "R. W. Bro. Coolidge in behalf of the visiting committee reported that they had visited St. Andrews' Lodge, of Boston ; Bethesda, at Brighton ; Star-of-Bethelem, of Chelsea ; and St. Paul's at Groton, at an expence of fifteen dollars and forty-four cents, and had been received with the usual civilities extended on such occasions.

Brothers Thacher, Cummings and Barton were appointed as the visiting committee for the present month."

December 7, 5854. "Bro. Coolidge in behalf of the visiting committee, reported that they had visited Lodges in the cities of Lowell and Lawrence, and in the states of Ohio and Pennsylvania, and he spoke in glowing terms of the success and prosperity of our institution.

The R. W. Master announced the appointment of Bros. Jones, Robbins and Atwood to constitute the visiting committee for the ensuing month."

March 1, 5855. "The visiting committee reported that they had visited our sister Lodges at New Bedford and Concord. Bros. Robbins, Nichols and W. P. Jones were appointed on that committee for this month."

In accordance with the authority given to him by the vote of March 2, 5854, the Master appointed a visiting deputation consisting of three Brethren, and issued to them a written commission, which was substantially as follows:

COLUMBIAN LODGE.

To the Worshipful Lodges within the Jurisdiction of the M.

*******   W. Grand Lodge of Free and Accepted Masons
* Seal. *   in the Commonwealth of Massachusetts.
******   Be it known, that whereas by Section 9, Article I,
J. T. H. Part Fourth of the Constitutions of the Grand Lodge,
Master. it is recommended that in order to preserve the same usages and customs, and establish uniformity of working in all the Lodges, and also to cultivate a good understanding among the Craft, some members of every Lodge should be deputed to visit the other Lodges as often as may be convenient; and whereas Columbian Lodge has authorized the Master thereof, to appoint from time to time such Deputations as he shall deem to be expedient:

Now, therefore, in consideration of the foregoing, the Master of Columbian Lodge does hereby constitute and appoint our —— —— ——, members of said Lodge, a Deputation for the purpose aforesaid, and to represent the said Lodge as aforesaid, until the —— day of —— next.

Confirming the acts of our Brethren in their capacity aforesaid, we pray that they may enjoy all the privileges and protection to which they are entitled.

In witness whereof, the Master has hereto subscribed his name, and caused the seal of the Lodge to be affixed this

A. L. 5854.

Attest,   .   *Secretary.*

Deputations were occasionally appointed by the Master between the sessions of the Lodge. All of them discharged the duties confided to them with alacrity; and they were uniformly received with kindness and consideration by the Fraternity whom they visited.

During the first fifteen years after the establishment of the Lodge, the custom prevailed of having refreshments at all meetings. The necessary stores and utensils for the purpose were provided under the direction of the Lodge, and kept in the custody of an officer called the Closet Steward. It should not be inferred that our brethren feasted or banqueted so frequently; what they partook of was of that simple character as to refresh them merely during their long sessions, and invigorate them for cheerful labor. The practice might, in a few cases, have led to excess; but its general effect was undoubtedly beneficial in promoting the social virtues. The expenses of refreshments were borne mutually by the members and visitors, the latter being required to pay a small fee. The amount of money received at each meeting, and the expenditures, were entered by the Secretary on the margin of the record book.

February 13, 5806. " Br. Benson moved for a committee to enquire into the expenditures of the Lodge for refreshments : whereon it was voted to choose a standing committee of three members to regulate the department of refreshments provided for the Lodge. Bro. Jno. W. Folsom, Bro. John Benson and Bro. John Swett were chosen the committee, who were instructed to report the result of their enquiry."

March 6, 5806 " The committee on the subject of refreshments, report as follows : the committee appointed to take into consideration the expenditure for liquors, candles, &c., in this Lodge, report, that in their opinion the Stewards should be considered as acting under the immediate directions of the Secretary in the absence of the Master, and that he shall at all times be responsible to the Master for the quantity and quality of the refreshments, &c., furnished from time to time;

and any complaints that may arise shall be communicated through the Master to the Secretary, who shall for the time being have the entire control thereof.

JNO. W. FOLSOM, ⎫
JNO. BENSON, ⎬ *Committee.*
JNO. SWETT, ⎭

Voted, To accept the report and that it be recorded."

This Lodge was one of the first of the Masonic bodies in Boston which discontinued the habitual use of refreshments. Except on rare occasions, the practice has, since 5810, been entirely suspended. Early in that year its discontinuance was agreed upon for four months, and at the expiration of that term refreshments were prohibited for another period of four months. At the close of the year the office of closet steward was virtually abolished, and the by-law demanding a fee of visitors rescinded.

January 4, 5810. " *Voted,* To dispense with refreshments and visitor's fees during the present and three following months ; and, also, to meet in the hall twice in each of the afore-mentioned months, viz.: first and third Thursdays in each for the purpose of lecturing, &c. It was further *Voted,* That the Union Society be respectfully invited to attend for the purposes alluded to."

April 19, 5810. *Voted,* "To continue the suspension of refreshments and visitor's fees during the four following months."

At the meeting of December 6, 5810, a committee reported several alterations of the by-laws, one of which was that " no refreshment shall, at any time, be used in the Lodge, except on particular occasions ; nor then, but by the special direction of the Master and Wardens." This continued to be the rule until 5821, when a by-law was adopted that " no refreshments shall be provided except by special vote of the Lodge from time to time." This is the present regulation on this subject. The occasions on which refreshments have been used since 5810, were generally on the annual visitations of the deputations of the Grand Lodge ; but during the past thirty years even this custom has but partially prevailed. The following record extracts are pertinent to this subject :

October 5, 5820. " On motion *Voted*, That the deputation from the M. W. Grand Lodge be received this year without a formal entertainment."

October 16, 5845. "Brothers Baxter, Tillson, and Baker were appointed a committee to make arrangements for his [D. D. G. M.] reception, with this restriction, however, that no intoxicating drinks shall be introduced at the entertainment."

May 3, 5855. "On motion of R. W. Bro. Coolidge, it was *Voted*, That refreshments be furnished at the next meeting."

With that point of Masonic etiquette relating to apparel, the brethren have cheerfully complied. A black or dark dress, a white apron and white gloves are what propriety demands in the Lodge-room as well as at public ceremonies. In the old constitutions, white stockings were prescribed as well as white gloves and aprons. Indeed, so important was personal appearance in the estimation of the founders of the institution that it was regulated by the original by-laws.

" That the greatest decency and good order may be observed, it is strongly recommended that every member appear cleanly dressed each Lodge night, and that no member presume to wear an apron, either in Lodge or at any procession, which has any paintings or decorations thereon, other than being lined, fringed or trimmed with ribbon ; the Lodge conceiving any paintings or emblematic decorations to be highly inconsistent with the Masonic Art.''

Though the clothing of the members was not afterwards provided for by special regulation, yet it was deemed a breach of propriety to be in assemblies of Masons in the variety of colors which custom outside the Lodge often sanctions, or to wear the fanciful and highly emblazoned regalia in which members of the Fraternity sometimes indulge. Through thoughtlessness or inattention, this mark of etiquette might have been occasionally disregarded; but as a general rule it has been punctiliously conformed to. Only at one meeting does it appear that there was cause to call attention to the subject.

April 6, 5843. "The R. W. Master took occasion to call the attention of the Brethren to some points of Masonic etiquette, which had latterly been somewhat disregarded. The officers of the Lodge were desired to appear in the Lodge properly clothed in their masonic dress, and with white gloves.

The deacons and such brethren as acted for them, were requested to announce to the Lodge, the name and masonic title of each brother as he entered. * * * * It was moreover suggested to the members, to avoid as far as possible any unnecessary motion while in the Lodge, and also to ask permission, when desirous of leaving it, of the presiding officer.''

The aprons worn by members for many years past are without decorations, except that they are edged with blue ribbon. Those worn by officers are beautifully painted with symbols appropriate to the rank of each. It would, however, be more consonant with the emblematic significance of the apron to omit all ornaments, save the trimming, leaving the officers to be distinguished by other badges.

CHAPTER XI.

PROVISION FOR FAMILIES OF DECEASED MEMBERS — FU-
NERALS — FUNERAL OF BRO. KINDNESS — PROCEEDINGS
ON THE DEATH OF MEMBERS — PROPOSAL TO BUY A
LOT IN MOUNT AUBURN — WASHINGTON'S FUNERAL —
HIS MASONIC LIFE AND CORRESPONDENCE — HIS POR-
TRAIT IN MASONIC TEMPLE. — WASHINGTON MONU-
MENT AT FREDERICKSBURGH.

The financial regulations relative to deceased
members have been of a character to provide immediately after their death for the necessities of
their families, in case they were left in destitute
circumstances; and the provision has been general, it having been extended to all whether rich
or poor. The operation of this rule has been humane, as it has sometimes carried relief where
want did not appear to exist. The original by-
laws contained nothing authorizing an appropriation of money for this purpose, but as early as
September 3, 5795, the following was added to
them as a by-law:

"In case of the death of a member, it shall be the duty of
the Master and Wardens, (before the funeral, if possible,) to
wait on the widow or nearest relation of the deceased member, or otherwise his administrator or assign, and present
her or them, the whole of said deceased's proportion of all
the stock of the Lodge, deducting therefrom whatever he may
have received before, if any, the same to be paid in cash, after deducting two and a half per cent for the use of the
Lodge."

By the by-laws adopted in 5799, power was
given to the majority of members at any meeting,

(two-thirds of all the members being present,) to grant the sum of twenty dollars on the application of a widow or orphan of a member. The regulation whereby the deceased's family or estate received a share of the stock of the Lodge does not, at that time, appear to have been existing; and probably the donation was a substitute for it. In 5803, the by-laws were altered so as to provide for a permanent fund for the benefit and relief of widows and orphans; and all monies that were derived from memberships, donations and assessments upon members were appropriated to that fund. Three trustees were chosen at the annual meeting to manage the fund and it was their duty, immediately upon the death of a member, to present to the legal heirs of the deceased his share of the fund. The by-laws adopted in 5808, declare that no money shall be voted from the funds of the Lodge when they amount to less than one thousand dollars, "except it be to a distressed member, his widow or orphans;" and on the decease of a member the treasurer was required to present to his widow or orphans, as soon as might be, the sum of twenty dollars. In 5812 an alteration of the by-laws reduced the sum to ten dollars to be paid by the treasurer, and in 5816 it was again made twenty dollars, to be paid by the same officer, by the order of the Master and Wardens. Also, in 5816, it was provided that no sum exceeding ten dollars should at any one time be voted to the widow and orphans of a deceased member, unless twenty members were present. From 5821 to the present time, it has been the duty of the Master and Wardens, upon the decease of a member, to present, forthwith, twenty dollars to his widow or orphans ; and donations could be voted to them from time to time, and in amount, according to the discretion of the Lodge, no by-law interfering to restrict their action.

According to ancient regulations no brother can be buried in Masonic form except he is a Master Mason ; and the rule in this jurisdiction is that his remains can be so interred only at his own special request, or by a dispensation obtained therefor from the Grand Master. The only instance of the interment of a member of the Lodge with full Masonic ceremonies, occurred soon after they were instituted. On the 9th of October, 5795, the funeral of Bro. N. Kindness took place, as related in the following extract, taken from the records :

November 16, 5795. " *Voted*, To accept and record the report of Br. Coles, respecting the funeral of our late worthy Br. Kindness, deceased. The following report of Bro. Coles was ordered to be recorded, viz. :

On the foregoing evening Bro. Coles asked leave to report as follows : On the 6th October, in the evening of said day, our late worthy Bro. Nicholas Kindness, departed this life after a few day's sickness. On the morning of the 7th, the R. W. Master was made acquainted with the same, who gave orders to the secretary to summons the Lodge to meet at the house of Br. Perkins, the same day at 11 o'clock : Also, the W. Master sent his love and respects to Bro. Merckell, President of the Columbian Society, requesting that he would be pleased to summons the Society to meet at the same time and place with the Lodge, both in convention, then and there to receive communications respecting the funeral of our late deceased Brother. The Lodge and Society accordingly met at the above time and place. At the request of the W. Masters, Bro. Coles then acquainted the Brethren then met in convention, that on the preceeding evening it had pleased the Great Architect of the World to take unto himself the soul of our late worthy Bro. Kindness ; and that his widow and

daughters had signified to him their inability to support the
expence of the funeral, and also requested the aid of the
Brethren.

The convention then *Voted*, That the whole of the expences
of the funeral in Masonic order should be borne by the Lodge
and Society; also any mourning that the widow shall be
pleased to ask for; and every other aid granted to her at
present. Bro. Coles was chosen to see the foregoing vote put
in execution; and, also, to superintend the funeral. Bro.
Coles accepted the appointment, and requested Bro. Merckell
to act as marshal in the arrangement of the procession, which
he accepted. The widow and daughters were provided with
all they requested, and on the 9th instant, in the afternoon,
at about 5 o'clock, the funeral moved in solemn order, pre-
ceeded by the Columbian Lodge and Columbian Society, together with a large number of brethren, including foreigners,
and an excellent band of music, also a fife and drum to relieve. The body was carried and the pall supported by
Brother Masons, and followed by mourners and acquaintances
and several gentlemen of the clergy,—all in regular order.
Thus the whole proceeded to the Stone Chapel, where the funeral dirge was played on the organ, and prayers were offered
by the Rev. Mr. Freeman. The body was then brought out
in the same order, carried to the church yard, and committed
to the grave, with the honors of Masonry. The Brethren
then returned to the church, unclothed, and retired. The
next day Bro. Coles proceeded to pay the bills; and on the
23d of the same month, (Oct.) the Lodge and Society met in
convention at Concert Hall, to arrange the assessment, and
receive the report of the expences. Bro. Churchill was chosen
chairman; Bro. Coles presented all the bills, which amounted
to twenty pounds, fifteen shillings and three pence. The bills
were all approved and accepted. On motion of Bro. Goldsbury, the thanks of the convention was voted to Bro. Coles
for his care and attention in superintending the whole proceedings; also the thanks of the same was voted to Bro.
Merckell for serving as marshal on the above occasion. The
expence was assessed on the following members, viz.: Bros.
Jos. Churchill, Jno. H. Merckell, Jno. Jenkins, Jas. Dodge,
Jno. Procter, S. Powell, Jno. Rittenhouse, Thos. Tannatt, S.
Hayden, Sam'l Gouldsbury, A. Orrick, Jno. W. Folsom,
James Eaton and Jno. Coles. Bro. McCorristine, Bros. Robert
Molineaux and Wallack, who were not members, requested
leave to contribute their equal parts of the expence, out of
love and respect to the memory of the deceased Brother.

The whole number assessed was seventeen; four dollars and six cents to each brother, making in all the above sum. Several Brothers of the band gave in their charges for the day, both out of respect to the memory of the deceased and to the honour of the Craft, viz.: Bro. Granger, Sheridan, Smink, Hardy, Sheffield, Feckner and Dontin, in all fourteen dollars.''

Bro. Kindness and Bro. John Coles were members by charter, and were made Master Masons at the first meeting, June 22, 5795. According to ancient usage, they not being Master Masons were not legal petitioners for a charter; and it is probable that the Grand Lodge were ignorant of their need of advancement, and that they themselves were unaware that their further progress in Masonry was a necessary qualification. The Lodge raised them, however, and did so as a consideration for valuable services in procuring the charter.

As has been observed the funeral of Bro. Kindness is the only one distinguished by all the formalities peculiar to the Order on such occasions. At other times these solemn rites may have been, in part, performed in the Lodge room; and members may have followed at the burial, but the records give no account of any other strictly Masonic interment. On the 22d of December, 5812, the Lodge met and opened in form, and then attended the funeral of Bro. Isaac Coolidge, Jr. They afterwards returned to the hall and adjourned; but it does not appear that they assisted further than to follow his body to the grave.

February 6, 5812. ''The R. W. Master drew the attention of the Lodge to its great loss by the death of the worthy Brother Samuel Baxter, which had taken place since the last meeting of the Lodge.

And after the Master had addressed the Lodge in a very able and solemn manner, it was *Voted*, That Bro. Jenkins, Moody and Sawyer be a committee to address a letter in be-

half of the Lodge to the widow of the said deceased brother,
and present her with twenty dollars."

December 22, 5812. "The members were summoned to
meet at half past one o'clock to attend the funeral of Bro.
Isaac Coolidge, Jr. The Lodge was then adjourned for that
purpose. After the usual cerermonies in honor of the deceased, they returned to the hall with a number of visitors,
and closed the Lodge at 5 o'clock."

The announcement to the Lodge of the death
of a member, has been usually followed by remarks from the Master and brethren, appropriate
to his character and the event ; and by resolutions
of sympathy for his family and friends. If an
officer, his station in the Lodge has been draped
in mourning to mark their respect for him, and to
awaken in his brethren a realizing sense of the
shortness of life, and to remind them that no dis-
tinctions among men can avert the arrow of death.

December 2, 5852. "The first three officers were appointed
a committee, to devise some plan of action to be taken by the
Lodge on the death of any of its members."

The votes which succeed, show the respect of
the Lodge for two most estimable men, and valuable members of the Fraternity. These brethren
were not affiliated with the Lodge, but were
endeared to them by their general Masonic
usefulness.

January 6, 5853. "R. W. Bro. Pickman announced the
death of R. W. Bro. F. E. White, past D. G. Master of the
M. W. G. Lodge, and on motion of R. W. Bro. Thacher, it
was voted to attend the funeral of our late Brother at St.
Paul's church, on Saturday next."

January 5, 5854. "R. W. Master announced the loss the
fraternity has sustained by the death of Br. Jonas Chickering,
a Brother distinguished for his great liberality, and upright
and exemplary character as a man and a mason."

In 5843 the Lodge submitted to the Lodges in this vicinity the project of purchasing a lot in Mount Auburn, as a burial place of stranger-brethren, and of members who might express a desire to be there interred After due consultation it was abandoned. The reasons for the rejection of so desirable an object are not stated ; but they were probably of a pecuniary nature. The present prosperous condition of the Order, would now render the plan more feasible ; and if it were undertaken by the Masonic Societies within the first Masonic district, would not be onerous upon any one of them.

November 2, 5843. " On motion of the Secretary, it was voted that Bros. G. G. Smith, Appleton, Sr., Baxter, the Secretary and Treasurer, be a committee to confer with the other Lodges in this vicinity, to obtain if possible their cöoperation in purchasing a lot in the cemetery of Mount Auburn, which lot shall be destined for the burial place of such stranger-brethren as may die in our City, and of such members of the fraternity as may express a wish to be there interred."

December 7, 5843. "The committee on the subject of a lot at Mount Auburn, asked further time which was granted,— on motion it was *Voted*, That this committee take such measures as they may deem necessary to have an early meeting of the various committees appointed on this subject by other Lodges."

March 7, 5844. "The committee on the subject of procuring a lot at Mount Auburn, reported that at a meeting of the several committees appointed to consider the matter, it was *Voted*, To indefinitely postpone the whole subject,—whereupon it was *Voted*, That Columbian Lodge accept the report, and discharge the committee from further action in the premises."

The funeral ceremonies of the Order that occurred, in Boston, in consequence of the death of the immortal Washington, and in honor of his Masonic character, as well as to commemorate his great private and public virtues, were most solemn and imposing. The whole Fraternity of the metropolis and vicinity united in the mournful pageant, and shared in the general grief at a nation's loss. On the morning of December 25, 5799, the following announcement of the death of Washington appeared in the Columbian Centinel newspaper:

"WASHINGTON IS NO MORE!

The editor yesterday received the following letter:

"*Alexandria, Sunday, December 15, 1799.*

DEAR SIR: It is with extreme pain I inform you, that Lieut. Gen. George Washington is no more!

I hear his complaint was the cramp; that he was sick twenty-four hours, and died last night at 12 o'clock.

I have just returned from the house of the Physician General of the United States, Dr. Clark, who has not yet returned from Mount Vernon, which prevents my being more particular.

All shops, &c., will be shut and no business done here to-morrow. We shall have a meeting this evening, for the purpose of making arrangements to show all the respect possible to the memory of the Saviour of our Country. I am, very respectfully, your obt. ser'nt,   JONATHAN SWIFT.

Maj. Benjamin Russell, Boston."

On the 28th of December the Grand Lodge issued the notice given below, which was published in the Centinel on the same date:

GRAND LODGE OF MASSACHUSETTS.

Boston, Dec. 28, 1799.

******
* Seal. *   To testify their veneration of the exalted char-
******   acter and preeminent virtues, and their respect
for the memory of their highly distinguished Brother, GEORGE WASHINGTON, deceased;—It is recommended to the Brethren of the Fraternity of Free and Accepted Masons in the Commonwealth of Massachusetts, to wear for the term of six weeks, commencing from the first day of January 1800, a crape on the left arm, interwoven with a narrow blue ribbon, running direct. By order of the Most Worshipful,

SAMUEL DUNN, ESQ.

DANIEL OLIVER, *Grand Sec'y.*

On the 15th January, 5800, the Grand Lodge proclaimed that the Masonic funeral procession would take place on the 22d day of February following ; but in consequence of arrangements having been made by the United States and State authorities to solemnize the event also on that day, the Grand Lodge anticipated the date first named for their procession, and assigned, instead, the 11th February.

GRAND FUNERAL PROCESSION.

****** * Seal. * ****** Information is hereby given that the Grand Lodge of the Commonwealth of Massachusetts, in ample form, will pay due FUNERAL HONORS to the memory of the preëminently enlightened ornament of the Craft, Brother GEORGE WASHINGTON, on Saturday, the 22d of February, 1800.

The solemnities will commence at 10 o'clock, A. M., and all the Brethren in the Commonwealth, and all visiting Brethren sojourning therein at that time, are hereby invited and enjoined to assist in the same. The Brethren are to be clad in plain white aprons and to wear white gloves.

A grand procession will move from the Old State house, in Boston, at half past 11 o'clock, to the Old South meeting house, where an EULOGY will be pronounced by the Hon. Br. Timothy Bigelow; after which the funeral relict will be deposited under the Stone Chapel, with ancient honors.

The officers of Lodges are requested to bring with them their respective jewels, shrouded in black crape.

By direction of the Most Worshipful

SAMUEL DUNN, *Grand Master of Massachusetts.*

DANIEL OLIVER, *Grand Secretary.*

Dated at Boston, 15th Jan., A. L. 5800.

MASONIC PROCESSION—ANTICIPATED.

****** * Seal. * ****** In consequence of the arrangements of the Governments of the United States and of this Commonwealth, devoting the 22d day of February next to " testify the grief of all the citizens thereof, for the death of General GEORGE WASHINGTON,"—

The GRAND PROCESSION, directed by the advertisement of the 15th, for the said 22d February, it is hereby notified, is to be anticipated ON TUESDAY, the 11th February next; when funeral Masonic honors will be paid to the Memory of the preeminently enlightened Ornament of the Craft, Brother GEORGE WASHINGTON,—of which anticipation all Free and Accepted Masons within this Commonwealth, and all visiting Brethren sojourning therein at the time, are requested to take due notice, and be governed accordingly.

The formation of the grand procession will commence at 10 o'clock; and at half past 11, will move from the Old State House to the Old South Meeting House, (with the consent of the proprietors,) where an Eulogy will be pronounced by the Hon. Brother Timothy Bigelow.

The officers of Lodges are requested to bring with them their jewels, the collars of which are to be shrouded in black crape. By direction of the Most Worshipful,

SAMUEL DUNN, *Grand Master of Massachusetts.*
DAN'L OLIVER, *Grand Secretary.*
Dated at Boston, 20th January, A. L. 5800.

FUNERAL OBSEQUIES OF THE ILLUSTRIOUS BROTHER WASHINGTON, AS SOLEMNIZED BY THE GRAND LODGE OF MASSACHUSETTS, FEBRUARY 11, 1800.

Agreeably to previous notice, the Grand Lodge of Massachusetts this day performed Masonic Funeral Services, in honor of the illustrious deceased Brother, GEORGE WASHINGTON. The tolling of the bells at 8 o'clock, commenced the ceremonies. At 11, a *Grand Procession*, composed of upwards of sixteen hundred brethren, was formed at the Old State House, and moved from thence in the following order :—

Two Grand Pursuivants,

clad in sable robes and weeds, mounted on elegant white horses, properly caparisoned, bearing an elliptical mourning arch, (fourteen feet in the clear,) with the sacred text in silver characters—" *Blessed are the dead which die in the Lord— for they do rest from their labors.*" The Pursuivants were supported by two continental veterans, in uniform, with their badges of merit.

A Deputy Marshal.

Nine Stewards of Lodges, with wands suitably shrouded.

Two Tylers.

Entered Apprentices of all Lodges.

Fellow Crafts.

Master Masons.

A Deputy Marshal.
Stewards of Lodges, with mourning staves.
Deacons of Lodges, with mourning wands.
Secretaries and Treasurers.
Junior and Past Junior Wardens.
Senior and Past Senior Wardens.
Past Masters.
The Chapter of Royal Arch Masons, as Past Masters.
Masters of Lodges.
An elderly Mason bearing an elegant figure of *Minerva*, on a
banner—emblem, " *Wisdom.*"
Three times three Sons of Masons, about 11 years of age,
bearing *Sprigs of Cassia;* the centre supporting
the banner of " *Strength.*"
A Mason's Son, bearing a banner emblematical of " *Beauty.*"
Nine Daughters of Masons, each bearing a basket of flowers.
☞ *The sons and daughters were clad in funeral uniforms.*
A Deputy Marshal.
A full band of Music.
The Masters of the three eldest Lodges, bearing three can-
dlesticks with candles, the right one extinguished.
The Rev. Clergy of the Fraternity.
A Master Mason, bearing a black Cushion, with the Holy
Writings, and a Grand Master's Jewel.
Eight relieving Tylers.

Pall Supporters.		Pall Supporters.
Rt. W. B. Scollay.	THE	Rt. W. B. Morton.
Rt. W. B. Bartlett.	U R N.	Rt. W. B. Revere.
Rt. W. B. Cutler.		Rt. W. B. Warren.

☞ The Funeral Insignia—A Pedestal, covered with a Pall,
the escutcheons of which were characteristic drawings on
satin, of *Faith, Hope, Charity, Brotherly Love, Relief,* and
Truth. The Pedestal, beside the Urn, which was upwards
of three feet in length, and which contained a relic* of the
illustrious Deceased, bore also a representation of the Genius
of Masonry, weeping over the Urn ; and other suitable
emblems. The whole of white marble composition. On
the Urn was this inscription, " *Sacred to the Memory of
Brother George Washington, raised to the all perfect Lodge,
Dec.* 14, 5799—' *Ripe in years and full of Glory.*'"

A Charger,
Properly and superbly caparisoned, led by two brethren.
Grand Marshal.

* A lock of the General's hair.

The most worshipful Brother Dunn, as chief mourner ;
attended by the Grand Deacons, and
Grand Sword Bearer.
The Deputy Grand Master.
Grand Wardens.
Grand Chaplain, and Orator.
Past Grand Officers.
Grand Treasurer and Secretary.
Three Grand Stewards, bearing an Arch, with the inscrip-
tion—'' *And their Works they do follow them.*''

☞The Grand Master, Pall Bearers, and Grand Officers, were
dressed in full mourning, with white scarfs and weeds.

☞Each Brother bore a sprig of Cassia, and every one wore
appropriate badges of mourning.

In this order the procession moved through several of the
principal streets, to the Old South Meeting-House, where the
solemnities commenced by an appropriate, fervent and judicious prayer, by the Rev. Dr. Eckley. To this succeeded the
following Odes, written by the Rev. Br. Harris, and sung by
Brother Dr. Fay, and a choir of Brethren.

Anniversary Ode.

Is this the Anniversary so dear,
The gayest festival in Freedom's year,
When millions met their gratitude to pay
To their Deliverer on his *natal day!*
And glad applauses echoed through the throng,
And festive joy inspired the choral song ;
It is! but ah, how chang'd! its joys are o'er!
Its Washington—its birthright is no more!

To civic triumphs, funeral rites succeed ;
To flowery garlands, this encircling weed ;
And to loud pæans sounding to the skies,
Deep solemn dirges, and heart rending sighs :
Whilst those who welcom'd once the morn's return,
Assemble now around its patron's urn.
How chang'd the day ! its gladsome scenes are o'er,
Its Washington—its birthright is no more.

An Eulogy, illustrative of the life, character, virtues, and
services of the glorious deceased, was then delivered by the
Hon Brother *Bigelow*, of Groton, which did justice to the
subject, and honor to the speaker. It contained an assem-

blage of chaste portraits of the illustrious WASHINGTON, drawn as a Warrior, a Statesman, a Citizen, a Christian, a Man, and a Mason—adorned with suitable improvements for direction.

The Grand Chaplain then pronounced a Benediction, and the solemnities of the house were finished by the following Masonic Dirge, by Rev. Brother Harris, sung by Brother Eaton, and the choir.

MASONIC DIRGE.

While every orator and bard displays
    The Hero's glory and the Patriot's fame,
And *all* the guardians of their country's praise,
    Revere his *greatness* and his *worth* proclaim.
We mourn the Man, made ours by tend'rest ties;
Their honor'd Chieftain, our lov'd Brother dies!

Come, then, the mystic rites no more delay,
    Deep silence reigns, the tapers dimly burn,
Wisdom and Fortitude the requiem pay,
    And Beauty strews fresh garlands round the urn.
A mason, brother; a Grand Master dies!
The *acacia sprig* designates where he lies.

As Love Fraternal leads our footsteps there,
    Again to weep, again to bid adieu;
Faith views the soul, releas'd from mortal care,
    Through spheres empyreal its blest course pursue.
Till it *the Lodge of perfect Light* attain,
There may we meet our WASHINGTON again!

From the Old South, the procession moved to the Stone Chapel, where an appropriate Funeral Service was performed by the Rev. Br. Bentley, Grand Chaplain, assisted by the Rev. Br. Dr. Walter. The flowers were then strewed, and the cassia deposited. The Brethren returned in procession to the Old State House, uncloathed, and separated.

EXTRACT FROM THE EULOGY.

" Having already contemplated such a variety of distinguishing features in this great and amiable character, does it still admit of addition? Is there room in the portrait for another trace of the faithful pencil, that will increase its beauty? Yes, my brethren, to us another and no less interesting view remains. Animated with a generous philanthropy, our deceased brother early sought admission into our ancient and honorable fraternity, at once to enable him to cherish with advantage this heavenly principle, and enlarge the sphere of its operation. He cultivated our art with sedulous attention, and never lost an opportunity of advancing the interest or promoting the honor of the *Craft*. While Commander-in-Chief of the American revolutionary army, he countenanced the establishment and encouraged the labors of a travelling Lodge among the military. He wisely considered it as a school of urbanity, well calculated to disseminate those mild virtues of the heart, so ornamental to the human character, and so peculiarly useful to correct the ferocity of soldiers, and alleviate the miseries of war. The cares of his high office engrossed too much of his time to admit of his engaging in the duties of the chair; yet he found frequent opportunities to visit the Lodge, and thought it no derogation from his dignity, there to stand on a *level* with the Brethren. True to our principles on all occasions, an incident once occurred which enabled him to display their influence to his foes. A body of American troops, in some successful rencontre with the enemy, possessed themselves, among other booty, of the jewels and furniture of a British travelling Lodge of Masons. This property was directed by the Commander-in-Chief to be returned under a flag of truce to its former proprietors, accompanied with a message, purporting that the Americans did not make war upon institutions of benevolence.

Of his attachment to our Order in general, you, my respected Brethren of the Most Worshipful Grand Lodge of this Commonwealth, have had personal knowledge. His answers to your repeated addresses, breathe throughout the spirit of brotherly love; and his affectionate return of thanks for the Book of Constitutions, which you presented him, and for the honor, as he was pleased to consider it, which you did him in the dedication, must be evidence highly satisfactory of the respectful estimation in which he held you. The information received from our Brethren, who had the happiness to be members of the Lodge over which he presided many years, and of which he died the Master, furnishes abundant proof of his persevering zeal for the prosperity of the institution. Constant and punctual in his attendance, scrupulous in his observance of the regulations of the Lodge, and solicitous at all times to communicate light and instruction, he discharged the duties of the chair with uncommon dignity and intelligence in all the mysteries of our art. Nothing can more highly con-

duce to the prosperity and honor of Masonry, than a successful imitation of this bright example. It cannot fail of its
effect upon our Brethren in its immediate neighborhood in the
south ; they will beautify their column. And shall we be
outdone in zeal? Placed geographically in the east, in a quarter of the Union from which the nation has been accustomed
to learn wisdom, it should be our peculiar care to diffuse light
through the temple of Masonry. As it is known that we
shared largely in the esteem and affection of our deceased
Brother, it is easy to perceive that our good conduct will itself
be an encomium on his memory. We see before us, among
the sad emblems of mortality, not only the sword which in
this neighborhood he drew in defence of his country, but also
the very attire which he has often worn as a Mason. How
devoutly is it to be wished, that these striking memorials may
stimulate us to a noble emulation ; that, like the mantle of
Elijah, they may inspire us with an unalterable attachment
to virtue and benevolence! This day witnesses to the world
in what veneration we hold the memory of departed greatness :
let not the solemnity be without its appropriate effect upon
ourselves. While with funeral pomp and Masonic honors, we
celebrate the obsequies of our deceased Brother, while we
bend with anguish over the urn which contains a part of what
was mortal in him,* let us like him remember, that we are
animated with a heavenly flame, which the chill damps of
death cannot extinguish; like him resolve to *square* our actions by the *rules* of *rectitude*, persevere in the *line* of our duty,
and restrain our passions within the *compass* of propriety,
knowing that the *all-seeing Eye* of our *Supreme Grand Master* above continually observes us : That when we shall have
performed the *task* assigned us here, we may like him be *called
from our work to the refreshments* which alone can satisfy our
immortal desires : That when we put off this earthly *cloathing*,
we may be arrayed with the garments of glory, put on the
jewels of light, and shine forever in the sublime *arch* above.''

R. W. Bro. Timothy Bigelow was born in Worcester, April 30, 5767, and died in Medford, May
18, 5821. He graduated at Harvard College in
1786, and commenced practice as a lawyer in
Groton, in 5789. In 5806, he removed to Med-

---

* A lock of the General's hair,

ford, of which town he continued a resident till
his death. His practice as a lawyer was very
great, not only before the courts of several coun-
ties of this State, but also of New Hampshire. It
is estimated in a biographical sketch in the American edition of Lempriere, that he argued fifteen
thousand causes. He was in one branch or
another of our State Government,—Representative, Senator, or Councillor,—for thirty years;
(though he died at the age of fifty-four;) was
speaker of the House for eleven years; and the
last speaker of the joint States of Massachusetts
and Maine. He was twice offered the nomination for Governor, and several times that for U. S.
Senator, by the Federal party, when in power.
He, however, would accept no office which would
withdraw him essentially from the profession
which he loved, and adorned. For hospitality,
public spirit, and refined and sparkling wit, he
was equalled by few of his contemporaries. Early
in life, (at the age of twenty-three,) he was initiated into Masonry, and took a deep and abiding
interest in the institution. He was at one time
Master of St. Paul's Lodge in Groton, and successively held important offices in the Grand
Lodge and Grand Chapter, including the highest
in each body. He was the father of Hon. and
W. Bro. John P. Bigelow, late Mayor of Boston,
and of Mrs. Lawrence, widow of the late Hon.
Abbot Lawrence. His father, who also was
named Timothy, was, in his day, an ardent Mason; and on one occasion assisted with Washington at the meeting of a Lodge. He was commander of the fifteenth Massachusetts regiment
in the revolutionary war with Great Britain. He

was born August 12, 5739, and died April 4, 5790. His great grandson, Bro. Prescott Bigelow, is a member of Columbian Lodge. Thus four successive generations of this distinguished family—father, son, grandson and great grandson—have received the honors of Masonry.

Columbian Lodge united with the other Masonic societies in the public ceremonies directed by the Grand Lodge; and their records contain the following votes:

February 6, 5800. " *Voted*, That Bros. Folsom, A. Stetson, Baxter, S. Stetson and Churchill be a committee to make arrangements with the Grand Lodge with respect to the funeral procession of General Washington, and that they be authorized to appropriate to the above mentioned purpose a sum not exceeding fifty dollars."

February 21, 5800. "The Lodge proceeded to take up the funeral expenses of our late Brother George Washington, and *Voted* twenty-five dollars from the stock of the Lodge."

Every thing pertaining to the life and character of so pure and good a man as Washington, should be held in the most sacred remembrance. As the man who was " first in war, first in peace and first in the hearts of his countrymen," his memory will ever be warmly cherished and justly reverenced; and his wisdom, patriotism and benevolence should be constantly presented as worthy of imitation. But when he is viewed as a Mason, whose attachment to the Order was unabated through the long period of nearly half a century, and ceasing only when his great earthly career was terminated, an additional interest is awakened among the Brethren to learn his history, and to know to what extent he mingled with the Fraternity, joined in their assemblies,

and promoted their interests. In a work purely
Masonic, therefore,—though its main object is to
recount the transaction of a particular society,—
space may properly be claimed to narrate, at some
length, the connection which so high an exem-
plar of human greatness has maintained with the
Institution.   The valuable lessons of his constancy and devotion to the tenets of Freemasonry
will not be confined to the present generation;
but will have, it may be hoped, an enduring influence upon the remotest posterity.

George Washington was born at Bridge's Creek,
in the County of Westmoreland, Virginia, on the
twenty-second day of February, (11th Feb. Old
Style,) 5732,—a few months before Henry Price,
of Boston, was appointed first Provincial Grand
Master of Free Masons for all North America,—
and died December 14, 5799.   He was initiated
into Masonry when very young, as he was not
twenty-one years old when he received his first
degree; but his second, however, he did not
obtain until he had arrived at a lawful age.   He
was initiated, passed and raised in Fredericksburg Lodge, No. 4, in Virginia, which was originally organized by authority of a Dispensation
from the Grand Lodge of Massachusetts.   There
are no means of "knowing how long it continued
to work under this Dispensation;" and "contrary
to the usual custom in such cases, the Lodge did
not take its charter from the Grand Lodge of Massachusetts, but from the Grand Lodge of Scotland."   The following interesting and important
facts were copied from the books of Fredericksburg Lodge, several years ago, by R. W. Bro.
Charles W. Moore:

"Nov. 4, 5752.—Received of Mr. George Washington, for his entrance, £2. 3."

"March 3, 5753.—George Washington passed Fellow Craft."

" Aug. 4, 5753.—George Washington raised Master Mason."

The Bible used at the initiation of Washington is now in the possession of Fredericksburg Lodge. It was seen by Bro. Moore, in July, 1848, when it was in a good state of preservation. It is a small quarto volume, beautifully printed on minion type. It bears on its title page the imprint: " 1668.—Printed at Cambridge, by John Field— Printer to the University."

In 1788, Washington headed a petition to the Grand Master of Virginia for a charter for a Lodge " by the name, title and designation of the Alexandria Lodge, No. 22." As is usual in such cases, the first petitioner is, either by appointment or election, made the Master. The records of that Lodge, previous to 5797, are lost or destroyed, and consequently cannot be produced in evidence on this point. After the death of Washington, the Lodge petitioned for a change of their name ; and a supplementary charter was granted, giving them the style of " Washington Lodge," which they bear to the present time.

To the most worthy Brother, R. W. Benj. B. French, who was for several years Grand Master of the Grand Lodge of the District of Columbia, are the Fraternity indebted for a faithful compendium of the Masonic life of Washington, given in an address delivered by him at the tomb of Washington, on the 24th of June, 5851. The following are extracts from this valuable production of Bro. French :

" George Washington was a Freemason—not of a day, a month, or a year, but of his whole adult life. On the 4th

day of November, 1752, a short time before he had reached
the age of twenty-one, he was initiated, as the records of the
Fredericksburg Lodge show, as an Apprentice; on the 3d of
March, 1753, nine days after he had attained his majority,
he passed the degree of Fellow Craft; and on the 4th of the
succeeding August, he was raised to the degree of a Master
Mason.

It may be proper to remark here that, from the earliest
Masonic period, even to this day, the precise age, *in years*, at
which a man may be initiated, is very indefinite.

By the general regulations of the Grand Lodge of England
of 1721, the period of life fixed was *twenty-five years;* but, in
what is termed "The Ancient Constitutions of Masonry,"
the term "*mature and discreet age*" is used. The custom
in this country has been to fix upon the time when, by our
laws, a man is authorized to act for himself—the age of
twenty-one years—although in some countries, under certain
circumstances, persons considerably under that age have been
considered of sufficiently "mature and discreet age" to be
admitted members of the Craft. It is reasonable to presume,
and has so been explained to me, that GEORGE WASHINGTON
was supposed to be more than twenty-one years of age at the
time of his application to Fredericksburg Lodge; that the
question was not as stated that he was not aware of the custom; and this presumption and explanation are corroborated
by the fact that he did not pass onward until nine days after
he was twenty-one years of age.

Circumstances, known to many of the Brethren present,
have led me to make this public explanation, in order to show
that, although the initiation of WASHINGTON was not in strict
conformity with the custom here, still that there was no real
departure from the ancient regulations; and also to show,
by implication, his early desire to comply with every Masonic
custom, by delaying the time of receiving the next degree
until after he had arrived at that age which the common law
prescribes as the mature age.

But the real 'mature age' of GEORGE WASHINGTON was
long previous to 1752, as the records of those times amply
show. Of him, at the age of sixteen, the pen of history records thus: 'And now, at sixteen years of age, in quest of
an honest maintenance, encountering intolerable toil, cheered
onward by being able to write to a school-boy friend, 'Dear
Richard, a doubloon is my constant gain every day, and sometimes six pistoles;' himself his own cook, having no spit but
a forked stick, no plate but a large chip, roaming over the

spurs of the Alleghanies, and along the banks of the Shenandoah, was this stripling surveyor, upon whom God had placed the rights and destinies of countless millions of men.'

And the records of Culpepper county show the following fact : ' 20 July, 1749, O. S., George Washington, gent., produced a commission from the President and Master of William and Mary College, appointing him to be surveyor of this county, which was read, and thereupon he took the usual oaths,' &c.

At the age of nineteen, he was appointed adjutant general, with the rank of major, in the Virginia militia ; and at the age of twenty, became executor of the large estates of his deceased brother, Lawrence Washington.

After considering the position which he occupied as a public man, at that early age, who would have stopped to inquire, in 1752, whether George Washington was twenty-one years of age ?

All these facts go conclusively to show the maturity of his age, and that he was worthy in every respect to enter upon the duties required by the rules of our Order.

Washington was, therefore, a Freemason during his entire adult life ; and no opportunity presented, during all the various and exciting scenes through which he passed, when he did not manifest to the world, both by his words and his acts, his confidence, his respect, and his Brotherly regard for the Fraternity.

Do not understand me as alluding to the fact of WASHINGTON's early initiation, and entering into this explanation of it, in view of making it a precedent. That illustrious man is probably the only one who was ever initiated, on this side the Atlantic, before he was twenty-one years of age ; at least no Masonic history, that I have ever read, shows that fact in any case except his ; and when *another* WASHINGTON shall appear on the stage of mortal existence, but not till then, I trust the whole body of Freemasons will cheerfully give their assent to its being quoted as a precedent, and adopted. But, as has been eloquently said by a most worthy Brother, ' No more WASHINGTONS shall come in our time. Mount Vernon shall not give back its sacred deposit to bless a nation ; and that human form has not yet been shaped to receive the ethereal fire to make it another WASHINGTON.'

Precious to us, my Brethren, is the character of WASHINGTON as a Freemason ; and of so much value was it admitted to be by the enemies of our Order, that many years have not gone by since the attempt was made to prove that he was not a Mason; or that, if he was, he renounced the Order. Having signally failed in this, the next effort was to deny that he ever attended Masonic Lodges, or took any interest in the labors of the Craft; and, in a letter to me, from an Anti-Mason of the city of Boston, in 1848, the opinion is fully expressed that WASHINGTON was never Master of a Lodge, and that he did not lay the corner stone of the Capitol of the United States as a Freemason.

Many of you have heard me discuss this matter very fully, and prove beyond a doubt, as I think, that WASHINGTON did lay that corner stone as a Freemason, and clothed in the regalia of a Freemason. Since that time, I addressed a letter to the venerable George Washington Parke Custis, from whom I received a prompt reply, from which I make the following extract: 'There is not the shadow of a doubt but that WASHINGTON officiated as Grand Master of Masons of the United States in laying the corner stone of the Capitol in 1793. He certainly wore the veritable apron now in possession of Alexandria Washington Lodge, No. 22, and such other insignia as was suitable to his exalted rank as a Mason. The apron, &c., was given to the Lodge, No. 22, by the executors of WASHINGTON, of whom I am sole survivor.'*

You will not fail to note the assertion by Mr. Custis, that he laid it as ' Grand Master of Masons of the United States.' The same allusion is made by Dr. Dick, in his eloquent address before Alexandria Lodge, on St. John's day, following the decease of WASHINGTON, from which I shall hereafter quote.

I will remark, that I have somewhere seen an authentic statement that some Grand Lodge, I believe that of Pennsylvania, during the Presidency of WASHINGTON, took some action in regard to the appointment of a Grand Master of the United States, and elected General WASHINGTON to that office; and this is doubtless to what Mr. Custis and Dr. Dick allude. The brief time that has been given me to prepare this address, has placed it out of my power to make the search for this statement, but I assure you there *is* such an one, for I have read it within the past year or two.

Mr. Custis, in the letter from which I have quoted, recom-

---

* And now, while reading the proof of this Address, on this 5th day of July, I will state, that the apron was worn by me yesterday at the ceremonies of laying the corner stone of the extension of the Capitol, Mr. Custis being present, and recognizing it, at once, as the apron presented by him, and worn by Washington. It was made and presented to Washington by the lady of Gen. Lafayette.—B. B. F.

mended me to apply to the venerable Daniel Carroll, then living, for further information, which I did. Mr. Carroll replied, that he was present, and saw WASHINGTON lay the corner stone; that he was surrounded by Masons, but he could not recollect whether he wore any regalia or not. But one of the oldest Freemasons in Washington, now living, was present, and well remembers that WASHINGTON was clothed in Masonic regalia.

These witnesses prove, beyond a doubt, that WASHINGTON *actually laid* the corner stone of the Capitol, clothed in the insignia of a Freemason, and disprove the ofttimes repeated Anti-Masonic assertion that it was laid by the Freemasons *in his presence*.

That he must have been the first Master of Alexandria Washington Lodge is as conclusive as anything of history can be. The charter of that Lodge was granted by Edmund Randolph, the Governor of Virginia, and Grand Master of the Grand Lodge of that State, on the 28th day of April, 1788, and is directed to ' our illustrious and well-beloved Brother, GEORGE WASHINGTON, Esq., late General and Commander-in-Chief of the forces of the United States of America, and our worthy Brethren Robert McCrea, William Hunter, Jr., and John Allison, together with such other Brethren as may be admitted to associate with them, to be a just, true and regular Lodge of Freemasons, by the name, title, and designation of the Alexandria Lodge, No. 22.'

This charter, dated at Richmond, under the seal of the Grand Lodge, and the bold and striking signature of Edmund Randolph, attested by William Waddell, as Grand Secretary, is now in possession of Alexandria Washington Lodge, in almost as perfect a state as when it came from the hands of Governor Randolph. Although WASHINGTON is not named in that charter *as Master of that Lodge*, what Mason is there, either here present or in these United States, who does not know, that, by universal Masonic usage, the first person named in every Masonic charter, or dispensation, is the Master. I do not believe a single instance has occurred, in the United States, where such has not been the case.

The records of that Lodge, prior to April, 1797, have been lost or destroyed ; but the record of December 16, 1799, contains the following words : ' Lodge of emergency; funeral Lodge called for the burial of General G. WASHINGTON, *first Master* of this Lodge, No. 22 ;' and there can be no more doubt that WASHINGTON was the first Master of that Lodge, than there is of the existence of such a Lodge !

*   *   *   *   *   *   *   *   *

Brother Scott, Past Grand Master of Virginia, in his able and eloquent address at the laying of the corner stone of the Washington Monument, at Richmond, on the 22d of February, 1850, said, 'Frequently, when surrounded by a brilliant staff, he would part from the gay assemblage, and seek the instruction of the Lodge. There lived, in 1842, in our sister state, Ohio, Captain Hugh Maloy, then ninety-three years old, who was initiated a Mason in the marquee of WASHING-TON, he officiating and presiding at the ceremony.'

Again, says Brother Scott, 'His military labors terminated on the heights of Yorktown. In that village was Lodge No. 9, where, after the siege had ended, WASHINGTON and LAFAY-ETTE, MARSHALL and NELSON, came together, and by their union bore abiding testimony to the beautiful tenets of Masonry.'

And speaking of Alexandria Washington Lodge, he says, 'of this Lodge WASHINGTON was a member, and was constant and punctual, and ever ready to communicate light and instruction.'

On the 19th June, 1784, WASHINGTON addressed a letter to Lodge No. 39, (Brook Lodge in Alexandria,) accepting an invitation to dine with them on the anniversary of St. John the Baptist.

On the 17th of August, 1790, he addressed a letter to King David's Lodge, in Newport, R. I., speaking in the highest terms of the principles on which the Masonic Fraternity is founded.

On the 2d of May, 1791, he addressed the Grand Lodge of South Carolina thus : 'I recognize with pleasure my relation to the Brethren of your society.' He then speaks of the Masonic Association as one 'whose principles lead to purity of morals, and are beneficial of action ;' and concludes by saying, 'I shall be happy on every occasion to evince my regard for the Fraternity.'

In 1793 and 1797, he replied in the warmest terms to addresses from the Grand Lodges of Massachusetts and Pennsylvania ; and is it likely, is it characteristic of the man, that he would have expressed himself, again and again, in such terms of approbation of the principles of Masonry ; have asserted his recognition of his relation to the Order, and his happiness on every occasion ; to evince his regard for the Fraternity, and never visited a Lodge?

On St. John the Evangelist's day, December 27, 1799, the Worshipful Master of Alexandria Lodge, Elisha C. Dick, delivered an eloquent address before the Lodge, from which, as it stands recorded on the Lodge records, I make the following extract :

' After having fulfilled the primary duties of the day, it has been heretofore our custom to indulge in festive gaiety ; but, on the present occasion, a cloud of sorrow surrounds our prospect ; a recent and heavy calamity has obstructed every avenue to mirth ; our great and good Grand Master is no more. He who so often united in our annual celebrations, is gone to return not again. He whose presence was wont to inspire surrounding multitudes with reverence and admiration ; he who was but lately the boast of his own country and the wonder of the world, now lies cold and prostrate in his tomb. Thus, my Brethren, is withdrawn from the treasury of the universal Lodge its brightest jewel.'

One of the oldest inhabitants of Alexandria, now living, a Freemason, has assured a worthy Brother, now present, that, as a member of Brook Lodge, No. 39, he had often met with General WASHINGTON in that Lodge.

All this incontrovertible evidence goes to show that WASHINGTON often mingled with the Craft in their public celebrations, and was present in their Lodges. And we cannot doubt that one or the other of the constructions I have given to his letter to Mr. Snyder is the true one ; and our departed Brother, to whose ashes we have come to-day to manifest our love, and our veneration for his memory, was a true and worthy Brother from the day of his initiation, in 1752, to the day when he yielded up his spirit to his Maker.

We have seen, from the record of Alexandria Lodge, that an emergent meeting was held for the burial of General WASHINGTON, and it is proper that I close this portion of these remarks by adding that, in accordance with the proceedings of the Lodge at that meeting, the remains of WASHINGTON were consigned to the tomb with Masonic honors. Among those who composed the procession to the tomb, according to the account given in the appendix to the Life of WASHINGTON, by Sparks, and copied from the very particular and interesting narrative of his last illness by Mr. Lear, an inmate of his household, appears ' Lodge No. 22 ;' and, of the services at the tomb, it is said ' The Masons performed their ceremonies, and the body was deposited in the vault.'

I have been thus particular, my respected Brethren, in gathering together and laying before you the evidences of the Masonic standing, character, and opinions of WASHINGTON, for the reason that no pains have been spared by the enemies of our Order to wrest from us the honor of calling him *our Brother*."

The Masonic correspondence of Washing'on was, about twenty years since, collected by R. W. Bro. C. W. Moore, and printed in pamphlet form ; and the greater portion of it, if not all, has been reprinted in the Magazine, edited by that Brother. The letters here given will suffice to exhibit the views and feelings of the distinguished writer in relation to Masonry.

Address of the Grand Lodge of Free and Accepted Masons of the Commonwealth of Massachusetts in North America, to their Brother, GEORGE WASHINGTON.

Whilst the historian is describing the career of your glory, and the inhabitants of an extensive empire are made happy in your unexampled exertions ; whilst some celebrate the Hero, so distinguished in liberating United America, and others the Patriot who presides over her councils ; a band of brothers, having always joined the acclamations of their countrymen, now testify their respect for those milder virtues which have ever graced the man.

Taught by the precepts of our Society, that *all its members stand upon a* LEVEL, we venture to assume this station, and to approach you with that freedom which diminishes our diffidence, without lessening our respect. Desirous to enlarge the boundaries of social happiness, and to vindicate the ceremonies of their Institution, this Grand Lodge has published "*A Book of Constitutions*," (and a copy for your acceptance accompanies this,) which, by discovering the principles that actuate, will speak the eulogy of the Society, though they fervently wish the conduct of its members may prove its higher commendation.

Convinced of his attachment to its cause, and readiness to encourage its benevolent designs, they have taken the liberty to dedicate this work to *one*, the qualities of whose heart, and the actions of whose life, have contributed to improve personal virtue, and extend throughout the world the most endearing cordialities : and they humbly hope he will pardon this freedom, and accept the tribute of their esteem and homage.

May the Supreme Architect of the Universe protect and bless you, give you length of days and increase of felicity in this world, and then receive you to the harmonious and exalted Society in Heaven !

JOHN CUTLER, G. M.

Boston,   JOSIAH BARTLETT, S. G. W.

Dec. 27, A. L. 1792.   MUNGO MACKAY, J. G. W.

To this address General Washington returned the following answer :

Answer to the GRAND LODGE *of Free and Accepted Masons of Massachusetts.*

Flattering as it may be to the human mind, and truly honorable as it is, to receive from our fellow citizens testimonies of approbation for exertions to promote the public welfare ; it is not less pleasing to know, that the milder virtues of the heart are highly respected by a Society whose liberal principles are founded in *the immutable laws of truth and justice.*

To enlarge the sphere of social happiness is worthy the *benevolent design* of a Masonic Institution ; and it is most fervently to be wished, that the conduct of every member of the Fraternity, as well as those publications that discover the principles which actuate them, may tend to convince mankind, that the grand object of Masonry is, to promote the happiness of the human race.

While I beg your acceptance of my thanks for the " *Book of Constitutions,*" which you have sent me, and for the honor you have done me in the dedication, permit me to assure you, that I feel all those emotions of gratitude which your affectionate address and cordial wishes are calculated to inspire ; and I sincerely pray, that the Great Architect of the Universe may bless you here, and receive you hereafter into his immortal temple !   GEO. WASHINGTON.

———

From Col. Watson to N. B. Haswell, Esq.

The history of the enclosed letter from General Washington, is as follows :

During the latter part of the American Revolution, a mercantile house was established, at the instance of Doct. FRANKLIN, at the city of Nantz, by ELKANAH WATSON, who associated himself with a French gentleman by the name of COSSOUL. The object of this house was to receive the consignment of all American vessels that escaped the English cruisers, and dispose of their cargoes of tobacco, &c., and return French fabrics of cotton, silk, &c. ; but more particularly to furnish supplies of arms and ammunition, for the Continental service.   *   *   *   *   *   *   *

Messrs. Watson & Cossoul, (the firm as above mentioned,) caused a magnificent set of *Masonic Ornaments* to be embroidered by the nuns of an adjacent Convent, who excelled in their execution of gold and silver tissue—and sent the same to Gen. Washington, with a letter of thanks for his glorious efforts in the cause of Independence, and noble sacrifice of his own preferment to the welfare of his country. The reply to that letter is the one herewith forwarded. *   *   *

Yours, respectfully,

CHARLES M. WATSON.

Hon. NATHAN B. HASWELL.

—

State of New York, Aug. 10, 1782.

GENTLEMEN—The Masonic ornaments which accompanied your brotherly address of the 23d of January last, tho' elegant in themselves, were rendered more valuable by the flattering sentiments, and affectionate manner, in which they were presented.

If my endeavors to arrest the evil with which the country was threatened by a deliberate plan of Tyranny, should be crowned with the success that is wished,—the praise is due to the *Grand Architect* of the Universe, who did not see fit to suffer his superstructure and justice to be subjected to the ambition of the Princes of this world, or to the rod of oppression in the hands of any person upon earth.

For your affectionate vows permit me to be grateful,—and offer mine for *true Brethren*, in all parts of the world; and to assure you of the sincerity with which I am,

Yours,   GEO. WASHINGTON.

Messrs. WATSON & COSSOUL, *East of Nantz.*

—

April 22, 1797. " At a meeting of Lodge No. 22, Ancient York Masons, at *Alexandria*, at which Gen. GEORGE WASHINGTON visited, the following address was presented from the chair :

Most Respected Brother,

The Ancient York Masons of Lodge No. 22, unanimously offer you their warmest congratulations on your retirement from your useful labors. Under the Supreme Architect of the Universe, you have been the Master Workman in erecting the Temple of Liberty, in the West, on the broad basis of equal rights. In your wise administration of the government of the United States, for the space of eight years, you have kept within the compass of our happy constitution and acted upon the square with foreign nations, and thereby preserved your country in peace, and promoted the prosperity and happiness of your fellow citizens. And now that you have retired from the labors of public life, to the refreshment of domestic tranquility, they ardently pray that you may long enjoy all the happiness which the Terrestrial Lodge can afford, and finally, be removed to a Celestial Lodge, where love, peace, and harmony forever reign, and where Cherubims and Seraphims shall hail you Brother.

By the unanimous desire of Lodge No. 22.

JAMES GILES, *Master*.

GEN. G. WASHINGTON.

—

Brothers of the Ancient York Masons of Lodge No. 22.

While my heart acknowledges, with brotherly love, your affectionate congratulations, on my retirement from the arduous toils of past years, my gratitude is no less excited by your kind wishes for my future happiness.

It has pleased the Supreme Architect of the Universe to make me an humble instrument to promote the welfare and happiness of my fellow men; my exertions have been abundantly recompensed by the kind partiality with which they have been received—and the assurance you give me, of your belief that I have acted upon the square in my public capacity, will be among my principal enjoyments in this terrestrial Lodge. GEO. WASHINGTON.

The toast of Bro. WASHINGTON was—

"The Lodge of Alexandria, and all Masons throughout the world."

———

LETTERS FROM THE GRAND LODGE OF MASSACHUSETTS TO MR. AND MRS. WASHINGTON.—THE GRAND LODGE OF MASSACHUSETTS TO THE LATE PRESIDENT WASHINGTON.

The East, the West, and the South, of the Grand Lodge of Ancient Free and Accepted Masons of the Commonwealth of Massachusetts, to their most worthy brother George Washington.

Wishing ever to be foremost in testimonials of respect and admiration for those virtues and services with which you

24*

have so long adorned and benefited our common country ; and not the last nor least to regret the cessation of them in the public councils of the Union ; your Brethren of the Grand Lodge embrace the earliest opportunity of greeting you in the calm retirement you have contemplated to yourself.

Though, as *Citizens*, they lose you in the active labors of political life, they hope as *Masons* to find you in the pleasing sphere of fraternal engagement. From the cares of State, and the fatigues of public business, our institution opens a recess, affording all the relief of tranquillity, the harmony of peace, and the refreshment of pleasure : of these may you partake in all their purity and satisfaction ; and we will assure ourselves that your attachment to this social plan will increase, and that, under the auspices of your encouragement, assistance, and patronage, the Craft will attain the highest ornament, perfection, and praise. And it is our ardent prayer, that when your light shall be no more visible in this Earthly Temple, you may be raised to the *all-perfect Lodge* above ; be seated on the right of the Supreme Architect of the Universe, and there receive the refreshment your labors have merited.

In behalf of the Grand Lodge, we subscribe ourselves, with the highest esteem, your affectionate Brethren,

PAUL REVERE, Grand Master.
ISAIAH THOMAS, Senior Grand Warden.
JOSEPH LAUGHTON, Jun. Grand Warden.
DANIEL OLIVER, Grand Secretary.
Boston, March 21, 1797.

—

GENERAL WASHINGTON'S REPLY TO THE GRAND LODGE OF MASSACHUSETTS.

To the Grand Lodge of Free and Accepted Masons in the Commonwealth of Massachusetts.

BROTHERS,

It was not until these few days, that I have been favored by the receipt of your affectionate address, dated in Boston the 21st of March.

For the favorable sentiments you have been pleased to express on the occasion of my past services, and for the regrets with which they are accompanied for the cessation of my public functions, I pray you to accept my best acknowledgments and gratitude.

No pleasure, except that which results from a consciousness of having, to the utmost of my abilities, discharged the trust which has been reposed in me by my country, can equal the satisfaction I feel from the unequivocal proofs I continually receive of its approbation of my public conduct; and I beg you to be assured, that the evidence thereof, which is exhibited by the Grand Lodge of Massachusetts, is not among the least pleasing or grateful to my feelings.

In that retirement which declining years induced me to seek, and which repose, to a mind long employed in public concerns, rendered necessary, my wishes that bounteous Providence will continue to bless and preserve our country in peace, and in the prosperity it has enjoyed, will be warm and sincere ; and my attachment to the Society of which we are Members, will dispose me always to contribute my best endeavors to promote the honor and interest of the *Craft*.

For the prayer you offer in my behalf, I entreat you to accept the thanks of a grateful heart, with the assurance of my fraternal regard, and best wishes for the honor, happiness and prosperity of all the members of the Grand Lodge of Massachusetts.   G. WASHINGTON.

FROM THE GRAND LODGE OF MASSACHUSETTS TO MRS. WASHINGTON. OCCASIONED BY THE DEATH OF THE GENERAL.

BOSTON, *January* 11, 1800.

MADAM,—The Grand Lodge of the Commonwealth of Massachusetts have deeply participated in the general grief of their fellow citizens, on the melancholy occasion of the death of their beloved *Washington*.

As Americans, they have lamented the loss of the Chief who had led their armies to victory, and their country to glory ; but as *Masons*, they have wept the dissolution of that endearing relation, by which they were enabled to call him their Friend and their Brother. They presume not to offer you those consolations which might alleviate the weight of common sorrows, for they are themselves inconsolable. The object of this address is, not to interrupt the sacred offices of grief like your's ; but, whilst they are mingling tears with each other on the common calamity, to condole with you on the irreparable misfortune which you have individually experienced.

To their expressions of sympathy on this solemn dispensation, the Grand Lodge have subjoined an order, that a *Golden Urn* be prepared as a deposit for a lock of hair, *an invaluable relique* of the Hero and the Patriot, whom their wishes would immortalize; and that it be preserved with the jewels and regalia of the Society.

Should this favor be granted, Madam, it will be cherished as the most precious jewel in the cabinet of the Lodge, as the memory of his virtues will forever be in the hearts of its members.—We have the honor to be, with the highest respect, your most obedient servants,   JOHN WARREN,
                                        PAUL REVERE,
                                        JOSIAH BARTLETT.
Mrs. MARTHA WASHINGTON.

—

MRS. WASHINGTON'S REPLY TO THE GRAND LODGE OF MASSACHUSETTS.

MOUNT VERNON, *January* 27, 1800.

GENTLEMEN,—Mrs. WASHINGTON has received with sensibility your letter of the 11th inst. enclosing a vote of the Grand Lodge of Massachusetts, requesting a *lock* of her deceased Husband's *hair*, to be preserved in a *Golden Urn*, with the jewels and regalia of the Grand Lodge.

In complying with this request, by sending the lock of hair, which you will find enclosed, Mrs. WASHINGTON begs me to assure you, that she views with gratitude the tributes of respect and affection paid to the memory of her dear deceased Husband; and receives, with a feeling heart, the expressions of sympathy contained in your letter.

With great respect and esteem, I have the honor to be, Gentlemen, your most obedient servant,

                                        TOBIAS LEAR.

JOHN WARREN,   ⎫
PAUL REVERE,   ⎬ *Past Grand Masters.*
JOSIAH BARTLETT. ⎭

The painting referred to in the letter of Bro. Parkman is now suspended in the south of the large hall. Samuel Parkman was an eminent merchant of Boston, who left at his death a large fortune. He was Treasurer of the Grand Lodge in 5792 and 5793, and, in 5794, Junior Grand Warden. The letter and votes relating to it are copied from the records of the Grand Lodge. Samuel Parkman was the son of Rev. Ebenezer

Parkman, of Westborough, Mass. He died in Boston, June 11, 5824, aged seventy-two years.

March 14, 5821. "The following letter directed to the M. W. Grand Master was read, viz.:

BOSTON, MARCH 5, 1821.

Sir.—Inclosed is an order on Mr. Doyle, at the Columbian Museum, for a full length picture of Washington. You will permit me, through you, to present this valuable painting to the Grand Lodge of Massachusetts, to be placed in their new hall, in State Street, that the Masonic family may hold in constant remembrance that inestimable character, who was the instrument in the hands of the Great Grand Master, in leading our country to independence and happiness.

I am, with esteem, Your mt. hble. Servant,

SAMUEL PARKMAN."

"*Voted*, unanimously, that the picture named in Bro. Parkman's letter be accepted, and placed according to his wishes.

"*Voted*, That the M. W. G. M. tender to Bro. Parkman the thanks of the Grand Lodge for his donation."

The following communication was received by Columbian Lodge in 5852. The appeal to the Masonic bodies throughout the United States was, very generally, favorably responded to; and it may be confidently expected that a Masonic monument will, at no distant day, be raised at Fredericksburg in conformity to the wishes of the Brethren of that place:—

GRAND LODGE OF MASSACHUSETTS. ⎱
Boston, Sept. 24, 1852. ⎰

DEAR SIR AND BROTHER:—At the quarterly communication of the Grand Lodge of Massachusetts, held on the 8th September instant, the W. Brother Robert J. Morrison, of Virginia, appeared and informed the Grand Lodge, officially, that Fredricksburg Lodge, No. 4, held at Fredericksburg, in Virginia, had determined to erect, in that place, a purely Masonic monument, to the memory of our late illustrious Brother Gen. GEORGE WASHINGTON; and to enable that Lodge to carry its determination into effect, an appeal for pecuniary aid was to be made to the whole Masonic Fraternity of the country. In pursuance of this latter determination, Brother Morrison, in behalf of the "*Executive Monumental Committee*" of Fredericksburg, made his appeal to the Grand Lodge, and through it to the Fraternity of this Commonwealth. The subject was referred to a Committee of the Grand Lodge, who, having carefully considered it, submitted the following report, which was *unanimously* adopted ;—

REPORT.

"In view of the importance of the call now made upon us, and in favor of which the feelings of every Brother will be more eloquent than words, your committee recommend the adoption of the following resolutions, viz. :—

"*Resolved*, That this Grand Lodge, as an evidence of its deep interest in the proposed plan, will contribute from its funds the sum of *one hundred dollars*.

"*Resolved*, That the Grand Secretary be directed to send Circulars to every Lodge in this jurisdiction, requesting their contributions as Lodges; and that each Lodge appoint a Committee to select subscriptions from its individual members.

EDWARD A. RAYMOND, ⎫
GEORGE G. SMITH, ⎬ *Committee.*"
WINSLOW LEWIS, ⎭

In pursuance of the instructions embraced in the last of the foregoing resolutions, this Circular is forwarded to you, with the request that you will cause it to be read before your Lodge, at your earliest convenience, that the Brethren may take such action in the premises as they may judge to be wise and proper.

The following Circular, issued by authority of Fredericksburg Lodge, will afford all the information, in respect to the character and purposes of the proposed measure, in the possession of the Grand Lodge, and all, it is believed, that will be deemed necessary to a correct understanding of the subject :

Fredericksburg, Vir., Aug. 25, 1852.

DEAR BROTHER :—On the 4th day of November, 1752, GEORGE WASHINGTON was initiated into the mysteries of Masonry, in Fredericksburg Lodge, No. 4. The 4th day of next November will be the centennial anniversary of that event. Comment upon this fact is unnecessary to excite the enthusiastic interest of the Fraternity, in a land where even infant lips lisp the name of Washington with reverence. At this peculiarly appropriate period, it is proposed to rear in the town of Fredericksburg, a MONUMENTAL MASONIC TEMPLE to his memory, in which a statue of our illustrious Brother, clothed in Masonic

Regalia, is to be placed. The Temple is designed only as a shrine for the statue, which is to be sculptured by Powers, or some other distinguished American artist. The oldest Monument of which man has any account was Masonic, and it was reared to tell to future generations the worth of an *" amiable, exemplary and distinguished character,"* when the Order was in its infancy, and before time had developed the benign and mighty influence it was to exert on human destiny.

A brief review of the past century will suggest what the active and patriotic exertions of Washington have accomplished for the human race. Even now his memory softens tyranny in distant lands, and strengthens the struggles of the oppressed. The privilege of paying a just tribute to the memory of this great and good Brother, and of promoting the interests of Masonry, by erecting a Monument to keep alive perpetually the recollection of a historical fact, of which the Craft must ever be proud, is now extended to American Masons. This is a period of preëminent prosperity and power to the Order, and the Executive Committee are confident that an appeal to the Fraternity of this country for contributions to this *" great and glorious work,"* will not be in vain.

We take the liberty of asking that you will present this matter, in an appropriate manner, to the Masonic body over which you preside, and that you will forward whatever amount it may contribute, to the Chairman of the Executive Monumental Committee. The Committee would request your body to appoint a Committee to solicit individual contributions on the 4th day of next November, for this purpose, from the Brethren within its jurisdiction, and to forward whatever may be obtained, to the same direction.

With sentiments of high regard, we are yours, Fraternally,

J. J. Young,
Geo. F. Carmichael,
J. J. Crew,
John W. Collins,   *Executive Monumental Committee.*
S. S. Howison,
F. Preston Wellford,
Robt. J. Morrison,

I am instructed by the M. W. Grand Master to say, that any sum which may be voted by your Lodge, or collected of the Brethren, may be forwarded to the R. W. Grand Treasurer, Hon. Thomas Tolman, No. 11 Court Street, Boston, who will, at the proper time, transmit it to the Executive Committee at Fredericksburg.

Respectfully and Fraternally,   Chas. W. Moore,
Grand Secretary Grand Lodge of Mass.

CHAPTER XII.

SOURCES OF INCOME. — FUNDS. — FINANCE REPORTS. —
PERMANENT FUND. — YEARLY BALANCES.

The pecuniary resources of the Lodge have
been mainly derived from fees for initiation and
for membership, and from periodical assessments
on members. Previous to 5810, each visitor contributed a small fee, but since then this has not
been required. The invested funds—now considerable in amount—have added to the means of the
treasury. Originally each member had an individual and convertible right in the funds of the
Lodge ; and at his death his share of the funds
could, under certain limitations, be withdrawn.
By regulations adopted September 3, 5795, the
widow or nearest relation, or otherwise the administrator or assign of a deceased member, was
entitled to his share of the stock after deducting
what portion of it he might have previously received, and two and a half per cent. for the use
of the Lodge; and if a member removed to the
distance of fifty miles from Boston, he could receive his proportion of the stock in cash, after deducting ten per cent. for the use of the Lodge;
but if he again took membership he was required
to refund the money so received. By the terms
of a by-law, passed December 3, 5795, it was
made a condition of membership that the applicant should pay a full and equal proportion of
what the stock would then give to each member

over and above the sum demanded for member-ship. The by-laws of 5799 are silent as to the individual right of members to the funds: but the Lodge could vote the sum of twenty dollars to the widow or orphan of a member.

At the meeting held December 1, 5803, the by-laws were amended so as to provide for a per-manent fund to be managed by three trustees. Monies derived from membership, donations and assessments upon members, were applied to the fund which was for the benefit of widows and orphans of deceased members. On the death of a member, his share of the fund was presented to his legal heirs; and if any member removed twenty miles from Boston, he could draw nine-tenths of his share, leaving ten per cent. for the benefit of the Lodge, provided he did not forfeit it by a breach of the rules relative to unbecoming conduct. Every Brother, admitted a member, de-posited a sum equal to a full share in the fund in addition to the sum paid for membership. The law was altered in 5806, requiring in each case, that a deposit of a sum equal to one half of a full share should be made for the fund additional to the sum paid for membership; and that a Brother thereafter admitted a member, who should with-draw his membership on account of removing more than twenty miles from Boston, should have the right to receive nine-tenths of a moiety of one share. This fund does not appear to have existed later than 5808. It was probably merged into the general fund during that year.

In 5808, it was provided that no money should be voted from the funds when it would reduce them below the sum of one thousand dollars, except for a distressed member, his widow or orphans; and in case of the removal of a member more than twenty miles from Boston, and the withdrawal of his membership, he could receive ten dollars as his proportion of the fund, if that sum did not exceed two-thirds of one share. In 5812, the regulation on the removal or withdrawing of a member remained the same as before, with the alteration, only, that the sum that could be then paid to him was five instead of ten dollars; and the widow or orphans of a member were presented with only ten dollars. At this time it was agreed that every member who had paid fifteen dollars for his membership, should be credited with five dollars for the payment of quarterages becoming due. The by-laws of 5816, fixed the sum on the removal or withdrawal at five dollars, or one-half of a membership; and authorized twenty dollars to be paid to the widow or orphans of a member. Since then the rules have not provided for the division of the funds, to any extent, on the removal of a member from Boston, or his withdrawal of membership; and the money presented to widows and orphans of members, has uniformly been a stipulated sum as a donation. The expulsion of a member, or his suspension from membership, has always deprived him of all claim to any portion of the funds. In the chapters in which reference is made to deceased members, to members and to initiates, much will be found bearing upon the subject of the finances, which is omitted here to avoid needless repetition.

The original by-laws required the Treasurer to exhibit the stock on the table, once in three months; and whenever the monies amounted to one hundred and fifty dollars, that he should inform the Lodge thereof, and one hundred dollars was to be appropriated to the stock of the Lodge. The remaining fifty dollars were to remain in the hands of that officer for immediate uses. The same provision exists in the code of 5799. The funds were, at first, loaned to the members by lot; but the practice did not result beneficially; and, therefore, in 5798, the report of a committee was accepted in which it was stated that the mode of loaning monies might "tend to interrupt the harmony and create disunion in the Lodge;" and they therefore recommended investing in such public stock as would be most safe and productive.

The first committee on accounts were appointed January 7, 5796; and in each succeeding year to the present time, the important duty of examining into the pecuniary condition of the Lodge has been regularly and faithfully attended to. The voluminous extracts from the records relating to the finances, will convey to the mind of the reader a clear idea of their management, and also of the difficulties with which the first members had to contend to provide the means which their benevolent designs rendered necessary.

January 7, 5796. " On motion, a committee was chosen to inspect the books of the Secretary and Treasurer, and to make a report at the next monthly meeting, at which time the stock is to be laid on the table; the committee to consist of three members, viz., Bros. Churchill, Eaton and Powell."

February 4, 5796. "The committee on books and accounts, made a report, which was accepted as per file.

A committee was chosen to consider the best mode of applying the cash in hand, and to report at next meeting. Bros.

Churchill, Coles, Perkins, Folsom and Powell were the committee.''

The following is the report above referred to;
it is in the files of 5796. It purports to be a
copy; but it may be questioned whether it is not
the only written report made by that committee.
They might, however, have made a rough sketch
of one, which the Secretary copied and attested.
It may be valued, notwithstanding, as the earliest
finance statement, even though the document on
file be a copy and not the original report.

" *Boston, February* 2, 1796.
The committee of the Columbian Lodge, appointed to audit
and examine the Treasurer's and Secretary's accounts, having
attended that service, report, that they find them fairly entered and stated, and the vouchers regular and complete.
Your committee also find that the Secretary has regularly
from time to time, paid into the hands of the Treasurer, the
monies collected in the Lodge, and that there now remains in
the hands of the Treasurer, (after deducting the expenses of
the meetings, and the stock and materials purchased for the
Lodge,) a balance of one hundred and fifteen dollars, twenty-
four cents, which remains to be appropriated. Your committee further find, that the whole stock of the Lodge amounts
to five hundred and ninety-three dollars, and thirty cents; so
that the proportion of each will make twenty dollars and
ninety-five cents. All which is submitted.
Signed,   JOSEPH CHURCHILL.
                                 SNELLING POWELL.
                                 JNO. PERKINS.
    True copy—Attest: JNO. COLES, *Sec'ry.*''

March 3, 5796. " The committee on money matters reported as per file, and was accepted. Bros. Churchill, Gouldsbury and Folsom were chosen a committee to procure bank
stock, or let the Lodge's money on hand to the best advantage they could. (N. B. This vote was reconsidered.)
" *Voted,* That at present, the money in hand shall be let to
Bro. ———, at lawful interest, with Bonds given to the
Master, in behalf of the Lodge.''

August 4, 5796. "The committee on accounts reported and accepted as per file, cash on hand as per report, laid on the table by the Secretary; its application was referred over to another meeting, and the money returned to the Treasurer."

August 9, 5796. " Voted, That the Treasurer be the person to let one hundred dollars, with proper good endorsers, by note.

Voted, That the above one hundred dollars shall be let by equal lot among the members (the Treasurer excepted) at six per cent. for one year, and Bro. —— drew the lot."

November 8, 5796. " Voted, To choose a committee to settle all accounts with the Secretary and Treasurer, and to report next monthly meeting. Bros. Churchill, Gouldsbury, Raymond, Hayden and Dodge, were chosen."

December 1, 5796. "The committee on accounts reported as per note on file; the report accepted.

Voted, That two hundred dollars be lent to Bro. ——, for one year, with ample security at six per cent.

Voted, That for the above money lent, the receiver give a note to the Master, and he to receipt with the Secretary."

" Boston, Nov. 28, 1796.

The committee appointed by the Columbian Lodge to audit and examine the Treasurer's and Secretary's books and accounts, having attended that service, beg leave to report, that they find them fairly stated, and the vouchers regular and complete. Your committee also find the Secretary has regularly from time to time, paid into the hands of the Treasurer, all the monies he has received, and that there now remains in the hands of the Treasurer, a balance of two hundred and fifty-four dollars, twenty-three cents. Your committee also find that the whole stock and apparatus of the Lodge amount to nine hundred forty-five dollars, and fifty-five cents.

JOSEPH CHURCHILL,
SAML. GOLDSBURY,
SAML. HAYDEN, } Committee.
JNO. RAYMOND,
JAMES DODGE,

True copy—Attest: JNO. COLES, Sec'ry."

June 2, 5797. "Motion was made and seconded, that the Treasurer be requested to lay a statement of the funds of the Lodge before them next Lodge night, which passed in the affirmative."

July 6, 5797. "Agreeably to a vote taken at the last monthly meeting, the Treasurer presented a statement of the finances of the Lodge, but as a petition from a distressed Brother remained to be taken up, and some other business, a motion was made and seconded that this statement be postponed acting upon till next Lodge night—passed in affirmative."

August 10, 5797. "The Report of the Treasurer was then taken up and read, whereupon it was unanimously *Voted*, That a committee of five members be appointed to take into consideration the said report, to examine the Treasurer and Secretary's books, to ascertain the sums due to individuals on account of membership, and settle and adjust all accounts of the Lodge, and to report at the next regular meeting.

For this purpose the following members were nominated and unanimously chosen, viz.—Bros. Coles, Goldsbury, Eaton, Dodge and Eames."

September 7, 5797. "The Committee on the Treasurer and Secretary's accounts, presented a Report, which was read. A motion was then made, to have the same recommitted to the same committee, for the purpose of making a statement of the debts and credits of the Lodge, both principal and interest, by way of account current, and to make report on the first Thursday of November next."

October 10, 5797. "A motion having been made (in consequence of the absence of some of the committee on the settlement of the Treasurer and Secretary's accounts,) that three members be added : nomination being called for, the Right Worshipful Master, Bros. Perkins and Stetson, were appointed."

November 2, 5797. "The committee to whom was recommitted the Report of the Treasurer and Secretary's accounts, &c., having completed the business, gave in a statement of the debts and credits, which was read, unanimously approved, and placed on the files."

The by-laws referred to in the vote given below, were probably those adopted February 12, 5797. This code, it will be remembered, is not now extant. What monies were refunded, it is not possible to determine satisfactorily.

November 2, 5797. "A motion was then made, that the Treasurer be directed to pay to the several members the monies to be refunded agreeably to the Bye-Laws, and to take receipts for the same. Passed in the affirmative."

February 1, 5798. "On a motion that there be a committee, to consist of three, appointed to inquire into the state and situation of the monies due to Columbian Lodge, and to make report on Thursday evening next: the following members were appointed, viz.—Bros. Eaton, Folsom and A. Stetson."

February 8, 5798. "On a motion, *Voted*, That Bro. —— be requested to pay into the Lodge, one hundred dollars at the next meeting, with interest thereon. The committee on loans appointed at the last meeting, reported progress and requested leave to sit again.
The Worshipful Master was added to the Committee."

October 4, 5798. "A motion was then made that a committee be appointed to audit the accounts of the Treasurer and Secretary, and to report at the next meeting.
The following Brethren were accordingly nominated and unanimously appointed, viz.: Bros. Churchill, Coles, Rittenhouse, Tannatt, and McCorristine."

Nov. 1, 5798. "At the request of the Treasurer, a motion was made that the Committee or a majority of them on the last year's accounts, resume their trust, correct any errors that may appear, and make report."

November 21, 5798. "Motion was made and seconded, that two members be added to the last year's committee, to revise and correct an error which has been pointed out by the Treasurer—passed in the affirmative, when Bros. Rittenhouse and Hayden were added.
On a motion that an additional member be added to the committee on accounts for the present year, passed in the affirmative; when Bro. Atwood was added."

December 6, 5798. "The committee appointed to take into consideration and examine the Treasurer's and Secretary's accounts, gave in a report which was unanimously accepted, and placed on the files.
The committee appointed to correct an error in the Treasurer's books for the year 1797, not having reported, were desired to meet as soon as possible to complete that business."

December 20, 5798. "The committee appointed to correct an error said to be made in the last year's report, gave in a statement of an error in favor of the Treasurer, for twenty-two dollars and forty-five cents, which was unanimously accepted.

A motion was made that a standing committee be appointed for the year ensuing, to consist of five members, who were nominated and unanimously chosen, viz.: Bros. Churchill, Folsom, Stetson, Perkins and Somes."

November 7, 5799. "A committee was chosen to audit the Treasurer and Secretary's accounts. Bros. Folsom, Rittenhouse and A. Stetson were chosen."

December 5, 5799. "The Lodge proceeded to hear the report of their committee, so far as respects the statement of the Treasurer's and Secretary's accounts, and the funds of the Lodge, which passed in the affirmative."

January 2, 5800. "The standing committee for the year past, reported that no particular business had been transacted the year past, except that monies received from time to time in the Lodge had been properly applied, by investing the same in the funds of the Lodge. Standing Committee for the year 1800, Bros. Folsom, Churchill, A. Stetson, S. Stetson, and Baxter."

January 16, 5800. "*Voted*, That those members who are delinquent in quarterages shall come forward and give their notes of hand, with an approved endorser, payable in four months with interest, provided nevertheless, that such notes shall not be considered as having exonerated them from a violation of the By-Laws in that case made and provided. (N. B. Those members only are included in the above vote, who are deficient for more than three quarters.)

"*Voted*, That the Secretary carry the above vote into execution, and that the notes be dated January 16, 1800."

January 8, 5801. "The committee for examining the Secretary and Treasurer's accounts brought in their report concerning the funds of the Lodge. Several Brothers expressed their minds on the subject, it accordingly passed and the Secretary was directed to file it, that any Brother finding himself dissatisfied may at any time have recourse to it."

November 5, 5801. "*Voted*, also, that a committee be appointed to take up the Treasurer's and Secretary's accounts, to consist of the following, viz.: the R. W. Master, Bros. A. Stetson, Baxter, Pons, and Jenks."

December 2, 5801. "The committee on accounts reported a statement of the yearly accounts and the funds of the Lodge."

November 4, 5802. "Bros. Thayer, Folsom, R. W. Master, Baxter and Kelly were appointed a committee to examine the Treasurer's and Secretary's accounts for the last year, and make report the next Lodge night. On motion, *Voted*, The same committee have power to adopt a plan to furnish the Lodge with supplies on a more economical plan than is now in operation."

November 18, 5802. "The committee appointed the last Lodge night gave in their report, (on file,) and after being read was unanimously accepted by a vote of the Lodge. On motion, *Voted*, The sum due from the Columbian Society to the Lodge be erased and considered as finally lost. The R. W. Master, Bros. Baxter and Folsom, were appointed a committee to loan the sum of four hundred dollars of the property of the Lodge, or a part thereof as they shall think proper, taking good security therefor."

January 6, 5803. "The By-Laws were read, the R. W. Master, Bros. Folsom and Baxter were appointed a committee to settle all accounts with the Grand Lodge. The committee appointed to loan the property of the Lodge, reported that they had attended that service, and loaned the amount agreeably to instructions from the Lodge."

November 14, 5803. "Bro. Baxter, W. Master, and Bro. Swett were appointed a committee to audit and settle the Secretary's and Treasurer's accounts for the year past."

November 21, 5803. "The committee appointed to audit the Secretary and Treasurer's accounts the last night, gave in their report, (see file,) which was accepted by vote of the Lodge. W. M. A. Stetson, Baxter and McDonnell were appointed a committee to provide for a fund, &c., and to alter the By-Laws accordingly. On motion, *Voted*, That the officers of Columbian Lodge, pay one year's quarterages in advance; also, that the Secretary request all members that are not officers to pay two quarters in advance."

December 1, 5803. "W. Bro. Stetson, Baxter and Crooker were appointed a committee to superintend the permanent fund."

" Boston, Dec. 12, 5803.

Duplicate,—Received of Amasa Stetson, Esq., late Master of Columbian Lodge, twelve and a half dollars for twenty-five initiates in the year 5800. Twenty-three and half dollars for forty-seven initiates in the year 5801, and one dollar and fifty cents for three initiates in 5802, under the old establishment; also fifty dollars for twenty-five initiates under the new regulations, to October 6, 5803, and thirty-two dollars for sixteen quarterages, from December 9, 5799, to December 12, 5803, as per return.   Jno. Boyle, *D. D. G. M.*

$119 50

18 75   deducted for twenty-five diplomas heretofore.
_____

$100 75   paid for under the new regulation."

" Boston, March 9, 5800.

Duplicate,—Received of Columbian Lodge, by the hand of their Master, nine dollars and fifty cents, being for nineteen initiates as per return for the year.

5799.—$9 50   Dan. Oliver, *Grand Sec'y.*"

July 5, 5804.   "R. W. Master, R. W. Bro. Stetson and R. W. Bro. Benson were appointed a committee to adjust all accounts with the Treasurer and Secretary."

The request in the succeeding vote was made in consequence of the death of the Treasurer, Bro. Samuel Stetson.

September 6, 5804.   "On motion, *Voted,* That R. W. Bro. Amasa Stetson be requested to receive the funds of Columbian Lodge, and act as Treasurer until the next regular choice of officers."

November 1, 5804.   "Bros. Baxter, Stetson, Folsom, Crooker and Benson were appointed a committee to audit the Secretary and Treasurer's accounts for the year past, and make a yearly report of all matters relative thereto at the next regular Lodge night."

December 6, 5804.   "The committee appointed the last regular Lodge night to audit the Secretary and Treasurer's accounts, attended that service, and gave in the following report, viz. :

That the amount of cash received for quarterages due before the establishment of the permanent fund, for initiations,

passings, and raisings, &c., for the last year
ending 28th November, 5804, is, ...$654 91
Six months interest on Cony's bond,.............. 12 00
Balance in Treasurer's hands, ... 28 70

$695 61

DISBURSEMENTS.

Viz. : For wines and other refreshments, Secretary's
fees, fuel and light, gloves, aprons, rent, fees to
the Grand Lodge, donations to distressed Brethren, &c., for the year past is.................. $553 33

CASH PAID GRAND LODGE.

Amount due before November 21st, 5803,......... 100 75
Balance in the hands of the Treasurer Nov. 28, 5804, 41 53

$695 61

STATE OF THE FUNDS.

Cash in the hands of the Treasurer, Nov. 28, 5804, $41 53
Cony's bond upon mortgage,.................... 400 00
Eleven months interest due thereon,............. 22 00

$463 53

Due from members for quarterages before January
1, 5804, ... $27 00
Bro. ———'s note,..................... $22 27
Three years and ten months interest on do.. 5 12 — 27 39
Bro. ———'s note, dated Aug. 11, 5796,
endorsed by ———,................. 100 00
Eight years 3½ months interest on do...... 49 75—149 75

$667 67

To be deducted, a small bill due to Mr. Jno. Cotton, for
painting. All of which is duly submitted by

        DANIEL BAXTER,   ⎤
        AMASA STETSON,   ⎥
        JNO. W. FOLSOM, ⎬ *Committee*
        JOHN BENSON,   ⎥
        TURNER CROOKER, ⎦

The above report was read and accepted by a vote of the
Lodge.

The trustees of the permanent fund made their yearly
report which was accepted by vote of the Lodge.

R. W. Master, R. W. Bro. A. Stetson and Bro.' Crooker were appointed Trustees for the management of the permanent fund.''

November 7, 5805. " *Voted*, That Bros. Folsom, Benson and Binney, be a committee to settle the accounts of the Treasurer and Secretary.''

December 5, 5805. "The committee appointed at the meeting of Columbian Lodge, on November 7, 5805, to audit, examine and settle the accounts of the Treasurer and Secretary for the year 5805, have attended that service, and ask leave to report, viz. : that they find the accounts of those officers accurately cast, properly stated, and fairly recorded with proper vouchers. That the monies paid into the hands of the Treasurer amount to three hundred and forty-three dollars and fifty-three cents, and his disbursements amount to four hundred and fifteen dollars and sixty cents; that there appears to have been added to the permanent fund in the year past the sum of one hundred and fifty-six dollars and fifty-nine cents, as will appear by the report of the committee on that institution.

There is now in the hands of the Treasurer a bond and mortgage of Cony's, for four hundred dollars, the interest of which has been regularly paid. All which is duly submitted.

AMOS BINNEY,   }
JNO. W. FOLSOM, } *Committee.*
JNO. BENSON,   }

Boston, Nov. 27, 5805.''

The above report was read and accepted by vote of the Lodge.

STATE OF THE PERMANENT FUND.

The trustees of the permanent fund beg leave to state for the information of their Brethren, that at the settlement of last year, that fund amounted to one hundred and two dollars and forty-three cents $102 43
Amount received since that time for memberships and quarterages,..............156 59
Thirteen months interest on 102,43 is..... 6 65—163 24

Due from members, 114,33. $265 67

All which is duly submitted,   D. BAXTER, }
                               A. STETSON, } *Trustees.*
                               T. CROOKER, }

Boston, Dec. 4, 5805.''

R. W. Baxter, Stetson and Bean were chosen Trustees for the management of the permanent fund, by written votes."

November 6, 5806. " *Voted*, That Bros. Crooker, Bean and Baxter be a committee to audit the accounts of the Treasurer and Secretary, for the last year, and report the next Lodge night.

Voted, That the above committee, together with Bros. Folsom and Stetson, take into consideration the expediency of altering the By-Laws so far as respects the amount to be paid for membership and steward's fees, and report the next meeting."

December 4, 5806. " The committee on accounts and on the By-Laws and permanent fund, reported as under.

The committee appointed to audit and settle the accounts of the Treasurer and Secretary, have attended to that service, and beg leave to report, that they find the accounts of those officers fairly stated and correctly cast, with the proper vouchers.

The receipts for the present year are five hundred and eighty-one dollars and fifty cents,..........	$581 50
Cony's note of mortgage,......................	400 00
Bro. ———'s note, one hundred dollars, and ten years' interest, sixty dollars,................	160 00
	$1,141 50
The expenditure for the present year, are five hundred and fifty-nine dollars and eighty cents,.....	$559 80
Balance due Treasurer for 5805,..............	72 07
	$631 87
Balance in hands of the Treasurer, five hundred nine dollars, sixty-three cents,..............	$509 63

> TURNER CROOKER, } *Committee.*
> STEPHEN BEAN, }

December 4, 5806.'

This report was twice read and unanimously accepted."

" A Report of the trustees of the permanent fund was then twice read for the information of the Lodge, in these words, viz.

The trustees for the management of the permanent fund,
beg leave to state for the information of their brethren, that
at the settlement last year, the fund amounted to $265 67
Amount received for memberships and quarterages
during the present year,..................... 182 33
Amount of interest received,...................   30 66
                                                 ———————
                                                 $478 66
Due from members,. 91 16
                                                 ———————
                                                 $569 82

The rapid progress of this fund promises to become very
respectable in a few years, if duly attended to. All which is
respectfully submitted.

AMASA STETSON, ——— ———, } *Committee.*

Boston, December 4, 5806.'

Ordered, That this report be entered on the records."

June 3, 5807. "Bro. Baxter proposed that the funds of
Columbian Lodge be called in and otherwise appropriated.

Voted, That the trustees of the permanent fund be a committee to confer with Bro. Thayer with respect to depositing
the funds with him, for the use of the hall, and to report the
next regular meeting."

July 2, 5807. "A report of the committee of conference
with Bro. Thayer, was read by Bro. Folsom, and accepted by
the Lodge.

Voted, That the Treasurer be directed to make a transfer of
the debts and mortgage, of which the Lodge funds consist, to
Bro. Seth Thayer."

November 6, 5807. "*Voted*, That a committee of three,
viz., Bros. Baxter, Phillips and Jenkins, be appointed to audit
and settle the accounts of the Secretary and Treasurer.

Voted, That the above committee be authorized to examine
and pass upon the bill presented by the steward, for refreshment furnished for the late special meeting, and if correct,
that the same be paid without delay."

January 7, 5808. "The committee appointed to audit and
settle the accounts of the Treasurer and Secretary, have
attended that service, and beg leave to report :

That they find the accounts of those officers to be fairly entered and correctly cast, with proper vouchers.

The committee likewise state for the information of the Lodge, that they have initiated thirty, crafted twenty-two, and raised to the sublime degree of Master Masons, twenty-one brethren, and that they have admitted ten respectable members.

The committee also find that the receipts of the Lodge, the year past, have been eight hundred and forty-six dollars and fifty cents,.................................. $846 50

Which, with the funds at the close of the year 1806, being 1125 50

Making the receipts of the Treasurer,............ $1972 00

That the expenses, together with the money loaned to Bro. Seth Thayer, amount to............. 1850 35

$121 65

Leaving a cash balance in the hands of the Treasurer, of one hundred and twenty-one dollars and sixty-five cents—adding to that amount, Bros. Thayer and ———'s notes, being ten hundred and sixty-six dollars,...................... 1066 00

Making the whole stock of the Lodge,........... $1187 65

Eight hundred and thirty-three dollars of which is in the permanent fund.

All which is duly submitted.

DANL. BAXTER, ⎫
EBENR. PHILLIPS, ⎬ *Committee.*
JOSEPH JENKINS, ⎭

The Report of the aforesaid committee was read, and accepted by a vote of the Lodge."

February 4, 5808. " *Voted*, That the Treasurer and Secretary be a committee to procure stores for the Lodge."

December 1, 5808. " The Lodge was opened in due form. The committee appointed at the last meeting of the Lodge, to settle the Treasurer and Secretary's accounts, have attended that duty, and find them fairly stated and correctly kept, with proper vouchers ; and beg leave to report that the receipts for

the last year, for initiating eight, crafting eleven, and raising
nine, together with quarterages, amount to...... $284 50
The interest received on loans, amount to........ 100 00
Received from permanent fund, as per new By-
Laws, ... 788 50
Cash in the hands of Bro. Thayer, on loan,...... 900 00

                                              $2073 00

The expenditures of the Lodge the last
  year have been.....................$292 63
Cash paid for one year's rent for the Hall, 100 00
Paid balance due from the Lodge, as per
  new By-Laws,..................... 681 35—1073 98

The whole funds of the Lodge are............... $992 02
There is due from members for quarterages,...... $111 00

All which is respectfully submitted for the consideration of
this R. W. Lodge.

　　　　　　EBENR. PHILLIPS, ⎫
　　　　　　DANL. BAXTER,　⎬ *Committee.*"
　　　　　　JOSEPH JENKINS, ⎭

February 6, 5812. "*Voted*, That Bros. Sawyier and
Moody be added to the committee, previously appointed for
investing the funds of the Lodge.

Voted, That the committee aforesaid be authorized to invest the funds of the Lodge in bank stock, if it can be obtained in advance, not exceeding five per cent. on the sum
actually paid in."

November 4, 5813. "On motion of Bro. Binney, *Voted*,
That the Secretary be instructed to pass to the credit of each
member of this Lodge, such sum as they shall have severally
paid over and above ten dollars for their memberships."

November 5, 5829. "Bros. G. G. Smith, Baxter, Jr.,
Johnson, Moody and Flint were appointed a committee to
confer with other committees from the several Masonic Societies, on the retrenchment of the expenses of the Lodge, with
power to make any alteration they may deem expedient."

Neither the records, books of accounts nor the files, furnish any more information respecting the annual statements of the finances to the year 5808, than is comprised in the foregoing copies of reports and extracts. The following figures represent the amount of the funds at the close of each financial year, beginning with the year 5809.

Year.	Amount.	Year.	Amount.	Year.	Amount.
5809	1,467,95	5825	1,958,27	5841	2,478,40
5810	1,236,06	5826	2,054,48	5842	2,555,16
5811	1,235,24	5827	2,000,00	5843	2,530,16
5812	1,265,34	5828	2,113,38	5844	2,583,49
5813	1,316,22	5829	2,137,50	5845	2,818,22
5814	1,434,43	5830	2,197,07	5846	2,709,86
5815	1,664,18	5831	2,317,89	5847	2,422,02
5816	1,412,85	5832	2,212,73	5848	2,418,94
5817	1,438,97	5833	2,339,31	5849	2,683,97
5818	1,437,48	5834	2,366,06	5850	3,231,33
5819	1,478,07	5835	2,422,90	5851	3,400,92
5820	1,211,67	5836	2,343,65	5852	3,769,90
5821	1,210,01	5837	2,305,40	5853	4,056,13
5822	1,349,71	5838	2,305,09	5854	4,664,78
5823	1,562,65	5839	2,321,76		
5824	1,520,99	5840	2,398,09		

At the close of the year 5855, the funds will probably exceed in amount the sum of five thousand dollars. The accumulation has been rapid since 5841, though the expenditure in charities has not been diminished. It may be said, indeed, that no worthy applicant for relief during that period, has been refused assistance.

CHAPTER XIII.

CHARITIES. — FIRE IN 5801. — CASE OF RELIEF TO A
WIDOW AND ORPHANS. — EXTRACTS RELATING TO
OTHER CASES. — PRISONERS OF WAR IN 5814. — BOARD
OF RELIEF. — DISASTER TO STEAMER RHODE ISLAND,
AND RESCUE OF TWO MEMBERS OF THE LODGE.

In tracing the acts of Columbian Lodge through
the ponderous volumes in which they are inscribed, nothing meets the eye more frequently
than the evidence that the members have ever
been ready to relieve the distresses of a worthy
Brother, and carry aid and consolation to his
widow and orphans.   Such deeds of benevolence
and kindness constitute the permanent honor and
true glory of the Lodge ; and, when registered by
the recording officer, though in simple and unos-
tentatious language, they irradiate and adorn the
pages of his labors, while they present to posterity
bright examples of faithful obedience to a leading
tenet of Freemasonry.   During the first years of
the society, the number of brethren was small ; —
and, as individuals, they were far from being rich ;
—yet their contributions for charitable purposes
were extensive.   The prayer of a worthy applicant for assistance was never refused, though the
amount of the gift might have been sometimes
contracted, not by the will, but because of the
diminished means of the donors.   In the bestow-
ment of relief to the destitute, it has been done
with a hearty wish to solace the recipient ; and,

without display, in a manner earnestly to assert, that

> " The widow's heart shall sing for joy,
> The orphan shall be glad."

But though the disbursements of the funds have been made with a liberal hand,—and at times they have not been restricted for want of ample means to satisfy all reasonable claims,—yet they have been out-measured by the practice of that higher charity which aims to soothe the unhappy, to sympathize with them in their misfortunes, to compassionate their miseries and restore peace to their troubled minds. When the cares, perplexities and adversities of life have caused dejection bordering on despair, it has been the kind word of encouragement and sympathy, and the active hand of fraternal interest and succour, that have inspired renewed efforts, and been the instruments of restored usefulness. To the foreign brother, cast upon the cold shores of the stranger, it has been the province of this nobler charity to take him by the hand and give him employment, where his efforts could provide for himself without his being subjected to the condition of the mendicant. It has been this charity which has prompted the brethren to fly to the relief of him who had the hand and the will to labor, and provide for him the field for his exertions. The amount of good done in this way by the Lodge, as such, and by individual members, cannot be estimated in money; it cannot be told; the work has been in secret, in unpretending quiet philanthropy which thought not of reward, or the approval of the world.

In the primal days of the institution it was not unfrequently the practice, when a petition for assistance was granted, for visitors to contribute, also, in aid of the supplicant; and, at such times, a convenient substitute for a "contribution box" was found in the hat of some brother present. The employment of the hat for this purpose was not peculiar to Masons, for at that time it was often brought into requisition for the same purpose, in meetings of every kind, so that the phrase "let the hat pass round," had the same significance as that more polite one of "a contribution will now be taken up." A few extracts from the records will show with what effect the hat passed round fifty-five years ago.

March 2, 5797. "On motion made and seconded from the visiting brethren, with the consent of the Master, *Voted*, That the hat pass among them for the further relief of the petitioner; passed unanimously, and it appeared that the sum of five dollars and ninety-five cents was also collected.

A motion was then made and seconded, that the Secretary be requested to take charge of the above sums, and to deliver the same to the petitioner, as soon as may be. Passed in the affirmative."

June 20, 5797. "A petition was presented by Bro. Coles, praying relief, whereupon it was unanimously *Voted*, That the sum of five dollars be paid to the petitioner by the Treasurer, in conformity to the By-Laws therein made and provided. Visiting brethren collected six dollars and eighteen cents."

January 3, 5799. "The hat was then called for by the visiting brethren, which being carried round among them, the additional sum of four dollars and forty-five cents was collected."

February 7, 5799. "The hat was then called for among the visiting brethren, when the sum of three dollars and twenty-three cents was collected."

June 6, 5799. "It was moved by the visiting brethren, that the hat go round. There was collected the sum of five dollars fifty-two cents."

The conflagration already referred to, (see page 143,) which occurred on the morning of Wednesday, December 16, 5801, was disastrous to several members of the Lodge, for whose relief measures were instituted at the meeting of January 7, 5802. A committee was appointed to inquire into their wants, who reported January 11, 5802. Their report was adopted and placed on file. The files do not now contain the report, and no means exist of determining the nature and extent of the assistance rendered. The disaster is thus noticed in the Columbian Centinel of December 16, 5801, the press having been stopped for the purpose:

"FIRE!

Wednesday morning, five o'clock.

It is with the most poignant regret we mention that a most tremendous fire is now raging in the north part of the town. It began at about two o'clock in a shop adjacent to the conflagration on Saturday evening. All the stores on Gardner's wharf, and all the dwelling-houses on both sides of the street, at the head of Gardner's and Gouldsbury's wharves, on the end of Cross street, four or five on the street to the northward, in Fore street, are now enveloped in flames, or are destroyed. A great many people have lost their all.

POSTCRIPT.

Six o'clock.—The fire is this moment got under command. About twenty houses and stores, as far as we can at this instant recollect, are destroyed—many of the stores with chief of their contents. The distressing disaster is generally attributed to design. The tide was out; and water was obtained with difficulty; and it is to the active exertions of the engine companies, firewards and citizens, that any limits have been prescribed to the destructive element."

January 7, 5802. "*Voted,* That a committee be appointed to inquire into the situation and circumstances of brethren of

this Lodge who have suffered by the late conflagration, as also
into the actual state of the finances of the Lodge, in order that
such relief may be given them as the state of the funds will
admit, and, also, take into consideration the propriety of dispensing with that part of the 25th Article of our By-Laws, so
far as relates to the application of money to distressed members ; and to request the R. W. Master and Wardens to summons a special Lodge as soon as they may be ready to report.

A committee was accordingly chosen, consisting of the following :—The R. W. Master, Br. Baxter, Br. Folsom, Br. S.
Stetson, and Br. Thayer. On motion, *Voted*, That the Secretary be requested to present a subscription to the brethren
of the Lodge, for the benefit of those members who have suffered by the late fire.''

January 11, 5802. '' On motion, *Voted*, That the Treasurer be requested to call for all the debts due to the Lodge,
within ninety days from this date, and when collected, lay the
same before the Lodge.

The committee appointed the last Lodge night, to inquire
into the situation and circumstances of brethren of this Lodge,
who have suffered by the late conflagration, as also into the
actual state of the finances of the Lodge, in order that such
relief may be given them, as the state of the funds will admit,
and, also, take into consideration the propriety of dispensing
with that part of the 25th Article of our By-Laws, so far as
it relates to the application of money to distressed members,
&c., reported that they have attended that service, and beg
leave to report. (See Report, on file.)

On motion, *Voted*, That the consideration of the Report lay
over until the next regular Lodge night, there not being a
sufficient number of members present to act thereon agreeably
to law. The Secretary was directed to note in the summons
for the next regular night, that the Report is to be taken up,
and the By-Laws to be acted upon.''

February 4, 5802. '' The report referred over to this evening was read and unanimously accepted. The R. W. Master, Bros. Folsom, Baxter, Thayer and S. Stetson, were appointed a committee to carry the report into execution.''

On the 19th December, the Centinel gives full
particulars of the calamity. Its effects were
mainly in Fish street, and upon Barrett's, Hitch-
born's, Burditt's, Gardner's, and Gouldsbury's

wharves. Fish street was a part of what is now called North street; and the wharves have given place to an extensive area of land which is at present covered with stores. Among the names of the sufferers are those of Joseph Churchill, Captain Amasa Stetson, Captain Samuel Stetson, Samuel Hayden and Samuel Jenks, all at that time members of Columbian Lodge. The house of Joseph Churchill, merchant; the shop of Samuel Stetson, dealer in shoes,—owned by Amasa Stetson; house occupied by Samuel Hayden, watch maker; and the shop of Samuel Jenks, blacksmith, were all numbered with the ruins. The sloops Charming Sally of Duck-Trap, and Franklin of Falmouth, bound to New York, and having three-fifths of her cargo on board, consisting of "fish, wine, chocolate, soap, medicine and small articles," were entirely destroyed, and several other vessels were damaged.

In 5810, the widow of a worthy deceased member, with her children, was desirous of visiting her friends who were in a foreign land; and being in destitute circumstances, she depended upon the Masonic friends of her husband for aid to enable her to gratify her wishes. They promptly responded to her request; obtained a passage for her; and provided an outfit calculated to render her and her children comfortable during the voyage. It will be observed that St. Andrew's chapter shared in the honor of this generous act.

June 7, 5810. "A petition from Mrs. —— ——, praying relief, was presented. *Voted*, To raise a committee to inquire into and supply her present wants; and report at next meeting the sum given, which was not to exceed ten dollars; and if further assistance, and what, was necessary. Bros.

Daniel Baxter and Samuel Smith were chosen a committee
for the above purpose.''

July 5, 5810. '' The committee on the petition of Mrs.
———, reported progress; and asked leave to report at a
future time. The request of this committee was complied
with.''

August 2, 5810. '' The committee on the business with
Mrs. ———, reported that they had advanced to her the ten
dollars allowed them to do at a former meeting. *Voted*, To
accept the report of the committee. Thanks were voted to
this committee for their services. *Voted*, That they continue
to be a committee for a longer term, to assist Mrs. ———, if
necessity require it, and that they present her fifteen dollars,
if and when expedient, and make report of their doings.''

September 6, 5810. '' *Voted*, To accept the report of the
committee on the business with Mrs. ———, and that it be
recorded.

REPORT.

The committee chosen by Columbian Lodge to alleviate the
distresses of the widow and children of our late Bro. ———,
by presenting them certain sums of money, according to
votes of said Lodge, and also to procure a passage for them to
Surinam, with deference state, that in coöperation with a committee from St. Andrew's Chapter for that purpose, they have
accomplished the above object, but not without expending
more money than was appropriated by said Lodge for that
purpose, as will appear by the following statement:

Cash advanced Mrs. ———,.....................	$ 25 00
Cash paid for bread,......................... ...	10 50
Cash paid Mrs. ———, for Mrs. ——— and chil-dren's board,.....	2 90
Cash paid for wine, eggs, butter, carriage and hack-hire, &c.,.................................	7 30
Cash paid for beef and bread,....................	7 36
Cash paid for meal, and washing floor,...........	1 75
Cash paid for sundries by J. B. Hammatt,........	34 25
Cash paid for same, by　　do.,..............	9 00
Cash paid for trucking, by　　do.,..............	2 00
Cash advanced Mrs. ———, by do.,............	15 00
	$115 06

That the committee from St. Andrews Chapter have paid fifty-one dollars of the above sum, thereby leaving sixty-four dollars and six cents, paid by your committee, and that they have received twenty-five dollars of the Secretary, which, deducted from the above sum, leaves thirty-nine dollars and six cents, for which no provision has been made.

DANIEL BAXTER, } *Committee.*"
SAMUEL SMITH, }

During the last war with Great Britain, the Fraternity were often called upon to assist prisoners of war, who were Masons. Owing to the town of Salem, Mass., being a depot for prisoners taken at sea, the brotherhood of that place were subjected to heavy expenditures to relieve this class of unfortunates ; and, therefore, in order to lessen the burden thus centered upon comparatively a few brethren, the Grand Lodge established a fund, called the prisoner's fund, to be made up from contributions from all the Lodges within the jurisdiction. The subject first came before Columbian Lodge, April 6, 5815 ; and was referred to a committee. The committee reported progress ; but they do not appear to have presented any final report, nor was there any further action in the matter taken by the Lodge. As the treaty of peace was ratified by the United States at the close of the month of February of that year, it is probable that any more proceedings were deemed unnecessary, and the committee were considered as discharged.

April 6, 5815. " A communication was received from the District D. G. Master, accompanying the annual return of the Grand Lodge, with duplicate blank returns. The said returns of the Grand Lodge, embracing the subject of the Prisoner's Fund ; which subject was referred to the Standing Committee."

May 4, 5815. "The Standing Committee reported progress on the subject of the Prisoner's Fund, and had leave to continue their attention to the subject."

The following communications from the Grand Lodge are on file :

CIRCULAR.

THE GRAND LODGE OF MASSACHUSETTS TO THE LODGES UNDER ITS JURISDICTION.

Right Worshipful, Worshipful and Beloved Brethren—The attention of the Masonic Fraternity has seldom been called to a more interesting subject than that submitted to our consideration by the officers and members of Essex Lodge. Indeed, our charities are never more characteristically and appropriately applied, than in mitigating the horrors of war, visiting the sick and the wounded, assuaging the agonies of bodily and mental distress, and supplying the hungry and the naked : and these offices of humanity we may discharge to the stranger and sojourner, and even "see through pity's melting eye a brother in a foe," without incurring the guilt or penalty of treason against either the laws of God or man.

The groaning of the prisoner has now reached our ears, and has not been disregarded by the Grand Lodge ; whose readiness to provide for those who are the immediate claimants on its sympathy, will it is hoped, meet the approbation, and receive the prompt support of our whole Masonic family.

The present object of our charities is to relieve the distresses of MASONS whom the fortune of war throws within the sphere of our attentions ; and although *their* duties as citizens of a country with whom we are at war may have compelled them to combat with *Brethren*, they have a powerful claim to our compassion. The moment the sword of the *Warrior* is sheathed, the feelings of the *Mason* return with redoubled force ; and *Charity*, displaying her banners of love, conducts the captive brother to the *Lodge*, the only "city of refuge."

The appropriation, granted at the benevolent instance of Essex Lodge, has been made in the fullest confidence that the Lodges under our jurisdiction, aided by those brethren who are blessed with affluence, will cheerfully engage in the charitable work of affording the means, (compatible with their ability) of replacing the grant in the funds of the Grand Lodge, and enabling it to dispense still greater charities, should the continuance of the war render them necessary.

For this purpose, Columbian Lodge is called upon to comply with the wishes of the Grand Lodge, as expressed by the acceptance of the Report hereto annexed.

The repeated relief, and instances of brotherly love which have been and still continue to be exercised towards our Brethren, carried prisoners of war to Great Britain and her dependencies, are gratefully acknowledged. It is our pride and consolation, that the fires of Masonic charities burn with fervor on transatlantic altars.

We most devoutly offer our prayers to the Supreme Architect of the Universe, for the return of peace ; and that the only point at issue among contending nations, may be a charitable emulation in the promotion and practice of those virtues which exalt and adorn our nature. But whatever may be the result of public measures, the Masonic institution will ever yield a respectful and loyal submission to their civil fathers. And the Grand Lodge take this opportunity of expressing a wish that the fraternity may eminently display to an admiring world the genuine and exalted principles of our royal craft, and exhibit the glorious specimens of the pure and disinterested love which Masons bear each other.

Per order of the Most Worshipful Grand Lodge of Massachusetts.

JOHN SOLEY, *Grand Secretary.*

Boston, December 27th, A. L. 5814.

At the annual communication of the M. W. Grand Lodge of Massachusetts, held at Masons' Hall, in Boston, Dec. 12th, 5814, a Representation from Essex Lodge, in Salem, was presented and read, in which it was stated, that Salem is the only place of *Depot*, within this Commonwealth, for prisoners of war captured at sea ; that the number of prisoners, though varied, has generally been large (at present upwards of three hundred) among whom there have been more or less of the Masonic family, who have not the means to render themselves comfortable, without soliciting the exercise of those charities which it is the peculiar province of the Masonic Institution to bestow. There being but one Lodge of Masons in Salem, the applications to Essex Lodge have been numerous, yet they have hitherto met with that attention becoming the principles which Masons profess. The effect has been a gradual and constant reduction of the funds of the Lodge, and appropriations have been diverted from the relief of its own indigent members, and those widows and orphans, who have long been pensioners on the bounty of the Lodge, for an annual pittance towards their support, to those claims which could not be resisted from their urgency, and the peculiar circumstances in which the applicants were placed. Essex Lodge, therefore, respectfully requests, that the M. W. Grand Lodge, will make an appropriation from its funds for the object under consideration, by which the burden will be equalized among the members of the Masonic family in this Commonwealth.

On motion, The subject was committed to the R. W. Brethren FRANCIS J. OLIVER, JOSEPH GEORGE SPRAGUE, ELIJAH MORSE, SHUBAEL BELL, and JONA. WHITNEY.

At the communication of the M. W. Grand Lodge, held for the installation of officers for the ensuing year, on the anniversary of the festival of St. John the Evangelist, Dec. 27, 5814, the following Report was presented, viz. :—

The Committee to whom was referred the Representation from Essex Lodge, relating to the situation and claims of prisoners of War, in Salem,

Respectfully report—That strongly impressed with the importance of the subject committed to them, and viewing it as an object highly interesting to the honor of the Grand Lodge, and calculated to excite the sympathy and best feelings of all the Lodges under this jurisdiction, they have unanimously agreed to recommend—

That the sum of five hundred dollars be appropriated to the relief of distressed prisoners of the Masonic family, who, in the course of the calamitous war in which our country is engaged, may be brought among us.

That the said sum be placed at the disposal of a Board of Commissioners, who are hereby authorized to dispense the same, with power to draw upon the Grand Treasurer for the whole, or any part thereof, as occasion may require.

That it shall be the duty of said Commissioners to exhibit, in writing, at every quarterly communication of the Grand Lodge, a statement, showing the sums which they have expended, the names of the prisoners whom they have relieved during the preceding quarter, and the names of the Lodges in which the said prisoners were initiated Masons, or of which they are members.

And, that every Lodge under this jurisdiction may have an opportunity of contributing to a fund, alike honorable and interesting to the whole fraternity, your committee further propose, that the following plan be adopted for reimbursing to the Grand Lodge the sums which may from time to time be advanced for this benevolent and truly Masonic object, viz.

A circular letter shall be addressed to the several Lodges under this jurisdiction, recommending to the Lodges in Boston, its vicinity and other populous places, to remit quarterly to the Grand Treasurer, during the continuance of the war, the amount of fees for initiating, passing and raising of one candidate, or in lieu thereof, the sum of thirty dollars annually; and requesting all the other Lodges to raise by contribution, assessment, or pay from their funds, the sum of ten dollars annually; the first annual contribution to be forthwith forwarded to the R. W. ANDREW SIGOURNEY, of Boston, Grand Treasurer. All which, with a copy of the proposed circular, is respectfully submitted.

FRANCIS J. OLIVER,
JOS. GEO. SPRAGUE,
ELIJAH MORSE, } *Committee.*
S. BELL,
JONA. WHITNEY,

The above report having been read, and accepted unanimously by the Grand Lodge, the following Brethren were appointed *commissioners of the prisoner's fund* for the year ensuing, viz.

R. W. JOSEPH BAKER, *of Salem.*
R. W. FRANCIS J. OLIVER, *of Boston.*
R. W. and Rev. WILLIAM BENTLEY, *of Salem.*
R. W. JAMES C. KING, *of Salem.*
R. W. RALPH H. FRENCH, *of Danvers.*
R. W. ABEL LAWRENCE, *of Salem.*
R. W. WILLIAM SWAN, *of Portland.*

Attest, JOHN SOLEY, *Grand Sec'y.*

PRISONERS' FUND.

The following Report on this subject was received, accepted and recorded.

Boston, Sept. 11, 5815.

The Commissioners of the "Prisoner's Fund," ask leave respectfully to make the following Report.

That pursuant to their commission, dated at Boston, the 23d of January, 5815, they were convoked by a public summons, and the Board organized, they proceeded to execute the sacred trust with which they had been charged by your Most Worshipful Body.

27*

They signified their readiness to receive applications for your distinguished charity, by advertisements in the public papers, and at their first meeting afterwards, they received from the prison ship and neighborhood in Salem, (the principal depot for prisoners of war in the Commonwealth) eighteen applications; the circumstances of which, having been properly investigated by a deputation of the commissioners, they were all admitted to share your bounty, according to their respective wants and circumstances. That your commissioners, agreeable to the vote of the Grand Lodge, which created them its almoners, drew on the R. W. Andrew Sigourney, Esq., for $150. That the arrival of the joyful news that peace was again restored to their bleeding country, which released the prisoner from his confinement, and restored him to his friends ; superceded the necessity for making any further appropriation, and of the amount already drawn for, only the sum of $131,68 was expended, and $18,32 has since been paid into the hands of the Grand Treasurer. The following are the names of the persons, and the sums which each respectively received, with the number and names of the Lodges to which they were reported to have belonged.

[*Here follow the names of eighteen British prisoners of war who received assistance; with the number of the Lodges to which they belonged, and their stations.*]

Your Commissioners cannot close this Report, without expressing the sentiments of gratitude exhibited by the recipients of your benevolence : nor without testifying their conviction, that this instance of the munificence of the Grand Lodge will be held in grateful recollection by its sister Grand Lodges in Europe, and that this discharge of one of the highest duties of the Order, is of a character to raise the reputation of the Craft in the view of all beholders.

Respectfully submitted,   J. BAKER, *Per Order.*

IN GRAND LODGE, *Voted*, That the thanks of this Grand Lodge be tendered to the Commissioners of the Prisoner's Fund, for the distinguished zeal and fidelity manifested by them in the discharge of their official duties, and for the ability and discernment displayed in all their proceedings, as delineated in the Report of their chairman, presented and accepted this evening. [Copy as recorded.]

To what has already been cited from the records in reference to charitable subjects, an extensive collection of extracts of a similar character might be added. It is not deemed important, however, to go further than to present the record of such proceedings as will show the variety of cases which have engaged the attention of the brethren. For this purpose, the subjoined quotations will be found sufficient:

March 3, 5814. "On motion, a committee consisting of Bros. Appleton, Howard and Morse was chosen to be called the committee on charity, to whom all petitions for charity are to be referred."

January 6, 5820. "The following letter was received from Bro. ——— ———.

Boston, January 6, 5820.

R. W. MASTER AND BRETHREN OF COLUMBIAN LODGE.—On the 3d day of June, 5813, it was *Voted* to present me with twenty dollars, which I received by a committee chosen for that purpose. I now have the means, and with much gratitude to my Brethren, return that sum to be united with the funds of the Lodge for charitable purposes.

Your friend and Brother, ——— ———."

February 3, 5820. "A committee was appointed consisting of the committee of charity, to confer with similar committees from other Lodges on the subject of granting relief to the brethren sufferers by the late fire at Savannah, that committee was invested with power to give from the funds of Columbian Lodge, a sum not exceeding fifty dollars if found expedient."

October 14, 5823. "A communication was received from the M. W. Grand Lodge, on the subject of establishing a Masonic asylum for female orphans,—read and committed to R. W. Bros. Daniel Baxter, David Moody and Samuel Smith."

November 7, 5844. "Bros. G. G. Smith, Baxter, Baker, Stevens and Thacher, were appointed a committee to consider and report on some plan to make more effective the charity of the Lodge."

May 1, 5845. "On motion of Bro. Stevens, *Voted*, That fifty dollars be placed at the disposal of a committee, to be distributed at their discretion among the Masonic sufferers by the late disastrous fire at Pittsburgh. Bros. Baker, the Secretary, and Stevens, were appointed the committee."

June 5, 5845. "The committee on the Pittsburgh sufferers made a report to the effect that no money was necessary to be distributed among the Masons in that place,—no Mason having materially suffered. On motion, it was *Voted* to send twenty-five dollars to the Lodge in Pittsburgh, to aid in the erection of a Masonic Hall."

April 2, 5846. "Bro. Smith, chairman of the committee on extending the charity of the Lodge, appointed November 7, 1844, submitted a report and resolutions,—report accepted, and resolutions laid on the table."

May 20, 5852, "A circular was received from the Grand Lodge of California, setting forth the amount and nature of its embarrassments, whereupon it was *Voted*, that the Treasurer be authorized to pay to the Grand Treasurer of M. W. Grand Lodge of Mass. the sum of twenty-five dollars, to be by him forwarded to the Grand Lodge of California."

September 15, 5853. "An application was received from the Board of Relief of New Orleans. On motion of Bro. Stevens, the R. W. Master was authorized to draw upon the Treasurer for the sum of fifty dollars."

October 5, 5854. "A communication from a committee of King Solomon's Lodge, of Waldoboro', Maine, in relation to the late disastrous fire at that place, was referred to the first three officers, with full powers."

October 11, 5854. "The committee to whom was referred the petition of King Solomon Lodge, of Waldoboro', Maine, reported that they had granted the sum of twenty-five dollars."

Early in the year 5819, measures were taken by the Masonic societies, in Boston, to form a board, consisting of delegates from each, to give aid to distressed brethren, and more particularly to the foreign or stranger brother; or to those who were not affiliated as members with any particular Masonic body in this vicinity. The operation of this board during a period of thirty-seven years, has been most beneficial, and evinces the wisdom and foresight of its founders. R. W.

Henry Purkett was the first president of the board, R. W. Benjamin B. Appleton the first treasurer, and R W. Thomas Power the first secretary. The original report of the .committee ably and urgently sets forth the reasons that prompted the establishment of this joint committee of relief. It is referred to in the records of the Lodge in these terms:

May 6, 5819. " A report was received from the committee of charity from the several Chapters and Lodges in Boston, assembled for the purpose of adopting a uniform plan, for the more effectual relief of distressed Masons, which was read, accepted and placed on file.

The sub-committee, appointed at a meeting of the committees of charity, from the several Chapters and Lodges in Boston, held at Mason's Hall, April 16th, A. L. 5819, to take into consideration the necessity and importance of adopting a general plan, for the more uniform and prompt relief of distressed brethren of the Masonic family, particularly strangers, who, through misfortunes of various kinds, are reduced to want and misery, and compelled through necessity to apply to their brethren for immediate relief, have attended to that duty, and Report:

From the experience of a number of years, many unfortunate brethren, who, from shipwreck and other unavoidable accidents, are thereby reduced to extreme distress, have been compelled to wait a long time for the meetings of the different Masonic bodies, before they could obtain a sum sufficient to carry them to their friends, or the nearest place, where they could obtain further assistance ; which delay has obliged them to expend the greater part of the money collected, to pay their board, while petitioning the different Masonic bodies, and compelled to leave the town with a less sum than was really necessary; in which case the different Masonic societies have expended more than double the necessary sum, and the applicant not so effectually relieved as he would have been with half the amount given on his first application. Besides his detention and loss of time, the trouble of making a number of applications, particularly should a Brother be in a poor state of health, (which is often the case) shows the necessity of a regular system of granting relief to the truly worthy, in season.

Charity, the foundation of our Order, should be so wisely
dispensed, and guarded, that the unworthy, or impostor, cannot obtain a share of those funds appropriated for the use of
the widow and fatherless, and the poor worthy Brother.

The poor we have always with us, but charity demands,
that the worthy distressed stranger, should have speedy relief,
which is consolation to the afflicted soul, in the hour of distress.

Your committee, do therefore recommend, that the different
Chapters and Lodges, of which this body are members, be requested to authorize their several committees of charity, to
form a board, and organize themselves, under certain rules
and regulations, agreeable to the laws and constitution of
Masonry, under the name of Boston Masonic Board for Relief,
whose duty it shall be to grant relief to poor and distressed
brethren, their widows and orphans; not interfering with the
claims any individual may have on any particular society by
reasons of being a member or initiate therein.

The foregoing Report was unanimously accepted by the
several committees on charity, convened at Masonic Hall, April
28th, A. L. 5819.   And ordered to be laid before the different
Masonic societies for their concurrence.

ELIAS HASKELL, *Secretary.*"

It is regretted that the names of the members
of the original committees composing the board,
and their proceedings at the time of organization,
cannot be placed before the reader. The first
records are not in possession of the present secretary, and he has no recollection of having ever
seen them. If not destroyed, they may be, perhaps, restored to the archives in which things no
more valuable are sacredly preserved. The oldest
record now extant, is of the proceedings of the
meeting, held January 7, 5828. The oldest book
of account extends to the year 5826. The first
by-laws were adopted July 19, 5819. They
were beautifully transcribed into the record-book,
commenced in 5828, by the late Bro. Charles A.
Spring, who was the secretary of the Board at
that time.

CONSTITUTION

OF THE

BOSTON MASONIC BOARD OF RELIEF,

ADOPTED JULY 19th, A. L. 5819.

—

PREAMBLE.—The committees of Charity from the M. W. Grand Lodge; St. Andrews, and St. Paul's, R. A. C's; St. John's, St. Andrew's, Massachusetts, Columbian and Mount Lebanon Lodges, pursuant to authority derived from their constituents, do form themselves, and their successors in office, into an association by the name of the BOSTON MASONIC BOARD OF RELIEF, having in view the more effectually to relieve strangers who are Masons, who may need assistance, and do therfore propose the following articles as the basis of our union, viz. :

ARTICLE FIRST.—The Board at their first regular meeting shall elect by ballot, a President and Secretary, to continue in office until the next annual meeting, and shall annually, afterwards, elect by ballot, a President and Secretary for the year ensuing.

ARTICLE SECOND.—The Board shall meet in addition to the annual meeting, once in every three months, or whenever requested by any monthly committee, or by any five members, and at any meeting shall be competent, (provided each Institution is represented) to transact such business as may legally be brought before them, not inconsistent with the usages of Masonry or the by-laws of any of their constituent societies.

ARTICLE THIRD.—There shall be a monthly committee selected, to consist of one representative from each committee forming a part of this board, to be selected by the committee of the Institution of which he is a member, said monthly committee shall meet once a week or oftener if necessary, at such time and place as they may agree upon, and it shall be their duty faithfully and diligently to inquire into the qualifications, circumstances, and necessities of every applicant for charity during the month for which they were appointed, and carefully to ascertain what sum of money will effectually relieve the applicant, and the best mode of bestowing the same, and it is expected said monthly committee will individually and punctually attend to the duty assigned them, and take measures to procure the sum they may consider necessary to relieve in any particular case, by conference among themselves and consistent with the authority vested in the committee of which they form a part. The President and Secretary shall be, ex-officio, members of each monthly committee.

ARTICLE FOURTH.—The Secretary shall keep a record of all the proceedings of the board, preserve all documents and reports made or acted upon in the board, and all petitions and receipts for donations, and shall also keep an accurate account of the sums granted by the committee of each institution, to the end that he may be able to issue to each committee a copy of any note or paper, and also a certificate as a voucher for the settlement of their annual accounts with their societies respectively, for the sums expended by them in charity.

—

The preceding amended as follows, April 2d, 5821. *Voted,* That the 2d Article be so amended as to dispense with the quarterly meetings, and that two thirds of the Masonic societies present shall be competent to transact any business relating to the board, at any meeting, and that an additional article be added as follows :

ARTICLE FIFTH.—No monies shall be granted by the monthly committee, unless four of the Masonic societies shall be represented at the time the donation is made.

Amended Jan. 2, 1826, *as follows. Voted,* That the By-Laws be so far amended as to require that a Treasurer to the Board be annually elected, and that this election be on the first Monday in January.

No further changes were made in the by-laws until 5836, when they were revised.

———

BY·LAWS

OF THE

BOSTON MASONIC BOARD OF RELIEF,

ADOPTED JANUARY 5th, 1836.

—

Masonic Temple, Boston, January 5th, 1836.—The committee appointed at the annual meeting of the Boston Masonic Board of Relief, to examine into their By-Laws, and ascertain if any alterations in the existing code are necessary for the convenience of the members, and to a better understanding of the same, and to report at a future meeting of said Board—have attended to that duty, and respectfully recommend the following Code of By-laws, for the future government of the " Boston Masonic Board of Relief."

PREAMBLE.

The Committees on Charity from the M. W. Grand Lodge, and M. E. Grand Chapter of the Commonwealth of Massachusetts, together with St. Andrew's, and St. Paul's Royal Arch Chapters; St. John's, St. Andrew's, Massachusetts, Columbian, and Mt. Lebanon Lodges—do, by and with the advice and consent of the respective Institutions they represent—form themselves into an association to be styled " The *Boston Masonic Board of Relief.*" The object of said association shall be, to relieve the distressed worthy Brother Master Mason, his widow or orphans.

Article 1st. The Boston Masonic Board of Relief shall hold their annual meeting on the first Tuesday evening in January, at which time they shall elect by ballot a President, Secretary, and Treasurer.

Article 2d. A regular meeting of said Board shall be held on the first Monday evening of every month ; and the members present shall constitute a quorum. Thus organized, they are hereby empowered to transact such business as may be consistent with their duties as members of said Board, and not repugnant to the usages, customs, and landmarks of the Craft.

Article 3d. The President, Secretary and Treasurer of said Board, shall constitute a Standing Committee, with authority to act upon such applications as may require immediate attention, and to make such grants as in their judgment shall be necessary.

Article 4th. It shall be the duty of the Secretary to keep a faithful record of the proceedings of all meetings of the Board ; to notify the members, in due season, of all stated and special meetings.

Article 5th. It shall be the duty of the Treasurer to obtain by draft drawn on Treasurers of the respective Institutions represented at this Board, for such sums of money, as may have been voted to be expended in charity ; and at the annual meeting of this Board, he shall render an account of all monies by him received and expended, as Treasurer of said Board.

Article 6th. It shall be the duty of the President to preside at all the meetings, and to preserve that order and regularity so indispensably necessary in all assemblies convened for the transaction of business.

Article 7th. The President is hereby empowered to call special meetings of any part, or the whole of this Board, whenever, in his judgment, necessity shall require it.

Masonic Temple, Boston, February 1st, 1836.—The undersigned, Committee, respectfully present to the Boston Masonic Board of Relief, the annexed Code of By-Laws for their consideration.   W. C. MARTIN, } *Committee.*
                                  DAVID PARKER, }
A true copy from the original manuscript.
         Attest :   W. C. MARTIN, *Secretary.*

Masonic Temple, Boston, February 1st, 1836.—At a regular meeting of the Boston Masonic Board of Relief, the preceding Code of By-Laws were received and read ; whereupon it was unanimously *Voted,* That the preceding Code of By-Laws be, and the same are hereby adopted by said Board, for their future government.
         Attest :   W. C. MARTIN, *Secretary.*

The by-laws now in force were adopted in 5844, and read as follows :

"At the Annual Meeting of the Boston Masonic Board of Relief, held at the Masonic Temple, on Tuesday evening, January 2d, 1844, Brothers Hamilton Willis, John Hews, and John Flint, were appointed a committee to revise the By-Laws of said Board, and to report thereon at the next regular meeting.

Masonic Temple, February 7th, 1844.—In Board of Relief, the above named committee made the following report on the revision of the By-Laws of said Board.

Masonic Temple, Boston, February 7th, 1844.
BY-LAWS OF THE BOSTON MASONIC BOARD OF RELIEF.

Article 1st. Boston Masonic Board of Relief shall hold their Annual Meeting on the first Tuesday evening in January successively, at which time they shall elect by ballot, a President, Secretary and Treasurer.

Article 2d. A regular meeting of said Board shall be held on the first Tuesday evening of every month, and the members present shall constitute a quorum. Thus organized, they are hereby empowered to transact such business as may be consistent with their duties, as members of said Board, and not repugnant to the usages, customs and landmarks of the Craft.

Article 3d. The President, Secretary and Treasurer of said Board shall constitute a standing committee, with authority to act upon all applications that may require immediate attention; with power to make such grants, not to exceed ten dollars on any one application, as in the judgment of the majority of said committee shall be deemed necessary; and to report at the next regular meeting of the Board.

Article 4th. The President of said Board is hereby empowered to call special meetings of this Board, whenever in his judgment the occasion shall require it.

Article 5th. It shall be the duty of the Secretary to keep a faithful record of the proceedings of all meetings of the Board, to notify the members of all stated and special meetings.

Article 6th. It shall be the duty of the Treasurer to obtain by draft drawn on the Treasurers of the respective Institutions represented at this Board, for such sums of money as may have been voted, to be expended in charity; and at the annual meeting of this Board, *he* shall render an account of all monies by him received and expended, as Treasurer of said Board.

Article 7th. It shall be the duty of the President to preside at all meetings, and to preserve that order and regularity so indispensably necessary in all assemblies, convened for the transaction of business.

Article 8th. It shall be the duty of all committees, who shall be appointed to dispense charities, to report at the subsequent meeting.

Article 9th. No member shall have more than one vote at this Board.

Article 10th. These By-Laws, nor any part, shall not hereafter be altered or amended, except at the regular annual meeting of this Board, at which due notice of the proposed alteration or amendment shall be given, at least one meeting previous to any action thereon, and then only by a two-third vote of members present, all voting.

Article 11th. These By-Laws, or any part, shall not be suspended, except by a vote of two-thirds of the members present, voting thereon; and such suspension shall not hold for more than one meeting, except by a new vote.''

The whole expenditure of the Board from its organization to January, 5855, amounts to the sum of thirteen thousand, seven hundred and twelve dollars and sixty-five cents, less a small balance remaining on hand at the commencement of that year.

From July, 5819 to January, 5829, there were expended,					$6,297 29
" Jan'y 5829 to	"	5839,	"	" "	2,650 96
" Jan'y 5839 to	"	5849,	"	" "	2,212 40
" Jan'y 5849 to	"	5855,	"	" "	2,552 00
			Total,		$13,712 65

The amount contributed by each society is as follows, viz. :

Grand Lodge,...............................	$2,994 06
Saint John's Lodge,..........................	1,205 26
Saint Andrew's Lodge,........................	1,401 91
Massachusetts Lodge,.........................	1,341 41
Columbian Lodge.............................	1,431 33
Mount Lebanon Lodge,........................	1,361 73
Grand R. A. Chapter,.........................	943 74
St. Andrew's R. A. Chapter,...................	1,402 66
St. Paul's R. A. Chapter,.....................	1,440 55
Boston Encampment of K. T.,..................	190 00
Total,..........$13,712 65	

That portion of the preceding statement which dates previous to 5829, was obtained from a table of receipts and expenditures entered with the records for that year.

On the morning of November 1, 5846, the steamboat Rhode Island, on her passage from Stonington to New York, when about forty miles from the latter place, met with a tremendous gale, lost her rudder, and was so much broken and disabled that she was driven on shore at a point near Huntington Light, on Long Island, within about three quarters of a mile of the beach, between which and the boat the surf was rolling heavily, rendering all intercourse with the beach impossible. An attempt was made to get a line on shore, by five hardy Nantucket whalemen,—who were among the passengers,—who manned the life boat and put off. When they were at a distance of only twenty rods from the steamer, a wave struck the life boat and washed them into the sea, but they gained the line and were thus drawn safely on board the steamer.

In this perilous condition, the storm increasing, Brothers William D. Coolidge, and John L. Dimmock, of Columbian Lodge, with about one hundred and twenty passengers, passed the day, expecting every hour that the boat would go to pieces. Signals of distress were made, but it seemed impossible that any thing could live in such a sea and surf. At about three o'clock, P. M., a whale boat was seen putting off to the steamer, manned by five resolute men,—four as oarsmen, and one at the helm. They, however, reached the wreck, and first took off the women and children. They continued their efforts, and had made the eighth trip to the steamer, when being exhausted, the boat was dashed to pieces on the beach, but all who were in her were saved by the efforts of persons upon the shore.

Brother Dimmock went ashore on the sixth and Brother Coolidge on the seventh trip. Some sixty or seventy passengers, exposed to the greatest peril, were compelled to remain in the steamer, because the boat-men were exhausted, their boat stove, and night had set in. It was impossible to continue any further endeavors to remove them that night; but they were all safely conveyed to the shore on the following morning.

Brother Coolidge on reaching the beach, was met and greeted, masonically, by Bro. Harvey Bishop, who sent him to his house, where he was warmed, fed and comforted. In expressing his admiration of the generous conduct of the man who guided the frail boat eight times through the surf, it was discovered that he was the son, or son-in-law, of Bro. Bishop—Capt. Samuel C. Bunce; for whom and for the noble men who aided him, Bros. Dimmock and Coolidge will ever feel deep and sincere gratitude. It was a truly self-sacrificing act, and most gallantly performed; exciting the admiration and thankfulness of all who beheld it.

The wife of Bro. Bishop asked her husband who it was that went out and guided the boat; he modestly replied, "it was our Samuel." It was a proud moment for the mother. At about midnight, Bro. Harvey said to Bro. Coolidge,—"My Brother, God has been very good to you to-day; come and kneel down by my side and let us thank Him together." On the following morning the passengers tendered to Capt. Bunce a handsome sum of money, which he declined; saying, "that he did not do that for money." They were, however, determined to testify to him in some suitable way their appreciation of his conduct, and did so at a meeting at the Astor house, in New York city. Columbian Lodge, also sent to them a suitable mark of their acknowledgment of the kindness of Capt. Bunce, and of the brotherly care which Bro. Bishop showed to their brethren in distress.

December 3, 5846. " Brother Junior Warden related to the Lodge a very interesting account of his escape at the late disaster of the steamer Rhode Island, and his reception on shore by Bro. Harvey Bishop.

On motion of R. W. Brother Smith, it was *Voted*, To present to Bro. Harvey Bishop, a Medal with a suitable inscription, for the kind and brotherly reception of Bro. Coolidge, and one to Mr. ———, son of Bro. Bishop, for his noble and manly exertions in rescuing Bros. Coolidge and Dimmock, passengers of the steamer Rhode Island, on the 1st day of November."

February 4, 5847. " R. W. Master, in behalf of the committee appointed for that purpose, reported that a Medal had been procured for Bro. Harvey Bishop, and one for Captain Samuel Bunce, in token of the respect of this Lodge for the valuable assistance rendered by them to our Brothers Coolidge and Dimmock, on the 1st November last."

The medals bore inscriptions as follows:—

" Presented by Columbian Lodge of Freemasons, Boston, to Capt. Samuel Bunce, for his heroism and courage in rescuing two of the members of this Lodge from imminent danger in the gale of November 1, 1846.—G. M. Thacher, W. M. ; P. C. Jones, S. W. ; Wm. D. Coolidge, J. W."

" Presented by Columbian Lodge of Freemasons, Boston, to Bro. Harvey Bishop, in acknowledgment of his brotherly kindness to a member of this Lodge, after the gale of Nov. 1, 1846."

The correspondence is presented entire, as it expresses sentiments which ought never to be lost sight of by Masons :

Masonic Hall, Boston, Feb. 25, 1847.

Capt. SAMUEL BUNCE,—Dear Sir,—We have heard from our brethren, Wm. D. Coolidge and J. L. Dimmock, of the noble daring evinced by yourself and others during the gale on the Sound, of Nov. 1st, 1846, and we hardly know which most to admire, the courage and skill which was shown during that exposure, or the goodness of heart which prompted the exercise of it.

It proves to us that there is a feeling of brotherhood in man, that he will go on foot and out of his way to help a fainting brother, and at the hazard of his own, save a brother's life.

Your conduct, and that of those who aided you in this noble effort, has taught us to love man better as our brother, and to remember him oftener in our prayers to the universal Father.

Wishing you and yours every happiness which Faith in God, Hope in immortality, and Charity and love to all mankind will give you, we ask your acceptance of the accompanying testimonial of our gratitude and respect, and remain in bonds of true affection and fellowship,   Your friends,

Signed,   GEO. M. THACHER,
                     PETER C. JONES,
                     WM. D. COOLIDGE.

Masonic Hall, Boston, Feb. 25, 1847.

Bro. HARVEY BISHOP,—Our brother, William D. Coolidge, has communicated to us the kindness and brotherly efforts of yourself and family, in relieving his wants after the exposure to which he was subjected in the gale of Nov. 1st, 1846, on the Sound.

We are glad to hear that he was met with the friendly grasp of a brother of our Order, and that he found a true Masonic heart in the hour of his need.

Wishing you and yours every happiness which Faith in God, Hope in immortality, and Charity to all mankind will give you, we ask your acceptance of the accompanying testimonial of our gratitude and brotherly love towards you, and remain in bonds of fraternal affection,

Signed,   GEO. M. THACHER, *M.*
                     PETER C. JONES, *S. W.*
                     WM. D. COOLIDGE, *J. W.*

North Port, March 2, 1847.

Gentlemen :—I acknowledge the receipt of a letter from you dated 22d inst., stating that you have had two Medals prepared, one for Harvey Bishop, Esq., and one for myself, for the exertions and kindness in your behalf, in rescuing yourselves and others who were on board the steamer Rhode Island, Nov. 1, 1846. At the time, I felt myself highly gratified, (and even honored,) as well as amply paid, by the many thanks that I received, while performing my *duty,* in helping to convey to the shore the unfortunate passengers. But if I have merited that mark of respect with which you are about to present me, I assure you, it shall be duly appreciated. I have only to regret, that my health at that time, did not permit me to make greater exertions in landing the passengers.

If you can send them by any one of your friends who may be coming to New York, who will leave them with Medad Platt & Co., 184 South street, they will be safe ; or, if you think best, you can send them by mail, addressed to me.

I acknowledge the receipt of two dollars from W. D. Coolidge, by H. Bishop, which were added to the funds of A. G. Mulford, to be distributed to those who rendered assistance on that occasion.

Gentlemen, if either of you should visit this place again, I should be highly gratified to have you call on me, that we may renew our acquaintance, whilst I remain,

Yours respectfully,   Saml. C. Bunce,
P. M. at North Port, L. I.

To Messrs. W. D. Coolidge and J. L. Dimmock, Boston, Mass.

North Port, October 1st, 1847.

William D. Coolidge, Esq.—Dear Sir—I received your letter dated Sept. 20th, and was pleased to hear from you. I told Capt. Samuel Bunce to write to you, and let you know that I received the Medal voted to me through your brotherly esteem, by Columbian Lodge, and I did intend to have written myself after. But you mentioned in the last letter I received from you, that you intended to visit Long Island this summer, so I kept putting it off, hoping that I should have the pleasure of seeing you here with us ; but as I have been disappointed in that, I could not verbally acknowledge the receipt of the Medal ; but I now do it by letter, and shall ever esteem it and the donors.

I should be pleased by your giving my respects to the brethren of " Columbian Lodge," and the following toast :

" Dear Brethren of the Columbian Lodge of Boston, I present you the TROWEL,—may it ever be kept bright, by spreading the cement of brotherly love and affection."

I shall expect to hear from you again, and I should like to know what evening your Lodge meets, so that I may keep you in remembrance.

We are all as well here as when you were with us, and I hope you and family are the same. Our dear friend, Brother Osborne, has been stationed up North River since last June.

Although I have been disappointed in not seeing you, I hope at some future time we will meet, and spend some time together ; but if Providence has ordered it otherwise, I hope we shall meet in Heaven.

Please give my love to Brother Taylor.

I remain, dear sir, your obliged friend and brother,

Harvey Bishop.

CHAPTER XIV.

THE VISIT OF LAFAYETTE TO THE UNITED STATES.—
HIS VISIT TO GRAND LODGE. — LAYING OF THE
CORNER STONE OF BUNKER HILL MONUMENT.—ITS
COMPLETION.—EXTRACT FROM HIS PUBLISHED AC-
COUNT OF THE CEREMONY. — HIS RECEPTION BY
MASONS IN ALEXANDRIA.

The great public event of the year 5824, was
the arrival of General Lafayette on a visit to this
country as the nation's guest. The government
of the United States, in conformity to the public
desire, had repeatedly solicited that distinguished
man to accept the hospitalities which the people
were anxious to extend to him, in acknowledge-
ment of his eminent services in the war of the
revolution. In compliance with this sentiment,
Lafayette determined, at the age of sixty-seven
years, once more to cross the ocean. He left
Paris early in July, 5824, accompanied by his son,
George Lafayette,—of whom the great Washington was god-father,—M. Levasseur, his secretary,
and one servant; and sailed from Havre on the
13th of that month in the ship Cadmus, bound to
New York. A national vessel of the U. S. was
placed at his disposal, but wishing to avoid all
appearance of ostentation, he chose a private
vessel. He arrived at Staten Island on the 15th
of August, and entered the city of New York the
day following, amidst the most enthusiastic demonstrations of public rejoicing. The press

throughout the Union announced his arrival ; the news spread with rapidity in every direction ; and preparations for his reception by the different states were at once commenced. During his sojourn of four days in New York, he was overwhelmed with invitations to visit numberless towns and cities. He left New York on the 20th of August and arrived in Boston, via New Haven, on the 24th, where he was received with great enthusiasm and splendor. On the 31st of August he departed from Boston on his great tour through the United States. At this time, railways did not exist : and, of course, a long journey by land required much time, and was besides, tedious and fatiguing. Still, such was the rapidity with which the General journeyed, that, at the expiration of twelve months after he landed upon the shores of America, he had been personally welcomed by nearly every state in the Union. On the 7th of September, 5825, he took leave of the authorities at Washington, preparatory to his return to France; and, receiving the affectionate farewell of the multitude assembled to witness his departure, he was escorted on board the steamer Mount Vernon, and conveyed to the U. S. frigate Brandywine, which awaited him at the mouth of the Potomac. His home-ward voyage, in this vessel, terminated on the 4th of October.

On the 5th of June, 5825, on his return from the South and West, he again visited Boston, for the purpose of assisting in the performances and festivities which were to mark the celebration of the battle of Bunker Hill, and the laying the cornerstone of the noble monument that now crowns the summit of that eminence. The seventeenth of June of that year, was distinguished more than ever before or since, for the extent, variety and brilliancy of the ceremonies with which it was honored. The whole population of New England seemed to have regarded the occasion as their festival; and the interest was general to make it one of joy and happiness. The presence of the illustrious Lafayette; the eloquence of the great Webster; the large and respectable body of Freemasons, clothed in their regalia; the banquet; the military; and the grand civic procession; attracted together an immense concourse of people, whose admiration of the display found utterance in enthusiastic plaudits.

The proceedings of the Masonic fraternity in honor of Brother Lafayette, as well as those in connection with the celebration, were of a highly interesting character. The Grand Lodge at their communication of December 8, 5824, adopted the following vote:

"On motion of R. W. Francis J. Oliver, *Voted*, That a committee of seven be appointed to prepare such arrangements for expression of gratitude and affection to our illustrious Brother La Fayette on his next visit to this city, as shall comport with the dignity of the Grand Lodge of Massachusetts, and is due to his distinguished services in the cause of our country and the freedom of men. The following were appointed on that committee: R. W. Francis J. Oliver, John Dixwell, Benjamin Russell, John Soley, Samuel P. P. Fay, Thomas Dennie, Joseph Baker."

The extracts taken from the books of Columbian Lodge show that they, also, participated in the general demonstrations of regard for the eminent brother. The official request of the Grand Master for them to accompany him on the seventeenth of June, is on file.

May 9th, 5825. "A communication was received from the Grand Lodge, requesting this Lodge to attend at the laying of the corner stone of the Bunker Hill Monument, on the 17th of June next. Whereupon it was *Voted*, That Columbian Lodge do attend on the above occasion, as a Lodge.

Voted, That Bros. D. Baxter, Jr., G. G. Smith, and H. D. Wolcott, be a committee to make such repairs in the regalia of the Lodge, as may be deemed necessary."

From the East of the Grand Lodge of Massachusetts. This 17th day of May, A. L. 5825. To the R. W. Master, W. Wardens and Members of Columbian Lodge, the M. W. Grand Master sends, greeting.

Whereas the Directors of the Bunker Hill Monument Association have requested the Grand Master of the Grand Lodge of Massachusetts to lay the corner stone of the contemplated Monument in ancient Masonic form, on the 17th of June next, with which request the Grand Master has consented to comply—You are hereby requested to accompany the Grand Master in the discharge of that duty on the day aforesaid, and bring with you, your jewels and badges of office.

Should you vote to attend as a Lodge, you are requested to send that information forthwith to the Grand Secretary.

There are some particulars to which the Grand Master requires your attention. All Master Masons should appear with white gloves, white aprons and blue sashes. The Grand Master, however, does not *order* this. A dark dress is recommended to be worn on the occasion above-named.

Several Lodges under the jurisdiction, will provide themselves with suitable banners, to be used on the occasion. Should you be desirous of adopting that measure, the Grand Secretary, on request, will furnish the size, form and emblems approved by the Grand Master. Notice will be given in the newspapers where you will assemble on the 17th.

For any further information on the subject, you will apply to the Grand Secretary.

By order of the M. W. Hon. JOHN ABBOT, Grand Master.

THOMAS POWER, *Grand Secretary.*

"A Special Meeting, June 17, 5825. Agreeably to an invitation from the R. W. Grand Lodge, the members of Columbian Lodge, with other invited brethren, assembled at the Hall of the Ancient and Honorable Artillery Company, at a quarter before 8 o'clock, A. M., and with the Grand and other Lodges, proceeded to Charlestown, and assisted in laying the corner stone of the Bunker Hill Monument."

At an early hour of the morning of the 17th, the Grand Lodge received Lafayette and the Grand Masters of other jurisdictions, in their apartments in the Old State House. The scene was in the highest degree grand and commanding. The account of this ceremony, and of the performances, afterwards, is taken from the records of the Grand Lodge.

"In Grand Lodge, M. W. John Abbot presiding. Delegations from the following Masonic Institutions, invited by the M. W. Grand Master, were successively introduced by the Grand Marshal, viz. :

Grand Lodge of Connecticut, R. W. James M. Goodwin, Junior Grand Warden and Suite.

Grand Lodge of New Hampshire, M. W. James F. Dana, Grand Master and Suite.

Grand Lodge of Rhode Island, M. W. John Carlisle, Grand Master and Suite.

Grand Lodge of Vermont, M. W. Phineas White, Grand Master and Suite.

Grand Encampment of Rhode Island and Massachusetts, M. W. Henry Fowle, Grand Master and Suite.

Grand Royal Arch Chapter of Massachusetts, M. E. Paul Dean, Grand High Priest and Suite.

Grand Royal Arch Chapter of Maine, E. Nathaniel Coffin, Dep. Grand High Priest and Suite.

M. W. Samuel J. Reed, Grand Master of the Grand Lodge of New Jersey, was present and introduced by the Grand Marshal.

The following R. W. Brethren, to wit, Benjamin Russell, Francis J. Oliver, Samuel P. P. Fay, John Dixwell, and Henry Purkett, were chosen a committee to wait upon R. W. Bro. Lafayette, and request him to visit the Grand Lodge.

At 15 minutes past 8 o'clock, A. M., the above committee attended R. W. Bro. Lafayette to the Hall, and introduced him to the M. W. Grand Master. The Grand Master then addressed Bro. Lafayette, who made a reply thereto.

The officers of the Grand Lodge and the several distinguished visitors above-named, were then successively introduced by the Grand Marshal to Bro. Lafayette.

Bro. Lafayette retired to join the civil procession.

At 9 o'clock, the M. W. Grand Master made known the request of the Bunker Hill Monument Association, that he would lay the corner stone of the contemplated Monument in ancient Masonic form. That in consequence thereof, he had caused the officers of the Grand Lodge to be called together to assist him in performing that duty; and that he had invited the presiding officers of the Grand Institutions in New England to be present with their officers.

The Grand Master directed the Grand Marshal to form a procession to repair to the Common, there to join the civil procession, and proceed to Bunker Hill, in Charlestown.

The Master Masons having assembled at Faneuil Hall, the Royal Arch Masons at Concert Hall, and the Knights Templars at the Armory and Refreshment Hall, the Grand Marshal, assisted by R. W. Bros. William Ingalls and Samuel L. Knapp, on horseback, with twelve other Deputy Marshals, on foot, formed a Grand Masonic Procession, in the following order :—

Two Grand Pursuivants;

Entered Apprentices;

Fellow Crafts;

Master Masons;

Tylers;

Stewards;

Junior Deacons;

Senior Deacons;

Marshals of Lodges;

Secretaries;

Treasurers;

Junior and Senior Wardens;

(Wardens' Banner;)

Past Masters :

(Past Masters' Banner;)

Grand Royal Arch Chapters of Maine, Vermont, New Hampshire, Massachusetts, Connecticut and Rhode Island;

Grand Encampments of Vermont, R. Island and Massachusetts;

Presiding Masters;

(Presiding Masters' Banner;)

Rev. Clergy of the Fraternity;

Grand Lodges of Maine, Vermont, Rhode Island, New Hampshire and Connecticut;

Music;

Grand Tyler;

Two Grand Stewards, with white rods;

Banner of the Order of Architecture; | Grand Lodge Banner; | Banner of the Implements of the Craft;

Silver Vessel with Wine; | Golden Vessel with Corn; | Silver Vessel with Oil;

Globe; | Principal Architect, with Square, Level and Plumb; | Globe;

District Deputy Grand Masters;

Rec. Grand Secretary; Grand Treasurer; Cor. G. Secretary;

G. Chaplain; Bible, Square and Compasses; G. Chaplain;

Past Grand Wardens;

Past Grand Masters;

Gr'd Marshal. {
Three Burning Tapers;
Senior Grand Warden; Deputy Grand Master; Junior Grand Warden;
Book of Constitutions;
Senior G. Deacon; GRAND MASTER; Junior G. Deacon;
}

Grand Sword Bearer;

Two Grand Stewards.

A number of Master Mason Lodges having provided themselves with appropriate banners, the Master Masons were arranged in divisions corresponding with the number of banners, which were placed in the intervals. A large proportion of the Master Masons were clothed with plain white aprons, white gloves and blue sashes.

The Grand Royal Arch Chapter of Maine appeared in full costume, with elegant banners. The Grand Royal Arch Chapter of Massachusetts was organized in ample form, and appeared with their elegant banner and flanking banners. A number of Chapters under the Grand Chapter of Massachusetts, several of which were provided with appropriate banners, were arranged under the Grand Chapter. All the Royal Arch Masons were arranged in procession, under R. W. Bro. Roulstone, their Marshal.

The Knights Templars appeared under the command of R. W. Bro. Henry Fowle, Dep. Gen. Grand Master of Knights Templars. They were in full dress, and displayed the banners of Knights Templars and Knights of the Red Cross. Six Knights, with lances, preceded, bearing on the points of their lances white pennants, on which were painted the names of the six New England States. A front and rear guard, and also the guards of the banners, were armed with lances. All the Knights Templars were arranged in procession, under R. W. Bro. William J. Whipple, their Marshal.

The Masonic Procession being formed in the foregoing order, proceeded to the Common, where a general procession was formed as follows :—

Military Escort ;
The Grand Lodge of Massachusetts ;
Survivors of Bunker Hill Battle, in open carriages ;
The President of Bunker Hill Monument Association ;
Chaplains ;
Directors and Officers of Bunker Hill Monument Association ;
The President of the United States, in a carriage ;
Gen. Lafayette, in a carriage ;
Officers of the Revolutionary Army ;
His Excellency the Governor of Massachusetts ;
Lieutenant Governor and Council ;
The Hon. the Senate and House of Representatives ;
Secretary and Treasurer ;
Governors of other States in the Union ;
Heads of Departments of the United States ;
Senators and Representatives of the United States ;
Judges of Supreme Court of United States and State Courts ;
Invited Strangers ;
Invited Guests ;
Presidents of Colleges and Clergy ;
Officers of the U. S. Army ;
Officers of the U. S. Navy ;
Officers of Militia ;
Members of the Association.

The procession then moved to Charlestown, and having arrived at the Square on which it was intended to erect the Monument, the whole was enclosed by the troops. Near the place intended for the corner stone, was erected by the Fraternity, a lofty Triumphal Arch, on which was inscribed the following :—' The Arts pay homage to Valor.' Through this Arch the whole body of Masons passed, and took up a position on the right of the Square, the Grand Master in front.

The President of the Association then requested the Grand Master to proceed and lay the Corner Stone. The Grand Master, accompanied by the Deputy Grand Master, Grand Wardens, Grand Treasurer and Secretaries, Grand Chaplain and Past Grand Masters, and attended by the Grand Marshal, advanced to the place intended, where the President of the Association and R. W. Bro. Lafayette met them. The Grand Marshal, by direction of the Grand Master, commanded silence to be observed during the ceremonies. The working tools were presented to the Grand Master, who applied them to the stone and passed them to R. W. Bro. Lafayette and the President of the Association, who severally applied them, and then the Grand Master declared it to be ' well formed, true and trusty.' The stone was then raised, and the Grand Chaplain repeated the following :—

' May the Great Architect of the Universe grant a blessing on this foundation stone, which we have now laid ; and by His Providence enable us to finish this and all our works with skill and success. Glory be to God in the highest.'

(Response by the Brethren.)

' As it was in the beginning, is now and ever shall be.'

The Grand Treasurer then placed under the stone a silver plate, on which was engraved the name of the Grand Master, the names of the officers of the Association, the time and occasion of laying the stone, etc.

The three vessels containing Corn, Wine and Oil, were presented to the Grand Master, who poured their contents in succession on the stone, and said :—

' May the all-bounteous Author of Nature bless the inhabitants of this place with all the necessaries, conveniences and comforts of life ; assist in the erecting and completing of this building ; protect the workmen against every accident ; and long preserve this structure from decay. And grant to us all, in needed supply, the Corn of nourishment, the Wine of refreshment and the Oil of joy.'

He then struck the stone thrice with his mallet, and the honors of Masonry were given.

The Grand Master delivered the working tools to Bro. Alexander Parris, the Master Workman, intrusting him with its superintendence and direction of the work.

The Fraternity then moved to seats prepared on the north side of the hill, in front of which was erected an extensive semi-circular building open in front, in the centre of which the Grand Master, the President of the Association and its officers were accommodated. An Oration was pronounced by the President of the Association.

A procession was then formed, which proceeded to an extensive range of tables, where refreshments were prepared.

The celebration of the completion of the Bunker Hill monument, occurred June 17, 5843,—on the sixty-eighth anniversary of the battle. The procession and ceremonies were grand, and characterized by much splendor. The President of the United States, Hon. John Tyler, with his suite, was present. Daniel Webster was the orator of the occasion, as he had been of that which commemorated the laying of the corner-stone of the edifice. There were about seven hundred Masons in the procession, who were marshalled by the present Grand Master, Winslow Lewis, M. D. On the 24th June, 5845, the fraternity assisted at what might be properly termed the Masonic completion of that structure. The ceremonies and festivities were under the auspices of King Solomon's Lodge of Charlestown. The ceremony of depositing a model of the original monument within the massive stone obelisk that now designates the battle-ground, was the main feature of the day. The original monument was erected by that Lodge, and the proceedings attending the placing of the model were properly directed by them. The chief marshal on this occasion, also, was Dr. Lewis, who was assisted by Bros. Newell A. Thompson and Peter C. Jones. Full accounts of these celebrations are given in Bro. Moore's Magazine.

After the return of Lafayette to France, his secretary, M. Levasseur, published an account of their travels in the United States. What he relates concerning the reception by the Grand Lodge, the public procession and the laying of the corner-stone, is in these words.:

Dès le matin du 17, la grand loge de Massachusetts s'était assemblée, et le général avait été la visiter. Des députations des grandes loges de Maine, New Hampshire, Rhode Island, Connecticut, Vermont et New Jersey, les officiers du chapitre et les chevaliers du temple, s'étaint réunis à eux, de tous les points de la Nouvelle-Angleterre, et l'on peut croire que c'st

la plus grande assemblee maçonnique qui ait eu lieu depuis la
fondation de l'ordre, puisqu'elle se composait de quatre à
cinq mille membres.

A dix heures, les maçons, seize compagnies d'infanterie, un
corps de cavalerie, les différentes corporations et les autorités,
se rendirent à l'hôtel de ville, où le cortége fut formé.

Les grands maîtres et députés de l'ordre maconique allèrent
prendre le général à la maison Lloyd oùil était logé, et où il
s'était rendu au sortir de la séance maçonnique.

Le cortége se mit en marche à dix heures et demi pour
Bunker's-Hill. Il était composé d'environ sept mille per-
sonnes. Deux cents officiers ou soldats de l'armée révolu-
tionnaire y figuraient; quarante vétérans de l'affaire de
Bunker's-Hill occupaient huit voitures, et portaient écrit sur
leur portrine: 17 *juin* 1775. Venait ensuite le général
Lafayette, dans une calèche attelée de quatre chevaux blancs.
Cette colonne s'avançait au son de la musique et des cloches,
au milieu de deux cents mille citoyens accourus de tous les
états de l'Union, tandis que des salves d'artillerie la saluaient
à de courts intervalles. Elle arriva à Bunker's-Hill à midi
et demi, et bientôt tout le monde fut placé dans un ordre
régulier, sur la colline où doit être élevé le monument,
témoignage de la reconnaissance nationale envers les premiers
héros de la révolution. * * * * * * *

Au meme lieu où combattirent leurs concitoyens, où
succomba Warren, les francs maçons d'Amerique ont voulu
élever un monument pour perpétuer la mémoire de ce
glorieux évènement. Toute la nation a pris part à ce noble
projet, et l'élève de Washington e été appelé pour solenniser,
par sa présence, cette cérémonie nationale.

Dans un coffre de fer furent mises des médailles et une
plaque d'argent, portant le programme de l'inauguration du
monument. La première pierre fut ensuite posée sur ce
coffre. Le grand maître ayant répandu du blé, du vin et de
l'huile sur la pierre, pendant que le chapelain prononçait une
bénédiction, donna ensuite l'ordre maçonnique d'achever la
construction du monument. Une salve d'artillerie annonça
la fin de cette partie de la cérémonie.

TRANSLATION.

Early on the morning of the 17th, the General attended a
meeting of the Grand Lodge of Massachusetts. Deputations
of the Grand Lodges of Maine, New Hampshire, Rhode
Island, Connecticut, Vermont and New Jersey, the officers of
the Chapter, and the Knights Templars, from all parts of

New England, were present: and it can be readily imagined that it was the greatest Masonic assemblage that had taken place since the Order was founded, since it was composed of four to five thousand members.

At ten o'clock, the masons, sixteen companies of infantry, a corps of cavalry, the various corporations and the authorities, repaired to the City Hall, where the procession was formed. The Grand Masters and deputations of the Masonic order, accompanied the General to his lodgings, in Lloyd's mansion, whither he went after leaving the Masonic meeting.

The procession moved at ten and a half o'clock for Bunker's Hill. It was composed of about seven thousand persons. Two hundred officers or soldiers of the revolutionary army were present; forty veterans of the battle of Bunker's Hill occupied eight carriages, and wore upon their breasts this inscription : ' 17th June, 1775.' Then came Gen. Lafayette in a calèche drawn by four white horses. This column advanced at the sound of music and of bells, in the midst of two hundred thousand citizens, gathered from all the states of the Union, whilst the roar of artillery was heard at short intervals. It arrived at Bunker's Hill at twelve and a half o'clock, and soon every body was placed in a regular order upon the hill, where the monument was to be raised, in testimony of the national gratitude towards the first heroes of the revolution. * * * * * * *

Upon the place where their fathers fought,—the same where Warren fell,—the Freemasons of America desired to erect a monument to perpetuate the memory of that glorious event. The whole nation has taken part in this noble project, and the pupil of Washington has been called upon to solemnize, by his presence, this national ceremony. Medals and a silver plate, bearing the programme of the inauguration of the monument, were deposited in an iron box. The first stone was then placed upon the box. The Grand Master, having poured corn, wine and oil upon the stone, whilst the chaplain pronounced a benediction, gave the Masonic order to complete the construction of the monument. The discharge of cannon announced the end of this portion of the ceremony.''

For the graphic description of the reception of brother Lafayette by the Masons of Alexandria, which is now for the first time presented in print, the brethren are under obligations to R. W. Bro. John B. Hammatt, who, at that time, was a resi-

dent of Alexandria, and was also the chairman of
the committee having charge of the ceremonies
of the reception. The first visit of Lafayette to
the city of Washington, was in the middle of
October, 5824; and his last, as has already been
stated, was in September, 5825; and it is probable, therefore, that the occasion delineated by
Bro. Hammatt, took place at the date last named.

"When our brother Lafayette visited the United States in
5824, on his arrival at Washington, the brethren of the
Masonic family in Alexandria being desirous to pay him some
attention, had a meeting and agreed to invite him to visit
them in that city in a Masonic manner. There were at
that time in Alexandria three Lodges and one Chapter, viz.:
1. Alexandria Washington Lodge, No. 22, W. Thomas
Simmes, Master. This Lodge was chartered by the Grand
Lodge of Virginia, and in the charter, Major Gen. George
Washington, late commander of the army of the United States
is named as the first Master; and in which office he served
several years. 2. Brooke Lodge, No. 2, chartered by the
Grand Lodge of the District of Columbia, W. Thomas Towers,
Master. 3. Evangelic Lodge, No. 8, John B. Hammatt,
Master, also chartered by the Grand Lodge of the District of
Columbia. 4. Brooke Chapter of R. A. Masons, chartered by
the Grand Chapter of the District of Columbia, R. W. John
B. Hammatt, High Priest. The chapter was composed of the
members of the Lodges in Alexandria.

These four societies appointed each its presiding officer to
constitute a committee to wait on brother Lafayette, and
make known to him the desire of the brethren of Alexandria;
and full powers were given to them to make all necessary arrangements. They consequently waited on him at Washington, and acquainted him with the object of their visit. He
replied that he was the Nation's Guest, and could not
accept any invitation until he had made his bow to the Governor of each state, for which purpose he should make a tour
through the states; that he should then return to Washington and spend some time as a private citizen; when, if it was
the desire of his brethren at Alexandria to then receive him,
he would be proud to visit them. After he had made the tour
of the states, and on his return to Washington, he informed
the committee of the fact, and that he was ready to comply

with their invitation. They immediately waited upon him and fixed the time for the visitation. It was agreed that he should be received in Washington Lodge, No. 22, as their hall was the largest and most convenient, besides it was the Lodge that his friend Washington had been connected with. Therefore, the members of the Lodges and the Chapter assembled there at the time assigned for the reception, and Washington Lodge was opened in due form, the Master, Dr. Simmes, presiding, and the members of the other bodies appearing as visitors.

At the time appointed, Lafayette, with those of his suite who were Masons, and several distinguished brethren from Washington, arrived, and were met in the reception room by the committee of arrangements. I inquired if he had his Masonic clothing with him; he said he had; and I then observed, that I was sorry for it, because the Lodge wished him to wear the badges I had in my hands. He at once recognized them, and in broken English exclaimed, emphatically and with emotion, that they were the clothing of his Brother Washington, and that he should be very proud to be allowed to wear it. He then remarked that when he returned to France, after the war of the Revolution, he was desirous to send some token to his friend, to remind him that he was not forgotten; and, that being unable to think of any thing that would be more acceptable to Washington, knowing his strong attachment to the Masonic Institution, he caused the sash, apron, collar and jewel to be prepared, and sent them to him in a box which he described. I told him that we knew the circumstance, and directed one of the stewards to fetch the box from the Lodge-room; and when it was presented to him he exclaimed, ' Ah, that is the very box!' I then informed him that the Lodge were acquainted with the fact that Washington wore the regalia during his life in remembrance of his friend in France; that, after his death, Mrs. Washington had presented the box and its contents to the Lodge; and that since that time the clothing had not been worn, but had been carefully kept in a glass case in the Lodge-room, and labelled—' the regalia of Brother Washington, presented by his friend General Lafayette;' and I further observed that it was the wish of the Lodge that he should appear in it on that occasion. When I put the sash and collar on him he said : ' My God, is it possible you will permit me to wear the regalia of my friend Washington! The queen of Great Britain; the emperor of France or Russia; nor any crowned head, could confer on me so high a compliment as

you now do ; it is far more highly prized by me than would
be the star and garter, or Roman eagle, or any other honor
that could be conferred on me.'   We then accompanied him
into the Lodge.   His reply to the address of the Master was
most appropriate.   He was then conducted around the hall
and introduced to each Brother.   Some considerable time was
spent in agreeable conversation, when a procession was
formed which escorted him to the hotel, where a dinner for
the company was provided ; also, rooms for Lafayette and
his attendants.   On the following afternoon he returned to
Washington.   During his visit, Washington Lodge made him
an honorary member, in order that he might be able to say
that he was a member of the same Lodge of which Washington
had also been a member.   When the committee entered the
Lodge with Lafayette, I observed to him that the Lodge
always associated him with their first Master ; that in the
East, over the chair, he would observe his friend ; and in the
West over the Senior Warden, he would see himself; and
that at every meeting they were associated in the minds of
the members.   The portraits thus brought to his attention
were excellent likenesses of Washington and Lafayette.''

CHAPTER XV.

BRIEF ACCOUNT OF GRAND LODGE.—PAUL REVERE.—
VISITS OF GRAND LODGE AND OF D. D. G. MASTERS.—
COMMUNICATION FROM GRAND LODGE OF ENGLAND.—
GRAND LECTURERS.— CORRESPONDENCE WITH GRAND
MASTER.—MASONIC CONVENTION.—LIBRARY.—RECORD
EXTRACTS.—PETITIONS FOR NEW LODGES.

From the " Saint John's Grand Lodge," con-
stituted at Boston, in 5733, originated the first
Lodges in Massachusetts, New Hampshire, Rhode
Island, Connecticut, New Jersey, Pennsylvania,
Maryland, Virginia, the Carolinas, Newfoundland,
Nova Scotia and several of the West India Islands.
The present Grand Lodge of Massachusetts, though
bearing a different title, are, by regular succession,
the same institution, and may, therefore, be justly
denominated the parent of Masonry in America.
A short account of the " St. John's Grand Lodge ;"
of "the Massachusetts Grand Lodge," instituted
in 5769; and of the present Saint Andrew's
Lodge, of Boston, whose charter was granted in
5756, by the Grand Lodge of Scotland, may be
interesting.

Upon the application of a number of brethren
residing in Boston, a commission, dated April 30,
5733, was granted by the Right Honorable and
Most Worshipful Anthony, Lord Viscount Montagu, Grand Master of Masons in England, by
which Henry Price, of Boston, was constituted and
appointed Provincial Grand Master for New Eng-

land.   In 5734, he received orders from the Grand
Lodge of England to establish Masonry in all
North America.   On the 30th July, 5733, the
Grand Master formed a Grand Lodge, and appointed R. W. Andrew Belcher, D. G. M.; R. W.
Thomas Kennelly, S. G. W.; and R. W. John
Quann, J. G. W., *pro tempore.*   This Grand Lodge
were organized under the designation of "Saint
John's Grand Lodge;" and were sometimes called
the "Grand Lodge of Modern Masons."   On the
day that this Lodge were constituted, they granted
a charter for a Lodge in Boston who were originally styled "the first Lodge in Boston," but
subsequently, "Saint John's Lodge;" which
name they still retain.   This is probably the
oldest subordinate Lodge in America.

In 5734, a petition was presented to Saint
John's Grand Lodge by Benjamin Franklin and
several brethren residing in Philadelphia, for a
constitution for holding a Lodge there, which
was granted, and R. W. Benjamin Franklin was
appointed their first Master.*   The Grand Masters
were as follows, viz., 5733, Henry Price; 5737,
Robert Tomlinson; 5744, Thomas Oxnard; 5755,
Jeremy Gridley; 5767, Henry Price, *pro tem.;*
5768, John Rowe; 5790, John Cutler, *pro tem.*

In 5756, a number of brethren petitioned the
Grand Lodge of Scotland for a charter of erection;
and their prayer having been granted, they received a charter, dated the 30th of November of
that year, from "Sholto Charles Douglas, Lord
Aberdour, Grand Master of the Free and Accepted
Masons of Scotland, with the consent of the

---

* Hist. R. W. Thaddeus M. Harris.

brethren of the Grand Lodge of Scotland," constituting and erecting them into "a Mason Lodge,
under the name, title and designation of the
Lodge of St. Andrew's, to be held in Boston, at
New England." This is the origin of the present
St. Andrew's Lodge. "The establishment of
this Lodge was discouraged and opposed by Saint
John's Grand Lodge, who imagined their jurisdiction infringed by the Grand Lodge of Scotland.
They therefore refused any communications or
visits from such members of St. Andrew's Lodge,
as had not formerly sat in their Lodges, and this
difficulty did not entirely subside for several
years." The Lodge were very successful, and
soon the roll of members contained the names of
many of the solid men of that time.

The flourishing condition of St. Andrew's
Lodge "soon led to great exertions for the establishment of an *Ancient* Grand Lodge in the prov-
inces;" and a commission was obtained from the
Right Honorable and Most Worshipful George,
Earle of Dalhousie, Grand Master of Masons in
Scotland, bearing date the 30th day of May, 5769,
appointing Joseph Warren to be Grand Master of
Masons in Boston, New England, and within one
hundred miles of the same." The Grand Master
organized afterwards the Grand Lodge by ap-
pointing R. W. Jeremiah French, S. G. W.; R. W.
P. Molesworth, J. G. W.; Thomas Crafts, Grand
Treasurer; William Palfrey, Grand Secretary.
A petition was granted in 5770, to establish a
new Lodge in Boston, under the designation of
"Massachusetts Lodge." In 5772, R. W. Joseph
Warren was appointed by the Grand Master of
Scotland, Grand Master of Masons for the conti-

nent of America. General Warren continued to be the Grand Master of this Grand Lodge until the time of his death on the 17th June, 5775. His successor was Joseph Webb who was elected in 5777, and served until 5778, when Dr. John Warren succeeded him. Brother Webb was again chosen in 5784, and continued in office until he died, in 5787, when Moses M. Hays was elected. Bro. Hays was the last G. Master of this Grand Lodge. In 5783, it was resolved that this Grand Lodge be hereafter known and called by the name of· "the Massachusetts Grand Lodge of Ancient Masons," also that the Grand Master, for the time being, be desired to call in all charters which were held under the jurisdiction of the late Grand Master Joseph Warren, Esq., and return the same with an endorsement thereon, expressive of their recognition of the power and authority of this Grand Lodge. St. Andrew's Lodge until now had been under the jurisdiction of this body, but on the 4th of March, 5784, "the G. Master communicated a letter from the Secretary of Saint Andrew's Lodge, expressing the determination of the brethren to retain their ancient charter from Scotland, and to consider themselves no longer subject to the control of this Grand Lodge."*

"At the communication of the Massachusetts Grand Lodge, held March 2. 5787, a committee was appointed to confer with Saint John's Grand Lodge, upon the subject of a perfect Masonic union throughout the Commonwealth of Massachusetts. This committee held a conference with the officers of the other Grand Lodge, soon after their appointment; but nothing of importance was effected.

At the meeting of the Massachusetts Grand Lodge of December 5, 5791, a committee was appointed, agreeably to

* Hist. R. W. Thaddeus M. Harris.

the vote passed at a former meeting, to confer with the officers
of Saint John's Grand Lodge, upon the subject of a complete
Masonic union throughout this Commonwealth, and to report
at the next quarterly communication.

A special meeting of Saint John's Grand Lodge having been
called, January 13, 5792, to consider the vote, and hear the
committee of the Massachusetts Grand Lodge respecting a
complete Masonic union throughout the Commonwealth:
whereupon, *Voted*, That a committee be chosen to confer with
said committee, and promote the proposed union, provided it
can be effected upon true Masonic principles.

In Saint John's Grand Lodge, March 2, 5792, the committee
appointed at the last meeting, for the purpose specified in the
votes then passed, report, That the joint committee, in pursuance of the trust reposed in them, have proceeded to draft a
number of rules and regulations for the organization and
government of a Grand Lodge, which they submit to the
deliberation of the Lodge. These being read by the Secretary,
it was *Voted*, unanimously, that the report of the committee
be accepted, and that a Grand Lodge be held on the Monday
then next, to carry the same into effect. Accordingly, on
March 5th, Saint John's Grand Lodge again met, and agreeably to the new Constitution, the Lodge proceeded to the
choice of seven electors, and nominated a list of candidates for
officers. After adjusting whatever else it was deemed proper
to attend to, previous to the intended incorporation, the
Lodge were closed in due form.

On the same day, March 5, 5792, in the Massachusetts
Grand Lodge, a Constitution and laws for associating the
two Grand Lodges, as agreed to by the Saint John's Grand
Lodge, were read, and deliberately considered, and the question for a concurrence being taken, the same were unanimously agreed to. The Grand Lodge then proceeded to
nominate a list of candidates for officers, and to appoint
electors as proposed in the said Constitution."

The first section of the first article of the new
Constitution declared the object of the union,
and the manner of organizing the new Grand
Lodge :

"In the year of Masonry 5792, the *Saint John's Grand
Lodge*, and the *Massachusetts Grand Lodge*, by their committee
of conference duly appointed, having deliberately considered

the present state of Masonry, and being desirous to promote
the benevolent designs of this ancient Fraternity ; do mutually agree in a complete Union of the Grand Lodges aforesaid :
And, that impartiality and candor may mark the original
proceedings of such coalition, each Grand Lodge shall assemble
at their respective places on the first Monday of March, and
shall nominate a Grand Master, Grand Wardens, Grand
Treasurer and Grand Secretary ; after which they shall each
appoint seven electors, to meet in convention, and from such
list of candidates to form a new Grand Lodge."

The fourteen electors were Paul Revere, Sam-
uel Barrett, James Jackson, Samuel Dunn, Job
Prince, Thomas Dennie, William Shaw, Thomas
Farrington, John Lowell, Aaron Dexter, William
Scollay, Samuel Bradford, William Little and
Caleb Swan.   On the 19th June, 5792, they assembled in convention agreeably to the Constitution, and after duly considering the respective
lists of candidates, they unanimously elected the
following brethren, officers of the Grand Lodge ;
M. W. John Cutler, G. M. ; R. W. Josiah Bartlett,
S. G. W. ; R. W. Mungo Mackay, J. G. W. ; Sam-
uel Parkman, Treasurer ; Thomas Farrington, G.
Secretary.   The R. W. Brother John Warren,
M. D. installed the Grand Master.   The title of
the Lodge was determined by the third article of
the Constitution, which declared that they " shall
forever hereafter be known by the name of *The
Grand Lodge of the Most Ancient and Honorable
Society of Free and Accepted Masons for the
Commonwealth of Massachusetts.*"   By the Constitutions adopted October 11, 5843, the title was
slightly changed.
    All the subordinate Lodges in Massachusetts,
commissioned by either of the Grand Masters or
Grand Lodges, acknowledged the jurisdiction of

the new organization. St. Andrew's maintained their allegiance to the Grand Lodge of Scotland until December 11, 5809, when they also became a member of a system designed to produce harmony and due Masonic subordination throughout the Commonwealth.

The powers of the Grand Lodge are concisely stated in the Constitutions, published in 5843.

" By the Ancient Constitutions and usages of Freemasonry, the Grand Lodge, as the supreme Masonic authority in this Commonwealth, is invested with certain original, essential and unalterable powers and privileges. Among these, is the power of enacting laws and regulations for the government of the Craft, and of altering, repealing and abrogating them : of establishing and preserving a uniform system of work and lectures ; of issuing dispensations and charters for new Lodges, and of suspending or revoking the same, for unmasonic conduct, the non-observance of the regulations of this Grand Lodge, the non-payment of dues, or other neglect of duty. The Grand Lodge has also the inherent power of investigating, regulating, and deciding, all matters relative to the Craft, or to particular Lodges, or to individual brothers ; which power it may exercise either in itself or by such delegated authority, as, in its wisdom and discretion, it may appoint : but in the Grand Lodge alone resides the power of revoking the charter of Lodges and expelling brethren from the Craft."

Brother Paul Revere, who was Grand Master when the Dispensation and Charter of Columbian Lodge were granted, was an active and zealous Mason. He was initiated in St. Andrew's Lodge, Sept. 4, 5760, and raised Jan'y 27, 5761 ; was elected S. Warden in Nov., 5764, and Master, Nov. 30, 5770. In "the Massachusetts Grand Lodge," in 5777, 5778, and 5779, he was Junior Grand Warden ; in 5780, 5781, 5782, and 5783, Senior Grand Warden ; and in 5784, 5790 and 5791, he was Deputy Grand Master. After the union, he became Grand Master, and served in that office during the years 5795, 5796 and 5797.

An interesting and ably written biography of Bro. Revere, may be found in Vol. III. of the New England Magazine, edited by Brother Joseph T. Buckingham. This work was discontinued some years since. An abridgment of the biography presents the following facts:

"Paul Revere, or Rivoire, as his ancestors wrote the name, was born in Boston, in December, 1734, O. S. (January 1, 1735,) and died there in May, 1818, aged 84. His grandfather emigrated from St. Foy, in France, to the island of Guernsey; and his father, at the age of thirteen, was sent by his friends from that island to Boston, to learn the trade of a goldsmith, where he afterwards married, and had several children, of whom Paul was the eldest. Young Revere was brought up by his father to the business of a goldsmith, and made himself very serviceable in the use of a graver. Having a natural taste for drawing, he made it his peculiar business to design and execute all engravings on the various kinds of silver plate then manufactured. In 1756, he received the appointment of Lieut. of Artillery, and was stationed at Fort Edward, on Lake George, the greater part of that year. After his return to Boston, he married, and commenced business, as a goldsmith, which, with engraving and other mechanical and manufacturing arts, were objects of industry, from time to time, during a long and active life. He was one of a club of young men, chiefly mechanics, who associated for the purpose of watching the movements of the British troops in Boston, and acted an important part in the events which occurred about the 19th April, 1775. He says, in a letter he wrote to the Corresponding Secretary of the Massachusetts Historical Society, 'We held our meetings at the Green Dragon tavern. We were so careful that our meetings should be kept secret, that every time we met, every person swore upon the Bible, that they would not discover any of our transactions, but to Messrs. Hancock, Adams, Doctors Warren, Church, and one or two more.

After the British evacuated Boston, a regiment of artillery was raised for the defence of the State. In this regiment he was appointed a Major, and afterwards a Lieutenant Colonel, and remained in the service until the peace. When the

British left Boston, they broke the trunnions of the cannon at Castle William, (Fort Independence,) and Washington called on Revere to render them useful—in which he succeeded by means of a newly contrived carriage. After the peace he resumed his business as a goldsmith. Subsequently he erected an air-furnace, in which he cast church bells and brass cannon. The manufacture of copper sheathing also engaged his attention, and he was successful in this undertaking. Colonel Revere was the first President of the Massachusetts Charitable Mechanic Association, instituted in 1795. At the time of his death he was connected with many other philanthropic associations, in all of which he was a munificent and useful member."

The first visit of the Grand Lodge to Columbian Lodge was on the occasion of the installation of officers which took place April 14, 5796, (see page 185.) The second was for the purpose of examining into the condition of the Lodge—a duty afterwards devolved upon District Deputy Grand Masters.

March 2, 5797. " The Worshipful Master then informed the brethren, that from information he had received the Grand Lodge of Massachusetts intended visiting the Columbian Lodge at the next monthly meeting, and accordingly gave directions for additional accommodations to be provided."

March 4, 5797. " The following members were unanimously appointed a committee to make the necessary arrangements for the reception of the Grand Lodge at the next meeting, viz. : the Worshipful Master, Bro. Folsom and Bro. Amasa Stetson."

April 6, 5797. " The Lodge then received a message from the Most Worshipful Grand Lodge of Massachusetts, that they were waiting to pay them a visit. A committee, consisting of the following members, were appointed to wait on the Grand Lodge, and to conduct them in form to the Columbian Lodge, viz. : Bro. Gouldsbury, Hayden, Eaton, Stetson and Folsom.

The Most Worshipful Grand Master, Paul Revere, then proceeded to open the Grand Lodge in due form, and at his request the Secretary proceeded to read the By-Laws and part of the proceedings of the Columbian Lodge; then the Most Worshipful Grand Master, in behalf of the Grand Lodge, addressed the Columbian Lodge, and expressed his entire approbation of the By-Laws and the proceedings read by the Secretary, at the close of which he introduced a few observations respecting the fines mentioned in our By-Laws, and though not objectionable, might nevertheless, upon a reconsideration and recurrence to other authorities, be found to be more Masonic to omit them. This was, however, submitted.

The Grand Lodge then proceeded to transact some business before them, which took up a few minutes, when the Most Worshipful Master called off the laborers, and refreshment was brought into the Hall.

The Most Worshipful then gave out a number of public and Masonic toasts; the intervals were filled by songs from several brothers, accompanied by a band of music, who assisted in paying the honors due to our most respectful guardians.

The Most Worshipful Grand Lodge retired at 10 o'clock, escorted by the committee, in the same manner they were received.

The Most Worshipful Grand Master, when the Lodge had arrived to the room prepared to receive them, gave a message to the Master and brethren of the Columbian Lodge by their committee, to return the thanks of the Grand Lodge for the very polite and distinguished mark of honor conferred upon them."

Two of the members having been expelled from the Lodge for sufficient cause as was supposed, they appealed to the Grand Lodge. The grounds of the expulsion were investigated by a committee of the Grand Lodge, whose proceedings are thus noticed in the records of Columbian Lodge.

January 5, 5797. " The committee from the Grand Lodge, consisting of Bros. Revere, Bartlett, Crocker, Dunn and Shaw, came in and took their seats. The subject of Bro. —— was taken up, and fairly and candidly discussed. On motion, *Voted*, That the certificate handed to the W. Master, by Bro. ——, be read.

On motion, *Voted*, To record the certificate presented by Bro. ——, which, in substance, is as follows, viz.

This may certify that by a vote passed in Grand Lodge, it is considered by said Grand Lodge, that —— —— is a member of Columbian Lodge.   DANL. OLIVER, *Gr. Sec'y.*

The committee on the subject of Bro. ——, were generally of opinion, that he has not just ground of complaint, or claim to membership in the Columbian Lodge, and recommended to him to make no further application to the Grand Lodge on that subject, and to rely on the Columbian for his being received or rejected."

The following is the account of the third visit of the Grand Lodge. The characteristics of these ceremonies should receive particular attention. The combining of festivals with them, led to social intercourse, and promoted cordiality among the brotherhood.

November 1, 5798. "A message then came in from the Grand Lodge that they were in waiting and ready to visit Columbian Lodge.

A motion was then made that a committee of five members be appointed, preceded by the stewards with their wands, to conduct the Grand Lodge to Columbian hall. The following brethren were accordingly nominated and appointed, viz.: Bros. Coles, McCorristine, Folsom, A. Stetson, Martin and Davidson.

On entering the hall the committee paid the usual honors to the Grand Lodge.

The Most Worshipful Grand Master [Josiah Bartlett] then took the chair and opened the Grand Lodge in due form.

The Right Worshipful Master then gave a lecture on Masonry.

The Most Worshipful Grand Master then addressed the brethren in a most animating and masterly manner, in which the true principles of the Craft were strikingly displayed, and in which the duties of the order were beautifully inculcated. He concluded with expressing his entire approbation of the records and proceedings of Columbian Lodge.

The brethren being called to refreshment, the Most Worshipful Grand Master gave several well adapted toasts. The Grand Lodge was then closed in due form, and the Right Worshipful Master resumed the chair, and for a toast gave ' the Grand Lodge of Massachusetts.'

The Grand Lodge then retired to Brother Merrian's, re-escorted by the committee of Columbian Lodge, who received the thanks of the Grand Lodge, from the Most Worshipful Grand Master, for their politeness and attention, which was reported by their chairman to the Right Worshipful Master and brethren present."

Further record extracts than those here appended, are unnecessary ; as they will, with what has been before cited, illustrate what proceedings have been deemed appropriate in the presence of the Grand Lodge and Grand Master :

March 6, 5806. "On motion of Bro. Benson, *Voted*, That the R. W. Master, R. W. Bro. Folsom, and W. Bro. Bean be a committee to inform the Most Worshipful Grand Master and officers of the Grand Lodge, that this Lodge will be happy of their company on Wednesday evening next. Also, to invite such brethren of other Lodges as they see proper. Likewise to make suitable arrangements for their reception."

March 12, 5806. "At eight o'clock the M. W. Grand Master Timothy Bigelow, and officers of the Grand Lodge, gave notice of their being ready to visit. A committee, consisting of Bros. Folsom, Walker, Crooker, Thayer and Perkins, were appointed to wait on the Grand Lodge and introduce them, which was done in due form. A Grand Lodge was then opened. The R. W. Master of Columbian Lodge, then called the Craft to refreshment, and again to labor. An address from the Most Worshipful Grand Master, on the nature, design, and tendency of the principles of Masonry was delivered, and received with the accustomed applause. The M. W. Grand Master and Grand officers then retired, preceded by the committee in due form. Bro. Benson suggested the propriety of this Lodge procuring for the use of the Right Worshipful Master a cocked hat. On motion, it was referred to the same committee that was raised on the subject of Past Masters' jewels."

March 5, 5807. "A committee of three, viz. : Bros. Baxter, Swett and Kelly, were appointed to introduce our M.W.G. Master Timothy Bigelow and other grand officers. The Grand Master delivered an appropriate address to the officers and members of Columbian Lodge, and retired with the usual formality."

February 2, 5843. "The Marshal introduced to Columbian Lodge, M. W. Augustus Peabody, Esq., G. M. of the Grand Lodge of Massachusetts."

The law for dividing the Commonwealth into Masonic districts, and authorizing the Grand Master to appoint District Deputy Grand Masters, was passed by the Grand Lodge in 5801. The first appointments according to its provisions were made in 5803. The first deputy for the first district, was R. W. John Boyle, who continued in the position four years. It has been usual for the incumbent to remain in office during the term of the Grand Master appointing him. The visits of the D. D. G. M. to the Lodge have been annual; generally just previous to the close of the financial year. The records describing the first visit of Bro. Boyle, are so circumstantial, that the objects of it, and the ceremonies attending it, will need no explanation. All the succeeding visitations have been characterized by like proceedings; and, indeed, the propriety of the transactions as they at first occurred, admits of little improvement. The reports mentioned in the letter of the D. D. G. Master, referred to expulsions of members by certain Lodges within the State.

"To COLUMBIAN LODGE :— *Boston, Oct.* 25, 5803.

Brethren,—By direction of the Grand Lodge, the foregoing reports are communicated for your information. I would also inform you that I propose to make my first official visit to your Lodge, on Thursday, Nov. 3d, at which time you will cause the blank return which I sent you in June last, to be filled up. I am your affectionate Brother,
JNO. BOYLE, *D. D. G. Master.*"

November 3, 5803. "R. W. Bro. Folsom, Bro. Alford Richardson and Emerald Wheeler, were appointed a committee to inform the D. D. G. Master, [John Boyle,] and his suit, that Columbian Lodge was ready to receive them.

The D. D. G. Master appeared, escorted by the committee. After the ceremony usually passed on such occasions, he took the Chair.

The R. W. D. D. G. Master delivered a short address to the officers and members of the Lodge, and ordered his commission read. After which he ordered the proceedings of the last evening and the By-Laws, to be read.

The R. W. Master gave a lecture on Masonry. The Lodge was then called off to refreshment, when the R. W. D. D. Grand Master gave several appropriate toasts. The Lodge was then called to labor, when the R. W. D. D. Grand Master rose, and delivered a short charge to the officers and members of Columbian Lodge, expressing at the same time, his entire approbation of the records, By-Laws and proceedings of Columbian Lodge. He then withdrew with his associates, escorted by the committee, preceded by the stewards with their wands.''

The communication from the Grand Lodge of England is presented as a memorial of the past. The only copy of it preserved is that on the record book. It furnishes proof of the vigilance of the grand body from which it emanated, to suppress imposition and insubordination, and protect the Masonic institution from the evil designs of its enemies.

September 1, 5803. '' The following communication from the Grand Lodge was read, and ordered to be recorded on the Lodge Books, and placed on the files of the Lodge.
' GRAND LODGE OF MASSACHUSETTS.
In quarterly communication, Boston, June 13th, 5803, the subsequent admonition of the Grand Lodge of Great Britain, having been read, on motion, it was *Voted*, That the Grand Corresponding Secretary communicate a copy thereof to the several Lodges under this jurisdiction, for their information and guidance. A copy of record.

JNO. PROCTOR, *G. R. Sec'y.*'

Grand Lodge of the most Ancient and Honorable Fraternity of Free and Accepted Masons of England, according to the old Constitutions, united with the most Ancient and Honorable Grand Lodges of Ireland and Scotland, America, &c.

Worshipful Sir and Brothers,—Beware of certificates with the following words engraved under an arch top, viz.—Lodge 57, Royal Naval Lodge of Independence, (Wapping,) of the most Ancient and Most Honorable Society of Free and Accepted Masons of England, according to the old Constitutions.

We have no such Lodge, nor ever had any such, under our Constitution.

The above certificates are in other respects an imitation and piracy, taken from our Lodge certificates, engraved with emblems of Masonry : the armorial bearings of our Right Worshipful Grand Lodge and Seal, fabricated by an expelled Mason, and intended to pass and impose upon our ancient Order, particularly in America. It has become necessary to guard against imposition and designs of those, who, to gratify the spleen of a disappointed individual, and cover nefarious practices of others, are most actively employed in vilifying and attempting to bring into disrepute, the ancient Craft in these kingdoms.

Our Right Worshipful Grand Lodge,—supported by the most zealous protection of his Grace the Duke of Athol, our most noble Grand Master, who defended the cause of Masonry in the late Parliament,—watchful to protect our ancient rights and privileges, and to preserve our inestimable resources and charities, I hope and trust,—under the protection of Divine Providence,—will long continue to us that increasing prosperity, so interesting and honorable to our most ancient fraternity.

I remain, Sir and Brothers, your obedient servant and faithful Brother in Masonry,

ROBT. LESLIE, *Grand Secretary.*"

A grand lecturer of the Grand Lodge was first appointed in 5805. The usefulness of such an officer in establishing uniformity of work by frequent lectures among the brethren, and instructing the new officers in their ceremonial duties, admits of no question. An experience of half a century, more than corroborates all that was predicted would result from it, when the office was established. Its creation does not appear to have received, at first, the hearty concurrence of all the Lodges; and the objections were probably moved by dislike to what might have been deemed an unnecessary innovation upon customs previously existing, and that the lecturer might infringe upon the prerogatives of others.

August 1, 5805. "An order from the Grand Lodge, appointing R. W. Bro. Benjamin Gleason, Lecturer and Instructor, authorizing him to visit and instruct the several Lodges under the jurisdiction of the Grand Lodge of Massachusetts, in Masonry, for the purpose of introducing a more accurate and uniform mode of working and lecturing, was received and read,—which producing some altercation,— *Voted*, That a committee of five be chosen to inquire more particularly into the subject, and make report at the next meeting. R. W. Master, W. Bro. Crooker, R. W. Bro. Folsom, W. Bro. Swett, and Bro. Jenkins, were accordingly chosen."

June 5, 5806. "On motion of Bro. Bean, *Voted*, That this Lodge will pay to Bro. Gleason, the Grand Lecturer, fifteen dollars for his services in instructing the members of the Lodge in the Lectures."

Bro. Gleason continued in the office several years. After he retired, it remained vacant until 5842. The brethren who since then have discharged the duties of lecturers, have been Gilbert Nurse, John R. Bradford, Horace G. Barrows, Charles B. Rogers, Charles Bates and William C. Martin; all workmen of rare skill and ability. A short notice of each will discover how much the Order is indebted to them through the manifold labors they have severally performed. The notice of Bro. Gleason was published by Mt. Lebanon Lodge, of Boston, in 5854, in connection with their by-laws.

"Benjamin Gleason, Esq. was a native of Boston, born in 1777, and graduated at Brown University in 1802. He originated a system of teaching astronomy and geography, which was at one time quite popular; he travelled through a large portion of the United States and Canada, giving lectures on this subject in the principal towns, and received various flattering testimonials of the gratification resulting from his labors. Bro. Gleason became a member of our [Mt. Lebanon] Lodge June 2, 1807, and was admitted an honorary member Sept. 7, 1813. He held the office of Senior Warden in 1808-9, and '10, and succeeded Samuel Thaxter as Master in January, 1811. He was subsequently Master of King Solomon's Lodge, in Charlestown, several years. In 1805, he was appointed Grand Lecturer of the Grand Lodge of Massachusetts, which office he ably filled for some years. He died in Concord, Mass., in September, 1847, aged 70 years. Bro. Gleason was well known in the Fraternity, during the active period of his life, as a zealous and well-informed Mason.''

R. W. Gilbert Nurse was born in Royalston, Worcester County, Mass. in 5798. He was initiated in Fredonia Lodge, Northboro', Mass. in 5822; was Master of Mount Lebanon Lodge in 5826, 5827 and 5843; Master of Naphtali Lodge, St. Louis, Mo. in 5839; High Priest of St. Paul's Chapter, in 5831; Grand Commander of the Boston Encampment of K. T. in 5836; Grand Lecturer in 5842 and 5843; District Deputy Grand Master of the first district, in 5843; Deputy Grand High Priest of Grand Chapter in 5848, '49; and has served as Secretary of St. Paul's Chapter, the convention of High Priests, and of the Grand Lodge of Perfection; Recorder of the Boston Encampment of K. T., and of the Grand Encampment of Mass. and R. I. He has, besides, filled many and various minor offices in the Grand Lodge, Grand Chapter and Grand Encampment.

R. W. Bro. John R. Bradford was born in Boston, September 19, 5790. He received his first and second degrees in Mt. Lebanon Lodge, Boston, March 2, 5813, and the third, the 6th of April following. He was admitted to membership therein July 6, 5813; served as Junior Deacon in 5815, 5816 and 5817; and was elected Junior Warden Jan. 3, 5820, and Senior Warden Dec. 26, 5820, and Dec. 31, 5821. The degrees of Mark Master, Past Master and M. E. Master were conferred upon him in St. Andrew's Chapter, April 19, 5815; and the Royal Arch degree, the 17th of May following. He was admitted a member Feb. 7, 5816, and an honorary member April 5, 5848. He was master of the first V. in 5816, of the second, in 5834 and 5835, and of the third, in 5836; he was P. S. in 5817, '38, '40, '41, '42, and '43; C. of the H. in 5827, '28, '29, '30 and '31; King in 5821; and High Priest in 5823, '24, '25, '32, '33 and '46. In the Grand Chapter, he acted on the committee of finance of that body in 5825, '26, '27, '28, '29, '30, '31, '46, '47, '48 and '50; as Grand Marshal in 5829, '30, '31, '32, '33, '34, '35, '36, '37, 38 and 39; as Grand Scribe in 5840; and as Grand King in 5841, '42 and '43. On the organization of the Boston Council of Royal and Select Masters, in 5817, Bro. Bradford served as secretary. He was appointed Sentinel of that body in 5817; was elected R. I. G. Master in 5824 and 5828; M. I. Grand Master in 5830, '31, '32, '33, '34, '35, '36, '37, '38, '39 and 40; and was C. of the Council in 5841 and 5842. In 5829 he was chosen Secretary of the board of directors of Masonic apartments, and served in that capacity several years. He was Junior Grand Warden of the Grand Lodge in 5846, '47 and '48. The many and important services which Bro. Bradford has rendered in so many positions of usefulness, has gained for him the sincere regard and affection of the brethren.

The old landmarks of the Order could never be departed from in the slightest degree without his sternest disapproval.

W. Bro. Horace G. Barrows, M. D., was born in Boston, June 20, 5816. He received the degrees in Masonry, in the 5837, in Fellowship Lodge, in the town of Bridgewater, Mass. From 5843 to 5850, he resided in Chelsea, Mass. He was one of the founders of Star-of-Bethlehem Lodge, in that town, and was appointed their first Master. He presided over them three years, and was their secretary one year. He served one term as marshal of Mt. Lebanon Lodge, Boston. He received the degrees in St. Paul's Chapter in 5843, and the orders of Knighthood in the Boston Encampment of K. T. during the same year, and is now the organist of the latter body. In 5844, Grand Master Peabody appointed him Grand Lecturer, in which capacity he acted one year. The ineffable degrees were conferred upon him, in 5845, in the Boston Grand Lodge of Perfection; and during one year he performed the duties of Grand Secretary of that body. During his connection with Masonry, he has devoted his best efforts to advance its prosperity, and has held, temporarily or permanently, all the offices in a Lodge. A few years since, he delivered a public lecture in Waltham, on the occasion of the installation of the officers of the Lodge in that town. The audience was large and intelligent, and the address was effective in removing prejudices against Masonry, which before had prevailed to considerable extent among the citizens of that place.

W. Bro. Charles B. Rogers was born in Cambridge, Mass., February 2, 5816. He was initiated in King Solomon's Lodge, Charlestown, Feb. 1, 5839; where he was passed Feb. 14, raised March 14, and elected a member April 11, of the same year. The offices in that Lodge in which he has served, are those of Secretary, J. Deacon, S. Warden and Master. That of Master he filled in 5844, 5845 and 5851 with great credit. He was Grand Lecturer from 5844 to 5849 inclusive. He was a member of the Masonic Convention, held in Boston in 5849. On the retirement of Bro. Rogers from the station of Grand Lecturer, the Grand Lodge at their communication in Dec. 5850, passed the following vote :

" *Resolved*, That the thanks of the Grand Lodge be presented to W. Bro. Charles B. Rogers, for the courteous, faithful and acceptable manner in which he has discharged the responsible duties of Grand Lecturer of this Grand Lodge, during the last seven years, and that a copy of this resolution be forwarded to him by the Grand Secretary, in token of the appreciation in which his past services are held by the brethren."

W. Bro. Charles Bates was born in Boston, January 23, 5812. He died April 3, 5852. He was initiated into Masonry in Mount Lebanon Lodge, Nov. 29, 5841, and admitted to membership April 25, 5842. He was elected Senior Deacon of that Lodge Dec. 26, 5842, and served two years ; elected Senior Warden Dec. 30, 5844, and acted as such one year ; and was elected Master, Dec. 30, 5846, which office he held four years. He was appointed Grand Lecturer of the G. R. A. Chapter of Mass. Sept. 11, 5849, and for the years 5850 and 5851; in 5851, to the rank of G. C. of the H. in the same body ; and remained in the station to the time of his decease.

When he died, he was one of the Grand Lecturers, and secretary of the Board of Directors of Masonic Apartments. His amiable disposition and excellent character endeared him not only to the fraternity, but, also to a large circle of friends in general society.

R. W. Bro. William C. Martin was born in Cambridge, Mass. June 28, 5792. There is no blank in his Masonic life, for from the time of his initiation until the present hour, it may be said that his labors have been unceasing. He was initiated in Mt. Lebanon Lodge, August 28, 5826, and raised Nov. 27, 5826, and has been their Tyler from December 30, 5833, to the present time. In that capacity, he has, the greater part of that period, acted for other Masonic institutions, in Boston. He received the degrees in St. Andrew's R. A. Chapter, and was admitted to membership therein, in 5828. In this body, he held a subordinate, though important station, from Oct. 1, 5828 to Oct., 5832. In 5852, he was elected High Priest of the Chapter, and served one year in the office. He was appointed Superintendent of Masonic Apartments, in Washington Hall, June 7, 5830, and with the exception of about one year, he has since then occupied the place. He received the order of Knighthood in the Boston Encampment in 5830; the degrees of Royal, Select and Super-excellent Masters, also, in 5830; the ineffable degrees and that of Prince of Jerusalem, in 5844; and the degrees in the Consistory to the 32d inclusive, soon after. He was admitted to membership in Columbian Lodge, February 7, 5839, where he was Senior Deacon three years; he was elected an honorary member in 5851 and was appointed to represent that Lodge at the State Convention, summoned by the M. W. Grand Lodge, in 5849; the objects of which were to correct, restore, and arrange the lectures and work of the first three degrees. The report of the Convention to the Grand Lodge, was accepted and adopted, and is the authorized work at the present time. In 5849, Brother Martin was commissioned as Grand Lecturer, which office he has ably filled to this time. Having, in 5851, been invited to take membership in St. John's Lodge, he was by his own request, discharged from active membership in Columbian Lodge. At the annual meeting of the former, in December of that year, he was chosen Master; he was reëlected in 5852; and again elected in 5853. Since October 8, 5852, he has been the Secretary of the Board of Directors of Masonic Apartments. The preceding statement of Bro. Martin's masonic relations and services, though embracing a wide range of duties and performances, does but partially include his sphere of action. His efforts to assist and instruct individual brethren; his charitable errands of relief; his valuable aid on committees; and other deeds almost enumerable, promotive of the interests of the Craft, are all well known to the brethren, and recollected by them with gratitude. By many of the younger members of the fraternity, his little office under the stairway of the Temple, will ever be remembered as the seminary where they have received from the "old man," lessons full of knowledge and understanding.

The following correspondence is important, as it shows how far the letter of the Constitutions of the Grand Lodge can be departed from in the case of an application for the degrees from a foreigner residing temporarily within the jurisdiction.

To the Most Worshipful George M. Randall, Grand Master of the Most Worshipful Grand Lodge of Ancient Free and Accepted Masons of the Commonwealth of Massachusetts:

I respectfully submit for your judgment whether a person who owes allegiance to a foreign country, which he regards as his home, and where there is a regular Grand Lodge, can receive the degrees in Masonry within this Masonic jurisdiction, without the written permission of the Grand Master of that Grand Lodge. As bearing upon this inquiry, I would respectfully invite your attention to Section 5 of Article III. of the Constitutions of the Grand Lodge of this Commonwealth, the concluding portion of which is in these words :— "Nor shall any candidate be received from any other State, (he being a resident thereof,) where a regular Grand Lodge is established, without the written permission of the Grand Master of the State." Two points of inquiry are here suggested : 1st, Does the word " State " refer to a foreign State, or is its application confined to the States of this Republic? 2d, Does the term, " being a resident," mean a fixed or legal residence, or only a temporary residence or sojourning?

The case to which this inquiry has reference, is that of the application for the degrees of a gentleman well known to many of our brethren, and who is highly respected.

I would respectfully solicit your reply at your earliest convenience, as it may be necessary to act on this application during the present week.

I am respectfully yours,   JOHN T. HEARD,
                                Master of Columbian Lodge.

Boston, Feb. 20, 1854.

OFFICE OF THE GRAND MASTER OF THE GRAND LODGE OF MASS.
                    Boston, February 21, 1854.

To the W. JOHN T. HEARD, Master of Columbian Lodge,—
Dear Sir,—Your letter of inquiry came to hand yesterday.

Touching the two points, on which you ask my opinion, I beg leave to say : *First.* The word " *State*" in the fifth Sect. of Art. III. of the Constitution of the Grand Lodge of Massachusetts, is to be understood as referring to *the States of this Union,* and *not* to foreign countries. *Second.* The expression, " *being a resident,*" is to be understood in the sense of a "fixed or legal residence," and does not apply to one who is only a temporary resident or sojourner.

The practice has been in this State, to confer the degrees on candidates who are subjects of the English Government, when found "worthy and well qualified."

With much regard, I am yours fraternally,

GEO. M. RANDALL,
Grand Master of the Grand Lodge of Massachusetts.

A Masonic Convention met in Boston, February 7, 5849, for the purpose of comparing, considering, determining and adopting a uniform system of work and lectures. By a vote of the Grand Lodge the Grand Master was authorized and requested to summon the Lodges to elect one delegate each, who, with the permanent members of the Grand Lodge, were to constitute the Convention. Proxies were not admitted, and the delegates were actual members of Lodges. About sixty delegates were present, and the session continued two days. M. W. Edward A. Raymond, who was then Grand Master, was President; R. W. and Rev. Geo. M. Randall, Vice President; and R. W. Charles W. Moore, Secretary. The lectures were exemplified by Bros. Martin, Rogers, Bates and Jarvis. The work and lectures as now existing in the jurisdiction, were adopted by the Convention and subsequently established by the Grand Lodge.

" *To the W. Master of Columbian Lodge.*

W. Brother,—At the regular communication of the M. W. Grand Lodge of Massachusetts, held at the Masonic Temple, in the city of Boston, on the evening of the 27th day of December, ultimo, it was

Voted, That the Grand Master be authorized and requested to summon the Lodges under this jurisdiction, to elect one delegate each from among the most experienced and able of their members, to meet the Permanent Members of this Grand Lodge, in Convention, at the Masonic Temple, in Boston, on the *first* WEDNESDAY in February next, for the purpose of comparing, considering, determining and adopting, a *uniform system of Work and Lectures* for all the Lodges throughout this Commonwealth.

Therefore, in pursuance of the foregoing vote, you are hereby required, at your earliest convenience, to call a meeting of all the members of your Lodge ; and they, when assembled in open Lodge, are hereby directed to elect from the ' most experienced and able' of their number, one delegate, to meet in Convention, at the Masonic Temple, in Boston, on WEDNESDAY, the 7th day of February next, at 11 o'clock in the forenoon, for the purpose contemplated by the preceding vote of our Grand Lodge.

And it is hereby further required, that the delegate so elected, shall be furnished with a certificate of his election, signed by the Secretary of the Lodge, certifying that he is a member thereof, and that he has been elected in the manner herein set forth ; and said certificate shall also bear the seal of his Lodge.

Given under my hand at the city of Boston, this 4th day of January, A. D. 1849, A. L. 5849.

EDWARD A. RAYMOND, Grand Master.

Attest: C. W. MOORE, *R. Grand Sec'ry.*

N. B. As it is probable that the Convention will occupy two or three days in their deliberations, the delegates are requested to make their arrangements accordingly. Proxies cannot be allowed.''

January 13, 5849. " A communication was received from the M. W. Grand Lodge, directing the Lodge to elect a delegate to the Masonic Convention to be held at the Masonic Temple, on the first Wednesday of February next.

On motion of R. W. Bro. Thacher, it was *Voted*, To postpone the election until the next meeting of the Lodge.''

January 19, 5849. "A committee were appointed to retire and report the name of some brother from those of the ' most experienced and able ' to represent this Lodge in the Masonic Convention, to be held on the 7th day of February next, who subsequently reported the name of Bro. William C. Martin, which report was accepted, and he was unanimously elected.''

The establishment of a Masonic library, embracing works historical of the Craft, and explanatory of the principles and objects of Masonry, is worthy of liberal encouragement. Under the patronage of the Grand Lodge, efficient means could be employed to advance the project with entire success. Already, under their auspices, a committee of intelligent and active brethren, have, within a short time, gathered together a considerable number of volumes, in various languages. Some of the books are very rare, so much so, that if they should be lost, they could not probably be replaced. In 5815, the Grand Lodge purchased that part of the library of the late R. W. Bro. Thaddeus M. Harris, composed of works on Masonry; but from that time, until within two years, the subject of a library has received but little attention from that body. It may now be expected that the collection of books will be steadily advanced, and if individual brethren should give their aid as they may have opportunity, it will not be long before a library will be formed that will be both honorable and beneficial to the fraternity. The action of Columbian Lodge on the communication from the committee of the Grand Lodge, is indicative of their approbation of the undertaking.

January 4, 5855. "A communication from the chairman of the Library Committee of the M. W. Grand Lodge was received, and the Secretary was directed to send a copy to each member of the Lodge.

[COMMUNICATION.]

The Committee on the formation of a Library for the Grand Lodge of Massachusetts, respectfully solicit the donation of books, pamphlets, manuscripts, &c., on the subject of Masonry. By forwarding to the undersigned, at 75 Boylston street, Boston, such as you may have in your possession and are willing to donate for the purpose indicated, you will confer an especial favor on the Grand Lodge.

WINSLOW LEWIS, *for the Committee.*
Boston, December, 1854."

A great number of extracts might be made from the records of the Lodge to evidence the respectful attitude they have ever maintained towards the parent institution. Their alacrity to obey every request of that body, and to promulgate and enjoin its edicts, evince an enlightened and praiseworthy subordination, without which the Masonic confederation would soon cease to exist. The following extracts will suffice to illustrate the justness of these remarks.

September 2, 5813. "The W. Master read the new Constitution of the Grand Lodge, lately adopted."

March 4, 5819. "A copy of the By-Laws of the Grand Lodge of Massachusetts, was received and read by the Marshal."

April 21, 5825. "A communication was received from the *Grand Lodge*, relative to the installation of its officers, &c."

December 7, 5843. "On motion of Bro. Baker, it was *Voted*, That Columbian Lodge cause to be procured five copies of the Constitution of the M. W. Grand Lodge recently published, and have them suitably bound, for the use of the Lodge."

January 4, 5849. "A report made to the Grand Lodge in relation to an application made in behalf of the Masonic College for orphans of Kentucky, was read and referred to Bros. Thacher, Jones and Baker, with full powers."

Some of the proceedings of the Lodge relative to petitions which they have received, for their consent to the formation of new Lodges, and the restoration of charters which had been surrendered, will be noticed in the record account, which has been copied to an extent to enable the inquirer to judge of them in a variety of cases.

May 2, 5805. "A committee from and in behalf of the Aurora Society in Cambridge, having presented to this Lodge a petition stating that they were desirous of erecting themselves into a Lodge, by obtaining a charter empowering them to work as such, and requesting of this Lodge their recommendation to the Grand Lodge, and assistance in procuring the same,—

Voted, That a committee be chosen to visit the Aurora Society, and if they think proper, recommend them to the Grand Lodge, and assist them in procuring a charter. R. W. Master, Bros. Benson, Crooker, Walker and Phillips, were accordingly chosen for said committee."

September 10, 5821. "The petition of Samuel Fisher and others, to the M. W. Grand Lodge, for a new Lodge in the town of Boston, was presented to this Lodge for their approbation, which, after proper discussion, inquiry and investigation, was unanimously granted."

November 6, 5845. "A communication addressed to the Lodge by certain brethren of East Boston, who are desirous of forming a new Lodge, was referred to Bros. Baxter, Baker and Tillson."

November 20, 5845. "The committee on a new Lodge at East Boston, reported in favor of the request of the petitioners."

February 5, 5846. "The application of a number of brothers of South Boston, for the consent of this Lodge for the establishment of a new Lodge at that place, was referred to R. W. Brothers Smith, Baxter and Baker."

March 5, 5846. "The committee on the application of Rev. Bro. E. M. P. Wells and others, for the establishment of a Lodge at South Boston, reported that this Lodge assent thereto, which recommendation was adopted."

December 4, 5851. "A communication was received from Bro. Joseph Richardson and twelve other brethren, formerly members of Old Colony Lodge at Hingham, asking the consent of Columbian Lodge for the restoration of their charter by the M. W. Grand Lodge. Whereupon it was *Voted*, That its consent be given, and it recommends the restoration of said charter by the R. W. Grand Lodge."

September 2, 5852. "A communication was received from R. W. Bro. Albert Case, D. D. Grand Master of the 5th D. in behalf of Plymouth Lodge, which was referred to the Finance Committee, with full powers."

October 7, 5852. "The R. W. Master, from the committee to whom was referred the application of R. W. Bro. Case, in behalf of Plymouth Lodge for assistance in procuring jewels, &c., reported that no further action was required, as those articles had been procured by the Grand Lodge."

CHAPTER XVI.

BOARD OF DIRECTORS OF MASONIC APARTMENTS.—
GRAND CHARITY FUND.—TRUSTEES OF THE TEMPLE.
—WATER CELEBRATION.—NEW STATE HOUSE.—SIGN
OF GREEN DRAGON TAVERN.—DEDICATION AT PHIL-
ADELPHIA.—DECLARATION IN 5831.

In the summer of 5817, all the Masonic bodies in Boston, occupied, for the first time, the same apartments, (see page 71,) and of course the care of them became a joint affair. Consequently, a general committee, constituted by a committee from each institution, were organized, September 25, 5817, under the style of *The Masonic Board of Directors of the Associated Societies in the Town of Boston*, for the management of the apartments, and matters pertaining to them that required the united control of the associated parties. The constitution for the government of the board is in these words:

" Whereas the committees from the several Masonic Societies, occupying the new Masonic Hall, in the Exchange Coffee
House, have unanimously *Voted*, that the presiding officers of
the said Societies for the time being, shall constitute a board
of directors for the management of the same, together with
all other matters and things appertaining to the general compact, as stated in the report of the said committees : The said
presiding officers having met and organized the Board, unanimously adopted the following rules for the regulation of their
proceedings :

First.—The M. W. Grand Master shall for the time being,
be President of the Board, and in case of his absence from
any cause, the chair to be supplied by nomination, and vote
of the Board.

Second.—A Secretary shall be elected annually, and oftener,
provided the person elected ceasing to be a member of the

Board, shall render it necessary. He shall notify the members of each meeting by order of the President.

Third.—The meetings of the Board shall be quarterly, on the Saturday preceding the regular communications of the Grand Lodge, at such an hour as the President shall direct.

Attest,   CHARLES C. NICHOLS, *Secretary.*"

In an account of the whole body of the Masonic fraternity of Boston, an extended notice of the transactions of this board would be desirable, in order to fully understand many things established in their capacity of joint tenants, and with respect to the ways and means by which the apartments have been controlled and furnished. It is designed now to do no more than to show what are the objects of the board and its organization. During the first five years after it was instituted, a general agent was appointed from among the members, who attended to its financial affairs,— to duties which are now intrusted to committees and to the superintendent. The first agent elected, was R. W. Z. G. Whitman, who declined serving. The vacancy was supplied by the choice of R. W. Andrew Sigourney, Esq. The office of Secretary has been filled, successively, by Bros. C. C. Nichols, Daniel L. Gibbens, Z. G. Whitman, Ferdinand E. White, David Parker, A. A. Dame, Joseph Eveleth, Gilbert Nurse, John R. Bradford, Charles W. Moore, Winslow Lewis, Jr., George M. Thacher, Daniel Harwood, Charles Bates and William C. Martin. The first superintendent was Bro. E. V. Glover. He was succeeded in 5818, by Bro. Ebenezer Oliver, who performed the duties until 5831, when Bro. W. C. Martin was chosen. With the exception of a period of about one year, he has continued in the position to the present time. On account of ill health, he resigned in

5848, and Bro. H. H. Tuttle acted in his stead from Sept. 8, 5848 to Sept. 18, 5849. In relation to the office of superintendent, the following report was made to the board, February 7, 5818.

" The committee on the subject of superintendent, report as follows :

The committee appointed to recommend some suitable person for superintendent of Masons' Hall, and to define his duties and compensation, have attended to the subject, and do recommend Elisha Vose Glover, as the most suitable person to fill the office of any who has made application for the same.

The committee also recommend that the following be the conditions of the engagement to be entered into by the said superintendent and the directors, viz. : He is to open and shut the hall at proper times, and thoroughly to clean the same on the day succeeding each meeting, and nicely to dust all seats and other furniture on the day of and previous to each meeting ; to procure all fuel, oil, and candles, and all refreshment when ordered by proper authority ; to light the hall and build the fires, and carefully extinguish the same at a proper time ; to take up and thoroughly shake all the carpets once in three months, if ordered by the directors, and scour all the floors, seats and platforms whenever it shall be necessary; in short, he is to keep every apartment, at all times, in a neat and decent condition, so that the whole premises can any day be viewed by strangers or others who are disposed to visit the same. He shall furnish vouchers, when practicable, for all articles procured by him ; shall charge each society no more than the original cost of articles procured ; he shall have no perquisites, but shall after each meeting dispose of all fragments according to directions of the presiding officer. He is to attend at each meeting to the presiding and other officers, furnishing them with and assisting them to put on and adjust their clothing, &c. The compensation to be allowed him is as follows :

For each meeting of the Grand Lodge,.............	$10 00
For each meeting of the Grand Chapter,...........	6 00
Common meeting of Lodges, Chapter or Encampment, with refreshment,......................	3 00
Each meeting of Chapter, Lodges, or Encampment for public installation,..........................	8 00
Each meeting of the above when no refreshments are had,......................................	2 00

Respectfully submitted,   JOSEPH JENKINS, *pr. order.*

On motion, *Voted*, unanimously, that the above report be accepted."

After the destruction of the Exchange Coffee House, November 3, 5818, provision was made for the re-occupation of Masons' Hall, in Ann street; (see page 85;) and the records of the board describe at length the terms on which it was to be held and conducted by the lessees, and also what societies participated in the arrangement : they are here admitted without abridgment. Saint John's Lodge came into the association, Feb. 5, 5819, on the terms proposed by the board.

Boston, February 1, A. L. 5819. " The committees of conference from the several Masonic Societies in Boston, viz., the M. W. Grand Lodge, M. E. Grand Chapter, The Boston Encampment of Knights' Templars, St. Andrew's and St. Paul's Chapters, St. Andrew's, Massachusetts, Columbian and Mt. Lebanon Lodges, and the Boston Council of Royal Masters, having hired the old Masons' Hall, in Ann street, and procured a lease thereof to Bros. J. Jenkins and Samuel Thaxter, sub-committee, and having established the rate of rent as follows, viz. :

Grand Lodge,	$32	St. Andrew's Lodge,	$24
Grand Chapter,	12	Massachusetts Lodge,	24
Boston Encampment,	8	Columbian Lodge,	24
Council of Royal Masters,	4	Mt. Lebanon Lodge,	24
St. Andrew's Chapter,	24		
St. Paul's Chapter,	24	Total,	$200

And that the repairs, taxes, &c., should be paid by the several societies in proportion to the rate of rent ; and having, also, constituted the presiding officers of each society for the time being, to be a Board of Directors to oversee and superintend the affairs of the general concern, with like powers and duties to the Board of Directors of the Masons' Hall, in the late Exchange Coffee House : The said Board of Directors so constituted, were requested to meet at said Hall, viz.
M. W. Francis J. Oliver, Esq., Grand Master of the G. Lodge;
M. E. James Prescott, Esq., G. H. Priest of the G. Chapter ;
M. E. Henry Fowle, Grand Commander of the Encampment ;
M. I. Joseph Jenkins, M. I. Master of the Council of Royal
· Masters ;
M. E. Joseph Jenkins, H. Priest of St. Andrew's Chapter ;

M. E. Paul Dean, H. Priest of St. Paul's Chapter;
R. W. Henry Fowle, Master of St. Andrew's Lodge;
R. W. Zach. G. Whitman, Master of Massachusetts Lodge;
R. W. Aaron Bean, Master of Columbian Lodge;
R. W. Charles Wells, Master of Mt. Lebanon Lodge;
Present, Brothers Fowle, Jenkins, Whitman and Bean.

Voted, That the same rules and regulations be adopted by this Board as those which governed the Board for the Exchange Coffee House Hall. Bro. Fowle was chosen moderator, the Grand Master, being absent. *Voted*, by ballot, that Bro. Z. G. Whitman be the secretary of the board. *Voted*, and chose Bro. Aaron Bean as general agent to collect and pay the rent, &c. *Voted*, and chose Bros. Whitman and Bean, a committee to search and enquire after the property belonging to the Masons' Hall, in the late Exchange Coffee House, and to cause such as they may find to be removed to the present hall. *Voted*, that said committee cause a correct inventory of all the property now owned in common to be taken, and exhibit the same to this Board. *Voted*, and chose Bros. Bean and Whitman a committee to audit the bills against the several societies in common, for the late hall in the Exchange, and, also, at the Commercial Coffee House, to settle the same and collect the proportions due from each society respectively.

It being represented that St. John's Lodge had expressed a wish to join in the hiring and use of Masons' hall, in Ann street, it was thereupon *Voted*, that they may be allowed to join the association, they paying a sum into the hands of the general agent equal to the sums paid by the other four Lodges for the expense of repairing and furnishing the hall, viz., sixty-five dollars and fifty-one cents, and also that they pay, annually, the sum of twenty-four dollars as rent, and the same sum as other Lodges for taxes, repairs, &c., for the benefit of the whole concern. *Voted*, that their application be referred to the general agent to agree with them pursuant to the above vote."

As the labors of the board became more defined and systematized, a revision of the by-laws, in 5822, was judged necessary:

" At an adjourned meeting of the Masonic Board of Directors, held at Masons' Hall, on Monday evening, 18th March, 5822, M. W. John Dixwell, President; R. W. Sam'l Smith, . of Columbian Lodge; R. W. D. L. Gibbens, of S. A. R. A.

Chapter; and R. W. David Parker, of St. Andrew's Lodge, were present.

The commitee appointed December 8, 5821, to revise the by-laws, having attended to that duty, respectfully report the following preamble and regulations:

Whereas at a meeting of the committees of the several Masonic Societies, occupying 'Masons' Hall,' in the Exchange Coffee House, in the year 5817,—the said committees having full powers to devise and carry into execution the best plan for the management of the concerns of the association—the said general committee did, by their unanimous vote, constitute and appoint the presiding officers for the time being, a Board of Directors for the management of all matters and things appertaining to the general compact as stated in the report of the several committees to their constituents:

And whereas the committees from the said societies, at a general meeting held at Masons' Hall, in Ann street, on the first day of February, 5819, (they being invested with similar powers,) did constitute and appoint the presiding officers of the several Masonic societies a Board of Directors, to oversee and superintend the general concern with the same powers and duties as the former Board; therefore *Resolved*, that the following shall be the rules and regulations for the government of the Board of Directors of Masons' Hall, in the Old State House, viz.:

Article. 1st.   The meetings of the Board of Directors shall be held quarterly, viz.: on the Friday preceding the meeting of the Grand Lodge in March, June, September and December, at such hour as the President shall direct.

Art. 2d.   The M. W. Grand Master of the Grand Lodge for the time being, shall be President of the Board, and in his absence, his place shall be supplied by nomination and vote of the members present.

Art. 3d.   A Secretary shall be chosen by ballot at the stated meeting, in March, annually, (and at any other meeting of the Board in case the Brother so chosen shall cease to be a member of the Board) who shall continue in office until a successor is chosen.   His duty shall be to notify the members of every meeting under direction of the President, and to record the proceedings of the Board.

Art. 4th.   Three members being present at any meeting of the Board, duly notified, shall constitute a quorum for the transaction of any business that may regularly come before them.

Art. 5th.   Special meetings may be called when in the

opinion of the President urgent business may render it expedient.

Art. 6th. A prudent and discreet Brother shall be chosen superintendent at the stated meeting, in March annually, and oftener when circumstances shall render it necessary, who shall have in charge the property belonging to the several societies not otherwise disposed of, the hall and all the property owned in common, shall keep the hall, furniture and regalia in neat and good order, shall attend all meetings of societies and committees, and perform all the services that may be required of him, and be subject to removal at the pleasure of this Board, and shall receive for his services such compensation as shall be deemed reasonable.

Art. 7th. These articles shall be subject to alteration or revision whenever it shall be thought expedient by a majority of the Board.

All which is respectfully submitted.

> D. L. GIBBENS, } *Committee.*
> DAVID PARKER, }

Voted, That the preceding report be accepted."

December 23, 5823. "The committee on the subject of the amendment of the By-Laws, made the following report: The undersigned, who were appointed at the last meeting of this Board, to consider the expediency of allowing to any member of this Board, who may represent more than one of the associated Masonic institutions occupying the hall in the Old State House, a vote for each institution which he may so represent, and if, in their opinion it is necessary, to report an amendment to the By-Laws to effect that object,—ask leave to report: that in the opinion of your committee it is equitable and just, and in accordance with the spirit of the regulations of the Board, that each institution should have a voice and a vote on all questions which may come before said Board. Your committee, therefore, suggest the propriety of adding the following article to the By-Laws.

Article.—Any member who may represent two or more Institutions at this Board, may claim and shall be allowed one vote for each Institution so represented.

Respectfully submitted. JOS. EVELETH, } *Committee.*"
JOHN R. BRADFORD, }

June 4, 5824. "The above report was accepted, and the addition to the by-laws proposed by the committee, was adopted as Article 8."

May, 12, 5825. " On motion, *Voted*, That in the absence of the presiding officer of any Masonic Institution represented at this Board, said Institution may be represented by some other officer :—provided, nevertheless, that no officer below the relative rank of Junior Warden of a blue Lodge, shall be admitted to a seat at this Board."

The powers and objects of the board of directors remain to day as they were originally. Modifications of the rules and regulations for their government, may have been adopted since 5824; but to prosecute further enquiry in this direction, would exceed the bounds assigned to this subject.

The Grand Charity Fund, established by the Grand Lodge over forty years ago, has now become an object of great importance. Through the fostering care of esteemed and honored brethren, it has assumed a magnitude that nearly approaches the amount which its founders contemplated. If the same watchfulness and protection that have been thus far exercised in the accumulation of the fund, shall be continued to its further increase, but a few years will elapse before the permanent resources of the grand institution will afford a reliable annual income for charitable purposes of several thousand dollars. The origin of the fund will be seen in the following extracts taken from the records of the Grand Lodge.

Grand Lodge, Dec. 11, 5809. " On motion, *Voted*, That a committee be chosen to consider and examine the fourth chapter of the rules and regulations of the Grand Lodge, and report a plan for carrying into execution a fund for charity. The following committee were chosen : R. W. John Soley, R. W. Shubael Bell, R. W. Benj. Russell, R. W. Francis J. Oliver, W. John Dixwell."

Grand Lodge, September 10, 5810. " R. W. John Soley, chairman of the committee on the establishment of the Charity Fund, made a report on the subject of their commission, which being read and discussed, it was moved and seconded, that the report be re-committed, and that they be directed to complete the same by the next quarterly communication."

Grand Lodge, December 10, 5810. "The committee on the Charity Fund made a report, which was read and ordered on file, to be acted upon at the future call of the Grand Lodge."

Grand Lodge, January 11, 5811. "The committee to whom was referred the important subject of devising ways and means for establishing a permanent Charity Fund for the Grand Lodge, produced the following report, which was read by the Grand Secretary, and is as follows:

The report of the Committee on the Charity Fund:

The committee appointed to devise the ways and means for a permanent Charity Fund, and to report a system for the government thereof, beg leave to recommend that the Grand Lodge pass the following resolutions, viz.:

First. A fund shall be established to be denominated *The Charity Fund of the Grand Lodge of Massachusetts.*

Second. This fund shall be raised by the appropriation of the sum of one thousand dollars in specie from the funds of the Grand Lodge, and supported by the fees and appropriations hereinafter named, and by such subscriptions and donations as shall be designated for this purpose.

Third. From and after the first Monday in March, A. L., 5811. one-fourth part of the quarterages paid to the Grand Lodge, shall be appropriated to the said fund.

Fourth. From and after the first Monday in March, 5811, one dollar shall be appropriated to said fund for each and every candidate who may be initiated by the Lodges under the jurisdiction of this Grand Lodge.

Fifth. One half of all donations made to the Grand Lodge, not specifically appropriated by the donors, shall be invested in said fund.

Sixth. The Charity Fund aforesaid shall be under the direction of a board of trustees, consisting of the M.W. Grand Master, R. W. Deputy Grand Master, Grand Treasurer, and four brethren who are not acting officers of the Grand Lodge, to be elected by ballot, and to constitute, during good behavior, a permanent part of the Board; and provided a vacancy should occur from death, resignation or any other cause, it shall be reported by the residue of the Board, to the

Grand Lodge at their next quarterly communication, at which time the vacancy shall be immediately filled.

Seventh. The Board of Trustees shall hold their meetings on the Monday preceding each quarterly communication of the Grand Lodge, and at such times as may be thought expedient; and a majority of the Board shall be necessary for every act, except that of adjournment.

Eighth. The Board of Trustees shall report their proceedings to the Grand Lodge at the next ensuing quarterly communication; and the Grand Secretary shall keep a separate book, in which shall be recorded all the proceedings of the Trustees that shall be reported by the Secretary of the Board.

Ninth. The Charity Fund shall be always in the safe keeping of the Grand Treasurer, under the direction of the Board of Trustees, and he shall invest the same in such stock as shall be most productive; and no loans, nor donations, shall be made from the principal of said fund, until the income thereof shall amount to three thousand dollars per annum.

Tenth. The Grand Treasurer shall have power to retain a year's interest arising from said fund, to be appropriated by the Board of Trustees to the relief of such poor and distressed Brethren, their widows and orphans, as they may consider worthy of assistance : and should there be any interest unappropriated at the end of the year, it shall be vested as heretofore provided, and ever after be considered as part of the principal of said fund.

Eleventh. The Grand Treasurer shall report to the Grand Lodge, at each and every communication, an account of all monies received, and appropriations made to the Charity fund and of all donations, and expenditures therefrom, which have arisen during the quarter. Be it further resolved, that from and after the passing the foregoing act, establishing a *Grand Charity Fund*, the fee to be paid to the Grand Lodge for the initiation of a candidate shall be three dollars.

It is further recommended : that the Grand Lodge appoint a committee to prepare an address to those individuals within its jurisdiction, whose state of property may enable them to subscribe liberally to the Charity Fund ; in which they shall represent the object of their application, and the purposes to be accomplished thereby.

That the same committee prepare an address to the several Lodges, to be forwarded by the Grand Secretary, that every individual of the Masonic family may have an opportunity to contribute in proportion to his ability to this grand object.

That the District Deputy Grand Masters be directed to appoint a committee in their respective districts, to designate the individuals proper to be addressed, and to wait upon them at a suitable time, to receive the result of their determination. The proceeds to be deposited with the District Deputy Grand Masters, and transmitted by them to the Grand Treasurer.

That all donations made to the Charity Fund, shall be recorded by the Grand Secretary in a book, to be appropriated solely for that purpose.

That the trustees of the Charity Fund, be directed to petition the Legislature for an incorporation of their Board.

All which is respectfully submitted.

JOHN SOLEY,
FRANIS J. OLIVER,
SHUBAEL BELL, } *Committee.*
JOHN DIXWELL,
BENJ. RUSSELL,

After mature discussion, it was, on motion, *Voted*, To accept all the eleven articles, as first designated in the report.

On motion, it was *Voted*, also, To accept the whole report as it now stands, except that clause which recommends the payment of an additional dollar by every new initiate.

On motion, it was farther *Voted*, That that article in the report, which goes to the exaction of one additional dollar from any initiate, be wholly expunged. * * *

The report on the Charity Fund was again resumed; and on motion, *Voted*, That a nominating committee should be appointed to bring in a nomination list, from which should be elected by ballot, as the report provides, four Brethren as trustees to the fund;—the three following Brethren were this committee, viz.: R. W. —— Moody, R. W. John Soley, R. W. Oliver Shead.

After a short retirement the committee returned and presented the following nominations, viz.: R. W. Josiah Bartlett, Esq. of Charlestown, R. W. Dr. John Warren, R. W. Thomas Dawes, Esq., and R. W. and Rev. John Elliot, of Boston; to these were afterwards added in the Lodge-room, R. W. Matthew Cobb of Portland, and R. W. Daniel Baxter of Boston.

It being conditioned in the report that the four trustees should be chosen by ballot, a committee was appointed to collect, sort and count the votes; and the R. W. Henry Fowle, G. Marshal, R. W. John B. Hammatt and R. W. Job Drew, G. Deacons, were this committee.

The ballot was accordingly taken, and on counting the votes, the R. W. Josiah Bartlett, P. M., R. W. Dr. John Warren, P. M., R. W. and Hon. Thomas Dawes, Esq., and the R. W. and Reverend John Elliot, were declared to be duly and constitutionally elected.

On motion, *Voted*, That a committee be now appointed by the M. W. Benj. Russell, Grand Master, *pro tem.*, from the chair, to complete that part of the report on the Charity Fund which involves addresses to the Legislature for incorporation ; to the prosperous and benevolent individuals of the Masonic Family ; and to the several Lodges under the jurisdiction, for the obtaining charitable donations, and all other duties designated in the report. The following R. W. Brethren were chosen, viz. : John Soley, of Charlestown, John Abbot, of ———, John Bartlett, of Charlestown, ——— Coffin, of Portland, and Ezra Ripley, of Concord.

On motion, *Voted*, That the Grand Secretary be directed to add a copy of the report of the committee on the Charity Fund, with the names of the four trustees, now elected, to the annual communication to be prepared for A. L. 5810.''

Grand Lodge, February 20, 5811. '' On motion, *Voted*, That two be added to the committee to address the Legislature of the State ; to obtain donations, &c., as provided and defined in the report of the committee on the Charity Fund as accepted by the Grand Lodge, and that they be nominated from the Chair. The Grand Master, *pro tem*, Francis J. Oliver, Esq., then nominated Rev. and R. W. Asa Eaton, Grand Chaplain, and R. W. Benjamin Russell, S. G. Warden.''

Grand Lodge, September 9, 5811. '' The committee appointed by Grand Lodge the 30th January last, to prepare an Address to such individuals within its jurisdiction as were in a state of prosperity, for liberal subscriptions to the Charity Fund and other purposes, as defined and recommended in the system of government for that Fund, were, by request of their chairman, and for reasons adduced by him, discharged from their commission.

On motion, *Voted*, That a new committee be now raised by nomination from the Chair, for the important purposes aforesaid—when the following R. W. Brethren were appointed, viz. : Josiah Bartlett, Past Grand Master ; Timothy Whiting, P. G. W. and P. D. D. M. 5th District ; Benjamin Russell, Jun. Gr. Warden ; Rev. Asa Eaton, Grand Chaplain; Rev. Thaddeus M. Harris, P. G. C. and P. C. G. S. On application to R. W. Brother Bartlett, he declined acceptance, and the R. W. Samuel Bradford, Deputy Grand Master, was chosen in his stead.''

Grand Lodge, December 9, 5811. "The committee to whom was referred the important duty of preparing an Address to the prosperous individuals of the Fraternity, for obtaining subscriptions to the Charity Fund, &c., were called upon to report. R. W. Benj. Russell, one of that committee, wished it might be delayed till R. W. and Rev. Brother Harris and other members should be present ; and leave was granted accordingly.''

December 27, 5811. "From the Constitutions of the Grand Lodge, adopted Anno Lucis, 5811—Chapter V. Of the Charity Fund.

SECT. 1. The Charity Fund established by the Grand Lodge, shall be styled ' The Charity Fund of the Grand Lodge of Massachusetts.'

SECT. 2. The fund shall be increased annually by adding thereto one-fourth part of the annual fees, and one-third part of all initiation fees paid the Grand Lodge by the Lodges under its jurisdiction.

SECT. 3. One half of all the donations made to the Grand Lodge, not specially appropriated by the donors, shall be added to said fund.

SECT. 4. The Charity Fund aforesaid, shall be under the direction of a Board of Trustees, consisting of the M. W. Grand Master, the R. W. Deputy Grand Master, Grand Treasurer and four brethren, who are not acting officers of the Grand Lodge, to be elected by ballot, and to constitute during good behavior a permanent part of the Board; and provided a vacancy should occur, from death, resignation or other cause, it shall be reported to the Grand Lodge at the next quarterly communication, at which time the vacancy shall be filled.

SECT. 5. The Board of Trustees shall hold their meetings on the Monday preceding each quarterly communication of the Grand Lodge, and at such other times as may be thought expedient ; and a majority of the Board shall be necessary for every act, except that of adjournment.

SECT. 6. The Board of Trustees shall appoint a Secretary, whose duty it shall be to make a correct record of the proceedings of the Board, and report the same to the Grand Lodge at every quarterly communication ; and each report made to the Grand Lodge, shall be signed by the Chairman of the Board.

The Grand Recording Secretary shall keep a separate book in which shall be recorded all the proceedings of the Trustees that shall be recorded by the Secretary of the Board.

SECT. 7. The Charity Fund shall be always in the safe keeping of the Grand Treasurer, under the direction of the Board of Trustees; and he shall vest the same in such stock, as shall be most productive; and no loans, nor donations, shall be made from the principal of said fund, until the income thereof shall amount to three thousand dollars per annum.

SECT. 8. The Grand Treasurer shall have power to retain a year's interest arising from said fund, to be appropriated by the Board of Trustees to the relief of such poor and distressed brethren, their widows and orphans, as they may consider worthy of assistance; but should there be any interest unappropriated at the end of the year, it shall be vested as heretofore provided, and ever be considered as principal of said fund.

SECT. 9. The Grand Treasurer shall report to the Grand Lodge at every quarterly communication, an account of all money received and appropriations made to the Charity Fund, and of all donations and expenditures therefrom, which have arisen during the quarter."

Grand Lodge, March 14, 5814. "Agreeably to order, the committee of finance have examined the accounts of the Grand Treasurer respecting the Charity Fund, and find them correctly kept and properly vouched. He has received from various sources during the year past, five hundred and seven dollars and nine cents, making the whole amount of the Charity Fund sixteen hundred and seventy-five dollars and sixty-one cents, in six per cent. stock. At the date of the Treasurer's account, the 11th December, 5813, the Charity Fund was indebted to him forty-two dollars and ninety-two cents, since which the receipts have enabled him to pay the balance then due, and he has a surplus, in addition to the above, of forty-eight dollars in cash. Respectfully submitted.

HENRY FOWLE,
JOHN B. HAMMATT,
JOHN DIXWELL."

The present regulations affecting the fund, are contained in the constitutions of the Grand Lodge adopted in 5843, and are as follows, being Art. 1, Part Second of the constitutions:

SECT. 1. The Charity Fund, established by the Grand Lodge, shall be styled "The Charity Fund of the Grand Lodge of Massachusetts."

SECT. 2 This Fund shall be increased annually, by adding thereto one-fourth part of the annual fees, and one dollar of all initiation fees, paid the Grand Lodge by the Lodges under its jurisdiction.

SECT. 3. The Charity Fund shall be held in the name of " the Master, Wardens and Members of the Grand Lodge ;" but shall be under the direction of a Board of Trustees, consisting of the Grand Master, Deputy Grand Master, Grand Wardens, Grand Treasurer, Recording Grand Secretary, and six brethren, who are not acting officers of the Grand Lodge, to be elected by ballot, for the term of three years, and to constitute, during that term, a permanent part of the Board ; and provided a vacancy should occur by death, resignation, or any other cause, it shall be reported to the Grand Lodge, at the next quarterly communication, at which time the vacancy shall be filled. The Board of Trustees thus constituted, shall be styled " The Trustees of the Charity Fund of the Grand Lodge of Massachusetts," who shall invest the accruing funds in the manner they shall deem most likely to be productive; and no donations in charity shall be made from the principal of s id fund, till the income thereof, at the rate of six per cent. shall amount to the sum of three thousand dollars per annum.

SECT. 4. The Trustees of the Charity Fund shall hold a meeting on the Monday preceding the annual communication of the Grand Lodge in December, and at such other times as may be thought expedient. A majority of the Board shall be necessary for every act, except that of adjournment.

SECT. 5. The Treasurer of the Grand Lodge shall be, ex officio, Treasurer of the Grand Charity Fund, unless the Trustees shall determine by vote to elect a special Treasurer, in which case the Treasurer so elected, shall give such bonds for the faithful discharge of his duties, as the Board may require.

SECT. 6. The Board of Trustees shall appoint a Secretary, whose duty it shall be to make a correct record of their proceedings, and report the same to the Grand Lodge at every annual communication ; and each report made to the Grand Lodge shall be signed by the Chairman of the Board.

SECT. 7. The interest arising annually from the fund, shall be appropriated as the Trustees shall direct, for the relief of such poor and distressed brethren, their widows and orphans, as they may consider worthy of assistance ; but all interest unappropriated at the end of the year, shall be added to the principal.

At the close of the year 5833, the Masonic Temple was sold to R. W. Robert G. Shaw, (see page 111,) just before the corporate privileges of the Grand Lodge were surrendered to the Legislature. Subsequently, he conveyed it to R. W. John Abbot, who, November 5, 5835, conveyed it to nine brethren, in trust. The deed by which this last conveyance was effected, is in these words:

INDENTURE of two parts made and concluded this fifth day of November, in the year of our Lord one thousand eight hundred and thirty-five, by and between JOHN ABBOT, of Boston, in the County of Suffolk, and Commonwealth of Massachusetts, Esq., of the first part, and Benjamin B. Appleton, merchant, John J. Loring, Esq., Daniel L. Gibbens, merchant, Jacob Amee, gentleman, Simon W. Robinson, Edward A. Raymond, and John Hews, merchants, and Winslow Lewis, Jr. and Joshua B. Flint, physicians, and all of said Boston, of the second part.

Whereas, the said John Abbot is seized in fee simple of certain real estate situate in said Boston, and hereinafter described, and is desirous of conveying the same to said parties of the second part, to be by them held upon certain trusts:

Now this Indenture witnesseth, That the said John Abbot, in consideration of the premises and of one dollar to him paid by the said parties of the second part, the receipt whereof is hereby acknowledged, and of the covenants on the part of the said parties of the second part to be kept and performed, and also for other good and valuable considerations him hereunto moving, doth hereby give, grant, bargain, sell, and convey to them the said parties of the second part and their heirs and assigns forever, as joint tenants however, and not as tenants in common, all that certain lot of land, with the buildings thereon standing, commonly called the Masonic Temple, situate in said Boston, bounded and described as follows, to wit: bounded northwesterly on Tremont-street sixty feet and half an inch; southwesterly on Temple Place ninety-four feet six inches; southeasterly on land now or late of Thomas Lee, sixty-five feet eight inches; and northeasterly on land belonging to the proprietors of St. Paul's Church ninety-one feet six inches—or however otherwise bounded or described—meaning to include all the land conveyed to Robert G. Shaw, by deed of the Master and Wardens and Members of the Grand Lodge of Massachusetts, a corporation duly established by authority of said Commonwealth of Massachusetts, dated December 26th, A. D. 1833, and recorded with Suffolk Deeds in lib. 375, fol. 62, and by said Robert G. Shaw conveyed to the said John Abbot by Deed dated October 14th, A. D. 1835—together with all the rights, easements, privileges, and appurtenances to the premises belonging, and subject to the provisions, restrictions, and limitations, under which the said John Abbot now holds the same. And subject also to two certain Deeds of Mortgage made by said corporation to the President and Fellows of Harvard College—one to secure the payment of fifteen thousand dollars with interest, the other to secure the payment of five thousand dollars with interest—which Deeds of Mortgage bear date respectively May 23, 1831, and April 16, 1832, and are recorded with Suffolk Deeds in lib. 352, fol. 280, and in lib. 358, fol. 226.

To have and to hold the same to them, the said parties of the second part, their heirs and assigns, to their own use and behoof forever, as joint tenants however, and not as tenants in common—and upon the trusts and to the intents and purposes and subject to the several provisions, limitations, powers and agreements following, to wit:

First.—The said parties of the second part shall from time to time lease and demise the said real estate to the most advantage as a whole, or in part and in such manner and on such terms as they or a majority of them shall deem expedient, and from the rents, profits, and income thereof shall be held to pay all charges and assessments for which said estate shall become liable—to cause the buildings standing on said land to be insured against loss by fire in such sum of money as may be considered reasonable—to keep said premises in good repair—altering or rebuilding the same in whole or in part, as may from time to time become necessary and proper. The amount which may at any time happen to be received by reason of any such policy of insurance, to be applied to repairing or rebuilding as aforesaid, and after first paying and discharging all premiums of insurance and all other costs, charges, and expenses whatever, which may arise in the execution of said trusts, shall, during each and every year of the continuance of said trust, pay the interest which may become due on any principal sum or sums of money which shall be charged upon said estate by any Deed or Deeds of Mortgage, and also the interest which may accrue upon the other sums of money now due and owing

from the Master, Wardens and Members of the Grand Lodge
of Massachusetts, as a voluntary association, to divers persons,
amounting in all to the sum of forty-seven thousand six hundred dollars principal, and the particulars of which are herewith furnished to said parties of the second part.

And after payment of the interest accrued upon said several
principal sums of money, the said parties of the second part
may, whenever it shall become necessary so to do, apply the
net balance of the rents, income and profits of said real estate
or any part thereof, toward the payment and satisfaction of
said principal sums of money or any of them—and otherwise
they shall pay the same to the person who during each and
every year shall be the Treasurer of the Grand Lodge of Massachusetts, elected and appointed in conformity to ancient
Masonic usage, by the voluntary association, which association
at the present time is composed of JOSHUA B. FLINT, Grand
Master ; Rev. PAUL DEAN, Deputy Grand Master ; ELIAS
HASKELL, Grand Senior Warden ; BENJAMIN B. APPLETON,
Grand Junior Warden ; JOHN J. LORING, Grand Treasurer,
all of said Boston, and CHARLES W. MOORE, Grand Secretary,
of Charlestown, in the County of Middlesex, together with
sundry other persons, now associated and known as the Master, Wardens and Members of the Grand Lodge of Massachusetts, whether said association shall continue to be, as now,
a voluntary association of individuals or otherwise. And shall
from time to time keep a true and accurate record of all their
acts and doings of and concerning the premises, and once in
each year present to said voluntary association an account in
writing shewing their receipts, expenditures and acts in the
said premises.

Secondly.—Whenever in the opinion of said parties of the
second part or of the majority of them, it shall become necessary or proper to pay off the whole or any part of the principal sum or sums of money which may be charged upon said
real estate by any existing Deed or Deeds of Mortgage, the
said parties of the second part or the majority of them are
hereby fully authorized and empowered so to do, and to convey the said real estate in fee simple discharged of all trusts,
by any new Deed or Deeds of Mortgage, conditioned for the
payment of any sum or sums of money not exceeding in all
the sum so paid off, upon such terms as to time of payment
and rate of interest as may be agreed upon, and so from time
to time whenever and as often as the like cases shall happen.

Thirdly.—If the aforesaid voluntary Masonic association
now known as the Master, Wardens and Members of the
Grand Lodge of Massachusetts, shall at any time hereafter by

the said name or any other become legally capable of taking and holding said real estate in fee simple, and said corporation shall at any meeting thereof legally holden elect so to do, then and in that case, the said real estate, subject to the mortgages and liens if any shall then exist thereon, shall be conveyed to said corporation, by a good and sufficient deed, to hold to said corporation, their successors and assigns to their own use forever in fee simple.

Fourthly.—If at any time the Master, Wardens and Members of the Grand Lodge aforesaid shall at a regular quarterly meeting require it, a proposition for that purpose having been made at a previous regular quarterly meeting and notice being given in the usual manner of such proposition, the said parties of the second part shall convey the premises aforesaid subject to the debts aforesaid to any person or persons and on such terms and conditions and for such uses as said Master, Wardens and Members shall appoint.

Fifthly.—If at any time the Master, Wardens and Members of the Grand Lodge aforesaid shall cease to exist, both as a voluntary association and a corporation and no transfer of the said real estate shall have been made, as is herein before provided, then and in that case, and for the period of five years thereafter the said parties of the second part shall hold said premises and faithfully apply the net annual income of the same to the extinguishment of any debt and incumbrances which may then exist thereon, and if during said period of five years a new Grand Lodge shall be formed, according to ancient Masonic usage, then and in that case, the said new Grand Lodge shall succeed to all rights, interests, privileges and incomes secured to the present Grand Lodge and the Treasurer of the said Grand Lodge for the use thereof by these presents.

Sixthly.—If during said period of five years no such new Grand Lodge shall be formed, then and in that case, the said real estate subject to the said debts and mortgages, if any, which shall then be charged thereon, shall be conveyed and transferred by good and sufficient instruments for that purpose to the Grand Lodge of the State of South Carolina, a corporation heretofore duly established by the said State of South Carolina, to be by said Grand Lodge of South Carolina used, improved, conveyed or disposed of, for such uses and purposes as shall be consistent with the principles of Freemasonry, and for no other uses and purposes whatever.

Seventhly.—And it is hereby agreed by and between the said parties of the first part and of the second part, that the parties of the second part, who are hereby constituted Trus-

tees for the purposes aforesaid, and any future Trustee or
Trustees who shall be associated with them, and the survivors
and survivor of them shall have a reasonable compensation for
their services that they may at all times reimburse themselves
out of said rents, profits and income for all expenses and charges
which they, or either of them may have incurred on account
of said premises and the execution of said trusts or any of
them—that neither of said Trustees shall be accountable for
the acts, omissions or receipts of any one of the others, or liable to make good any more sum or sums of money than shall
actually have come into his own hands nor be answerable
for any other matter or thing whatsoever which may arise in
the execution of said trusts unless it shall happen by or through
his own neglect or wilful default.

And inasmuch as it may happen from time to time that one
or more of said Trustees appointed by these presents shall become unable to execute said trusts or shall die before all of
them are executed or shall desire to relinquish the same, then
and in every such case it shall and may be lawful and a duty
to and for the said continuing and surviving Trustees, or a
major part of them, to nominate to the said Masonic association now known as the Master, Wardens and Members of the
Grand Lodge of Massachusetts, whether existing as a corporation recognized by law or as a voluntary association of individuals, a suitable person to be a new Trustee in the place and
stead of each Trustee so dying or relinquishing or unable to
discharge said trusts, and so from time to time, when and so
often as during said trusts, or any of them, the like cases, or
any of them shall happen ; and if the said person so nominated shall be approved by the said Grand Lodge of Massachusetts, whether it be a voluntary association of individuals,
or a corporation established by law, and the person so approved shall accept of said trusts, then and in every such case
the said real estate shall be conveyed so and in such manner
as that the same, subject to any mortgage or mortgages or
liens, which may then lawfully exist thereon, shall be fully
and legally vested in such continuing and surviving Trustees,
and in the new Trustee so nominated and approved as aforesaid, to hold upon the trusts hereinbefore mentioned, or such
of them as shall then exist or be capable of taking effect.
And furthermore, in case the said Grand Lodge of Massachusetts shall cease to exist for the said term of five years, or for
any less number of years, and during such term, while there
shall be no Grand Lodge of Massachusetts, if the office of any
one of the said Trustees shall become vacant by reason of or
from any one of the causes aforesaid, then and in every such

case it shall be the duty of, and incumbent upon the continuing, or surviving Trustees, as soon as may be, to appoint some suitable person to be a Trustee in the place and stead of the Trustee who may have died, resigned, or become unable to discharge said trusts as aforesaid ; and upon the said person, so appointed as aforesaid, signifying to the said continuing or surviving Trustees, his acceptance of said trusts, the said real estate shall be conveyed as above is provided in such manner, as that the same, subject to any mortgage, mortgages or liens thereon, shall be fully and legally vested in such continuing and surviving Trustees and in the Trustee so appointed as aforesaid, to hold upon the trusts, or such of them as may then exist, or be capable of taking effect as aforesaid.

And each person who shall from time to time be nominated by said continuing or surviving Trustees and approved by the said Grand Lodge, or who shall be appointed by said continuing or surviving Trustees, when there may be no Grand Lodge, and who shall accept said trusts, shall and may thenceforth have all the rights and powers and be subject and liable to perform all the duties enjoined and required by these presents of the Trustees hereinbefore named and appointed. And the said parties of the second part, each for himself severally, and his heirs, executors and administrators, and not jointly or one for the others of them, do covenant, promise, and agree to and with the said John Abbot, his heirs, executors, administrators, and assigns, that each of them the said parties of the second part will severally faithfully perform and fulfil from time to time and at all times all and singular the said trusts according to the true intent and meaning of these presents, and will make, execute, acknowledge, and deliver good and sufficient conveyances by way of mortgage or otherwise, and generally will do and perform any and all other acts and things that may be necessary or proper to the full and faithful execution of each and every the trusts aforesaid.

In witness whereof, the said parties have hereto interchangeably set their hands and seals the year and day first above written.　　　　　　　(Signed)

JOHN ABBOT.　　　　　　　SIMON W. ROBINSON,
BENJAMIN B. APPLETON,　　EDWARD A. RAYMOND,
JOHN J. LORING,　　　　　　JOHN HEWS,
DANIEL L. GIBBENS,　　　　WINSLOW LEWIS, JR.
JACOB AMEE,　　　　　　　JOSHUA B. FLINT.

Signed, sealed and delivered ⎞
　　in presence of　　　　　⎠

Suffolk, ss. Nov. 5, A. D. 1835. Then personally appeared the above named John Abbot and acknowledged the foregoing instrument to be his free act and deed.''
   Before me, THOMAS W. PHILLIPS, *Justice of the Peace.*''

The rules and regulations here presented, have been adopted by the trustees in order to give efficiency to their own acts, and ensure a faithful supervision over the Temple.

" *Organization and By-Laws of the Trustees of the Masonic Temple.*

Whereas by a deed bearing date October, 1835, the subscribers are constituted Trustees of a certain property committed to their care by the Hon. John Abbot, of Boston, to be held and improved by them, for certain purposes set forth in said deed, and whereas we have severally accepted said Trusts, and entered upon the execution of them—therefore, in order to secure formal, regular, and consistent proceedings on the premises, we adopt, for our government therein, the following *Organization and By-Laws.*

JOHN J. LORING,
BENJ. B. APPLETON,
DANL. L. GIBBENS,
JACOB AMEE,
S. W. ROBINSON,   } *Trustees.*
EDWARD A. RAYMOND,
JOHN HEWS,
WINSLOW LEWIS, JR.
JOSHUA B. FLINT,

SECTION 1.—NAME.
Article 1. The name and style of this Board shall be ' The Trustees of the Masonic Temple.'

SECTION 2.—OFFICERS AND THEIR DUTIES.
Article 1. The officers of the Board shall be a *Chairman, Treasurer* and *Secretary*, who shall each be elected by ballot, at the annual meeting in January, and shall hold and exercise their respective offices without salary, while others are regularly elected in their stead.
Art. 2. In case of the death, resignation or removal of either of the officers during the year, the Board shall proceed to fill the vacancy by ballot, at the first quarterly meeting after it occurs.

Art. 3. Any officer of the Board may be removed for misdemeanor by a vote of two thirds of the members at a special meeting called for that purpose, and duly notified accordingly.

Art. 4. The *Chairman* shall preside at the meetings, receive and put all questions for the consideration of the Board, preserve order and decorum in its deliberations, by the application of usual parliamentary rules, so far as they may be applicable and necessary, and have a determining vote in cases of equal division; in his absence, the *Chair* shall be occupied by that member among those present at the time of assembling, whose name may be at or nearest to the head of the list of Trustees, as subscribed on the original indenture.

Art. 5. The *Treasurer* shall have charge of all deeds, notes, and other evidences of property belonging to the estate, and shall receive all the rents, profits and income of the same from the Superintendent, or from other persons who may be indebted, and shall carefully keep or improve them for the benefit of the estate. He shall pay all demands against the same which are presented with the written approbation of the Committee of Finance. He shall keep a plain and faithful account of all his receipts and disbursements, and shall transfer to his successor in office, when so directed by the Board, all the property, and evidences of property, belonging to the estate which may be in his possession at the time of any such change, together with all the books and papers relating to the same. It shall also be his duty, at the quarterly meeting in January annually, to present to the Board a complete and audited account, and in the course of ten days thereafter, to pay over such portion of the balance then in his hands as they may direct, to the Treasurer of the Grand Lodge. At each quarterly meeting he shall also report generally on the state of his department, and take advice of the Board as to the disposition to be made of any funds which may have accumulated in his hands.

Art. 6. The *Treasurer* shall, under the direction of the Board, execute all the leases and the contracts, which may require the formal attestation of their signatures.

Art. 7. It shall be the duty of the Treasurer to give bonds in the sum of one thousand dollars, for the faithful performance of the duties of his office.

Art. 8. The Secretary shall keep a faithful record of the doings of the Board at its regular and special meetings, in a suitable book to be procured for that purpose. He shall send written or printed notices of all meetings to each member, and shall have charge of all papers, letters, &c. which are not by the By-Laws of the Board, or a special vote of the same, intrusted to the Treasurer, and shall transfer them to his successor in office when so directed by the Board.

SECTION 3.—MEETINGS.

Article 1. The Board shall hold quarterly meetings on the first Monday of January, April, July and October annually. And the Chairman shall call special meetings whenever so directed by a vote of the Board, or requested to do so by a written application of any three members specifying the business for which the meeting is desired.

SECTION 4.—SUPERINTENDENT.

Article 1. At the quarterly meeting in January, the Board shall appoint a suitable person for Superintendent of the Temple, who shall have the immediate charge of the premises ; shall negotiate for the rent of the apartments under the advice of the Board, or of any committee appointed for that purpose ; shall collect rents and dues of the tenants, and pay the same forthwith to the Treasurer, and attend to other matters and things in the premises, as he may be particularly instructed at the time of accepting the appointment, and from time to time thereafter.

Art. 2. The Superintendent shall receive such compensation for his services as the Board shall annually determine to be just and proper.

SECTION 5.—COMMITTEES.

Article 1. There shall be chosen at the quarterly meeting in October annually, a committee for examining and auditing the Treasurer's accounts, and at each quarterly meeting, a committee of supervision for the three months following, whose duty it shall be to visit the Temple frequently, and direct the Superintendent in behalf of the Board, in respect to any arrangements or alterations which may require immediate attention. This committee shall report at the end of the quarter whatever of importance shall have been done under their direction, during their term of service.

Art. 2. At the regular meeting in January, there shall be appointed a Committee of Finance, who shall examine and approve all demands against the estate, before they are paid by the Treasurer.

SECTION 6.—ALTERATION OF BY-LAWS.

Article 1. These By-Laws, or any of them, may be altered at any quarterly meeting of the Board, notice having been given at a previous meeting and in the notifications, of the intended alteration, and a majority of the whole Board voting in favor of it.''

January 2, 5837. '' The Committee on the duties of the *Superintendent*, made the following report, which was accepted.

The committee appointed to prepare rules establishing the duties of the Superintendent of the Masonic Temple, ask leave to recommend the following requirements :—

1st. He shall open the building every morning at such an hour as shall be convenient to all the tenants, and shall close the same every evening after the occupants have retired.

2d. He shall be in or about the building as much of his time as possible, and see that order and cleanliness are observed in the public entries and passages, and, in general, shall exercise such supervision and acts of attention as shall promote every reasonable accommodation of the tenants, as well as the security and improvement of the premises.

3d. During one hour of each day, (Sabbaths excepted,) viz. from one to two o'clock in the afternoon, he shall be found in the apartment occupied by the Trustees for their meetings, and a notice of this shall be placed in a conspicuous place, at the entrance of the building.

4th. He may negotiate and conclude engagements for the occupation and use of any room in the building, for a single day or evening ; but when wanted for a longer term, he shall consult the gentleman who may be the Committee of Supervision for the time.

5th. He shall collect all the rents and income of the estate, and pay them as soon as received, to the Treasurer.

6th. He shall distribute the notifications for the quarterly meetings of the Board of Trustees, as a part of his regular duty. For special and extraordinary meetings, he may charge fifty cents for delivering the notices, and at all meetings of the Board, he shall open and light their room, and warm it when necessary, and take charge of it after their adjournment.

7th. In case of illness, or other necessary cause of absence, the Superintendent may employ a substitute, himself being responsible for the good conduct of his deputy.

8th. The Superintendent shall always be a Master Mason, and will be regarded, and is expected to regard himself, as the confidential agent of the Board of Trustees.

For the Committee.   J. B. FLINT, *Chairman*.''

June 10, 5839. '' The committee to whom was referred the subject of Rules and Regulations, made a report which was accepted, and voted to be copied, as follows :—

1st. It shall be the duty of the Treasurer to collect and receive the rents and income from the permanent tenants of the Temple, having a regular account with each, in a book to be kept for that purpose.

2d. There shall be a committee chosen annually, to whom all applications for the use of the Lecture room, and other rooms in the Temple, may be made. It shall be the duty of said committee to form such rules and regulations for letting the Lecture Room, and give such directions to the Superintendent, as will afford the greatest facilities to strangers and others who apply for the use of it, (being first approved by this Board,) and a book shall be kept in the Trustees' Room, in which every engagement of the Lecture room shall be forthwith entered, stating to whom, for what purpose, the terms, time, &c. for the use of the Trustees only. All applications for the permanent occupancy of any room in the Temple, shall be submitted to the Board.

For the Committee.   ENOCH HOBART, *Chairman.*"

March 1, 5841. "The Committee on the By-Laws made the following report, which was accepted.

The committee appointed to consider the expediency of altering the By-Laws of this Board, in relation to the time of holding its stated meetings, ask leave to recommend the following alterations, viz. The annual meeting of the Board shall, in future, be held on the first Monday of December, and the quarterly meetings on the first Monday of March, June and September, and that the several articles of the By-Laws be made to conform to this recommendation, by substituting the months of December, March, June and September, in place of January, April, July and October, wherever they may occur.   Respectfully submitted by

S. W. ROBINSON,   } *Committee.*"
ENOCH HOBART,   }

December 6, 5847. "*Voted*, That at the next meeting of the Board, the members consider the expediency of changing Sect. 3, Art. 1, of the By-Laws, so that the word 'Monday' in that Article, shall be changed for Tuesday.

Attest,   WINSLOW LEWIS, JR., *Secretary.*"

March 6, 5848. "The alteration in the By-Laws proposed at the last meeting was adopted."

December 6, 5853. "On motion, the By-Laws were referred to Bros. Loring and Moore for revision."

January 3, 5854. " The committee on amendment of the By-Laws, reported that the 1st Sect. of the 3d Art. be so amended, as that it shall read as follows :—

The Board shall hold an annual meeting on the first Tuesday in December, and the President shall call special meetings whenever so directed by vote of the Board, or requested to do so by a written application of any three members, they specifying the business for which the meeting is desired."

The trustees met at the South Bank, Boston, November 5, 5835, and organized by the choice of R. W. John J. Loring as chairman *pro tempore*, and of R. W. Winslow Lewis, Jr., as secretary *pro tempore*. They then proceeded to the election of permanent officers, and R. W. Benjamin B. Appleton was chosen chairman, R. W. Simon W. Robinson, treasurer, and R. W. John Hews, secretary. In consequence of their declining to serve, a new election took place, November 16, 5835, which resulted in favor of R. W. Edward A. Raymond for chairman, R. W. Benjamin B. Appleton for treasurer, and R. W. Winslow Lewis, Jr. for secretary.

Bro. Raymond served as chairman until the close of the year 5839, when R. W. Daniel L. Gibbens was elected, and continued in the office until December 1, 5847. R. W. Enoch Hobart succeeded him, and performed the duties of the chair to December 3, 5850, when Bro. Raymond was again elected. This last named Brother still occupies the station.

Bro. Appleton was annually elected to the post of treasurer up to the time of his death, in 5844. On the 6th of May of that year, Brother S. W. Robinson was chosen as his successor, and he has performed the duties of the position ever since.

Bro. Lewis served as secretary until March 6,

5849, when he resigned on account of ill health. R. W. John Hews was elected to succeed him. On Bro. Hews declining to be again chosen, December 8, 5851, the choice fell upon R. W. Charles W. Moore, who is the present secretary.

R. W. William C. Martin has been the super-intendent of the Temple, from the time of the organization of the Board to the present day.

August 6, 5838, Brother Enoch Hobart was chosen trustee on the part of the board of trustees to fill the vacancy occasioned by the resignation of R. W. Bro. Joshua B. Flint.

May 6, 5844, R. W. Ruel Baker was elected trustee by the Board, in place of Bro. Appleton, deceased.

March 3, 5845, R. W. William Eaton was elected trustee, to fill the vacancy caused by the death of R. W. Jacob Amee.

March 6, 5848, The Board chose R. W. Gardner Greenleaf, a trustee, to take the place made vacant by the decease of Bro. Baker.

March 4, 5851, Bro. C. W. Moore succeeded Bro. Lewis who had resigned.

June 3, 5854, R. W. Lucius R. Paige was made the successor of Bro. Gibbens. R. W. Thomas Tolman was chosen trustee, December 6, 5853, but declined the office on account of his business and other engagements.

The Board of Trustees now consists of Bros. John J. Loring, Simon W. Robinson, Edward A. Raymond, John Hews, Enoch Hobart, William Eaton, Gardner Greenleaf, Charles W. Moore and Lucius R. Paige. During the twenty years that the Board has existed, it has held one hun-dred and twenty-eight meetings, the records of which clearly demonstrate a diligent and faithful discharge of the great trust. The time and labor of the trustees have been rendered gratuitously, although by the deed of trust it is provided that they shall have a reasonable compensation for their services. The fraternity of Massachusetts have much cause for rejoicing that the management of their Temple has been entrusted to men of ability, fidelity and experience.

In the fall of 5848, the celebration of the introduction of Cochituate water into Boston took place. It was a jubilee in which the people of Boston and of the surrounding country generally participated. The weather was delightful, and possessed all the bland and placid qualities which characterize so much of the autumnal season of New England. The procession of the occasion was very extensive, and was composed of many divisions, embracing numerous and various societies. The Masonic fraternity were invited; and contributed much to the display. The letter of invitation to Columbian Lodge, and that part of the procession containing the division assigned to Masons, may properly be added to this brief notice of that event:

" *October* 5, 1848.

Sir,—The City Government of Boston intend to celebrate the introduction of pure water from Lake Cochituate into the city, on the 25th of October, by a public Procession, and other ceremonies suited to the occasion. You, with the members of your Lodge, are respectfully invited to join in the same. JOSIAH QUINCY, JR.
BENJAMIN SEAVER,
JOHN P. OBER,
WILLIAM D. COOLIDGE,
JOHN P. PUTNAM,
Committee on Invitations.

To P. C. JONES, Esq., Master of Columbian Lodge.

DIVISION THREE.

UNDER THE DIRECTION OF

Col. N. A. THOMPSON, chief marshal.

Aid.　　　　　　　　　　　　　　　Aid.

Major George M. Thacher.　　　　Hamilton Willis.

CONSISTING OF MASONIC FRATERNITY.

Grand Lodge, Grand and subordinate Encampments, and
subordinate Lodges, throughout the States of

MASSACHUSETTS, MAINE, NEW HAMPSHIRE, VERMONT, RHODE
ISLAND AND CONNECTICUT.

INDEPENDENT ORDER OF ODD FELLOWS.

Grand Lodge, Grand and subordinate Encampments, and
subordinate Lodges throughout the States of

MASSACHUSETTS, MAINE, NEW HAMPSHIRE, VERMONT, RHODE
ISLAND AND CONNECTICUT.

Order of United Americans.

Ancient Order of Druids.

Council of the Star in the East."

Soon after Columbian Lodge received their
Dispensation, they were summoned, with the fraternity generally, to take part with the Grand
Lodge in laying the corner-stone of the present
State House of this Commonwealth, which, for
some time, was called the New State House. The
ceremonies took place on the 4th July, 5795.
The call of the Grand Lodge was published in
the Columbian Centinel newspaper.

"GRAND LODGE.

Agreeably to an invitation of the Governor, and the Agents
of the Commonwealth, the Grand Lodge will assist his
Excellency in laying the foundation Stone of the New State
House, This Day, the 20th Anniversary of the Independence
of the United States. A procession will be formed in the
Representatives' Chamber, at 10 o'clock. The Lodges under
the jurisdiction, the Brethren of the Craft resident in the
jurisdiction, and sojourning Brethren, are invited to attend
properly Clothed.

By order of the M. W. Grand Master.

Boston, July 4, 5795.　　　　Daniel Oliver, *G. Sec.*"

The procession was composed as follows :

" Independent Fusileers.
Martial Music.
Two Tylers.
The CORNER STONE,
[On a truck, decorated with ribbons, drawn by 15 white horses, each with a leader.]
Operative Masons.
Grand Marshal.
Stewards, with Staves.
Entered Apprentices, and Fellow-Crafts.
Three Master Masons, bearing the *Square, Level* and *Plumb-Rule.*
Three Stewards bearing *Corn, Wine* and *Oil.*
Master Masons.
Officers of Lodges, in their respective Jewels.
Past Masters, Royal Arch, &c.
Grand Tyler.
Band of Music—decorated.
Grand Stewards.
Grand Deacons, with Wands.
Grand Treasurer, and Grand Secretary.
Past Grand Wardens.
Grand Senior and Junior Wardens.
Past Deputy Grand Masters.
Past Grand Masters.
Rev. Clergy—Brothers.
Grand Master, attended by the Deputy Grand Master, and Grand Stewards.
Deputy Grand Marshal.
Sheriff of *Suffolk.*
The Agents of the Commonwealth.
His Excellency the Governor.
His Honor the Lieutenant Governor.
Adjutant-General, Quarter Master General.
Hon. Council.
Members of Legislature.
Clergy, and Strangers of distinction."

The inscription on the plate deposited under the stone, was in these words:

" This corner stone of a building intended for the use of the Legislature

and Executive Branches of Government of the
Commonwealth of Massachusetts,
was laid by
His Excellency Samuel Adams, Esq.
Governor of said Commonwealth,
assisted by the Most Worshipful Paul Revere,
Grand Master,
and the Right Worshipful William Scollay,
Deputy Grand Master,
The Grand Wardens and Brethren
Of the Grand Lodge of Massachusetts,
on the 4th day of July,
An. Dom. 1795,
A. L. 5795.
Being the 20th anniversary of American Independence."

While making extensive repairs to the foundation of the State House during the month of
August, 5855, it was found necessary to provide a
new corner stone, and consequently to replace the
plate deposited under the original stone. This
was accomplished without public display by the
M. W. Grand Master, in the presence of the Governor of the Commonwealth, the President of the
Senate, members of the Executive Council, the
heads of the departments of State, and other gentlemen. A very interesting account of the first
and second laying of the corner-stone of this
edifice, is given in Bro. Moore's Magazine, Vol.
XIV, No. 12, from which the following extract is
taken, it being the new inscription upon the
plate :—

" The Corner Stone of the Capitol
having been removed in consequence of alteration and
additions to the building,
the original deposit, together with this inscription,
is replaced by
The Most Worshipful Winslow Lewis, M. D.
Grand Master,
and other Officers and Brethren of
The Grand Lodge of Massachusetts,

in presence of
Ilis Excellency Henry J. Gardner,
Governor of the Commonwealth,
on the 11th day of August, A. D. 1855.
A. L. 5855.

JOSEPH R. RICHARDS,
SAMUEL K. HUTCHINSON, } *Commissioners.*"
GEORGE M. THACHER,

Reference has already been made to the Green
Dragon Tavern, (see page 52,) where Columbian
Lodge held one of their meetings, and which was
owned and occupied by St. Andrew's Lodge for
many years. Whatever, therefore, relates to its
history will not be without interest to the fraternity of this locality; and for this reason a recent
report of a committee of St. Andrew's Lodge, de-
scriptive of the old sign of this noted Inn, which
is supposed to be destroyed, and of a new one
lately provided to resemble the original, may be
appropriately given in this relation:

"*St. Andrew's Lodge, Nov.* 8, 1855.
The committee appointed to make diligent search for the
old Green Dragon Sign, and in case of failure in finding the
same, to prepare a model of one as like the original as possible,
have attended to the duty assigned to them, and respectfully

REPORT :

That after having made inquiries of all persons whom they
thought might in any degree be likely to know anything of
the old figure or of its whereabouts, and having also made
very diligent search in all places where it might be supposed
to be laid away or concealed; and having entirely failed of
obtaining the slightest clew to its present condition, and
despairing of ever being able to discover what had become of
the original sign, after spending more than eighteen months
in inquiries and fruitless search, have prepared a model, which
they have caused to be carved in a truly artistic and work-
manly manner in durable sandstone, by a skilful person in
the employ of Mr. Thomas J. Bayley, of this city. They
have also caused the same to be inserted in the front wall

(near Hanover Street) of the brick building lately erected on the site of the Green Dragon estate on Union Street.

The sculpture was placed in situation on the first of the present month. In general features it resembles the old copper sign, as far as the memory of those who retained any knowledge of it could point out. The artist has, however, with commendable pride, made it a very sightly and creditable production, and wherein memory failed he has supplied the defect from a very beautiful and costly work of art, representing the patron saint of England, St. George, and his usual accompaniment, the Dragon, designed and executed by an eminent member of the Royal Academy of Great Britain, by direction of his Royal Highness Prince Albert. The monster represented is entirely fabulous, and is variously delineated by artists. The Dragon of heraldry assumes one form, and its varieties others. The old English Dragon, which is constantly associated with St. George, is seldom depicted in the same manner. Our Dragon, as it now appears, is undoubtedly one of the finest models of the monster now to be seen; and, in the opinion of the committee, marks a spot which should never be forgotten, as one of the early meeting places of St. Andrew's Lodge, and as memorable for its connection with many of the events of the American Revolution, and which they trust will not derogate from the interest which we entertain for the estate.

Respectfully submitted,   JOHN RAYNER,
                               EZEKIEL BATES.''

The dedication of the magnificent Masonic Hall in Philadelphia, October 26, 5855, was witnessed by the Grand Master of Massachusetts and about twenty brethren of his jurisdiction, including several members of the Grand Lodge, and the Master and several Past Masters and members of Columbian Lodge. The records of the Lodge refer to the occasion, as follows:

October 4, 5855. "The R. W. Master gave a very interesting account of the dedication of the new Masonic Hall in Philadelphia on the 26th ult., the banquet, the visit to Integrity Lodge in that city, &c. Among the many thousand brethren present, from all parts of the Union, were W. Bros. Geo. M. Thacher, P. C. Jones, W. D. Coolidge, J. T. Heard

B. Stevens, Bros. J. A. Cummings, Wm. Parker Jones and Joseph Trenkle, all of Columbian Lodge, most of whom were honored by the M. W. Grand Master [M. W. Winslow Lewis, of Massachusetts] with Jewels of the Grand Lodge."

That most remarkable movement against Masonry which controlled the politics of several of the States of the Union twenty-five years ago, and so severely tested the courage and integrity of the members of the Order during several years, demands a more lengthened notice of its rise and progress than this work will admit of, to convey an adequate conception of its extent and virulence, and do justice to the fortitude and fidelity of the brethren. The period of Anti-Masonry abounds with instruction and warning, and a full and faithful history of it ought to be in the hand of every brother. Its origin was the abduction of William Morgan in September 5826, which it was alleged was the work of Freemasons, who hoped thereby to suppress the publication of a work in which he intended to reveal the secrets of Masonry. Morgan was a native of Virginia, and had previous to his disappearance resided three years in Batavia, in the State of New York. From evidence adduced in the trials of several persons convicted of being accessory to his abduction, it appeared that he was conducted to Fort Niagara on the border of that State, but in relation to his subsequent fate nothing was elicited. From that time to the present no trace of him has been found. The persons engaged in this high-handed affair, if Masons, were so only in name, for the principles of the Order, had they known them, would have restrained them from the commission of a crime which is as much the abhorence of Masonry as it is opposed to divine and human laws. Every Mason is taught to strictly obey the moral law ; to be a peaceable citizen ; to pay proper respect to the civil migistrate ; to conform to the laws of the country in which he resides ; and before a man is made a Mason he is informed that his duties to his God, his country, his neighbor and himself, are in no way compromised by his Masonic obligations. This act charged upon Masons, afforded ground for attack against the Masonic institution, and every effort was made to show that it was planned and executed by the fraternity, generally, of the neighborhood where it occurred. It was averred that it was in accordance with the rules and requirements of Masonry thus to deal with a false member, and in conformity with the commands of those who occupied high positions in the Order. It gave to malevolence a pretext for the gratification of the worst feelings. By the distortion of facts, by exaggerated, false and scandalous statements, constantly disseminated through an excited community, it was designed to overturn and destroy a society, notwithstanding it included among its members many of the good and wise and patriotic of the country—men whose characters were above reproach, and who had occupied the first rank in public and private esteem. A blind, self-righteous, uncharitable fanaticism fanned the flame of excitement into a persecution at once malignant and unsparing, which became more effective through the machinations of demagogues who sought to turn the prejudices of the community to the promotion of their plans of ambition.

This was the position of Anti-Masonry throughout the State of New York in 5827. The same views and feelings entertained there, were soon spread over the New England States, and the persecution of the brethren was no less severe here than it had been there. It also became a political engine here with more or less success to aspirants for political preferment; and in several States Anti-Masonic Governors and Legislatures were alternately chosen and defeated as the public mind happened to be affected. An Anti-Masonic candidate for the Presidency was run in 5832, with however, but little success, as at that time the sober, second thought of the people had begun to be exercised, and a partial reaction had commenced, consequent upon the manifest injustice of the accusations which had been made against the fraternity.

In 5831, when the excitement was in its meridian, and the brethren of Massachusetts were subjected to the grossest personal insults, and the most scandalous charges were preferred against them as a body, and when flagrant violations against their rights as citizens were threatened, they felt that some measures should be taken to repel the attacks to which they were thus wantonly and constantly exposed. Hitherto, they had maintained silence ; the work of detraction they had suffered to pass unnoticed, and with a courage and forbearance which men only can exercise who are conscious of their integrity, they had borne the pitiless storm of a heartless and fanatical persecution in silent dignity and meek submission. Justice to themselves, to their families and friends, to the community of which they were members, demanded a denial, at least, of what had been so sedulously urged against them as Masons—to maintain silence longer, would be construed into a tacit admission that the criminations of their assailants were well founded and justifiable. The subject was accordingly brought before the Grand Lodge. That body were divided as to the propriety of going before the public to meet charges made by Anti-Masons. The proposition was, however, entertained, and a committee were appointed to report some paper adapted to the exigency, for publication. Various plans were reported, but none of them meeting with acceptance, the subject was at last postponed. The uproar of accusation continuing without abatement, and the brethren being daily importuned by their friends to oppose some statement to the course of their opponents, the subject of a protest was introduced before the Boston Encampment of Knights Templars, a body of true and estimable men, and devoted Masons. A declaration, or protest, written by Companion Charles W. Moore, was unanimously adopted by that society. Though it had been intended that the paper should be signed only by the members of the body in which it originated, such was the desire among the brethren generally, to unite with them in the promulgation of the sentiments it embodied, that it was determined that all might become parties to it who were so inclined. Without any efforts having been made to obtain signatures, fourteen hundred and seventy-two of the brethren in Massachusetts, in the course of a few days, had appended their names to the document, of whom four hundred and thirty-seven were residents of Boston. It was then printed and circulated. Subsequently, many other signatures were added, until finally, they reached the number of about sixteen hundred. The brethren in Connecticut and Rhode Island having procured copies of the protest, very generally signed it. About six thousand Masons in New England participated in this act of self-defence. The firm stand thus taken by the brotherhood was attended with the most salutary effects. It evidenced that the great body of the fraternity were not intimidated by the attitude of their enemies, and were faithful to the noble institution which was so ruthlessly assailed. These facts afforded encouragement to those who had faltered, and stimulated all in the reliance that truth would ultimately prevail, and their rights would be reëstablished. From that time, Anti-Masonry began to decline, and in the course of a few years it became utterly extinct.

The protest is here subjoined, with the names of the brethren of Boston, only, attached to it. It will be observed, that among the names are those of many members of Columbian Lodge.

DECLARATION
OF THE
FREEMASONS OF BOSTON AND VICINITY.

PRESENTED TO THE PUBLIC DEC. 31, A.D. 1831.

WHILE the public mind remained in the high state of excitement, to which it had been carried by the partial and inflammatory representations of certain offences, committed by a few misguided members of the Masonic Institution, in a sister State; it seemed to the undersigned [residents of Boston and vicinity] to be expedient to refrain from a public declaration of their principles or engagements, as Masons. But believing the time now to be fully come, when their fellow citizens will receive, with candor, if not with satisfaction, A SOLEMN AND UNEQUIVOCAL DENIAL OF THE ALLEGATIONS, which, during the last five years, in consequence of their connexion with the Masonic Fraternity, have been reiterated against them, they respectfully ask permission to invite attention to the subjoined

DECLARATION.

Whereas, it has been frequently asserted and published to the world, that in the several degrees of Freemasonry, as they are conferred in the United States, the candidate, on his initiation and subsequent advancement, binds himself, by oath, to sustain his Masonic brethren in acts, which are at variance with the fundamental principles of morality, and incompatible with his duty as a good and faithful citizen; in justice therefore to themselves, and with a view to establish TRUTH and expose IMPOSITION, the undersigned, many of us the recipients of every degree of Freemasonry, known and acknowledged in this country, do most SOLEMNLY DENY the existence of any such obligations in the Masonic Institution, so far as our knowledge respectively extends. And we as SOLEMNLY AVER that, no person is admitted to the Institution, without first being made acquainted with the nature of the obligations which he will be required to incur and assume.

FREEMASONRY secures its members in the freedom of thought and of speech, and permits each and every one to act according to the dictates of his own conscience in matters of religion, and of his personal preferences in matters of politics. It neither knows, nor does it assume to inflict, upon its erring members, however wide may be their aberrations from duty, any penalties or punishments, other than those of ADMONITION, SUSPENSION, and EXPULSION.

The obligations of the Institution require of its members a strict obedience to the laws of God and of man. So far from being bound by any engagements inconsistent with the happiness and prosperity of the Nation, every citizen, who becomes a Mason, is doubly bound to be true to his GOD, to his COUNTRY, and to his FELLOW-MEN. In the language of the "Ancient Constitutions" of the Order, which are printed and open for public inspection, and which are used as text-books in all the Lodges, he is "required to keep and obey the MORAL LAW; to be a quiet and peaceable citizen; true to his government and just to his country."

MASONRY disdains the making of proselytes. She opens the portals of her asylum to those only, who seek admission, with the recommendation of a character unspotted by immorality and vice. She simply requires of the candidate, his assent to one great fundamental religious truth—THE EXISTENCE AND PROVIDENCE OF GOD ; and a practical acknowledgment of those infallible doctrines for the government of life, which are written by the finger of God, on the heart of man.

Entertaining such sentiments, as MASONS, as CITIZENS, as CHRISTIANS, and as MORAL MEN, and deeply impressed with the conviction that the **Masonic Institution** has been, and may continue to be, productive of great good to their fellow-men : and having "received the laws of the society, and its accumulated funds, in sacred trust for charitable uses," the undersigned can neither renounce nor abandon it. We most cordially unite with our brethren of Salem and vicinity, in the declaration and hope that, "should the people of this country become so infatuated as to deprive Masons of their civil rights, in violation of their written constitutions, and the wholesome spirit of just laws and free governments, a vast majority of the Fraternity will still remain firm, confiding in God and the rectitude of their intentions, for consolation, under the trials to which they may be exposed."

BOSTON.	Jonas Chickering	Joel Nason
Thos. Melvill	Charles Newman	Ebenezer Oliver
Thos. Dennie	Alex. H. Jennings	Samuel Goodrich
Thomas K. Jones	David Orr	John Peters
Robert G. Shaw	B. D. Baldwin	John A. Lamson
Geo. Blake	Geo. Blackburn	John Flint
Benjamin Whitman	John M. Whidden	Wm. Bradford
Daniel Baxter	John Robinson, Jr.	P. Allen
Henry Farnum	William Gutterson	Samuel Brewer, Jr.
(Rev.) Asa Eaton	William M. Stedman	Cory Cook
Thomas Blake	Nestor Houghton	Eph. M. Cunningham
Thomas Power	Warren Fisher	Simeon Dunbar
John J. Loring	E. Williams, Jr.	David Manley
Samuel F. Coolidge	Calvin Ellis	Peter Dunbar
Eliphalet Williams	Albert Williams	L. H. Osgood
Abraham A. Dame	Marshall S. Perry	Jno. B. Derby
Gideon Snow	Elias B. Thayer	Abijah Patch
Edward Eldridge	Luther Thayer, Jr.	Gera Jenkins
N. F. Cunningham	B. M. Nevers	Samuel Howe
N. T. Eldridge	Samuel Morrill	Joseph Stockwell
James K. Mills	John L. Phillips	Stephen Locke
Winslow Lewis	Edward Bugbee	J. P. Robinson
Benjamin Russell	Jos. T. Buckingham	Samuel A. Allen
Francis J. Oliver	Stephen Codman	William Palfry
John Dixwell	Amos Cotting	John K. Simpson
David Henshaw	Daniel Dole	Luther Faulkner
Augustus Peabody	Joseph Jones, Jr.	Joseph Eveleth
(Rev.) Paul Dean	James E. Cooley	Jacob Amee
John Suter	John Bigelow	Robert Lash

William Ingalls
Harrison Gray
Adam W. Thaxter
Daniel L. Gibbens
Samuel Curtis
John J. Low
Thomas A. Dexter
E. L. Eliot
Abner Bourne
(Rev.) Jona. Greenleaf
Amos Bridges
Nathan Crafts
Joseph Blanchard
John T. Dingley
Joseph Converse
Daniel R. Newhall
Job Tower
Amos Coolidge
James Hunt
John Augustus
Wm. W. Motley
Jon. Bowditch, Jr.
Martin Bangs
Samuel Sweetser
Alonzo Crosby
Josh. Holden
Thomas Crehore
John Baker
Abel P. Baker
John Bacon.
Josiah Baldwin
David Parker
Martin Tylor
Francis Welch
Edward Shaw
Joseph Jones
William Nye
(Rev.) John L. Blake
Tristram Haynes
W. B. Annin
W. Philpot
John Chadwick
Joseph Jenkins
Richard W. Bayley
James Cushing
Daniel Stone
Nicholas Little
Wm. Emerson
Jno. Benson
Jos. Baker
James W. Gates
H. Daggett
John Banchor
Wm. McClennen
Lewis Lerow

Thos. M. Vinson
James Estabrook
Saml. Eveleth
Josiah Dunham
Ebenezer Stevens
Benj. Whipple
John D. Dyer
Josiah Newhall
Ezra Mudge
Josiah Dunham, Jr.
James A. Dickson
Henry Purkitt
Benjamin Smith
Thomas B. Wales
Charles Wells
Daniel Baxter, Jr.
J. S. Hastings
John Dwight
Isaac P. Osgood
Justin Field
Marshall P. Wilder
(Rev.) E. M. P. Wells
John Brazer Davis
J. B. Brown
Abel Baker
Nathl. Winsor, Jun.
Henry N. Fullerton
Wm. Lang
L. M. Walter
Ambrose Morell
Willard Felt
Wm. Rowson
Josiah L. C. Amee
Horace Dupee
Robert Keith
James Holbrook
Simon W. Robinson
Henry Robinson
Ensign Sargent
Eben. Scott
Chas. Williams
John R. Bradford
John Punchard
Jas. Johnson
Nathan Fessenden
Galen Holmes
Simon Wilkinson
Wm. Adams
Thomas Wait
Charles G. Hall
L. Snow
Marshal Keith
W. C. Martin
W. H. Neville
Amos Stevens

Fred. LeCain
Thomas J. Stone
Seth T. Thayer
Isaac Stevens
Nathl. Hammond
Andrew H. Ward
Oliver Fletcher
Abraham T. Lowe
James B. Richardson
Sumner Crosby
Elias Haskell
Alfred Dutch
Clement Willis
M. Roulstone
Peter Stephenson
David Tillson
Ezekiel Bates
Jeremiah Foster
Abiel Buttrick
Jeremiah Washburn
Francis L. Bates
Obadiah Kendall
John Wedger
Geo. W. Foster
John Park
Amherst Eaton
Salmon Washburn
John Allen
Wm. Crombie
(Rev.) Ed. T. Taylor
John B. Wells
L. Lawrenson
Gideon Eldridge
Benj. Converse
Elijah Williams
Ferdinand E. White
James Foster
Benj. Stevens
Thos. Wetmore
John Wilson
Joseph H. Lord
John Wheelwright
James Wilson
Charles Hubbard
S. B. Barrell
Wm. Hilliard, Jr.
F. P. Leverett
J. Vincent Brown
Samuel Kneeland
Abraham Millet, Jr.
Leach Harris
Warren Bowker
Richard Witherell
J. C. Tebbetts.
Thos. Waterman

Jeremiah Prichard
Wyatt Richards
Benj. I. Leeds
Ruel Baker
Edwin Barnes
Wm. Knapp
Jacob Page
James Mann
John Green
J. A. Pollard
Giles T. Crocket
George G. Smith
Ward Litchfield
Eleazer G. House
Nathaniel Hill
Wm. Eaton
Reuben T. Robinson
Timothy Fessenden
Ephraim Nute
Geo. W. Crockett
Josiah Bradlee
Francis Fisher
Isaiah Bangs
Jona. Howard
John J. Valentine
Elisha V. Glover
Joshua B. Flint
Hugh H. Tuttle
Wm. V. Kent
Leonard Battelle
Jos. Goodwin
Isaiah Rogers
Isaac K. Wise
Nathl. Bryant
Levi Whitney
Geo. Dodge
Luke Baldwin
Lewis A. Lauriat
A. Steuart
Wm. Stewart
Wm. Bachellor
Jona. Parker
Benj. Wood, 2d.
Jos. Goodwin
Jona. Whitney
John Gale
Thos. Holden
Thos. L. Chase
Samuel Cabot
Thomas W. Phillips
Edward A. Raymond
Charles W. Moore
William Parker
S. C. Thwing
Jno. Kennedy

Chas. Henshaw
Abel Phelps
Joseph Cheney
Jacob Bacon
Edward Prescott
Seth Thaxter
John Vose
Josiah Stedman
Charles Adams
Geo. W. Lloyd
John Rayner
Samuel Thaxter
John P. Bigelow
Winslow Lewis, Jr.
John Doak
Pliny Clap
Thomas Simpson
D. Kimball
David Putnam
James Pierce
Enos Briggs
Warren Wild
Bodwell Sargent
Geo. Bacon
Fred. Wentworth
J. W. Welch
Joseph F. Hill
Chas. W. Taylor
Alex. Parris
Henry H. Barton
Ebenr. Leman
Hazen Morse
Martin Wilder
Timothy Eaton
James Williams
Wm. Reed
Chas. Lyon
Elijah T. Weatherbee
Jedediah Tuttle
(Rev.) S. Streeter
Chas. C. Nichols
Jared Lincoln
Augustus Reed
C. Gayton Pickman
John B. Hammatt
Wm. Bittle
John Sowdon
Asa Adams
Ebenr. Waters
Joseph Grelee
Josiah Haskell
William Capen
Timothy Claxton
(Rev.) Samuel Barrett
Robert Bradford

Gardner Greenleaf
John Hews
Gilbert Nurse
Nahum Capen
Nathl. Greenough
Prentiss Hobbs
Phineas Sprague
M. S. Parker
N. Daggett
Josiah Vose
Edwin Sevey
D. Moody
Enoch Hobart
Benj. B. Appleton
Silas Bullard
Benj. Smith, Jr.
Josiah Willard
James Barry, Jr.
Francis R. Bigelow
Wm. Belknap
Martin Burr
Nathan Foster
Geo. Carpenter
Wm. W. Wood
Wm. H. Howard
George Page
Loring Newcomb
Daniel D. Brodhead
Ebenezer B. Foster
Jerome V. C. Smith
John Foster
Timothy Johnson
Nathl. Harris
Josiah Pierce
Elijah Trask, Jr.
Geo. Robinson
Wm. Shattuck
E. Parsons.
Wm. Wilkins
John S. Tyler
Edwin Adams
Saml. Adams
John Hammond
Willard Clough
Cornelius Hersey
Jacob Todd
John B. Andrews
Stephen Peabody
Wm. Parker
J. Smallidge
Wm. Loring
Jedediah Barker
Henry Bowen
Abel Bowen
Wm. Bell

Cornelius Driscoll	John White	Joel Shipley
James H. Gavett	Samuel Gragg	C. Southworth
Bela Greenwood	Nathan Fessenden	Amos Binney
J. F. Kimball	Joseph Wheeler	Thos. Jordan
Saml. Smith	Samuel Millard	Gurdon Steele
Wm. Wright	Dana Fay	Joseph Bassett
Wm. Barry	Richard D. Tucker	Manuel Francis.

The American Quarterly Review of March, 5830,—the time when the excitement was most rife,—contains an able and candid article on Anti-Masonry; it being a notice of *"A Narrative of the Anti-Masonic Excitement in the western part of the State of New York, during the years* 1826, 1827, 1828, *and part of* 1829. By HENRY BROWN, *Counsellor at Law:* Batavia, New York: pp. 244: 1829." The reviewer, who was not a Mason, treats his subject at great length. The following extracts will afford specimens of his style and views:

" This is the first connected and rational account we have seen of the rise and progress of *Anti-Masonry* in our country. It exhibits with candor, temper and clearness, the history of what is called Public Excitement; a species of madness, which, having for the most part its origin in the best feelings of our nature, almost always degenerates into an instrument in the hands of designing men, either of political or religious persecution.

" The sentiment which gives rise to public excitement, if not always virtuous, is generally mistaken for virtue. But such is the nature of man, and such the perversion to which his best feelings are liable; such the dominion which cunning and hypocrisy too often acquire over the imagination, when overheated by enthusiasm, that it has almost always happened, in every age and country, that the stream, however pure in its source, has been diverted to purposes of misery and mischief. Sometimes it rolls its destructive energies over all who stand in the way of its progress; and at others, turning short in its course, it overwhelms those who were the first to poison its waters and stimulate its fury.

" However the subject of anti-masonry may have become connected with the strife of party, we certainly shall not consider it in the light of a political question. Its temporary influence in the great struggles of ambition, is to us a matter of subordinate interest. We view it in a wider sphere of action, and in its more permanent consequences. We consider the uses to which this excitement has been prostituted, as disgraceful to the character of the country; as furnishing decisive proof that there are sufficient materials of ignorance and fanaticism among us, with which to fashion the implements of proscription and persecution. We contemplate it as paving the way for bigotry and hypocrisy to intrude themselves into our political system, and poison the spring of our liberties at its very source; as a daring attempt, in short, to make the love of justice and the detestation of crime subservient to the purposes of injustice and oppression, and bring back the people of the United States to the threshold of bigotry and intolerance. For these reasons it is, that we consider the subject as highly important, and not on the score of its incidental connection with politics. * * *

" The spark which lighted this mighty flame, fell in the village of Batavia, in the western part of the State of New York; and was struck out by a little miserable contention, which, according to our author, originated in the rivalry of two village newspapers. But it fell among combustibles, it would seem, and by degrees became a devouring conflagration. * * * * * * * *

" The reader will perhaps feel some curiosity to know the contents of these celebrated papers of Morgan, which occasioned all these acts of violence. They were afterwards published under the title of ' Illustrations of Masonry,' and consist principally in disclosures of the manner of initiation, and the oaths of the different candidates for degrees. Not being masons ourselves, we cannot judge of their truth or falsehood; but whether true or not, we are free to confess there is nothing in them, but what indicates, with sufficient clearness, that masonry is nothing more than a tie of brotherhood, instituted for purposes of benevolence. These disclosures derive little claim to our belief, however, from the circumstance of their being made by persons who had belonged to the fraternity of masons, and consequently carrying with them the violation of a voluntary oath. * * *

" Having thus given a sketch of the prominent features and principal transactions of this mortifying exhibition of the facility with which the best feelings of our nature may be perverted to the worst purposes, we will proceed to offer some reflections on the subject. We call it a mortifying exhibition,

not because the feelings of the people rose in just indignation
against a series of unjustifiable acts, ending in the forcible
seizure of a citizen, and his disappearance under circumstances
carrying with them strong suspicion of his being murdered.
Such a feeling does honor to the moral sense of a community;
it is the source of much that is good within us, since the
detestation of guilt in others, is one of the strongest securities
for our own innocence.   Had this honest and virtuous excitement confined its operation within just limits, and extended
no farther than to the pursuit and punishment of the actors
in this mysterious drama, but one sentiment of approbation
would have arisen in the minds of all.   But when we see this
virtuous feeling, diverted from its just and proper direction;
overflowing its bounds, and with undistinguishing fury involving the innocent with the guilty; denouncing a whole class
and denomination of men, spread through every part of the
Union, who by no possibility could have participated in these
offences, and who have publicly disclaimed and condemned
them and their actors; when we see them proscribed and dis-
franchised, religiously and politically, one and all, we cannot
but lament and pity the extremes to which virtue may sometimes be impelled in the pursuit of the most praiseworthy
objects.

    " We had hoped never to have lived to witness any of these
extraordinary panics and excitements, which other ages and
nations, and unfortunately our own, have offered to the contemplation of posterity; and which posterity wonders at and
despises, until it beholds them again repeated under its own
eyes, and is compelled to sit down with the mortifying conviction, that human nature is the same everywhere and at all
times.   Certain it is, that the love of justice, the sentiment of
piety, and the detestation of crime, have too often led mankind into excesses incompatible with them all, insomuch that
had not these feelings of justice and piety been derived from a
higher source, and sustained in our hearts by a higher power,
the crimes of which they have in all ages been made the
pretext, would have banished them from the face of the
earth.   *   *   *   *   *   *   *   *   *

    " That the sweeping proscription of the masons, and the
wide extension of anti-masonry, are in a great degree owing
to the intrusion of some selfish purpose, which has diverted
this excitement, in its origin perfectly pure, from its just
object, and appropriate sphere of action, no one we think who
reads Mr. Brown's book will doubt for a moment.   That
intruding principle seems to have been a curious combination

of religious and political ambition. For some reason or other, which has never presented itself distinctly to our understandings, masonry has, in various ages and countries, been peculiarly obnoxious to the church, although one would imagine, that, charity and benevolence being the basis of both, they would naturally be linked together in the bond of brotherhood. It is probable, we think, that the secrecy affected by the fraternity has been and still continues to be at the root of this prejudice against masonry. Mankind, and justly too, since common experience sanctions it, are prone to believe that where there is mystery all cannot be right. Secrecy, we all know, is necessary at times; but where there is secrecy, without any known cause, we are apt to believe there must be some cause which it would be dangerous to disclose. Hence probably the thousand idle reports concerning the nature and objects of masonry; hence the persecutions it has undergone in various countries; and hence the facility with which the good people of the western part of New York have fallen into the projects of wily politicians and ambitious clerks. * * * * * * *

"A number of other important considerations, arising out of the subject, crowd upon us; but we have already reached the utmost limits of the space allowed to this article. It was our intention to give a few quotations from the anti masonic publications of various kinds, with which the nation has been scandalized and insulted of late, as furnishing additional evidence of the designs of the party, and the spirit by which it is animated. Above all, we purposed to lay before our readers, some curious extracts from the Anti-Masonic Almanac, in which, the different months are designated, not by the good old agricultural emblems, but by the prominent scenes in the supposed murder of Morgan, represented in all the horrors of wood engravings. It was also our design to remark, in terms of just reprehension, on the conduct of some of the members of the masonic fraternity, who, after having voluntarily taken the oaths of secrecy prescribed as one of the conditions of admittance, afterwards as voluntarily came forward, and perjured themselves in the face of the world, by declaring all they knew. But we have now only room for a very few words on the work before us.

"The author has executed his task in a manner to entitle him to the thanks of all rational persons. The narrative is clear, precise, and particular; abounding in just principles, correct feelings, candid admissions, and manly censures of both masons and anti-masons, where Mr. Brown thinks them wrong. It is singularly impartial, considering it was written in the midst of the fires of persecution and proscription, and displays an intimate acquaintance with the history of similar excitements in different countries. We therefore strongly recommend it to attention, as a salutary antidote to the epidemic which seems to be spreading itself in all directions throughout this many headed, many minded republic."

————oo————

CHAPTER XVII.

MEMBERS. — LIFE MEMBERS. — HONORARY MEMBERS. — DELINQUENT MEMBERS. — INITIATES. — VISITORS.

The number of original members whose names are inserted in the Dispensation and Charter, was seventeen. The original by-laws limited the number of members to thirty ; and those adopted in 5799 and 5808, provided for fifty. Seventy members were allowed by the code of 5816, while that of 5821, abolished all limitation to the number ; and since then no restriction has existed. There are three classes of memberships, i. e. active, life, and honorary. The only difference in the first two classes is that the active is subject to quarterages or periodical fees, whilst the life member purchases exemption from them during life by the payment of a specified sum. In all other respects these two classes are alike ; they are alike as to the duties required of them by the Lodge, and as to the privileges they enjoy. Honorary membership is conferred upon those persons who have by long and faithful services in Masonry won the respect and esteem of the Lodge; or who, while they have proved themselves meritorious as Masons, have also become honorably distinguished in their other relations with their fellow men. It gives no vote in the business affairs of the Lodge.

Neither the records nor the files of the Lodge afford the means of determining the exact number of members at any time previous to 5813. An approximation to it might be realized after a careful and laborious analysis of the books of account, but the result would be far from satisfactory, especially if the object should be to present annual lists of members during the eighteen years. The subjoined extract from a report of a committee states who were members in 5813.

December 2, 5813. "Your Committee further report that, in their opinion, no person ought to be considered a member of this Lodge, excepting

Bro. John W. Folsom,
" Seth Thayer,
" Daniel Johnson,
" Snelling Powell,
" Stephen Bean,
" Daniel Baxter,
" Joseph Jenkins,
" Scammell Penniman,
" Amos Binney,
" Josiah Vose,
" Charles Tuttle,
" John Park,
" Calvin Howe,
" Jonathan Howard,
" Daniel C. Brown,
" Samuel Smith,
" David Moody,

Bro. Samuel B. Jarvis,
" Ezekiel Little,
" Nathaniel Heard,
" Elisha V. Glover,
" George Bender, Jr.
" B. B. Appleton,
" Samuel R. Green,
" Oliver Mills,
" Perley Fairbanks,
" John Leman,
" Elisha Brimhall,
" Elijah Morse,
" Ezra Stone,
" Thomas Bruce,
" Horace Collamore,
" Jason Braman,
" Willard Clough.

Making in all, thirty-four members, the first of whom is not subject to quarterages."

The table here given, showing the number of members in each year, is compiled from the yearly reports of the finance committee which are made in the month of December. These reports are entered with the records.

5813,	33 active members—1 honorary member—(John W. Folsom.)					
5814,	34 "	"	1 "	"	"	"
5815,	45 "	"	1 "	"	"	"
5816,	54 "	"	2 "	" (J. W. Folsom, Paul Dean.)		
5817,	52 "	"	2 "	" "	"	
5818,	59 "	"	3 "	" (Folsom, Dean, Cotting.)		
5819,	59 "	"	3 "	" "	"	"
5820,	57 "	"	3 "	" "	"	"
5821,	62 "	"	3 "	" "	"	"
5822,	66 "	"	4 "	" (Folsom, Dean, Cotting, Sabine.)		
5823,	57 "	"	3 "	" (Folsom, Dean, Sabine.)		
5824,	60 "	"	3 "	" "	"	"
5825,	70 "	"	3 "	" 7 life members.		
5826,	65 "	"	3 "	" 8 "	"	
5827,	56 "	"	3 "	" 8 "	"	
5828,	52 "	"	3 "	" 9 "	"	
5829,	48 "	"	3 "	" 10 "	"	
5830,	42 "	"	3 "	" 9 "	"	
5831,	40 "	"	3 "	" 9 "	"	
5832,	38 "	"	3 "	" 9 "	"	
5833,	38 "	"	3 "	" 7 "	"	
5834,	34 "	"	3 "	" 7 "	"	
5835,	36 "	"	3 "	" 7 "	"	
5836,	(yearly report not recorded, nor is it on file.)					
5837,	"	"	"	"	"	"
5838,	"	"	"	"	"	"
5839,	39 active members—3 honorary members—6 Life members.					
5840,	34 "	"	6 "	"	6 "	"
5841,	40 "	"	11 honorary and life members.			
5842,	41 "	"	9 "	" "	"	
5843,	43 "	"	10 "	" "	"	"
5844,	54 "	"	9 "	" "	"	"
5845,	67 "	" /	9 "	" "	"	"
5846,	83 "	"	6 honorary members—5 life members.			
5847,	82 "	"	7 "	"	5 "	"
5848,	82 "	"	8 "	"	5 "	"
5849,	85 "	"	10 "	"	6 "	"
5850,	105 "	"	9 "	"	6 "	"
5851,	114 "	"	9 "	"	8 "	"
5852,	125 "	"	9 - "	"	7 "	"
5853,	135 "	"	9 "	"	7 "	"
5854,	154 "	"	9 "	"	7 "	"

The number of members enrolled, December 6, 5855, was two hundred and eight, of whom sixteen were honorary members. Several of the honorary members were also life members. The acceptance of the complimentary membership deprives no one upon whom it is bestowed of any right to participate in the affairs of the Lodge, which he had previously enjoyed.

Originally, an applicant for membership was required to stand proposed one month before he could be balloted for, and if no more than three negatives appeared against him he was admitted. This rule applied to all applicants, whether they were made in Columbian Lodge or elsewhere. But this regulation existed only for a few months. On the 16th November 5795, it was so altered as to require a unanimous vote. At the meeting of March 22, 5796, the by-law for members to stand one month proposed on the book before they could be admitted, was suspended by a vote of the Lodge for that night, when brethren were balloted for and made members. The abrupt suspension of the by-law here cited, does not appear to conflict with the letter of the law as it then existed, though it did undoubtedly militate against the spirit of it. In 5803, candidates could be voted for if proposed at a previous meeting. In 5808, every candidate for membership stood proposed on the records one meeting previous to his being balloted for; and a unanimous ballot was required. This rule has prevailed up to the present time. Written applications for membership were first demanded in 5816. The by-laws of 5821, provided that the name of an applicant for membership should be inserted on the notifications for the meeting at which the application was to be acted upon, and this practice still continues. The names of brothers desirous to become members were, in 5806, referred to a committee of inquiry, of not more than five nor less than three members ; and though it was not enjoined by succeeding by-laws until 5854, yet the importance of such reference has been recognized by the practice of the Lodge up to the present time.

The first by-laws obliged every brother made
in the Lodge, on his becoming a member, to pay
three pounds; and every brother not so made, on
his being admitted a member, to pay four pounds,
ten shillings. These fees, in 5799, were five and
seven dollars, respectively. In 5808, the fee for
membership, without reference as to where the
brother was made a Mason, was fifteen dollars;
and this was the sum until 5812, when it was
changed to ten dollars. The sum of ten dollars
continued to be the admission fee until 5835,
when it was altered to five dollars. In 5853, five
dollars were demanded of a brother who received
degrees in Columbian Lodge, and ten dollars from
him who received them in another Lodge. This
latter provision is that which at present exists.

The quarterage, at first, was four shillings and
six pence. From 5799 to 5803, it was seventy-
five cents; from 5803 to 5810, it was one dollar.
From that time to 5821, it was fifty cents. Since
5821, the assessments have been sixteen and two-
thirds-cents monthly, or equal to fifty cents each
quarter year. The penalty for non-payment of
assessments has uniformily been the forfeiture of
membership. Neglect to pay quarterages for
three successive quarters, after being called for,
forever forfeited privileges of membership, and all
right to the Lodge's stock, unless satisfactory reasons could be given to the Lodge for the delinquency, were the provisions of the first by-laws
in relation to this subject. The by-laws of 5799,
Art. 13, declare it to be the duty of the Secretary
to call regularly on each member for his quarterages, when due, by notice on the summons;
should any member be found deficient to the
amount of three quarters, the Secretary was to

report the same to the Lodge on the next regular meeting, and a record was to be made of the same. It was also the duty of the Secretary to inform such delinquent member or members, in writing, that unless said arrearages were discharged previous to the next regular meeting of the Lodge, report should be made, and his name erased from the books; and he was no longer considered a member. Failure to pay three quarterages, successively, worked a forfeiture by the by-laws of 5808; and four quarters arrearages caused a like result in 5816. Since 5821, a member neglecting to pay his periodical dues for eighteen months, could be voted out of the Lodge, by a majority of members present. Seafaring brethren were not subject to the penalty, except when at home. In the earlier years of the Lodge, members were subject to contribute to the funds beyond their payments in fees, as has already been stated in another chapter. Brethren on being admitted to membership have always been required to subscribe their names to the by-laws.

The first life memberships were conferred in 5825. The first written provisions therefor were in the constitution and by-laws adopted in 5821. In 5825, the form of a certificate was agreed upon. As a full compensation for all assessments any member could pay twenty dollars; which would exempt him from all periodical dues during his life. The same regulation exists at the present time.

September 15, 5825. " *Voted*, That Bros. Baxter, Jr., G. G. Smith, S. Smith and N. Williams be a committee to draft a form of certificate for Life membership."

October 6, 5825. " The committee appointed to draft a form of certificate for Life membership, made the following report of a form :

COLUMBIAN LODGE.

This certifies that Brother ——— ——— has paid the sum of TWENTY DOLLARS, which constitutes him a member of COLUMBIAN LODGE during life, or so long as said Lodge may esteem him worthy of this honor ; and that he is not liable to any periodical assessments in future.

——— ———, *Master.*

Boston, 5855.''   ——— ———, *Secretary.*

The first permanent regulations in relation to honorary memberships are contained in the constitution adopted in 5S21. It is therein declared, that no brother shall be made an honorary member unless his name for such membership shall be on the notifications for the meeting at which the application is to be acted upon, and he be unanimously accepted. Previous to that time, but five members of this class had been admitted. The same regulations have been continued to the present day. The first action of the Lodge in relation to honorary members was on the 2d December, 5802, and is recorded in these words:

" *Voted,* That the R. W. Bro. Churchill and R. W. Bro. Folsom, having severally presided as Masters of this Lodge, be hereafter exempted from the payment of quarterages, and that they be considered as honorary members.''

The following table presents a correct list of all brothers who have been made honorary members.

Joseph Churchill,	admitted	5802	Wm. M. Stedman,	admitted	5847
John W. Folsom,	"	5802	Warren Fisher,	"	5847
John Perkins,	"	5809	David Tillson,	"	5847
Paul Dean,	"	5816	Mordecai M. Wallis,	"	5849
John R. Cotting,	"	5818	Edward Prescott,	"	5849
James Sabine,	"	5822	William C. Martin,	"	5851
Daniel Baxter, Sr.	"	5825	Asa Eaton,	"	5855
John Leman,	"	5837	Samuel Smith,	"	5855
Joshua B. Flint,	"	5840	Joseph R. Chandler,	"	5855
Benj. B. Appleton, Sr.	"	5840	Daniel Baxter, Jr.	"	5855
George G. Smith,	"	5840	Benjamin Stevens,	"	5855
Ammi Cutter,	"	5845	Edward T. Taylor,	"	5855
Joseph Jones,	"	5846	George M. Randall,	"	5855

Notices of W. Bros. Joseph Churchill, John W. Folsom, Daniel Baxter, Sr., Joshua B. Flint, Benjamin B. Appleton, Sr., George G. Smith, David Tillson, Samuel Smith, and Daniel Baxter, Jr., will be found in the chapter devoted to Masters. An outline of the life of Bro. Eaton, is on pages 189 and 190; and a sketch of the masonic services of Bro. Martin, is on pages 365 and 366.

John Perkins, the third on the honorary list, was born in Saxony, one of the German States, and came to this country when a young man. He was made a mason in St. John's Lodge in 5766, and was one of the original members of Columbian Lodge. He was a very active member. It was at his house that the Lodge held four of their meetings in 5795, (see page 50.) It was he who presented the Charter to the Lodge at their meeting of August 9, 5796. At the meeting of January 1, 5807, the thanks of the Lodge were voted to him for his services as Marshal on that evening. He was the first elected Junior Warden, to which office he was installed April 14, 5796. He served as Senior Deacon in 5798. During the last years of his life, he resided at Waldoboro, Me., where he died about thirty years ago.

R. W. and Rev. Paul Dean was born in Barnard, Windsor County, Vt., on the 28th of March, 5783. He passed his youth in agricultural labor, in attending common schools, in academic and biblical studies, and in school teaching. In the year 5806, he commenced the Christian ministry at Montpelier, Vt.; from thence, in 5810, he removed to New Hartford, N. Y.; and, in 5813, he came to reside in Boston. He was for many

years the pastor of the first Universalist Church
in Boston, and subsequently, he was settled over
the Bulfinch street church, where he officiated for
considerable time. Of late years, he has resided
in Framingham, Mass. He early became a life-
member of the American Bible Society, and of
the American Colonization Society. This faithful
teacher in the Christian Church, has also been a
devoted and earnest Mason. Bro. Dean was
initiated, passed and raised in Center Lodge, No.
6, at East Rutland, Vt., during the winter of
5805. He received the chapter degrees in Horeb
R. A. Chapter, No. 7, at New Hartford, N. Y., in
the year 5811. The degrees of Royal and Select
Master, and the Templar degrees were conferred
upon him in Boston. He was admitted to Honorary Membership in Columbian Lodge, April 4,
5816, and officiated as their Chaplain, in 5817,
'18, '19, '20, '25, '26, '27, '29, '34, '35 and '36.
He has served as G. Chaplain of the Grand
Lodge; was D. D. G. M. of the 1st District, in
5821, 5822 and 5823; Deputy Grand Master, in
5835, 5836 and 5837; and Grand Master of Massachusetts, in 5838, 5839 and 5840. He has held
membership in St. Paul's R. A. Chapter, the
Grand Chapter, the convention of High Priests,
the General Grand R. A. Chapter of the United
States, in the Boston Encampment of K. T., and
in the General Grand Encampment of the U. S.
He has served as Prelate in the G. G. Encampment; in the G. G. Chapter, as Chaplain, King
and High Priest; in the Grand Council of Royal
and Select Masters for Mass., as M. I. Grand
Master; in the Grand Chapter of Mass., as Deputy
and Grand High Priest; in the convention of

High Priests, as President; and in St. Paul's R. A. Chapter, in 5818, '19 and '20, as High Priest. The numerous Masonic services which Bro. Dean has rendered in the various stations he has filled, richly entitle him to the high estimation in which he is held by his brethren.

Rev. Bro. John R. Cotting was made a Mason April 4, 5816, and admitted as an honorary member, January 15, 5818. He resigned his membership five years afterwards, as will appear by the subjoined letter:—

To the Right Worshipful Master, Wardens and Brethren of Columbian Lodge.

Brethren,—About five years since, you did me the honor to elect me a member of your Lodge, about the same time St. Andrew's Lodge conferred the same honor. I did not then know that it was incompatible with the rules of the Grand Lodge, for a brother to be an honorary member of more than one Lodge ; lately I have learned that this is made a question in your Lodge. To prevent any further discussion on the subject, I request that my name may be erased from your list of honorary members. The brethren will do me the justice to accept the assurance of my warmest gratitude, for the repeated honors and favors they have conferred upon me ; with my sincere prayers for the honor, respectability and increase of their Lodge.

With sentiments of affection and esteem,

J. R. COTTING.

Boston, March 4, 1823.

The incompatibility referred to, does not now exist. Honorary membership carrying with it no right to vote on the financial or other business concerns of a Lodge, it being of a complimentary character merely, can be conferred on a brother by any number of Lodges. Active membership cannot be held in more than one Lodge at the same time.

Rev. Bro. James Sabine was born in Fareham, Hants, Eng., May 26, 5774. He lost his mother at the early age of five years, and was subsequently in the charge of an aunt whose severity induced him to leave her while yet a boy, and repair to London, where he found employment in the establishment of a book-binder. The information which he here obtained came to be of much service to him in after life, when he sought exercise from the duties of study and composition by converting his numerous pamphlets—gathered during many years—into a series of well-bound volumes, with which his library was stocked. His family are not advised at what period he became pious, as there is no record to show, but as early as his seventeenth year, he must have entered the classical and theological school of Hoxton, near London, belonging to the dissenters, then under the presidency of Dr. Simpson ; for he was in the ministry when he was at the age of twenty-one, i. e. 5795. After officiating in England, in different places, he left his native land with his family in 5816, and became the pastor of the Independent Chapel in St. Johns, Newfoundland, until 5818, when, in consequence of the great conflagration that had consumed two-thirds of the city, he sailed with his family for Boston, where he arrived in the summer of that year. After serving as a Congregational clergyman, and being instrumental in building two churches in Boston, he was induced, in 5828, to join the Episcopal church, and was ordained by Bishop Griswold in 5830. Soon after, he removed to Bethel in Vermont, and became rector of Christ Church, over which he officiated fifteen years, until his death, which took place at his son-in-law's, Dr. John Smith's, at Randolph, on the second day of October, 5845. Ann Davenport, his wife, died in Bethel, October 2, 5837. Their remains lie in one grave in the churchyard belonging to Christ Church, Bethel, over which their sorrowing and affectionate children have placed a suitable head-stone, as a memorial of departed worth. In Masonry, Brother Sabine took a deep interest, which in no degree abated during his life. He was initiated in Columbian Lodge, August 3, 5820; was admitted to honorary membership, April 4, 5822; and served as Chaplain in 5825, '26, '27, '28, '29 and '30. He was made a member of St. Andrew's R. A. Chapter, March 19, 5823, of which body he was Scribe in 5823 and 5824, and King in 5825. He was a member of the British Charitable Society. In whatever sphere he acted, he was earnest and sincere, and there are many in this community who remember him as a true friend and faithful Christian teacher.

Brother John Leman was initiated and became a member October 3, 5811, and an honorary member May 4, 5837. He was made a member of St. Andrew's R. A. Chapter, December 25, 5811. He was, also, in 5820, a member of the Massachusetts Charitable Mechanic Association. He was born in Reading, Mass. November 2, 5775, and died in Boston, October 7, 5841. His remains were buried in the Copps Hill Cemetery. He was a most worthy man, and excellent Mason.

Bro. Ammi Cutter, who was one of the earliest initiates of the Lodge, was born in Cambridge, September 7, 5777. He was initiated October 4, 5798, and received as a member November 7,

5799. He was Senior Steward in 5800, Junior Deacon in 5801, and Secretary in 5802, 5803 and 5804. Honorary membership was conferred upon him in 5845. He died April 4, 5850, and was buried in the town of his nativity. During the long period in which he was connected with the Masonic fraternity, he ever manifested a deep interest in their welfare. On the announcement of his death, the Lodge passed the following resolves : —

" *Whereas*, It has pleased the all-wise Disposer to call home to himself the spirit of our venerable and beloved brother, Ammi Cutter, and

Whereas, Our brother had endeared himself to the Masonic fraternity and to Columbian Lodge in particular, by his many virtues and by his constant devotion to its interests and welfare through a long life ; therefore

Resolved, That while in this event, the death of our oldest brother, we are grieved for his loss, we desire to be grateful that we were so long permitted to be gladdened by his presence and counsels, and rest in the full belief that he has exchanged the feebleness of age and the flesh for a seat in the Celestial Lodge above.

Resolved, That these resolutions be entered on our records, and a copy of the same be transmitted to the family of the deceased, with the assurance of our heart-felt sympathy in their bereavement."

Bro. Joseph Jones was initiated Feb. 6, 5800, passed February 21, 5800, raised November 22, 5821, and made a member April 4, 5822. On account of the high esteem with which they regarded him, the Lodge, in 5845, conferred honorary membership upon him. He was, in 5801, a member of the Massachusetts Charitable Mechanic Association, and belonged to the British Charitable Society at the time of his decease. He was born in Halifax, N. S. March 15, 5768, and came to Boston with his parents when six months old.

He died in Boston, April 25, 5851, and was buried in his tomb on Copps Hill.

Bro. William M. Stedman was born in Weston, Mass., where he now resides. He was initiated March 7, 5816, admitted to membership November 7, 5816, and to honorary membership March 5, 5846.

Bro. Warren Fisher was born in Sharon, Mass., May 30, 5794. He now resides in Roxbury, Mass., but his business is in Boston. He was initiated October 2, 5823, admitted a member November 4, 5824, and to honorary membership in 5847.

One of the oldest surviving members, is the venerable Brother Mordecai L. Wallis. He was made a Mason February 18, 5808, a member August 3, 5815, and an honorary member May 3, 5849. He was born in Cohassett, February 1, 5779. He came to Boston at the age of fourteen, and apprenticed himself to Mr. John Homer, mason. He commenced business as an operative mason, on his own account, at twenty-two years of age, and was engaged in that employment, in Boston, for fifty years. He has been a member of the Republican Institution since October, 5819, and also of the Massachusetts Charitable Mechanic Association since Jan. 2, 5834. He belonged to the Boston Fire Department a number of years previous to 5812. He is appreciated by the Lodge for his modest but sterling worth. They cherish him as a connecting link with the brethren far back in the past.

Bro. Edward Prescott received his first instruction in Masonry, April 4, 5816, was made a member, November 7, 5846, and an honorary member, May 3, 5849.

R. W. and Hon. Joseph R. Chandler is a native of Kingston, Plymouth County, Mass. He was reared to mercantile business, but early became a teacher. He was for twenty-five years the editor of that highly respectable and influential daily newspaper, the United States Gazette, published in Philadelphia. He was during seventeen years a member of the Councils of that city; was a member of the convention that framed the present Constitution of Pennsylvania; and for six years, (three terms) he represented Philadelphia in the Congress of the United States. He has been, also, distinguished as a Mason. He was initiated in Columbian Lodge, October 28, 5813; elected a member, February 3, 5814; and Junior Steward, in 5815. Subsequently, after his removal to Philadelphia, he held the office of Master of Phœnix Lodge, No. 130; Master of Columbia Mark Lodge; High Priest of R. A. Chapter, No. 52; Grand High Priest of the Grand Chapter, all in that city; and of Grand Master of the Grand Lodge of Pennsylvania for two years, also the subordinate offices in each body. He has, besides, delivered numerous addresses to the masonic brethren, which were characterized by great ability and pure and elevated sentiments. His adherence to masonry continued steadfast during the anti-masonic period, though his prominence marked him out as an object for direct personal attack. He met his assailants nobly, and triumphantly vindicated and sustained that institution of which he is one of the brightest ornaments. Columbian Lodge have honored themselves in plac-

ing his name upon the roll of honorary members.
At the celebration of St. John's Day, by the Morning Star Lodge at Worcester, in 5847, the following letter from Bro. Chandler was read :

" Philadelphia, June 18, 5847.

Dear Brethren,—Yours, inviting me to join in the Masonic Festival on the approaching St. John's Day, was duly received. So much do I enjoy these gatherings of the Fraternity, that though I was apprehensive that important business would demand my presence elsewhere on that day, still I was unwilling to decline accepting your invitation, while there remained a hope that I might be with'you. I am, however, now constrained to express a belief that I shall be deprived of the pleasure you have proposed to me. I shall, however, remember you on that day, and wish for all blessings upon your festival.

It is to me a source of great joy that the good cause of the Fraternity is prospering with you, and while I desire its prosperity, I most heartily wish to see the Order respected for the character, as well as for the number of its members ; and in such a community as yours, I am sure Masonry will have claims on the good opinions of the world by the worth of her children. May our brethren at all times and in all places remember, that charity, (social and fraternal affection,) is the bond of our union.

With deep gratitude for the kind remembrance of my brethren in Worcester, and with fraternal respect,

I am yours, truly,   Jos. R. Chandler.

To Messrs. Case, Chenery and others, Committee, &c."

W. Bro. Benjamin Stevens was born in Boston, April 16, 5790—on the spot on Washington street where stood the piano-forte establishment of Messrs. Jonas Chickering & Sons, lately consumed by fire. He has been a most useful citizen, having done the State and city important service. Under the old town government of Boston, he was clerk of ward twelve, four or five years, and warden of the same ward two years. Under the city government he was warden of ward twelve, four years, and of ward eleven, two years. He was a member of the board of health during the mayoralty of Hon. J. Quincy, Sr. ; and of the primary school committee, two or three years; he served as an inspector of ward eleven one year, and of ward twelve two years ; and was a member of the Common Council from the same ward in 5828. He, for a period of four years, represented Boston in the House of Representatives of Massachusetts. In a note addressed to a friend, he humorously observes—"I served my country in the war of 1812, along with Bro. John McLellan ; and commanded Fort Strong at East Boston, with the enormous force of a sergeant's guard." But the great public service which he has rendered, however, has been the long and most faithful performance of the duties of Sergeant-at-Arms of the General Court of Massachusetts. First elected in 5835, it is now more than twenty years that he has filled the station with the highest honor to himself, and to the entire acceptance of the very large number of individuals who, as legislators, have been assembled at the capitol during that time. As a Mason, Bro. Stevens enjoys the affectionate regard of his brethren. He was made a Mason, April 17, 5817 ; was admitted a member of the Lodge, June 5th of that year, and elected Junior Steward in 5818. He served as Marshal—an office to which his agreeable manners and knowledge of the etiquette belonging to a Lodge, eminently fitted him—during the years 5819, 5820, 5821, 5822, 5842, 5845 and 5846. He became a life-member in 5826 ; and the Lodge have lately complimented him with honorary membership. He was an original member of St.

Paul's Chapter. In the Grand Lodge, Bro. Stevens has for several years held various subordinate, but important positions.

Rev. Bro. Edward T. Taylor was admitted a member April 2, 5846, and served as Chaplain in 5847, 5848, 5849, 5850, 5851, 5852 and 5853. The compliment of honorary membership has lately been voted to him. He was born in Richmond, Va., December 25, 5793, but has lived in Boston between forty and fifty years. He .was made a Mason in Duxbury, Mass., in 5819, in the Lodge of which the Hon. Seth Sprague was then the Master. He aided in forming the Star-in-the-East Lodge at New Bedford. This is not the place to attempt to give an account of Brother Taylor's long and devoted services in the Christian church, and of his untiring interest in promoting the temporal and spiritual welfare of the sailor. His early life was spent at sea, which enabled him to observe the exposure of seamen to immorality and vice ; and he sought to ameliorate their condition, by removing temptations to which they were subject when on shore. A large portion of his life has been thus employed ; and many there are who have been made better and happier through his humane and philanthropic efforts. He has ever felt a warm interest in Masonry. In the dark days which beset the institution, he was one of its staunchest defenders and supporters.

Rev. and R. W. Bro. George M. Randall was born in the town of Warren, Rhode Island, on the 23d of November, 5810, and is a graduate of Brown University of the class of 5835. He graduated at the General Theological Seminary of the Protestant Episcopal Church in New York city, in 5838, and during that year took charge of the parish of the Church of the Ascension, Fall River, Mass. He removed to Boston in May, 5844, to take the rectorship of the Church of the Messiah, in which he has continued to the present time. He was made a Mason in Washington Lodge, No. 3, at Warren, R. I. in 5845, and received the chapter degrees in the same town the following year. He was Chaplain of the Grand Lodge of Massachusetts in 5846; D. D. G. M. of the first District in 5848; Deputy Grand Master in 5849, 5850 and 5851; and Grand Master in 5852, 5853 and 5854. He was admitted a member of Columbian Lodge, and acted as their Junior Chaplain in 5852 and 5853. He has been their orator on several occasions. He is a ready and eloquent speaker, and his addresses before the Lodge, and also before the Grand Lodge in his capacity of Grand Master, have commanded the undivided attention of all who heard him. His administration as Grand Master was highly successful.

Notices of the lives of many other brethren, living and dead, especially of those long connected with the Lodge, would interest the reader; but the bounds to which these pages are confined, will exclude them, with a few exceptions.

Bro. Amos Binney was initiated January 3, 5805, and admitted a member May 2, 5805. He served as Secretary in 5806; as Treasurer in 5807 and 5808; as Junior Warden in 5809; and as Marshal in 5812. He was a most useful and active member, and performed much service on committees. The subjoined account of him has been furnished by a member of his family:

"Col. Amos Binney, of Boston, the son of Amos and Mary (Prentice) Binney, was born in Hull, Mass., April 15, 1778. His father Amos, born in 1745, was the son of Amos Binney, Senior, born 1711, and wife of Rebecca (Loring), of Hull. Amos Binney, Sr. was son of Dea. John Binney, born 1680, and his wife Hannah Paine. Dea. John was the son of the first ancestor in America, John, and wife Mercy, who were in Hull, Mass., 1682, and probably came from Hull, Eng. or vicinity; as the Binneys of Hull, Eng. and vicinity have been buried in Worksop, Nottinghamshire, some 200 to 250 years, as stated lately by Thomas Binney, now of Hull, Eng.

Col. Binney's mother was a daughter of the Rev. Solomon Prentice, of Grafton, Mass., a well educated and energetic woman, and from whóm he derived much of her character and knowledge. He married in Boston, Feb. 21, 1799, Hannah, daughter of Nath. and Mary (Gray) Dolliver. He died in Boston, at his residence corner of Hancock and Mount Vernon streets, January 11, 1833, aged 55. His father died when he was only five years old, He was of so attentive and steady a character as to be able to assist his mother at a very early age. At the age of sixteen or seventeen, he came to Boston, about 1793, to select a business for himself. He chose that of a wheelwright, with a Mr. Hill, but this being too mechanical, in a year or two he engaged with Messrs. Lord & Kimball, brewers, of Roxbury, for a short time only; afterwards he kept school in Hull for six months, then returned to Boston as clerk to a Mr. Thoro, in the West India Goods line, Long wharf. He was a partner with a Mr. Clark, same wharf, in the Savannah trade, where Mr. B. went to purchase cotton. On his return, he found it was sold to a man who proved a rogue, who resold it, pocketed the money and failed. After losing all, Mr. B. again commenced business by himself as a merchant, about 1798. He and his brother John boarded with their mother in Brattle street. The Boston Directory, 1810, says Amos Binney, W. I. Goods store, 3 Broad street, house Snow Hill street. He also gave his attention to the settlement of estates in Probate Court, to the satisfaction of the judge. The late Gideon Snow a few years since informed the writer, that Mr. B. settled the estate of Mr. Thwing, and after examining large piles of accounts and papers, discovered great wrong, and secured to his children considerable property. Mr. Snow said, though he was a Federalist, and Mr. Binney a Democrat in politics, they were good friends; and when Mr. B. endured the great persecutions and trials while Navy Agent, Mr. Snow met him one day, at the time Mr. B. was perplexed and anxious, and said—' Don't you mind it, Mr. B., all know you to be incapable of these things charged against you, and you will come out of the furnace the brighter for it;' and he did. The result proved the truth of it.

In 1808–10 he was appointed a captain of the Legionary Brigade, and in 1812, Navy Agent for the port of Boston, which office he held until 1826. In 1813, he was elected Lieutenant Colonel of the 1st Regiment of Infantry, 3d Brigade, 1st Division Massachusetts Militia, Caleb Strong being Governor. Afterwards he was elected Colonel.

When he took the Navy Agency, there was no system to the Navy, or any branch of it. It was in bad repute, and thought but little of as an arm of defence against the power of England. The war, too, was opposed by a strong party. In the war of 1812, his exertions in the office were unceasing, day and night, and at times very severe and trying. The government funds were not forthcoming for many weeks at a time, and to meet the pressing demands he incurred for the Navy, he often had to pledge all his own and those of his brother, and borrowed largely of all his friends who would trust the Government. Among them was the late honorable merchant, William Gray, who was clear-sighted enough to discern brighter days, and freely responded to Mr. B's calls for money for the public service. It was mainly owing to Mr. B's great exertions, ably seconded by Com. Hull, that the frigate Constitution " Old Ironsides" was fitted out in season to meet the Guerriere. On this occasion she must have remained in ordinary, had not the means to fit her for sea, recruit her crew and supply her stores, been furnished upon the personal responsibility of the Navy Agent. This victory gave confidence to the friends of the Navy, and proved that England was not invincible on the ocean. The only means he could get were Treasury notes, which his friends were obliged to dispose of at such discount as they could. For several years his accounts show large balances against the Government, at the end of each quarter.

Since 1826, he attended to other business, in which he was prosperous. He did much to develope the resources of the mineral wealth of the country, which, in his youth, in an extensive pedestrian tour throughout New England, he examined. He started the Vermont Copperas Works, in Strafford, Vt., of which he was President; assisted in the working of coal in Worcester county, Mass.; and in various iron and other mines. As President, he took the management of the Worcester Railroad; and was President of the Market Bank, Boston.

He saved Joy's building from fire, in a large conflagration, by procuring and nailing over it all the bales of blankets he could obtain. Several pieces of plate, presented to him, mark the appreciation of his various services. He was largely interested in real estate, in and around Boston. He assisted both by his services, advice, and money, many churches and schools, as well as individuals. His judgment was acute and penetrating. He was enterprising and industrious, devoting but few hours to repose. He was an early and steady patron of American manufactures. He had the satisfaction of living down political animosity, and became known to the whole community as an honest, upright, able and energetic man, possessing extraordinary talents for business, with a sound and discriminating judgment, displayed in the numerous corporations and public institutions, of which he had been a member.

He was charitable and liberal, and a sincere Christian, a member of the Independent Methodist Church. As early as 1797, he made piety the chief and best thing to be obtained in this life, and never swerved from its principles, or his duty. Regular in his attendance at church, on the Sabbath, both forenoon and afternoon, he put away all worldly employments. At his funeral were present, among others, the venerable "Father" Taylor, and the pastor of the African Church, both of whom lost in him a friend.

Of eleven children, but four survive. Col. Binney was of good personal appearance; rather stout, dark complexion, black hair and eyes. An excellent portrait of him is preserved in his family. His means of education were so small in youth, that it may be truly said, he educated himself, and was a self-made man.''

Bro. Benjamin Marshall Nevers, was born in that part of Woburn, Mass., which is now the town of Burlington, August 18, 5789. He was initiated May 4, 5815; admitted to membership, October 6, 5815; elected Senior Steward for 5819; and Junior Deacon for 5820. He has remained constant in the faith, and no one in the Lodge is esteemed more than he is, for amiability of character, and fraternal interest in their prosperity. Capt. Nevers was admitted to membership in the Ancient and Honorable Artillery Company in 5818, and was a Lieutenant in that corps in 5827.

Bro. David Henshaw was made a Mason, October 6, 5814. At a previous meeting, he was proposed for initiation by Bro. Joseph R. Chandler, according to the records:

September 1, 5814. "Bro. Chandler presented the application of Mr. David Henshaw, praying to be admitted into the Masonic Order."

Membership was conferred upon him March 6, 5817. He became afterwards a life-member. He was a firm supporter of the Masonic institution, and anti-masonry met with his sternest condemnation. The following letter is plain spoken, and to the point—where an opponent was to be dealt with, his epithets were unsparing, yet to his friends he was the gentlest of men:

" *Leicester, May* 20, 5847.

Gents :—I am obliged for your kind invitation to attend the celebration by the Morning Star Lodge of Worcester, on the 24th of June. I am about leaving on a journey for a few weeks, and should I return in season, I shall do myself the honor of being present at your celebration.

Allow me to congratulate the Brethren on the prosperous state of this charitable Institution. Those of the Brethren who stood firm, fearless and unmoved during the hot persecution of the Order, and amidst apostacy and treachery, in years past, cannot but feel satisfied with their own course, and gratified with the present condition and prospect of the Fraternity.

Very respectfully, your obedient servent,

DAVID HENSHAW.

To the Committee of the Morning Star Lodge, Worcester."

Bro. Henshaw was born in Leicester, Mass., April 2, 5791, and died there November 11, 5852. During the more active part of his life, he resided in Boston. He was a merchant, and followed the trade of druggist in Boston, by which he accumulated an ample competency. He was upright in all his transactions, and left an honorable reputation as a merchant of integrity and ability. In 5826, he was a senator from Suffolk county, and a member of the Massachusetts Board for Internal Improvement. He was, in 5834, a government director of the United States Bank. From April 14, 5829, to February, 5838, he was the Collector of the Port of Boston, the manifold duties of which position he discharged with the approbation of the entire mercantile community. The office of Secretary of the Navy of the United States, he occupied in 5833–4, but political considerations prevented his confirmation by the U. S. Senate, much to the regret of all who knew his eminent fitness for the station. After his retirement from public life, he visited Europe; but his usefulness was in some degree impaired by a disease which caused him great bodily suffering. But his strong and active mind never prevented his feeling a lively interest in passing events of general concern. He was an able writer, and the productions of his pen would, if collected, make a most valuable and instructive volume. The proceedings of Columbian Lodge, consequent upon his death, were as follows :—

December 2, 5852. " Bro. Stevens announced the death of Bro. DAVID HENSHAW, whereupon Bros. Stevens, Schouler and Adams, were appointed a committee to retire and report suitable resolutions; who subsequently reported the following Preamble and Resolutions.

Whereas it has pleased the Great Architect of the Universe, the Maker and Creator of all things, to remove by death, our late distinguished brother and member of Columbian Lodge— the Hon. David Henshaw—and to take him to Himself:

And whereas our late distinguished brother was one of the oldest members of our Fraternity, in this Commonwealth, distinguished alike by the purity of his life, his good faith as a Free and Accepted Mason, and his ability in the civil services of the State and nation;—Therefore be it, by this, the Columbian Lodge of Boston,

Resolved, That in the departure of our friend and brother to that ' bourne from whence no traveller returns,' we feel our loss, and lament that one who, while living, bore himself so well, and cast by the excellence of his life and the prominence of his position, so great an honor upon the Masonic Fraternity, should have been taken from us.

Resolved, That as a mark of our esteem and regard for our late brother, and sorrow for his decease, that the usual badge of mourning be placed upon the altar for the ensuing three months, and that this Preamble and these resolutions be entered upon the records of this Lodge, and a certified copy be transmitted by the Secretary to Brother Joseph W. Ward, with a request that he communicate the same to the family of the deceased. BENJAMIN STEVENS, WILLIAM SCHOULER, CHARLES B. F. ADAMS, } *Committee.*"

Bro. Amos Cotting was initiated January 18, 5821, and admitted a member of the Lodge March 1, 5821. He became a life-member Dec. 4, 5828. He was one of the signers of the protest issued by the Fraternity in 5831, and has always been firm in his loyalty to the institution. He was born in Marlboro, May 27, 5797.

Bro. Horace Collamore was born in Scituate, (now South Scituate,) Mass., Nov. 4, 5791. His father was a farmer, in moderate circumstances, and frequently represented the town in General Court. Horace was the youngest of eight children who survived infancy. He received the common school education of the day—working on the farm in summer, and attending the District School in winter. In the spring of 5807, he went to Boston to learn a trade of Belcher &

Eastburn, merchant tailors, in Court street, and remained with them some six months, when they suspended business, and he returned to the paternal roof and again attended the District School during the winter. In the succeeding spring, he returned to the city to attend in a dry goods store in Marlboro' street, (now Washington,) where he remained for something more than a year. This employer having, also, suspended business, he returned to the country, determined to finish his education, and study a profession. He attended the Academy at Hanover, studied the languages, taught District Schools, &c., until the spring of 1811, when his brother, then of the firm of Hastings & Collamore, prevailed on him to go to the city once more. He remained with that firm until November, 5812, when he commenced the crockery and glass-ware business on his own account, at No. 64 Court street. One year afterwards, he removed to No. 48 Marlboro street, corner of Franklin street, where he continued in business until he left the city in 5821, on account of declining health. He was married to Laura Briggs, of Pembroke, Sept. 20, 5821.

He was initiated in Columbian Lodge in 5813, and became a member of the same soon after. In 5816, he received the degree of Royal Arch Mason. In 5821, he purchased the farm on which he now lives, and removed to Pembroke, where he has since devoted his time to farming, keeping a country store, &c. In 5829, he was chosen Master of Phœnix Lodge, in Hanover, an adjoining town, which Lodge a year or two afterwards surrendered their charter, in consequence of the Anti-Masonic excitement. During the same year, he was appointed Postmaster of Pembroke, which office he now holds. For several years, he was Brigade Major and Inspector of the 1st Brigade, 5th Division, Massachusetts Militia.

In 5841 and '42, he represented that town in the General Court; in 5853, was chosen to the Senate from Plymouth District; has for several years held the offices of Justice of the Peace, and Justice of the Peace and of the Quorum. He has been a member and officer in the Plymouth County Agricultural Society from its infancy; has been Supervisor for several years, and is now one of its Vice Presidents. He is Chairman of the Board of Selectmen of the town of Pembroke, which office he has held for several years. He has had eleven children, ten of whom are now living, and has twelve grand-children. In 5819, Bro. Collamore presented to the Lodge, two splendid Masonic pitchers, which are still in their possession, (see page 234.) They were manufactured in Staffordshire, Eng., agreeably to his order. By reference to the proceedings of the Lodge, forty years ago, it will be seen that he mingled regularly with the brethren; and the interest he then took in Masonry, remains undiminished.

The delinquency of members to pay their dues, occasioned some trouble to the Lodge for a short time after its institution, but since then, a general promptness to respond to this obligation demands honorable notice. Non-attendance at meetings has, now and then, given cause of complaint, though this important duty has, on the whole, been discharged with remarkable fidelity. The members seem to have been fully sensible of their responsibility in this respect; and of their engagements as Masons, to watch over the interests of the Lodge, and, by rightly influencing their action, to promote the welfare of the Fraternity.

July 7, 5796. " *Voted*, That those members who mostly are absent, from time to time, are to be notified by the Secretary, when he compares the records; and that unless they attend in future, or give proper excuse, the Lodge is in duty bound to expel any one or more of such members for not attending to their summons.",

July 25, 5796. " On motion, *Voted*, That the Lodge adjourn till tomorrow night, to take into consideration the delinquent members, and act thereon."

July 26, 5796. " The debates on members attending, referred over to next regular Lodge night."

August 4, 5796. " Bro. Coles reported that he had sent a copy of the note respecting the attendance of members, passed the 7th July last, to those members whom it concerns. This was referred to a special Lodge."

March 15, 5800. " *Voted*, That if any of those members who are delinquent in quarterages will come forward and state to the Lodge their inability to discharge the same, they shall be relinquished and still be considered as members of the Lodge, provided they appear within four months from January 16th, 1800; after which time they cannot be considered members agreeably to the By-Laws made and provided."

October 2, 5800. " *Voted*, That the Secretary call again on delinquent members, and inform them that unless they settle their arrearages, their names will be erased as members of Columbian Lodge."

June 3, 5802. " The Treasurer reported that he had called on the persons indebted to Columbian Lodge, but could not obtain payment. Bros. Jenks, Baxter and McDonnell were appointed a committee to alter or amend the 28th Article of the By-Laws, and report to the Lodge the next regular night."

December 20, 5821. " Brothers Jenkins, Baxter and Appleton were appointed a committee to consider the claims of long absent members to their standing in the Lodge."

"The committee on the subject of delinquent members, chosen at the regular communication in January last, having attended to the duties assigned them; recommend, that,

In consideration of the favorable condition of the finances of the Lodge, and of the peculiar circumstances of the whole Institution at the present time, that no order be taken on the subject, and that the provision in the 1st Article of the By-Laws, which authorizes the discharge of any member who neglects to pay 'his periodical dues for eighteen months,' be suspended in the instance of such members as have come under this rule up to the first of November last.

And the committee further recommend that all sums now due the Lodge for quarterages, be remitted to members owing them; provided, however, that any such member thus indebted, be first solicited by the Secretary, to pay the same, and in case of his want of ability or inclination, that his accounts be cancelled.

On the subject of Bro. ―― ――'s application for a discharge from the Lodge, the committee would report, that in their opinion it is inexpedient to act thereon; Bro. ―― having been understood by one of the committee to express a willingness to continue a member.

All which is respectfully submitted.

DAVID TILLSON,
RUEL BAKER, } Committee.
SAMUEL A. ALLEN,

Boston, April 7th, 5836."

The law of the Lodge relative to candidates for the degrees has undergone very little change. The first provisions, those existing in 5795, were, that every candidate for initiation should stand proposed one month, and obtain the unanimous consent of the brethren present at the meeting at which his application was to be acted upon. If two negatives appeared against him no further proceedings could be had at that time; but if there was only one negative, he could have the benefit of a second and third ballot. If after rejection, he were proposed again, his second application was proceeded with as if he had never been mentioned in the Lodge. The fee for the degrees was three pounds, sixteen shillings and six pence. Every brother made in the Lodge could be passed whenever the Master should judge him to be deserving of it; but if he were not so made, he was required to obtain the unanimous consent of the brethren present, at a meeting legal for that purpose. The fee for this degree alone, was eighteen shillings. A candidate for the degree of M. M. was examined before the Lodge as to his proficiency in masonic knowledge, and could not be raised without a unanimous vote of the members of the Lodge present. The fee demanded from him if he had been made in Columbian Lodge was one pound, four shillings; and one pound, ten shillings if he had not been so made.

The regulations of 5799 as to candidates for the degrees, slightly differed from those previously existing. The term of probation was the same; and unanimous consent demanded. Three negatives appearing against an applicant, further proceedings were stayed; but if there were only one or two negatives, he could have the benefit of a second trial. If rejected and re-proposed, the proceedings commenced *de novo.* The fee was seventeen dollars. The degree of F. C. was conferred according to the old rule. The fee was two dollars for a brother not made in the Lodge. No change of the previous law was made as to raising; excepting that the fee was altered to three dollars, if the candidate had been made in the Lodge, and to five dollars, if he had been made in another Lodge.

At a meeting of the Lodge, February 4, 5802,

it was voted, "that the regulations of the Grand
Lodge render it indispensably necessary to alter
the price of making a Mason to fifteen dollars,
including the two dollars required by the Grand
Lodge for every initiate; that the price of passing
to the degree of F. C. be two dollars; that every
brother raised to the Sublime Degree of Master
shall pay three dollars; that the secretary shall
receive for every certificate (notwithstanding the
regulations of the Grand Lodge,) one dollar, exclusive of the parchment; and that the secretary
be directed to alter the table of fees accordingly."

At the meeting of December 1, 5803, the regulations were altered so as to provide that a candidate could be proposed at a "previous meeting,"
instead of "standing proposed one month."

The regulations established in 5808, provided
that every member who proposed a candidate for
initiation, should deposit with the secretary five
dollars, which were placed to the credit of the
candidate. At the next meeting the ballot took
place, and if it was unanimously in favor of the
candidate, he received the first degree, and paid
fifteen dollars. If he were accepted, and refused
to attend for initiation, he forfeited the deposit of
five dollars; if rejected, the money was refunded
to him. A candidate once rejected, could be again
proposed; but if rejected a second time he could
have "no more trials." Candidates for the second
degree, if made in the Lodge, could be passed on
the recommendation of the Master, by paying two
dollars; but if made in another Lodge, unanimous consent by ballot and the same charge were
necessary. Every regular F. C. could be raised
after obtaining unanimous consent by ballot and

paying three dollars into the treasury, and three dollars to the secretary, which would entitle him to a diploma.

At the communication of December 5, 5811, it was decreed that every candidate for initiation shall make application in writing; should be balloted for at the next meeting; and, if accepted, pay fifteen dollars to the secretary for the funds of the Lodge.

Candidates for initiation by the law of 5816, made their applications in writing, and were balloted for at the next meeting; if accepted, they received the first degree, paid fifteen dollars to the funds of the Lodge, and a fee of one dollar to the secretary. An applicant for the degree of F. C., if made in Columbian Lodge, and recommended by the Master, was passed, on the payment of two dollars. If not made in the Lodge, he was required to obtain unanimous consent, and pay the same fee. To raise a brother, unanimous consent was necessary; and the payment of six dollars for the funds, and three dollars to the secretary, which entitled him to a diploma. The fees for the secretary were abolished July 2, 5818, and he was allowed instead two dollars and fifty cents.

The by-laws adopted in 5821, provided that each candidate for the degrees should make a printed or written application stating the place of his birth, his age, residence and occupation; and that it should enclose the sum of fifteen dollars. The application was read in open Lodge; if he were rejected the money was returned to him; if accepted, on receiving the first degree he was required to pay the further sum of eight dollars, when he was entitled to the second degree, upon

the recommendation of the Master, and to the
third, by a unanimous vote of the members present.   Any brother who had received the first degree in another Lodge, and desired the second and
third, paid eight dollars ; and he who obtained
the third degree only, was charged six dollars.
The secretary received one dollar for each diploma, which was paid for by the recipient.

The latest regulations respecting candidates for
degrees—the by-laws of 5854—provide that each
candidate make a printed or written application
at a stated meeting, setting forth his place of birth,
his residence, age and occupation.   He is required
to pay thirty dollars, which are to be returned to
him if he is not accepted.   Any brother having
had the first degree, or the first and second degrees
conferred upon him in another Lodge, can receive
the other degrees or degree, by applying as other
candidates are required to do, and paying for each
degree ten dollars.   A unanimous vote to confer
the degree is requisite.   A brother on being raised
to the degree of M. M. is entitled to a diploma, for
which he is charged one dollar.   It is not regular
to give more than one degree to the same individual on the same day, nor at a less interval than
one month from the time of receiving a previous
degree.   A strict inquiry by a committee shall be
made into the moral character of every candidate.
If an applicant has been rejected by another Lodge,
he cannot be initiated into Columbian Lodge without a recommendation from six members of the
Lodge where he was rejected, of whom the Masters and Wardens of such Lodge shall be three.
No person residing in a town within this Commonwealth, wherein a Lodge is held, can be

admitted a candidate, without the approbation of the Master and Wardens of a Lodge in the town of his residence ; nor can he be received from any other State, he being a resident thereof, where a regular Grand Lodge is established, without the written permission of the Grand Master of such State. No E. A. or F. C., initiated or passed in another Lodge within the United States, can be passed or raised without the consent of the Master and Wardens of the Lodge in which he was first admitted. No petition for degrees can be withdrawn unless the report of the investigating committee be favorable.

In cases of emergency, the dispensation of the Grand Master, or of his Deputy, has been obtained to supersede the requirement that candidates should stand proposed a given term, before they could be initiated. Candidates made in a Lodge specially called for the purpose, have paid the expenses therefor in addition to the usual fees. The names of candidates for degrees have always been entered on the summons or notifications of the members of the Lodge. The whole number of persons upon whom degrees had been conferred to June 7, 5855, was one thousand and thirty-five, of whom nine hundred and forty-five received all the degrees in Columbian Lodge. The following quotations from the records are pertinent to this subject :—

July 6, 5815. "An application for initiation was presented from the following gentlemen of the United States Navy, through the medium of Bro. Amos Binney, viz :— James H. Clark, Purser ; Lawrence Kearney, Lieutenant Com'g ; John A. Kearney, Surgeon ; Abraham S. Ten Eyck, Lieut. ; Benjamin W. Boothe, Lieut. ; Elisha Peck, Sailing Master ; William Hall, Captain's Mate ; William Laughton, Lieut. ; and Joseph Wragg, Lieut."

July 10, 5815. "Ballots were taken for the following gentlemen, viz. ; James H. Clark, John A. Kearney, Lawrence Kearney, Benjamin W. Boothe, William Hall, Abraham S. Ten Eyck, Elisha Peck, Asheton Y. Humphreys, and John Hamilton, and they were severally and unanimously accepted."

February 7, 5822. "R. W. Bros. Baxter, Jr., Fisher, Cobb, G. G. Smith, and Stevens, were appointed a committee, to consider and report the manner best calculated to furnish this Lodge with Masonic information."

September 23, 5825. " *Voted*, That the thanks of the Lodge be presented to R. W. Bro. D. L. Childs, for his services to the Lodge as an interpreter, during the ceremony of the initiation of E. F. B. Mundrucŭ and J. F. de Mello."

September 7, 5826. "Brothers G. G. Smith, Appleton and S. Smith, were appointed a committee to confer with the committee from Mt. Lebanon Lodge, to propose a plan by which information may be given to all the members of all the Lodges in this city, when application is made for the degrees."

October 5, 5826. "The joint committee of all the Lodges in this city, appointed to report a plan by which information may be given to the members of the subordinate institutions in the city, when application is made for the degrees, made a report, which was accepted and placed on the file."

June 15, 5843. " *Voted*, That a suggestion of the R. W. M. as to the expediency of fixing a 'Box' in the ante-room, wherein shall be placed regularly the names of all candidates for initiation and membership, together with the committees on such applications,—be referred to a committee composed of the three first officers of the Lodge, with authority to take such action on the subject, as they may think proper."

February 1, 5844. "The committee on a 'Box,' or frame, to contain the names of the individuals proposed for initiation or membership, reported that it had been procured, and would be placed in the ante-room prior to the next meeting. Accepted."

The brethren who are mentioned below, were initiated in Columbian Lodge.

The venerable and most worthy R. W. Bro. John B. Hammatt, is probably the oldest surviving

initiate of the Lodge, he having received the first
degree August 7, 5800. He was passed and
raised August 21, of the same year. He was
admitted to membership in St. John's Lodge, in
November, 5801, and elected Master thereof in
5810. He was exalted to R. A. Masonry in St.
Andrew's Chapter in 5801, and became a member
June 9, 5802. He filled the office of King in that
body in 5808, 5809 and 5813, and of that of High
Priest in 5810 and 5811. In the Grand Lodge,
he was appointed a Steward, in 5802, by R. W.
Isaiah Thomas; a Deacon, in 5807, by R. W.
Timothy Bigelow; was elected J. G. Warden in
December, 5811, and S. G. Warden in December,
5814. He was knighted in the Boston Encampment in 5805, and admitted to membership therein,
in 5806. Bro. Hammatt removed to Alexandria,
D. C. in 5815, and returned to Boston in 5830.
While in Alexandria, he was commissioned by
the Grand Lodge of Virginia, as D. Dep'y Grand
Master, in which capacity he visited fourteen
Lodges in his District. At the end of the year,
he declined a reappointment. He was at the time
a member of Alexandria Washington Lodge, No.
22, which, as Bro. H. remarks in a note to a
friend, was "the Lodge that Gen. Washington
presided over for several years, he having been
named in the charter as the first Master." In
5818, he was appointed by the Grand Chapter of
Maryland and District of Columbia, as the first
High Priest of Potomac Chapter in Georgetown,
which station he held three years, when he was
called to preside over Brook Chapter, in Alexandria, who received a charter from the same Grand
Chapter. In 5820, he was elected Master of

Evangelic Lodge in Alexandria, and served two or three years. In 5826, he was elected Deputy Grand High Priest of the Grand Chapter of the District of Columbia, over which body R. W. William W. Seaton was at the time Grand High Priest. They both retained their offices until 5830. While in the Grand Chapter, Bro. H. was appointed Grand Lecturer by the Grand Lodge of the District of Columbia. After his return to Boston, in 5830, he was appointed Deputy Grand Master by R. W. Augustus Peabody; he served as Grand Commander of the Boston Encampment of K. T.; Grand H. P. of the Grand Chapter of Massachusetts; and as Grand Master of the Grand Encampment of Massachusetts and Rhode Island.

Brother Hammatt was born in Boston, (on Hanover street, where Blackstone street now crosses it,) June 12, 5778. In 5792, he began to serve as an apprentice to Moses Grant, upholsterer and paper-stainer, who kept on Union street; and in 5799, he commenced business on his own account, on the same street. His exemplary and useful career through a long life, has justly earned for him the high esteem in which he is universally regarded.

Bro. Nahum Capen was born April 1, 5804, in the town of Canton, Norfolk county, Mass., and received the first degrees of Masonry in Columbian Lodge, under peculiar and very interesting circumstances. The occasion was deemed an extraordinary one, as may be inferred from the fact, that the degrees were conferred upon him in presence of the officers of the Grand Lodge—the Grand Master presiding. The origin of this distinction, which stands alone in the history of the

Masonic institution, in the United States, may be briefly stated.

In 5826 or 5827, at the time of the Morgan excitement, Bro. Capen was applied to, he being connected with a large publishing house, to publish the Secrets of Freemasonry, being promised large profits if he would consent to give to the work the influence of his firm, and take measures to insure it an extensive circulation.

Instead of yielding to the temptation, he solicited a statement of motives from the author for pursuing such a course ; and being favorably impressed by what he knew of the institution, to favor and defend it, he prevailed upon the applicant to abandon his purpose, as a wicked one, and to consent to submit his case as one of want, to the good judgment of the government of the Grand Lodge. After much and patient investigation, the erring brother confessed his error, and earnestly and repeatedly, with tears of gladness, thanked his benefactor for saving him from shame and degradation, and the institution from the scandal of the world. Resolutions of thanks were passed and tendered to Bro. Capen, for the course which he pursued, and as a mark of respect, the degrees were conferred upon him as an honorary distinction ; he having expressed a determination to become a member of the Order. The Chapter Degrees, and those of Knights Templars, were also conferred upon him, and for the same reasons. These meetings were attended by a few of the leading Masons of the Commonwealth, and were rendered intensely interesting by the peculiar circumstances which occasioned them.

In Dec., 5833, Bro. Capen was appointed by Grand Master Abbot, Corresponding Secretary of the Grand Lodge, which office he held until Dec., 5840. While holding this office, he visited Europe in 5835, and officially communicated with the Grand Lodge of England. He delivered a communication from the Master of the Grand Lodge of Massachusetts, to the Master of the Grand Lodge of England—the late Duke of Sussex. The account of his visit to Kensington Palace was made on his return, and may be found on the files of the Grand Lodge.

As might be supposed, one who was ready to defend Masonry, unasked, and before he became a member, would not be likely to prove a silent or inactive observer of events, after he was made a brother, under circumstances of so much interest. His Masonic life was commenced in the midst of the Anti-Masonic war, and he made numerous contributions to the press, and continued to exert himself on all proper occasions, so long as Anti-Masonry was kept alive.

In 5829, he delivered an address before the Constellation Lodge, Dedham, Mass., at their public celebration, June 24, which was printed in Boston, and republished in Albany, N. Y., for general distribution. He wrote an elaborate reply to the letter of the Hon. Richard Rush, of Pa., which was continued in six successive numbers of the Boston Masonic Mirror, and which was republished, in a cheap form for general distribution, in Lancaster, Pa. He was the author of the Appeal to the Masons of Vermont, and in 5833, he replied to the Hon. William Wirt, in the Boston Masonic Mirror; and in 5837 he delivered the

Annual Address before the Grand Lodge, at the public installation of officers at the Masonic Temple.

Bro. Capen wrote the biography of Dr. Gall, and edited his works—translated from the French in six volumes—and the biography of Spurzheim, and edited his works published in the United States. He was principal editor of the Annals of Phrenology, in 2 volumes, 8vo. He edited the writings of the late Judge Woodbury, in 3 vols., and the Massachusetts State Record, from 5847 to 5851, 3 volumes. He was one of the first to write on the subject of International Copy-right, in the United States, and was the author of a letter to Hon. John Davis, of the United States Senate, respecting the U. S. Census—and the Census Board was originated by his suggestion. He is the author of other works, on Science, History, Political Economy, &c., &c. The following are some of the public journals to which he has occasionally contributed articles on Political Economy, Science, Education, &c., &c.

Boston Daily Advertiser, Boston Daily Post, Boston Courier, Boston Atlas, Boston Palladium, Boston Evening Gazette, Workingman's Advocate, Jackson Republican, American Traveller, Boston Times, Boston Spectator, Bay State Democrat, Masonic Mirror, Mason Magazine, Pennsylvanian, Phila., Washington Union, National Intelligencer, Washington Star, etc., etc., etc.

M. W. Bro. Winslow Lewis, M. D., the present Grand Master of Massachusetts, was initiated in Columbian Lodge, November 3, 5830, passed January 6, 5831, and raised February 3, 5831. By the following extract from the records, it appears that he did not receive his diploma at the time when he was first entitled to it:

July 3, 5845. "The Secretary was authorized to issue a Diploma to Bro. Winslow Lewis, Jr., who received his third degree in February 5831, in this Lodge, and to affix to it the names of the then officers of the Lodge."

He is a member of St. John's Lodge, St. Paul's Chapter, Council of Royal and Select Masters, Boston Encampment, Grand Chapter, Grand Encampment, affiliated member of the "Loge clement—Amitie," at Paris, and honorary member of Pythagoras Lodge, No. 86, at New York. He has been Sen. Warden of St. John's Lodge, High Priest of St. Paul's Chapter, Commander of the Boston Encampment, Grand King of the Grand Chapter, Grand Generalissimo of the Grand Encampment, Corresponding Grand Secretary of the Grand Lodge, a Trustee of the Grand Charity Fund, a Trustee of the Masonic Temple, and Deputy Grand Master of the Grand Lodge. This enumeration does not evidence the extent of his official services, as he has also held many subordinate stations. His unremitting and arduous efforts to advance the welfare of the brotherhood, have endeared him to them in bonds which cannot be sundered; and the elevated position which he now so ably fills, he justly merits. In speaking recently of his regard for the Masonic institution, he remarked, that "truth and my feelings prompt the declaration that in Masonry I have found the best friends, the best social ties and comforts; and that the 'whitest' hours of my life (apart from my family,) have been when surrounded by 'Brothers,' and around that Altar, where heart beats responsive to heart, and all 'mingle into bliss.'"

Bro. Lewis is the son of the late R. W. Winslow Lewis,—who was also a valuable member of the Masonic fraternity,—and was born in Boston, July 8, 5799. He was educated at Harvard University, and was a member of the class of 5819. He received the degree of M. D., in 5822. He is a Counsellor of the Massachusetts Medical Society ; a member of the American Medical Society, at Paris, and consulting surgeon of the Massachusetts General Hospital. As a surgeon, he undoubtedly stands at the head of his profession in Massachusetts. Dr. Lewis has entered but little into politics, probably because the asperities of that sphere are repulsive to his amiable and genial nature. He was a member of the Common Council of Boston in 5839, and he represented that city in the Legislature in 5836, 5852 and 5853.

During the fifteen years immediately succeeding the establishment of the Lodge, visitors were required to pay a fee. It being at that time the custom to provide refreshments on Lodge nights, of which all the brethren present were expected to partake, rendered the charge a just and proper one. The practice of having refreshments prevailed in all Lodges. The amount of the fee at first demanded, was two shillings from every "brother belonging to town or its vicinities." Foreigners were not subject to the requirement on their first visit to the Lodge. In 5795, November 16, the fee was raised to "two shillings, three pence, or three-eights of a dollar." At the meeting of May 7, 5896, it was advanced to half a dollar. According to the by-laws of 5799, no brother was required to pay a visiting fee the first time he appeared in the Lodge, but all

other visitors paid three shillings, unless excused by the Master.   By the by-laws adopted
in 5808, every visitor was obliged to pay fifty
cents, unless excused by the Master.   In 5809,
the by-laws were so far altered, that no fee
should be received from a brother for his first
visit.   At the meeting of December 6, 5810,
every worthy brother wishing to visit the Lodge,
was "admitted and made welcome, without money
and without price."   This last provision constitutes an article in the by-laws of 5816; but as this
custom as to visitors had become obsolete, in
consequence of refreshments being no longer provided by the Lodge, excepting on rare occasions,
the by-laws, afterwards adopted, contain no provision for admittance fees from visiting brethren.

CHAPTER XVIII.

WARDENS. — TREASURER. — SECRETARY. — DEACONS. — STEWARDS. — CHAPLAIN. — MARSHAL. — INSIDE SENTINEL. — TYLER. — CLOSET STEWARD. — ORGANIST. — EXTRACTS.

By the general regulations of the Grand Lodge of England, in 5720, in case of sickness, death or necessary absence of the Master, the Senior Warden acted as Master *pro tempore*, if no Brother was present who had been Master of that Lodge before; for in that case the absent Master's authority reverted to the last Master then present; though he could not act until the said Senior Warden had congregated the Lodge, or, in his absence, the Junior Warden. At a later day, in this country, when the Master was absent, a Past Master, only, could confer degrees, but the Wardens presided over all other transactions. Afterwards, though the regulations did not prohibit the work to be done by the Wardens, yet it was judged due by courtesy to a Past Master, if present, that they should invite him to preside. The rule that now prevails, and which has existed for many years, is that the Senior Warden governs in the absence of the Master, and when both of those officers are absent, the duty of governing devolves upon the Junior Warden; and the authority of the presiding Warden extends for the time being over all the transactions of the Lodge.

To some extent, the by-laws of Columbian Lodge have required and still require the advice and consent of the Wardens to certain acts of the Master. Power to call Lodges of emergency was vested in the Master and Wardens until 5821, when it was given to the Master alone, in whom it has since resided. Certain subordinate officers have either been chosen by the Master and Wardens, or appointed by the Master with the advice and consent of the Wardens; and in 5816, the fees of the Tyler were determined by the Master and Wardens, within a maximum sum fixed by the Lodge. The Wardens have seats in the Grand Lodge, and each has a vote therein on all questions.

The names of the brethren who have filled the office of Senior Warden, from the origin of the Lodge to the present time, are—Jas. Eaton, Samuel Goldsbury, John Rittenhouse, Amasa Stetson, Daniel Baxter, Sr., William J. McDonnell, Turner Crooker, Stephen Bean, Ebenezer Phillips, Joseph Jenkins, Samuel Smith, David Moody, Nathaniel Heard, Elijah Morse, Benjamin B. Appleton, Sr., Elisha V. Glover, Daniel Baxter, Jr., Francis Fisher, George G. Smith, Henry D. Wolcott, David Tillson, William H. Neville, William Bittle, Samuel A. Allen, Andrew H. Ward, George M. Thacher, Peter C. Jones, William W. Baker, Wm. D. Coolidge, John T. Heard, Preston A. Ames, William B. Fowle, Jr., and Robert L. Robbins.

The following extracts from the records relating to this office communicate facts of interest:

October 4, 5798. " The following toast was given from the chair, the lights being previously extinguished, and the Senior Warden's seat made vacant, which gave proper solemnity to the occasion :—' To the memory, and much respected but now departed friend and brother, James Eaton, late Senior Warden of this Lodge, whose mortal part though now made food for worms, his immortal, we trust, has a place in that Lodge, where presides eternally the Grand Master of the Universe.' Bro. Eaton departed this life at Newport."

February 3, 5814. " Previous to proceeding to business, W. Bro. Morse called the attention of the brethren to the great loss the Lodge had sustained, by the death of our late Bro. Nath. Heard, who had deceased since the last meeting. Several select sentences were read from the Book of Constitutions, suited to the occasion, after which the following resolve was passed, and ordered to be recorded, viz. :—

Resolved, That, in token of the respect which we owe to the memory of our deceased brother, Nath. Heard, who was not only a useful member of this Lodge, from having sustained important offices for many years, but an honor to the Craft, we will dress the furniture and clothing of the Lodge in mourning for three months from this date."

March 3, 5814. " The office of Senior Warden being vacant by the death of Bro. Heard, the Lodge proceeded to fill said vacancy. The votes being called for, it appeared that Bro. E. Morse was unanimously elected. Bro. Glover was chosen Junior Warden, Bros. Stone and Collamore, Senior and Junior Deacons, and Bros. Braman and Chandler, Stewards. The officers were then installed into their respective stations, in due form."

January 15, 5818. " The Right Worshipful Master then adverted to one of the reasons for calling this meeting, viz. : The vacancy in the Senior Warden's department, occasioned by the resignation of Br. E. Morse, who had recently been appointed by the Grand Lodge their Corresponding Secretary. W. Bro. Morse had requested him to apologise for his absence this evening, and also to tender to this Lodge his warmest wishes for its interests, honor, harmony and happiness, and to say that his heart was with them, and his person should be present at their meetings, as often as his other duties would permit."

December 6, 5838. " The death of our worthy and esteemed brother and late Senior Warden, was announced from the Chair; and, on motion of Bro. G. G. Smith, it was *Voted*, That the two senior officers of the Lodge, with Brothers

Smith, Appleton and S. A. Allen, be a committee to address a suitable letter to the family of our deceased Brother William Bittle."

December 20, 5838. " *Voted*, That R. W. Brothers G. G. Smith and Appleton, be a committee to consider and report on the subject of a funeral service, in token of our respect and esteem for our departed brother and late Senior Warden, William Bittle. *Voted*, That the three first officers be added to the last named committee."

January 3, 5839. " The committee on the subject of Bro. Bittle's death, reported that in their opinion it was not advisable to take any order thereon."

" *Newton*, April 27, 1842.

B. B. APPLETON, Jr., Secretary of Columbian Lodge.

My Brother,—Will you have the goodness to lay this communication before the Lodge? Having removed from the city, distance and other engagements will prevent my regular attendance for the future, at your stated meetings; at least it is too certain to be so, for me to think of retaining and discharging my official duties therein, with punctuality so necessary and requisite, in one, whose duty it is to look well to the west. I therefore deem it my duty to resign the station of Senior Warden of Columbian Lodge, and desire this communication may be considered as my resignation. I will meet with you when I can, and whether absent or present, will coöperate with you for the good of Masonry, and Columbian Lodge in particular.

The future prospects of our Order brighten, as we advance ; its moral health has greatly improved, by reason of some having gone out from us, who were never of us. That purification has proved of service to the Fraternity, while the seceders and defamers, like unclean birds, now find favor with none. No man, now, as formerly, glories in being known as an Anti-Mason. That appellation has become a by-word and a reproach—a reptile name, so unpopular as to be now disowned by all. The past is full of instruction for the future. That the Fraternity may profit by it, and ever hold on to that which is good and true, is the ardent wish, and shall have, unto the end, the unwavering support of your friend and Brother Mason,   ANDREW H. WARD."

" On motion, it was voted unanimously, that the thanks of Columbian Lodge be presented to Bro. A. H. Ward, for the able, zealous and faithful manner in which he has discharged the duties of its Senior Warden during his continuance in that office."

October 5, 5854. "A communication was received from W. Preston A. Ames, resigning the office of Senior Warden, which was laid upon the table."

The office of Junior Warden has been filled by Bros. John Rittenhouse, John Perkins, Samuel Hayden, Amasa Stetson, Daniel Baxter, Sr., Samuel Stetson, Elisha Tower, Joseph Kelly, Turner Crooker, John Swett, Ebenezer Phillips, Joseph Jenkins, Amos Binney, David Moody, Nathaniel Heard, Elijah Morse, Oliver Mills, Benjamin B. Appleton, Sr., Calvin Howe, Daniel Baxter, Jr., Francis Fisher, Geo. G. Smith, Henry D. Walcott, Jason Braman, Joshua B. Flint, Caleb Coburn, Peter Johnson, David Tillson, William H. Neville, Wm. Bittle, James Hunt, Joseph Grelee, Samuel A. Allen, Benjamin Converse, George M. Thacher, Jonathan Towne, John R. Dow, Wm. D. Coolidge, Nahum Ball, John T. Heard, Preston A. Ames, William B. Fowle, Jr., Robert L. Robbins, and John Stetson. The only Junior Warden who died while in office was Bro. Calvin Howe:

November 5, 5821. "R. W. Bro. Stevens announced the death of our worthy Bro. and late Junior Warden, R. W. Calvin Howe. R. W. Bros. Appleton, Fisk and Baxter were appointed a committee to report what measures shall be adopted by the Lodge, to evince its respect for the deceased, and they reported as follows:

Voted, That the brethren of Columbian Lodge will attend the funeral of our late respected brother and member, Calvin Howe, tomorrow afternoon, at 2 o'clock, and will meet for that purpose, at the house of Bro. Daniel Baxter, Jr., in South Bennett street.

Voted, That the Chaplain of the Lodge be invited to attend at Bro. Baxter's, and that solemn services be performed on the occasion, before the brethren.

Voted, That each brother be requested to provide himself with a suitable badge of mourning on the occasion. *Voted*, That the Tyler notify verbally all the members not present. Accepted unanimously.

R. W. Bros. Baxter, Dean and Jenkins were then appointed a committee to address a letter of condolence to the widow of the deceased, expressive of their regret at the loss the Lodge has sustained by this melancholy event, and their sympathy in her bereavement."

The duties of Treasurer have been nearly the same during the existence of the Lodge. Only eleven individuals have occupied the station, viz., Bros. Samuel Hayden, John W. Folsom, Amasa Stetson, Joseph Churchill, Samuel Stetson, Amos Binney, Turner Crooker, Daniel Baxter, Sr., Benj. B. Appleton, Sr., Ruel Baker and John Bigelow. Bro. Baxter was in this office twenty-three years. This extract is from the records:

August 2, 5804. " The following toast was given from the chair :—' To the memory of our respected but now departed brother, S. Stetson, (late Treasurer of this Lodge.) May his virtues be rewarded in Heaven.' "

The by-laws have uniformly provided that the Treasurer should give a bond to the Master and Wardens. In order to meet legal difficulties, the bond now existing is given to a member of the Lodge, as trustee. The form of the bond is as follows:

" *Know all men by these presents*, That I, ——— ——— of Boston, ———, as principal, and ——, ——— ——— and ——— ———, are holden and stand firmly bound and obliged unto ——— ———, of Boston aforesaid, ——— in the full and just sum of —— —— dollars. to be paid unto the said ——— ———, his executors, administrators, and assigns : to the which payment, well and truly to be made, we bind ourselves, our heirs, executors, and administrators jointly and severally, firmly by these presents.

Witness our hands and seals.

Dated the first day of March, in the year of our Lord, one thousand eight hundred and fifty-five.

The condition of this obligation is such, that whereas the above bounden —— —— has been elected, and now is the Treasurer of the Columbian Lodge of Freemasons, established in Boston, and duly organized according to the customs of the Order : And whereas by reason of said office, he will receive into his hands, divers sums of money : and divers chattels, and other things, the property of said Lodge. And whereas the said —— may from time to time hereafter, be elected to fill said office of Treasurer : Now then, if the said —— ——, his executors, or administrators, at any time upon request to him or them to be made, shall make and give unto such person or committee, as may be appointed by said Lodge, by vote at a meeting of said Lodge, held in the usual and customary manner, a just and true account of all such sum or sums of money, goods, chattels, and other things as have come, or at any time may come into his hands, charge or possession as Treasurer, either during his present term of office, or during any future term of office, for which he may be elected, and shall also pay and deliver over to his successor in office, or to any other person duly authorized by vote of Columbian Lodge as aforesaid, to receive the same, and in default of such successor, then to the said ——, his executors, administrators or assigns, all such sums of money, goods, chattels, property, certificates of stock, and other things which shall appear to be in his hands as Treasurer, or to have been received by him as Treasurer, during his present and during any future, and any previous term of his office as Treasurer, excepting such sums as have been lawfully accounted for, or by due authority paid out for the use of said Lodge.

Then this obligation to be void; otherwise to be in full force and virtue. It is understood and agreed, that this bond is given to and taken by the said —— in trust, for the benefit of Columbian Lodge, and its present and future members, according to the customs and by-laws, regulating the affairs of said Lodge.

Signed, sealed and } —— ——, delivered, in presence of } —— ——,, —— —— } —— ——.,,

The services of Secretary have been performed by Bros. John Coles, John W. Folsom, Samuel

Stetson, Jonathan F. Sleeper, Wm. J. McDonnell,
Ammi Cutter, Stephen Bean, Amos Binney, John
M. Dunham, Josiah Vose, Ezekiel Little, Nathaniel
Sawyier, Benjamin B. Appleton, Sr., Joseph Jen-
kins, Isaac McGaw, Gershom Cobb, Ebenezer W.
Hayward, Nathaniel Williams, Samuel A. Allen,
Joseph W. Ward, Benjamin B. Appleton, Jr., John
McClellan and Charles E. W. Dimmock.

The fees of the Secretary, in 5795, were six
shillings for every person made a Mason, and
twelve shillings for every certificate. The first
by-laws rendered it obligatory upon the Secretary
to inform the Lodge of any breach of them that
might come to his knowledge, under the penalty
of paying forty shillings should he neglect to do
it. In 5797, his fees were six shillings for making, and a like sum for issuing a certificate. The
by-laws of 5799 allowed him one dollar for every
person made a Mason, and two dollars for every
certificate, exclusive of parchment. This last fee
was altered February 4, 5802, to one dollar, exclusive of parchment; but in the following year
it was restored to two dollars. The by-laws of
5808, entitled the Secretary to one dollar for each
initiation, and three dollars for each Brother raised
to the degree of M. M., but no charge could be
made for the diploma, and the same fees were
allowed by the code of 5816. At the meeting
held July 2, 5818, two dollars and fifty cents
were allowed for each meeting instead of the fees
previously authorized. In 5821, the same compensation for each meeting was continued, and a
fee of one dollar allowed for diploma, and this
regulation has prevailed to this day.

May 7, 5818. "The record of the preceding meeting was read by the Secretary, after which he informed the Lodge that he had in contemplation a journey, and expected to be absent a number of months, and requested the Lodge to accept his resignation of the office of Secretary, and appoint a committee to examine and settle his accounts. The Lodge with much regret complied with his request, and appointed R. W. Master, Senior and Junior Wardens, a committee to audit said accounts."

June 4, 5818. "The committee appointed to examine the accounts of the late Secretary, J. McGaw, reported that he had performed every part of his duty in a style of elegance and correctness, which do him much credit, and entitle him to the cordial thanks and approbation of the Lodge."

July 2, 5818. "The members were requested to bring in their votes for Secretary, and Bro. Gershom Cobb had eighteen votes, it being the whole number given in. The R. W. Master was requested to inform Bro. Cobb of his election."

R. W. Charles W. Moore, though not a member of the Lodge, acted as their Secretary at the meeting of April 6, 5837. The record reads:

"The Secretary being absent, R. W. Bro. Charles W. Moore was requested to officiate as Secretary, *pro tempore.*"

The many and eminent services which, for more than thirty years, this distinguished brother has rendered to Masonry as a member and officer in various societies of the Order, and as a writer and editor, demand a more enlarged notice than can be included in a work of this description; they require, rather, a volume exclusively devoted to their consideration. A succinct statement of them is all that can be done, in this relation, for the information and gratification of the reader.

Brother Moore was born in Boston, March 29, 5801. He was proposed for the degrees in Massachusetts Lodge, in February, 5822, and he intended to have been initiated in that Lodge on the evening of his twenty-first birth day. He was, however, called to the state of Maine, and was initiated, on the recommendation of Mass. Lodge or their committee, in Kennebec Lodge, in April or May following. In October, 5822, he was admitted a member of St. Andrew's Lodge, Boston, and in the following month was placed in office. He was elected Master of that Lodge in 5833, but having, in 5834, been elected Recording Grand Secretary of the Grand Lodge, he was under the necessity of resigning the office of Master—the two being incompatible. He was, however, the same evening, elected Secretary of St. Andrew's Lodge, which place he held for sixteen years, when he resigned. In 5825, he was made a R. A. Mason in St. Andrew's Chapter, and having filled most of the offices in that body, he was, in 5840, chosen their High Priest. He was, subsequently, elected G. H. Priest of the Grand Chapter, in which he had previously sustained nearly all of the subordinate offices, including that of G. Lecturer. He was made a Knight Templar in the Boston Encampment, in 5830, or about that time, and filled most of the offices therein. He was their Grand Commander in 5837. He has also been the G. Commander of the De Molay Encampment of Boston. In 5841, he served as Grand Master of the G. Encampment of Mass. and R. I., and held the station about three years. In 5832, or thereabouts, he received the Royal and Select Master's degrees in the Boston Council, over whom he presided for ten or twelve years. He is now the third officer in the Grand Council of the State. The thirty-third degree of the Scotch Rite was conferred upon him in 5848, and he is now the G. Sec. Gen. of the Supreme Council Thirty-third for the Northern Jurisdiction of the U. S. He has also occupied various offices in the G. G. Encampment of the U. S., and is at this time their third officer.

When he was elected R. G. Secretary of the Grand Lodge, in 5834, it was the moment when the anti-masonic excitement was raging with its greatest violence in this State, and his first official act was to attest the Memorial, (written by him,) surrendering to the Legislature the Act of Incorporation of the Grand Lodge. (See page 111.) This act of surrender originated with him, and he may proudly look upon it as one of the most important and beneficial performances of his masonic life. He was the author of the Declaration given in the preceding chapter. Indeed, nearly all of the more important papers that have emanated from the Grand Lodge for many years, were, in full or in part, the work of his pen. It need only be suggested that the twenty-one years, during which he has been Secretary of the G. Lodge, have been the most trying and important in their history, to be able to appreciate the responsibilities and labors that have necessarily devolved upon him. And it should be a source of gratification to the fraternity to know that the grand institution has maintained her integrity and high respectability and influence, untarnished and unimpaired.

Bro. Moore was also Secretary of the Board of Trustees of the Grand Charity Fund, sixteen years, and is now a member and Secretary of the Board of Trustees of the Masonic Temple. In short, he has filled nearly every office in a Lodge, Chapter and Encampment, holding each several

years. During the long time that has passed since
he became a Mason, it is doubtful whether he has
been out of office; but, on the contrary, he has
rarely failed to occupy less than three or four, and
frequently five or six official stations at the same
time. At the present moment he holds three Sec-
retaryships, and three or four other offices in
different bodies—all non-paying, excepting that
of Sec'y of G. Lodge. He is also an honorary
member of several Masonic Societies, grand and
subordinate, at home and abroad. There has been
no Masonic movement of importance for thirty years
past in which he has not taken an active part.

In 5825, he established the "Masonic Mirror"
in this city, and continued it until 5835. In it
he fought the battle of Anti-masonic times, which
lasted from 5827 to 5834–5, and raged with mad
violence. In 5834 he was prosecuted for libel.
This afforded him an opportunity to establish, in
a judicial form, the iniquity of the persecution and
the profligate character of its managers. The
trial broke down the High Priest of Anti-masonry
and his supporters, and from that time the public
opinion assumed a healthful tone. The fight was
over, and it only remained to clear the field of the
wounded. The conflict left Bro. Moore with
broken health and exhausted means. The Mirror
was therefore united with, or merged in the Bun-
ker-Hill Aurora, with which he was associated as
co-editor, doing up what little fighting remained
to be done—killing off the stragglers!

Bro. Moore also published in 5828–9, two volumes of the "Amaranth, or Masonic Garland," a
work exclusively Masonic—a History of Freemasonry, several pamphlets, &c., &c. In 5841, he

started the excellent Masonic Magazine, which he still conducts, and which is invaluable, not only as a vehicle for general Masonic information, but as a most able expounder of Masonic law. Bro. Moore has probably written more on the subject of Masonry than any other man living or dead. His productions are distinguished for perspicuity, force and ability; and his articles on Masonic jurisprudence that have appeared so frequently in his Magazine, evince a profound knowledge of the ancient common law of the Order, as well as of the more modern regulations established in the various jurisdictions for its government.

Bro. John McClellan has performed the duties of Secretary during the last ten years—a term longer than that of either of his predecessors. He was installed in the office January 1, 5846, and completed his last year of service December 31, 5855, having been annually elected with great cordiality. While in office he recorded the transactions of one hundred and forty-nine meetings, and experienced a constantly increasing accumulation of duties consequent upon the growth of the Lodge,—from seventy-six to two hundred and eight members. The following extracts from the records relate to him, and convey a merited compliment to a faithful officer :

October 1, 5846. " R. W. Bro. Baxter informed the Lodge that the Secretary had prepared a book containing the names of all persons who have received the degrees and taken membership in this Lodge, from the granting of the dispensation by the Grand Lodge in 1795, to the present time ; whereupon it was voted, that the thanks of the Lodge be presented to that officer for the same."

January 7, 5847. " R. W. Master, in behalf of the committee appointed for that purpose, reported that a very splendid mantle clock had been presented to the Secretary."

Bro. McClellan was born in Providence, R. I., February 28, 5813, and was initiated in Columbian Lodge, April 4, 5844. He was Secretary of the Boston G. L. of Perfection eight years ; has been Treasurer of the Boston Masonic Board of Relief, eight years, in which office he now is. He is High Priest of St. Andrew's R. A. Chapter; Senior Warden of the Boston Encampment of K. T. ; one of the Stewards of the Grand Lodge of Massachusetts ; Marshal of the Boston Council of Royal and Select Masters ; G. Generalissimo of the G. Encampment of K. T. and dependant orders of Mass. and R. I. ; and officer and member of the Council of Princes of Jerusalem, and an officer and member of the Sov. Grand Consistory of the 32d degree. He has held besides, many subordinate stations in the bodies above named.

According to the original regulations of the Lodge, the Deacons were elected by hand vote. In 5799, they were chosen by ballot, and this rule has been continued to the present time. The office of Deacon is not an old one ; but it existed before the Lodge was established. It is one of the most important stations in every Lodge. The remarks here appended are taken from the " Book of the Lodge," by Dr. Oliver, and published in England a few years since :

" The Lodges in the early part of the last century were worked by three principal officers only ; and the present assistant officers were then unknown. In fact the office of a Deacon does not appear of any great importance in the business of Masonry ; and I suspect that it was not introduced till near the expiration of the century. I am not prepared to name the exact date, because I have not convenient access to any Lodge Minute Books which are earlier than the commencement of the present century ; but I shall approximate very nearly to it if I state it to be between the years 1785 and

1790. In the primitive Lodges the Worshipful Master stood in the East, and *both* the Wardens were placed in the West. This disposition of the chief officers is evident from every copy of the Lectures down to the year 1784 ; and the old Masonic song, which is still used, proclaims the fact.

> In the West see *the Wardens* submissively stand,
> The Master to aid, and obey his command ;
> The intent of his signal we perfectly know,
> And we ne'er take offence when he gives us a blow.

A Continental writer of the period says to the same effect. Lorsqu'on se met a table, le Venerable s'assied le premier en haut du cote de l'Orient. Le premier et second Surveillans se placent vis-a-vis le Venerable a l'Occident.

The station in the South was occupied by the Senior Entered Apprentice, and his business was ' to obey the instructions of the Master, and to welcome the visiting brethren, after due proof, first had and obtained, that they were Masons.' This latter duty was transferred to the Junior Warden when he was placed in the South on the appointment of Deacons, as attendants on the two chief officers ; and in a copy of the Lectures which were used about the close of the 18th century, the Junior Warden's office, amongst other important matters, is said to include ' the examination of visitors.' While in the same lectures, the office of the deacons is simply explained to be, the one ' to carry messages from the Master to the Senior Warden ; and the other, ' to carry messages from the Senior to the Junior Warden, that they may be regularly dispersed round the Lodge.' The Junior Entered Apprentice was placed in the North ' to prevent the intrusion of cowans and eavesdroppers ;' and his duty, at the above period was transferred to the Tyler. It will also be remembered that from the revival of Masonry in 1717, no Lodge was competent to confer more than one degree; and the Entered Apprentice was entitled to vote on all questions, even in the Grand Lodge. The Senior Entered Apprentice was therefore an important personage, and qualified for the office of a Warden ; but he could not be elected to the Chair of the Lodge until he had been passed to the degree of a Fellow Craft in Grand Lodge. In some Lodges, down to the year 1780, the above two officers were denominated Senior and Junior Stewards.

In 1745, the officers of the Lodges on the Continent are thus described. — Every private Lodge possesses the power of choosing its Master (Venerable) from its own members, by a plurality of voices. In France, however, this was frequently a life office. There were also two other principal officers appointed by the Master, and called Wardens (Surveillans.) It was their duty to see that the regulations of the order were observed by the members ; to superintend the ceremonies and lectures under the directions of the Master. Each Lodge had also a Treasurer to whom were entrusted the funds of the Lodge, of which he was obliged to render an account to the brethren in an especial Lodge holden for the purpose on the first Sunday in every month. It had also a Secretary to record the deliberations of the Lodge, of which he was obliged to make a report periodically to the Grand Secretary. The office of a Deacon is not named.

There is no mention of Deacons in any of the early Constitutions of Masonry ; whether edited by Hunter, Senex, and Hooke, (1723 ;) ditto Anderson, (1725, 1738 ;) Cole, (1728, 1751 ;) Watts, (1730 :) Spratt, (1751 ;) Entick, (1756, 1767 ;) Kearsley, (1769 ;) Dermott, (1756, 1778 ;) or Noorthouck, (1784.) In the year 1731, it was declared in Grand Lodge, that the Grand Master, his Deputy, and the Wardens, were the only Grand Officers ; and in 1768 a fund being raised towards building a Freemason's Hall, each Grand Officer was subjected to an annual payment in proportion to the dignity of his office. Amongst these offices the Deacons are not registered, although the list extends down to the Grand Sword Bearer ; nor are they mentioned in it at all.

In the details of the Procession which took place at the dedication of the above Hall, although Northouck has particularized the situation of every officer who was present on the occasion, down to the Tyler, no Deacons occur. It is clear therefore, that in 1776, Deacons were unknown as Masonic office bearers. Again, in the Edition of Preston's Illustrations dated 1781, where he gives directions for the investiture of the several officers of a Lodge in his description of the ceremony of installation, no mention is made of the Deacons, while we find them introduced into a subsequent edition of the same work. In the Masonic Miscellanies of Stephen Jones (1797,) he describes the above ceremony ; and also inserts the order of a procession at funerals, in neither of which is the office of a Deacon to be found. These repeated examples cannot fail to prove satisfactorily that Deacons were not considered necessary in working the business of a Lodge before the very latter end of the 18th century.

At this period the number of Masons had increased considerably, and some additional officers appeared to be necessary to assist in the government of the Lodges. The office of a

Deacon was therefore instituted ; and as there were two Wardens, the same number of Deacons were appointed as their immediate deputies and assistants, and the representatives of all absent craftsmen. The Stewards are now considered as assistants to the Deacons, and the representatives of all absent Entered Apprentices. The duties attached to the office of a Deacon are, ' to convey messages, to obey commands, and to assist at initiations, and in the general practice of the rites and ceremonies of the order.' The Jewel of their office is a dove, as an emblem of peace, and characteristic of their duties ; and their badges are two columns, which are entrusted to them at their investiture ; and when the work of Masonry in the Lodge is carrying on, the Senior Deacon's column is raised ; and when the Lodge is called from labor to refreshment, that of the Junior Deacon is raised, and the other lowered. In the old Lodges these badges were called ' Truncheons ;' and an inventory of the furniture belonging to a Lodge at Chester, taken in the year 1761, mentions among other things, ' two Truncheons for the Wardens.' "

The first code of by-laws provided for the election of Stewards by hand vote, but since the by-laws of 5799 were adopted, the choice has been determined by ballot. In 5775 and until 5799, the Stewards were required to furnish the tables when directed by the Master, and at the annual meeting to exhibit, in writing, to the Master, an inventory of the furniture and utensils of the Lodge, the same to be delivered to their successors, and a copy of it to the Secretary for record. In 5799, their duty is limited to furnishing the tables under the direction of the Master. From and after 5808 until 5821, no by-law enjoined any duty upon them. Neither since 5821, has there been any special service demanded of them ; the subsequent by-laws declaring, in general, that they were under the orders of the Master and Wardens, but particularly under the direction of the Jr. Warden. The code of 5799, exempted them from quarterages when they attended the Lodge, which privilege they did not enjoy when absent; but this provision exists in neither of the other codes. Before the custom of providing refreshments was discontinued, in 5810, it is probable that the Stewards performed certain duties in connection therewith, which were a consideration for exemption from assessments.

Until 5854, no by-law existed in relation to the office of Chaplain. Until 5817, the duties of that officer were discharged by the Master or by some clerical brother who might chance to be in attendance. R. W. and Rev. Paul Dean was the first Chaplain, in which capacity he acted for many years. For several years there were two Chaplains. The brethren who have · held this office are Paul Dean, James Sabine, Edward T. Taylor, Henry W. Adams, George M. Randall, and Henry A. Miles.

Rev. Bro. Henry A. Miles D. D., was born in Grafton, Worcester County, Mass., May 30, 5809. He graduated at Brown University, in 5829, and at the Divinity College in Cambridge in 5832. He was ordained pastor of the Unitarian Church in Hallowell, Me., December 19, 5832, and installed pastor of the South Congregational Church in Lowell, December 14, 5836. In May 5853, he was appointed General Secretary of the American Unitarian Association, and removed to Boston in the autumn of that year. He was raised to the degree of Master Mason, February 26, 5846, in Pentucket Lodge in Lowell, having immediately before taken the preceding degrees after the usual interval between each. He became a R. A. Mason in Mount Horeb Chapter in Lowell, December 27,

5847, and was admitted to membership in Columbian Lodge in. 5854. Soon after he became a member, he was appointed to the office of Chaplain, which office he has most acceptably filled to the present time.

In relation to the office of Marshal the by-laws were silent until 5854. Previous to 5809, this officer was appointed for special occasions only. In the chapter on the origin of the Lodge, mention was made of Bro. John H. Merckell, who was President of the Columbian Society in 5795. He was the Marshal on the occasion of the burial of Bro. Kindness — see page 252. John Henry Merkll, no doubt the same individual, was a member of St. Andrew's R. A. Chapter, May 26, 5791.

Bro. Snelling Powell acted as Marshal in directing the procession when the Lodge left Concert Hall for Market Square, May 5, 5796, (see page 54.) Bro. Henry Purkett officiated May 23, 5800, when the Lodge removed from Market Square to Ann Street. Bro. John Perkins received a vote of thanks for his services as Marshal at the installation of officers, January 1, 5807. At the installation of January 5, 5809, Bro. Stephen Bean was Marshal, and since then the office has been filled regularly, with a few exceptions. The office since 5809, has been occupied by Bros. Thomas Wiley, George Bender, Jr., Amos Binney, John Park, Elisha V. Glover, Elijah Morse, Aaron Bean, Benjamin Stevens, Joshua B. Flint, Francis Fisher, Benjamin B. Appleton, Sr., Daniel Baxter, Jr., George G. Smith, Joel Nason, Ruel Baker, Jonathan Towne, E. Smith, Jr., Newell A. Thompson,

Joseph Hall, Joseph L. Ross, Geo. M. Thacher, J. W. Barton, Wm. Rogers and Wm. H. Mackintosh.

Bro. Snelling Powell was probably made a Mason in England, before he came to this country. He was an original member of C. L. He was Marshal on the occasion of the removal of the Lodge, May 5, 5796, as has been remarked, and was Senior Warden in 5795 and 5796. He was, also, an original member of St. Paul's R. A. Chapter. The following obituary notice of him appeared in the New England Galaxy of Friday, April 13, 5821. Bro. Powell never was a Master of Columbian Lodge, and it is doubtful whether he ever served in that capacity in any Lodge. He was buried under Trinity Church, Boston :

" Died, in this town on Sunday morning last, after a distressing illness of many weeks, Mr. SNELLING POWELL, aged 63.

Mr. Powell was born in Carmarthen in Wales. His father, Mr. S. Powell, was manager of a theatre, and had a respectable company and circuit in that part of Great Britain. Mr. Powell began his theatrical career at an early age, performing the parts usually assigned to children. We have understood that he was also bred to the profession of a printer. It is probable, however, that this was pursued during his minority rather as a matter of convenience, or temporary profit, than with an intention of making it a permanent profession. He brought with him to America a printing apparatus ; among these articles was a small press suitable for striking off cards, bills, &c., which we believe is now in the possession of J. Mycall, Esq., Cambridge, and which is a specimen of neat and elegant workmanship. Mr. Powell performed when very young at Bath and Weymouth, and was sometime in a company with Mr. Warren, now of the Philadelphia theatre. We have been told too that he was the hero of another company in some of the provincial theatres, in which Mr. Green began his theatrical life. He came to Boston in 1793, with his brother, Charles Stuart Powell, formerly of the theatre royal Covent Garden, and the first manager of a regular theatrical establishment in Boston. The year after his arrival he married Miss Harrison, (the present Mrs. Powell) who was at that time the admired and unrivalled heroine of his brother's company. He continued connected with the Boston theatre, with the exception of one season only, we believe, either as actor or manager, till his death. He became the sole lessee of the theatre in 1803, and in 1806 he renewed the lease jointly with Messrs. Bernard and Dickson. The prosperity of the establishment may be dated from the period when he first became manager ; for a number of years previous, the concern had been in a state of bankruptcy, and five different managers, J. B. Williamson, Harper & Co., Hodgkinson, Barrett, and Whitlock, had failed in their attempts and sunk an immense amount of property. For several years immediately succeeding the commencement of his management, the theatre was a fashionable resort, and consequently a source of pecuniary profit ; and it must have been by the wise and prudent economy of management only, during that time, that Mr. Powell could have rendered himself able to sustain the losses of later years without involving himself in absolute bankruptcy.

As an *actor* Mr. Powell was hardly known to those who frequent the theatre at the present day. For the last sixteen years he had never appeared on the stage but in cases of emergency, and for six or seven years he had relinquished playing altogether. This could not have been owing to a declension of powers ; for we recollect that one of his latest performances was a representation of Farmer Ashfield, in which he displayed with uncommon accuracy and richness, the rude simplicity and native excellence of heart which peculiarly distinguish that character. In early life he performed Belcour, Sir George Airy, Doricourt, Floriville, and the leading characters in light and genteel comedy. The first time the writer saw him was in the character of Major Sturgeon, in Foote's comedy of The Mayor of Garratt ; and so vivid is our present recollection of his performance, that we should be disposed to mistrust our judgment, and attribute our admiration to the power of novelty and first impressions, did we not know that others, whose maturity of judgment could not be deceived, had given him a high rank among the actors of that day. His smart flippant valets, such as Lissardo, Spatterdash, &c., were allowed by the late Mr. Hodgkinson to be the neatest that he had seen in America, and during his management he always assigned those parts to Mr. Powell. His Romeo, Richmond, Barnwell, and similar characters in tragedy, are often spoken of by the old play-going people as always respectable and often excellent.

As a citizen and a neighbor Mr. Powell was respected and

esteemed ; and deservedly so, for he was a man of responsibility and integrity.   Though born in a foreign land, he had
passed nearly half of a longer life than is usually allotted to
man, in this town ; and had imbibed a respect for our feelings,
our habits, our manners, and our prejudices ; he felt an interest in our institutions ; he loved our country, for it was his
by adoption, it was the native land of his children, it was endeared to him as the scene of many friendships and associations ; it was here that he had found friends, a home, and a
country ; it was here that he had prepared a tomb.   He had
seen something of the vicissitudes of life.   When he arrived
in Boston, violent prejudices existed against the establishment
of a theatre ; players were viewed by some of the narrow-
minded bigots of that period as hardly entitled to the common
privileges of humanity, and even the more liberal almost
dreaded contamination from their approach.   Mr. Powell was
prudent enough to pursue a course of upright and gentleman-
ly conduct, and he was fortunate enough to conciliate, by that
course, the refined and the liberal, and if he could not win
the favor of the uncandid and uncharitable, he did at least
disarm their enmity of some portion of its malignity, and soften
the obstinacy of the ignorant.   It is not too much to attribute
to the private worth and respectability of Mr. and Mrs. Powell
the credit of having dissipated much of the prejudice which
characterized our puritannic townsmen in 1795.   They have
at least proved that actors do not *necessarily* belong to the inferior ranks of society ; for they have been examples of industry and prudence rising from a depressed condition to affluence
and respectability.

    Mr. Powell was a much esteemed member of the Masonic
fraternity.   He was one of the original petitioners for the
charters of Columbian Lodge, and St. Paul's R. A. Chapter,
and had repeatedly held the office of Master in the Lodge.
His generosity had here often been tried and never found wanting.   His memory will be dear to every Masonic brother ; and
his alms and labors, fresh and fragrant as the cassia which
blooms on his grave, we trust will go up as a memorial

> To the *Great Architect* divine,
> In that Grand Lodge that's far awa'."

Col. Henry Purkett, or Purkitt, was born in
Boston, March 18, 5755, and died there March 3,
5846, aged 91 years.   He was apprenticed to Samuel Peck, cooper.   He was present when the

famous tea-party performed their daring act, on the 16th of December, 5773, and assisted them on that occasion. Bro. Purkett was made a Mason in St. Andrew's Lodge, Boston, December 15, 5795, and admitted a member therein, January 14, 5799, which he continued to be until the time of his death, a period of forty-seven years. He was a member of St. Andrew's R. A. Chapter, in 5798, and Scribe in 5804, and an original member of the Boston Encampment of K. T. He was the first President of the Boston Masonic Board of Relief, and in 5820, Grand C. General of the Grand Encampment of Mass. and R. I. He was an original member of the Mass. Char. Mec. Association. It may be truly said of him, that he lived respected and died regretted.

The by-laws of 5816 are the first which refer to the office of Inside Sentinel. He was appointed by the Master and Wardens, and it was declared to be his duty to see that no brother passed or repassed without the permission of the Master. The mode of his appointment and his duties remain unchanged. He has always been exempted from quarterages. There is no record that the office was filled earlier than 5820, when Brother Luman Streeter was appointed to it. His successors have been Bros. Charles Tuttle, Isaac Spear, Jedediah Barker, Daniel Whitney, Joseph Grelee, J. Towne, Wm. W. Wood and Gilbert Simonds. From 5832 to 5844, the station was unoccupied.

The station of Closet Steward was abolished many years since. He was an appointed officer, and his duties, as defined by the by-laws of 5799, were to take care of the stores, and report them to the Treasurer from time to time, so that the closet

might be properly supplied ; to keep the room
and utensils in cleanly order ; to extinguish the
fires and lights ; to dispose of the keys under the
direction of the Master ; and to attend on committees when required.   No one except a member of
the Lodge could fill the place.   The by-laws of
5808, authorize the Master and Wardens to appoint
some discreet brother as Superintendent and Closet
Steward, who should take care of the Jewels, keep
the hall clean, and provide refreshments under their
direction.   In 5810, when refreshments were excluded, his duties were to take care of the regalia,
keep the hall clean, kindle the fires, and light the
candles.   The same services were assigned to him
in 5816.   In 5821, his sphere was somewhat
enlarged ; it being his province at that time to
keep a list and have the care of the Jewels, clothing, and furniture of the rooms ; at each meeting,
to deposit the Jewels at their respective stations ;
at the close of the meetings, to collect and secure
the same ; and to have charge of the lights, fuel,
hall and rooms.   It will be observed that the
duties by the Closet Steward since 5810, are now
performed by the Superintendent and Tyler.   The
compensation of the Closet Steward as fixed by
the by-laws, was, at first, six shillings for each
meeting ; in 5799, it was two dollars ; in 5806,
it was one dollar ; in 5808, two dollars, and nothing more by way of perquisites ; in 5810 and 5816,
not exceeding one dollar and fifty cents ; and in
5821, it was to be according to the arrangement
made with him by the presiding officers of the
several Masonic Societies who constituted the
Boston Board of Directors.   The brethren who
served in this position, were Alexander Davidson
and Ebenezer Oliver.

The Tyler has been appointed by the Master, and his duties continue to be the same as when the Lodge was chartered, i. e. to tyle the Lodge, to deliver notifications to the members, and to be subject to the direction of the Master. The by-laws previous to 5808, forbade his being a member of the Lodge. His fees, originally, were three shillings for notifying members, three shillings for tyling each night, two shillings for every person made a Mason, and two shillings for every Brother made a M. Mason. At the meeting of January 5, 5797, they were altered, from the old to the new currency, to fifty cents for tyling, fifty cents for notifying, and to thirty-three cents for each making and raising. In 5808, they were fixed at fifty cents for notifying, seventy-five cents for tyling, fifty cents for each initiation and fifty cents for every raising ; and in 5810, the amount of them was determined by the Master and Wardens, but could not exceed two dollars for each meeting. In 5816, they could not be more than one dollar and fifty cents for each meeting, and were liable to be less should the Master and Wardens order it. The by-laws of 5821, provide that the Closet Steward and Tyler be allowed a compensation, to be arranged by the Boston Board of Directors. These two offices were probably held at that time by the same individual. For many years previous to 5854, the Tyler was allowed three dollars and fifty cents for each meeting ; and since the 28th of November of that year, he has received five dollars for delivering the notifications, superintending and tyling. The Tylers have been Bros. ⸻ Jones, Henry Wickham, ⸻ Bunton, Ebenezer Mountford, Ebenezer Oliver, E.

V. Glover and William C. Martin. The quotations from the records here given are testimonials highly complimentary to Bro. Martin.

February 7, 5839. "On motion of R. W. Bro. George G. Smith, (of which he had given notice at a previous meeting,) it was *Voted*, That an account of the signal and important services rendered at various times to Columbian Lodge by Brother Martin, the seventeenth article of the By-Laws requiring the payment of five dollars for the privileges of membership, be in this case suspended."

The following, alludes to the gift of a handsome lamp by the Lodge:

September 7, 5843. "The R. W. Master in offering the lamp, paid a merited tribute to the many services Bro. Martin had rendered the Lodge, for a long series of years. Brother Martin responded appropriately. The ceremonies were of an unusually interesting character."

May 21, 5846. "R. W. Master from the committee appointed to make Brother Wm. C. Martin a donation, reported that the committee had presented him with a mantle clock, of the value of twenty dollars."

Since 5842, when the organ in the upper hall, where the Lodge then met, was presented by R. W. Edward A. Raymond for the use of the societies occupying the Temple, it has been the practice for the Master to appoint an organist. The organ in the lower hall where meetings are now held, is so deficient in quality and power, as to offer no attraction to the musician, and to its defects may be attributed in no small degree the repeated unsuccessful attempts that have been made to form a choir from among the members. Music in a Lodge-room is most important, and every facility to provide it, should be granted. The Grand Lodge being fully sensible of this, have appointed a committee on the subject of procuring another organ. The present organist is Bro. J. H. Wilcox. Record extracts pertaining to this subject are here appended :

December 7, 5843. " *Voted*, That R. W. Thomas Power be requested to wait upon Br. Geo. W. Lloyd, and request him to accept the office of organist to the Lodge,—and also to authorize him in behalf of the Lodge to form a choir from amongst its members."

October 3, 5844. " At the suggestion of the R. W. Master it was *Voted*, That Bros. Tillson, Thacher, and Coolidge, be a committee to take into consideration the formation of a choir from among the members of the Lodge."

October 2, 5845. " The music committee were authorized to employ an organist."

Not one of the books named in the subjoined extracts is now in the possession of the Lodge. The portraits are photograph likenesses of the Past Masters.

February 3, 5803. " On a motion, *Voted*, That five copies of Bro. Gurley's Oration, be deposited in the the archives of the Lodge, under the direction of the Secretary, for the use of the members of the Lodge."

November 7, 5805. " *Voted*, To purchase four volumes of Bro. Harris' Masonic Sermons for the use of the Lodge, to be paid for out of the funds of the Lodge."

September 3, 5812. " The Secretary presented a communication from Brother John Lathrop, Jr., containing a prospectus of a Free Mason's Annual Anthology.

Voted, That the Secretary be requested to subscribe for one copy for the Lodge, and likewise to furnish such matter from the records of the Lodge for said publication as he may think necessary."

October 2, 5817. " The proposal by Bro. Luke Eastman, for publishing Masonic Melodies, was presented for subscriber's names, received two, and was returned to Bro. Little."

June 7, 5855. " Bros. Robbins, McClellan and Mackintosh, were appointed a committee with full powers to procure the portraits of the Past Masters of the Lodge."

CHAPTER XIX.

MASTERS. — CONCLUSION.

The Master of a Lodge is invested with great power, and upon him the government mainly depends. He obligates himself before his installation to conform to the ancient charges and regulations of the Order, to the rules and constitutions of the Grand Lodge, and the by-laws of his Lodge, and within their limits his authority is supreme during the term for which he is elected. Should it be arbitrarily exercised, or he prove incompetent to perform his duties, or from any other cause however flagrant, become unfit for his station, it is not in the power of the Lodge to remove him. Their complaints must be carried before the Grand Master or Grand Lodge, who alone can depose him. Happily, Columbian Lodge and their Masters have always worked together in harmony and unity. There is not an instance on record of the slightest disagreement.

Including the present incumbent, there have been twenty-two Masters, eleven of whom, only, are now living. In the succeeding pages it has been attempted to present an outline of the biography of each of them. The attempt has not, in several cases, been attended with the success desired; still, important facts relating to each individual have been obtained which may be most valuable at some future time.

W. Joseph Churchill.

Brother Churchill, the first Master, was probably born in Plymouth. His father's name was Jesse, who had four sons—Jesse, David, Simon and Joseph. Mr. John D. Churchill, of Plymouth, states, October 25, 5855, that "Joseph lived in Boston some years, came to Plymouth about 1803 or 1804, and in the same year went to the South, (Richmond,) as near as I (he) can ascertain. His father and family moved to Ohio about 1815." Enquiries have been made at Richmond Va., and at Marietta, Ohio, in the hope of obtaining some information respecting Brother Churchill, but thus far they have proved unavailing. He was, no doubt, a merchant when he resided in Boston. There are bills on file which warrant this conclusion. The Boston Directory for 5803, contains the name of " Joseph Churchill, merchant, North Row, Fish Street ;" and a person of this name was a sufferer by a large fire in Fish Street, (see page 307.) Bro. Churchill headed the petition to the Grand Lodge for a warrant to establish Columbian Lodge, was their first Master, and served them as such in 5795–96–97 and 98. He was their Treasurer in 5799 and 5800. He was elected an honorary member, December 2, 5802.

W. John W. Folsom.

Brother Folsom was born in Exeter, N. H., and died in Boston in 5823, aged sixty-six or sixty-eight years. He was raised in Columbian Lodge in Aug. 5795, and admitted to membership Aug. 8, 5795. He was Treasurer in 5796, Secretary in 5797 and 5798, and Master in 5799, 5800 and

5801. He was the first Secretary of the Mass. Char. Mec. Association, and served five years. He was a member of the Board of Health of Boston in 5803, a Coroner from 5803 to 5817, and a Justice of the Peace from 5817 to 5822. In the Boston Directory of 5789, he is entered as " printer and book-seller, Union Street."

W. Amasa Stetson.

Bro. Stetson was initiated in Columbian Lodge December 8, 5795, and made a member March 22, 5796. He was Treasurer in 5797, 5798, 5805 and 5806 ; Junior Warden in 5799 ; Senior Warden in 5800 and 5801 ; and Master in 5802–3. He was born in Randolph, March 26, 5769. The following account of him is from " *A Geneological and Biographical Sketch of the Name and Family of Stetson ; from the year* 1534 *to the year* 1847. *By John Stetson Barry.*'

" Amasa, son of John, m. Rebecca, daughter of Joseph and Rebecca Kettell, of Boston, and grand-daughter of the Rev. Thomos Prentice, formerly of Charlestown, Mass. She was b. Aug. 25, 1775, and m. Aug. 21, 1798. Mr. Stetson had no children. He commenced life, as a poor boy, and learned the shoemaker's trade, which was the trade of his father. He afterwards went to Boston, and engaged in the shoe business, with his brother Samuel. By that close application and strict economy, for which he was always distinguished, his business prospered, and his circumstances began to improve. He was a man much esteemed wherever known ; and during the last war held the office of Commissary for the district of Massachusetts ; and has held the office of Senator in the same State. His property was very large ; the assets at his death, which occurred Aug. 2, 1844, being over $500,000 ; and his liberality was in proportion to his ability. He gave to the town of Randolph the sum of $10,000, for the erection of a Hall, which occupies a conspicuous station in the western part of the town ; and $10,000, for the endowment of a School, to be kept in the Hall ; also $100 towards building a face wall in front of the burying-ground, on North Street, in which his father and mother lie. The town of Stetson, in Maine, was named from him, and a short time before his death he caused a church to be erected there, for the use of all denominations. It was finished at the time of his last visit to the place ; and what is a little singular, the first time the bell was ever tolled, was for his death. He resided in Dorchester, and the splendid clock on the church of the Rev. Mr. Hall, which was his place of worship, was a present from him, and cost $700. Many acts of private munificence might be recorded here ; and a large circle of relatives and friends have reason to remember him with thankfulness and gratitude. A pleasing circumstance connected with the school founded by him in Randolph, may be noticed here. Soon after its establishment, all the scholars, accompanied by their teacher, made a visit to Mr. Stetson, at his residence ; and it being the winter season, the scholars had both the ride, and an opportunity to see the man to whom they were so greatly indebted. He received them with his accustomed hospitality, and on their departure, they gave three cheers for his health and happiness. A full length portrait of Mr. Stetson, by Frothingham, of Charlestown, graces the Town Hall in Randolph, and one of the most excellent and striking likenesses it was ever my privilege to look upon, is in the house of his widow at Dorchester. His body lies in the Dorchester burying-ground ; and over his remains stands a chaste and elegant monument of white marble ; a most appropriate and touching memento of the affection of his surviving partner."

W. Daniel Baxter, Sr.

Bro. Baxter was born in Braintree, Mass., (since Quincy,) March 1, 5758. He removed to Boston early in the year 5794, and died there, after a lingering illness of nearly three years, July 22, 5836. His widow still lives at the advanced age of ninety-three years. He was a Selectman of the town of Boston several years; and an Alderman of the city of Boston in 5823 and 5824. He was two years a Senator of Massachusetts, from Suffolk County. In the militia he served as captain of

an independent company in Quincy during the
revolution. He was made a Mason in Old Colony
Lodge, Hingham. He was admitted a member of
Columbian Lodge June 6, 5799; served as Junior
Warden in 5800; as Senior Warden in 5802 and
5803; as Master in 5804, 5805, 5806 and 5809;
and as Treasurer, twenty-three years, beginning
with the year 5811, and terminating with that of
5833. He was admitted a member of St. Andrew's
R. A. Chapter in 5807, and was their Scribe in
5809. In 5818, he resigned his membership in
that Chapter, and became one of the original members of St. Paul's R. A. Chapter, with whom he
continued until his death. He was also a member
of the Council of Royal Masters, and of the Boston
Encampment of K. T. The records refer to this
faithful member and officer as follows:

January 1, 5807. "The thanks of the Lodge was voted to
Br. Baxter for his faithful services while Master of Columbian
Lodge. *Voted*, also, That Bro. Swett's toast be recorded as a
monument of our respect as follows:
'Our dear illustrious and enlightened Right W. Past
Master Daniel Baxter, who has for three years past filled the
oriental chair with dignity, punctuality and honor to this
Lodge, therefore it is our ardent prayer for his reward, that
when his light shall be no more visible in this earthly Lodge,
he may be raised to the all perfect Lodge above, and seated
on the right of the Supreme Architect of the Universe, and
there receive the refreshment his labors have merited,—so
mote it be.'"

January 2, 5823. "At the installation of each officer an
appropriate address and charge were given, in a style manly,
friendly and Masonic. The one deserving particular notice
and record, was that to our long tried and venerable friend
R. W. Bro. Treasurer,—the recipient and faithful guardian
of our funds, the feeling almoner and dispenser of our charities,—the father of our present R. W. Master.
The father first led the son to the fane of friendship and
brotherly love, the son by a correct course of conduct induced

and encouraged by the example of the father, has risen to an office the highest in the gift of Columbian Lodge. And in his address expresses himself in a manner indicative of his obligations, his feelings, his gratitude, to the author of his existence, and means of his present elevation. A listening auditory 'heard and was pleased.' Such scenes are calculated to impress on the minds of every Mason, 'how pleasant it is for Brothers to dwell together in unity,' and to inculcate the noble maxim, that among us no contention should arise but that of 'who best can work, who best agree.' "

January 6, 5825. " R. W. Daniel Baxter, Esq. was unanimously admitted honorary member of Columbian Lodge.

Voted, That an honorary jewel with an appropriate inscription be presented to our R. W. Bro. Baxter, and that he be requested to wear the same while attending to his duties in the Lodge.

On motion of R. W. Bro. Samuel Smith, *Voted*, That the three first officers elect, be a committee to furnish a suitable jewel to be presented to our R. W. Bro. Baxter."

On the presentation of the Jewel referred to above, which occurred January 27, 5825, W. Bro. Daniel Baxter, Jr., the son of the recipient, who was then Master, delivered a feeling and appropriate address, which will be found in another part of this chapter.

January 2, 5834. "R. W. George G. Smith, B. B. Appleton and Baker, were chosen a committee to consider the expediency of presenting our R. W. Bro. Daniel Baxter, Sen., for a long series of years Treasurer of this Lodge, with some testimonial of our gratitude and respect."

December 4, 5834. " The committee chosen some time since on the subject of a donation to our respected Past Master and Treasurer, R. W. Bro. Daniel Baxter, Sen., reported, that after a long conversation with Bro. Baxter, the object having been made known to him, he positively declined any other token of our good feelings and gratitude, than a simple vote of thanks, should the Lodge deem his services worthy of such ; whereupon, it was unanimously *Voted*, That the sincere and heartfelt thanks of Columbian Lodge be presented to our highly esteemed past Treasurer, R. W. Bro. Daniel Baxter, for his invaluable services during the term of twenty-three years, while he held that office, and that the Secretary be requested to transmit this vote to Bro. Baxter."

W. STEPHEN BEAN.

W. Bro. Stephen Bean, A. B., brother of W. Bro. Aaron Bean, who died in the station of Master in 5820, was born in Brentwood, N. H, in 5772 ; fitted for College with Rev. Isaac Smith, of Gilmanton; graduated at Dartmouth College in 5798 ; taught the academy in Salisbury ; was in mercantile business in Boston, where he married a woman of considerable wealth, and died there December 10, 5825, aged 53 years. It is not known where he was initiated. He was admitted a member of C. L. July 5, 5804, and withdrew March 5, 5818. He was Secretary in 5805 ; Senior Warden in 5806 ; and Master 5807 and 5808. Membership in St. Andrew's Chapter was conferred upon him April 12, 5806. The History of Gilmanton states that he was in mercantile business in Boston, while the History of the Ancient and Honorable Artillery Company, in which he was admitted a member in 5806, records him as a lawyer.

R. W. JOSEPH JENKINS.

Bro. Jenkins was born in Barre, Mass., Nov. 11, 5781, and died in Boston, Oct. 11, 5851. His remains were buried in Forest Hills Cemetery, Roxbury. He left his father's house when about fourteen years of age, to live with an elder brother in Boston, and learn the carpenter's trade. It has been said that he held, in Boston, every grade of commissioned officer in the militia, from Ensign to Colonel. In the History of the Ancient and Honorable Artillery Company, he is mentioned as a member of that body in 5810, and is referred to as follows:

" Lieut. Col. Joseph Jenkins, Boston, housewright, officer of militia; lieut. Colonel of the third regiment. He was a reflective and self-taught man—very industrious, and had a numerous family. Misfortunes in business rendered him poor. He then entered into a large contract with the U. S. Government to build their custom house and other public buildings at New Orleans, and became independent. Alderman, representative, and a distinguished Free-Mason."

He was a member of the first Board of Aldermen of the city of Boston, and of the Mass. Char. M. Association in 5810, and Vice President of the Association in the years 5825 and 5826. He was a Representative from Boston in the General Court of Mass. in 5823 and 5824. He was made a Mason in C. L., April 4, 5804; admitted a member July 5, 5804; served as Junior Deacon in 5806; as Junior Warden in 5807 and 5808; as Senior Warden in 5809; as Secretary in 5815 and as Master in 5810, '11, '12, '13, '17 and '18. He was admitted to membership in St. Andrew's R. A. Chapter Oct. 21, 5809, was Scribe in 5812, and High Priest in 5817 and 5818. In 5819, he was M. I. Master of the Council of Royal Masters. He was J. G. W. of the Grand Lodge in 5819, and Grand Master in 5830, 5831 and 5832. This last office he held when the Masonic Temple was built, and during the time when the Anti-masonic excitement was greatest. In this brief sketch it is impossible to display the extent and variety of Bro. Jenkins' masonic services; a mere outline of them is all that can be here presented. He filled probably high stations in other Masonic bodies than those above named ; and it is certain he occupied many subordinate offices in all which have been particularly mentioned. The records of C. L., which have been liberally introduced into this volume, show abundantly that he was a most active and useful member and officer. He also delivered many addresses, Masonic and otherwise, some of which were printed. He pronounced a funeral oration in 5820, on the death of W. Bro. Aaron Bean, who died while he held the office of Master. It is believed that his first published address was delivered before the Mass. Char. Mec. Asso. in December 5819. In June 5822, he addressed Mount Zion Lodge, and his remarks on that occasion, it is believed, were also published. His addresses to the Lodge, when he was Master, and before the Grand Lodge, when he was Grand Master, were always dignified and appropriate, and expressed sentiments of sound morality and Masonic excellence. The following is from the records of Columbian Lodge :

January 7, 5819. " The committee empowered to express in a suitable manner the thanks of this Lodge to R. W. Joseph Jenkins, for his services as Master the past two years—Report : That they have procured from him the Past Master's Jewel, presented to him on his vacating the chair in 5813 ; on which they find engraved the following, viz. : " *Presented to R. W. Joseph Jenkins, by the unanimous vote of Columbian Lodge, for his distinguished and successful services as Master, from December, 5809 to December, 5813.*" [See page 228.] To which your committee add the following, viz. : " *The thanks of Columbian Lodge were again unanimously voted to R. W. Jos. Jenkins, for his renewed, faithful, distinguished and successful services as Master, from December, 5816, to December, 5818.*" Your committee have also caused the same to be engraved on the Jewel, to be again presented to their much respected R. W. Joseph Jenkins, by the Master elect, R. W. A. Bean, on his taking the chair.

All which is respectfully submitted by your committee.

DANIEL BAXTER,
DAVID MOODY.

Boston, Jan. 7, 5819.

This report was unanimously accepted."

W. DAVID MOODY.

Bro. Moody was born in Newbury, (parish of Byfield,) Mass., February 10, 5783, and died in Boston, December 2, 5832. The first William Moody and three sons—Samuel, Joshua and Caleb, —came from England about 5633, and settled in Ipswich in 5635, and from thence removed to Newbury. David was the youngest son of Capt. Paul Moody, who descended from the eldest Samuel. David was educated by his eldest brother, Samuel, at Hallowell, Maine. In early life he spent some little time in St. Vincent, (W. I.) On his return he settled in Boston. During the war with Great Britain, 5812, he was a Lieutenant in a company in Boston, and was stationed on Governor's Island, (in Boston harbor.) In 5812, he was admitted a member of the An. and Hon. Ar. Co., and is recorded in the history of the company thus :

"Capt. David Moody ; Boston, housewright. A distinguished architect and engineer in the improvement of Lowell. Representative from Boston, and died in 1832, aged 50."

After peace was declared, he went to Waltham as superintendent of the out-door work of the Boston and Waltham Manufacturing Company, and remained in their employ until the Boston and Roxbury Mill-dam was commenced. He was employed with Mr. Uriah Cotton, the originator of that then great work, and after the death of Mr. Cotton, he was appointed in his place, and finished the work. He then engaged with Mr. Gray in the iron-works, and continued so connected until the time of his death. He was initiated in C. L., Nov. 19, 5807, and admitted a member May 4, 5809. He served as Junior Warden in 5810, 5811 and 5830; as Senior Warden in 5812 and 5813; and as Master in 5814. He presided while Master only six times. A silver pitcher was presented to him by the Grand Lodge about the year 5831, as a token of their appreciation of the services he had rendered to them in the purchase of the land for the Masonic Temple, and erection of that edifice. In 5828, he was a member of the Common Council of Boston from ward six.

December 6, 5832. " On motion of our R. W. Bro. G. G. Smith, it was *Voted*, That the R. W. Master and W. Senior Warden, be added to a former committee, (consisting of Bros. Tillson, W. Fisher and Allen) for the purpose of taking such notice of the death of our late esteemed Brother and Past Master, David Moody, as may seem proper."

December 29, 5832. " A committee on the subject of the decease of our late Brother David Moody, reported, that our Rev. and R. W. Brother Paul Dean, had accepted an invitation to pronounce an eulogium at such time as the Lodge should direct.

Voted, That the same committee be authorized to make such arrangement in relation to the above subject as they may deem expedient and proper."

February 7, 5833. " Pursuant to previous arrangements, the Lodge and visiting Brethren attended to an Eulogium pronounced by R. W. Bro. Paul Dean, on occasion of the death of our late esteemed Brethren, David Moody and Amos Binney.

On motion of R. W. Bro. Jenkins, *Voted*, That the thanks of Columbian Lodge be presented to our R. W. Bro. Dean for the address delivered this evening; and that a copy of the same be requested to be placed on the files of the Lodge.

Voted, That the three first officers of the Lodge, with Bros. G. G. Smith and Appleton, be a committee to convey the sentiments of the Lodge to the families of our deceased Brethren, Moody and Binney, in such a manner as they may deem proper."

R. W. Elijah Morse.

Bro. Morse was admitted a member October 15, 5812. He was Senior Deacon in 5813, Junior Warden in 5814, and Master in 5815. On the 2d of February 5815, he resigned the office of Master, in consequence of his having received the appointment of D. D. G. M. of the first district. The proceedings of the Lodge will be observed by the following extract from the records:

February 2, 5815. "The R. W. Master, Elijah Morse, announced to the Lodge that he had been honored by the M. W. G. Master, with an appointment to the office of District Deputy Grand Master for the first Masonic district in the Commonwealth of Massachusetts, and could not, constitutionally, retain his station as Master of Columbian Lodge; and in a very feeling and affectionate manner he resigned that office from which he had no doubt anticipated much pleasure and satisfaction, and the Lodge equal profit and respectability.

At this interesting event, the members of Columbian Lodge, actuated by those sentiments which always pay just tribute to worth, under whatever circumstances, unanimously expressed their feelings in the following resolution:

Resolved, That while we rejoice at the honorable promotion of our Right W. Master—while Columbian Lodge joyfully exults at the eminence to which fame hath exalted her son,— we sincerely regret that so bright a luminary is thus suddenly taken from our temple of love, and although our Brother is honorably impelled to quit our labors for more important duties, we rejoice that our work will continue to receive his inspection, our meetings his frequent attention, and ourselves his kind affections.

On motion, *Voted*, That Bros. Jenkins, Baxter, Appleton, Mills and Smith, be a committee to consider the subject of a new election."

Bro. Appleton, Sr., was elected in his place, March 2, 5815. The office of D. D. G. M. was filled by Bro. Morse during the years 5815 and 5816. He again became Senior Warden, and served in 5817 and 5818. In 5816 he acted as Marshal. He was Corresponding G. Secretary of the Grand Lodge in 5818 and 5819; Grand Treasurer in 5820, '21, '22, '23, '24, '25 and '26; and Deputy Grand Master in 5830. He was admitted to membership in St. Andrew's R. A. Chapter, October 30, 5816. He was born (probably in Medway,) September 10, 5785. He was a member of the legal profession, and practised in Boston. He represented ward seven in the Common Council in 5824–5. The notice of him here given is taken from the " Memorial of the Morses," by Rev. Abner Morse, A. M.

" Elijah Morse, Esq., graduated with distinguished honors in his class, which has furnished such men as Rev. Dr. Ide, of Medford, and Rev. Dr. Burgess, of Dedham, and others advantageously known. He commenced the study of law with Judge Thatcher, of Thomastown, Me., and finished with Timothy Bigelow, of Boston, whose office and a share of its emoluments passed immediately into his hands on being admitted to the bar. He married the daughter of Dr. Jackson, M.D., Edinburgh, whose father was one of the Aldermen of London, and passed his remaining days in Boston, in the practice of his profession, welcoming numerous acquaintances to the hospitalities of his house. He consented, at a sacrifice, to represent Boston one year in the General Court, but declined a second nomination. He was a member of the City Council at the time of his death, and also one of the standing committee of the bar, with Samuel Hubbard, W. D. Sohier, John Pickering, Charles G. Loring, John R. Adan and James T. Austin. ' When his death was reported, a special meeting of the bar was held, and a resolution adopted to testify their respect for him by attending his funeral. This being declined on behalf of his family, whereupon it was motioned by John Pickering, Esq., and voted that the bar of Suffolk are deeply impressed with the lamented decease of their late Brother, Elijah Morse, Esq. His urbanity of manners and active usefulness will be testified by all, while his zeal and fidelity to his clients will be appreciated by those who met with him in the walks of his profession. *Voted,* That the foregoing resolution be transmitted to his family as a testimonial of sincere sympathy in their loss of a father and a husband, who united the virtues of private to the energies of active life.

Attest, JOSIAH QUINCY.' "

R. W. BENJAMIN B. APPLETON, SR.

This R. W. Bro. was born in Boston, May 8, 5781, and died there April 23, 5844. He was made in C. L., March 1, 5810 ; admitted a member November 15, in the same year ; served as Junior Steward in 5811 ; as Junior Deacon in 5812 ; as Secretary in 5813 and 5814 ; as Junior Warden in 5817 and 5818 ; as Senior Warden in 5815, '28, '30, '31 and '32 ; as Marshal in 5826 and 5827 ; as Treasurer in 5834, '35, '36, '37, '38, '39 and '40 ; and as Master in 5816 and 5818. But few members have served the Lodge in so many ways requiring time and labor, as Bro. Appleton. His transcript of the records, (see pages 175 and 176,) embracing the period of the first thirteen years after the Lodge was established, should alone render him endeared to them. Had not that work been performed, it is more than probable that the means of tracing their early history would long since have been obliterated ; but to his energy, perseverence and promptness, a contingency so lamentable has been averted. In the Grand Lodge, he was Junior Grand Warden in 5834, 5835 and 5836, and Senior Grand Warden in 5837. He was the Treasurer, and a Trustee of the Board of Trustees of the Masonic Temple from 5835 until his death. He was a hard-ware importing merchant, and was brought up with Peter Bazin, with whom he became a partner. He was afterwards in business alone until 5837. In politics he was a Federalist of the old school, and a firm and uncompromising Whig. He was a member of the Common Council of Boston from ward seven, when he died, also a member of the British Charitable Society. The following extracts are from the records of C. L. :

> May 2, 5844. " The R. W. M. announced to the Lodge the great loss the Fraternity had met with since the last meeting, in the sudden death of our respected Brother, R. W. Benjamin B. Appleton.
> The three first officers were appointed a committee to address a letter of condolence to the family, and to make arrangements for religious services to be performed in the Lodge Room at such time as they may deem best, in memory of our deceased Brother."

> May 16, 5844. " The committee appointed to make arrangements for religious ceremonies on the decease of P. M. Benjamin B. Appleton, reported, That in their opinion owing to the lateness of the season and the approaching adjournment of the Lodge, it was inexpedient that these ceremonies should take place, which report was accepted."

The following resolutions occasioned by the death of Bro. Appleton, were unanimously adopted at the meeting of the Trustees of the Masonic Temple, held May 6, 5844:

> " *Resolved*, That the Board of Trustees of the Masonic Temple deeply sympathize in the loss which they, as well as the Masonic Institution in general have sustained in the sudden decease of their late Brother and member, Benjamin B. Appleton, Esq. That associated with them from the first organization of the Board, their mutual communion has been uniformly of a pleasing character—and that the memory of that union now broken by death, shall ever be cherished by the surviving associates.

Resolved, That in the important trust confided to him as Treasurer of this Board, he has always evinced a continued vigilance and an unwearied zeal to promote the best interests of this department of the Masonic Institution, diligently attendant on, and faithfully fulfilling every duty incumbent on that office.

Resolved, That the Secretary transmit the above resolutions to the family of the deceased."

W. AARON BEAN.

Bro. Aaron Bean, A. B. (brother of Stephen, fifth Master,) was born in Brentwood, N. H., in 5779; fitted for college partly with Rev. Mr. Smith of Gilmanton, and partly at Gilmanton Academy, and graduated at Dartmouth College in 5804. He became a Boston merchant, married a niece of his brother Stephen's wife, and died April 4, 5820, in his 41st year, leaving a widow and two children. Membership was conferred upon him in C. L. June 5, 5817. Where he was initiated is unknown. He was Marshal in 5818, and was elected Master for the years 5819 and 5820, but died while in office, April 4, 5820. He was a member of St. Andrew's R. A. Chapter, January 21, 5818, and an original member of St. Paul's R. A. Chapter. The record proceedings in relation to the death of Bro. Bean are given entire :

April 6, 5820. " At a regular meeting of Columbian Lodge, at Mason's Hall, Ann Street, Boston, on Thursday evening. at half-past five o'clock, P. M., the Lodge was declared duly organized by the Marshal, with the exception of the R. W. Master. R. W. Joseph Jenkins, past presiding Master, then arose and announced the melancholy event of the decease of our R. W. and truly beloved Brother and Master, AARON BEAN, ESQ., who departed this life on the 4th inst., at 6 o'clock, P. M. He then assisted in opening the Lodge. The government of the Lodge was then entrusted to the W. Senior Warden, who directed the members to assemble around the alter, from which the Throne of Grace was addressed in an appropriate, solemn, affecting and truly Christian prayer, by the R. W. and Rev. Paul Dean, Chaplain to the Lodge. The Brethren present appeared impressed with but one sentiment, that of unfeigned grief for the loss of a member so valuable and useful. This feeling was so unequivocally expressed as to testify in the strongest manner the virtues of the deceased, the estimation in which he was held, and the affection of all the Brothers towards him.

It was agreed that the ordinary business of the evening be suspended, and on motion, the following resolutions were brought forward, and unanimously adopted.

Resolved, That Columbian Lodge have learned with great grief the recent death of their R. W. and beloved Master, Aaron Bean, Esq., and that they will adopt all proper measures in testimony of their deep regret, and the high estimation in which they held the virtues and usefulness of their deceased Brother.

Resolved, That the members of this Lodge will attend the funeral of their lamented Brother to-morrow, at four o'clock, P. M., and on that occasion, and on the four following Sabbaths, will wear crape on the left arm ; the implements and dresses of the Lodge, the Master's chair and pedestal be shrouded in black for three months.

Resolved, That a committee of three be appointed to express the feelings of the Lodge in a letter of condolence to the widow of our beloved Brother and worthy Master, whose sudden death has deprived an interesting family of its chief support and comfort ; Columbian Lodge of one of its most valuable members; the Fraternity of a distinguished ornament, and the community of a most correct and worthy man.

Resolved, That a committee be appointed to consider the most proper method of expressing our regret for the loss we have sustained in the death of our R. W. beloved Master, with power to make such arrangements as they shall deem expedient.

The last two resolutions were committed to R. W. and Rev, Paul Dean, R. W. Joseph Jenkins, and R. W. Samuel Smith."

April 20, 5820. "The records of the last meeting were read by the Secretary.

This evening was set apart purposely to notice in some solemn manner the lamented death of our late R. W. Master, friend and Brother, Aaron Bean, Esq. Of course no work was brought forward.

The ceremonies of the evening commenced 1st, with prayer, by R. W. and Rev. Paul Dean, Chaplain to the Lodge.

2d. Hymn by the Brethren.

3d. An Address on the occasion by R. W. and P. M. Joseph Jenkins.

4th. Hymn by the Brethren.

5th. Prayer by R. W. Chaplain.

After the ceremonies were closed, a motion was made, seconded and carried, that a committee be chosen to wait on R. W. Bro. Jenkins, and express to him the cordial thanks of the members of Columbian Lodge, for the chaste, elegant and appropriate eulogy delivered by him this evening, on the much lamented event of the death of R. W. and beloved Master, Aaron Bean, Esq. That the committee be instructed to request of Bro. Jenkins a copy of his address for the press ; that said committee be requested to confer with the committee from St. Paul's R. A. Chapter, appointed for the same purpose, and to make provisions that this address with the one to be presented by St. Paul's Chapter, be handsomely bound together, and presented in conjunction with that committee, to the widow of the deceased. R. W. and Rev. Paul Dean, R. W. Samuel Smith, and R. W. Daniel Baxter, were appointed as the committee."

April 27, 5820. " A committee were chosen to take into consideration the expediency of chosing a Master to fill the vacancy occasioned by the death of our late R. W. Master, and to report at the next meeting. The committee on this subject, were Bros. Baxter, Appleton, Jenkins, Glover, and Cobb."

May 4, 5820. " The Committee on R. W. Bro. Jenkins' address, reported that they had caused two hundred and sixty-five copies to be printed. The Lodge voted fifty copies to Bro. Jenkins, two copies to each member, and the remainder to be disposed of by the committee."

" The committee chosen at the last meeting, on elections, made the following report, which was accepted, viz :

The committee raised to consider the propriety of electing a new Master to fill the vacancy occasioned by the death of R. W. Bro. Bean, having attended to the subject,

REPORT:

That in their opinion it is expedient for the Lodge to proceed as soon as convenient to the election of a Master, and to fill such other vacancies as may occur at the time of such election, and that as soon thereafter as may be, the Secretary make out duplicate returns of all officers so elected, and communicate one of them to the M. W. Grand Lodge, and place the other on our files.   Submitted respectfully,

JOSEPH JENKINS,
E. V. GLOVER,   } Committee.
G. COBB,

June 1, 5820. "Agreeably to a resolve of the last meeting, the Lodge at nine o'clock, went into committee of the whole for the choice of a Master. Bros. Baxter, Howard, and Gordon were appointed a committee to collect, count and sort the votes. This committee reported,

R. W. Bro. Samuel Smith unanimously elected Master.
R. W. Bro. Daniel Baxter   "   "   S. Warden.
R. W. Bro. Joel Nason   "   "   J. Warden.
R. W. Bro. Elisha V. Glover   "   "   S. Deacon.

The R. W. Master elect was then introduced to the R. W. P. M. Joseph Jenkins, who in a solemn, impressive and pleasing manner, installed and conducted him to the chair of Solomon."

The following letter is from the son of Brother Bean :

"Boston, Jan., 1856.

Dear Sir,—After our conversation respecting my father's birth place, I addressed a letter to my brother at Weare, N. H., requesting him to make enquiries of Aunt Ruth Raymond, the only surviving sister of my father, and she gives the following account: 'I was about six years old when they left Brentwood, and Aaron was a year old. We went on horseback—mother carried Aaron in her lap, and I rode behind on a pillion. Aaron lived with friend Hoyt, (a worthy Quaker of Gilmanton,) from the age of nine to fifteen; then went to work on the farm at home.' He graduated 1804, from Dartmouth, and went to Boston, and was usher in the Franklin school, under Dr. Asa Bullard. Afterwards he went into the grocery business with Mr. Gulliver, under the firm of Gulliver & Bean, Merchants Row.

Respectfully your obt. servt.   AARON H. BEAN.

W. Samuel Smith.

Bro. Samuel Smith was born in Westford, Mass., November 17, 5780. He was made a Mason in Massachusetts Lodge in 5804 or 5805. Membership was conferred upon him in C. L. November 6, 5807, life-membership in 5827, and honorary membership in 5855. He served as Senior Deacon in 5808, 5809, 5817 and 5818 ; as Senior Warden in 5810, 5811, 5819 and 5820; and as Master in 5820, after the death of Bro. Bean, and in 5821 and 5822. For a period of many years he was most active and useful, both as a member and officer. He was an original member of St. Paul's R. A. Chapter.

W. Daniel Baxter, Jr.

Bro. Baxter was born in Quincy, Mass., September 18, 5792. His present residence is in Newton, Mass. He was a member of the House of Representatives of Massachusetts six or seven years. He was initiated in Columbian Lodge March 7, 5816, and membership was conferred upon him November 7, 5816. He was Junior Steward in 5817 and 5827; Junior Deacon in 5818 ; Junior Warden in 5819 and 5820 ; Senior Warden in 5821, 5822 and 5829 ; Marshal in 5828, and Master in 5823, 5824 and 5825. He has been a life member many years, and was made an honorary member in 5855. He was an original member of St Paul's Chapter, and belongs to the Boston Encampment, and Council of Royal Masters. Of the eighteen original members of St. Paul's Chapter, nine of them were members of Columbian Lodge, i. e., Bros. Paul Dean, Daniel

Baxter, Sr., Samuel Smith, Elisha V. Glover, Nathaniel Hammond, Daniel Baxter, Jr., Snelling Powell, Aaron Bean, and Benjamin Stevens. The address of Bro. Baxter to his father on the presentation of a jewel voted by the Lodge to the latter, has been referred to. It is here given entire as copied on the records, together with the proceedings of the Lodge relating to it :

January 27, 5825. "On motion of R. W. Bro. Samuel Smith, *Voted* unanimously, That the address made by the presiding Master to R. W. and Past Master Daniel Baxter, Sr., and on account of the presentation of Past Master's Jewel as voted at the last meeting, be recorded with the doings of the Lodge."

" At a special meeting of Columbian Lodge, held on Thursday evening, January 27, 5825, it was unanimously *Voted*, that the following address from the R. W. Master to his father on his installation, for the fifteenth time into the office of Treasurer, be placed upon the records.

ADDRESS.

Treasurer : By the unanimous vote of the members of Columbian Lodge, you have been this evening elected honorary member ; not, Sir, as a reward for the important services you have performed during the twenty-five years you have been associated with them; for they are sensible they can confer no honor that would not come infinitely short of those services; but they have done it, to express in the only way the regulations of the Lodge will allow, their gratitude and affection.

They recollect the standing of Columbian Lodge in 5799 ; they contemplate what *she now is*, and turn their eyes to you as one of her principal benefactors. They remember, Sir, that during your membership, you have had the offices of Senior and Junior Warden four years ; of Master, five ; and of Treasurer, fourteen ; and that for all those services, you have neither expected nor received any compensation. It was you, Sir, who first proposed the abolishment of refreshment, and led the way to that glorious epoch in the history of our Lodges, which has convinced the world that it is the pure morality of Free Masonry which we love, and not its dissipations. Columbian Lodge may well look to you as one of her benefactors, who has done so much and so faithfully; who has discharged every Masonic duty with so much zeal and promptitude; who has so eminently assisted in leading her on to respectability and honor.

I have now the pleasure of investing you with the jewel, the badge of your office as Treasurer. It is customary for the presiding officer on the investment of those who serve in offices under him, to give instruction relative to their several duties; but how, my venerated and beloved father, can I perform that duty? Can one who from his earliest infancy has looked up to you for advice, instruction and example, attempt to direct your performance of any duty? If the members of this Lodge have cause of gratitude and love towards you, how much more, Sir, have I, who have always enjoyed your friendship and paternal love; who have constantly been in the habit of receiving proofs of your love and affection! Nor will that affection be withdrawn; the kind interest expressed every day for my welfare, can never be forgotten; and as this is the last public opportunity I shall ever have, you will now accept assurances of my present love, gratitude and affection.

As Treasurer of Columbian Lodge, follow your own example, and then, indeed, will the ' *widows* heart be made to *leap for joy;* ' the distressed Brother be sure of prompt relief; the lonely orphan rise up and call you blessed; and the grateful tears of age, penury and distress, reward your labors. Your place is on the right of the Master."

R. W. GEORGE G. SMITH.

Bro. Smith was born in Danvers, now South Danvers, Essex Co., Mass., September 8, 5795. He was initiated in C. L. November 4, 5819, admitted a member May 5, 5820, and to honorary membership May 7, 5840. He served as Senior Deacon in 5821, '22, '33 and '35; as Marshal in 5830 and 5834; as Junior Warden in 5823 and 5824; as Senior Warden in 5825, and as Master in 5826, '27, '29, '42, '43, '44 and '45. No other presiding officer has served so many terms as Bro. Smith. Soon after he left the chair in 5845, he became the Master of Massachusetts Lodge, he having been invited to join them with that view. He was Deputy Grand Master of the G. Lodge in 5838, 5839 and 5840. He has delivered Masonic addresses on various occasions, which have had the elegant and useful impress of his cultivated and well stored mind. At installations, he has often presided both in C. L. and other Lodges, (see pages 195 and 200,) and his graceful manner and impressive remarks, in the ceremonies attending them, have always elicited unbounded admiration. He was a member of the school committee in 5837 and 5838, and the warden of ward nine in 5843 and 5844. He was admitted a member of the Mass. Char. Mec. Asso. in 5831, and presided over that body in 5845, 5846 and 5847. He was in 5846, the resident representative of St. John's Lodge, No. 1, in New York, to C. L. The following are extracts from the records :

April 2, 5840. " The R. W. Master in behalf of the committee appointed for that purpose, presented to our R. W. Past Master, George G. Smith, his Jewel, re-inscribed in accordance with a vote of the Lodge to that effect."

January 1, 5846. " *Voted*, That the three first officers be a committee to cause to be engraven upon the Past Master's Jewel of our late Master, the approbation of the Lodge for his distinguished services in its behalf during the past three years."

November 5, 5846. " The Right Worshipful Master informed the Lodge of the appointment of R. W. Bro. G. G. Smith, as the representative of St. John's Lodge, No. 1, of New York, to this Lodge, and made the appointment of R. W. Bro. Elias W. Nexen, of St. John's Lodge, as the representative of this Lodge for St. John's Lodge of New York."

R. W. Joshua B. Flint.

Bro. Flint, M. D., was born in Cohasset, Mass. His father was the clergyman of that town previous to the time when it was divided into parishes. He was made a Mason in C. L., November 20, 5822, admitted a member March 6, 5823, and an honorary member in 5840. He served as Marshal in 5824; as Senior Deacon in 5825 and 5826; as Junior Warden in 5827; and as Master in 5828, 5830, 5831, 5832 and 5833. The latter office he resigned October 20, 5828, on account of leaving the country; and again October 3, 5833, probably because he had been appointed D. D. G. Master. He was the D. D. G. Master of the first district in 5833, 5834 and 5835; and Grand Master in 5836 and 5837. The highest degree taken by him in Masonry is that of M. M. He has delivered several Masonic addresses at the request of brethren; one at the centennial celebration of St. John's Lodge, one for St. John's day, at Concord, and several before Columbian Lodge. Brother Flint writes under a recent date :

" My early and intimate connexion with Masonry and masons, in Boston, has supplied me with some of the most agreeable reminiscences of my life, as well as with some of the most precious friendships which I still enjoy. Especially is this remark true with respect to Columbian Lodge, within whose hallowed precincts that connexion was formed, and whose partial brethren kindly led me up, step by step, in official progress, to that position which has entitled me to the consideration implied in the interrogatories you have proposed.

That position, moreover, is memorable to me, for having rendered me eligible to the Grand Mastership,—an office to which I was elected at an earlier age, both as a Mason and a man, than any one before or after me. That office at all times an eminently honorable and dignified one, was esteemed by me peculiarly honorable to myself, in view of the circum-

stances and considerations which determined my selection.
The institution was in the midst of a bitter persecution; many
of those who had been entrusted with responsible offices had
been seduced by the allurements of political ambition, and
betrayed the interests that had been committed to them by a
confiding fraternity, under assurances and engagements to
fidelity which only the baseness of desperate villany could
disregard. 'We must refrain from our usual practice of
devoting to the G. Mastership some brother, whose distinction, in public life, blended itself becomingly and favorably
with the highest masonic dignity,' said the brethern—' we
ca'nt trust such candidates for political promotion — we
must find a man who has no such temptation, and on whose
fidelity we can rely.' Herein was the special honor of the
office as it was conferred upon me. 'He will not betray us,'
said that vote of the brethren of the G. Lodge who had known
me well, a vote by which I was placed in the most responsible
and dignified masonic position in the Commonwealth. This
assurance of their confidence was better than the office, and
has been felt by me, to be so, ever since. *   *   *   *   *
During a large part of my masonic experience in Boston,
the institution was passing through the ordeal of a relentless
persecution. It 'tried the spirits.' It showed that many
weak, and some wicked persons had unfortunately found admission to an institution, where the one class is almost as
much out of place as the other. The former were too easily
frightened or coaxed into a renunciation of their Masonic
vows—the latter took their 'thirty pieces of silver,' gave the
treacherous kiss, and imitated their great prototype in all but
the contrition which was his only redeeming trait. But it
showed also that there were good men and true, worthy disci-
ples of that ancient Masonic martyr whom they had all once
personified. With an intelligent appreciation of their rights
as citizens, and a lively sense of their Masonic obligations,
these men were unmoved alike by legislative dictation, the
denunciations of the press, the counsel of time-serving friends,
and by every other form of action which the impertinent ras-
cality of anti-masonry assumed. They were 'true as steel'—
those Masons of Boston and Massachusetts, who breasted that
storm, and defied those who raised and ruled it. I shall
always honor and love them, and be proud in the recollection
of having been even one of the least of so resolute and faithful
a band.''

Bro. Flint was fitted for Harvard University at

home, and graduated with the class of 5820. Soon after leaving the university, he became the assistant master of the English classical school in Boston, in which service he remained two years. At the end of that time he commenced the study of medicine, as private pupil of Dr. John C. Warren, matriculating as a student in the medical department of Harvard University. He received the degree of M. D., after completing the usual term of pupilage, and was immediately selected as a candidate for practice in Boston, where he resided until 5837.

During that year he received an invitation from the managers of the Louisville Medical Institute, then just going into operation, to occupy the chair of surgery, in its first Faculty. He accepted the proposal, removed to Louisville, and has been there in the practice of his profession ever since. At the end of three years, he resigned his chair in the Institute, and a few years afterwards, accepted the professorship of surgery in the Kentucky School of Medicine, at its commencement a department of the Masonic College at Lagrange. He is still a member of the Faculty of the same school, which is now an independent institution.

While in Boston, he was for a number of years, physician of the county penitentiary institutions, and was appointed one of the medical commission to visit New York in 5832, for the purpose of making observations in the then novel pestilence—cholera. In 5827 or 5828, he established a course of popular lectures on anatomy—the first, it is believed, in the country, or even in the world, where that science was taught publicly, and to miscellaneous classes, illustrated by actual dissections.

At the time when an effort was to be made in
the legislature of Massachusetts, to legalize the
study of anatomy, he was elected as a representative from Boston, with a special view to the services which a medical gentleman interested on
that subject, and well-informed respecting it,
might render in its behalf.   He was on the committee that proposed a report and submitted a project of law, which led to the first legislative action
promotive of human dissection, or the dissection
of human bodies, which, probably, ever took
place.   He was continued in the legislature three
years.   He was, also, several times elected to the
Common Council of Boston, from the fourth ward,
where he ˙ resided.   The following letter and
extracts are taken from the records :

                              " *Boston*, *October* 20, 1828.
To the Officers and Brethren of Columbian Lodge:
    Prudential considerations which I am not at liberty to disre-
gard, make it necessary for me to be absent from our city and
country for several months to come, and as one of the last
and interesting duties awaiting my departure, I hasten to
resign the charter of our Lodge, as well as the office, by virtue
of which I have lately held it, to those from whom I receive
them.
    While I am happy at all times to acknowledge with grati-
tude the repeated marks of respect and confidence, which the
members of Columbian Lodge have shown me in the way of
official honors, it becomes me on this occasion, especially, to
express my regret, that those favors have not met with a
more adequate return than can be found in the very imperfect
services which it has been my power to render you.
    The circumstances which occasioned my protracted absence,
during the last quarter, are probably known to you, and will
excuse my dereliction of duty at that time—while for the rest
I must depend for my apology on the exercise of that crown-
ing Masonic virtue, Charity, which covers a multitude of
faults.   In the mean time, I ask the benefit of your prayers
and benediction during my voyage and absence and assure you

in turn, that the hope of enjoying together again the sober and solid satisfaction of our Masonic intercourse, will be among the most delightful anticipations connected with my return. Your friend and Brother, JOSHUA B. FLINT.

December 4, 5828. "Bros. G. G. Smith, Baxter, Jr. and Johnson, were appointed a committee to procure a Past Master's Jewel, for our late Master, J. B. Flint."

October 3, 5833. "R. W. J. B. Flint, took this opportunity to tender his resignation of the chair of Columbian Lodge."

December 4, 5834. "R W. Bro. Flint then favored the Lodge with a short but pertinent address, on the subject of our *Masonic duties*, and the present condition of the institution. He congratulated the Brethren on the prospect of a speedy deliverance from anti-*masonic* persecution, and urged us to *vigilance*, and good faith in our Masonic relations."

W. DAVID TILLSON.

Bro. Tillson was born in Bridgewater, Mass. July 29, 5797. He was initiated in C. L. April 5, 5821, and admitted to membership November 9, 5824. He was elected an honorary member in 5847. He served as Junior Deacon in 5828 and 5829; as Senior Deacon in 5830; a Junior Warden in 5831 and 5832; as Senior Warden in 5833, 5839 and 5840; and as Master in 5834, 5835 and 5836. He is a "good man and true," and failed not in the battle of the persecution, heroically to maintain his ground in the South, West or East, or wherever else duty called him. He is the Master of the new Lodge lately established at Woburn, Mass. He was admitted a member of the Mass. Char. Mec. Asso. in 5829, and was a Trustee of that Society in 5846, 5847 and 5848. The following vote of the Lodge was passed on his retirement from the chair:

January 5, 5837. "On motion of Bro. Daniel Baxter, *Voted*, That our R. W. Brother and late Master, David Tillson, be presented with the collar and jewel of a Past Master, and Bros. B. Appleton and George G. Smith, were appointed a committee to present the same."

W. RUEL BAKER.

This Bro. was born in Sudbury, Mass., July 19, 5792, and died in Boston, January 17, 5848. His remains were interred in Mount Auburn. He was the youngest son of John Baker, who served in the revolutionary war, and was engaged in the battle of Bunker Hill. He was made a Mason in C. L. May 5, 5825, and a member December 29, of that year. He filled the station of Senior Steward in 5827, '33, '34 and '35; of Marshal in 5836; of Master in 5837, '38, '39 and '40; and of Treasurer in 5841, '42, '43, '44, '45, '46, '47, and '48, or until the time of his death. He was one of the Grand Stewards in the Grand Lodge in 5841 and 5844. He was admitted to membership in St. Andrew's R. A. Chapter May 7, 5828; served as Scribe in 5834 and 5835; as King in 5836 and 5837; as High Priest in 5838 and 5839. He was for a time the presiding officer of the Boston Encampment, G. Master of the Grand Encampment of Mass. and R. I., and an officer in the Council of the 33d degree. In the Board of Relief he was a most active and useful member. In 5844, he was chosen a member of the Board of Trustees of the Masonic Temple, in the place of Bro. Appleton, and held the position until the time of his decease. During the last war with England, Bro. Baker served in the militia, and was stationed in Boston harbor. At the close of the war he received an honorable discharge. He afterwards became the Lieut. Colonel of the 3d Regiment of the Mass. Militia. He was admitted a member of the An. and Hon. Ar. Co. in 5819:

"Lieut. Col. Ruel Baker, Boston, painter: born at Sudbury. Lieut. Colonel of the third regiment; Lieut. of the Artillery Co., 1824."

He became a member of the Mass. Char. Mec. Asso. in 5831, and represented ward eleven in the Common Council in 5833, 5834 and 5835, also ward ten, in 5839, 5840 and 5841. A funeral sermon was preached at his obsequies by Rev. David Fosdick, at the Hollis Street Church. The attendance at the funeral was very numerous, embracing the members of various Masonic institutions, of the Mass. Char. Mec. Asso., and of other societies to which the deceased belonged. The following resolves are copied from the records of C. L. :

February 3, 5848. "W. Brother Coolidge announced the death of our R. W. Bro. Ruel Baker, in an eloquent and impressive manner, and offered the following resolutions, which were unanimously adopted :

Whereas, it has pleased the Almighty Dispenser of events, to call home to himself the spirit of our late Brother Ruel Baker ;—therefore,

Resolved, That the sad event which has deprived us of a Brother, honored and beloved throughout the Masonic family, calls on us, the members of Columbian Lodge, particularly, to bring to mind his many virtues, and to try to emulate his usefulness and fidelity.

Resolved, That in parting with our friend, we feel the deepest assurance that a life of so much excellence has not closed without leaving us the hope of a glorious immortality, and that if we can exemplify in our lives as he did, the principles of our Order, we have the blessed hope of meeting him again in the Celestial Lodge above.

Resolved, That we tender to the widow and family of our late Brother, the assurances of our deep sympathy in their bereavement, that our tears flow with theirs, and that our

hearts are stricken also, and to those of our own household
who are called to mourn the loss of a father, we would unite
in the tenderest expressions of sorrow, at the loss of one to
whom we all looked up as to a Masonic father and friend.

Resolved, That these resolutions be placed at length upon
our records, and a copy of the same transmitted to the family
of our deceased Brother."

At the annual election, December 19, 5840, Bro.
Samuel A. Allen was chosen Master, but he declined accepting the office, when W. Bro. Ruel Baker
was chosen in his stead.

January 2, 5840. " The records having been read, Bro.
Smith in behalf of the committee who were chosen to wait on
Brother Allen, to inform him of his election as Master, report-
ed that Bro. Allen declined serving.

Bro. Joseph Grelee having declined serving as Junior Warden, the Lodge went into a new choice, and Bro. Samuel A.
Allen was chosen to fill that vacancy."

Bro. Allen was born in Charlestown. Mass, Oct.
5, 5801. He was made a Mason in C. L. November 1, 5827, and admitted a member December 3,
5830. He faithfully performed the labors of Secretary for a long time, i. e., in 5832, '33, '34, '35,
'36, '37, '38 and '39. He was Junior Warden in
5840, and Senior Warden in 5841. He became a
member of the An. and Hon. Ar. Co. in 5836:

" Maj. Samuel A. Allen, Boston, trader. Brigade Major,
Adjutant of Ar. Co. 1839. Author of the humorous and
spirited circular in behalf of the Lancers, occasioned by the
riot in 1842."

W. George M. Thacher.

Bro. Thacher was born in Boston, March 5,
5809. He was initiated in C. L. November 5840,
and made a member January 7, 5841. He served
as Junior Warden in 5842; as Senior Warden in

5843, 5844 and 5845; as Master in 5846 and 5847 ; and as Marshal in 5850 and 5851. He was S. W. of the Boston Encampment in 5851 and 5852. In the Grand Lodge he was G. Pursuivant in 5852, G. S. Bearer in 5853, and G. Marshal in 5854. He was appointed the representative of Ark Lodge, N. Y. in 5848 :

September 7, 5848. " A communication was received from Ark Lodge, No 33, of Geneva, N. Y., recommending R. W. Bro. Enos Barnes, as the representative of Columbian Lodge to that Lodge, and asking the nomination of some one as a suitable person to represent that Lodge in Columbian Lodge ; whereupon, R. W. Bro. Enos Barnes was appointed as the representative of Columbian to Ark Lodge, and R. W. Bro. G. M. Thacher, was recommended to Ark Lodge, as the representative from that Lodge to Columbian."

Bro. Thacher was elected a member of the An. and Hon. Ar. Co. in 5839 :

" Maj. George M. Thacher, Boston, merchant, Adjutant of Ar. Co. 1840. Staff of Gen. Howe, son of Hon. P. O. Thacher; born at Boston, March 5, 5809."

He served as Div. Quarter Master, Mass. Militia, from 5839 to 5850, and is now the Senior *Aide-de-camp* of Gov. Gardner. He has held various commissions under the State government, and is a member of the Board of Commissioners for the enlargement of the State House. In 5854, he was Knighted by the King of Denmark for long and faithful services as Consul. He is a Senator of Suffolk County in the General Court of Massachusetts; a member of the Mass. Char. Fire Society, and of the Society of the Cincinnati of Massachusetts.

W. Peter C. Jones.

Bro. Jones was born in Charlestown, Mass., August 10, 5808, and came to reside in Boston in the autumn of 5822. He was made a Mason in C. L. April 1, 5841, and admitted a member June 3, 5841. He served as Junior Deacon in 5842; Senior Deacon in 5843, 5844 and 5845; as Senior Warden in 5846 and 5847; and as Master in 5848 and 5849. In St. Andrew's R. A. Chapter he was admitted a member March 2, 5842, and officiated as Scribe in 5844, as King in 5845 and 5846, and as High Priest in 5847 and 5848. He held the third office in the Boston Encampment two years. In 5837 he was elected assistant engineer of the Boston Fire Department, and continued in the office until he resigned in 5847. He was an active member of that department for more than twenty years. He was a member of the Common Council from ward nine in the years 5850, 5851 and 5852; and Trustee of the Mass. Char. Mec. Asso. about two years. In 5854 he was chosen one of the directors of the House of Industry and Reformation. He is now (5856,) a representative from Boston in the General Court of Massachusetts.

W. William W. Baker.

Bro. Baker, (son of Ruel) was born in Boston, May 4, 5822, and educated at Lexington, Mass. He was initiated in C. L. January 6, 5845, and made a member May 1, 5845. He officiated as Senior Deacon in 5846 and 5847; as Senior Warden in 5848 and 5849; and as Master in 5850 and 5851. He was High Priest of St. Andrew's

R. A. Chapter in 5850 and 5851; Generalissimo of the Boston Encampment in 5850, 5851 and 5852; G. M. of the G. Lodge of Perfection in 5849, 5850 and 5851; and a member of the Board of Relief several years. He has filled several minor offices in the city government, and under the new organization of the Boston School Committee in 5854, was elected to that body for three years. He was a member of the Boston Light Infantry Company from 5839 to 5849, and during a part of that time he served as clerk of the company.

W. WILLIAM D. COOLIDGE.

Bro. Coolidge was born in Boston, February 15, 5808. His first lesson in Masonry he received in C. L. January 6, 5842, and membership was conferred upon him May 19, in the same year. He was Junior Steward in 5843 and 5844; Junior Deacon in 5845; Junior Warden 5846 5847 and 5848; Senior warden in 5850 and 5851; and Master in 5852 and 5853. In the Grand Lodge he has served as G. Steward, G. Sword Bearer, and and Grand Marshal; the latter station he now occupies. On the revival, in 5854, of the practice of appointing Visiting Deputations to represent C. Lodge in the sister institutions, he took a leading, active and most useful part. As chairman of several of the deputations, he rendered them effectual for the objects for which they were established. He was a member of the Common Council for ward five in 5847 and 5848, and a representative of Boston in 5849, in the General Court of Mass.

R. W. John T. Heard.

Bro. Heard was born in Boston, May 4, 5809. Bro. John Perkins, an original member of C. L., was his maternal grandfather, (see page 427.) He was initiated in Columbian Lodge, February 20, 5845; admitted to membership May 1, 5845; officiated as Junior Deacon in 5846 and 5847; as Junior Warden in 5850 and 5851; as Senior Warden in 5852 and 5853; and as Master in 5854 and 5855. He was admitted a life member January 19, 5855. He received the chapter degrees in St. Andrew's R. A. Chapter, and was knighted in the Boston Encampment. Of the last named body he is a member. He was Grand Marshal of the Grand Lodge two terms; and in December 5855, was elected Senior Grand Warden. In 5850, he was a director of the House of Industry and Reformation; and in 5851, a member of the Cochituate Water Board. In 5851, he was commissioned as Senior *Aide-de-camp* of the Governor of Massachusetts. In 5853, he was appointed by Gov. Clifford one of the Board of Commissioners for the enlargement of the State House; and in 5854, by Gov. Washburn, a commissioner for the establishment of the State Hospital at Rainsford Island, both of which positions he declined.

W. William B. Fowle, Jr.

Bro. Fowle, was born in Boston, July 27, 5826. He was made a Mason in C. L. March 7, 5850, passed April 8, and raised May 2, in the same year. He was admitted to membership June 6, 5850. He served as Senior Steward in 5851 ; as Senior Deacon in 5852 ; as Junior Warden in 5854 ; and as Senior Warden in 5855. At the annual meeting December 6, 5855, he was unanimously elected Master, in which office he was installed December 31, 5855. The installation was public, and made the fifth of that character in the history of the Lodge. The retiring Master installed the new Master, who, with grace and effect, conducted the remainder of the ceremonies. R. W. George M. Randall, delivered an interesting address, and beautiful and appropriate music was performed by a choir who volunteered for the occasion. Bro. Fowle is a member of St. Paul's R. A. Chapter, and was J. G. W. of the Boston G. L. of Perfection.

The preceding pages contain nearly all the transactions of Columbian Lodge that can properly be published, or which the members would care to have presented even to themselves alone. Nearly every subject suggested by the records has been introduced, excepting, of course, those which can never be revealed but among Masons. Information of a purely personal nature, mainly relating to petitions of candidates and for relief, has been excluded, though much is supplied concerning the first class of petitioners, by the catalogue of initiates and members, prepared by the Secretary. It is regretted that the means were not more ample for furnishing fuller biographical notices in some cases, and that various documents of interest could not be produced owing to the imperfection of the files of papers. The copious extracts from the records demonstrate that the purpose entertained at the commencement of the work—to let the record speak for itself—has been fully accomplished.

When the manuscript for the first two chapters was placed in the printer's hands in March last, it was supposed that the historical account might reach one hundred and fifty pages, and the size of the page was determined accordingly. Had the magnitude of the undertaking been anticipated, the mechanical arrangement would have been different. The first seven chapters were printed previous to the middle of June. During the warm season but little was done either in printing or preparing copy, so that it follows that over three hundred pages of historical matter have been produced since the middle of September. A good deal of delay in the publication has been occasioned by the difficulty of obtaining information concerning persons. The value of the work consists in the additional means it affords of preserving what may be termed the vital part of the written proceedings of the Lodge, which is thereby multiplied from one copy to five hundred.

It is a source of joyful congratulation that the career of the Lodge has been so honorable, so true to Masonic propriety and excellence, and so free from the evidences of human infirmity : may their future testify to their continued fidelity to the principles of Masonry.

January 19, *A. L.* 5856.

CATALOGUE

OF THE

OFFICERS OF COLUMBIAN LODGE.

5795 TO 5856.

ABBREVIATIONS : S. W. for Senior Warden; J. W. for Junior Warden; T. for Treasurer; S. for Secretary; S. D. for Senior Deacon; J. D. for Junior Deacon; S. S. for Senior Steward; J. S. for Junior Steward; I. S. for Inside Sentinel ; C. S. for Closet Steward.

5795.

First meeting under Dispensation, June 22, 5795.
Joseph Churchill, Master.

James Eaton, S. W.	John Rittenhouse, J. W.
Samuel Hayden, T.	John Coles, S.
Snelling Powell, S. D.	James Dodge, J. D.
Nicholas Kindness, S. S.	Thomas Leatham, J. S.
—— Jones, Tyler.	

5796.

Election December 3, 5795, Installation April 14, 5796.
Joseph Churchill, Master.

James Eaton, S. W.	John Perkins, J. W.
John W. Folsom, T.	John Coles, S.
Snelling Powell, S. D.	Samuel Gouldsbury, J. D.
John Rittenhouse, S. S.	Thomas Tannatt, J. S.
Henry Wickham, Tyler.	

5797.

Election December 1, 5796, Installation December 31, 5796.
Joseph Churchill, Master.

Samuel Gouldsbury, S. W.	Samuel Hayden, J. W.
Amasa Stetson, T.	John W. Folsom, S.
James Dodge, S. D.	John Raymond, J. D.
John Martin, S. S.	A Davidson, J. S.
—— Bunton, Tyler.	

5798.

Election December 7, 5797, Installation January 4, 5798.

Joseph Churchill, Master.

* James Eaton, S. W.
Amasa Stetson, T.
John Perkins, S. D.
John Martin, S. S.
Alexander Davidson, C. S.

John Rittenhouse, J. W.
John W. Folsom, S.
John Coles, J. D.
Thomas Tannatt, J. S.
Ebenezer Mountford, Tyler.

* Died in office.

5799.

Election December 6, 5798, Installation December 20, 5798.

John W. Folsom, Master.

John Rittenhouse, S. W.
Joseph Churchill, T.
Samuel Hayden, S. D.
John Martin, S. S.
Alexander Davidson, C. S.

Amasa Stetson, J. W.
Samuel Stetson, S.
Thomas Tannatt, J. D.
John Green, J. S.
Ebenezer Mountford, Tyler.

5800.

Election December 5, 5799, Installation January 2, 5800.

John W. Folsom, Master.

Amasa Stetson, S. W.
Joseph Churchill, T.
John Green, S. D.
Ammi Cutter, S. S.
Alexander Davidson, C. S.

Daniel Baxter, J. W.
Jonathan F. Sleeper, S.
Thomas Pons, J. D.
William J. McDonnell, J. S.
Ebenezer Mountford, Tyler.

5801.

Election December 4, 5800, Installation December 18, 5800.

John W. Folsom, Master.

Amasa Stetson, S. W.
Samuel Stetson, T.
Thomas Pons, S. D.
Seth Thayer, S. S.
Alexander Davidson, C. S.

Samuel Stetson, J. W.
William J. McDonnell, S.
Ammi Cutter, J. D.
Elisha Tower, J. S.
Ebenezer Mountford, Tyler.

5802.

Election December 3, 5801, Installation same evening.

Amasa Stetson, Master.

Daniel Baxter, S. W.
Samuel Stetson, T.
Thomas Pons, S. D.
Samuel Jenks, S. S.
Alexander Davidson, C. S.

Elisha Tower, J. W.
Ammi Cutter, S.
John Swett, J. D.
Scammel Penniman, J. S.
Ebenezer Mountford, Tyler.

5803.

Election December 2, 5802, Installation same evening.
Amasa Stetson, Master.

Daniel Baxter, S. W.
Samuel Stetson, T.
John Swett, S. D.
Samuel Jenks, S. S.
Alexander Davidson, C. S.

Joseph Kelly, J. W.
Ammi Cutter, S.
Turner Crooker, J. D.
Daniel Johnson J. S.
Ebenezer Mountford Tyler.

5804.

Election December 1, 5803, Installation same evening.
Daniel Baxter, Master.

William J. McDonnell, S. W.
*Samuel Stetson. T.
John Swett, S. D.
Abraham Jenkins, S. S.
Alexander Davidson, C. S.

Turner Crooker, J. W.
Ammi Cutter, S.
Daniel Johnson, J. D.
Edward Cutter, J. S.
Ebenezer Mountford, Tyler.

* Died in office, and Amasa Stetson acted as his successor.

5805.

Election December 6, 5804, * Installation December 27, 5804.
Daniel Baxter, Master.

Turner Crooker, S. W.
Amasa Stetson, T.
Abraham Jenkins, S. D.
Oliver Ware, S. S.
Alexander Davidson, C. S.

John Swett, J. W.
Stephen Bean, S.
Ebenezer Phillips, J. D.
Archibald Dunlap, J. S.
Ebenezer Mountford, Tyler.

* Address by Master at Installation.

5806.

Election December 5, 5805, Installation same evening.
Daniel Baxter, Master.

Stephen Bean, S. W.
Amasa Stetson, T.
Aaron Allchorus S. D.
Lewis Stearns, S. S.
Alexander Davidson, C. S.

Ebenezer Phillips, J. W.
Amos Binney, S.
Joseph Jenkins, J. D.
Thomas Kidder, J. S.
Ebenezer Mountford, Tyler.

5807.

Election December 4, 5806, Installation January 1, 5807.
Stephen Bean, Master.

Ebenezer Phillips, S. W.
Amos Binney, T.
Aaron Allchorus, S. D.
Noah Porter, S. S.

Joseph Jenkins, J. W.
John M. Dunham, S.
Josiah Vose, J. D.
Charles Tuttle, J. S.

5808.

Election December 3, 5807, Installation January 7, 5808.

Stephen Bean, Master.

Ebenezer Phillips, S. W.
Amos Binney, T.
Samuel Smith, S. D.
Samuel Hayden, S. S.

Joseph Jenkins, J. W.
* Josiah Vose, S.
† Charles Tuttle, J. D.
Nathaniel Hammond, J. S.

* John M. Dunham elected Secretary, but declined the office.

† Calvin Howe elected J. D., but declined the office.

5809.

Election December 1, 5808, Installation January 5, 5809.

Daniel Baxter, Master.

* Joseph Jenkins, S. W.
Turner Crooker, T.
Samuel Smith, S. D.
John Park, S. S.
‡ Stephen Bean, Marshal.

Amos Binney, J. W.
Josiah Vose, S.
† Charles Tuttle, J. D.
Thomas Willey, J. S.
Ebenezer Mountford, Tyler.

* In place of E. Phillips who declined.

† In place of Calvin Howe who declined.

‡ Appointed Marshal for Installation January 5, 5809.

5810.

Election December 7, 5809, * Installation January 4, 5810.

Joseph Jenkins, Master.

Samuel Smith, S. W.
† Turner Crooker, T.
Charles Tuttle, S. D.
Samuel Baxter, S. S.

David Moody, J. W.
Ezekiel Little, S.
John Park, J. D.
Samuel B. Jarvis, J. S.

Thomas Willey, Marshal.

* Address by Joseph Jenkins.

† Treasurer resigned July 5, 5-10. D. Baxter succeeded.

5811.

Election December 6, 5810, Installation December 27, 5810.*

Joseph Jenkins, Master.

Samuel Smith, S. W.
Daniel Baxter, T.
Nathaniel Heard, S. D.
Elisha V. Glover, S. S.
George Bender, Jr., Marshal.

David Moody, J. W.
Nathaniel Sawyier, S.
Samuel Baxter, J. D.
Benjamin B. Appleton, J. S.
Ebenezer Oliver, C. S. and Tyler.

* Address by Master.

5812.

Election December 5, 5811, Installation January 2, 5812.
Joseph Jenkins, Master.

David Moody, S. W.
Daniel Baxter, T.
Elisha V. Glover, S. D.
George Bender, Jr., S. S.

Nathaniel Heard, J. W.
Nathaniel Sawyier, S.
Benjamin B. Appleton, J. D.
Ezekiel Little, J. S.

Amos Binney, Marshal.

5813.

Election December 3, 5812, * Installation January 7, 5313.
Joseph Jenkins, Master.

David Moody, S. W.
Daniel Baxter, T.
Elijah Morse, S. D.
Perley Fairbanks, S. S.

Nathaniel Heard, J. W.
Benjamin B. Appleton, S.
Oliver Mills, J. D.
Ezra Stone, J. S.

John Park, Marshal.

* Female visitation, Address by E. Morse.

5814.

Election December 2, 5813, Installation same evening.
David Moody, Master.

* Nathaniel Heard, S. W.
Daniel Baxter, T.
Elisha V. Glover, S. D.
Horace Collamore, S. S.

Elijah Morse, J. W.
Benjamin B. Appleton, S.
Ezra Stone, J. D.
Jason Braman, J. S.

John Park, Marshal.

* Died in office March 3, 5814. E. Morse was elected S. W.; E. V. Glover, J. W.; Ezra Stone and H. Collamore, S. and J. Deacons, and Jason Braman and Joseph R. Chandler, S. and J. Stewards. The Master, D. Moody, presided but six times during the year.

5815.

Election December 1, 5814, Installation December 8, 5814.
* Elijah Morse, Master.

Benjamin B. Appleton, S. W.
Daniel Baxter, T.
Ezra Stone, S. D.
Jason Braman, S. S.
Elisha V. Glover, Marshal.

† Oliver Mills, J. W.
Joseph Jenkins, S.
Horace Collamore, J. D.
Joseph R. Chandler, J. S.
Ebenezer Oliver, Tyler.

* The Master, E. Morse, resigned, he having received the appointment of D. D. G. M. 1st District, and Benjamin B. Appleton was elected March 2, 5815.

† E. V. Glover was elected S. W., but declined serving.

5816.

Election December 7, 5815, Installation January 4, 5816.

Benjamin B. Appleton, Master.

Elisha V. Glover, S. W.
Daniel Baxter, T.
Ezra Stone, S. D.
Nathaniel Hammond, S. S.

Oliver Mills, J. W.
Ezekiel Little, S.
Jason Braman, J. D.
Elisha Brimhall, J. S.

Elijah Morse, Marshal:

5817.

Election December 5, 5816, Installation December 19, 5816.*

Joseph Jenkins, Master.

Elijah Morse, S. W.
Daniel Baxter, T.
Samuel Smith, S. D.
George Guild, S. S.
Paul Dean, Chaplain.

Benjamin B. Appleton, J. W.
Isaac McGaw, S.
Nathaniel Hammond, J. D.
Daniel Baxter, Jr., J. S.
E. V. Glover, Tyler.

* Address, &c.

5818.

Election December 4, 5817, Installation (public,) December 22, 5817.

Joseph Jenkins, Master.

* Elijah Morse, S. W.
Daniel Baxter, T.
Samuel Smith, S. D.
Joel Nason, S. S.
Paul Dean, Chaplain.

Benjamin B. Appleton, J. W.
† Isaac McGaw, S.
Daniel Baxter, Jr. J. D.
Benjamin Stevens, J. S.
Aaron Bean, Marshal.

Ebenezer Oliver, Tyler.

* January 15, 5818; Bro. Morse resigned.

† July 2, 5818, Secretary resigned, Gershom Cobb elected. January 7, 5819. Thanks to B. B. Appleton and Calvin Howe, for acting as S. W. anl J. W., the past year.

5819.

Election December 2, 5818, Installation January 7, 5819.

Aaron Bean, Master.

Samuel Smith, S. W.
Daniel Baxter, T.
Joel Nason, S. D.
Benjamin M. Nevers, S. S.
Paul Dean, Chaplain.

Daniel Baxter, Jr., J. W.
Gershom Cobb, S.
Alva Spear, J. D.
Luther Corey, J. S.
Benjamin Stevens, Marshal.

5820.

Election December 2, 5819, Installation February 17, 5820.

* Aaron Bean, Master.

Samuel Smith, S. W.

Daniel Baxter, T.

Joel Nason, S. D.

Luther Corey, S. S.

Paul Dean, Chaplain.

Leuman Streeter, I. S.

Daniel Baxter, Jr., J. W.

Gershom Cobb, S.

Benjamin M. Nevers, J. D.

Cornelius Cowing, J. S.

Benjamin Stevens, Marshal.

Ebenezer Oliver, Tyler.

* April 6, 5820. See records relative to the death of the Master, Aaron Bean. June 1, 5820. Samuel Smith was elected Master, Daniel Baxter, Jr., S. W., Joel Nason, J. W., and Elisha V. Glover, S. D.

5821.

Election December 7, 5820, Installation January 4, 5821.

Samuel Smith, Master.

Daniel Baxter, Jr., S. W.

Daniel Baxter, T.

George G. Smith, S. D.

Luther Corey, S. S.

Leuman Streeter, I. S.

Francis Fisher, J. W.

Gershom Cobb, S.

Jason Braman, J. D.

Nehemiah Lovejoy, J. S.

Benjamin Stevens, Marshal.

Ebenezer Oliver, Tyler.

5822.

Election December 6, 5821, Installation December 20, 5821.

Samuel Smith, Master.

Daniel Baxter, Jr., S. W.

Daniel Baxter, T.

George G. Smith, S. D.

Luther Corey, S. S.

Benjamin Stevens, S. Marshal.

Amos Cotting, J. Marshal.

Francis Fisher, J. W.

Gershom Cobb, S.

Jason Braman, J. D.

Ebenezer W. Hayward, J. S.

Charles Tuttle, I. S.

Ebenezer Oliver, Tyler.

5823.

Election December 5, 5822, * Installation January 2, 5823.

Daniel Baxter, Jr., Master.

Francis Fisher, S. W.

Daniel Baxter, T.

Luther Corey, S. D.

Samuel Dennis, S. S.

E. V. Glover, Marshal.

George G. Smith, J. W.

Gershom Cobb, S.

Jason Braman, J. D.

Henry D. Wolcott, J. S.

Isaac Spear, I. S.

Ebenezer Oliver, Tyler.

* Address by Master.

5824.

Election December 4, 5823, Installation January 1, 5824.
Daniel Baxter, Jr., Master.

Francis Fisher, S. W.
Daniel Baxter, T.
Henry D. Wolcott, S. D.
William H. Neville, S. S.
Joshua B. Flint, Marshal.

George G. Smith, J. W.
Gershom Cobb, S.
Jason Braman, J. D.
William Bittle, J. S.
Isaac Spear, I. S.

Ebenezer Oliver, C. S. and Tyler.

5825.

Election December 2, 5824, Installation January 6, 5825.
Daniel Baxter, Jr., Master.

George G. Smith, S. W.
Daniel Baxter, T.
Joshua B. Flint, S. D.
William H. Neville, S. S.
Paul Dean,   } Chaplains.
James Sabine,   }

Henry D. Walcott, J. W.
* Ebenezer W. Hayward, S.
Jason Braman, J. D.
William Bittle, J. S.
Francis Fisher, Marshal.
Isaac Spear, I. S.

Ebenezer Oliver, Tyler.

* E. W. Hayward resigned the office of Secretary, and May 5, 5825, N. Williams was elected.

5826.

Election December 1, 5825, Installation January 5, 5826.
George G. Smith, Master.

Henry D. Walcott, S. W.
Daniel Baxter, T.
Joshua B. Flint, S. D.
W. H. Neville, S. S.
Paul Dean,   } Chaplains.
James Sabine,   }

Jason Braman, J. W.
Nathaniel Williams, S.
Caleb Coburn, J. D.
D. Whitney, J. S.
Benjamin B. Appleton, Marshal.
Jedediah Barker, I. S.

Ebenezer Oliver, C. S. and Tyler.

5827.

Election December 7, 5826, Installation January 4, 5827.
George G. Smith, Master.

H. D. Walcott, S. W.
Daniel Baxter, T.
C. Coburn, S. D.
Ruel Baker, S. S.
Paul Dean,   } Chaplains.
James Sabine,   }

Daniel Whitney, I. S.
Joshua B. Flint, J. W.
N. Williams, S.
William V. Kent, J. D.
Daniel Baxter, Jr., J. S.
B. B. Appleton, Marshal.

Ebenezer Oliver, Tyler.

5828.

Election December 6, 5827, Installation January 3, 5828.

* Joshua B. Flint, Master.

Benjamin B. Appleton, S. W.	Caleb Coburn, J. W.
Daniel Baxter, T.	N. Williams, S.
Luther Corey, S. D.	David Tillson, J. D.
William Bittle, S. S.	John Glover, J. S.
James Sabine, Chaplain.	Daniel Baxter, Jr., Marshal.

Ebenezer Oliver, Tyler.

* He resigned October 20, 5828.

5829.

Election December 4, 5828, Installation January 1, 5829.

George G. Smith, Master.

Daniel Baxter, Jr., S. W.	Peter Johnson, J. W.
Daniel Baxter, T.	N. Williams, S.
H. D. Wolcott, S. D.	David Tillson, J. D.
Wm. H. Neville, S. S.	William Bittle, J. S.
Paul Dean, } Chaplains.	Joseph Greele, I. S.
James Sabine, }	E. Oliver, Tyler.

5830.

Election December 3, 5829, Installation January 7, 5830.

Joshua B. Flint, Master.

Benjamin B. Appleton, S. W.	David Moody, J. W.
Daniel Baxter, T.	N. Williams, S.
David Tillson, S. D.	W. H. Neville, J. D.
William Bittle, S. S.	George H. Cunningham, J. S.
James Sabine, Chaplain.	George G. Smith, Marshal.
J. Towne, I. S.	E. Oliver, Tyler.

5831.

Election December 3, 5830, Installation January 6, 5831.

Joshua B. Flint, Master.

B. B. Appleton, S. W.	David Tillson, J. W.
Daniel Baxter, T.	N. Williams, S.
Wm. H. Neville, S. D.	Wm. Bittle, J. D.
George H. Cunningham, S. S.	George Bartlett, J. S.
J. Towne, I. S.	E. Oliver, Tyler.

5832.

Election December 1, 5831, Installation January 5, 5832.

Joshua B. Flint, Master.

Benjamin B. Appleton, S. W.	David Tillson, J. W.
Daniel Baxter, T.	Samuel A. Allen, S.
Wm. H. Neville, S. D.	William Bittle, J. D.
Joseph Greele, S. S.	Jonathan Towne, J. S.

5833.

Election December 29, 5832, Installation February 7, 5833.

* Joshua B. Flint, Master.

David Tillson, S. W.
Daniel Baxter, T.
George G. Smith, S: D.
Ruel Baker, S. S.

William H. Neville, J. W.
Samuel A. Allen, S.
William Bittle, J. D.
Joseph Greele, J. S.

William C. Martin, Tyler.

* October 3, 5833, he resigned.

5834.

Election December 19, 5833, Installation January 2, 5834.

David Tillson, Master.

William H. Neville, S. W.
Benjamin B. Appleton, T.
Joel Nason, S. D.
Ruel Baker, S. S.
Paul Dean, Chaplain.

William Bittle, J. W.
Samuel A. Allen, S.
Joseph Greele, J. D.
David Marden, J. S.
George G. Smith, Marshal.

William C. Martin, Tyler.

5835.

Election December 4, 5834, Installation January 1, 5835.

David Tillson, Master.

William H. Neville, S. W.
Benjamin B. Appleton, T.
George G. Smith, S. D.
Ruel Baker, S. S.
Paul Dean, Chaplain.

William Bittle, J. W.
Samuel A. Allen, S.
Joseph Greele, J. D.
David Marden, J. S.
Joel Nason, Marshal.

William C. Martin, Tyler.

5836.

Election December 3, 5835, Installation January 7, 5836.

David Tillson, Master.

William H. Neville, S. W.
Benjamin B. Appleton, T.
Joseph Greele, S. D.
Josiah Haskell, S. S.
Paul Dean, Chaplain.

William Bittle, J. W.
S. A. Allen, S.
Elisha V. Glover, J. D.
James Hunt, J. S.
Ruel Baker, Marshal.

William C. Martin, Tyler.

5837.

Election December 15, 5836, Installation January 5, 5837

Ruel Baker, Master.

William Bittle, S. W.
Benjamin B. Appleton, T.
Joseph Greele, S. D.
Benjamin Converse, S. S.

James Hunt, J. W.
Samuel A. Allen, S.
Josiah Haskell, J. D.
Charles J. F. Allen, J. S.

William C. Martin, Tyler.

5838.

Election December 7, 5837, Installation January 4, 5838.
Ruel Baker, Master.

William Bittle, S. W.
Benjamin B. Appleton, T.
Joseph Greele, S. D.
Benjamin Converse, S. S.
Jonathan Towne, Marshal.

James Hunt, J. W.
Samuel A. Allen, S.
Josiah Haskell, J. D.
David Marden, J. S.
William C. Martin, Tyler.

5839.

Election December 20, 5838, Installation January 3, 5839.
Ruel Baker, Master.

David Tilson, S. W.
Benjamin B. Appleton, T.
Josiah Haskell, S. D.
W. G. Edwards, S. S.

Joseph Greele, J. W.
Samuel A. Allen, S.
Benjamin Converse, J. D.
W. B. Hawes, J. S.

William C. Martin, Tyler.

5840.

Election December 19, 5839, Installation February 6, 5840.
* Ruel Baker, Master.

David Tilson, S. W.
Benjamin B. Appleton, T.
Josiah Haskell, S. D.
W. G. Edwards, S. S.

Samuel A. Allen, J. W.
Joseph W. Ward, S.
W. B. Hawes, J. D.
John Fox, J. S.

* Samuel A. Allen was elected Master, but declined serving, and R. Baker was chosen January 2, 5840.

5841.

Election December 3, 5840, Installation January 7, 5841.
Benjamin B. Appleton, Master.

Samuel A. Allen, S. W.
Ruel Baker, T.
William C. Martin, S. D.
George W. Lloyd, S. S.

Benjamin Converse, J. W.
Joseph W. Ward, S.
William Hawes, J. D.
Wildes P. Walker, J. S.

5842.

Election December 16, 5841, Installation January 6, 5842.
George G. Smith, Master.

* Andrew H. Ward, S. W.
Ruel Baker, T.
Jonathan Towne, S. D.
William B. Hawes, S. S.
Benjamin Stevens, Marshal.

George M. Thacher, J. W.
Benjamin B. Appleton, Jr., S.
Peter C. Jones, J. D.
Wildes P. Walker, J. S.
William C. Martin, Tyler.

* A. H. Ward resigned April 27, 5842.

5843.

Election December 9, 5842, Installation same evening.
George G. Smith, Master.

George M. Thacher, S. W.
Ruel Baker, T.
Peter C. Jones, S. D.
William B. Hawes, S. S.
E. Smith, Jr., Marshal.

Jonathan Towne, J. W.
Benjamin B. Appleton, Jr., S.
John R. Dow, J. D.
William D. Coolidge, J. S.
William C. Martin, Tyler.

5844.

Election December 15, 5843, Installation same evening.
George G. Smith, Master.

George M. Thacher, S. W.
Ruel Baker, T.
Peter C. Jones, S. D.
William B. Hawes, S. S.
E. Smith, Jr., Marshal.

Jonathan Towne, J. W.
Benjamin B. Appleton, Jr., S.
John R. Dow, J. D.
William D. Coolidge, J. S.
William W. Wood, I. S.
William C. Martin, Tyler.

5845.

Election December 19, 5844, Installation same evening.
George G. Smith, Master.

George M. Thacher, S. W.
Ruel Baker, T.
Peter C. Jones, S. D.
Ebenezer Smith, Jr., S. S.
Benjamin Stevens, Marshal.

John R. Dow, J. W.
Benjamin B. Appleton, Jr., S.
William D. Coolidge, J. D.
E. F. Follansbee, J. S.
William W. Wood, I. S.
William C. Martin, Tyler.

5846.

Election December 13, 5845, Installation January 1, 5846.
George M. Thacher, Master.

Peter C. Jones, S. W.
Ruel Baker, T.
William W. Baker, S. D.
George Tucker, S. S.
Benjamin Stevens, Marshal.

William D. Coolidge, J. W.
John McClellan S.
John T. Heard, J. D.
Hiram Simmons, J. S.
William W. Wood, I. S.
William C. Martin, Tyler.

5847.

Election December 10, 5846, Installation (public) January 21, 5847.

George M. Thacher, Master.

Peter C. Jones, S. W.	William D. Coolidge, J. W.
Ruel Baker, T.	John McClellan, S.
William W. Baker, S. D.	John T. Heard, J. D.
George Tucker, S. S.	Hiram Simmons, J. S.
Edward T. Taylor, Chaplain.	Newell A. Thompson, Marshal.
William W. Wood, I. S.	William C. Martin, Tyler.

5848.

Election December 2, 5847, Installation January 6, 5848.

Peter C. Jones, Master.

William W. Baker, S. W.	William D. Coolidge, J. W.
* Ruel Baker, T.	John McClellan, S.
Nahum Ball, S. D.	Levi Bates, J. D.
James A. Dupee, S. S.	Hiram Simmons, J. S.
Edward T. Taylor, Chaplain.	Joseph Hall, Marshal.
William W. Wood, I. S.	William C. Martin, Tyler.

* Died January 17, 5848, John Bigelow elected April 6th, 5848.

5849.

Election Dec. 7, 5848, Installation Jan. 4, 5849.

Peter C. Jones, Master.

William W. Baker, S. W.	Nahum Ball, J. W.
John Bigelow, T.	John McClellan, S.
Levi Bates, S. D.	James A. Dupee, J. D.
Henry Blaney, S. S.	George Stimpson, Jr., J. S.
Edward T. Taylor, Chaplain.	Joseph L. Ross, Marshal.
William W. Wood, I. S.	William C. Martin, Tyler.

H. G. Barrus, Organist.

5850.

Election December 6, 5849, Installation (public,) December 21, 5849.

William W. Baker, Master.

William D. Coolidge, S. W.	John T. Heard, J. W.
John Bigelow, T.	John McClellan, S.
James A. Dupee, S. D.	Charles L. Thayer, J. D.
Preston A. Ames, S. S.	George Stimpson, Jr., J. S.
Edward T. Taylor, Chaplain,	George M. Thacher, Marshal.
William W. Wood, I. S.	William C. Martin, Tyler.

5851.

Election December 5, 5850, Installation same evening.

William W. Baker, Master.

William D. Coolidge, S. W.
John Bigelow, T.
Preston A. Ames, S. D.
William B. Fowle, Jr., S. S.
Edward T. Taylor, } Chaplains.
Henry W. Adams, }
John T. Heard, J. W.
John McClellan, S.
Charles B. F. Adams, J. D.
George Stimpson, Jr., J. S.
George M. Thacher, Marshal.
William W. Wood, I. S.
William C. Martin, Tyler.

5852.

Election December 4, 5851, Installation January 1, 5852.

William D. Coolidge, Master.

John T. Heard, S. W.
John Bigelow, T.
William B. Fowle, Jr., S. D.
M. D. Parker, S. S.
Edward T. Taylor, } Chaplains.
George M. Randall, }
Preston A. Ames, J. W.
John McClellan, S.
Robert L. Robbins, J. D.
John A. Cummings, J. S.
William W. Wood, I. S.
J. W. Barton, Marshal.
William C. Martin, Tyler.

5853.

Election December 2, 5852, Installation January 6, 5853.

William D. Coolidge, Master.

John T. Heard, S. W.
John Bigelow, T.
William B. Fowle, Jr., S. D.
M. D. Parker, S. S.
Edward T. Taylor, } Chaplains.
George M. Randall, }
Preston A. Ames, J. W.
John McClellan, S.
Robert L. Robbins, J. D.
John A Cummings, J. S.
William W. Wood, I. S.
J. W. Barton, Marshal.
William C. Martin, Tyler.

5854.

Election December 1, 5853, Installation January 5, 5854.

John T. Heard, Master.

Preston A. Ames, S. W.
John Bigelow, T.
Robert L. Robbins, S. D.
Lemuel S. Williams, S. S.
Henry A. Miles, Chaplain.
William W. Wood, I. S.
William B. Fowle, Jr., J. W.
John McClellan, S.
John Stetson, J. D.
Charles U. Cotting, J. S.
William Rogers, Marshal.
William C. Martin, Tyler.

5855.

Election December 7, 5854, Installation same evening.
John T. Heard, Master.

William B. Fowle, Jr., S. W.
John Bigelow, T.
John Stetson, S. D.
Sylvester Trull, S. S.
Henry A. Miles, Chaplain.
William W. Wood, I. S.

Robert L. Robbins, J. W.
John McClellan, S.
Charles E. Buckingham, J. D.
William P. Jones, J. S.
William Rogers, Marshal.
William C. Martin, Tyler.

5856.

Election December 6, 5855, Installation (public,) December 31, 5855.
William B. Fowle, Jr., Master.

Robert L. Robbins, S. W.
John Bigelow, T.
Charles E. Buckingham, S. D.
William P. Jones, S. S.
Henry A. Miles, Chaplain.
Gilbert Simonds, I. S.

John Stetson, J. W.
Charles E. W. Dimmock, S.
Sylvester Trull, J. D.
Thomas J. Lee, J. S.
William H. Mackintosh, Marshal.
William C. Martin, Tyler.

CATALOGUE

OF THE

MEMBERS OF COLUMBIAN LODGE,

JANUARY 3, A. L. 5856.

---

* Life Members.   † Honorary Members.   ‡ Life and Honorary Members.

Preston A. Ames.
Chas. B. F. Adams.
James A. Abbott.
H. C. Ahlborn.
Gilbert Atwood.
‡Daniel Baxter.
Sewell B. Bond.
Charles Bridgham.
Levi Bates.
George Bancroft.
Wm. P. Brown.
John Bigelow.
Wm. W. Baker.
Jabez W. Barton.
Nahum Ball.
Thacher Beal.
Daniel D. Brodhead.
Cyrus Buttrick.
E. D. Brigham.
Prescott Bigelow.
Ivory Bean.
Joseph Barnard.
J. Q. A. Bean.
Asa O. Butman.
Wm. Bogle.
Richard Briggs.
·C. E. Buckingham.
George O. Brastow.
Wm. R. Barton.
Robert Bickford.

John H. Bradbury.
Wm. H. Brown.
John F. Bates.
*Amos Cotting.
†Joseph R. Chandler.
Wm. D. Coolidge.
John A. Cummings.
Thomas Conery.
J. H. Cheever.
Charles U. Cotting.
Amos W. Cross.
Uriah H. Coffin.
Thomas E. Chickering.
Wm. Clapp.
Chas. E. Caneday.
†Paul Dean.
John R. Dow.
John L. Dimmock.
James Dillon.
Peter Dunbar.
Benj. H. Dixon,
Henry F. Durant.
John Dutton.
G. L. Drinkwater.
S. A. Denio.
W. W. Delano.
Wm. F. Davis.
Moses T. Davis.
C. E. W. Dimmock.
†Asa Eaton.

Francis F. Emery.
†Warren Fisher.
†Joshua B. Flint.
George Foster.
Ezra Forristall.
Wm. B. Fowle, Jr.
Eben B. Foster.
Isaac D. Farnsworth.
Wm. M. Fleming.
Wolf C. J. Fries.
Geo. A. Fields.
Jonas H. French.
H. W. Fuller.
Oliver M. Foster.
Jonas Fitch.
Gardner Greenleaf.
George Greig.
Joseph Grafton, Jr.
Robert Greer.
Jos. B. Glover.
John Gile.
John E. Gowan
Joel Golthwait.
Jos. M. Gibbens.
W. T. Grammar.
Franklin E. Gregory.
*John T. Heard.
John C. Hammond.
William Heywood.
Jos. J. Hewes.
Sylvester Hunt.
Geo. A. Hill.
J. S. Hill.
Francis D. Hall.
Adin Hall.
Peter C. Jones.
Harvey Jewell.
Wm. P. Jones.
Joseph S. Jones.
George S. Jones.
Carmi E. King.
Geo. P. King.
Slade Luther.
Rufus Leighton.

James W. Lee.
Thomas J. Lee,
Geo. Lovejoy.
A. Lothrop.
†Wm. C. Martin.
John McClellan.
Robert McGill.
Judson Murdock.
Wm. B. May.
Alfred Mudge.
Wm. H. Mackintosh.
Henry A. Miles.
John J. Mann.
Peter McIntyre.
Henry Niebuhr.
D. W. Nutting.
Benj. M. Nevers.
Lewis W. Nute.
Robert C. Nichols.
†Edward Prescott.
Joseph Pratt.
M. D. Parker.
Geo. W. Patten.
Edw'd Palgemeyer.
John D. Parker.
Geo. S. Potter.
Edward G. Parker.
Isaiah Rogers.
Benj. G. Russell.
Joseph L. Ross.
A. P. Richardson.
Thos. W. Robinson.
Robt. L. Bobbins.
Geo. C. Rand.
J. A. Richards.
C. G. Ripley.
†Geo. M. Randall.
Wm. Rogers.
Wm. H. Rand.
Sam'l E. Robbins.
Francis Richards.
‡Sam'l Smith.
‡Benj. Stevens.
†Geo. G. Smith.

Geo. W. Smith.
†Wm. M. Stedman.
Hiram Simmons.
Chas. A. Smith.
Eben'r Smith.
†Geo. Stimpson, Jr.
Isaac Sweetser.
Wm. M. Stedman, Jr.
D. N. Skillings.
Wm. Schouler.
Wm. C. Starbuck.
John Stetson.
Gilbert Simonds.
J. T. Spalding.
Geo. P. Sanger.
S. S. Seavey.
Josiah A. Stearns.
James M. Shute.
Wm. H. Sargent.
Benj. F. Stevens.
†David Tillson.
Geo. M. Thacher.
Chas. Thacher.
Newell A. Thompson.
Geo. Tucker.
Chas. L. Thayer.
Sam'l G. Tower.
Benj. F. Tenney.
†Edward T. Taylor.
John L. Tucker.

Holbert Taylor.
Sylvester Trull.
Jos. Trenkle,
Enos H. Tucker, Jr.
Chas. Thompson, Jr.
Wm. O. Taylor.
Moses Tenney, Jr.
Alfred T. Turner.
Spencer A. Turner.
†M. L. Wallis.
Wm. W. Wood.
Jos. W. Wright.
James S. Wiggin.
Jos. W. Wheelwright.
Wm. P. Winchester.
Silas Warren.
Wm. W. Warren.
Jos. J. Whiting.
*William Ward.
*Jos. W. Ward.
L. S. Williams.
Geo. A. Wadleigh.
Elbridge Wason.
Sewall Warner.
Henry T. Woods.
Aaron D. Weld, Jr.
John H. Wilcox.
F. L. Washburn.
Alex'r Williams.
Miles Washburn.

CATALOGUE

OF

INITIATES AND MEMBERS

OF

Columbian Lodge;

FROM THE ORIGIN OF THE LODGE TO JANUARY 1, 5856.

PREPARED BY

Bro. JOHN McCLELLAN,

SECRETARY FROM JAN. 1, 5846, TO DEC. 31, 5856.

——o——

For Original Members see Charter.

NAMES.	BY WHOM PROPOSED.	INITIATED.	CRAFTED.	RAISED.	MEMBERSHIP.
Atwood, Alexander D.	J. Coles,	March 3, 1796,	October 28, 1796,	Nov. 8, 1796,	May 4, 1797.
Ankins, John	Martin,	May 5, 1796,	July 9, 1796,	Sept. 1, 1796,	
Atkins, Edward		July 25, 1796,	Nov. 8, 1796,		
Alden, Alpheus	Raymond,	Dec. 7, 1797,	March 1, 1798,	April 11, 1798,	
Atkins, Joseph		August 1, 1799,	July 8, 1800,	July 8, 1800,	
Adams, John	Hayden,	February 6, 1800,	Feb. 21, 1800,	April 2, 1800,	
Appleton, Thomas			Sept. 4, 1800,	Sept. 4, 1800,	
Adams, Joseph	.	January 8, 1801,	Feb. 18, 1801,		Dec. 3, 1801.
Albree, Samuel					Nov. 8, 1807.
Anderson, James		July 7, 1803,	July 13, 1803,	July 13, 1803,	May 2, 1805.
Ayres, Lemuel		January 3, 1805,	January 3, 1805,	March 7, 1805,	
Allen, Nathan		October 2, 1806,	Nov. 6, 1806,	Nov. 6, 1806,	
Allen, Joseph Jr.		April 2, 1807,	April 2, 1807,	April 7, 1807,	
Appleton, Benjamin B.	J. Jenkins,	March 1, 1810,	March 15, 1810,	March 15, 1810,	April 19, 1810.
Allen, John	Hammond,	June 3, 1819,	July 1, 1819,	July 1, 1819,	Nov. 15, 1810.
Allen, Alexander	Streeter,	April 27, 1820,	April 27, 1820,		
Adams, Charles	Fisher,	February 1, 1821,	February 1, 1821,	Feb. 22, 1821,	
Adams, Laban	Baxter, Jr.	June 7, 1821,	July 5, 1821,	Nov. 5, 1821,	
Adams, Ward		June 6, 1822,	June 14, 1822,	June 14, 1822,	
Atwood, James		Feb. 10, 1824,	Feb. 10, 1824,	Feb. 13, 1824,	
Amee, Josiah L. C.	Jones,	January 27, 1825,	January 27, 1825,	Feb. 3, 1825,	
Angier, John	Bittle,	Nov. 3, 1825,	Nov. 3, 1825,	Nov. 3, 1825,	
Allen, Samuel A.	Flint,	Nov. 1, 1827,	Nov. 1, 1827,	Nov. 1, 1827,	Dec. 3, 1830.
Allen, Charles J. F.	G. G. Smith,				Dec. 1, 1836.
Adams, Charles W.	S. A. Allen,	Sept. 17, 1839,	Sept. 17, 1839,	Sept. 17, 1839,	
Adams, Isaac	R. Baker,				Dec. 5, 1839.
Appleton, Benjamin B. Jr.	W. Ward,	March 5, 1841,	April 1, 1841,	May 6, 1841,	June 3, 1841.
Abbott, Ed. West	G. M. Thacher,	March 4, 1847,	March 4, 1847,	March 4, 1847,	
Ames, Preston Adams	"				October 4, 1849.
Argyrus, Basiluis		Nov. 4, 1849,	Nov. 14, 1849,	Nov. 14, 1849,	

Name	Proposer			
Adams, Charles B. F.	G. M. Thacher,	April 4, 1850,	April 18, 1850,	June 6, 1850.
Armington, Horace E.	J. A. Cummings,	April 4, 1850,	May 2, 1850.	
Adams, Henry W.	J. McClellan,	April 18, 1850,	April 18, 1850,	June 6, 1850.
Abbott, James A.	W. W. Baker,	Mass. Lodge,	Mass. Lodge,	Sept. 5, 1850.
Ahlborn, Henry C.	P. A. Ames,	January 6, 1852,	February 3, 1853,	March 3, 1853.
Adams, William	J. L. Ross,	April 7, 1853,	April 23, 1853,	
Atwood, Gilbert	John Stetson,	Dec. 1, 1853,	January 5, 1854,	Feb. 2, 1854.
Bunton, Samuel	J. Coles,	January 7, 1796,	June 3, 1796.	
Bacon, Josiah	J. Martin,	Dec. 18, 1795,		
Bacon, John	S. Raymond,	Dec. 18, 1795,		
Blackman, Andrew	Martin,	February 4, 1796,	October 19, 1798.	
Burnham, Thomas S.	"	January 7, 1796,	March 3, 1796.	
Butts, Richard		January 7, 1796,	January 8, 1796.	
Bourley, Charles	Churchill,	January 7, 1796,	January 8, 1796.	
Barker, Nathaniel	Folsom,	June 2, 1796,	June 3, 1796.	
Benson, Joseph		June 2, 1796,	June 3, 1796.	
Baker, John	Folsom,	July 7, 1796,	Sept. 1, 1796.	
Burr, Peter	Eaton,	Nov. 24, 1796,	Dec. 1, 1796.	
Bargum, Frederick W.	Martin,		May 4, 1797.	
Beckman, George			June 23, 1797.	
Bailey, John		July 6, 1797,	July 11, 1797.	June 6, 1799.
Blaney, Joseph	Folsom,	April 5, 1798,		June 6, 1799.
Baxter, Daniel	Martin,	Feb. 7, 1799,		
Bateman, Francis	A. Stetson,			
Butler, Henry S.	"	July 3, 1800,	January 17, 1801.	
Bottomly, John		January 8, 1801,	May 26, 1801.	
Blanchard, Frederick		February 5, 1801,		
Berlois, Thomas	Mountford,	May 7, 1801,	August 13, 1801.	
Bord, Stephen		July 2, 1801,	March 4, 1802.	
Buckley, Stephen		July 30, 1801,	January 7, 1802.	
Bartlett, John		Nov. 5, 1801,		
Ballard, Joshua Jr.	Rittenhouse,	February 4, 1802,	March 4, 1802,	March 27, 1802.

NAMES.	BY WHOM PROPOSED.	INITIATED.	CRAFTED.	RAISED.	MEMBERSHIP.
Barry, William	Albree,	March 27, 1802,	March 27, 1802,	October 6, 1802.	April 7, 1803.
Brown, Joseph		April 1, 1802,	May 6, 1802,	October 6, 1802.	
Bull, John	A. Cutter, Jr.	May 6, 1802,	May 8, 1802,	October 8, 1802.	
Bottomly, Abraham	"	June 3, 1802,	July 8, 1802,	July 8, 1802.	
Blanchard, Stephen	"	July 1, 1802,	July 8, 1802,	July 8, 1802.	
Babbit, Ira					July 1, 1802.
Bayley, Joseph Allen	S. Stetson,	Sept. 2, 1802,	Sept. 2, 1802,	Sept. 8, 1802.	
Baxter, William	D. Baxter,	Nov. 4, 1802,	Nov. 4, 1802,	Feb. 3, 1803.	
Benson, John	John Sweet,	Nov. 14, 1803,	Nov. 14, 1803,	Nov. 21, 1803.	January 6, 1803.
Blake, John	"				
Bean, Stephen	"	January 3, 1805,	January 3, 1805,	March 7, 1805.	July 5, 1804.
Binney, Amos		Sept. 5, 1805,	Sept, 5, 1805,	October 3, 1805.	May 2, 1805.
Bodge, Nathan	Davidson,	February 6, 1806,	Feb, 13, 1806,	May 1, 1806.	
Burnham, Elisha		April 24, 1806,	May 15, 1806,	May 24, 1806.	
Barrus, Rufus L.		February 5, 1807,			
Bean, Asa		June 3, 1807,	Nov. 6, 1807,	June 2, 1808.	
Baker, Abel	Vose,	Nov. 19, 1807,	January 7, 1808,	January 21, 1808.	October 1, 1807.
Brown, Daniel C.	Jenkins,	Dec. 9, 1808,	January 5, 1809,	January 6, 1809.	August 3, 1809.
Baxter, Samuel		January 5, 1809,	January 5, 1809,	January 6, 1809.	
Babcock, Alvin	Hayden,	August 3, 1809,	Sept. 7, 1809,	October 12, 1809.	
Belknap, Ebenezer	"	May 3, 1810,	May 3, 1810,	June 7, 1810,	
Benard, Peter					
Brown, John B.	Mountford,	March 7, 1811,	April 4, 1811,	April 4, 1811,	Dec. 19, 1816.
Bender, George Jr.	Sawyer,	June 4, 1812,	June 4, 1812,	July 6, 1812.	Nov. 15, 1810.
Brimhall, Elisha	Jenkins,	Dec. 3, 1812,	Dec. 17, 1812,	February 4, 1813,	March 5, 1812.
Bell, Edward	Johnson,	Dec. 17, 1812,	Dec. 17, 1812,	February 4, 1813,	
Braman, Jason	Park,				October 28, 1813.
Bruce, Thomas	"	in Vermont,	in Vermont,	June 16, 1814.	
Baldwin, Daniel	Stone,	Dec. 1, 1814,			May 6, 1813.
Barker, Samuel P.	Chandler,		April 6, 1815,	April 6, 1815.	

Name	Proposed by				
Bacon, Jacob	Glover,	July 6, 1815,	July 12, 1815,	July 12, 1815.	
Boothe, B. W. (U. S. N.)	A. Binney,	July 10, 1815,	July 12, "	July 12, "	
Baxter, Daniel Jr.	George Guild,	March 7, 1816,	April 4, 1816,	May 6, 1816.	Nov. 7, 1816.
Bancroft, Joseph	Glover,	Aug. 15, 1816,	Aug. 15, "	Sept. 5, "	Dec. 19, "
Belcher, David	Leman,	Oct. 3, 1816,	Nov. 7, "	Dec. 5, "	
Bent, Buckly	Cobb,	Jan. 2, 1817,	Jan. 9, 1817,	Feb. 6, 1817.	
Bissell, Harvey	Hammond,	Feb. 2, 1817,	Feb. 6, "	Oct. 1, 1818.	
Bittle, William	McGaw,	Jan. 9, 1817,	Jan. 9, "	March 6, 1817.	
Barker, Jedediah	Jenkins,	March 20, 1817,	April 17, "	May 1, "	April 3, 1817.
Brooks, John	J. Jenkins,				July 3, "
Bean, Aaron					June 5, 1817.
Blake, Samuel	B. Stearns,	Jan. 1, 1818,	Jan. 1, 1818,	Jan. 15, 1818.	
Bryant, Nathaniel	Braman,	March 5, 1818,	April 16, "	March 19, 1818.	Nov. 13, 1819.
Ballard, Eleazer	Streeter,	Bethel L., N. H.			
Bean, Joshua	A. Bean,	April 2, 1818,	April 16, 1818,	May 7, "	
Butterfield, Charles		April 2, 1818,	April 16, "		
Bullard, Charles A.	Johnson,	April 16, 1818,	April 16, "	Oct. 1, 1818.	
Broadbent, Augustus	S. Smith,	Aug. 6, 1818,	Oct. 1, "	Oct. 1, "	
Brown, John	Mason,	Jan. 21, 1819,	Jan. 21, 1819,	Jan. 21, 1819.	
Bemis, Isaac	Cobb,	March 4, 1819,	April 1, "	April 1, "	
Brown, Oliver P.	"	Aug. 3, 1820,	Aug. 10, 1820,	Aug. 10, 1820.	Feb. 22, 1821.
Blodgett, Nathan	Streeter,	March 1, 1821,	March 10, 1821,	March 15, 1821.	
Blanchard, Joseph	G. G. Smith,	March 7, 1822,	March 7, 1822,	April 4, 1822.	
Bowditch, Jonathan, Jr.	D. Baxter, Jr.	June 5, 1823,	June 5, 1823,	July 3, 1823.	May 7, 1835.
Bates, Levi, (Weymouth.)	Dis.	Aug. 5, 1823,	Sept. 4, 1824.	Sept. 4, "	Jan. 5, 1826.
Battles, Benjamin	Baxter, Jr.	Oct. 7, 1824,	Oct. 7, 1824.		
Baker, Ruel	"	May 5, 1825,	May 9, 1825,	May 9, 1825.	
Bates, Francis L.	Wallis,	May 5, 1825,	May 9, "	May 9, "	Dec. 29, 1825.
Brackett, Ebenezer	Dis.	Aug. 4, 1825,	Aug. 10, "		
Bartum, Jos. Pluta, Rev.	Flint,	Nov. 3, 1825,	Nov. 3, "	Nov. 3, 1825.	
Battiste, John	Baxter, Jr.	Nov. 3, 1825,	Nov. 3, "	Nov. 8, "	
Bessom, Jonas	Cunningham,	Feb. 2, 1826,	Feb. 8, 1826,	Feb. 8, 1826.	

47

NAMES.	BY WHOM PROPOSED.	INITIATED.	CRAFTED.	RAISED.	MEMBERSHIP.
Brown, William	Dis.	Jan. 19, 1826,	Jan. 19, 1826,	Jan. 19, 1826.	
Brooks, James Ellis	"	Jan. 19, 1826,	Jan, 19, "	Jan. 19, "	
Booth, Henry P.	Freeman,	June 1, 1826,	July 6, "	July 6, "	
Belknap, William		Sept. 7, 1826,	Sept. 7, "	Oct. 5, "	
Bartlett, George	C. Eaton,	Aug. 7, 1828,	Oct. 2, 1828,	Nov. 6, 1828,	Dec. 4, 1828.
Bergman, Charles 'de	S. A. Allen,	April 13, 1838,	April 13, 1838,	April 13, 1838,	Oct. 4, 1838.
Braman, Jarvis		June 3, 1841,	June 8, 1841,	June 8, 1841,	March 3, 1842.
Bowen, Wilbur R.	R. Baker,	Dec. 2, 1841,	Feb. 3, 1842,	March 3, 1842,	
Bond, Sewall B.		Jan. 6, 1842,	Feb. 3, "	March 3, "	
Bridgham, Charles	W. W. Wood,				Dec. 1, 1842.
Bates, Levi	Nichols,	Oct. 5, 1843,	Oct. 5, 1843,	Nov. 2, 1843,	Feb 2, 1843.
Burrowscale, John	R. Baker,	Dec. 4, 1843,	Jan. 4, 1844,	Feb. 1, 1844,	Jan. 4, 1844.
Bancroft, George	"	April 4, 1844,	May 2, "	June 6, "	March 7, "
Baker, William W.	"	Jan. 6, 1845,	Feb. 6, 1845,	Feb. 25, 1845,	Sept. 5, 1845.
Brown, William P.	G. W. Smith,	Jan. 16, 1845,	Feb. 6, "	Feb. 25, "	May 1, "
Bigelow, John	D. Tillson,				April 3, "
Barton, Jabez W.	B. Stearns,	Dec. 4, 1845,	Dec. 18, 1845,	Jan, 15, 1846,	April 3, "
Beal, Thacher	J. McClellan,				June 5, 1845.
Ball, Nahum	Joseph Hall,				Feb. 5, 1846.
Baker, Benjamin F.	R. Baker,	Dec. 13, 1845,	Dec. 18, 1845,	Jan. 15, 1846,	Nov. 6, 1845.
Brown, James L. (Capt.)	J. R. Dow,	May 6, 1847,	May 6, 1847,	May 6, 1847,	March 5, 1846.
Blaney, Henry	Wm. W. Baker,	Oct. 7, 1847,	Nov. 18, "	Dec. 2, "	
Broadhead, Daniel D.	G. M. Thacher,				Feb. 3, 1848.
Buttrick, Cyrus	Samuel A. Allen,	May 4, 1848,	July 6, 1848,	Sept. 7, 1848,	Jan. 6, "
Brigham, Elijah D.	G. M. Thacher,	June 7, 1849,	Sept. 15, 1849,	Nov. 14, 1849,	July 5, 1849.
Bigelow, Prescott	" " "	Feb. 7, 1850,	March 7, 1850,	March 21, 1850,	May 2, 1850.
Bean, Ivory	J. L. Ross,	March 20, "	April 4, "	May 2, "	May 2, "
Bacon, Stuben T.	J. McClellan,	June 20, "	June 20, "	June 21, "	June 6, "
Bean, John Q. A.	W. B. Fowle, Jr.	Oct. 3, "	Nov. 21, "	Jan. 2, 1851,	Feb. 6, 1851.
Barnard, Joseph	John T. Heard,	Mt. Lebanon,	Mt. Lebanon,	Mt. Lebanon,	Oct. 31, "

Name	Proposer	Jan. 2, 1851,	Dec. 20, 1851,	Dec. 20, 1851.	Jan. 15, 1852.
Butman, Asa O.	G. M. Thacher,	Jan. 2, 1851,	Dec. 20, 1851,	Dec. 20, 1851.	Jan. 15, 1852.
Bogle, William	Wm. Schouler,				Jan. 15, "
Bickford, Robert	Geo. Stimpson, Jr.	Feb. 5, 1852,	April 9, 1852,	June 6, 1854,	Dec. 7, 1854.
Briggs, Richard	J. A. Cummings,	May 20, "	June 3, "	July 1, 1852,	Nov. 4, 1852.
Bigelow, Samuel C.	J. Bigelow,	March 3, 1853,	March 11, 1853,	March 11, 1853.	
Brastow, George O.	B. F. Tenney,	Feb. 2, 1854,	March 2, 1854,	April 14, 1854,	May 4, 1854.
Buckingham, Charles E.	J. W. Barton,	Feb. 2, "	May 4, "	April 14, "	May 4, "
Barton, William R.	J. McClellan.	March 2, "	Nov. 28, "	June 2, "	Sept. 7, "
Baxter, James F. G.	Geo. Stimpson, Jr.	Nov. 5, "		Jun. 6, 1855.	
Bogle, James	Wm. M. Fleming,	April 2, 1855,	Oct. 9, 1855,	Oct. 19, "	
Bates, John F.	D. Tillson,	May 11, "	May 30, "	June 7, "	Sept. 6, 1855.
Bradbury, John H.	J. D. Parker,	May 11, "	May 30, "	June 7, "	Sept. 6, "
Butler, George	G. S. Potter,	May 11, "	May 30, "	June 7, "	
Brown, William H.	W. W. Baker,	May 30, "	May 30, "	June 7, "	Sept. 6, 1855.
Coles, John	J. Perkins,	Nov. 5, 1795,	Nov. 5, 1795,	May 22, 1795.	
Conning, Richard	"	Nov. 5, "		May 12, 1796.	
Cleland, Robert	Coles,	Dec. 5, "	Dec. 5, "	Nov. 10, 1795.	
Clark, Marsh	Perkins,	Dec. 18, "	Dec. 15, "	Dec. 11, "	
Chapman, Samuel	Churchill,	June 27, 1796,	July 9, 1796,	Sept. 1, 1796.	
Claghorn, George		Nov. 3, "		March 4, 1797.	
Carnes, Thomas	Martin,	Feb. 2, 1797,	Nov. 16, 1796.		
Croswell, Elisha	Dodge,	Nov. 16, 1796,	June 20, 1797.		
Carrol, Jared	Coles,		Sept. 7, "		
Collins, Israel G.	"				
Clark, ———					
Campbell, Ronal	Hayden,	Aug. 3, 1797,	Oct. 19, 1798,	Sept. 20, 1799,	Nov. 7, 1799.
Cutter, Ammi	Martin,	Oct. 4, 1798,	Feb. 14, 1799,	Feb. 19, "	
Cannon, James		Feb. 14, 1799,			
Cowdin, Robert	N. Seaver,	Feb. 14, "	Sept. 5, "	Sept. 4, 1800.	Dec. - 4, 1800.
Caten, John	Hayden,	Sept. 5, "			
Crocker, Turner		Feb. 6, 1800.			
Connor, Michael		Jan. 8, 1801,	March 19, 1801,	March 19, 1801.	

NAMES.	BY WHOM PROPOSED.	INITIATED.	CRAFTED.	RAISED.	MEMBERSHIP.
Cutter, Edward		Oct. 1, 1801,	Oct. 1, 1801,	Oct. 15, 1801.	May 6, 1802.
Caro, Nicholas		July 30, "	July 30, "	Aug. 13, "	
Copeland, Smith	A. Cutter, Jr.	Aug. 5, 1802.			
Cushing, Josiah		July 7, 1803,	Sept. 1, 1803,	Sept. 1, 1803.	
Collier, Peleg		May 3, 1804,	May 3, 1804,	May 5, 1804.	
Curtis, Samuel	Baxter,	March 12, 1806,	March 12, 1806,	April 24, 1806.	March 20, 1817.
Cobb, Gershom	Sweet,	April 17, "	April 17, "	May 1, "	
Chenev, Joseph, Jr.	Allchorus,	May 22, "	May 22, "	May 24, "	
Copp, William		Feb. 5, 1807.			
Chickering, Farnum	Hare,	Nov. 3, 1808,	Nov. 3, 1808,	Feb. 16, 1809.	
Coolidge, Luther	Vose,	March 2, 1809,	March 6, 1809,	April 6, "	Oct. 5, 1809.
Coolidge, Isaac	John Park,	Oct. 5, "	Oct. 12, "	Nov. 16, "	
Crocker, Asa	Vose,	Jan. 18, 1810,	Feb. 1, 1810.	March 15, 1810.	
Crocker, David	J. Vose,	Feb. 15, "	Feb. 15, "	May 17, "	
Cogswell, William	E. Little,	April 5, "	April 19, "	Nov. 28, 1811.	
Chapin, Seth	D. Baxter,	Sept. 6, "	Sept. 6, "	Feb. 4, 1813.	Oct. 28, 1813.
Clongh, Willard	Park,	Dec. 3, 1812,	Dec. 17, 1812,	June 3, 1814,	Aug. 5, "
Collamore, Horace	Morse,	March 4, 1813,	April 1, 1813,	Jan. 6, "	Feb. 3, 1814.
Chandler, Joseph R.	Collamore,	Oct. 28, "	Nov. 4, "	July 12, 1815.	
Clark, Jas. H. (U. S. N.)	Binny,	July 10, 1815,	July 12, 1815,	July 12, "	
Chidistee, Thomas		July 12, "	July 12, "	Nov. 2, "	
Cobb, Enos	J. Jenkins,	Sept. 7, "	Sept. 7, "	May 6, 1816,	Jan. 4, 1816.
Cotting, John R. (Rev.)	E. Little,	April 4, 1816,	April 4, 1816,	May 8, 1817,	Jan. 15, 1818.
Corey, Luther	D. Baxter, Jr.	March 20, 1817,	April 10, 1817,	Aug. 6, "	Feb. 5, "
Clark, Amos (Rev.)	A. Cotting,	July 3, "	Aug. 6, "	Aug 6, "	
Chapin, Aaron	D. Baxter, Jr.	July 3, "	Aug. 6, "	Aug 6, "	
Cowing, Cornelius		Feb. 5, 1818,	March 5, 1818,	March 10, 1818,	Nov. 5, 1818.
Converse, Benjamin	Cory,	Dec. 2, 1819,	Jan. 6, 1820,	Feb. 17, 1820,	May 7, 1835.
Converse, Joseph	Cobb,	March 2, 1820,	March 2, 1821,	Oct. 5, "	
Converse, Adolphus B.	Braman,	Dec. 7, "	March 1, 1821,	March 21, 1821.	

Name	Proposed by / Remarks	Initiated	Passed	Raised	Member
Cotting, Amos	Moody,	Jan. 18, 1821,	Feb. 1, 1821,	Feb. 22, 1821,	March 6, 1828.
Cary, Lewis	G. G. Smith,	Dec. 6, "	Jan. 3, 1822,	Feb. 15, 1822,	Feb. 10, 1824.
Cook, Corey	Leman,	May 2, 1822,	May 2, "	May 10, "	Feb. 10, "
Coburn, Caleb		May 6, 1822,	May 14, 1822,	May 14, "	Feb. 10, "
Craft, Nathan F.		June 6, "	June 14, "	June 14, "	
Cotting, William	Baxter, Jr.	June 7, "	June 20, "	June 20, "	
Cheney, Parson		Nov. 28, "	Nov. 28, "	Nov. 28, "	
Clark, Moses (Rev.)		Nov. 16, "	Nov. 16, "	Nov. 16, "	
Cheney, Carmel	L. Corey,	Dec. 6, 1823,	Dec. 6, 1823,	Dec. 6, 1823.	
Clesby, Joseph	Dis.	Feb. 6, "	Feb. 6, "	Feb. 6, "	
Claflin, Calvin	"	Feb. 14, "	Feb. 14, "	Feb. 14, "	
Coggins, George	"	March 3, "	March 8, "	March 3, "	
Child, Hugh	P. Dean,	April 10, "	April 10, "	April 3, "	
Crooker, Charles	Moody,	Oct. 5, 1824,	Oct. 5, 1824,	Oct. 4, 1824,	
Crooker, Ralph	Fisk,	Feb. 2, 1824,	Feb. 7, 1824,	Feb. 9, "	
Cunningham, George H.	"	Sept. 9, "	Sept. 9, "	Sept. 9, "	
Coburn, Hiram	Bittle,	Nov. 9, "	Nov. 9, "	Nov. 3, 1825.	
Chapin, Alden B.	Baxter, Jr.	Jan. 27, 1825,	Jan. 27, 1825,	Feb. 20, "	Dec. 5, 1825.
Coolidge, Amos	Dis.	Oct. 10, "	Oct. 10, "	Oct. 26, "	Sept. 15, "
Conha, J. F. 'de	Moody,	Oct. 26, "	Oct. 26, "	Oct. 26, "	
Crooker, Herman A.	Dis.	Feb. 2, 1826,	Feb. 2, 1826,	March 2, 1826.	
Capen, Nahum	Wise,	Sept. 6, 1827,	Sept 6, 1827,	Sept. 6, 1827.	
Cook, Rufus R.	"	April 3, 1828,	April 3, 1828,	June 5, 1828.	
Coolidge, Wm. D.	R. Baker,	Feb. 6, 1842,	Feb. 6, 1842,	March 3, 1842.	May 19, 1842.
Cook, Benjamin F.	"	March 5, 1846,	May 7, 1846,	May 21, 1846.	Sept. 3, 1846.
Cummings, John A.	N. A. Thompson,	April 17, "	May 7, "	June 4, "	May 7, "
Curtis, George J.	C. D. Coolidge,	Dec. 7, 1848,	Jan. 4, 1849,	Feb. 1, 1849.	
Culbertson, Nathaniel Y.	J. McClellan,	in Maine,			Feb. 7, 1850.
Crowell, Henry G.	P. A. Ames,	Sept. 5, 1850,	Oct. 3, 1850,	Nov. 7, 1850,	
Conery, Thomas	C. Buttrick,	Nov. 21, "	Nov. 21, "	Dec. 5, "	Jan. 2, 1851.
Clark, Orange (Rev.)	G. M. Thacher,	Jan. 1, 1852,	March 4, 1852,	May 20, 1852,	
Cheever, John H.	J. McClellan,				June 3, 1852.

NAMES.	BY WHOM PROPOSED.	INITIATED.	CRAFTED.	RAISED.	MEMBERSHIP.
Cotting, Charles U.	J. A. Dupee,	Dec. 2, 1852,	Jan. 6, 1853,	Feb. 3, 1853,	April 7, 1853.
Coffin, Uriah H.	Silas Warren,	April 23, 1853,	June 2, "	June 2, "	March 2, 1854.
Cheever, David W.	J. McClellan,	April 23, "	April 23, "	April 23, "	
Cross, Amos W.	C. Buttrick,	Mt. Lebanon,	Mt. Lebanon,	Mt. Lebanon.	Dec. 1, 1853.
Chickering, Thomas E.	George M. Thacher,	Feb. 2, 1854,	March 2, 1854,	April 14, 1854,	May 4, 1854.
Clapp, William	C. E. King,	Feb. 2, "	March 2, "	April 14, "	May 19, "
Caneday, Charles E.	J. T. Spalding,	Nov. 2, "	Nov. 28, "	Jan. 19, 1855,	Feb. 16, 1855.
Dixon,				Jan. 18, 1796.	
Davidson, Alexander	J. Coles,	April 7, 1796,	June 3, 1796,	June 3, 1796.	July 7, 1796.
Dyer, John		July 25, 1796.	Oct. 28, 1796,	Oct. 28, 1796.	
Durant, John B.	Martin,	Sept. 10, 1896,	Sept. 7, 1797,	Sept. 7, 1797.	
Dunlap, John	Folsom,	Aug, 3, 1797,	June 21, 1798,	June 21, 1798.	
Dover, Chas.	Hayden,	April 5, 1798.	Nov. 21, 1798,	Feb. 19, 1799.	
Davenport, Thomas	Tennant,	April 5, 1798,	Nov. 21, 1798,	Nov. 26, 1798.	
Donnellan, John	McCorestine,	Nov. 21, 1798,	April 2, 1801,	Sept. 17, 1801,	
Dennis, Benj.	Martin,	Nov. 21, 1798,	July 8, 1802,	July 8, 1802.	
Dunham, John M.		March 4, 1801,	Nov. 2, 1803,	Sept. 1, 1803.	Oct. 25, 1808.
Dexter, G. B.		July 1, 1802,	June 7, 1804,	Sept. 8, 1803.	
Dockindorf, Thos.			June 5, 1806,	June 11, 1804,	
Dunlap, Archibald		Oct. 6, 1803,	Nov. 21, 1807,	Sept. 30, 1806.	Jan. 5, 1804.
Dunlap, John		June 7, 1804,	Nov. 12, 1808.	Nov. 21, 1807.	June 2, 1808.
Dunlap, James		June 5, 1806,	May 3, 1808,	Jan. 6, 1809.	
Dunham, Josiah			Nov. 3, 1808,	Jan. 17, 1811.	
Davis, Samuel			Jan. 3, 1811,	July 1, 1813,	
Dunton, Daniel	Cutter,	May 1, 1808,	April 1, 1813,	Nov. 2, 1815,	
Dennet, Asa	Jenkins,	Nov. 3, 1808,	Sept. 7, 1815,		
Draper, Jeremiah	Morse,	Nov. 15, 1810,	Jan. 3, 1811,		March 3, 1814.
Dennis, Samuel	Hammond,	March 4, 1813,	April 1, 1813,		Dec. 7, 1815.
Dean, Paul, (Rev.)		Aug. 3, 1815,	Sept. 7, 1815,		April 4, 1816.
Dimond, Benjamin	McGaw,	March 20, 1817,	April 10, 1817,	Honorary May 1, 1817.	

Name					
Darling, Sylvester	Stetson,	Oct. 2, 1817,	Nov. 27, 1817,	Nov. 27, 1817.	Feb. 4, 1819.
Dupee, Horace		Feb. 5, 1818,	March 5, 1818,	March 19, 1819,	July 1, 1824.
Davidson, Edward	Jones,	March 4, 1824,	April 1, 1824,	April 1, 1824,	
Dingley, John T.	Spear,	Nov. 9, 1824,	Nov. 9, 1824,	Nov. 9, 1824.	
Drew, Valorus	Fisk,	Feb. 3, 1825,	March 3, 1825,	March 3, 1825.	
Dana, William	Dis.	April 7, 1825,	April 7, 1825,	April 7, "	
Davis, Eben'r	Dis.	June 2, 1825,	June 25, 1825,	June 25, "	
Dunham, Josiah, Jr.	Amee,	Sept. 15, 1825,	Sept. 15, 1825,	Sept. 15, "	Jan. 4, 1827.
Dorado, Antonio	Dis.	Oct. 20, 1825,	Oct. 20, 1825,	Oct. 20, "	
Dudley, Truworthy	D. Tilson,	June 1, 1826,	June 15, 1826,	June 15, 1826.	
Darling, Thomas H.	G. G. Smith,	Nov. 1, 1826,	Nov. 10, 1826,	Nov. 10, "	
Delano, Ezekiel	Coburn,	May 24, 1827,	June 7, 1827,	June 7, 1827,	Jan. 3, 1828.
Dow, John R.	R. Baker,	Jan. 6, 1842,	Feb. 3, 1842,	March 3, 1842,	May 19, 1842.
Dillon, James	Nichols,	Jan. 6, 1845,	Feb. 6, 1845,	Feb. 25, 1845.	April 3, 1845.
Denny, R. S.	W. Ward,	May 1, 1845.		Nov. 6, 1845.	Dec. 4, 1845.
Dimmock, John L.	G. M. Thacher,	June 5, 1845.	Oct. 16, 1845,	June 3, 1847.	April 2, 1846.
Dunbar, Peter	Jos. Hall,	April 1, 1847,	May 7, 1847,	May 1, 1851,	Sept. 2, 1847.
Dupee, James A.	P. C. Jones,	Feb. 6, 1851,	March 6, 1851,	Dec. 20, 1851,	Jan. 6, 1848.
Dixon, Ben. Homer	G. M. Thacher,	Nov. 6, 1851,	Dec. 16, 1851,	St. Andrews L.	Jan. 15, 1852.
Drinkwater, Geo. L.	J. Barton,	In St. Andrews L.	St. Andrews L.	Oct. 7, 1852,	Jan. 15, "
Dutton, John	M. D. Parker,	May 6, 1852,	June 3, 1852,	July 1, 1852,	Dec. 20, 1851.
Durant, Henry F.	J. McClellan,	May 6, 1852,	June 3, 1852,	Jan. 19, 1855,	Nov. 4, 1852.
Denio, Sylvanus A.	S. G. Tower,	Oct. 11, 1854,	Oct. 26, 1854,	Oct. 9, 1855,	Nov. 4, "
Delano, Wm. W.	W. W. Baker,	May 11, 1855,	Sept. 21, 1855,		Feb. 16, 1855.
Davis, Wm. F.	G. B. F. Adams,				May 3, 1855.
Davis, Moses T.	H. T. Wood,				Dec. 6, 1855.
Dimmock, Chas. E. W.	W. B. Fowle, Jr.				
Eames, Samuel					
Ellis, Wm.		June 2, 1796,	June 3, 1796,	June 3, 1796,	Nov. 8, 1796.
Enson, James		April 6, 1798,	April 6, 1798,	June 21, 1798.	
Eaton, David M.	Jenks,	Jan. 1, 1801,	Feb. 19, 1801,	Feb. 19, 1801.	April 2, 1800.
Eastman, Zebina		March 4, "	March 19, "		

NAMES.	BY WHOM PROPOSED.	INITIATED.	CRAFTED.	RAISED.	MEMBERSHIP.
Enos, Joseph	Crooker,	Jan. 19, 1804,	Feb. 9, 1804,	Feb. 9, 1804,	May 1, 1806.
Everett, Nathaniel	Davidson,	Nov. 21, 1805,	Nov. 29, 1805,	Jan. 2, 1806.	
Eych, A. S., Ten.	A. Binney,	July 10, 1815,	July 12, 1815,	July 12, 1815.	
Ellis, Charles	W. Clough,	April 3, 1817.			
Evans, Richard S.	J. Nason,	Sept. 3, 1818,	Oct. 1, 1818,	Nov. 19, 1818,	July 1, 1819.
Ellis, Abner	Streeter,	June 3, 1819,	July 22, 1819,	Nov. 18, 1819.	
Elliot, Eph. L.	Hayward,	May 15, 1821,	May 17, 1821,	May 22, 1821.	
Elwell, Joshua	Jones,	May 15, 1824,	May 15, 1824,	May 15, 1824.	
Eaton, Calvin	Fisk,	May 5, 1825,	July 7, 1825,	July 7, 1825,	Dec. 1, 1825.
Ellis, Benjamin	Dis.	Feb. 2, 1826,	Feb. 8, 1826,	Feb. 8, 1826,	
Eaton, Wm.	E. B. Foster,	April 5, 1827,	June 7, 1827,	June 7, 1827.	
Edwards, Wm. G.	D. Tillson,				Dec. 1, 1836.
Evans, Thomas L.	P. C. Jones,	Nov. 20, 1845,	Dec. 18, 1845,	Jan. 15, 1846.	
Ellison, Wm.	J. McClellan,	March 5, 1846,	May 7, 1846,	May 21, 1846.	
Eames, Ithamer B.	J. Stetson,	June 1, 1854,	June 6, 1854,	June 6, 1854.	April 5, 1555.
Emery, Francis F.	J. J. Whiting,	Oct. 11, 1854,	Oct. 26, "	Jan. 19, 1855,	Dec. 6, 1855.
Eaton, Asa					Aug. 8, 1795.
Folsom, John W.	Perkins,	Nov. 3, 1796,	Nov. 8, 1796,	Aug. 8, 1795,	
Fisher, Thomas	Eaton,	Nov. 24, 1796,	Nov. 24, "	Jan. 7, 1797.	
Freeman, Jeremiah	Folsom,	Oct. 5, 1797,	Oct. 10, 1797,	Oct. 10, 1797.	
Foley, John	Rittenhouse,	Nov. 21, 1798,	Nov. 26, 1798,	Nov. 26, 1798.	
Fitzgerald, David		Aug. 8, 1799,	Aug. 8, 1799,	Aug. 13, 1799.	
Frost, John	Baxter,	May 1, 1800,	May 1, 1800,	Sept. 18, 1800.	
Flinn, Wm.		Feb. 5, 1801,	March 19, 1801,	May 19, 1801.	
Fretta, Philip		May 6, 1802,	May 6, 1802,	Sept. 8, 1802.	
Fitzpatrick, Peter	A. Cutter,	Jan. 19, 1804.			
Folsom, Peter					
Ford, Joseph	Tuttle,	April 2, 1807,	April 2, 1807,	April 7, 1807.	
Foster, James		Feb. 3, 1809,	Feb. 16, 1809,	July 6, 1809.	

Name					By
Field, Justin	April 5, 1810,	April 19, 1810,	Nov. 17, 1810.	Oct. 3, 1811.	Jenkins,
Fairbanks, Perley	Aug. 15, 1816,	Aug. 15, 1816,	Sept. 5, 1816.	Dec. 4, 1817.	Streeter,
French, John	Oct. 24, 1816,	Oct. 24, 1816.		Feb. 3. 1820.	
Farnsworth, Samuel	April 10, 1817,	April 10, 1817,	May 8, 1817,		Nason,
Fisk, Sewell	April 4, 1818,	April 2, 1818,	May 8, "		Nason,
French, Joseph	July 3, "	Oct. 1, "	Aug. 10, 1818.		J. Wise,
French, Jonas	Oct. 3, 1821.	Nov. 20, 1821,	Nov. 19, "		Wm. Stedman,
Fisher, Francis	July 20, 1822,	Nov. 2, 1822,	Nov. 5, 1821.	March 6, 1823.	F. Fisher,
French, Eben	Nov. 2, 1823,	Oct. 2, 1823,	Nov. 20, 1822,		Colborn,
Flint, J. B.	Oct. 2, 1823,		Oct. 14, 1823,		
Fisher, Warren	May 5, 1825,	May 9, 1825,	May 9, 1825.	Nov. 4, 1824.	Fisk,
Fisk, David	Oct. 1, "	Oct. 10, "	Oct. 20, "		Baxter, Jr.
Freeman, John	April 6, 1826,	April 17, 1826,	April 17, 1826.		Bittle,
Farnsworth, B. F. (Rev.)	April 6, "	April 17, "	April 17, "		S. Smith,
Foster, Eben B.	May 16, 1844,	June 16, 1844,	June 6, 1844,	Sept. 5, 1844.	J. McClellan,
Follansbee, Edward F.	Nov. 27, "	Nov. 27, "	Nov. 27, "		Dis.
Franz, Fred'k W.	April 3, 1845,	July 9, 1845,	Sept. 18, 1845,	Nov. 6, 1845.	G. M. Thacher,
Foster, George	Feb. 5, 1846,	March 5, 1846,	April 2, 1846,	May 7, 1846.	W. W. Baker,
Fay, Chas. Fuller	March 7, 1850,	April 18, 1850,	May 2, 1850,	June 6, 1850.	J. L. Dimmock,
Fowle, Wm. B., Jr.	March 7, "	April 4, 1850,	May 2, "	June 6, "	G. W. Smith,
Forrestall, Ezra	Dec. 4, 1851,			April 3, 1851.	J. McClellan,
Farnsworth, Isaac D.	Nov. 4, 1852,	Jan. 1, 1852,	March 4, 1852,		A. T. Thorup,
Fries, C. J. Wolf	Feb. 3, 1853,	Jan. 14, 1853,	Jan. 14, 1853,	April 1, 1852.	J. A. Cummings,
French, Samuel L.		March 11, 1853,	April 23, 1853.		W. W. Baker,
Fleming, Wm. M.	Feb. 2, 1854, S. B.	March 2, 1854,	May 19, 1854,	Feb. 2, 1854.	P. C. Jones,
French, Jonas H.	Feb. 2, 1854, St. Paul's	Nov. 28, 1854,		April 6, 1854.	Wm. P. Jones,
Fields, Geo. A.	Nov. 2, 1854, Hampden L'ge.			June 1, "	J. L. Dimmock,
Fuller, Henry Weld	St. Paul's,		Jan. 19, 1855,	June 1, "	J. McClellan,
Foster, Oliver M.				Feb. 16, 1855.	B. Stevens,
Fitch, Jonas				Feb. 1, "	Rittenhouse.
Gale, Calvin				Dec. 6, "	
Gore, Grunman	May 5, 1796,	May 12, 1796,	May 12, 1796.		Martin,

NAMES.	BY WHOM PROPOSED.	INITIATED.	CRAFTED.	RAISED.	MEMBERSHIP.
Godshall, William		July 25, 1796,	Aug. 4, 1796,	Aug. 4, 1796.	
Graham, George	Coles,	Nov. 24, "	Nov. 24, "	Dec. 1, 1797,	
Green, John B.	Eaton,	June 1, 1797,	July 11, 1797,	Sept. 7, 1797,	April 5, 1798.
Gregory, William		Nov. 21, 1798,	Nov. 21, 1798,	Nov. 26, 1798.	
Gross, Asahel		April 16, 1800,	April 16, 1800.	Nov. 6, 1800.	
Greenough, Nathaniel, Jr.	Folsom,	Aug. 7, "	Aug. 21, "	Nov. 6, "	
Gillerase, James		Oct. 2, "	Nov. 6, "	Feb. 4, 1802.	
Gay, Peyton		Oct. 2, "	July 30, 1801,	May 26, 1801.	
Gilman, Peter	Tower,	March 4, 1801,	April 2, "	Feb. 3, 1803.	
Gleason, J. W.		Oct. 6, 1802,	Nov 4, 1802,	March 15, 1804.	
Getty, Francis	J. Benson,	March 1, 1804,	March 1, 1804,	May 5, "	
Gordon, William		May 3, "	May 3, "	May 24, 1806.	
Greeley, Daniel	Sweet,	Nov. 29, 1805,	Nov. 29, 1805,	July 6, 1809.	
Gouldsbury, Samuel		May 22, 1806,	May 22, 1806,	Oct. 12, "	
Greenwood, James		May 4, 1809,	June 1, 1809,		
Glover, Elisha V.	Vose,	Aug. 3, "	Sept. 7, "		Sept. 20, 1810.
Gilbert, John N.	Little,	Jan. 3, 1811,	June 6, 1811.		Jan. 3, 1811.
Greene, Samuel R.	Sawyer,	July 2, 1812,	July 9, 1812,	July 9, 1812.	
Godsor, Benjamin	Jenkins,	Jan. 6, 1814,	Feb. 3, 1814,	Feb. 3, 1814.	June 9, 1814.
Gray, Charles		June 9, "	June 9, "	June 16, "	Jan. 5, 1815.
Guild, George	Baxter,	Oct. 3, 1816,	Nov. 17, 1816,	Jan. 9, 1817.	
Gill, Moses	Little,	Sept. 3, 1818,	Oct. 1, 1818,	Nov. 19, 1818.	
Garvin, Andrew	Hammond,	Feb. 4, 1819,	Feb. 4, 1819,	Feb. 4, 1819.	
Gibbs, Freeman	Streeter,	July 22, "	July 22, "	Aug. 5, "	
Gifford, Pardon A.	"	Feb. 7, 1822,	Feb. 7, 1822,	May 10, 1822.	
Galvin, George J.	Paine,	Sept. 2, 1821,	Sept. 26, 1821,	Sept. 26, 1821.	
Greene, B. H.	Cotting,	Jan. 6, 1825,	Jan. 6, 1825.		
Gay, Amasa	S. Fisk,	Dec. 10, 1824,	Dec. 12, 1824,	Jan. 27, 1825,	April 7, 1825.
Glover, John	Coburn,	Dec. 1, 1825,	Dec. 5, 1825,	Jan. 5, 1826,	
Greenleaf, Gardner	Peirce,				March 7, 1844.

Name					
Gill, James B.	Baxter, Jr.,	Nov. 3, 1825,	Nov. 3, 1825,	Nov. 8, 1825.	March 6, 1828.
Greele, Joseph	Coburn,	Feb. 2, 1826,	Feb. 8, 1826,	Feb. 8, 1826.	Jan. 6, 1827.
Garland, John	R. Baker,	Feb. 2, "	Feb. 8, "	Feb. 8, "	Feb. 4, 1841.
Griswold, Albert	W. B. Hanes,				April 2, 1846.
Greig, George	J. L. Dimmock,				Oct. 3, 1850.
Grafton, Joseph, Jr.	G. M. Thacher,	Nov. 4, 1847,	Nov. 18, 1847,	Nov. 18, 1847.	
Goss, Emery	J. Braman,	March 2, 1848,	April 6, 1848,	Sept. 7, 1848.	
Glover, Joseph B.	W. M. Stedman, Jr.,	Feb. 7, 1850,	March 7, 1850,	March 21, 1850.	
Greer, Robert	J. McClellan,	in Mt. Lebanon.	in Mt. Lebanon.	in Mt. Lebanon.	
Greene, O. H. P.					
Gile, John	E. Forristall,	June 5, 1851,	June 5, 1851,	Oct. 2, 1851.	May 2, 1850.
Gowan, John E.	E. B. Foster,	May 4, 1854,	Oct. 26, 1854,	Oct. 26, 1854.	May 2, "
Goldthwait, Joel	J. A. Cummings,	Feb. 16, 1855,	March 1, 1855,	April 13, 1855.	Oct. 3, 1851.
Grammer, William T.	D. Tillson,	May 11, "	May 30, "	June 7, "	Dec. 4, 1851.
Gregory, Franklin E.	J. D. Parker,	May 11, "	May 30, "	June 7, "	Dec. 7, 1854.
Gibbens, Joseph M.	B. Stevens,	May 11, "	May 30, "	June 7, "	May 3, 1855.
Howe, Thomas	Martin,	June 27, 1796.	July 9, 1796,	July 9, 1796.	Sept. 6, "
Homes, Robert	Martin,	June 27, "	Oct. 28, "	Nov. 8, "	Sept. 6, "
Hoyt, Charles	Goldsbury,	Oct. 28, "	Nov. 16, "		Sept. 6, "
Howland, Nath'l	Coles,	Nov. 16, "			
Howard, Oliver	A. Stetson,	Oct. 5, 1797,	Oct. 10, 1797,	Oct. 10, 1797.	
Hurley, John	Hayden,	Nov. 2, "	March 1, 1798,		
Herault, John		April 5, 1798,	April 6, "	June 7, 1798.	
Hall, John		Oct. 2, "	Oct. 19, "		
Holland, Thomas		June 19, 1799,	June 11, 1799,	April 6, "	
Harris, John H.		June 6, "	June 11, "		
Hoyt, Stephen		Nov. 11, "	Nov. 7, "	Nov. 9, 1799.	
Hannagan, John	S. Stetson,	May 7, "	May 1, 1800,		
Hilton, John		May 1, 1800,	May 1, "	Sept. 18, 1800.	
Hammatt, John B.	Folsom,	May 1, "	Aug. 21, "	Aug. 21, 1800.	
Harvey, Wm.		Aug. 7, "	Sept. 4, "		
Howe, James		Jan. 8, 1801,	Feb. 18, 1801.		

NAMES.	BY WHOM PROPOSED.	INITIATED.	CRAFTED.	RAISED.	MEMBERSHIP.
Higgins, Esekiel H.		Jan. 17, 1801,	Jan. 17, 1801,		
Hayden, John		May 7, "	May 26, "	May 26, 1801.	
Higgins, Joshua		Nov. 27, "	Nov. 27, "	Jan. 7, 1802.	
Humphrer, Richard		Aug. 6, 1804.	Sept. 3, "		
Haskell, Caleb		Jan. 5, "			
Hunt, Timothy	A. Cutter, Jr.	June 7, "	June 7, 1804,	June 11, 1804.	
Hamblen, William		Nov. 24, "	Nov. 24, "		
Hyer, Henry	Porter,	April 3, 1806,	April 17, 1806,	April 24, 1806,	not recorded.
Hayden, Sam'l	Thayer,	Sept. 30, "	Oct. 30, "	Oct. 30, "	Sept. 10, 1807.
Howard, Jonathan	Kidder,	March 5, 1807,	April 2, 1807,	April 27, 1807,	Sept. 10, "
Hammond, Nath.		March 5, "	March 12, "	April 27, "	Nov. 6, "
Howe, Calvin					March 12, "
Hunt, John		Nov. 12, 1807,	Nov. 21, 1807,	Nov. 21, 1807.	
Harrington, Jona.	Perkins,	Feb. 3, 1809,	Feb. 16, 1809.		
Haven, George	Baxter,	Nov. 16, 1810,	Jan. 4, 1810,	Jan. 18, 1810.	
Heard, Nathaniel	Vose,	April 19, "	April 19, "	May 17, "	Sept. 20, 1810.
Hayward, John	Sawyer,	Nov 15, "			
Homes, Nath'l B.	Jos. Jenkins,	March 5, 1812,	April 2, 1812,	May 14, 1812,	
Hooton, Jonathan, Jr.	B. B. Appleton,	March 5, "	April 2, "	May 14, "	
Henshaw, David	B. B. Appleton,	Oct. 6, 1814,	Nov. 3, 1814,	Nov. 3, 1814,	Nov. 2, 1815.
Hall, Wm.	Jos. R. Chandler,	July 10, 1815,	July 12, 1815,	July 12, 1815.	
Humphries, Ashton T.	Binney,	July 10, "	July 12, "	July 12, "	March 6, 1817.
Hamilton, John		July 10, "	July 12, "	July 12, "	
Hixon, George	Baxter, Jr.	Oct. 3, 1816,	Nov. 7, 1816,	Dec. 6, 1816.	
Hastings, Joseph	Jenkins,	Oct. 2, 1817,	Jan. 1, 1818,	May 7, 1818.	
Homes, Josiah W.	B. Sterns,	Jan. 1, 1828,	Jan. 1, "	Jan. 1, "	
Hoxie, John, (Capt.)	D. Baxter, Jr.	Nov. 5, "	Nov. 5, "	Nov. 19, "	
Hadlock, Coburn,	French,	Dec. 7, 1820,	Jan. 4, 1821,	Feb. 21, 1821.	
Hayward, Eben'r W.	Baxter, Jr.	Feb. 1, 1821,	Feb. 1, "	Feb. 22, "	
Harding, Newell	Nason,	Feb. 15, "	Feb. 15,	Feb. 22, "	

Name	Proposed by				
Holmes, William	J. Barker	May 3, 1821,	May 17, 1821,	May 22, 1821.	
Hunter, James G.	Lovejoy	May 3, "	May 17, "	May 22, "	
Hall, Andrew	Haddock	Oct. 4, "	Oct. 4, "	Dec. 20, "	
Holbrook, Samuel F.	Leman	Sept. 6, "	Oct. 3, "	Dec. 20, "	
Hale, Nathan		Oct. 3, 1822,	Oct. 3, 1822,	Oct. 3, 1822.	
Hall, Andrew	Fisk	March 14, 1823,	March 14, 1823,	April 8, 1823.	
Hills, Parker	Dis.	Oct. 2, "	Oct. 2, "	Oct. 14, "	
Haynes, Tristram	Wise	Jan. 1, 1824,	Jan. 1, 1824,	Feb. 13, 1824.	
Honey, R. T.	Bittle	May 1, "	May 1, "	May 1, "	
Hammond, John	Fisk	April 1, "	April 1, "	May 6, "	
Harris, Nathaniel	"	Sept. 2, "	Oct. 7, "	Nov. 9, "	
Haskell, Josiah		Nov. 9, "	Nov. 9, "	Nov. 9, "	
Hall, Adin	Spear	May 5, 1825,	May 9, 1825,	May 9, 1825.	Feb. 6, 1834.
Howard, William	Fisk		May 17, 1856,	April 17, 1826.	Dec. 5, 1844.
Hallett, Robert B.	Nason				
Henshaw, Charles	Dis.	May 1, 1828,	May 1, 1828,	May 1, 1828.	
Hunt, James	Baxter, Jr.				
Hawes, William B.	Haskell				
Hathorne, Eben					
Hall, Joseph	S. A. Allen	Feb. 20, 1845,	Feb. 20, 1845,	March 6, 1845,	Feb. 4, 1830.
Heard, John T.	T. S. Nichols	Sept. 18, "	Sept. 18, "	Sept. 18, "	March 5, 1835.
Hammond, John C.	Wm. Ward	Oct. 1, 1846,	Dec. 3, 1846,	Jan. 7, 1847,	Dec. 6, 1838.
Howe, William	G. W. Smith	Nov. 5, "	Feb. 3, "	Jan. 7, "	May 29, 1840.
Hersey, Warren A.	T. S. Nichols	Jan. 4, 1849,	Sept. 1, 1849,	March 1, 1849,	Jan. 2, 1845.
Hall, Joseph Parkman	John McClellan	July 5, "	Nov. 15, "	Oct. 4, "	May 1, "
Hayward, William	Joseph Hall	Oct. 2, 1851,	April 6, 1851,	Dec. 9, 1851,	Sept. 3, 1846.
Hewes, Joseph J.	J. W. Barton	April 1, 1852,	Feb. 9, 1852,	April 9, 1852,	
Hilton, Gustavus A.	John McClellan	Star of Beth.	Star of Beth.	Star of Beth.	Feb. 4, 1847.
Hunt, Sylvester	"	Jan. 4, 1855,	Feb. 1, 1855,	June 7, 1855,	
Hill, George A.	P. C. Jones	Feb. 1, "	March 30, "	April 13, "	Jan. 3, 1850.
Hill, Seneca J.	C. B. F. Adams	March 1, "		Oct. 9, "	Dec. 20, 1851.
Hardwick, Charles F.	" " " " W. B. Fowle				April 6, 1854.

NAMES.	BY WHOM PROPOSED.	INITIATED.	CRAFTED.	RAISED.	MEMBERSHIP.
Hall, Francis D.	W. D. Coolidge,	May 11, 1855,	May 30, 1855,	June 7, 1855,	Sept. 6, 1855.
Hall, John R.	R. C. Nichols,	Nov. 1, "			
Irons, Nicholas	James,	March 1, 1810,	May 3, 1810,	May 17, 1810,	
Ingerson, John	Delano,	Sept. 24, 1831,	Sept. 24, 1831,	Sept. 24, 1831,	
James, John		Nov. 5, 1795,	Nov. 5, 1795,	Dec. 5, 1795,	
Jones, Joseph	Hayden,	Feb. 6, 1800,	Feb. 21, 1800,	Nov. 22, 1821,	April 4, 1822,
Jenks, S.					May 1, 1800.
Johns, Samuel		June 27, 1800,	June 27, 1800,		
Jones, William		Feb. 5, 1801,	Feb. 19, 1801,	Feb. 19, 1801.	
Jacobs, Thomas		July 2, "			
Johns, St. Summers		Nov. 27, "	Nov. 27, 1801.		Dec. 3, 1801.
Johnson, Daniel					
Jenkins, Abraham					
Johns, St. H. R. S.		Nov. 27, 1801,	Nov. 27, 1801.		April 1, 1802.
Jenkins, Joseph	A. Jenkins,	April 4, 1804,	April 4, 1804,	May 5, 1804,	July 5, 1804.
Jeffrey, Archibald	Davidson,	May 15, 1806,	May 15, 1806,	May 24, 1806,	
Jenks, John	Martin,	March 17, 1808,	May 12, 1808,	June 2, 1808,	
Jarvis, Samuel B.	Jenkins,	Feb. 3, 1809,	Feb. 16, 1809,	April 6, 1809,	Sept. 7, 1809.
Jenkins, Charles	Smith,	Oct. 5, "			
Jewett, John		Nov. 2, "	Nov. 2, 1809,	Nov. 16, 1809.	
Johnson, Phillip	McGaw,	Dec. 2, 1813.			
Jenkins, John F.	Jenkins,	April 3, 1817,	Aug. 6, 1817,	Aug. 6, 1817,	
Jones, Daniel	S. Smith,	Jan. 1, 1818,	Jan. 1, 1818,	March 10, 1818.	
Jewett, Samuel G.	E. French,	March 1, 1821,	March 1, 1821,	March 15, 1821.	
Johnson, Nathan	Jones,	June 6, 1822,	June 14, 1822,	June 14, 1822,	
Joy, Joseph A.	Baxter, Jr.	Feb. 10, 1824,	Feb. 10, 1824,	Feb. 13, 1824,	
Jones, Nathaniel	Pierce,	Feb. 10, "	Feb. 10, "	Feb. 13, "	
Jordon, Andrew	R. Baker,	Oct. 10, 1825,	Oct. 10, 1825,	Oct. 20, 1825,	
Johnson, Peter	" "				Jan. 3, 1828.
Jones, Peter C.		April 1, 1841,	April 1, 1841,	May 6, 1841,	June 3, 1841.

Name	Proposed by				
Jewell, Harvey	J. L. Dimmock,	Nov. 3, 1853,	Dec. 9, 1853,	Jan. 5, 1854,	Feb. 2, 1854.
Jones, William P.	J. McClellan,	Dec. 1, "	Dec. 9, "	Jan. 5, "	Feb. 2, "
Jones, Joseph S.	P. C. Jones,	April 6, 1854,	June 6, 1854,	Sept. 7, 1854,	Oct. 5, "
Jones, George S.	G. M. Thacher,	May 11, 1855,	May 30, 1855,	June 7, 1855,	Sept. 6, 1855.
Jewell, Lyman B.	John Stetson,	Nov. 1, "			
Kindness, Nicholas					
Knowles, Paul	Perkins,	June 27, 1796,	July 9, 1796,	Aug. 4, 1796.	
Kook, John	Martin,	July 7, "	July 9, "	June 22, 1795	
Kennedy, Peter	Martin, "	Feb. 6, 1800,	March 6, 1800,	March 15, 1800,	
Kelly, Joseph Jr.	Stetson,	Nov. 6, "	Nov. 6, "	Nov. 6, "	Dec. 3, 1801.
Kidder, Thomas		Oct. 6, 1803,	Oct. 25, "	Aug. 21, 1803,	Jan. 5, 1804.
Kelly, Henry	J. Vose,	May 7, 1812,	June 4, 1812,	July 6, 1812.	
Kearney, John A. (U.S.N.)	A. Binny,	July 10, 1815,	July 10, 1815,	July 12, 1815.	
Kearney, Lawrence,	A. Binny, "	July 10, "	July 10, "	March 12, "	
Kidder, Ephraim	D. Baxter, Jr.	Feb. 5, 1818,	March 19, 1818,	Feb. 19, 1818.	
Kettridge, Jesseniah, Jr.	D. Baxter, "	Feb. 7, 1822,	Feb. 7, 1822,	March 15, 1822.	
Kean, Benjamin, Jr.	Dis.	Feb. 5, 1824,	Feb. 5, 1824,	March 4, 1824.	
Kehr, William	Kent,	Feb. 10, "	Feb. 10, "	July 1, "	Jan. 27, 1825.
Kent, William V.	Baxter, Jr.	June 15, 1826,	June 15, 1826,	June 15, 1826,	Nov. 7, 1826.
Kingman, Edward, Jr.	Bowditch,	April 17, 1846,	May 7, 1846,	June 4, 1846,	Sept. 3, 1846.
King, Carmi E.	N. A. Thompson,	Mass. Lodge,	Mass. Lodge,	Mass. Lodge.	
Kingsley, Elias	T. S. Nichols,	Feb. 5, 1852,	March 4, 1852,	April 9, 1852,	Oct. 1, "
Kennison, Josiah F.	A. P. Richardson,	Feb. 2, 1854,	March 2, 1854,	April 14, 1854.	Dec. 7, 1854.
King, George P.	M. D. Parker,	Oct. 4, 1855,	Oct. 9, 1855,	Oct. 9, 1855.	
Keating, Thomas H.	H. T. Woods,	Jan. 6, 1796,	Feb. 4, 1796.	Jan. 25, 1802	
Loring, Mathew	Perkins,	Jan. 7, "	Oct. 28, 1796,	Oct. 28, 1796,	
Loud, Edmund	Martin,	April 7, "	Jan. 7, 1797,	Feb. 9, 1797,	
Lincoln Nathaniel	Martin, "	Sept. 10, "	Feb. 2, "	Feb. 9, "	
Lailson, Philip	Folsom,	Sept. 10, "			
Langley, William	Folsom, "	Jan. 7, 1797,			
Leroy, Marion	Folsom, "	Jan. 26, "			
Lincoln, Cornelius	Churchill,				

NAMES.	BY WHOM PROPOSED.	INITIATED.	CRAFTED.	RAISED.	MEMBERSHIP.
Lynch, William		Feb. 5, 1801,	Feb. 19, 1801,	Feb. 24, 1801,	
Lynch, John		July 2, "	July 2, "	July 6, "	
Loup, Lewis F. 'le			July 6, "	Aug. 6, "	
Lombard, Israel		Jan. 11, 1802,	Jan. 11, 1802,	Jan. 25, 1802,	
Lombard, Lewis		Jan. 25, "	Jan. 25, "	June 3, "	
LaParrele, Israel		March 24, 1804,	March 24, 1804.		
Lincoln, Hesekiah	Watson,	April 4, 1805,	June 6, 1805,	Sept. 26, 1805.	Oct. 5, 1809.
Leonard, Linus R.		Aug. 6, 1807,	Sept. 10, 1807,	Nov. 8, 1807,	
Little, Ezekiel		Nov. 6, "	Nov. 6, "	Nov. 8, "	
Lakeman, Israel	Park,	Feb. 7, 1811,	March 7, 1811,	April 4, 1811.	Oct. 3, 1811.
Lemon, John	Jenkins,		Oct. 6, 1815,	Nov. 2, 1815.	Jan. 1, 1818.
Lovejoy, Nehemiah	Braman,	Sept. 4, 1817,	Jan. 1, 1818.	Aug. 10, 1818.	
Lovejoy, Warren	Morse,	Oct, 2, "	Nov. 27, 1817,	Nov. 27, 1817.	
Lane, Calvin	J. Barker,	Feb. 3, 1820,	Feb. 3, 1820,	Feb. 17, 1820.	Jan. 4, 1821.
Leland, Caleb W.	Cobb,	March 2, "	March 2, "	May 4, "	
Lamson John A.	Braman,	Dec. 16, 1822,	Dec. 16, 1822,	Dec. 16, 1822.	Jan. 6, 1842.
Lawrence, Jonathan	D. Baxter, Jr.	Feb. 10, 1824,	Feb. 10, 1824,	Feb. 13, 1824.	
Leighton, Rufus	" "	Oct. 10, 1825,	Oct. 10, 1825,	Oct. 20, 1825.	
Lewis, David	" "	Nov. 8, "	Dec. 5, "	Jan. 5, 1826.	
Latouch, Bertrand	Pierce,	Nov. 3, 1830,	Jan. 6, 1831,	Feb. 3, 1831.	
Lewis, Winslow, Jr.	Flint,				
Loyd, George W.	R. Baker,	June 1, 1843,	June 1, 1843,	June 15, 1843.	Oct. 1, 1840.
Laporte, Count Chas. F.	E. Smith,	Dec. 7, "	Jan. 4, 1844.	Feb. 1, 1844.	
Luther, Slade	R. Baker,	March 3, 1853,	April 7, 1853,	May 5, 1853,	March 7, 1844.
Lee, James W.	J. McClellan,	April 14, 1854,	June 6, 1854,	June 6, 1854.	June 2, 1853.
Lang, W. J. C.	J. W. Barton,	June 1, "	Sept. 7, "	April 13, 1855,	
Lathrop, Augustus	Samuel G. Tower,	June 11, 1854,	Oct 26, "	Oct. 26, 1854.	May 3, 1855.
Lyon, Joseph	J. McClellan,	Oct. 11, 1854,	Feb. 1, 1855,	Jan. 19, 1855,	
Lee, Thomas J.	Joseph J. Whiting,	Jan. 4, 1855,		May 13, "	Feb. 16, "
Lovejoy, George	C. Buttrick,				May 3, "

Name					
May, A. De	Nov. 10, 1795,	Nov. 10, 1795,	July 2, 1795.	Perkins,	Dec. 3, 1795.
Martin, John	June 2, 1796,	June 3, 1796,	Nov. 10, "	Churchill,	
Moore, Jonathan	March 22, "	March 22, "	June 3, 1796.	Hayden,	
Meagher, John	Nov. 3, 1797,	Jan. 7, 1797,	March 27, "	"	
Miller, James	Jan. 7, "	May 4, "	Jan. 7, 1797.		
McNamara, Francis T.	March 2, "	May 10, 1798,	June 2, "	Martin,	
Montfort, Ebenezer	Dec. 7, "	March 6, 1800,	Nov. 2, "	Perkins,	
Mutzenberghen, John	April 11, 1798,	Nov. 21, 1798,	Nov. 9, 1799.	Hayden,	
Merchant, Samuel	May 3, "	March 6, 1800,	March 15, 1800.	Churchill,	
Meriam, Zadock	Nov. 21, "	May 9, 1799,	Nov. 26, 1798.	Tennant,	
Mood, Henry	Dec. 6, "	April 30, 1800,	Aug. 21, 1800.	Raymond,	
Meriam, Peter	May 2, 1799,	July 16, 1801,	May 7, 1799.	Hayden,	
McDonald, William J.	April 16, 1800,	Sept. 8, "	Aug. 13, 1801.	Rittenhouse,	Oct. 3, 1799.
Marsh, Mathias	July 30, 1801,	Oct. 1, "	Sept. 17, "		
Michelon, Glodeus	Aug. 6, "	Oct. 1, "	Oct. 13, "		
Mallet, Francis	Aug. 6, "	Sept. 3, "	Jan. 11, 1802.		
Marshall, Thomas	Aug. 6, "	May 6, 1802,	Nov. 18, 1802.		
Mayall, Robert	Sept. 3, "	Sept. 6, 1804,	Oct. 11, 1804.		
McCormic, Robert	May 6, 1802,	Oct. 11, "	Oct. 11, "		
Mentor, Jeremiah	March 1, 1804.	Jan. 8, 1805,	Jan. 4, 1805.		
McKown, John	Aug. 2, "	March 6, 1806,	April 7, 1807.		
McAllaster, James	Aug. 11, "	March 12, 1807,	Jan. 21, 1808.	Arch. Dunlap,	
McAllaster, Benjamin	Jan. 3, 1805,	April 7, "	Feb. 16, 1809.	"	
Miller, Robert	Feb. 6, 1806,	Jan. 7, 1808,	April 9, 1808.		
McPhiel, John	March 12, 1807,	Feb. 16, 1809,	Nov. 1, 1810,	Davidson,	
Marshall, Moses	Oct. 1, "	April 7, 1808,	Jan. 6, 1809.	Baxter,	
Morse, William	Nov. 19, "	Nov. 1, 1810,		Mountfort,	
Moody, David	Nov. 19, "				
Martin, William	April 7, 1808,				
Martin, Peter	Oct. 4, 1810,				May 4, 1809.
McGaw, Isaac				Howard,	April 4, 1816.
Morse, Silas					

48*

NAMES.	BY WHOM PROPOSED.	INITIATED.	CRAFTED.	RAISED.	MEMBERSHIP.
Morse, Elijah	Joseph Jenkins,				Oct. 15, 1812.
Mills, Oliver					Feb. 7, 1811.
Manzouco, Captain					
Morse, Moses L.	Moody,	May 5, 1814,	May 28, 1814,	June 2, 1814,	
May, Daniel	Streeter,	" 2, "	June 9, "	June 16, "	
Merrett, Timothy (Rev.)	James Wise,	May 2, 1816,	May 2, 1816,	May 6, 1816,	
Merrill, Nathaniel W.		Oct. 2, 1817,	Nov. 27, 1817,	Nov. 27, 1817,	
Morton, Isaac	Streeter,	June 1, 1820,	March 19, 1818,	March 19, 1818,	
Mason, John	Fiske,	Dec. 7, "	June 3, 1820,	June 3, 1820,	
Mecum, Charles	Nason,	Jan. 18, 1821,	Jan. 4, 1821,	Nov. 5, 1821,	
Mayhew, Nathaniel	G. G. Smith,	May 3, "	Feb. 1, "	Feb. 22, "	
McKenny, Andrew	D. Baxter, Jr.,	Oct. 2, 1823,	May 17, "	May 22, "	
Marston, John C.	William Pierce,	Nov. 7, "	Oct. 2, 1823,	Oct. 14, 1823,	
Morse, James	Jones,	March 4, 1824,	Nov. 7, "	Nov. 7, 1824,	April 7, 1825.
Marden, David	Baxter, Jr.,	Oct. 7, "	April 1, 1824,	April 1, "	
Morten, James M.	"	Oct. 10, 1825,	Oct. 7, "	Nov. 4, "	
Mundrucu, E. F. B.	Dis.	Sept. 23, "	Oct. 10, 1825,	Oct. 20, 1825,	
Melto, 'de, J. F.	"	Sept. 23, "	Sept. 23, "	Sept. 23, "	
Mann, Joshua	Coburn,	Dec. 5, "	Sept. 23, "	Sept. 23, "	
Mayo, M. H.	"	Sept. 7, 1826,	Dec. 5, "	Jan. 5, 1826,	
Martin, William C.	G. G. Smith,	Mt. Lebanon,	Sept. 7, 1826,	Oct. 5, "	Feb. 7, 1839.
McGill, Robert	R. Baker,	June 3, 1841,	Mt. Lebanon,	Mt. Lebanon,	Jan. 16, 1845.
Mallow, William	P. C. Jones,	May 4, 1843,	Oct. 7, 1841,	Oct. 7, 1841,	
McClellan, John	J. R. Dow,	April 4, 1844,	May 4, 1843,	June 15, 1843,	
McLellan, Samuel	J. Braman,		May 2, 1844,	June 6, 1844,	Sept. 5, 1844.
Moore, Augustus L.	R. Baker,	Feb. 20, 1845,	Feb. 20, 1845,	March 6, 1845,	Nov. 7, "
Murdock, Judson	J. McClellan,				April 3, 1845.
Melvin, Alonzo A.	"	June 1, 1848,	July 6, 1848,	Sept. 7, 1848,	Nov. 20, "
Merrill, Annis		May 12, 1849,	May 12, 1849,	May 12, 1849,	Jan. 4, 1849.
Messer, William W.	C. E. King,	June 20, 1850,	June 20, 1850,	June 21, 1850,	Oct. 31, 1850.

Name					
May, William B.	J. McClellan,	Oct. 3, 1850,	Nov. 21, 1850,	Feb. 6, 1851,	March 6, 1851.
McIntyre, Peter,	J. T. Heard,	Oct. 31, "	April 3, 1851,	May 5, 1851,	Dec. 4, "
Mudge, Alfred	Peter C. Jones,	March 3, 1853,	April 7, 1853,	May 5, 1853,	June 2, 1853.
Merwin, Timothy G.	P. A. Ames,	June 1, 1854,	June 6, 1854,	June 6, 1854,	
Mann, John J.	E. B. Foster,	Nov. 2, 1809,	Nov. 28, "	Jan. 19, 1855,	
McIntyre, James	P. McIntyre,	Sept. 21, 1855,	Sept. 21, 1855,	Oct. 9, 1855.	Feb. 16, 1855.
Nichols, John	Raymond,	Feb. 9, 1797.			
Nance, John Webb		Aug. 15, 1799,	Aug. 15, 1799,	Sept. 20, 1799.	
Nesmeth, Thomas		Sept 5, "	Sept. 5, 1799,	Aug. 5, 1802,	
Newell, Jabez		Jan. 1, 1801,	Feb. 19, 1801,		
Nicholson, Thomas		Jan. 17, "	Jan. 17, 1801,		
Nicholson, Thomas W.		July 2, "	July 6, "		
Nathan, Moses	J. Perkins,	March 27, 1801,	March 27, "	April 1, 1802.	May 2, 1805.
Neal, John O.	Cutter,	Dec. 1, 1803,	March 15, 1804,	March 15, 1804.	
Nelson, John	S. Smith,	Jan. 19, 1804,	Feb. 9, 1804,	Feb. 9, "	
Noble, John F.	Vose,	Oct. 5, 1809,	Nov. 2, 1809,	Nov. 16, 1809.	Nov. 2, 1815.
Newell, Montgomery	Little,	Dec. 7, 1809,	Jan. 4, 1810.	Jan. 18, 1810.	
Nason, Joel	Park,	Oct. 15, 1812,	Dec. 17, 1812.	Feb. 4, 1813,	
Nichols, Luther W.	W. Clough,	Dec. 3, "	Dec. 17, "	Feb. 4, "	
Nevers, Benj. M.	Streeter,	May 4, 1815,	June 1, 1815,	Aug. 3, 1815.	Oct. 6, 1815.
Norton, Robert,	Wm. Bittle,	June 1, 1820,	June 3, 1820,	June 3, 1820.	Feb. 15, 1822.
Neville, Wm. H.	Baxter, Jr.	May 17, 1821,	May 17, 1821,	May 22, 1821,	
Norris, Benj.	Baxter, Jr.	Oct. 6, "	Oct. 6, 1821,	Nov. 5, "	
Nepson, Daniel	R. Baker,	Nov. 20, 1822,	Nov. 20, 1822,	Nov. 20, 1822.	
Nerris, Eben'r W.	Fisk,	May 4, 1826,	July 6, 1826,	July 6, 1826.	
Nichols, Martin		Feb. 1, 1827,	Feb. 1, 1827,	Feb. 1, 1827.	
Neibuhr, Henry					
Nichols, Timothy S.	R. Baker,	Nov. 3, 1842,	Dec. 1, 1842.	Jan. 5, 1843.	March 5, 1841.
Nutting, Daniel W.	P. A. Ames,	In Maine,			Feb. 2, 1843.
Nute, Lewis W.	J. McClellan,	Feb. 5, 1852,	April 4, 1852,	April 9, 1852,	March 7, 1850.
Nichols, Robert C.	E. B. Foster,	April 6, 1854,	June 4, 1854,	June 6, 1854,	April 6, 1854.
Orr, Edward		May 7, 1801,	June 4, 1801,	June 4, 1801.	Sept. 7, 1854.

NAMES.	BY WHOM PROPOSED.	INITIATED.	CRAFTED.	RAISED.	MEMBERSHIP.
Orcutt, Samuel	Brown,	Feb. 9, 1809,	Feb. 16, 1809,	July 6, 1809.	
Ornes, Don F. De		Oct. 29, 1814,	Oct. 29, 1814,	Nov. 3, 1814.	
Owen, James	Baxter,	April 3, 1828,	April 3, 1828,	June 5, 1828.	
Parker, John	J. Coles,	April 7, 1796,	June 3, 1796,	June 3, 1796.	
Pendleton, Oliver	J. Martin,	Nov. 3, "			
Payson, Benjamin	Churchill,	Jan. 26, 1797,	Feb. 2, 1797,	March 4, 1797.	
Pomroy, Zadok	Folsom,	March 2, "	May 4, "	May 4, "	
Perry, Wm.	Folsom,	Jan. 4, 1798,	Feb. 1, 1798,	July 5, 1798.	
Pomroy, Daniel	Coles,	Feb. 1, "	Feb. 1, "		
Parsons, Andrew		March 7, 1799,	March 7, 1799.		
Pons, Thomas	A. Stetson,	April 4, "	April 4, 1800,	May 9, 1799,	June 6, 1799.
Penniman, Scammel	Sleeper,	March 2, 1800,	April 6, "	Aug 21, 1800,	Dec. 4, 1800.
Penniman, Silas		Oct. 6, 1800,	Nov. 18, 1801,	Dec. 18, "	Feb. 19, 1801.
Packard, Charles		Jan. 8, 1801,	Feb. 30, "	April 16, 1801,	
Pouten, Louis		July 30, "	July 5, "	Aug. 13, "	
Patch, Abraham		Nov. 5, "	Nov. 2, 1803,	Jan. 7, 1802,	Oct. 4, 1804.
Parker, Ichabod		Nov. 4, 1802.	June 3, 1805,	Oct. 6, 1803,	Jan. 6, 1803.
Phillips, Eben'r		Jan. 5, 1804.	Jan. 6, 1804,	Jan. 3, 1805.	
Pollard, Joseph		Sept. 6, "	Sept. 11, "	Feb. 7, "	
Parsons, James		Oct. 4, "	Oct. 5, 1805,	Oct. 11, "	
Paul, Hosea		Aug. 1, 1805.	Sept. 29, 1805,	Sept. 26, "	
Potter, Noah	J. Jenkins,	Nov. 21, 1805.	Nov. 13, 1806,	Jan. 2, 1806.	Dec. 5, 1805.
Pollard, Isaac	Davidson,	Feb. 6, 1806.	Feb. 13, "	April 3, "	
Park, Benjamin	Johnson,	Feb. 13, "	Feb. 15, "	April 3, "	
Polly, John	Dunlap,	May 1, "	May 7, "	June 5, 1807.	
Penn, Wm.		July 3, "	Aug. 12, 1807,	Oct. 2, 1806,	
Park, John	J. Jenkins,	March 12, 1807,	March 12, "	April 7, 1807,	
Penniman, Elisha	S. Hayden,	March 12, "	March 6, "		Feb. 5, 1807.
Penniman, William	S. Hayden,				
Peterson, Chas.	J. Shaw,	Oct. 1, "	Nov. 27, "		

Name					
Page, John Green	J. Shaw,	Oct. 1, 1807,	Nov. 6, 1807,	Nov. 27, 1807.	
Pulsifer, Stephen Bean	Sweet,	Nov. 2, 1809,	Nov. 2, 1809,	Nov. 16, 1809.	
Pratt, James, Jr.	Little,	May 3, 1810,	May 3, 1810,	May 17, 1810.	
Peters, Dyer	Sawyer,	Jan. 3, 1811,	Jan. 3, 1811,	Jan. 17, 1811.	
Peters, John				Jan. 17, "	
Parmenter, Samuel					
Peck, Elisha, (U. S. N.)	A. Binney,	Aug. 5, 1813,	Oct. 7, 1813,	Nov. 4, 1813.	Nov. 7, 1816.
Parker, Foxhall A. "	A. Binney,	July 12, 1815,	July 12, 1815,	July 12, 1815.	
Prescott, Edward	Baxter,	July 12, 1815,	July 12, "	July 12, "	May 6, 1819.
Pope, Calvin J.					
Paine, Asa Warren	Smith,	April 4, 1816,	April 4, 1816,	May 6, 1816.	
Peabody, Thomas	Barker,	Feb. 5, 1818,	March 5, 1818,	March 10, 1818.	
Pratt, Benjamin	Moody,	Sept. 3, "	Oct. 1, "	Nov. 19, 1819.	
Parris, Alexander	Cobb,	Sept. 2, 1819,	Nov. 13, 1819,	Nov. 13, 1820.	
Perley, Josiah	Fiske,	Dec. 2, "	Jan. 6, 1820,	June 3, "	
Peirce, James	Fisher,	Jan. 6, 1820,	Feb. 3, "	Feb. 17, "	
Pratt, Cornelius					
Pratt, Joseph	D. Baxter, Jr.	July 12, 1820,	July 12, "	July 12, "	Jan. 4, 1844.
Pratt, Daniel, Jr.	W. Pierce,	Jan. 18, 1821,	Feb. 1, 1821,	Feb. 22, 1821.	
Porter, Zachariah B.	Weld,	May 25, 1822,	May 25, 1822,	May 25, 1822.	
Peirce, Wm.	Coburn,	Oct. 1, 1823,	Oct. 2, 1823,	Oct. 14, 1823.	April 27, 1825.
Page, Jacob	French,	Jan. 1, 1824,	Jan. 1, 1824,	Feb. 13, 1824.	
Park, Thomas D.	R. Baker,	Nov. 9, "	Nov. 9, "	Nov. 9, "	Dec. 5, 1844.
Pike, Wm. B.	J. W. Ward,	June 2, 1825,	July 7, 1825,	July 7, 1825.	June 5, 1845.
Pomroy Thomas M.	J. McClellan,	Jan. 4, 1844,	Jan. 4, 1844,	Feb. 1, 1844.	Sept. 3, 1846.
Penniman James F.	Jos. L. Ross,	Dec. 5, "	Feb. 20, 1845,	May 1, 1845.	
Pope, John	Nahum Ball,	Jan. 1, 1846,	March 5, 1846,	Sept. 4, 1846.	Oct. 3, 1850,
Patten, Geo. W.	H. Blaney,	Jan. 13, 1849,	Jan. 13, 1849,	Jan. 13, 1849.	Sept. 5, 1850.
Parker, M. D.	W. W. Baker,	Feb. 1, "	March 1, "	March 1, 1849,	Jan. 15, 1852.
Palgemeyer, Edward	G. W. Patten,	June 20, 1850,	June 20, 1850,	June 21, 1850,	
Parker, John D.	J. W. Barton,	Feb. 2, 1854,	March 2, 1854,	April 14, 1854,	May 4, 1854.
Potter, Geo. S.	E. B. Foster,	April 6, 1854,	May 4, 1854,	Oct. 26, 1854,	Dec. 7, 1854.

NAMES.	BY WHOM PROPOSED.	INITIATED.	CRAFTED.	RAISED.	MEMBERSHIP.
Parker, Edward G.	O. H. P. Green,	April 14, 1854,	Oct. 26, 1854,	Oct. 26, 1854,	Dec. 7, 1854.
Potter, James B.	John D. Parker,	April 5, 1855,	Sept. 21, 1855,	Oct. 9, 1855.	
Park, Wm. D.	W. B. Fowle, Jr.	Sept. 21, 1855,	" "	Oct. 9, "	
Quiser, Jacob	Eaton,	Feb. 2, 1797,	Feb. 2, 1797,	June 2, 1797.	
Rice, Matthew		Nov. 5, 1795,	Nov. 5, 1795,	Nov. 10, 1795,	Nov. 16, 1795.
Richards, Josiah	Raymond,	Dec. 3, "	Dec. 5, "	Dec. 11, "	
Redman, James	Perkins,	Jan. 6, 1796,	Feb. 4, 1796,		
Robinson, Joseph	Coles,	March 3, "	Sept. 20, 1810,	Sept. 20, 1810.	
Rich, Benjamin	Somes,	Nov. 3, "	Nov. 8, 1796,	Nov. 8, 1796.	
Rice, Benjamin	Churchill,	Jan. 26, 1797,	Feb. 2, 1797,	Feb. 9, 1797.	
Rogers, William		July 6, "	July 11, "	Oct. 10, "	
Rover, ——			April 6, 1798,	April 6, 1798.	
Ridgway, Philip R.	Martin,	Oct. 4, 1798,	Oct. 19, "	Jan. 16, 1800.	
Rogers, Andrew		Nov. 7, 1799,	Nov. 7, 1799,	Nov. 9, 1799.	
Rogers, Zenos		April 16, 1800,	April 16, 1800,	Dec. 18, 1800.	
Richardson, Alford		Feb. 5, 1801.	Feb. 19, 1801,	March 19, 1801.	Dec. 3, 1801.
Richards, Henry		Nov. 27, "			
Rice, John		Jan. 19, 1804,	March 4, 1804,	March 15, 1804.	
Redman, John	Perkins,	Jan. 3, 1805,	Jan. 3, 1805,	Feb. 7, 1805.	
Russell, George		April 17, 1806,	April 17, 1806,	May 17, 1810.	
Rogers, S.	E. Little,			Oct. 15, 1812.	
Richie, Samuel K.	Jenkins,	Oct. 1, 1812,	Oct. 1, 1812,	Feb. 4, 1813.	Sept. 2, 1813.
Roberts, John		May 6, 1813,	July 1, 1813,	Aug. 5, "	
Read, Eleazer		May 28, 1814,	May 28, 1814,	May 30, 1814.	
Robles, Jose 'de,		In N. Hamphire.	July 12, 1815,	July 12, 1815.	
Roberts, William H.	Morse,	March 7, 1816,	May 2, 1816,	June 6, 1816.	Nov. 7, 1816.
Rogers, Samuel		March 20, 1817,	June 5, 1817,	Aug. 6, 1817.	
Rogers, Richard W.	Morse,	April 3, "	April 17, "	May 1, "	
Reed, George	Park,	Feb. 5, 1818,	March 5, 1818,	Aug. 10, 1818.	
Reed, Augustus	Davis,				

Name	Proposer				
Reynolds, Stephen	J. Barker	Nov. 20, 1822,	Nov. 20, 1822,	Nov. 20, 1822.	
Rice, Emery	Wise	Feb. 10, 1824,	Feb. 10, 1824,	Feb. 13, 1824.	
Rogers, Joseph S.	Fisk	Jan. 27, 1825,	Jan. 27, 1825,	Feb. 3, 1825.	
Robinson, William P.	French	Aug. 4, 1825,	Aug. 10, "		
Rougel, Joaquin	Child	Nov. 29, 1825,	Nov. 29, "		
Rogers, Isaiah	Whitney	Aug. 3, 1826,	Sept. 7, 1826,	Dec. 29, 1825,	April 3, 1845.
Ritchie, James	J. Borrowscale	Oct. 16, 1845,	March 5, 1846,	Oct. 10, 1826,	Feb. 5, 1846.
Russell, Benjamin G.	T. S. Nichols	Nov. 20, "	Dec. 18, 1845,	Oct. 21, 1846,	Sept. 3, 1847.
Roberts, John L.	S. Luther	April 17, 1846,	May 7, 1846,	May 15, "	May 6, 1848.
Ross, Joseph L.	Joseph Hall	Feb. 4, 1847,	March 4, 1847,	Jan. 4, "	Oct. 5, 1848.
Richardson, Aaron P.	C. E. King, (Dis.)	July 29, "	July 29, "	June 1, 1847,	Feb. 1, 1849.
Richardson, Nathaniel	Daniel Baxter	April 6, 1848,	May 4, 1848,	April 29, "	Feb. 6, 1851.
Rand, George Curtis	Joseph Hall	May 3, 1849,	May 3, 1849,	July 1, 1848,	Oct. 3, 1850.
Robinson, Thomas W.	James S. Wiggin	Feb. 7, 1850,	March 7, 1850,	June 21, 1849,	April 6, 1854.
Robbins, Samuel E.	J. McClellan	Feb. 7, "	March 7, "	June 21, 1850,	March 6, 1851.
Richards, J. Avery	"	Oct. 3, "	Nov. 21, "	March 18, "	Feb. 6, "
Robbins, Robert L.	J. T. Heard	Oct. 31, "	Nov. 21, "	April 6, 1851,	Sept. 4, "
Ripley, Christopher Gore	J. W. Barton	April 3, 1851,	June 5, 1851,	Feb. 8, 1850,	Dec. 20, "
Randall, George M. (Rev.)	W. W. Baker	April 1, 1852,	July 3, 1852,	Dec. 3, 1851,	Dec. 2, 1852.
Rogers, William	J. A. Cummings	Sept. 15, 1853,	Jan. 6, 1853,	July 1, 1852,	April 6, 1854.
Rand, William H.	George C. Rand	Feb. 16, 1855,	April 5, 1855,	Aug. 5, 1854,	May 3, 1855.
Richards, Francis	W. W. Baker	Aug. 16, 1855,	Dec. 16, 1855,	Dec. 13, 1855,	
Stetson, George		Dec. 11, 1795,	July 18, 1795,	July 18, 1795.	
Saunders, Joseph		Dec. 18, "	Jan. 18, "	Dec. 3, 1796,	
Stetson, Amasa	Raymond	Jan. 6, 1796,	Jan. 18, "	March 18, "	Nov. 8, 1796.
Somes, John	Perkins	Jan. 6, "	Feb. 4, "	Jan. 4, "	
Stoddard, Samuel	"	Jan. 6, "	Jan. 8, "	Feb. 8, "	
Small, Nathaniel		Jan. 27, "	Jan. 9, "	Jan. 1, "	
Stetson, Samuel	Raymond	June 7, "	Sept. 9, "		
Snow, Gideon	Martin	July 7, "	July 9, "		
Stetson, Benjamin	A. Stetson	Oct. 5, 1797,	Oct. 4, 1798,	Oct. 4, 1798.	
Small, Gamaliel	Raymond	Oct. 5, 1797,	Oct. 10, 1797,	Oct. 10, 1797.	

NAMES.	BY WHOM PROPOSED.	INITIATED.	CRAFTED.	RAISED.	MEMBERSHIP.
Smith, William	Rittenhouse,	Dec. 7, 1797,	Feb. 1, 1798,	Feb. 1, 1798.	June 6, 1799.
Seaver, Nathaniel		Feb. 1, 1798,	Feb. 1, "	April 11, "	
Stanton, Latham		March 1, "	March 1, "	Oct. 3, 1799.	
Spear, Samuel	Martin,	May 3, "	Sept. 5, "	Nov. 26, 1798.	
Snow, Ephriam	Raymond,	Nov. 21, "	Nov. 21, "	May 7, 1799.	
Stewart, David		May 2, 1799,	May 7, 1799,	Sept. 20, "	Nov. 7, 1799.
Sleeper, Jonathan F.	Folsom,	July 4, "	Sept. 5, "	Sept. 20, "	
Scott, Edward		Aug. 7, 1800,	Aug. 15, "	Dec. 18, 1800,	Feb. 19, 1801.
Sweet, John	Stetson,	Aug. 7, 1800,	Aug. 21, 1800,		
Swan, Thomas, Jr.		Feb. 24, 1801,	Feb. 24, 1801.	Jan. 4, 1805.	May 2, 1805.
Sweet, Jabez	Tower,	March 4, "	April 2, 1801.	Feb. 3, 1803.	
Swan, William	McDonnel	April 2, "	Dec. 6, 1804,	Feb. 9, 1804.	
Sweet, Jabez,		March 6, "	Sept. 3, "	May 8, "	
Solages, Francis		Aug. 4, 1802,	Nov. 4, 1802,	April 3, 1806.	
Spear, Daniel	Crooker,	Nov. 19, 1804,	Feb. 9, 1804,	Oct. 24, "	
Stearns, Lewis	A. Davidson,	Jan. 24, "	March 24, "	Nov. 12, 1807.	
Shaw, John	"	March 24, "	Feb. 13, 1806,	Nov. 12, 1807.	
Sute, Benjamin	Baxter	Jan. 2, 1806,	March 12, "	Jan. 21, 1808.	
Steadman, Josiah		March 12, "	Sept. 10, 1807,	Jan. 6, 1809.	
Scource, John R.		Sept. 10, 1807,	Nov. 6, 1807.	Nov. 16, "	Nov. 6, 1807.
Shattuck, Joel		Oct. 1, "	Nov. 6 1807,	Feb. 1, 1810,	
Smith, Samuel	Bean,	Nov. 6, 1807,	Dec. 3, "		
Snelling, Josiah		Nov. 27, 1808,	Jan. 5, 1809,		
Stevens, Jonathan		Sept. 1, 1809,	Oct. 12, "		
Stevens, Solon	S. Bean,	Sept. 7, "			
Simpson, John K.	S. Smith,				Dec. 2, 1824.
Sawyer, Nathaniel	S. Bean,				Feb. 15, 1810.
Stone, Ezra					Sept. 20, "
Sanger, Avery	Jenkins,	May 2, 1811,	May 2, 1811,	May 2, 1811.	
Stewart, Glaudus	"	July 2, 1812,	July 9, 1812,	July 9, 1812.	

Name	Proposed by				
Streeter, Leman	Leman,	May 1, 1815,	June 1, 1815,	Aug. 3, 1815,	Oct. 6, 1815.
Shaw, Simson	Collamore,	Oct. 6, "	Oct. 6, 1815,	Nov. 2, "	
Smith, Joel, Jr.		Mar. 7, 1816,	Apr. 4, 1816,	May 6, 1816,	Jan. 15, 1818.
Stedman, William M.	Geo. Guild,	Mar. 7, "	May 9, 1817,	May 6, 1817,	Nov. 7, 1816.
Sullaway, John		Juny. 2, 1817,	Jan. 17, "	Feb. 8, "	
Stevens, Benjamin	D. Baxter, Jr.,	Apr. 17, "	April 1, "	May 8, "	June 5, 1817.
Spear, Alba	J. Braman,	May 1, "	May 22, 1819,	July 1, 1817,	Dec. 4, 1817.
Spear, John	Barker,	Nov. 6, 1819,	July 22, "	Jan. 6, 1820,	March 15, 1821.
Swift, Clark	Streeter,	May 22, "	July 13, "	July 5, 1819,	
Southworth, James	Braman,	July 4, "	Nov. 13, "	Aug. 13, "	
Somerby, Eben	Park,	Nov. 4, "	Nov. 7, 1820,	Nov. 13, "	
Smith, George G.	Cobb,	Nov. 3, 1820,	Sept. 7, 1821,	Sept. 7, 1820,	May, 1820.
Sabine, James (Rev.)	Jenkins,	Aug. 18, 1821,	Feb. 6, 1823,	Feb. 23, 1821,	April 4, 1822.
Swift, William	Fisher,	Juny. 1, "	Feb. 4, "	Feb. 6, 1823,	
Sprague, Luther, Jr.	J. Braman,	Nov. 7, 1823,	Sept. 10, "	Sept. 4, "	
Shaw, Edward	N. Lovejoy,	Aug. 10, "	Oct. 3, 1824,	Oct. 14, "	
Sharon, Daniel		Oct. 3, 1824,	Oct. 3, 1825,	Feb. 3, 1824,	Nov. 7, 1828.
Sceva, Henry	Dennis,	Oct. 3, 1825,	Feb. 27, "	Mar. 3, 1825,	
Shwab, John G.	S. Smith,	Feb. 27, "	Jan. 25, "	Feb. 3, "	
Sargent, Hosea	Fisk,	Jan. 25, "	June 1, "	June 25, "	
Stockwell, Lemah	Dis.	June 15, "	Sept. 15, 1826,	Oct. 20, "	
Savage, James S.	Spear,	July 15, 1826,	Sept. 17, "	Sept. 15, 1825,	
Smith, Amos	Dis.	Sept. 6, "	June 15, "	June 15, 1826,	
Sibley, J. W.	Baxter, Jr.	June 1, "	April 7, "	April 17, 1826,	April 17, 1826.
Sinclair, James	S. Smith,	April 7, "	June 10, "	June 15, "	Nov. 2, "
Salmon, William		June 2, "	Sept. 2, 1840,	Oct. 10, "	
Stacy, Henry C. R.	Braman.	Sept. 2, 1840,	Nov. 1, 1841,	Nov. 10, "	
Sears, Eben	Prescott,	Nov. 1, 1841,	April 5, 1842,	May 7, 1840,	
Simpson, John K.	W. Ward,	April 1, 1841,	April 4, 1844,	June 8, 1841,	May 29, 1840.
Smith, Ebenezer, Jr.	" "	April 7, 1842,		May 19, 1842,	Dec. 2, 1841.
Simmons, Hiram	R. Baker,	April 7, 1843,		Feb. 1, 1844,	Dec. 1, 1842.
Slack, Samuel R.	Hawes,	Dec. 7, 1843,	Jan. 4, 1844,		

NAMES.	BY WHOM PROPOSED.	INITIATED.	CRAFTED.	RAISED.	MEMBERSHIP.
Smith, George W.	R. Baker,	Dec. 7, 1843,	Jan. 4, 1844,	Feb. 1, 1844,	March 7, 1844.
Smith, Ralph	G. M. Thacher,	Dec. 5, 1844.	Jan. 2, 1845,	Feb. 25, 1845,	" 4, "
Smith, Joseph Belknap	J. McClellan,				
Stearns, William	Tillson,	Oct. 16, 1845,	Dec. 4, 1845,	Jan. 15, 1846,	April 3, 1845.
Schnieder, Valentine	Neibuhr,	Nov. 20, "	Dec. 18, "	15, "	March 5, 1846.
Smith, Charles Ashton	J. McClellan,	Nov. 5, 1846,	Dec. 3, 1846,	Jan. 7, 1847,	Feb. 5, "
Smith, Ebenezer	"	Oct. 7, 1847,	Dec. 2, 1847,	Jan. 6, 1848,	Feb. 5, "
Stimpson, George, Jr.	Joseph Hall,	In Roxbury.	In Roxbury.	In Roxbury.	March 3, 1847.
Sweetser, Isaac	P. C. Jones,	In Maine.	In Maine.	In Maine.	Jan. 3, 1848.
Stedman, Wm. M., Jr.	W. W. Baker,	Nov. 1, 1849,	Dec. 6, 1849,	Dec. 6, 1849,	Jan. 4, 1849.
Skillings, David N.	Jos. L. Ross,	St. Andrews.	St. Andrews.	St. Andrews.	March 1, "
Schouler, William	W. W. Baker,	Jan. 1, 1852,	Jan. 15, 1852,	Jan. 15, 1852.	Feb. 7, 1850.
Starbuck, W. C.	B. Stearns,	Jan. 1, "	Jan. 15, "	March 4, 1852,	May 2, 1850.
Snow, John F.	J. McClellan,	May 6, "	June 3, 1852,	July 1, 1852,	Oct. 3, "
Stetson, John	W. W. Baker,	May 6, "	June 3, 1852,	July 1, 1852,	April 1, 1852.
Spaulding, Jonathan T.	P. C. Jones,	Jan. 14, 1853,	Jan. 14, 1853,	Jan. 14, 1853.	Oct. 7, 1852.
Simonds, Gilbert	J. Q. A. Bean,	Sept. 1, "	March 2, 1854,	April 14, 1854,	Nov. 4, 1852.
Shortridge, George E.	P. A. Ames,	Nov. 3, "	Dec. 9, 1853,	May 19, 1854.	May 4, 1854.
Sanger, George P.	Geo. M. Thacher,	May 4, 1854,	June 6, 1854,	Oct. 26, 1854,	Dec. 7, 1854.
Sennott, George E.	J. McClellan,	June 1, 1854,	June 6, 1854,	June 6, 1854.	June 6, 1854.
Stearns, Josiah A.	J. W. Barton,	Nov. 2, 1854,	Nov. 28, 1854,	Jan. 19, 1855,	April 5, 1855.
Sherman, Edwin A.	W. W. Wood,	April 5, 1855,	Sept. 21, 1855,	June 7, 1855,	Sept. 6, 1855.
Seavey, Stephen S.	W. W. Baker,	May 11, "	May 30, 1855,	June 7, 1855,	Sept. 6, 1855.
Shute, James M.	George O. Brastow,	May 11, "	May 30, "	Oct. 9, 1855,	
Skery, Amory T.	John B. Parker,	March 1, "	Oct. 9, 1855,	Dec. 5, 1795.	
Sargent, William H.	Geo. A. Wadleigh,	Nov. 5, 1795,	Nov. 5, 1795,		
Stevens, Benjamin F.	B. Stevens,	Feb. 4, 1796,	Feb. 4, 1796,		
Stanton, Samuel	W. Bogle,				
Tuttle, Jacob	Hayden,				
Turner, Gannett	Rittenhouse,				

Name					
Tower, Elisha	Folsom,	July 25, 1796,	Sept. 7, 1797,	Sept 7, 1797,	Oct. 3, 1799.
Tuttle, Charles		Jan. 4, 1798,	Feb. 1, 1798,	July 5, 1798,	May 1, 1806.
Treadwell, Moses		Feb. 6, 1800,	Feb. 21, 1800,	Feb. 21, 1800,	Dec. 4, 1800.
Thayer, Seth		July 3, "	July 3, "	Sept. 4, 1800,	
Treferthen, Benjamin					
Trajetta, Philip					Feb. 5, 1807.
Tyler, Joseph					
Todd, Robert					
Trow, Daniel		Dec. 4, "	Mar. 19, 1801,	March 19, 1801,	
Thomas, Nathaniel	Jenkins,	Feb. 5, 1801,	Feb. 9, 1804,	Feb. 9, 1804,	
Town, Ethol	Binny,	Dec. 6, 1804,	Dec. 6, "	Jan. 4, 1805,	
Tufts, Amos	Jenkins,	July 3, 1805,	Sept. 26, 1805,	Oct. 3, 1805,	
Taggard, Henry		Apr. 17, 1806,	Apr. 17, 1806,	May 1. 1806.	
Turner, Peter	J. Barker, Jr.	Oct. 5, 1809,	Oct. 12, 1809,	Nov. 16, 1809.	
Thaxter, Seth	D. Baxter, Jr.	Feb. 7, 1811,	Mar. 7, 1811,	April 4, 1811.	Nov. 9, 1824.
Tillson, David	Corey,	Jan. 15, 1818,	Jan. 15, 1818,	Jan. 15, 1818.	Apr. 3, 1823.
Topleff, Samuel	D. Baxter, Jr.	Apr. 2, "	Apr. 16, "	May 7, 1818.	
Town, Jonathan		Dec. 7, 1820,	Jan. 4, 1821,	Feb. 22, 1821.	
Towle, Frederick	Fisk,	April 5, 1821,	May 17, "	May 22, 1821.	
Thayer, Elias B.	Baxter, Jr.	Nov. 22, "	Nov. 22, "	Dec. 20, 1821.	
Thompson, Calvin	Whitney,	Nov. 9, 1824,	Nov. 9, 1824,	Nov. 9, 1824.	
Thompson, Jas. W. (Rev.)	J. B. Flint,	Dec. 5, 1825,	Dec. 5, 1825,	Jan. 5, 1826.	
Thacher, George M.	W. Ward,	Feb. 2, 1826,	Feb. 8, 1826,	Feb. 8, 1826.	
Thacher, Charles	J. W. Ward,	Oct. 11, 1830,	Oct. 11, 1830,	Oct. 11, 1830.	
Town, Nathan W.	Dis.	Nov. 5, 1840,	Nov. 5, 1840,	Dec. 3, 1840.	Jan. 7, 1841.
Thompson, Newell A.	J. R. Dow,	Oct, 5, 1843,	Oct. 5, 1843,	Nov. 7, 1844.	Feb. 4, "
Tucker, George	Baxter,	Feb. 20, 1845,	Feb. 20, 1845,	Feb. 25, 1845.	April 3, 1845.
Taylor, Edward T.	"	Feb. 20, "	Feb. 20, "	March 6, 1845.	June 5, "
Thayer, Charles Lowell	W. W. Baker,	Apr. 5, 1849,	May 3, 1849,	May 12, 1849.	April 2, 1846.
Tubbs, Alfred L.	Preston A. Ames,	Nov. 1, "	Nov. 14, "	Dec. 6, 1849.	July 3, 1849.
Tukey, Francis	Geo. M. Thacher,	Feb. 7, 1850,	Mar. 7, 1850,	March 21, 1850.	Jan. 2, 1850.
Tower, Samuel G.	George W. Smith,	Mar. 7, "	Apr. 4, 1850,	May 2, 1850.	May 2, 1850.

NAMES.	BY WHOM PROPOSED.	INITIATED.	CRAFTED.	RAISED.	MEMBERSHIP.
Tenny, Benjamin F.	Geo. M. Thacher,	April 4, 1850.	Apr. 4, 1850.	May 2, 1850,	June 6, 1850.
Tucker, John L.	" " "	Nov. 21, "	Nov. 21, "	Feb. 6, 1851,	March 6, 1851.
Thorup, Andreas T.	" " "				April 3, "
Taylor, Holbert	M. D. Parker,	May 6, 1850,	June 3, 1652,	Oct. 7, 1852,	Nov. 4, 1852.
Trull, Sylvester	Amos W. Cross.	Feb. 2, 1854.	Mar. 2, 1854,	April 14, 1854,	May 4, 1854.
Trenkle, Joseph	J. A. Dupee,	April 6, 1854,	May 4, 1854,	June 6, 1854,	Sept. 7, 1854.
Taylor, William O.	J. W. Lee,	April 6, 1854,	May 4, 1854,	June 7, 1854,	Sept. 6, 1855.
Tucker, Enos H., Jr.	J. McClellan,	June 1, 1854,	Sept. 7, "	Sept. 26, 1854,	Dec. 7, 1854.
Thompson, Charles, Jr.	Wm. Heywood,	Oct. 11, 1854,	Nov. 28, "	Oct. 19, 1855,	Feb. 16, 1855.
Turner, Alfred T.	B. Stearns,	May 11, 1855,	May 30, 1855,	Jan. 7, 1855,	Sept. 6, 1855.
Tenny, Moses, Jr.	G. O. Brastow.	May 11, 1855,	May 30, "	June 7, 1855,	Sept. 6, 1855.
Turner, Spencer A.	B. M. Nevers,			June 7, 1855,	Oct. 4, 1855.
Ungar, Philip	Phillips,	Oct. 26, 1806,	Oct. 26, 1806,	Nov. 1, 1806.	
Urann, Nath'l C.	Appleton,	May 7, 1812,	July 9, 1182,	July 9, 1812.	
Vincent, George	Sleeper,	Feb. 6, 1800,	Feb. 21, 1800,	Feb. 21, 1800,	Feb. 19, 1801.
Vose, Peter	Rittenhouse,	May 6, 1802.			
Vose, Josiah	Baxter,	March 12, 1806,	March 12, 1806,	April 3, 1806,	May 1, 1806.
Vose, Edward		Nov. 19, 1807,	Jan. 7, 1808.	Jan. 21, 1808.	
Vose, Jeremiah	D. Baxter,	April 4, 1816,	April 7, 1816,	Feb. 6, 1817.	
Virgin, Charles, (Rev.)	Wise,	March 5, 1818,	March 5, 1818,	March 10, 1818.	
Valentine, Elmer	G. Cobb,	Jan. 2, 1823,	Feb. 6, 1823,	Feb. 6, 1823.	
Vincent, James R.	W. W. Baker,	Sept. 15, 1849,	Sept. 15, 1849,	Sept. 15, 1849,	
Wallack, Samson H.	J. Perkins,	Sept. 3, 1795,	Oct. 2, 1795,	Dec. 5, 1795.	March 7, 1850.
Wellington, Samuel	Martin,	Jan. 7, 1796.			
Wood, Jonas	Martin,	Jan. 7, 1796,	Feb. 4, 1796.	March 3, 1796.	
Washburn, Thomas	Coles,	Oct. 28, 1796,	Oct. 28, 1796.		
Wales, Jones	Dodge,	March 2, 1797,	May 4, 1797.	June 2, 1797.	
Walman, Lawrence		June 20, 1797,	June 23, 1797,	June 23, "	
Whittington, William	Stetson,	Feb. 7, 1799,	March 7, 1799,	March 7, 1799,	April 4, 1799.
White, Samuel	Martin,	Sept. 5, 1799,	Sept. 5, 1799,	Jan. 16, 1800,	May 7, 1801.

Name	Proposer				
Walker, John		June 5, 1800,	June 5, 1800,	Sept. 18, 1800.	
Williams, Samuel		Feb. 5, 1801,	July 8, 1800,	July 8, "	
Waters, Samuel		Feb. 24, 1801,	Feb. 18, 1801,	March 19, 1801, "	
Waters, Josiah, Jr.		April 2, 1801,	Feb. 24, 1801,	April 16, "	July 1, 1802.
Wetherell, William		Aug. 6, 1801,	April 2, 1801,	May 26, "	
Webster, Ruben	McDonnel,	Aug. 5, 1802,	Aug. 11, 1802,	Jan. 11, 1802. "	
Ware, Oliver		Sept. 2, 1802,	Aug. 5, 1802,	Sept. 8, "	Jan. 5, 1804.
Wheeler, Emerald		Nov. 4, 1802,	Sept. 2, "	Sept. 8, "	April 7, 1803.
Winn, Nathan	Daniel Johnson,	April 7, 1803,	Sept. 2, "	Jan. 5, 1804.	
Watson, Eben'r	J. Jenkins,	Oct. 6, 1803,	Nov. 4, "	July 13, 1803,	
Warren, Ephraim		Nov. 14, 1803,	April 13, 1803,	Jan. 5, 1804.	Oct. 25, 1808.
Whitney, John		Dec. 8, 1803,	Oct. 6, 1804.	Dec. 15, 1803.	
Wilder, Samson V. S.		April 1, 1804,	Nov. 14, 1803,	July 5, 1804.	
Warren, William		Nov. 1, 1801,	Dec. 8, 1803,		
Walker, Charles		March 6, 1806,	April 1, 1804,		
Williams, Lawrence M.	Rittenhouse,	March 5, 1807,	Nov. 24, 1844.	July 5, 1804.	July 5, 1804.
Wriford, Abel		March 12, 1807,	March 6, 1806.	Nov. 8, 1807.	
Wightman, Thomas	S. Bean,	April 2, 1807,	March 7, 1807,	April 7, "	
Wiley, Thomas		Aug. 6, 1807,	March 12, 1807,	April 7, "	Sept. 10, 1807.
White, John	S. Hayden,	Nov. 19, 1807,	April 21, "	Nov. 21, 1807.	Feb. 8, 1809.
Wilkins, Abijah		Feb. 18, 1808,	Aug. 6, 1807,	Nov. 15, 1810.	
Wetherby, Samuel	Charles Tuttle,	Feb. 18, 1808,	Nov. 19, 1807,	June 2, 1808,	
Webb, Elisha		Oct. 5, 1809,	Feb. 7, 1808,	Nov. 16, 1809.	
Wallis, Mordecai L.	Vose,	Dec. 19, 1811,	Feb. 3, 1808,	Jan. 2, 1812,	Aug. 8, 1815.
Willard, Solomon	Amos Binney,	Dec. 19, 1811,	Oct. 12, 1809,	Jan. 2, "	
Webb, Jonathan	E. Little,	Jan. 2, 1812,	Dec. 19, 1811,	Jan. 6, 1814.	
Webb, David	E. Little,	Oct. 7, 1813,	Dec. 19, 1811,	June 16, "	
Wilson, Abiel	Jenkins,	June 2, 1814,	Jan. 2, 1812,	Aug. 3, 1815.	
Wilson, Jesse		Jan. 5, 1815,	Oct. 4, 1813,		
Wheelock, John G.			June 9, 1814,		
Whiting, Eben			Aug. 6, 1815,		
Wise, James					April 6, 1855.

NAMES.	BY WHOM PROPOSED.	INITIATED.	CRAFTED.	RAISED.	MEMBERSHIP.
Whitney, Daniel W.	Clough,	Nov. 7, 1816,	Nov. 7, 1816,	Dec. 5, 1816.	
Wrigley, Joseph	Enos Cobb,	Jan. 9, 1817,	Jan. 9, 1817,	Jan. 9, 1817.	
Whitney, Wm. T.	E. Morse,	April 10, 1817,	April 10, 1817,	April 17, "	
Woodbury, Jacob					
Wheeler, Asa, Jr.	A. Spear,	May 17, 1817,	May 17, 1817,	May 17, "	
Woodbury, Asa	Leman,	Sept. 3, 1818,	Nov. 5, 1818.	Dec. 17, 1818.	
Weld, Frederic	Fisk,	Dec. 2, 1818,	Dec. 17, 1818,	Feb. 22, 1821.	March 15, 1821.
Whittier, Asa		Jan. 18, 1821,	Feb. 1, 1821,		April 19, 1821.
Williams, Nathaniel					
Wolcott, Calvin, (Rev.)	S. Smith.	Jan. 3, 1822,	Jan. 3, 1822,	Jan. 3, 1822.	
Wolcott, Henry D.	Baxter, Jr.	Dec. 6, 1821,	Feb. 15, 1822,	Feb. 15, 1822,	May 2, 1822.
Wilber, Asa	G. G. Smith,	Jan. 3, 1822,	Jan. 3, 1822,	Jan. 3, "	
Whittemore, Thos. (Rev.)	L. Cory,	Jan. 3, 1822,	Jan. 3, 1822,	May 10, "	
Woods, Moses		May 13, 1822,	May 2, 1822,	Aug. 13, "	
White, Linmon	D. Baxter, Jr.	Aug. 13, 1822,	Aug. 13, 1822,	Oct. 14, 1823.	Feb. 3, 1825.
Whitney, Daniel	J. Town,	Oct. 10, 1823,	Oct 10, 1823,	Feb. 13, 1824.	
Weston, Alden B.	G. G. Smith,	Feb. 5, 1824,	Feb. 5, 1824,	Oct. 10, 1826.	
White, Alvin	Freeman,	Oct. 5, 1826,	Oct. 5, 1826,	Jan. 6, 1827.	
Ward, William	S. A. Allen,	Nov. 5, 1826,	Jan. 6, 1827,	Feb. 7, 1839.	April 4, 1839.
Ward, Joseph W.	S. A. Allen,	Dec. 6, 1838,	Feb. 3, 1839,	Feb. 7, "	April 4, "
Ward, John T.	S. A. Allen,	Dec. 6, 1838,	Feb. 7, 1839,	March 7, 1840,	May 2, 1840,
Whiting, William	W. Ward,	Dec. 6, 1838,	March 7, 1839,	May 7, "	May 29, "
Walker, Wildes P.	W. Ward,	March 5, 1840,	April 2, 1840,	May 7, "	May 29, "
Wood, William W.	W. C. Martin,	April 2, 1840,	April 2, "		June 8, 1841.
Ward, Andrew H.	J. W. Ward,				
Wright, John	E. Smith, Jr.	Feb. 2, 1843,	March 2, 1843,	April 6, 1843,	Sept. 7, 1843.
Wilkinson, Warren	P. C. Jones,				Oct. 5, 1843.
Williams, Thomas A.	P. C. Jones,	May 16, 1844,	May 16, 1844,	June 6, 1844,	Sept. 5, 1844.
Williams, Benj. E.	Wood,	Dec. 5, 1844,	Jun. 2, 1845,	March 6, 1845,	April 3, 1845.
Wilder, Marshal P, Jr.	G. G. Smith,	Feb. 5, 1846,	March 5, 1846,	April 2, 1846,	May 7, 1846.

Name	Recommended by					
Wright, Joseph W.	Jos. Hall.	Jan. 19, 1849,	Jan. 19, 1849,	Jan. 19, 1849.	Jan. 19, 1849.	May 7, 1846.
Wilder, Lucius J.	M. P. Wilder, Jr.	July 5, 1849,	Aug. 2, 1849,	Aug. 2, "	Sept. 6, "	Feb. 7, 1850.
Wood, William B.	J. McClellan,	July 1, 1849,	Aug. 2, 1849,	Aug. 2, "	Oct. 4, "	Nov. 1, 1849.
Wiggin, James S.	J. L. Dimmock,	Dec. 28, 1849,	Dec. 28, 1849,	Dec. 28, "	Dec. 28, "	Oct. 31, 1850.
Winchester, Wm. P. Jr.	J. W. Barton,	Jun. 3, 1850,	April 4, 1850,	April 4, 1850,	April 18, 1850,	Oct. 3, 1850.
Wheelwright, Jos. W.	J. McClellan,	April 4, 1850,	April 4, 1850,	April 4, "	May 2, "	June 6, 1850.
Wentworth, Wm. H.	L. Bates,	Oct. 31, 1850,	Nov. 21, 1850,	Nov. 21, "	Jan. 2, 1851,	Feb. 6, 1851.
Whiting, Joseph J.	J. McClellan,					Jan. 2, 1851.
Warren, Silas	W. W. Baker,	Feb. 6, 1851,	March 6, 1851,	March 6, 1851,	May 1, 1851,	Nov. 3, 1853.
Wason, Elbridge	J. Barnard,	St. Andrews,	St. Andrews,	St. Andrews,	St. Andrews,	Feb. 6, 1851.
Warren, William W.	W. Schouler,				May	May 1, "
Ward, William	J. McClellan,				May	May 1, "
Ward, Jos. W.	J. McClellan,				June	June 2, 1853.
Williams, Lemuel S.	R. L. Robbins,	Feb. 3, 1853,	March 11, 1853,	March 11, 1853,	May 5, 1853,	Oct. 6, 1853.
Wadleigh, Geo. A.	N. Ball,	May 5, 1853,	June 2, 1853,	June 2, 1853,	June 2, 1853,	Dec. 7, 1854.
Warner, Sewall	C. E. King,	June 1, 1854,	Sept. 7, 1854,	Sept. 7, 1854,	Oct. 26, 1854,	Feb. 16, 1855.
Weld, Aaron D. Jr.	J. McClellan,	Nov. 2, 1854,	Nov. 28, "	Nov. 28, "	Dec. 19, 1855,	May 3, 1855.
Washburn, Fred'k L.	W. W. Baker,	Jun. 4, 1855,	Feb. 1, 1855,	Feb. 1, 1855,	Jan. 13, "	May 3, 1855.
Wilcox, John H.	G. M. Thacher,	Jan. 1, 1855,	Feb. 1, "	Feb. 1, "	April 13, "	May 3, 1855.
Williams, Alexander	W. W. Baker,	Feb. 1, 1855,	March 1, "	March 1, "	April 13, "	Feb. 1, 1855.
Woods, Henry T.	J. McClellan,	St. Andrews,	St. Andrews,	St. Andrews,	April 13, "	
Woods, Joseph W.	G. N. Thacher,	Oct. 4, 1855,	Oct. 9, 1855.	Oct. 9, 1855.	St. Andrews,	Nov. 1, 1855.
Washburn, Miles	J. W. Lee.				Oct. 9, 1855.	
Young, Henry,	J. Martin,	Nov. 3, 1796.				Nov. 1, 1855.
Yates, George	Baxter,	Sept. 4, 1806,	Sept. 4, 1806.	Sept. 4, 1806.		
Young, James		Nov. 13, 1819,	Nov. 13, 1819.	Nov. 13, 1819.	Nov. 13, 1849.	Nov. 13, 1849.

CATALOGUE

OF THE

GRAND MASTERS,

DEPUTY GRAND MASTERS,

SENIOR AND JUNIOR GRAND WARDENS,

GRAND TREASURERS,

RECORDING AND CORRESPONDING
GRAND SECRETARIES,

AND

DISTRICT DEPUTY GRAND MASTERS OF THE
FIRST DISTRICT,

OF THE

Grand Lodge of Massachusetts,

FROM 5792 TO 5855.

OFFICERS OF THE GRAND LODGE.

5792.

John Cutler, G. M.
Josiah Bartlett, S. G. W.
Samuel Parkman, G. T.

John Lowell, D. G. M.
Mungo Mackay, J. G. W.
Thomas Farrington, G. S.

5793.

John Cutler, G. M.
Josiah Bartlett, S. G. W.
Samuel Parkman, G. T.

John Lowell, D. G. M.
Mungo Mackay, J. G. W.
Thomas Farrington, G. S.

5794.

John Cutler, G. M.
Mungo Mackay, S. G. W.
William Little, G. T.

Josiah Bartlett, D. G. M.
Samuel Parkman, J. G. W.
Samuel Colesworthy, Jr., G. S.

5795.

Paul Revere, G. M.
Isaiah Thomas, S. G. W.
William Little, G. T.

William Scollay, D. G. M.
Richard Salter, J. G. W.
Daniel Oliver, G. S.

5796.

Paul Revere, G. M.
Isaiah Thomas, S. G. W.
William Little, G. T.

William Scollay, D. G. M.
Joseph Laughton, J. G. W.
Daniel Oliver, G. S.

5797.

Paul Revere, G. M.
Isaiah Thomas, S. G. W.
William Little, G. T.

Samuel Dunn, D. G. M.
Joseph Laughton, J. G. W.
Daniel Oliver, G. S.

5798.

Josiah Bartlett, G. M.
Joseph Laughton, S. G. W.
Thomas Dennie, G. T.

Samuel Dunn, D. G. M.
William Little, J. G. W.
Daniel Oliver, G. S.

5799.

Josiah Bartlett, G. M.
Joseph Laughton, S. G. W.
Allen Crocker, G. T.

Samuel Dunn, D. G. M.
John Boyle, J. G. W.
Daniel Oliver, G. S.

5800.

Samuel Dunn, G. M.
John Boyle, S. G. W.
Allen Crocker, G. T.

Joseph Laughton, D. G. M.
Thrddeus M. Harris, J. G. W.
Daniel Oliver, G. S.

5801.

Samuel Dunn, G. M.
John Boyle, S. G. W.
Allen Crocker, G. T.

Joseph Laughton, D. G. M.
Isaac Hurd, J. G. W.
Daniel Oliver, G. S.

5802.

Samuel Dunn, G. M.
John Boyle, S. G. W.
Allen Crocker, G. T.

Joseph Laughton, D. G. M.
Isaac Hurd, J. G. W.
John Proctor, G. S.

5803.

Isaiah Thomas, G. M.
Isaac Hurd, S. G. W.
Allen Crocker, G. T.

Simon Elliot, D. G. M.
Timothy Bigelow, J. G. W.
John Proctor, R. G. S.

Thaddeus M. Harris, C. G. S.
John Boyle, D. D. G. M., 1st District.

5804.

Isaiah Thomas, G. M.
Timothy Bigelow, S. G. W.
Allen Crocker, G. T.

Simon Elliot. D. G. M.
John Soley, J. G. W.
John Proctor, R. G. S.

Thaddeus M. Harris, C. G. S.
John Boyle, D. D. G. M., 1st District.

5805.

Isaiah Thomas, G. M.
Timothy Bigelow, S. G. W.
Allen Crocker, G. T.

Simon Elliot, D. G. M.
John Soley, J. G. W.
John Proctor, R. G. S.

Thaddeus M. Harris, C. G. S.
John Boyle, D. D. G. M., 1st District.

5806.

Timothy Bigelow, G. M.
John Soley, S. G. W.
Allen Crocker, G. T.

Simon Elliot, D. G. M.
Shubael Bell, J. G. W.
John Proctor, R. G. S.

Thaddeus M. Harris, C. G. S.
John Boyle, D. D. G. M., 1st District.

5807.

Timothy Bigelow, G. M.
John Soley, S. G. W.
Allen Crocker, G. T.

Simon Elliot, D. G. M.
Shubael Bell, J. G. W.
John Proctor, R. G. S.

Thaddeus M. Harris, C. G. S.
Daniel Davis, D. D. G. M., 1st District.

5808.

Timothy Bigelow, G. M.
Shubael Bell, S. G. W.
Allen Crocker, G. T.

Simon Elliot, D. G. M.
Henry Fowle, J. G. W.
John Proctor, R. G. S.

Thaddeus M. Harris, C. G. S.
Daniel Davis, D. D. G. M., 1st District.

5809.

Isaiah Thomas, G. M.
Henry Fowle, S. G. W.
Allen Crocker, G. T.

John Boyle, D. G. M.
Francis J. Oliver, J. G. W.
John Proctor, R. G. S.

Thaddeus M. Harris, C. G. S.
Henry M. Lisle, D. D. G. M., 1st District.

5810.

Josiah Bartlett, G. M.
Francis J. Oliver, S. G. W.
Andrew Sigourney, G. T.

John Boyle, D. G. M.
Oliver Prescott, J. G. W.
John Proctor, R. G. S.

Thaddeus M. Harris, C. G. S.
Shubael Bell, D. D. G. M., 1st District.

5811.

Timothy Bigelow, G. M.
Francis J. Oliver, S. G. W.
Andrew Sigourney, G. T.

Samuel Bradford, D. G. M.
Benjamin Russell, J. G. W.
John Proctor, R. G. S.

John Bartlett, C. G. S.
John Dixwell, D. D. G. M., 1st District.

5812.

Timothy Bigelow, G. M.
Francis J. Oliver. S. G. W.
Andrew Sigourney, G. T.

Thaddeus M. Harris, D. G. M.
Benjamin Russell, J. G. W.
John Soley, R. G. S.

John Dixwell, D. D. G. M., 1st District.

5813.

Timothy Bigelow, G. M.
Benjamin Russell, S. G. W.
Andrew Sigourney, G. T.

Francis J. Oliver, D. G. M.
John Abbot, J. G. W.
John Soley, R. G. S.

Thaddeus M. Harris, C. G. S.
Asa Peabody, D. D. G. M., 1st District.

5814.

Benjamin Russell, G. M.
John Abbot, S. G. W.
Andrew Sigourney, G. T.
Francis J. Oliver, D. G. M.
John B. Hammatt, J. G. W.
John Soley, R. G. S.
Thaddeus M. Harris, C. G. S.
Asa Peabody, D. D. G. M., 1st District.

5815.

Benjamin Russell, G. M.
John B. Hammatt, S. G. W.
Andrew Sigourney, G. T.
Francis J. Oliver, D. G. M.
Joseph Baker, J. G. W.
John Soley, R. G. S.
Thaddeus M. Harris, C. G. S.
Elijah Morse, D. D. G. M., 1st District.

5816.

Benjamin Russell, G. M.
Augustus Peabody, S. G. W.
Andrew Sigourney, G. T.
Francis J. Oliver, D. G. M.
Ralph H. French, J. G. W.
John Soley, R. G. S.
John Bartlett, C. G. S.
Elijah Morse, D. D. G. M., 1st District.

5817.

Francis J. Oliver, G. M.
Augustus Peabody, S. G. W.
Andrew Sigourney, G. T.
John Dixwell, D. G. M.
Ralph H. French, J. G. W.
John Soley, R. G. S.
Edward Turner, C. G. S.
Samuel P. P. Fay, D. D. G. M., 1st District.

5818.

Francis J. Oliver, G. M.
Caleb Butler, S. G. W.
Andrew Sigourney, G. T.
John Dixwell, D. G. M.
James C. King, J. G. W.
John Soley, R. G. S.
Elijah Morse, C. G. S.
Thomas Power, D. D. G. M., 1st District.

5819.

Francis J. Oliver, G. M.
Caleb Butler, S. G. W.
Andrew Sigourney, G. T.
Samuel P. P. Fay, D. G. M.
Joseph Jenkins, J. G. W.
John Soley, R. G. S.
Elijah Morse, C. G. S.
Thomas Power, D. D. G. M., 1st District.

5820.

Samuel P. P. Fay, G. M.
Andrew Sigourney, S. G. W.
Elijah Morse, G. T.
Asa Eaton, D. G. M.
Thomas Cole, J. G. W.
John Soley, R. G. S.
Thomas Power, C. G. S.
Samuel J. Gardner, D. D. G. M., 1st District.

5821.

John Dixwell, G. M.
Thomas Cole, S. G, W.
Elijah Morse, G. T.
John Abbot, D. G. M.
Elijah Crane, J. G. W.
Thomas Power, R. G. S.
Cheever Felch, C. G. S.
Paul Dean, D. D. G. M., 1st District.

5822.

John Dixwell, G. M.
Thomas Cole, S. G. W.
Elijah Morse, G. T.
John Abbot, D. G. M.
Elijah Crane, J. G. W.
Thomas Power, R. G. S.
Warren Peirce, C. G. S.
Paul Dean, D. D. G. M., 1st District.

5823.

John Dixwell, G. M.
Elijah Crane, S. G. W.
Elijah Morse, G. T.
John Abbot, D. G. M.
Samuel Thaxter, J. G. W.
Thomas Power, R. G. S.
Asa Bullard, C. G. S.
Paul Dean, D. D. G. M., 1st District.

5824.

John Abbot, G. M.
Samuel Thaxter, S. G. W.
Elijah Morse, G. T.
Caleb Butler, D. G. M.
John Keyes, J. G. W.
Thomas Power, R. G. S.
John J. Loring, C. G. S.
Asa Bullard, D. D. G. M., 1st District.

5825.

John Abbot, G. M.
Samuel Thaxter, S. G. W.
Elijah Morse, G. T.
Caleb Butler, D. G. M.
John Keyes, J. G. W.
Thomas Power, R. G. S.
John J. Loring. C. G. S.
Asa Bullard, D. D. G. M., 1st District.

5826.

John Abbot G. M.
Samuel Thaxter, S. G. W.
Elijah Morse, G. T.
Caleb Butler, D. G. M.
John Keyes, J. G. W.
Thomas Power, R. G. S.
John J. Loring, C. G. S.
Abraham A. Dame, D. D. G. M., 1st District.

5827.

John Soley, G. M.
John Keyes, S. G. W.
John J. Loring, G. T.
John Bartlett, D. G. M.
John Mills, J. G. W.
Thomas Power, R. G. S.
William J. Whipple, C. G. S.
Abraham A. Dame, D. D. G. M., 1st District.

5828.

John Soley, G. M.   John Bartlett, D. G. M.
John Keyes, S G. W.   Henry Purkit, J. G. W.
John J. Loring, G. T.   Thomas Power, R. G. S.
           William J. Whipple, C. G. S.
     Abraham A. Dame, D. D. G. M., 1st District.

5829.

John Soley, G. M.   John Bartlett, D. G. M.
Seth Sprague, Jr., S. G. W.   Abraham A. Dame, J. G. W.
John J. Loring, G. T.   Thomas Power, R. G. S.
           William J. Whipple, C. G. S.
       Charles Wells, D. D. G. M., 1st District.

5830.

Joseph Jenkins, G. M.   Elijah Morse, D. G. M.
Abraham A. Dame, S. G. W.   William J. Whipple, J. G. W.
John J. Loring, G. T.   Thomas Power, R. G. S.
              Asa Eaton, C. G. S.
     Joseph Eveleth, D. D. G. M., 1st District.

5831.

Joseph Jenkins, G. M.   William Hilliard, D. G. M.
Abraham A. Dame, S. G. W.   William J. Whipple, J. G. W.
John J. Loring, G. T.   Thomas Power, R. G. S.
              Asa Eaton, C. G. S.
       Harrison Gray, D. D. G. M., 1st District.

5832.

Joseph Jenkins, G. M.   David Wilder, D. G. M.
Abraham A. Dame, S. G. W.   William J. Whipple, J. G. W.
John J. Loring, G. T.   Thomas Power, R. G. S.
              Asa Eaton, C. G. S.
       Harrison Gray, D. D. G. M., 1st District.

5833.

Elijah Crane, G. M.   Abraham A. Dame, D. G. M.
William J. Whipple, S. G. W.   James A. Dickson, J. G. W.
John J. Loring, G. T.   Thomas Power, R. G. S.
              Asa Eaton, C. G. S.
       Joshua B. Flint, D. D. G. M., 1st District.

5834.

John Abbot, G. M.   Abraham A. Dame, D. G. M.
Elias Haskell, S. G. W.   Benjamin B. Appleton, J. G. W.
John J. Loring, G. T.   Thomas Power, R. G. S.
       ·   Nahum Capen, C. G. S.
       Joshua B. Flint, D. D. G. M., 1st District.

5835.

Joshua B. Flint, G. M.
Elias Haskell, S. G. W.
John J. Loring, G. T.

Paul Dean, D. G. M.
Benjamin B. Appleton, J. G. W.
Charles W. Moore, R. G. S.

Nahum Capen, C. G. S.
Simon W. Robinson, D. D. G. M., 1st District.

5836.

Joshua B. Flint, G. M.
Elias Haskell, S. G. W.
John J. Loring, G. T.

Paul Dean, D. G. M.
Benjamin B. Appleton, J. G. W.
Charles W. Moore, R. G. S.

Nahum Capen, C. G. S.
Simon W. Robinson, D. D. G. M., 1st District.

5837.

Joshua B. Flint, G. M.
Benjamin B. Appleton, S. G. W.
John J. Loring, G. T.

Paul Dean, D. G. M.
Simon W. Robinson, J. G. W.
Charles W. Moore, R. G. S.

Nahum Capen, C. G. S.
Henry H. Barton, D. D. G. M., 1st District.

5838.

Paul Dean, G. M.
Simon W. Robinson, S. G. W.
John J. Loring, G. T.

George G. Smith, D. G. M.
C. Gayton Pickman, J G. W.
Charles W. Moore, R. G. S.

Nahum Capen, C. G. S.
Henry H. Barton, D. D. G, M., 1st District.

5839.

Paul Dean, G. M.
Simon W. Robinson, S. G. W.
John J. Loring, G. T.

George G. Smith, D. G. M.
C. Gayton Pickman, J. G. W.
Charles W. Moore, R. G. S.

Nahum Capen, C. G. S.
Daniel Harwood, D. D. G. M., 1st District.

5840.

Paul Dean, G. M.
Simon W. Robinson, S. G. W.
John J. Loring, G. T.

George G. Smith, D. G. M.
C. Gayton Pickman, J. G. W.
Charles W. Moore, R. G. S.

Nahum Capen, C. G. S.
Thomas Tolman, D. D. G. M., 1st District.

5841.

Caleb Butler, G. M.
Thomas Tolman, S. G. W.
John J. Loring, G. T.

Simon W. Robinson, D. G. M.
Winslow Lewis, Sn., J. G. W.
Charles W. Moore, R. G. S.

Winslow Lewis, Jr., C. G. S.
Samuel Eveleth, D. D. G. M., 1st District.

5842.

Caleb Butler, G. M.
Thomas Tolman, S. G. W.
John J. Loring, G. T.

Simon W. Robinson, D. G. M.
Winslow Lewis, Sn., J. G. W.
Charles W. Moore, R. G. S.

Winslow Lewis, Jr., C. G. S.
Samuel Eveleth, D. D. G. M., 1st District.

5843.

Augustus Peabody, G. M.
Thomas Tolman, S. G. W.
John J. Loring, G. T.

Simon W. Robinson, D. G. M.
Winslow Lewis, Sn.,, J. G. W.*
Charles W. Moore, R. G. S.

Winslow Lewis, Jr., C. G. S.
Gilbert Nurse, D. D. G. M., 1st District.

* Died in May, 1850.

5844.

Augustus Peabody, G. M.
Robert Lash, S. G. W.
John J. Loring, G. T.

John B. Hammatt, D. G. M.
Thomas Power, J. G. W.
Charles W. Moore, R. G. S.

Winslow Lewis, Jr., C. G. S.
E. M. P. Wells, D. D. G. M., 1st District.

5845.

Augustus Peabody, G. M.
Robert Keith, S. G. W.
John J. Loring, G. T.

E. M. P. Wells, D. G. M.
John Hews, J. G. W.
Charles W. Moore, R. G. S.

Benjamin Huntoon, C. G. S.
Addison Searle, D. D. G. M., 1st District.

5846.

Simon W. Robinson, G. M.
Edward A. Raymond, S. G. W.
John J. Loring, G. T.

Winslow Lewis, Jr., D. G. M.
John R. Bradford, J. G. W.
Charles W. Moore, R. G. S.

Benjamin Huntoon, C. G. S.
Addison Searle, D. D. G. M., 1st District.

5847.

Simon W. Robinson, G. M.
Edward A. Raymond, S. G. W.
John J. Loring, G. T.

Winslow Lewis, Jr., D. G. M.
John R. Bradford, J. G. W.
Charles W. Moore, R. G. S.

Benjamin Huntoon, C. G. S.
Addison Searle, D. D. G. M., 1st District.

5848.

Simon W. Robinson, G. M.
Edward A. Raymond, S. G. W.
John J. Loring, G. T.

Ferdinand E. White, D. G. M.
John R. Bradford, J. G. W.
Charles W. Moore, R. G. S.

Benjamin Huntoon, C. G. S.
George M. Randall, D. D. G. M., 1st District.

5849.

Edward A. Raymond, G. M.
John J. Loring, S. G. W.
Thomas Tolman, G. T.
George M. Randall, D. G. M.
Thomas M. Vinson, J. G. W.
Charles W. Moore, R. G. S.
Samuel Barrett, C. G. S.
C. Gayton Pickman, D. D. G. M., 1st District.

5850.

Edward A. Raymond, G M.
Thomas M. Vinson, S. G. W.
Thomas Tolman, G. T.
George M. Randall, D. G. M.
Asa T. Newhall, J. G. W.
Charles W. Moore, R. G. S.
Samuel Barrett, C. G. S.
Stephen Lovell, D. D. G. M., 1st District.

5851.

Edward A. Raymond, G. M.
Thomas M. Vinson, S. G. W.
Thomas Tolman, G. T.
George M. Randall, D. G. M.
William Eaton, J. G. W.
Charles W. Moore, R. G. S.
Samuel Barrett, C. G. S.
Stephen Lovell, D. D. G. M., 1st District.

5852.

George M. Randall, G. M.
William Ferson, S. G. W.
Thomas Tolman, G. T.
Lucius R. Paige, D. G. M.
John Flint, J. G. W.
Charles W. Moore, R. G. S.
Jonas A. Marshall, C. G. S.
Jerome V. C. Smith, D. D. G. M., 1st District.

5853.

George M. Randall, G. M.
Daniel Harwood, S. G. W.
Thomas Tolman, G. T.
Lucius R. Paige, D. G. M.
Benjamin Huntoon, J. G. W.
Charles W. Moore, R. G. S.
Jonas A. Marshall, C. G. S.
Jerome V. C. Smith, D. D. G. M., 1st District.

5854.

George M. Randall, G. M.
Richard S. Spofford, S. G. W.
Thomas Tolman, G. T.
Lucius R. Paige, D. G. M.
Jonas A. Marshall, J. G. W.
Charles W. Moore, R. G. S.
John H. Sheppard, C. G. S.
Jerome V. C. Smith, D. D. G. M., 1st District.

5855.

Winslow Lewis, G. M.
William C. Plunkett, S. G. W.
Thomas Tolman, G. T.
Abraham Low, D. G. M.
Samuel K. Hutchinson, J. G. W.
Charles W. Moore, R. G. S.
John H. Sheppard, C. G. S.
Henry G. Clark, D. D. G. M., 1st District.

5856.

Winslow Lewis, G. M.
John T. Heard, S. G. W.
Thomas Tolman, G. T.

Abraham, T. Low, D. G. M.
Charles R. Train, J. G. W.
Charles W. Moore, R. G. S.

John H. Sheppard, C. G. S.
Henry G. Clark, D. D. G. M., 1st District.

ERRATA.

Page 86, 22d, line, for L. G. Whitman, read Z. G. Whitman.
" 124, 9th, "   " Affords,   "   Afford.
" 132, 28th, "   " John James,   "   John Somes.
" 135, 13th, "   " H. Stetson,   "   A. Stetson.
" 145, 27th, "   " Wm. S. McDonnell, " Wm. J. McDonnell.
" 152, 17th, "   " John Barker,   "   John Park.
" 155, 12th, "   " Fee,   "   Degree.
" 163, 8th, "   " Received,   "   Benewed.
" 164, 14th, "   " Foster,   "   Fisher.
" 170, 19th, "   " Greeley,   "   Greele.
" 355, 13th, "   " Festivals,   "   Festivities.
" 366, 25th, "   " Enumerable,   "   Innumerable.
" 426, 30th, "   " Mordecai M.   "   Mordecai L.
" 446, 32d, "   " This important duty, " The important duty of at-
                                                       [tendance.
" 544, 6th, "   Geo. Stimpson, Jr. is a life, not an honorary, member.

www.ingramcontent.com/pod-product-compliance
Lightning Source LLC
Chambersburg PA
CBHW032336280326
41935CB00008B/356